# CHILD WELFARE SERVICES

## A SOURCEBOOK

Alfred Kadushin

# Child Welfare Services

## A SOURCEBOOK

*The Macmillan Company*
*Collier-Macmillan Limited, London*

# To Sylvia

First Printing

Library of Congress catalog card number: 79–88841

THE MACMILLAN COMPANY
866 Third Avenue, New York, New York 10022
COLLIER-MACMILLAN CANADA, LTD., TORONTO, ONTARIO

Printed in the United States of America

The editor is grateful to the authors and publishers of the following articles for permission to reprint:

Bernice Boehm, "Protective Services for Neglected Children," *Social Work Practice*, 1967. Copyright © 1967, National Conference on Social Welfare, Columbus, Ohio.

Harriet C. Wilson, "Problem Families and the Concept of Immaturity," *Case Conference*, Vol. 6, No. 5 (October 1959).

Leontine R. Young, "An Interim Report on an Experimental Program of Protective Service," *Child Welfare*, Vol. 45 (July, 1966).

Edith Varon, "Communication: Client, Community, and Agency." Reprinted with permission of the National Association of Social Workers, from *Social Work*, Vol. 9, No. 2 (April, 1964), pp. 51–57.

Paul E. Weinberger and Peggy J. Smith, "The Disposition of Child Neglect Cases Referred by Caseworkers to a Juvenile Court," *Child Welfare*, Vol. 45 (October, 1966).

Joseph B. Kelly, "What Protective Services Can Do," *Child Welfare*, Vol. 38 (April, 1959).

Jane McFerran, "Parents' Groups in Protective Services," *Children*, Vol. 5 (November–December, 1958).

Children's Aid Society of New York, "Nine- to Twenty-four-Hour Homemaker Service Project," *Child Welfare*, Vol. 41 (March–April, 1962).

Bessie Mae Jones, "A Demonstration Homemaker Project," *Child Welfare*, Vol. 43 (March, 1964).

Irene L. Arnold and Lawrence Goodman, "Homemaker Services to Families with Young Retarded Children," *Children*, Vol. 13 (July–August, 1966).

Miriam Shames, "Use of Homemaker Service in Families That Neglect Their Children." Reprinted with permission of the National Association of Social Workers, from *Social Work*, Vol. 9, No. 1 (January, 1964), pp. 12–18.

John Hansen and Kathryn Pemberton, "Day Care Services for Families with Mothers Working at Home," *Child Welfare*, Vol. 42 (April, 1963).

Elizabeth K. Radinsky, "Followup Study on Family Day Care Services," *Child Welfare*, Vol. 43 (June, 1964).

Frank A. Foley, "Family Day Care for Children," *Children*, Vol. 13 (July–August, 1966).

F. Davidson, "Day-Care Centres in Paris and Its Suburbs," World Health Organization, *Public Health Papers*, No. 24.

Kenneth Dick, "What People Think About Foster Care," *Children*, Vol. 8 (March–April, 1961).

John Wakeford, "Fostering—A Sociological Perspective," *The British Journal of Sociology*, Vol. 14, No. 4 (December, 1963).

Patricia Garland, "Public Assistance Families: A Resource for Foster Care," *Child Welfare*, Vol. 40 (September, 1961).

Martin Wolins, "The Problem of Choice in Foster Home Finding." Reprinted with permission of the National Association of Social Workers, from *Social Work*, Vol. 4 (October, 1959), pp. 40–48.

Eliezer D. Jaffe, "Correlations of Differential Placement Outcome for Dependent Children in Israel," *Social Service Review*, Vol. 41 (December, 1967).

H. F. Dingmam, C. D. Windle, and S. J. Brown, "Prediction of Child-Rearing Attitudes," *Child Welfare*, Vol. 41 (September, 1962).

David Fanshel, "Specializations Within the Foster Parent Role: A Research Report," Vol. 40 (March, 1961).

Mignon Sauber, "Preplacement Situations of Families, Data for Planning Services," *Child Welfare*, Vol. 46 (October, 1967).

Shirley Jenkins, "Duration of Foster Care: Some Relevant Antecedent Variables," *Child Welfare*, Vol. 46 (October, 1967).

Walter Ambinder, Laura Fireman, Douglas Sargent, and David Wineman, "Role Phenomena and Foster Care for Disturbed Children," *American Journal of Orthopsychiatry*, Vol. 32, No. 1 (January, 1962), pp. 32–39. Copyright the American Orthopsychiatric Association, Inc. Reproduced by permission.

Walter J. Ambinder and Douglas A. Sargent, "Foster Parents' Techniques of Management of Preadolescent Boys' Deviant Behavior," *Child Welfare*, Vol. 44 (February, 1965).

Alfred Kadushin, "The Legally Adoptable, Unadoptable Child," *Child Welfare*, Vol. 37 (December, 1958).

Elizabeth G. Meier, "Current Circumstances of Former Foster Children," *Child Welfare*, Vol. 44 (April, 1965).

Kenneth W. Watson and Harold Boverman, "Preadolescent Foster Children in Group Discussions," *Children*, Vol. 15 (March–April, 1968).

Elizabeth Herzog and Rose Bernstein, "Why So Few Negro Adoptions?" *Children*, Vol. 12 (January–February, 1965).

Donald Brieland, "An Experimental Study of the Selection of Adoptive Parents at Intake," Child Welfare League of America, New York (May, 1969).

Trudy Bradley, "An Exploration of Caseworkers' Perceptions of Adoptive Applicants," *Child Welfare*, Vol. 45 (October, 1966).

Velma L. Jordan and William F. Little, "Early Comments on Single-Parent Adoptive Homes," *Child Welfare*, Vol. 45 (November, 1966).

Chicago Region Child Care Association, "Subsidized Adoption." Published by Child Care Association of Illinois, 1518 Fifth Avenue, Moline, Ill. 61265.

Harvey L. Gochros, "A Study of the Caseworker-Adoptive Parent Relationship in Postplacement Services," *Child Welfare*, Vol. 46 (June, 1967).

H. David Kirk, "A Dilemma of Adopted Parenthood: Incongruous Role Obligations," *Journal of Marriage and the Family*, Vol. 21, No. 4 (November, 1959), pp. 316–26.

Jerome D. Goodman, Richard M. Silberstein, and Wallace Mandell, "Adopted Children Brought to Child Psychiatric Clinic," *Archives of General Psychiatry*, Vol. 9 (November, 1963).

Lilian Ripple, "A Follow-Up Study of Adopted Children," *Social Service Review*, Vol. 42 (December, 1968).

Alfred Kadushin, "Reversibility of Trauma: A Follow-Up Study of Children Adopted When Older." Reprinted with permission of the National Association of Social Workers, from *Social Work*, Vol. 12, No. 4 (October, 1967), pp. 22–23.

Catherine R. Collier and Anne Campbell, "A Post-adoption Discussion Series," *Social Casework*, Vol. 41 (April, 1960).

Edith M. Chappelear and Joyce E. Fried. "Helping Adopting Couples Come to Grips with Their New Parental Roles," *Children*, Vol. 14 (November–December, 1967).

Reprinted with permission from Anthony I. Schuham, Rodney M. Coe and Naomi I. Rae-Grant, "Some Social-Psychological Variables Influencing Parental Acceptance of Residential Treatment for Their Emotionally Disturbed Children," *Journal of Child Psychology and Psychiatry*, Vol. 5 (1964). Reprinted by permission of Pergamon Press.

Howard W. Polsky, "Changing Delinquent Subcultures: A Social-Psychological Approach." Reprinted with permission of the National Association of Social Workers, from *Social Work*, Vol. 4, No. 4 (October, 1959).

Irving Piliavin, "Conflict Between Cottage Parents and Caseworkers," *Social Service Review*, Vol. 37 (January, 1963).

Armin Klein, Ellin Kofsky and William Klien, "Behavior and Its Changes in the Residential Treatment of Children: A Preliminary Report," *Psychotherapy*, Vol. 3 (1966).

Henry S. Maas, "The Young Adult Adjustment of Twenty Wartime Residential Nursery Children," *Child Welfare*, Vol. 42 (February, 1963).

Rosalyn Saltz, "Evaluation of a Foster-Grandparent Program," Merrill Palmer Institute, Detroit, Michigan (May, 1967).

Alvin E. Winder, Lindo Ferrini, and George E. Gaby, "Group Therapy with Parents of Children in a Residential Treatment Center," *Child Welfare*, Vol. 44 (May, 1965).

Martin Wolins, "Another View of Group Care," *Child Welfare*, Vol. 44 (January, 1965).

# Preface

THERE are currently available several textbooks on child welfare services. The texts are useful for teaching in-service and university courses in child welfare and for providing a source of information for interested practitioners. However, no textbook can do justice to the wealth of material on child welfare. The relevant materials are widely scattered in conference proceedings, in technical journals representing a wide assortment of professions, in government publications, and in the reports of special meetings. It was felt that a sourcebook which conveniently made available the most pertinent of this material would be a helpful supplementary tool for those interested in teaching and learning about child welfare. It is also anticipated that the wider familiarity with such writings will help develop a deeper understanding and appreciation of the activities of child welfare services.

At the outset a fundamental distinction needs to be made between a child-development sourcebook and a child welfare services sourcebook. Admittedly there is some overlap, but the child-development sourcebook emphasizes research concerned primarily with the biological, psychological, and social development of the child. The child welfare sourcebook, on the other hand, emphasizes research concerned primarily with the antecedents, concomitants, and consequences of child welfare services offered to children as well as research regarding the nature of such services.

Piaget's material on the development of children's patterns of thinking, the research by Spitz on the smiling response of children, and Sears' work on identification in childhood would be appropriate for a child-development reader but inappropriate for a reader on child welfare services. The development, however, of children (child development) living in an institution (child welfare service) is a point at which these two areas can overlap.

Having distinguished between a child-development and a child welfare services sourcebook, one must distinguish between the general activities which affect the welfare of children and the more restricted activities of child welfare services.

Selection of material for the sourcebook was based on a definition of child welfare services within the context of the profession of social work. It is primarily concerned with child welfare services performed by those who are child welfare social workers and who are employed by institutions. organizations, and agencies under social work auspices. This, however, is only a beginning in defining parameters. Within the profession of social work itself there is considerable controversy over what child welfare service is, or what it should be. Some see the principal responsibility of child welfare social work as a concern with those children and families struggling with particular problems for which particular child welfare services are an appropriately helpful response. Others see the responsibility of child welfare social work as studying, understanding, and changing the basic socioeconomic pathologies which adversely affect all children in all families. Some champion a "residual" approach to service and focus concern on those children in families where there is some breakdown in normal functioning; others advocate an "institutional" orientation to child welfare services and see such services as "social utilities" required for all children in all families. Some see a specialized concern with the child's welfare as encouraging fragmentation; they prefer a wider approach centering on the family, of which the child is only one member.

There is controversy regarding the way in which the variety of child welfare services might best be categorized. Some prefer a dual categorization of (1) "services to children in their own home," which covers day care, homemaker service, protective services, family-agency or child-guidance-clinic services and income-maintenance programs, and (2) "services to children outside their own home," which includes foster-family care, adoptions, and institutionalization. Others, including the Child Welfare League of America, prefer a breakdown in terms of supportive services (family service, child-guidance clinic, protective services), supplementary services (day care, homemaker service, income-maintenance service), and substitute service (foster-family care, adoption, institutional child care).

There is controversy about the organization of delivery of service and about the relative balance of child welfare social work professionals, paraprofessionals, and aides.

Some previously controversial questions have been resolved. There seems to be, for instance, general agreement that child welfare social workers should be multiskilled, part caseworker, part group worker, and if not a community organizer, at least perceptive and sensitive to factors in the client's situation which need community organization attention. However, some controversial questions of concern to the general field of social work are given little attention in the child welfare social work literature. There is, as yet, little debate about the relative efficacy of a psychoanalytically oriented approach as compared with behavioral modification procedures as these relate to child welfare services..

The sourcebook reflects a residual, child- and family-change orientation following the Child Welfare League's categorization of services (supportive, supplementary, substitutive) rather than an "institutional," social-action orientation based on some alternative categorization of service. This is primarily a consequence of the fact that any sourcebook or reader reflects what is available in the literature, and what is available in the literature is based on yesterday's (or at best, today's) practice. It also reflects, in part, the prejudice of the editor.

While fighting for what is best for all children, we should do our best for those limited groups of children for whom we have been assigned responsibility and for whom the profession is accountable. We recognize that the welfare of the child is related to the welfare of the family, which in turn is related to the welfare of the local community, the state, the nation, and the world. However, a specialized focus on the child, through child welfare social work services, is legitimate in that it makes for conceptual clarity and an accrual of practical wisdom and cumulative knowledge derived from experience in working with a particular group of clients who have similar characteristics and problems. Such specialization provides a "workable focus for directing social work practice efforts." It provides a limited concern of primary responsibility which permits the development of a professional level of competence.

Child welfare social workers may in the near future become undifferentiated staff members of multiservice neighborhood centers serving the family, and through the family the child, in an unfragmented manner by providing coordinated, integrated services. However, the services discussed in this sourcebook will be among the services that will be needed in the new service system. The skills required to help the client use such services effectively will be the skills the child welfare social worker (or whatever his new designation) will need to have learned, perhaps through source material included here.

Whatever the future nature of the service delivery system, the deployment of welfare personnel, the administrative arrangements, the designation applied to the workers, the social policies implemented, and social utilities available, the problems faced by families with children will continue, with changing emphasis, to be essentially those encountered today. Despite any envisioned changes it is likely that protective services, day care, home-maker service, adoption, foster-family care, institutional care, and parent–child counseling will be among the services that child welfare social workers will be called on to provide.

It is true that the present residually focused, case-oriented child welfare system serves only a very limited segment of the nation's children. The desirable response is not to abolish the services that have been developed and that are discussed in this sourcebook, but to extend them to all those children who might, and can, use these services and who are presently not being reached.

The services included for discussion here are not all the services necessary for implementing an effective and comprehensive social-planning blueprint for the welfare of children. Although they are not in themselves sufficient to meet the needs of children, each of these services will be a necessary unit of any all-embracing plan which might ultimately be established. Such services are among some of the essential building blocks for a more comprehensive edifice for the welfare of children. Hence, attention to such specialized services is desirable.

These considerations suggest the general point of view which guided selection of the contents of the sourcebook. There were some other, more specific, kinds of criteria which determined the exclusion of some articles and inclusion of others. Recency of publication, availability, concern for diversification both as to source and content, originality, and general applicability of content were among the criteria for inclusion. The most important criteria, however, were research orientation and concern for factual specificity. Many articles in the field make general statements of dubious validity, use words and terms imprecisely, and enumerate conclusions categorically. Those articles which reported research or attempted to cite research in the presentation were given preference. Many undergraduate and graduate social work students are more scholarly than is the literature of the field, and they are impatient with and irreverent toward it. Consequently, selection of material reflected an effort to emphasize available research regarding each of the child welfare services. This principal criterion for selection is based on a conviction that if we as child welfare social work practitioners are to become truly professional, if we are to do our job in the most efficient and most effective manner and do it more competently than anyone else, then we need valid generalizations based on research. Without such content, professional schools of social work are a sham and professional training for child welfare social work is a deception.

Although primary emphasis in selection has been on research orientation, secondary criteria have dictated giving some preference to productive new approaches to child welfare services, to the multimethod responsibility of the child welfare worker, and to widening perspectives by including some of the child welfare experience of other countries. An ideal article for selection in terms of these criteria would be a research study of a multimethod approach in the perspective of our own experience as compared with that of other countries.

Although our principal audience is the child welfare social worker and the student preparing for such employment, this audience has not been our exclusive concern. The sourcebook is also of value to the intelligent, community-conscious laymen concerned with services to children and to professionals in other fields—medicine, law, nursing, teaching—whose own work brings them in contact with child welfare services.

A tentative listing of contents for the sourcebook was originally sent to some forty teachers, consultants, practitioners, researchers, and administrators in the child welfare field. These included people affiliated with public and private agencies here and in England. A request was made that they review the tentative listing, critically evaluate the proposed reader content, and suggest alternative desirable items for inclusion. Some 70 per cent of the group responded with suggestions. On the basis of these responses the listing was revised and reduced.

I should like very much to thank Mildred Arnold, Earl Beatt, Samuel Berman, Donald Brieland, Dorothy Daly, David Fanshel, Ursula Gallagher, Beatrice Garrett, Paul Glasser, Martin Gula, Norman Herstein, Elizabeth Herzog, Gertrude Hoffman, Gladys Lawson, Henry Maas, Bernice Madison, Henry Maier, Elizabeth Mansfield, Norman Polansky, Leon Richman, Mignon Sauber, Olive Stevenson, Milton Willner, Corinne Wolfe, and Martin Wolins. They were extremely helpful; any mistakes in rejecting suggestions are exclusively my own.

*A. K.*

# Contents

## Section IV
## Adoption Services

## Section V
## The Child-Caring Institution

# Section I

## Protective Services

ONE OF THE MOST frequently encountered problems faced by child-welfare social workers is the problem of neglect. Indeed a nation-wide study of child-welfare problems conducted by the federal government within the past decade came to the conclusion that it was the single most important child-welfare problem. Protection of children from physical, social, and emotional neglect is the responsibility of protective services. It is a very difficult assignment. Parents are frequently neglectful because they themselves are deprived, harassed, overburdened. Protective services are most effective in serving children through meeting parental needs. But many of these parents offer limited personal, social, and economic potentialities with which to build a healthier family environment for children. Their attitude toward the child-welfare service worker frequently reflects a generous measure of distrust, hostility, resistance, and limited motivation. Work with these families generally requires a modification of traditional social-work approaches in the direction of more concrete services, more explicit expectation, more direct advice. It requires easy accessibility to, and availability of, a rich network of community resources and services. The problem is made more complex for the child-welfare worker because of the need in protective services to exercise authority in protecting the child and because the community is undecided as to the equitable balance between the privileges of parents and the rights of children.

There is a growing recognition that many children suffer from community neglect of damaging social conditions that are deleterious to healthy growth and development. Congressional investigations and reports by concerned citizens testify to the existence of childhood malnutrition and starvation as a consequence of community neglect.

One instance of community neglect is the failure to make available explicit protective services to all children. Currently, many areas of the country lack child-welfare workers with an assigned protective-service function. The police frequently fill the gap created by community neglect. The 1962 Social Security amendments, however, require that all states have a plan for protective services for all children operational by 1975.

Child abuse has been a focus of considerable concern during the past few years. Supported by a widespread consensus, which is rare in dealing with any social problem, a law was passed in every state within a three-year period making it mandatory that professionals officially report any instance of suspected abuse. Recent statistics indicate that although the community is right to be concerned about any and every instance of child abuse, this actually is a problem affecting only a very limited number of children—some 6,000 in 1967.[1] It is a dramatic problem and is

---

[1] David Gil, *Nationwide Survey of Legally Reported Physical Abuse of Children*, No.

one that is highly visible rather than extensive. The readings, therefore, focus on neglect as the principal concern to child-welfare social workers in protective-service agencies.

15, Papers in Social Welfare, Florence Heller Graduate School for Advanced Studies in Social Welfare, Brandeis University, 1968.

# 1

❰ The following research study explores the attitudes of influential groups in the community regarding the situations they considered to require protective services. In further refining the definition of neglect, the study reviewed the neglect complaints actually received over a period of time. This indicated the nature of the situation and the kind of family actually viewed by the community as neglectful.

# Protective Services
# for Neglected Children

*Bernice Boehm*

The problem of neglect and abuse has been identified as our most important child welfare problem and a major cause for placement of children in foster care In a nationwide survey by the U.S. Children's Bureau, neglect was found to be the principal problem for 43 percent of all children in foster care under public auspices and for 17 percent of those in foster care under voluntary auspices; it appeared among the first three problems for almost 50 percent of all children receiving child welfare services from public agencies and for more than 20 percent of those who were receiving services from voluntary agencies.[1] The growing concern over child neglect has resulted in new protective legislation and in the rapid development of protective services, primarily under public auspices/ although many communities offer little more than lip service. This poses an imperative need for an expansion of knowledge and substantive research in the area of neglect to enable social workers to carry the heavy responsibility for decision-making that is inherent in protective services; and to develop models of family behavior which can serve as a framework for the assessment of family functioning in determining the extent of neglect and in considering the potential need for removal of the child from his family.

Research in protective services was carried out in the Twin Cities, Minneapolis and St. Paul,[2] a large urban area with a population of more than

---

[1] Helen R. Jeter, *Children, Problems, and Services to Child Welfare Programs* (Washington, D.C.: U.S. Government Printing Office, 1963), pp. 2, 4, and 5.

[2] The research was carried out under the auspices of the Minnesota Department of Public Welfare and financed by the National Institute of Mental Health, Applied Research Branch, Project MH 596–02.

4

a million. Protective legislation in Minnesota is broad and comprehensive and makes it mandatory to channel complaints of child neglect or abuse through the welfare department for investigation and treatment. This enabled the researchers to secure complete coverage of neglect complaints, active cases, and decision-making in protective situations during the period of study.

In protective services a heavy responsibility for decision-making rests with the social worker, since the request for service does not come from the family itself but results from community concern about the mistreatment or inadequate care of the child. This process conflicts with strongly held values and cherished legal rights against the invasion of privacy; and intervention requires authorization by legislation or by special charters granted to voluntary agencies.

Throughout the period of service, the social worker is faced with a vital question and a critical decision. Can the family be helped to improve its pattern of child rearing, or is the situation so hazardous to the child that plans must be made to remove him from the home? The responsibility for making such a decision is overwhelming, since placement may be necessary despite the opposition of the parent, and may entail initiation of legal action for custody or guardianship of the child. Because of the social control function of protective service, its legal enforcibility, bearing with it the potential for removal of the child from the family, the identification of the model of family functioning used for protective intervention and placement decisions is crucial.

These, then, were the focal questions of our research: How are decisions for placement made? What criteria are used by the social worker in determining whether or not placement is needed? How does he evaluate the adequacy of the family to continue the care of the child? Are such decisions reached on the basis of clearly determined criteria, or are they random, capricious decisions based on single pieces of behavior or individual judgment, and differing from worker to worker?

## THE ROLE OF THE COMMUNITY

Protective services operate as one part of a larger system, a system whose major components are the community, the family, the child, and the social agency. The first step in the sequence of decision-making rests with the community, since recognition of the existence of neglect and the request for service do not come from the client himself, but from the community. Thus the first step in decision-making has already been taken before the social agency enters into the situation.

Like other social services, protective service is both an expression of the humanitarian values of society and an exercise of social control, providing help to the child who is neglected, exploited, or abused as well as protection to society through the control of deviant behavior. Neglect, as a concept, is culturally defined, and each community identifies for itself, explicitly or implicitly, the child-rearing behaviors of which it disapproves and those which it considers harmful. Responsibility for the initial decision about the need for protective service rests first with the community when it perceives and refers situations to the agency in which it has vested the responsibility for protective action, and second with the agency which investigates the referral, determines whether protective intervention is needed, and decides upon the treatment plan for each family accepted for service. The crucial role of the community in this process is readily apparent. Through its selection of situations for referral to the protective agency it sets up the boundaries within which protective action can take place and establishes a culturally sanctioned definition of neglect that expresses the community's values, norms, and assumption of responsibility. The study of the community's definition of neglect, and its willingness to sanction protective intervention, thus became the first focus of the research.

In order to determine the kinds and types of situations which the community considered harmful to children and the kinds of situations in which protective intervention would receive support, questionnaires were mailed to a stratified sample of community groups that, experience showed, play a significant role in the referral and disposition of neglect complaints. This included professions concerned with child care: medicine, law, education, nursing, social work, the police, and the clergy, as well as community policy-makers, such as legislators and agency board members. The rate of response was 81 percent of the total, and approximately fourteen hundred completed questionnaires were used in the analysis of community attitudes.

The respondents were presented with vignettes typical of problems frequently found in protective referrals. Three general classifications were chosen: (1) situations involving physical neglect or abuse of a child; (2) situations of emotional neglect evidencing disturbance in the parent-child relationship, with overt manifestations of emotional disturbance in the child; (3) situations where the parents' behavior violated community norms and values, but where no emotional neglect, physical neglect, or abuse were apparent. The purpose of this inquiry was to determine the type of situation in which members of the community would approve of protective intervention, regardless of the family's resistance to seeking help.

Fairly clear patterns of community opinions and convictions emerged from these responses. There was strong consensus for protective action in situations involving physical hazard to the child. Situations involving emotional neglect drew equally strong consensus; however, a large majority opposed protective action.

Here are typical examples from each group.

> Mrs. Pitts has two daughters, ages 7 and 9. The children have lice and suffer from impetigo, an infectious skin disease. Mrs. Pitt has not kept clinic appointments or carried out the doctor's instructions.

This situation received the strongest support for protective intervention, with more than 80 percent of the respondents favoring intervention as a necessary action.

Let us contrast this with a situation illustrating emotional disturbance:

> Jerry, a boy of 11, keeps to himself at school, does not play with other children, and seldom speaks to anyone. His teachers consider him tense and troubled. The parents have been asked to take Jerry to a guidance clinic, but have refused to keep the appointments because they do not feel the boy is having serious problems.

Approximately 75 percent of the respondents were opposed to protective action in this case. Here are two situations in which evidence of damage already exists. In one, the children have an unpleasant but not serious physical ailment; in the other, a tense, severely withdrawn child has emotional problems that appear to be more severe than the medical problem posed by the little girls. Impetigo is contagious, however, and it is interesting to speculate upon the influence of this factor in the community's strong positive sanction for protective intervention. On the other hand, the long-range effects and community hazards resulting from the emotional disturbance of Jerry appear to be either less clearly perceived or of less concern. It is evident, then, despite the inclusion of "emotional neglect" in Minnesota's protective legislation, that the community does not consider this a significant factor in its formulation and use of the intervention model of family behavior, and provides little support or sanction for protective intervention when the child's emotional well-being is at stake.

The third type of situation, where parental delinquency and deviant behavior were present, and where socialization of the child rather than physical or emotional neglect was involved, received less sanction for protective action than might have been anticipated. Somewhat less than 50 percent of the respondents considered protective action necessary:

> Mrs. Young is a divorced woman with three children under school age. She is fond of the children and gives them good physical care. She is sexually promiscuous, however, and often has had men staying overnight at her apartment.

The community sanction for protective intervention was approved by only 45 percent of the respondents. However, several respondents stated that they endorsed protective action "only if she is receiving AFCD." This strange concept of a double standard of morality is most revealing.

*Characteristics of Referred Families.* The study of community attitudes had been based upon hypothetical cases focusing completely upon selected family behaviors. We next went to the agency to study the families who were actually referred for protective service. What were the characteristics of these families? Was there any linkage between these characteristics and the situations for which the community approved protective intervention?

Two major questions were explored: Do these families represent a cross section of the total population of the community, or do they differ from the general population in their family structure and socioeconomic characteristics as well as in their child-rearing behavior? What is the relationship between the demographic and socioeconomic characteristics of the families and the community's perception and appraisal of their behavior?

Within recent years more attention has been focused upon socioeconomic factors and their significance in shaping family functioning with particular reference to child-rearing patterns.[3] These factors have been shown to operate as cultural determinants, carrying with them prescribed value judgments, patterns of aspiration, and other patterns of social functioning. Although their major impact upon the child occurs through his experience within the primary family group, they also have a cumulative effect in providing him with both opportunity for, and restriction of, specific modes of behavior in the school among peer groups and in other secondary group memberships. Consequently, we might anticipate that the socioeconomic characteristics of the referred families would have implications for possible causal factors entering into the neglect or abuse of the child, or for the pattern of services needed by the child and his family.

The analysis for the total intake, numbering 183 complaints over a two-month period in the Twin Cities, showed a marked pattern of differentiation between the families involved in neglect complaints and the general population of the community. The preponderance of the neglect families came from the lowest socioeconomic strata, and differed from the general population in a significantly higher incidence of broken homes, minority group membership, lower income and education, substandard housing and neighborhood, and large family size. Although educated, economically advantaged families were also found among the referrals, these were the rare exceptions, and more likely to involve situations of physical abuse with overt manifestations of severe emotional disturbance.

---

[3] See Walter B. Miller, "Implications of Urban Lower-Class Culture for Social Work," *Social Service Review,* XXXIII (1959), 219–36; Herbert J. Gans, *The Urban Villagers* (New York: Free Press of Glencoe, 1962).

In our society the most typical family structure is the intact home in which the child lives with both parents. In the general population of the Twin Cities[4] 93 percent of the families with children under eighteen years of age consist of a home with two parents. In the neglect complaint families, on the other hand, only 40 percent have two parents in the home.

In the general population, only 3 percent of the families are dependent upon general relief or public assistance; in the neglect complaint families, 42 percent receive assistance. The preponderance of the population, both in the general community and in neglect families, is Caucasian, but the proportion of nonwhite neglect families is almost three times that in the general population. In the general population fewer than 10 percent of the husbands are in unskilled or service occupations; in the neglect families, more than 50 percent are in this occupational group. In the general population approximately 17 percent of the families live in a high-delinquency area;[5] in the neglect families, approximately 50 percent live in these areas. As might be anticipated from these statistics, the great majority of the families involved in the neglect complaints had had extensive contact with the welfare department and other social agencies prior to the current complaint.

The second step, then, in the community's perception and assessment of family inadequacy and its definition of the intervention model is to single out the families who belong to the lower socioeconomic strata in our society. The marked contrast between the socioeconomic status of the neglect families and that of the community in general raises the legitimate question of possible bias on the part of a predominantly middle-class group toward those of lower status. Do neglect complaints and protective intervention represent a tendency to interpret deviance from middle-class norms as pathological or harmful to the child when they may be, indeed, a reflection of differing subcultural practices and norms? This question, which the current research cannot answer, merits further consideration and research. However, it is important to recall the community's response to the questionnaire, since the selection of cases for protective intervention was based upon case illustrations from which all indication of socioeconomic status was deliberately omitted. The high priority accorded to physical neglect by the community for the intervention model inevitably results in the referral of families most vulnerable to this kind of problem, and in the selection of families where neglect is most visible.

The families have often been referred to as "multiproblem families"; but perhaps it would be more relevant to the issue of child neglect to describe them as "multiple-stress families," since life in the great major-

---

[4] Data based upon U.S. Census of 1960.
[5] Based upon census tract statistics for juvenile arrests.

ity of these families follows an involved, multidimensional pattern of stress. The stress and hardship caused by inadequate income are too obvious to require discussion. In addition, there are also stresses resulting from minority group membership, high delinquency environment, low job status, marital tension, and the stigma attached by the community to the status of relief client. Furthermore, when these stresses are compounded by the psychological stress inherent in the one-parent family, where the mother assumes the total responsibility for management, guidance, and physical care, lacking adequate emotional as well as financial support, the resultant stress is often overwhelming. However, little attention has been given to the alleviation of stress in such families, even though their prevalence in neglect caseloads marks them as a group of high vulnerability.

## PLACEMENT DECISIONS

In order to study the criteria used in reaching decisions for the separation of child and family in cases of child neglect, we went directly to the protective service agencies in the Twin Cities, and studied actual decisions rather than hypothetical cases. The basic data for the study were secured from 200 active neglect cases: 100 children who were separated from their families after the study began; and 100 children whose placement was not under consideration since the social worker believed it possible to work effectively within the family setting. The placement cases were not preselected but were taken in consecutive order as placement occurred until the desired number was reached. The nonplacement cases, on the other hand, were selected from the caseloads of the same workers who were responsible for the placement cases, and were matched as closely as possible to the placement cases by age and sex. The nonplacement cases were classified by the workers into two levels of adequacy: families who were "reasonably adequate" and families who were "marginal." Nonplacement cases were included only if they had been active with the agency for six months or more, so that there would have been sufficient contact with the family to reach a decision against placement.

Two major assumptions guided this study. First, we assumed that although criteria for evaluation of family inadequacy had not yet been made explicit, there was a likelihood that implicit criteria might be evident in the decisions of the social workers. Second, we assumed, because of general social work values, and the explicit practice philosophy voiced by the agency, that a child would be separated from his family only when the hazards to his welfare were considered too great to permit him to remain in his own home. Thus, the comparison between the placement and nonplacement cases would be based upon the workers' assessment of parental adequacy, and would yield the general dimensions used in the assessment of family adequacy as well as identify the crucial dimensions involved in the placement decision.

Only brief mention can be made here of the methodology used in comparing the placement and nonplacement cases. Families were rated on behavioral items drawn from lists submitted by workers in the protective agencies and selected from their own caseloads. These lists, originally containing approximately 2500 items, were reduced to 140 items through elimination of similar or duplicate behaviors. The process used for rating was the Q-sort,[6] which required the workers to select a specified number of items in five categories ranging from behaviors "most like the family" to those "most unlike the family." This enabled us to assign a numerical value of 1 through 5 for each item, and to determine differential scores and profiles for each family.

In order to reach a level of generality which could not be provided by individual item behaviors, these items were then subjected to factor analysis[7] to determine whether or not the correlation among items could identify clusters that could be grouped into recognizable behavioral patterns or dimensions. The large number of behaviors rated by the caseworkers of these 200 families was found to yield 12 discrete behavioral dimensions. These factors or behavioral dimensions then classified for us the kinds of general behavioral patterns that.caseworkers look at when they assess neglect, and the kinds of questions they ask themselves in deciding on the level of adequacy of specific families. The content of these behavioral factors is revealing and answers our first question: Do social workers base their decisions on a global adjustment of family adequacy, or are there generalizable but definable criteria which they consider important and use as a basis for decision-making?

Each factor or behavioral dimension consisted of several items. Two factors deal with general family behavior. The first concerns household management: Is the home clean? Are the children adequately nourished and clothed? Do they receive good physical care and appropriate discipline? The second deals with the family's insight into the problem: Does the family have an understanding of its problem? Does the family cooperate with the agency in trying to improve its child-rearing practices? We found that placement cases had significantly lower scores on these factors than the nonplacement cases.

The next four behavioral factors deal specifically with the behavior of the father. The first has been termed "interest and affection of the father": Does the father show interest and involvement with his family and a desire to keep the family together? The second concerns delinquent behavior on the part of the father: Is his behavior characterized by alco-

---

[6] For a more detailed description of this methodology, see William Stephenson, *The Study of Behavior* (Chicago: University of Chicago Press, 1953); Norman A. Polansky, "Techniques for Ordering Cases," in Polansky, ed., *Social Work Research* (Chicago: University of Chicago Press, 1960), pp. 164–66.

[7] Since the factors reproduce the common variance of the initial set of items, this reduces the data to a smaller set of variables with a minimum loss of information.

holism and sexual promiscuity? The third has been termed "impulse control of the father": Does the father evidence physical violence toward his wife and children? The fourth concerns the father's over-all emotional adjustment: Does he show signs of marked emotional disturbance with internalized symptoms of depressed, withdrawn behavior? Of the four factors dealing with the father, only the first plays a part in the placement decision. Families who score low on this factor are highly likely to have children who go into placement. Otherwise, the father's behavior shows no difference between the two groups and thus may be assumed to have no significant effect upon the placement decision.

Four factors describing behavior of the mother show a close similarity to those used to evaluate the father's behavior. The first of these has to do with the mother's interest and affection for the family: Does the mother lack motivation or desire for keeping the family together? Does she seem overwhelmed by her family responsibility? The second factor deals with the mother's acting-out behavior: Does she show evidences of sexual promiscuity or alcoholism? The third factor deals with the mother's impulse control: Does she exhibit hostile, punitive behavior toward the children? The fourth maternal factor deals with the mother's emotional disturbance: Does she show signs of severe depression or withdrawn behavior? Although these questions closely parallel those that are asked about the father, we find that evaluation of the mother, unlike that of the father, plays a very strong role in the decision for placement. And children in the placement group come from families that have a significantly lower score on every aspect of maternal behavior than do the children in the nonplacement group, except for delinquent behavior of the mother which appears to play no part in the placement decision.

It is particularly important to emphasize the important role of maternal behavior. Obviously, these results indicate that primacy in reaching the decision for placement is given to the question of whether or not the children are getting good maternal care. The father's behavior has far less significance in determining whether or not the child can remain with his family. This is true regardless of whether the father is in the home or out of the home. In fact, in many instances when the child is in a two-parent family, and the decision is made to leave him in his own home, the worker is likely to classify this as a "marginal" situation. It is almost as if the worker were asking: "Why should neglect exist in a home where there are two parents, and the stress of the one-parent home is not present?" We have already spoken of the fact that the majority of families referred for protective service come from one-parent families. When we find that the decision for a placement is based largely on an evaluation of the maternal care of the child, we gain additionally strong reinforcement for our conviction that more study and help are essential for the purpose of strengthening family functioning in the one-parent family, and for developing a creative, readily available community-support system for alleviation of financial, environmental, and psychological stresses inherent in the single-parent family.

The remaining two factors concern the behavior of the children. These show a gross division into two major patterns: the neurotic child, characterized by withdrawn or frightened behavior; and the acting-out child whose behavior is characterized by delinquency. It is of interest to note that neither of these dimensions plays any part in the placement decision, and the placed and nonplaced children show no significant differences in the incidence of behavior problems of either sort.

As a second step in the caseworker's assessment of family adequacy, we sought to discover whether the behavioral dimensions that entered into the placement decision would also enter into the worker's placement plan, and the prognosis for the duration of placement. At the time of placement, the caseworkers were asked to classify each case into one of three categories:

1. The child will need temporary placement of less than one year.
2. The child will need placement for longer than one year, but will probably eventually return to his family.
3. The child will need permanent placement until he is self-sufficient or is placed into adoption.

The following research questions were posed: Is there a constant relationship between the scores on the behavioral scales and the length of time that the child is considered to require placement? Do the families where placement is seen as a temporary measure for less than one year show more "desirable" behavior, as indicated by scores on the twelve factors, than the families where placement will be needed for a longer period, or where placement is seen as a permanent measure? Our assumption was that prognosis of the duration of placement would also be a reflection of family adequacy and could be measured by the same behavioral scales that differentiated between the placement and nonplacement cases. In essence, we were trying to refine our assessment model so that it would show varying levels along a continuum of family adequacy.

We found, however, that the three prognoses for duration of placement differed significantly on only one behavioral dimension. This was the scale that measured the mother's affection for the children and her desire to keep the family together. This would indicate that the major behavioral determinant affecting the perceived length of placement is the social worker's assessment of the mother's desire to have the child returned to her, or else a function of attributes not measured by the behavior scales that enter into the original decision for placement.

## MODELS OF FAMILY BEHAVIOR

When the study was first begun it was entitled, "The Family Adequacy Study." Now we speak of "family inadequacy." The transition from one to the other may seem a small thing, but it answers an important question which had been an issue since we began to consider decisions in protective service. A basic question that required exploration concerned the model of family behavior which was to serve as the framework for evaluating each family. Obviously, we cannot use the "ideal" family as a frame of reference or evaluate families by their deviation from ideal parental behavior. The "ideal family" could not serve as the bench mark for evaluation since social work, in serving families where neglect already existed, had to determine whether or not the inadequacies were of such a nature as to preclude the possibility of healthful development for the child.

Many models of healthy family functioning have been developed by family sociologists, and these include a far wider range of behavior than those which entered into the evaluation of the families in the protective caseloads. Models of healthy family functioning stress the significance of good marital relationships, sound economic functioning, good sibling relationships, and participation in community activities. Such models of family behavior might be called "aspiration models," since they express our aspirations for healthy family functioning. Most of us would agree, however, that inadequacies in most of these areas would not be justifiable grounds for protective action, nor would they enter into the definition of neglect. It would be highly unlikely that unemployment, financial need, lack of community participation, or even an unhappy marriage would be considered as valid grounds for a "neglect complaint" and recommendation for protective services.

In contrast, the intervention model consists only of behavior relating to the child-rearing functions of the family, and community sanction for protective intervention is given only with regard to relatively gross, and presumably hazardous, inadequacies in child-rearing behaviors. It is apparent from the behavioral dimensions used by the social workers for evaluation that they had this charge clearly in mind.

Emphasis has been placed upon the need for middle-range theory in social work, having a closer relationship to the problem-solving tasks of the profession, than might be found in theory on a higher level of abstraction. The present research would bear this out, indicating that in the assessment of family adequacy it becomes important to raise the question: "Adequate for what?" The contrast between the intervention model with its limited range of behaviors and the more generalized models of family functioning which encompass the total range of desirable family behaviors is striking, and the two types of family models should be used differentially in accordance with the auspice, purpose, and social-control function of the service that is being enforced or sought by the agency. The intervention model to be used for family assessment in protective services differs sharply from the model used in assessment and determination of service goals in an agency where the family voluntarily seeks help on problems of family functioning. To be sure, the protective case may, in the course of service, evolve into one where broader goals may be sought and the scope and purpose of services widened. Here the aspiration model may become relevant to the purpose at hand and the assessment of the family. However, the expansion of goals and services can be justified only if the family itself is in accord with the change in the scope and purpose of the service, and cannot be enforced under the guise of "protective service."

It also becomes apparent that the concept of family adequacy is not a unitary concept; that is, adequacy and inadequacy cannot be measured as different points on a continuum. There are attributes entering into the assessment of inadequacy, attributes such as physical violence of the parent or delinquent behavior of the parent, which can only be used to measure the extent of family inadequacy, whereas *non*delinquent behavior or *non*violence cannot be quantified to assess levels of family adequacy. In the adequate family it is only important that these behaviors be *nonexistent*.

Industrial research has shown that the attributes which measure job satisfaction are often quite different from those which measure job dissatisfaction.[8] For example, financial compensation is a factor that applies to both satisfaction and dissatisfaction and varies directly with the job satisfaction-dissatisfaction continuum. On the other hand, the human relations aspects of the job, associated with working conditions and attitudes of co-workers, may be prime factors in the satisfaction and happiness of the worker but play little part in job dissatisfaction, and measurement of these factors will not vary directly along a job satisfaction-dissatisfaction continuum. However, in the assessment of family behaviors, we tend to think of family adequacy as measurable along a single continuum, sometimes using attributes for assessment which are irrelevant to the determination of family inadequacy for child-rearing. This may be tied in with the social workers' goals for providing each child with an opportunity to develop to his fullest potential, and may thus offer the temptation to use protective service in a manner that is unwarranted or incompatible with its legal enforcibility.

## IMPLICATIONS FOR SERVICE

The inputs that have gone into the actual placement decision made by the protective agency consist of the values held by the community and the

---

[8] See R. Carlson et al., *The Measurement of Employment Satisfaction* (Minneapolis: Industrial Relations Center, University of Minnesota, 1962).

social agency, and information derived from actual observation of the family and child as well as from other sources of factual data. However, it would be unfortunate if the decision process were to stop at this point. Each decision is not only an outcome of the decision-making process, but becomes input data for later decision-making, by providing feedback by which the decision can be monitored and evaluated. This becomes particularly important when the outcome decisions can be classified in a priority system of desirability. We have professed our conviction that it is preferable to retain a child in his own home, and our obligation to strengthen the home wherever possible so that it meets minimum standards of adequacy. It thus becomes imperative to consider the data that have provided the input for the decision to place the child. What clues or guidelines do they provide to patterns of service that can serve a preventive function, so that the family can be strengthened and the child kept in his own home?

The socioeconomic characteristics of the families and children most vulnerable to neglect and abuse have already been discussed, as well as their implications for family stress and breakdown. Creative measures are needed to provide the community support necessary to insure adequate parental functioning in such families. Perhaps the approaches used by the field of public health can suggest more effective directions for the delivery of preventive services. Although services such as homemaking and day care have been tried in protective cases, they have not been widespread and have met with limited success. In all instances, these services have been used within the traditional definition of protective services; that is, as treatment for families in which severe neglect has already occurred. A focus upon stress rather than problem would lead to a planned concentration of services for a vulnerable group and would require that these services be made readily available and easily accessible and that special efforts be made to demonstrate their value to the population at risk so that they will use the services on a voluntary basis. This approach is similar to the "public utility" approach strongly espoused by Kahn.[9]

The community and the social agency may indeed be wise in maintaining a stringent definition of neglect and in limiting involuntary protective intervention to the enforcement of minimum standards, since this protects strongly cherished values of individual freedom and enables the protective service to maintain the legal authority and backing necessary for effective functioning. It is to be hoped, of course, that the definition of neglect will undergo modification as new knowledge is acquired and demonstrated. The protection of children cannot be left entirely to protective service, however, since this service can be called into action only when dysfunctioning

---

[9] Alfred J. Kahn, *Planning Community Services for Children in Trouble* (New York: Columbia University Press, 1963).

is severe. Protection as a total concept goes beyond the limitations of neglect and protective service. It calls for a strong linkage between protective service and the other community health and welfare services so that special areas of stress and vulnerability can be identified and an effective network of resources and services can be provided to alleviate stress and to prevent neglect, or at least to treat the problem when it is still in an incipient stage.

# 2

❪ Based on a research study of neglectful families in England, the author discusses the usefulness of the concept of immaturity in "explaining" child neglect. As in Boehm's article the attempt here is to discuss the research findings on the socioeconomic characteristics of neglectful families.

# Problem Families and the Concept of Immaturity

*Harriett C. Wilson*

It is perhaps an advance in diagnostic thinking that the problem family is no longer explained primarily in terms of mental subnormality and temperamental instability (Blacker, 1952), but that, instead, the concept of immaturity has been introduced as the main causative determinant. Rankin (1958), for instance, says that "it would not be unreasonable if we describe problem families . . . as persons suffering from chronically unstable or abnormally immature personalities the effect of which is their 'problem family' status." Bodman (1958) states that "among professional social workers the concept of psychopathic personality is falling into disuse, and is in process of being replaced by the concept of emotional immaturity." Ratcliff (1958), in discussing personality factors in the problem family, speaks of a "pattern of immaturity" which he believes is fundamental. The problem is thus lifted out of the therapeutically sterile field of biological determinism and placed in the field of psychiatric understanding of personality, with much wider opportunities for treatment.

It may, perhaps, at this stage not be out of place to consider some of the difficulties that arise in using a concept such as that of immaturity. These appear to be on three levels. The first concerns a definition of the concept; the second its applicability to the group and its specificity; and the third concerns the function of immaturity in the problem family syndrome. The questions to be asked are:

1. What do we mean by immaturity in connection with problem families?
2. Is it a characteristic found in the group generally, and only in the group, but not elsewhere?
3. What role does this concept play as a causative influence? If immaturity is really found to exist generally in the group, does that *ipso facto* mean that it is the essential factor in family breakdown? Or, could what appears to be immaturity be interpreted as frustration reaction to external obstacles which are insurmountable?

It is at once obvious that the answer to the latter question depends to a large degree on the definition of the term immaturity; i.e., if used indiscriminately to include regression as well as emotional retardation the causal implications cannot be clearly stated.

A definition of the concept "immaturity" as generally used in this context has been offered by Ratcliff (1958). He says that members of problem families "seem not to learn very much from experience. They change quickly and easily in mood and attitude. They appear to be very susceptible to suggestions and ideas but unable to sustain those ideas for very long . . . I suspect that very often what workers have regarded as intellectual backwardness is really this pattern of immature behavior appearing so much out of keeping with 'what one would expect from people of that age.'" In another place Ratcliff also suggests that these families make incessant demands on various social agencies. The degree of immaturity shown by various members of the family varies considerably, not only from one person to another, but also from one life situation to another. For an understanding of the reasons for this immaturity Ratcliff offers the explanation of a childhood background of much insecurity. "They have received some mothering and mother-love, but they have experienced an unstable pattern of handling and attitudes with no very clear-cut relationship within which the child could identify and mould himself. They have known no really emotionally secure setting in which they could develop beyond a certain stage of maturity." It is obvious that Ratcliff's interpretation is that of inadequate gratification of early dependency needs which have led to arrested emotional development. This, he argues, can only be dealt with by some form of "satisfactory relationship therapy."

Ratcliff does not consider the alternative interpretation of problem-family behaviour as an expression of regressive responses to particular stress situations, an omission which, if generally accepted, would be of great importance in the future orientation of the social worker.

In an attempt to answer the first set of questions posed above, and in particular the question concerning specificity of the concept, we are hampered by lack of knowledge derived from a systematic investigation on the psychiatric level. All literature, so far, is impressionistic. On the basis of a sociological study of 52 families in Cardiff the writer would like to offer a number of observations on the sociological level which may aid discussion on the psychiatric level. The case material consisted of the hardest core of a total group of 157 families who had been referred to the Coordination Committee during the first three years of its existence. The method of selection and collection of information is described more fully elsewhere (Wilson, 1958). It appeared from this study that a large proportion of the families had to face extreme stress situations for considerable periods, which could not entirely or even partially be explained in terms of inevitable consequences of immature personalities. On the contrary, it appeared that in a number of cases external conditions were such that even the most mature and resourceful person would probably not be able to cope without support from outside the family. One of the more interesting results of this survey was that in the great majority of cases links with kin either had been severed, or no longer existed because of death or separation. There was, therefore, no relative who would perform the various supporting services in the family setting which are normally taken for granted.

The most important single factor that determines living patterns is the father's ability to work. Two fathers were old-age pensioners, two other families were fatherless. Of the remaining 48, 14 were physically disabled, and a further 13 suffered from chronic ill health. One was mentally deficient, and seven were receiving or had received treatment for mental illness. The remaining 13 were of normal health. While the physically disabled, the mentally deficient, and the mentally ill person presents his own problem of handicap, which has not yet found a happy solution in the community, it suffices to say here that it would be premature to tackle these sections within the problem-family group as in need of casework therapy. It may well be that the frustrations resulting from these disabilities in a setting of little, if any, material comfort gradually affect the parental personalities and bring about regressive characteristics. These cannot be dealt with any other way than by a good therapeutic relationship. But would it not be of greater importance at this stage to concentrate on the special needs arising out of these disabilities, and provide, for instance, sheltered work opportunities and routine supports for the families of these disabled men?

The 13 men suffering from ill-health may, on the other hand, be the type which is so often at present referred to as the emotionally retarded, the immature personality. In particular in the case of five men with duodenal and gastric ulcers, and possibly three with chronic chests, the indications are that there is a defence mechanism at work in an individual who cannot bear the responsibilities of adult life. It is interesting, however, that two of the men with ulcers do manage to keep a good work record, but one of them has eight, the other ten children to bring up.

The most interesting group is perhaps that of the men of good health who have, for some reason, managed to become the fathers of problem families. Are they immature? First of all, what do their work records tell us? Not one of the men in this group is permanently unemployed. Three of them have indifferent records, frequent changes interspersed with lengthy periods of unemployment. The indications here are that one of them, a man with frequent prison sentences for minor offences, is probably the immature type, and a second one, also with considerable spells of voluntary unemployment, might be. The third man works in the docks as a boiler scaler, a job which, while it lasts, brings in good money, but which also brings with it lengthy spells of unemployment. This man brings up 11 children.

There are ten men of good health who all show good steady work records. As far as their ability to shoulder the responsibilities of family maintenance is concerned we cannot consider them as immature. There are a number of indications that in these cases the primary reason for failure to cope is to be found either in the incapacity of the wife, or the large size of family. One mother of a family of eight children is mentally ill and has had treatment. Another one is mentally retarded, and four of her six children have had to be removed for neglect. There are three mothers (with five, six, and seven children respectively) who suffer from chronic ill-health. One is a diabetic who neglects her diet and has frequent blackouts, another has severe hernia, and the third has had treatment for anaemia and undernourishment. This leaves five men with good work records whose wives are of normal health.

In some ways this section is the most interesting sociologically, as it demonstrates most clearly the impact of economic stress on family life. They are all the families with the largest number of children, four of them having 11, and the fifth ten children. None of the men are of a calibre that would enable them to have a skilled occupation, and the incomes for the rather rougher types of unskilled labourer do not normally exceed £8-9 per week. The unskilled builders' labourer, for instance, who has little chance of overtime or bonus work, would normally bring home not more than £7 after deduction of insurance payments. He is also subject to the weather and long spells of unemployment in the winter. Family allowances for a family of, say, eight children under 15 add another £3 8s. If this family were on National Assistance, total income would exceed this. The payments of the National Assistance Board vary according to the ages of the children and rent; if, for instance, this family had two children under five, three children between the ages of five and 11, and three children between the ages of 11 and 16, and if the minimum of 16s. were paid towards rent, this family's total payments would be £11 12s., which is 24s. above the normal working income. We must assume that N.A.B. allowances are based on some estimate of a subsistence minimum. The income per head in the large family with a low-income earner is, therefore, substantially below subsistence level; how far below depends on numbers and ages of children.

The National Assistance Board has powers to deduct part of the allowances payable to an applicant so as to keep his spending income some 5s. to 10s. below his normal spending wage. The effect of this regulation on that section of men in the research set who were unemployed was that they, too, had to manage on incomes below subsistence level, and some of them on substantially lower ones. The plight of those on long-term state-maintained incomes has been discussed in this Journal by Shaw (1958) and Bowerbank (1958); none of the cases mentioned, however, were subject to the above-mentioned discretionary deductions. If it is so difficult, as Shaw says, "as to be nearly impossible to live within income on statutory allowances when the interruption to earnings has lasted for more than 12 months," then, one may ask, how much more difficult is it to live on an income which is below, and sometimes substantially below, that discussed by Shaw?

The first consideration, therefore, in such cases should be: is this family faced with an undue amount of economic strain which, through its insolubility, creates continuous frustration situations? If that is found to be the case, no amount of casework therapy with a bias towards situational adjustment can substantially alter the frustration situation. Towle (1955) stresses the importance of measures to relieve the sources of pressure and of strain so that the economic burden carried by an adult is more nearly commensurate with his capacity, as "it is generally agreed that lack of basic economic security heightens the stress of parenthood and intensifies relationship problems. One may expect in families where there is economic strain more regressive responses on the part of the parents. . . . Because the demands of adult life are likely to be more consistently inescapable than those in adolescence and because the personality is more rigidly formed, retreats to more satisfying life periods of the past may bring a more lasting fixation."

The third question posed at the beginning of this article—that concerning the functional role of the concept of immaturity—might, therefore, be answered in the following way. A parental attitude is frequently found in the group which closely resembles that of emotional retardation, but may be no more than a regressive response to economic and psychological strain. In many cases physical disabilities, mental handicaps, and economic insecurity have prevented the parent from developing an acceptable pattern of life and have exposed him to continuous frustration situations. Although it is very likely that in a number of cases the diagnosis would be that of emotional retardation due to emotional starvation in childhood, we cannot assume that this is always the case, and we cannot, therefore, accept the concept of immaturity as always being causally connected with the problem family syndrome.

The first set of questions—concerning the generality of immaturity and its specificity—is much more difficult to answer. If we say that an attitude resembling emotional retardation is frequently found among problem families, do we mean that such an attitude is not normally found in other families? Here again, we are handicapped by the fact that no comparative investigations have been undertaken. One thing is certain, and that is the fact that emotional retardation is not in itself sufficient cause for a problem-family way of living. The Cardiff findings suggest that one of the essential features by which the research set differed from the norm was the absence of kin in daily life and particularly in crisis situations. This could not always be seen as a by-product, so to speak, of immaturity, as it was not necessarily a break caused by friction, but in a number of cases it was due to death or distance. To end on a subjective note, we are all more or less immature in various life situations, and one of the external factors which retard maturation would be the absence of the comfort-giving figure in a crisis. This coupled with economic strain—caused by low income per head, or disabilities which cause long-term unemployment, or disabilities of the mother which necessitate frequent assistance from the father and therefore create a short wage packet—brings about a situation in which regressive processes work on a personality that may or may not already have traits of emotional retardation.

Finally, we should ask not only how far does the individual adjust to his environment, but how far does society provide the proper environment for the development of mental health? "A healthy society," in the words of Fromm (1956), "furthers man's capacity to love his fellow men, to work creatively, to develop his reason and objectivity, to have a sense of self which is based on the experience of his own productive powers. An unhealthy society is one which creates mutual hostility, distrust, which transforms man into an instrument of use and exploitation for others, which deprives him of a sense of self. . . ." Which environment is the one, we may ask, in which our problem-family fathers grow up?

## REFERENCES

Blacker, C. P. (Editor), 1952. Problem Families—Five Enquiries. London.
Bodman, F., 1958. *Case Conference*, 5, 99–104.
Bowerbank, M., 1958. *Case Conference*, 4, 283–287.

Fromm, E., 1956. The Sane Society. London.
Rankin, T. G., 1958. The Problem Family. I.S.T.D. London.
Ratcliff, T. A., 1958. The Problem Family. I.S.T.D. London.
Shaw, L., 1958. *Case Conference*, 4, 247–251.
Towle, C., 1955. Common Human Needs. American Association of Social Workers, New York.
Wilson, H. C., 1958. *British Journal of Delinquency*, 9, 94–104.

# 3

❪ The following article describes a program which integrates casework, group work, and education for protective-service families. The tentative findings of the experimental program are reported and indicate that much can be done to arrest family disorganization and prevent damage to the children.

# An Interim Report on
# an Experimental Program
# of Protective Service

*Leontine R. Young*

Family disorganization is increasingly recognized as one of the major social diseases of our time. Its roots are to be found in the interlocking and interacting elements that have created modern society, i.e., technology, urbanization, the population explosion, population mobility, and rapid social change. They have precipitated an increase in demands for success and achievement. The impact of these forces has understandably been greatest upon those groups least prepared for this acceleration of change and the resultant necessity for new adaptations.[1] Lack of education, poverty, and slums have been precipitating and interacting elements of a disorganization that encompasses almost every area of life, although this does not mean that every family living under these circumstances is necessarily dis-

---

[1] *The Negro Family: The Case for National Action* (Washington, D.C.: Office of Planning and Research, Department of Labor, 1965).

organized.[2] It does mean that any such family is exposed consistently to the virulence of its contagion and that many families will inevitably succumb to it. There is, of course, ample evidence that this has already happened.

If one accepts the premise that the family is the primary socializing institution of society, then its disorganization must produce a range of social, economic, and emotional ills. However diverse they may appear in form, substance, and effect, their etiology is interwoven into a common core. These ills add their own disintegrating influence to the existent disorganization and set up a cycle of deterioration. The family and its members make their own adaptations to a pathological environment; and, in turn, these adaptations add to the disorganization and a pathology of the environment. Even when these adaptations are functional in immediate terms for members of the family, they tend to be dysfunctional for the family as a unit and for the extended future.[3]

The life-style patterns of poverty-level families have been described by a growing number of studies;[4] and although there is general agreement about the broad configurations of these life styles, there are increasing warnings that it is probably erroneous to consider a single subculture of the poor. For example, Chilman has observed that "subcultures of poverty" is a better term than "culture of poverty."[5] Although research that distinguishes various ethnic, regional, religious, and nationality poverty groups from each other is generally lacking, it is more than likely that there are variations on the central theme of the subculture of poverty. And Herzog points out that "the culture of poverty is a very useful concept, if and only if it is used with discrimination, with recognition that poverty is a subculture, and with avoidance of the cookie-cutter approach."[6]

There is clear evidence that there are marked degrees of disorganization within the large faceless group known as "the poor." For some families within this group, lack of opportunity may be the predominant factor and access to opportunity the only needed cure. For other families, lack of opportunity may combine with varying degrees of inability to utilize oppor-

---

[2] Gordon F. Lewis, "Implications of the Sociological Concept of Security for Social Work Practice," *Social Casework*, XLVI (1965), 621–625; and Herbert J. Gans, "Redefining the Settlement's Function for the War on Poverty," *Social Work*, IX, No. 4 (1964), 3–12.

[3] Leonard Schneiderman, "Value Orientation Preferences of Chronic Relief Recipients," *Social Work*, IX, No. 3 (1964), 13–18.

[4] For an excellent comparison of child-rearing and family life patterns reported to be conducive to successful adaptation to our predominantly middle-class society with "child-rearing and family life patterns reported to be more characteristic of the very poor," see Catherine S. Chilman, "Social Work Practice with Very Poor Families," *Welfare in Review*, IV, No. 1 (1966), 13–22.

[5] Catherine S. Chilman, "Child-Rearing and Family Relationship Patterns of the Very Poor," *Welfare in Review*, III, No. 1 (1965), 9.

[6] Elizabeth Herzog, "Some Assumptions about the Poor," *Social Service Review*, XXXVII (1963), 395.

tunity, at least without special help. It is with this latter group of families that this project—instituted in the fall of 1962—is concerned.

## FAMILIES IN THE PROJECT

The families studied in this project demonstrate many behaviors common to the studies of poverty-level families, but there is often an exaggeration of many of these characteristics. This could be expected, since they are selected by the criterion of child neglect. This neglect is sufficiently severe and consistent to have attracted attention from schools, health agencies, and other community resources and, consequently, precipitated their referral to this agency. They do not, however, represent the most severe group—defined by consistent underfeeding that endangers the health and even the life of the children. Our experience with neglect of this severity resulted in referral for foster home placement in 100 percent of the cases. The child neglect present in this population shows faulty feeding in terms of inadequate diet, irregular meals, and poor food preparation. Closely related to this are lack of family routines, inconsistent income management that fails to provide for the essentials of family care, neglect of medical problems, and consistent lack of cleanliness in both care of the children and of the household. (This does not mean that all of these factors are necessarily present in every family. One or more of them are present, and in some families all of them.)

In short, these are families so disorganized as to precipitate community action but not so extreme in behavior as to endanger the lives of the children. Chronic health problems are common, but near-starvation is not usual.[7] Poverty is an omnipresent condition. Of 125 families in the project, 77 percent are receiving some form of public assistance; 98.5 percent have an income of $4000 or less. Since the average family size is eight people— and many have 10 or 12 children—the economic limitation is bitterly real. Educational level is low, and illiteracy not uncommon.

Apathy is the predominant attitude of these families toward life. Actions tend to be impulsive and sporadic rather than purposeful and consistent. Planning is largely confined to the immediate situation and precludes goals requiring continued effort. Standards of behavior tend to be minimal and often show decreasing authority and consistency. In almost every case, there is a marked lack of family cohesion, that is, members tend to see themselves as victims of the demands of other family members rather than as a unit from which each may draw strength and fulfillment. This inevi-

---

[7] Note: Although the agency accepts some cases of child abuse, abuse is not used as a criterion of family disorganization since it represents a pathology of a particular type and not one necessarily relevant to the problems discussed here. [*See* Leontine Young, *Wednesday's Children* (New York: McGraw-Hill Book Co., 1964).] The agency operates a small child-placement program for children removed from homes characterized by severe abuse or severe neglect.

tably gives rise to chronic friction and frustration and further weakens the ability of the family to act with any consistent direction. Under these circumstances, responsibility tends to become erratic and discontinuous.

For example, one father who was regularly employed at a minimal wage gave half of his earnings to the support of his wife and six children. The other half he considered his own to be used for whatever purposes he chose. As he explained, "I earn the money, and I should have half of it to spend on myself." The obvious fact that half of his income could not provide for the family needs was disregarded.

In a somewhat extreme form, this father illustrated a factor true of nearly all the families: their concept of responsibility differs decidedly from that approved by the dominant culture. Responsibility is seen as narrow in scope, highly specific in nature, and largely oblivious of consequence. In other words, what happens beyond the recognized specific limits of obligation is not seen as personally connected or caused. It is simply there, like an "act of God." Lack of clear role definitions on the part of husband and wife, and of parents and children must be a contributory element in this sharply segmented concept of responsibility.

Although this is a comprehensible adaptation in the context of the specific situation, its impact upon family life and particularly upon children is deleterious and often catastrophic. All of these described characteristics can be viewed with validity as adaptations to a pathological environment. Unfortunately they also have a pathological effect upon family life and most especially upon children. They are highly dysfunctional for the kind of change required for admission to the dominant culture around them.[8] They combine into that disorganization characterized by a lack of life structure that tends to exaggerate personal weaknesses and prevent directed use of strengths. Thus, disorder tends to overflow into almost every area of life and to dissipate both potentialities and opportunities.

When this situation combines with the realities of inadequate opportunity, racial prejudice, meager education, and lack of skills, it is not surprising that the deteriorating family is a primary problem. The family lacks both the internal and the external means for building a life style and structure that would provide a way out of this cycle of misery and hopelessness. Personal concepts of self-worth are so low that there is little soil in which motivation for a better life can grow to the strength required for continued effort and struggle.

### THE PROJECT AND ITS PROGRAMS

This project was evolved out of the observed needs and problems of this specific group of families. (I use the word "evolved" advisedly because its

---

[8] Florence R. Kluckhohn and Fred L. Stodtbeck, *Variations in Value Orientations* (Evanston, Ill.: Row, Peterson and Co., 1961).

programs were developed as a consequence of firsthand observation, and they continue to change and modify as new observation and study dictate.) The program as a whole is based on certain specific premises:

1. Since these families show a failure of initiative, we would assume responsibility, not only by going to them, but by providing direction in the solution of urgent and immediate problems.
2. Since lack of order was a major obstacle in their lives, we would concentrate on developing the means of helping families achieve some order in whatever life area should prove most accessible.
3. We assumed that some motivation that could be used for change was present, even though it might not be motivation for change as this is commonly understood.
4. Because both passivity and lack of knowledge hamper these families in reaching, using, and coordinating segmented community resources, we would attempt to combine services in one place under one auspice; and where this could not be done, we would take responsibility for sharing with the families the effort of reaching and coordinating resources.
5. Since members of the family tended to see personal needs as paramount and often hostile to the needs of other family members, we would concentrate on services to individual family members and integrate these efforts toward the goal of family unity.
6. Our treatment goals were long range, viz., to help parents achieve as much stability as possible and to provide children with compensation for what their homes could not give them.

We did not delude ourselves that such compensation would or could be adequate in any but a highly relative sense, but we also knew that children, when given a chance, have a great capacity for using opportunity for their own growth. We did not and do not assume that whatever progress families may make is necessarily internalized to a point where further outside support and help is unnecessary. This may prove to be the case with some families, but we have no conclusive evidence of it at this point. Our assumption remains that we will continue service to these families, although not necessarily of the same intensity, until the children are grown.

The present program is comprised of three main divisions: casework, education, and groupwork; all three are closely integrated by a common goal.

### Casework

The caseworker receives the family directly after the intake study. He usually meets the family at a point of crisis, since this often precipitated the referral, and begins with the immediate concrete needs—whether these be for financial assistance, housing, medical care, emergency planning for children, or any of the host of problems that can beset a family in these circumstances. Whatever the precipitating emergency, the caseworker concentrates on family financial needs, resources and planning, health problems of every member of the family, housing, household practices, and school problems as well as any specific problems of immediate urgency. This phase of the work is the most time consuming and most demanding period. It is quite probably also the most important. A caseworker may see one or another member of the family as often as five times a week, and most of these contacts involve visiting in the home, taking children to clinics, seeking out needed resources, and helping families to use them. On the average, this period lasts about six months.

During this time, the caseworker assumes the major share of the initiative, but in activities that are of immediate concern to the family. If he finds 12 people living in four rooms, he acts to help them find better housing. If he finds serious health problems, he moves to get medical care. He does not tell the parents they ought to do this. He helps them do it. If they were truly unwilling, there would be little he could do. In our experience with this particular group, that is rarely the case. On the contrary, suspicious and fearful as they usually are, and hostile as they sometimes are, they use this period to test the caseworker's willingness to help and his genuine concern for them. They do not trust words; they are convinced by actions. They follow the caseworker at first, then slowly they begin to participate. Their dependence, which underlies the passivity, is increasingly attached to the caseworker. Despite caseworkers' past fear of dependence as a major motivation, it proves to be a powerful motivation that can be used constructively when it is understood and directed toward purposes beneficial to the people themselves.

The goals of this first phase are (1) to bring some order out of chaos, (2) to give the family opportunity to learn through experience that they can trust the caseworker and the agency, and (3) to help them take the first steps in the direction of long-range planning. The mother who cleans her house until it shines to please the caseworker and to win his praise, the father who agrees to try planning the use of his weekly earnings, and the youngster who follows up on plans for special tutoring help are all expressing in their own ways that some change is occurring. The change is still incipient, tenuous, inconsistent in expression. For us it is the first indication that it may be possible.

### Education

Early in the contact, the caseworker calls on other agency services to help. Children of 3 and 4 are placed in the agency preschool. Since our parents are rarely motivated by interest in the education of their children and are, in any case, not likely to be consistent in responsibility, transportation of the children is necessarily provided by the agency. In the beginning phase of work with a family, it may even be necessary to bring clothing and dress the children if they are to come regularly. Most parents are willing for their children to attend pre-school if this does not require consistent effort on their part. The children attend a full day's session and come five days a week.

As early as 3, these young ones reflect the attitudes prevalent at home. Hyperactive, unable at the beginning even to listen to a brief story, they run from one distraction to another and lack any concept of accomplishment. They will be involved, for example, in cutting or pasting not because they want to make something, but because "the lady told me to." Success is staying out of trouble with the adults, and failure is the reverse. Both learning and the growth of healthy relationships to others are severely handicapped by these basic attitudes. Although inability to wait for gratification of a desire is (within limits) normal for any 3-year-old, for these particular 3-year-olds delay becomes synonymous with denial and orderly process with deprivation. Concepts of self—if they can be said to exist in any formulated fashion—are generally so low as to constitute virtually a negation of self.[9]

The goals of the preschool are threefold. Most important is the attempt to change basic attitudes toward other people and toward themselves. If they can learn to see adults as protectors of strength and consistency, other children as fellow participants, and themselves as people of value, the preschool will have accomplished its major objective. Although all these qualities are necessarily relative, the great necessity is to make a beginning, one that can be developed by growth and promoted by continuing help.

The second goal is the establishment of routines and standards for everyday activities. Order has been alien in the environment of these children, and there has been a dearth of mutual expectations in their homes. That they eat at certain times every day according to certain procedures, that they engage in certain activities at definite stated times, that rules are consistent, and that adults as well as children follow orderly processes introduces the comfort of some certainties, as well as the protection of defined limits, into the confusion of their lives.

The third objective is the specific effort to open up new areas of knowledge to children who have been severely restricted in their awareness of the world around them. Usually, they lack the information taken for granted by the more fortunate child; and this, in turn, contributes to their belief in their own stupidity when they reach the conventional schoolroom. Stimulation of curiosity, exposure to new worlds, and expansion of perception are integral parts of this objective.

Obviously, all these goals are interlocking and interdependent. The children themselves respond with the flexibility and wonderful growth

---

[9] John E. Hansan and Kathryn Pemberton, "Day Care: A Therapeutic Milieu," *Child Welfare*, XLIV (1965), 149–155.

potential of their years. They love the school and regard vacations away from it as interludes to be terminated as quickly as possible. Even illness becomes a kind of punishment because it keeps them away from school. This is contributory evidence that children do prefer order to confusion.[10]

School-age children, we found, were often having trouble in school. Some of them were failing or working at such a minimal level that future failure was almost certain. Truancy was common and behavior disturbances in the classroom frequent. Even more disturbing was the attitude of apathy on the part of many of the children, an indifference too often echoed by the parents. These youngsters reflected the family problems and epitomized the attitudes observable in the preschoolers.

To meet this problem, a tutoring program was inaugurated. It is staffed by volunteers, some of them high school students. One paid person, trained in special education, supervises the program and tutors some of the adolescents, whereas the volunteers are directly responsible for the teaching. On the basis of one tutor to one student, the stress is again on continuity and the quality of relationships. Children are picked up at their schools and brought to the agency on one or, for those requiring it, two afternoons a week. The stress is on reading and arithmetic—the two subject areas of greatest need. The goals, like those of the preschool, are attitudinal as well as educational in the more formal sense. Children experience personal attention, personal concern for their progress, and personal pride in their achievements. In many cases, the relationship between teacher and student becomes one of deep satisfaction to both.

### Groupwork

Because these children rarely belonged to any organized groups, their need for recreation was acute. They tended to play on the streets and to rely on the haphazard, often destructive activities of their immediate environment. Moreover, few of them would participate with any continuity in available community groups, including those of the school. Their own feelings of defeat, of apathy, operated to bar them from even the resources that were available to them. Because of this, we initiated a summer day camp, which included children from 3 to 7 in one division and children from 7 to 15 in another.

As in the educational programs, the goals were to provide a new kind of living experience, to open up new horizons, and to modify attitudes. This was a camp on wheels—the children went to the beach, to a lake, and to parks. They learned new games and crafts; they put on plays, engaged in group projects, developed new interests. Appointed monitors were responsible for gathering all the children at a set collection point, at a set time.

---

[10] Eleanor Hosley, "Culturally Deprived Children in Day-Care Programs," *Children*, X (1963), 172–179.

The agency bus picked them up at these points and brought them to a central location where they had breakfast. Most of them came hungry. Then, with box lunches, they were off for the day.

Out of their enthusiasm, as well as their needs, grew the beginnings of a year-round group program for them. Still in its developmental stage, this program includes groups for parents as well as children and, like the other services, is an integral part of the total project. Although the groups are still too new to permit final conclusions, we have observed some interesting developments.

Mothers who had seemingly reached a plateau in their progress have responded with new enthusiasm to small groups. They come to the agency and never miss a meeting. They are often early and reluctant to leave. They eat together, plan projects of interest to the members, and talk freely to one another. One woman—who had always had trouble keeping herself and her family clean—had begun to arrive neatly dressed, her hair combed, her person clean. At the same time, her youngster in preschool came bathed and in clean clothes. Another woman announced to the group that she had not intended to come because she was in such a bad temper that she yelled at everyone. She took the bus to go to the store and then found she had bought a transfer for the bus passing the agency. As she explained, she thought she should use the transfer since she had already bought it. The other mothers described their bad days and how they felt; and over coffee, the bad temper vanished in a newly felt relaxation.

The children use the groups not only for recreation, but for stimulation and education. Some of them begin to show growing identification with the group leader. One adolescent boy, who had two alcoholic parents, said sadly to the leader of his group, "I don't want to be like my father when I grow up. I want to be like you." The boy was right. It was his only chance. With many of these youngsters, the agency must seek unceasingly to compensate for what their parents cannot give.

## Coordination of Services

The caseworker is responsible for the coordination of all services to the family. This is vital if its individual members are to make continued and effective use of these services. Thus progress by the children can precipitate new conflicts in the home and active opposition by the parents unless their understanding and participation keeps pace with that progress. A preschooler goes home and asks, "Why don't we use paper napkins? At school we have napkins." A boy of 12 complains that he has no place to study. Children come home with new ideas, new aspirations. Although these are indications of progress for the children, to the parents they can represent undesirable changes.

The common assumption that parents would welcome such changes in their children and would even learn from their children may be correct for better organized families, but it has not proved valid with this particular group. Much more frequent has been parental jealousy of children and even resentment of the degree of attention paid to them. Parents remark openly, "You pay more attention to the children than you do to me," or "No one ever helped me like that when I was a kid." Here speaks the deprivation of their own past as well as their damaged and limited concept of parenthood. Unless continuing and concentrated help is given parents, these attitudes can congeal into effective obstruction of help for the children and into hostility that can only militate against their own hope for a better future.

In essence, this program seeks to tackle three basic problems of this group of families: lack of integration, lack of continuity, and lack of initiative. The agency takes the initiative for the family, gradually relinquishing it as the family can, and does, assume more. The agency provides the integration for the family, while encouraging the family in its own ability to achieve purpose and planning. The agency provides continuity as a part of its own planning, with the long-range goal of ultimately enabling families to establish their own continuity of effort and balance.

## RESULTS OF THE PROJECT

Although the program is still too new to permit of definitive conclusions, certain trends have become visible. In addition, structured observations can now be made with the way clear to their refinement in the future.

1. Deterioration is checked in 90 percent of the families by the end of the first year. The families may show some transient and sporadic change for better or for worse, but the most certain factor is that there is no evidence of continuing deterioration. This is also the most intensive period of service by the caseworker. It is not unusual for a caseworker to visit a family as much as three times a week, to carry major responsibility for getting family members to health clinics, and to meet a succession of crises. And when children are in preschool, an agency member is in the home five days a week and is responsible for immediately reporting any incipient trouble or problem to the caseworker. When school-age children are also participating in tutoring and club groups, there is further weekly contact with the children.

This saturation of service varies in length according to the circumstances of the individual family, but in general it ceases to be necessary by the end of one year. It is usually possible to begin its diminution after six months, the criteria being (1) the reduction of crises to the point that a family discusses problems with the caseworker before a crisis occurs, (2) the growing confidence of family members in the caseworker and the agency as demonstrated by their willingness to use the judgment and leadership of the caseworker, and (3) increasing order and routine in the family's everyday life.

During this same period, the children may and frequently do show considerably more progress. By the end of the first year in preschool, they have lost much of their hyperactivity, have developed some concept of purpose and displayed growing continuity in achieving it, have made positive relationships with teachers, and have taken a big step in making learning possible. Of the children in tutoring groups, 75 percent have improved their grades in school to the point of passing at the end of one year. The continuance and further development of this gain, however, is heavily dependent upon the overall progress of the family.

2. During the second year, a majority of the families—an estimated 55 percent to 60 percent—show progress in at least one area of family functioning. Not surprisingly, the first areas are income management and household practices. There is a large element of education present in both, as well as tangible and relatively immediate gratifications for both mother and father. Often a mother begins to take pride in her house for the first time. In one such case, the caseworker gave the family a set of dishes that had been admired by the mother. This mother not only keeps them displayed on open shelves, but carefully dusts them each day. The need for beauty is important, and one long-starved in families like these.

As this kind of order continues, there is a lessening of other tensions. There are fewer precipitating occasions for dissension and fewer incitements to complain. In turn, this permits more attention and more energy to be channeled into activities that are constructive. Thus, in one family where the mother and father fought bitterly, each blaming the other for the family's misery, and where the father increasingly turned to the solace of alcohol, the improvement in money management and household care gave incentive to both parents. The father gained in status within the family as he used the available income with more judgment and reduced his drinking. The mother took a part-time job in the evenings because she could now trust her husband to stay with the children and to participate in family responsibility.

This second year, therefore, is a period of moving toward some new adaptations. The family has developed confidence in the agency, and its members have gained enough self-confidence to attempt some new activities. This can be seen in the growing number of parents who come to the office to see the caseworker, thus reducing the amount of home visiting necessary. It can be seen in the parents who enter retraining courses and follow through on the acquisition of new skills. It can be seen in the increased attention to how they look and pride in their appearance. It can be seen in the new interest that brought 70 percent of the parents to the opening program of the summer day camp. It can be seen in the changing attitudes of children, the drop in truancy rates, the zest for creative activities, the reduction in delinquency, and the rechanneling of aggression from destructive outlets to constructive leadership.

At the same time, families develop new needs that are the logical outcome of their movement into new adaptations. Mothers begin to break their isolation and express interest in new activities that reflect new attitudes. A group of mothers recently and spontaneously began to plan "sweet 16" parties for their daughters, to discuss what could be saved from their budgets to pay for the parties, and to plan two and three months ahead. The interest in parties for their daughters and the independent planning are new.

Although the caseworker continues to carry responsibility for the family, he is now able to be more of a resource for family members when they need him than the initiator of activity. It seems likely that in the near future, casework loads will be divided into three sections according to the level of stability achieved by families. Thus, 5 families—during the initial period—may be equivalent in workload to 25 or 30 families at the stage where groups assume major responsibility.

3. The program is yet too new for any considerable number of families to be observed over the total three year period, but there is enough available evidence to provide clues to the future. The most important trend is the growth of family cohesion. In their actions, parents show a broadening concept of responsibility toward their children, and this is accompanied by an increased interest in their own achievements.

The same father who once retained half his salary for himself now has an additional part-time job and provides for the family's essential needs. Once illiterate, he is now learning to read and write in night school. The mother now keeps her home well, cooks regular meals, and cares for her children. Now she wants to go to school and is becoming interested in community participation. There has been a marked reduction of marital conflict and a growth of family sharing.

Interest in community activities seems to be a third area of change in these families. For the first time, several have joined churches and begun to participate in organized groups.

These families have, in most cases, also voluntarily limited the increase of family size. The importance of this cannot be exaggerated. No amount of service, however skilled, can compensate for the disorganization introduced by a continuing growth of family size in the face of an inadequate income and a continually increasing burden of responsibility. The agency has actively encouraged family planning and has assisted mothers in reaching resources such as Planned Parenthood. The result has been that —for the first time—families could plan for the future, see a way to encompass their problems, and move toward a better life. The advent of a new baby every year augmented reality problems to a point where far more mature parents than these might well have resigned themselves to apathy. It is probably valid to say that those parents who have faced this problem are well on their way to a permanent change of life style.

## SUMMARY

This is a project that places primary emphasis on comprehensiveness and continuity as a means of reversing the cycle of disorganization. It is concerned with, the integration of casework, education, group-work, and services adapted to the changing needs of individual family members and to the family as a unit. It has relied heavily upon the concept of compensation—that is, developing strengths that may compensate for weaknesses and, in time, diminish the effects of those weaknesses. The concept is borrowed from the field of medicine and has proved to be useful. We have applied it both in program and in casework technique. Essentially, this involves (1) a clear and specific diagnosis of areas of strength and of weakness in individual family members, (2) awareness of the process of interaction created by these strengths and weaknesses within a particular environmental situation, and (3) concentration of support upon the areas of strength. This approach places emphasis upon structural change and its maintenance through agency support. Whether it will be influential with adults in effecting internalization of such change cannot, at this point, be predicted.

Thus, in one family there has been great improvement in the marital situation. This is the result of a combination of factors that have enabled the father to carry through on a retraining project and the mother to take a part-time job in the evenings, with the assurance that the father will be responsible for the children in her absence. The financial, housing, educational, and recreational circumstances have improved, easing many of the precipitates of marital friction. The home life is far more gratifying to parents and children. This does not mean that the marital relationship is necessarily changed. So far the changes are structural, and lack of open friction is not the same as a positive human relationship. That may or may not be possible. In the meantime, the compensating improvements and gratifications, and the more stable family behavior are proving of tremendous help to both parents and children.

With the children, it is hoped that much more can be done. The prevention of such incapacitating damage, the development of positive areas and strengths would render the internalization of a more constructive life pattern possible and even probable. Since we know no specific cure for the social and psychological disease known as disorganization, the only present alternative would seem to be to arrest its development and to compensate in accessible areas for its ravages.

Further and more exact evaluation will be required to test the reliability of observations and to determine major trends over a period of time. For example, a detailed schedule of specific and individual behaviors will be checked according to each service on a scale of family functioning.[11] Since these schedules will be completed every three months and will cover almost every member of a family, they should serve both as a valuable coordinating device and as a means of collecting and organizing the data of observation. Specifically, it will be possible to document whether a change in one area—as for example, a child in preschool—is accompanied by changes in other areas and what over a period of time is the predominant direction of change. In time, this should become a device by means of which the process of family interaction can be charted. It would provide clues to the kinds of family imbalance precipitated by continued agency intervention and if and how such imbalances may be resolved by the evolution of new and more productive family adaptations. There are many questions to be answered, but the old feeling of hopelessness on the part of families and social workers alike is yielding to the conviction that there is much that can be done.

# 4

❲ The following research report is based on interviews with former protective-service clients and a group of nonclient neighbors. The research attempted to obtain data on factors determining the protective-service client's perception of the agency and the problems in communication between the protective-service worker and client.

# Communications: Client, Community, and Agency

*Edith Varon*

The purpose of the study on which this paper is based was to gain an understanding of the communication between a protective agency and its clientele, as it was influenced by similarities or differences in values and

---

11 The scale is adapted from Geismar's Scale of Family Functioning. *See* Ludwig L. Geismar and Beverly Ayres, *Measuring Family Functioning*, mimeographed (St. Paul, Minn.: Family Centered Project, Greater St. Paul Community Chest and Councils, 1960).

standards, and through the effect of the community attitude on the client. Communication is a key social process. It is through an analysis of it that the functioning of a social agency can best be understood. This position is in keeping with Norbert Wiener's statement, "Society can only be understood through a study of the messages and the communication facilities which belong to it."[1]

Communication is a process in which, when it is truly effective, the senders and recipients of messages give them the same interpretation. Words, concepts—symbols—mean the same thing to different individuals when they have the same frame of reference. It is by evaluating the congruence of their frames of reference, therefore, that one can assess their ability to communicate.

The agency that was the subject of this study, the Massachusetts Society for the Prevention of Cruelty to Children, engages in protective services, a form of "aggressive casework." In this situation, it is the agency that approaches the client, rather than the client who is seeking help. Consequently, it was assumed that the agency must adapt to the client. Furthermore, the client must be understood as a member of his community, for his frame of reference will to some extent be determined by the values of the community in which he lives.

The word "community" has many meanings. For the purposes of this paper is meant a geographic neighborhood where the residents not only live close to one another but also have so much in common that ties are readily formed among them. Their life styles are similar. They have comparable attitudes toward marriage and the family, comparable ways of relating to friends as well as to relatives, the clergy, schools, and employers. They have comparable problems in making ends meet. Their sources of income differ, but within a narrow range; their jobs require roughly the same levels of education and the same kinds of vocational or professional skills. As a consequence, neighbors in such a community share the same experiences and have standards and values sufficiently the same to enable them to give the same interpretation to what each expresses. Hence, they "communicate." The process of communication is largely verbal, but the spoken word is often replaced or supplemented by nonverbal means—through glances, bodily postures, shared activities, or the giving or withholding of material things.

## DESIGN OF THE STUDY

Such considerations as these lay behind the study on which this paper is based. It took place in two small areas of greater Boston containing a total of eight census tracts. These were working-class areas, in the sense that occupations in skilled, semiskilled, and unskilled labor predominated

---

[1] *The Human Use of Human Beings—Cybernetics and Society* (New York: Doubleday Anchor Books, 1954), p. 16.

and a fair percentage of residents received some form of assistance. Neighborhood populations were predominantly Catholic: Yankee, Irish, and East European, with a sprinkling of Negroes. Each area was dominated by a large housing project surrounded by rather rundown, low-rental multiple dwellings accommodating three, six, or eight families. These formed self-contained communities—one in particular, as it was bounded on all sides by highways. Since the results of the survey did not differ significantly in the two areas, they will be presented as one.

Interviews were held with former clients and nonclients in order to obtain data on factors that affected their perception of the agency, and the standards and values to which the agency worker would have to accommodate himself in order to communicate with clients. The questions asked, therefore, dealt with experiences with and perceptions of social agencies, how they were seen in the structure of society and as instruments of the relationship between social classes, analogous questions about the MSPCC, who could be expected to make referrals to it, questions about the court—its role in situations of neglect and individuals' feelings about it, and, finally, questions to obtain social data about the informants. Agency workers were asked parallel questions, starting with their perceptions of clients. Community leaders were asked about their perceptions of the agency, their standards of child care, definition of neglect, and handling of referrals to the agency.

An attempt was made to obtain not a representative sampling, but the total population of former clients of the MSPCC in this area within the period January 1959 to September 1960, excluding only the mentally ill or those who had left town. Out of a total of twenty-four former clients in this area, only thirteen agreed to participate in the study, even though as many as five revisits were made to the others in an attempt to involve them. Those who agreed were seen an average of three times in unstructured interviews. A total of fifty neighbors living three, six, or nine dwelling units away were seen once.[2] Also interviewed were such agents of social control as the housing project manager, the police, and the neighborhood clergy. Through these parallel interviews community attitudes toward the agency were derived. Six field and two intake workers of the agency were interviewed on the same issues, in order to evaluate the points of agreement between agency worker, the client, and the community. Only highlights of the results can be reported here.

## CHARACTERISTICS OF THE COMMUNITY

From the interviews with former clients and nonclients living nearby some of the attitudes prevailing in the community can be extrapolated.

---

[2] Ann Andrus, Dwight Dale, Patti Dessler Ewen, Nancy Meyer, and Nina Scheider, "Community Orientations Toward the MSPCC." Unpublished master's thesis, Boston University School of Social Work, 1961.

There is, of course, no simple attitude; each is subject to variations and can be represented on a continuum. One might generalize that on one dimension the attitudes toward social agencies vary from pessimistic—expecting bad things to happen—to optimistic—expecting good things to happen. The former clients had probably had more bad experiences than the nonclients, and they had more pessimistic expectations. Of the nonclients, those who had had experiences with social agencies other than the MSPCC also seemed more pessimistic than those who had had no agency experiences.

Another dimension deals with perceptions. Again there is a range, from perceiving in simple terms only what is here and now to a deeper perception including facts that cannot be seen immediately but must be conjured up by an intellectual process, e.g., the function of a social agency or the relation of supervisors to workers. Those who perceived primarily in terms of what was immediately present had only vague notions about social agencies, which they evaluated in terms of the workers with whom they had had contact. Although many contributed to chest drives, they thought of social agencies as being run by "the government" and generally thought of their functions as being to meet material needs. Few had thought of the structure of agencies or of society.

On the whole, these people lacked not only knowledge but also curiosity about agencies. They reacted to the agency worker rather than the agency.[3] They reacted to the individual, the close-at-hand, rather than to abstractions, and their emotional investment was in the community. At the same time, they tended to react in an "all-or-none" way, with strong, unmixed feelings and decided opinions.

It is significant that, among former clients, those who had more sophistication about social agencies knew about their different functions—supervision, high case loads, and even overlapping agency functions. They could understand mixed feelings and conceive of an authority that was simultaneously benevolent and coercive.

Within the community all these people usually know a great deal about what is going on, in sharp contrast to their lack of knowledge of the larger society and its institutions. The importance of neighbors and of talk—gossip—comes out clearly in interviews. A picture emerges in which almost everyone fears gossip, yet participates in it to some extent. The gossip itself establishes a neighborhood code of what is or is not permissible, and by deterring residents from violating the neighborhood code acts as a superego, which is a powerful force. In other words, there is communication on vital issues, and one outcome of this is that, through this exchange, the neighborhood maintains certain values and attitudes.

---

[3] This is in agreement with the findings of Leonard Schatzman and Anselm Strauss, "Social Class and Modes of Communication," *American Journal of Sociology,* Vol. 60, No. 4 (January 1955), pp. 329–338.

Neighbors seem to be well aware of who is working and who is not, whether children are hungry to the point of begging for food, cold for lack of proper clothing, left unsupervised while their parents go either shopping or partying. Social workers are quickly recognized, and neighbors note whom they visit. There is considerable talk about social workers and agencies, which plays an important part in molding the image of the agencies, to which clients later react. Not infrequently neighbors entered during the interviews—sometimes by the former client's special invitation—to join in a vigorous discussion about social agencies, using this opportunity to let out their distress over past experiences.

These working-class people live economically marginal lives. Five of the thirteen former clients were receiving financial help, as were four of the fifty nonclients. In keeping with this insecurity, they place high value on material things such as food, clothing, and shelter—for themselves, their children, their neighbors. Good mothering is defined by them in these terms; it is failure to provide for material needs that constitutes neglect. Attention to emotional needs is included as a part of good mothering, but failure in this regard is not seen as neglect.

When they see that others are in need, they do not turn to social agencies. Their impulse is to do something about it personally. A number of instances were cited of children who were roaming the streets being taken in or fed when they were seen foraging in trash barrels. This warm impulse gives way to resentment, however, if the situation remains unimproved, and they begin to feel imposed on. The help they give is unplanned and sporadic, and does not usually include finding ways of changing the source of the trouble. When nonclients were asked what they would do if the situation were one of neglect, the most common answer was, "Go to the police." Next came "Do something myself," and after that the church, relatives, and neighbors. Last mentioned were the social agencies.

The material gathered from interviews contains not explanations, but suggestions as to why there is this reluctance to turn to social agencies. Out of forty-four nonclients who described the function of a social worker, half thought it was investigatory, and thirteen used the same words, "It's the same thing over and over: she asks questions, wants to know where the children are." Twelve attributed a helping function to the social worker, and ten a combination of the two. Of the eleven former clients who refused to participate in the study, seven showed fearful attitudes toward social workers. They dared not refuse an interview outright, but made appointments and then were "not at home." When those who participated were asked to explain this behavior, they said, "It's like the bill collector." One added, "Social workers . . . are like the police, but not the good side of the police. . . ." Former clients described social workers as "nosy," but to them this meant not only interfering and asking questions, but doing so with the intention of hurting, of "taking away that welfare aid." Social workers were often identified with public welfare workers, as well as with police officers and prison wardens.

These, then, are some of the general characteristics of the community within which the clients of this protective agency live, and they provide the background against which it operates. The worker given a complaint to investigate is faced with a client who is to some degree affected by attitudes and values such as these.[4]

## PUNITIVE IMAGE OF AGENCY

Agency policy was to take complaints either over the phone or in person, obtaining enough details to be reasonably certain there actually was a situation of neglect. The complainant was encouraged to identify himself, but he frequently did not; in most cases he remained anonymous to the referred family even if he identified himself to the agency. Many complainants stated that if they were questioned, they would deny having made the complaint.

Once the complaint was accepted, a letter was sent to the referred family explaining the function of the agency in investigating neglect cases and advising that a worker would visit. The referred parents usually wanted to talk about the complainant, but the workers refused to become involved in this. Four of the six field workers interviewed felt that the anonymity of the complainant created a barrier to communication that was frequently insuperable.

The problems noted by the workers were the counterpart of the attitudes of residents toward referrals to the agency. Although less familiar than the welfare department or the Salvation Army, the agency was well known in the community, where it was seen as punitive. It had originally dealt with neglect by removing the child from the home; within the last fifteen years, however, it had been attempting to save the home and also to remedy emotional neglect. Nevertheless, most of the community leaders interviewed saw its function as one of removing the child when they themselves had determined by their own standards that this was the only recourse. This attitude was echoed among nonclients; twenty-nine referred to removal of children as a function of the agency, while only seven referred to correction of the home situation—although fifteen lived near former clients who had been helped. Among the former clients

---

[4] For a discussion of working-class values, *see* Martin B. Loeb, "Social Class and the American Social System," *Social Work*, Vol. 6, No. 2 (April 1961), pp. 12–17. Loeb sees the function of social work as transmitting middle-class values to working-class clients.

themselves this image continued to linger on, and not one said he would make a referral to the agency.

There may be many reasons for this punitive image—in the nature of the residents themselves as well as in the history of the agency. One former client laid it to the nature of the gossip that takes place: "It's only the bitterness that gets passed along." Fear of what the neighbors would think was a prominent obstacle to referral among the nonclients. Guilt was also found, and finally there was the prevalence of a punitive, authoritarian attitude among these persons themselves. They made such comments as, "A mother like that doesn't deserve to have her child." Some saw agency intervention as punishment, and asked, "Why take it out on the child?" because they saw separation as a severe trauma for the child.

The close relationship between the former client's attitude toward referrals and community attitudes was brought out by many responses. A nonclient, for example, gave as his reason for hesitating to refer: "I'd be killed going out the door." Another exploded, "I wouldn't do that to my worst enemy!" A referral was almost universally seen as an inimical act, the purpose of which was to remove the children from the home, the gravest threat that could be made to a parent. This was recognized by complainants who refused to be identified to the referred families.

The response of those who have been referred is, naturally, to want to know who the "enemy" is. Those who can identify the source of the complaint relax. Others remain distrustful of their neighbors and anxious about the agency. When one cannot identify the enemy, everyone becomes suspect, and relationships within the community are disrupted. From this point of view, it would have been important to be able to assess the degree of alienation from the community of those former clients who refused to participate, and whether this alienation was affected by their contact with the agency.

The questions about referrals, by eliciting this punitive image, brought into the open what may be the greatest impediment to communication between the agency and its clients. The circumstances making referrals possible, in other words, would roughly coincide with the elements making communication possible. Willingness to make referrals could be a manifestation of communication. Fundamental disagreement on the function of the agency proved to be a block to both communication and referrals. The information gathered about the standards and values of the residents could be useful in communication only if there were agreement on the benevolent purpose of the agency when it intervened in a case. Disagreement, in the parlance of the theoreticians, acts like "noise" in a communications system; it prevents the parties from hearing the messages being sent and comparison of the content of the messages, therefore, cannot even be begun.

## FACTORS AFFECTING ACCEPTANCE OF AGENCY

An analysis of the thirteen informants indicated that five had been helped by the agency, three had been unaffected by it, and five were still disturbed at the time of the study. The analysis further indicated some factors associated with these outcomes.

A corollary to the attitude toward referrals was the need to know the identity of the complainant. Among those who were helped, there was a combination of the client's being aware of where the complaint came from and of not being identified with the working-class community. These women did not want to raise their children in this neighborhood and wanted them to have more education than they themselves had. Furthermore, they were mostly strong individuals who could assume a position of leadership with their friends and have the courage to disagree with them as to the nature of the agency. They also had the courage to disagree with the worker, whereas others showed a passive, compliant front and told their true feelings to their friends later.

Those who did not accept the agency worker were also those who did not know the identity of the complainant. They tended to accept the standards and values of the community, one of which was rejection of the agency. Their relationships in the community were so important and supportive to them that they could not relinquish them in favor of an agency that they did not feel they could trust.

The type of reaction to referral appears to stem from this universal need to know the source of potential danger, coupled with the vulnerability and sense of impotence that characterize these persons. These traits manifested themselves indirectly in the way the former clients handled the incident. They attributed the complainant's motivation to spite, something done out of envy, but what was envied was something that made the individual feel vulnerable, such as being on AFDC or having a job.

More directly, the vulnerability and impotence came out in discussion of the courts. The predominant attitude in this area toward the courts was a hopeless one, sometimes expressed as "The parent has no hope, once the case has gone to court." Seven nonclients thought the parents' right, when they were taken to court, was a right to "a second chance." Several of the former clients had had experiences in court. Their attitudes varied from feeling shame at the thought of court, to one that "it is supposed to stand for justice . . . but the poor women don't stand a chance." Agency workers, on the other hand, indicated that it was important to them to know they had the backing of the court; they had a sense of power, and expected the judge to act in accordance with their recommendations. "Of course," said one, "sometimes you get a lousy decision," meaning that sometimes it is the client who wins the case.

This statement means one thing when we are concerned with the welfare of a particular child, but another when we consider that there appears to be a generalized feeling of impotence in this one segment of the population. It is understandable that someone feeling so impotent might enter a complaint in order to use the power of the agency against someone he wanted to hurt. This feeling would also lead the complainant to want to conceal his identity. Not knowing who made the complaint enhances the feelings of vulnerability and impotence of the referred parent in addition to impeding communication with the agency.

There is a vicious cycle in progress, and we may question how it affects the patterns of relationships, the way of life of the families about whom we are concerned. Further, we are forced to ask ourselves whether such middle-class values as education, steady employment, or better living conditions, which are predicated on being oriented to the future, are not also predicated on having some sense of power and whether these values can be transmitted to the working class without modification of the feeling of impotence.

### QUESTIONS FOR CONSIDERATION

When the client of the protective agency is viewed in the context of a working-class community, the questions that result are different in kind from those that are based on interactions with the client alone. They suggest that we may need to rethink some of the ways in which protective services are offered, at the level of community organization as well as at the level of direct service.

The study revealed that the protective agency has to contend with negative attitudes toward social workers that can be traced, in part at least, to the investigatory function of the public assistance worker. The agency therefore has a direct stake in the modification of the administration of public assistance. On the other hand, the residents of the community turn more readily for help to the police and the clergy; the agency should perhaps consider finding ways of working more closely with these latter.

Only a fraction of the former clients interviewed appeared able to conceptualize something as complex as an authority that is simultaneously coercive and benevolent. This creates problems for the agency. A related problem is whether the coercive use of authority should be concentrated in the protective agency, which can then be used as a "bogeyman" by people in the community.

At the level of direct service, the questions raised by the study have to do with the congruence between agency policy and the psychology of the community that influences the client. For example, how can services be offered without enhancing the vulnerability and sense of impotence of the client? Can services be extended in ways that will avoid the present danger of disrupting the client's relationships in the community? Is it advisable to continue to conceal the identity of the complainant from the referred family? Perhaps the screening done at intake can procure enough data on such items as the family attitude toward education, their aspirations, and their relative ability to cope with difficult situations, to give clues to their value systems and the kind of casework service they can use.

In the community, at all levels, there was support for agency intervention when the situation was a drastic one such as children abandoned in their homes. In such cases, the protective agency would have community backing. In less drastic situations there now exists a divergent opinion between the agency and the community. The helpful services the agency offers are identified by the community as punitive, and rejected. The working-class values placed on the meeting of physical needs only partially coincide with the values of professional casework practiced in the agency. There might be agreement if help were offered with baby sitters, with money, with the problems of a one-parent family. Could this be done, and done in a setting with which the client can identify without feeling he has damaged his self-esteem, as has been done in settlement houses? It must not be forgotten that situations classified as child neglect most often have other ramifications, and could be defined and helped differently in other settings. When the situation is not drastic, then, and the family's values are such that they are identified with and rooted in the working-class community, the questions revolve around the problem of achieving a more benevolent identification in the community by offering help within the value system of the clients.

This study should be replicated in other working-class areas throughout the country to determine further what attitudes exist and affect clientele of protective agencies.

# 5

❡ The following research study presents data regarding the frequency with which judges accept the requests for petitions submitted by social workers alleging neglect. The article includes an analysis of the factors associated with different court decisions.

# The Disposition of Child Neglect Cases Referred by Caseworkers to a Juvenile Court

*Paul E. Weinberger and Peggy J. Smith*

Protective service, "the name given to the service initiated when the protection of . . . children falls to the community,"[1] has been the subject of rapidly increasing attention and study by the social work profession. Neglect has now been identified as our single most important child welfare problem, although this recognition has been long in coming.

A major problem in child neglect situations is the absence of standards or criteria for authoritative intervention when a child's health and welfare are threatened. Welfare agencies and the courts do not necessarily share a common conceptual framework for assessing child neglect. Much of the confusion in protective service between the courts and social welfare agencies stems from the legal emphasis on parental rights and the social work emphasis on parental responsibilities.[2]

This article will describe a study that analyzed the disposition of cases referred by family aid caseworkers in public assistance to the Juvenile Court of Los Angeles County on behalf of neglected children whose parents were receiving financial aid. The focus of the study was to identify factors that led the court to take action as requested by caseworkers and to compare these outcomes with cases in which court action did not conform to the intent of the petition filed by social caseworkers.

---

[1] Henrietta L. Gordon, *Casework Services for Children* (Boston: Houghton Mifflin Co., 1956), p. 371.

[2] See Leontine Young, *Wednesday's Children* (New York: McGraw-Hill Book Co., 1964), p. 109.

## THEORETICAL CONSIDERATIONS

Because of its focus on enhancing social functioning within the context of the family, the social work profession has generally been averse to separating a child from his parents. Where evidence of child neglect is noted in public assistance caseloads, an effort is made to transfer such cases to child neglect units. In these special units, experienced child welfare workers maintain frequent contact with families where child care is inadequate, and through guidance and advice, they try to obviate the need for requesting court action. Boehm, for example, notes that "the preferred mode of treatment in protective situations is treatment in the child's own home, where the goal is improvement of family interaction and social functioning so that the child can remain with his family."[3]

Where ameliorative measures fail and the family environment is considered hazardous for the welfare of the child, a child neglect worker files a petition asking for removal of the child from the home and placement in foster care. The filing of the petition follows a close study of the family situation, including a diagnostic evaluation of parental adequacy and the ability of the family to modify existing patterns of behavior. The recommendation that the child be removed from the home by court authority is a last resort and is used when the parent or guardian refuses to care for the child responsibly and also refuses voluntary placement.

Requests for placement are forwarded to the Probation Department for investigation under a brief cover letter noting the section of the Juvenile Court Law that appears in violation and the primary reason for the request. The Probation Department may reject the request because of insufficient evidence, elect to provide noncourt supervision up to six months, or refer the matter to court for a disposition hearing.

This study is concerned with the outcome of petitions filed for alleged violation of Sections 600 A and B of the California Juvenile Court Law, which reads as follows:

A. (Said child) is in need of prior and effective parental care and control and has no parent or guardian, or has no parent or guardian willing to exercise or capable of exercising such care and control, or has no parent or guardian actually exercising such care and control. . . . B. or whose home is an unfit

---

[3] Boehm, "An Assessment of Family Adequacy in Protective Cases," *Child Welfare*, Vol. 41, Jan. 1962, p. 11. On the other hand, Rose comments that such programs of intervention in the child's home are valuable to prevent a total breakdown of family functioning, but fail to bring the dependent child to attention at a period of greatest vulnerability to developmental deviation. "Children and parents in circular destructive interaction frequently cannot be helped except through separation; often it is otherwise not even possible to identify the various facets of the problem." John A. Rose, "Delayed Recognition of Childhood Emotional Disorders," *Child Welfare*, XXXVIII, No. 10 (1959), 10.

place for him by reason of neglect, cruelty, or depravity of either of his parents or of his guardian or other person in whose custody or care he is.[4]

## HYPOTHESES

Two hypotheses about the disposition of child neglect cases were advanced:

1. Such reality factors as large number of children per family and older aged children would influence the court to reject the caseworker's request for placement.
2. The court would sustain placement requests where there is widespread, tangible evidence that parental behavior is endangering the physical safety and well-being of the child(ren) involved.

## STUDY PLAN

This study was conducted in the Los Angeles County Bureau of Public Assistance. Study findings are based on a detailed content analysis of requests for petitions to the Juvenile Court alleging violations of Section 600 A and B of the Juvenile Court Law. The petitions reviewed for this research were submitted by child neglect workers on behalf of neglected children receiving public assistance.

The study population included all such requests submitted in Los Angeles County between July 1, 1963 and June 30, 1964. An unduplicated count of all petitions indicated that a total of 40 families were involved in neglect petitions. The research procedure involved abstraction of factual and descriptive data from the petitions submitted to the court so as to obtain detailed information about the families involved in neglect proceedings, as well as the child neglect workers' reasons for requesting court intervention. Data on the disposition of the petitions were also abstracted.

Twenty-eight of the 40 families studied were headed by the mother only (five of whom had never been married) and 1 by the father only; in 11 families, either both parents or the mother and a stepfather were in the home. None of the 48 adults[5] named in the requests was employed at the time the request was submitted. It appeared that none had been employed, including the fathers, during the period of time covered by the summary.

Few of the children in these families had known contact or relationship with their natural fathers. Fifty-six different natural fathers were

---

[4] *State of California Welfare and Institutions Code and Laws Relating to Social Welfare* (Sacramento: State of California, Documents Printing Section, 1963), Division 2, Part 1, Chapter 2, Article 5.

[5] The whereabouts of three mothers was unknown at the time petitions were filed.

named in the 40 family cases included in the study. The whereabouts of two-thirds of these natural fathers was either unknown or known to be outside of Los Angeles County.

Of particular interest was the finding that one-half (20) of the families had only one or two children. (The common perception of the family with multiple problems, where neglect situations are likely to be found, is that of a large family with five or more children.)[6] Sixteen families had three to five children, and only four families had six or more children.

## DISPOSITION OF PETITIONS
## AND RELATED FINDINGS

Of the 40 cases in which child neglect workers saw the need for court intervention on behalf of the child, it was recommended that children be placed outside of the parental home in 38 cases. In the case of two predelinquent girls, the recommendation was for placement or court protection of the children in their own homes. The actual disposition of cases is shown in Table I.

In 13 out of 40 requests, the caseworker's recommendation for placement of a child outside the home was confirmed by the County Probation Department and sustained by the court. All agencies agreed that neglect existed in sufficient degree to warrant separation of child and parent.

TABLE I. Disposition of Requests for Placement

| Disposition | Number | Percent |
|---|---|---|
| Placement confirmed by Probation Department and sustained by court | 13 | 32.5 |
| Noncourt supervision by Probation Department in parental home | 16 | 40.0 |
| Placement and probation denied | 11 | 27.5 |
| Total number of cases | 40 | 100.0 |

The second group of 16 cases consisted of situations in which the Probation Department either confirmed the need for placement outside the home, but the court rejected this recommendation and extended noncourt supervision to the family, or in which the Probation Department disagreed with the caseworker and recommended noncourt supervision of the child in the parental home. In effect, these requests were partially sustained since the children were declared wards of the court even though

---

[6] Young, *op. cit.*, p. 69.

TABLE II. Age of Children as Related to Disposition

| Age | Placement Sustained | Noncourt Supervision | Placement and Probation Denied |
|---|---|---|---|
| 1 month–6 years | 18 | 17 | 14 |
| 7 years–12 years | 13 | 15 | 13 |
| 13 years–18 years | 9 | 10 | 9 |
| Total number of children | 40 | 42 | 36 |

they were returned home. It was hoped that the presence of an authoritative agency, the Probation Department, would motivate the parent(s) to improve standards of child care sufficiently so as not to warrant subsequent court action.

A third group of 11 cases consisted of those in which, during or after investigation, the Probation Department rejected the caseworker's recommendation for placement in violation of either Section 600 A or B of the Juvenile Court Law. These requests were usually rejected on grounds of "insufficient evidence" to support a neglect petition. In these instances, the caseworker's assessment of neglect was not supported by the Probation Department, which did not refer the request to court for a disposition hearing.

The hypothesis predicting that a large number of children per family would influence the court to reject a caseworker's request for placement was not upheld. The mean number of children per family was 3.1 for cases in which the court ordered placement, it was 2.6 for families that received noncourt supervision, and it was 3.3 for families in which the caseworker's request was denied in its entirety. Application of a t-test showed that the mean number of children did not differ significantly among the three disposition groups. Nor was the age of the children involved in petitions a factor associated with the outcome of the request for placement, as Table II indicates.

### Parental Behavior

From a reading of petition summaries, it became evident that the caseworker's decision to request court intervention aimed at placement of the children was related to behavior problems of the parents. The bulk of evidence presented served to document the existence of detrimental parental behavior patterns and to show the adverse effects such behavior had on the children. Three types of family patterns were identified.

The largest category contained what the caseworker frequently termed the inadequate or immature parent. This group included the physically ill, the mentally dull, the immature personality, and the parent who was seemingly unaware of the cultural and social expectations for child care and guidance. Over two-fifths of the families in the study fell into this category. Most of the families were noticed by the community and the caseworker because of the behavior of the children themselves. It was the parents' inadequate response, or lack of response, to their children's behavior that directed the attention of the caseworker to the parents' inability to perform their parental duties.

The second category presented a somewhat different picture. It comprised the parents who had been diagnosed by some source other than the caseworker as being severely emotionally disturbed or mentally ill. There were 14 families in this category. For the most part, the children in these situations did not act out in an antisocial or delinquent manner. The complaints from the school—if any—described strange, withdrawn, maladjusted children who frequently had trouble achieving their potential. The home conditions might or might not be poor. The parent's behavior itself was largely responsible for community attention to the family, and evidence supporting the adverse effects on the children had to be sought primarily by the caseworker.

The third category contained families in which one or both of the parents were alcoholic. This category did not include parents who were known to drink occasionally, but rather those who drank consistently to the point where they were unable to provide minimum standards of child care. Although mental illness and inadequacy were frequently alluded to in the request, alcoholism was cited as being the primary cause of neglect. To the community, these families appeared quite similar to the first category. Complaints by relatives were common among these families and were largely responsible for clarifying for the caseworker whether the drinking problem was severe and repetitive, or sporadic. The physical condition of the home and of the children was usually very poor. School complaints of excessive absenteeism and poor child hygiene were frequent. Many of these children behaved in an aggressive, acting-out fashion, thereby attracting attention to the family. Usually, along with the children's acting out, the parents attracted attention on their own.

There appeared to be a tendency, which could not be statistically assessed,[7] for the court to intervene most actively in cases where the parent's current drinking problem was associated with a neglect situation;

---

[7] More than 20 percent of the cells in this table had an expected frequency of less than five. A $\chi^2$ test could therefore not be used since data did not meet the requirements for use of this test. For a discussion of the appropriate uses of the $\chi^2$ test, *see* Sidney Siegel, *Nonparametric Statistics* (New York: McGraw-Hill Book Co., 1956), p. 110.

TABLE III. Behavior Patterns of Parents as Related to Disposition of Requests

| Behavior Pattern | Placement Sustained | Noncourt Supervision | Placement and Probation Denied | Total |
|---|---|---|---|---|
| Alcoholism | 6 | 2 | 1 | 9 |
| Emotional instability | 5 | 5 | 4 | 14 |
| Immature personality | 2 | 9 | 6 | 17 |
| Total number of cases | 13 | 16 | 11 | 40 |

TABLE IV. Effect of Parental Behavior on Children as Related to Disposition

| Effect of Parental Behavior | Placement Sustained | Noncourt Supervision | Placement and Probation Denied | Total |
|---|---|---|---|---|
| Physical abuse or urgent need of protection[a] | 9 | 5 | 4 | 18 |
| Adverse health and development predicted | 4 | 11 | 7 | 22 |
| Total number of cases | 13 | 16 | 11 | 40 |

$\chi^2 = 4.64$, 2 df, $p < .10$ (two-tailed).

[a] Physical abuse or urgent need of protection includes situations in which a child is physically abused or his life is threatened, as in cases of diagnosed severe malnutrition.

whereas the implications of parental emotional problems or personal immaturity for the welfare of the child were given relatively less consideration (see Table III). A tendency by the court to give greater weight to overt physical abuse as against potential harm to the child's future development was also noted, as is shown in Table IV.

For the guidance of its caseworkers, the Los Angeles County Bureau of Public Assistance publishes a statement that explores in general terms what constitutes adequate child care in such areas as food, shelter, housekeeping, clothing, child hygiene, medical care, school attendance, and supervision of children.[8] Instances of inadequate parental performance in one or more of these areas of child care are used as documentation for child neglect petitions.

The hypothesis predicting that the court would recommend placement in situations in which evidence of danger to the safety and well-being of the child could be documented was upheld. Instances of poor child care were tabulated for all 40 cases, and a median test was performed to determine whether a larger number of items of poor child care was

[8] *Expectations of Child Care in ANC/GR Family Situations* (Los Angeles: Los Angeles County Bureau of Public Assistance, 1963).

TABLE V. Incidence of Neglect as Related to Disposition

| Incidence of Neglect | Placement Sustained | Noncourt Supervision | Placement and Probation Denied | Total[a] |
|---|---|---|---|---|
| 6 or less items of poor child care | 3 | 10 | 8 | 21 |
| 7 or more items of poor child care | 8 | 6 | 3 | 17 |
| Total number of cases | 11 | 16 | 11 | 38 |

$\chi^2 = 5.02$, 2 df, $p = \frac{1}{2}$ (.10) $= p < .05$ (one-tailed).
[a] This information was not available for two cases.

TABLE VI. Police Involvement in Support of Request as Related to Disposition

| Police Action | Placement Sustained | Noncourt Supervision | Placement and Probation Denied | Total |
|---|---|---|---|---|
| Police involvement | 11 | 6 | 3 | 20 |
| No police involvement | 2 | 10 | 8 | 20 |
| Total number of cases | 13 | 16 | 11 | 40 |

$\chi^2 = 9.50$, 2 df, $p < .01$ (two-tailed).

associated with a court decision to remove children from such homes (see Table V).

The differences among the three groups were statistically significant and indicate that cases involving a larger number of instances of "poor" child care were sustained for placement by the Juvenile Court more frequently than those involving fewer items of "poor" child care. Documented evidence of child neglect was significantly associated with the decision of the court for placement of the neglected child away from the home.

### Police Involvement

Another factor associated with the court's decision to sustain placement of the child away from the home was in relation to cases in which the police were directly involved or supported a caseworker's decision to request a petition. In some instances, police involvement resulted from the behavior of a parent, and the welfare of the child was either acted upon by the police, or the implications of the situation were conveyed by the police to the Bureau of Public Assistance.

A $\chi^2$ test showed that police involvement was significantly associated with the court's decision to support the caseworker's recommendation for placement (Table VI). Further underscoring the association between police involvement in neglect cases and the decision of the court to sustain placement was the finding that in seven cases in which the police had removed children from the home at the time of the court hearing, all seven cases were decided in favor of placement away from home.

Over one-third of the parents had been previously charged with neglect. This fact was not significantly associated with court disposition of cases.

## SUMMARY

A retrospective study of the outcome of petitions filed with the Juvenile Court by child welfare workers on behalf of neglected children whose parents were receiving public assistance indicated that social work requests for placement outside the home were followed in less than one-third of the cases studied. Both the Probation Department, which investigated all families, and the court frequently failed to accept social work recommendations.

The lack of consensus among the three institutions involved in neglect situations—i.e., the Juvenile Court, the Probation Department, and the Bureau of Public Assistance—was analyzed in relation to a number of hypotheses the study sought to test. It was found that court decisions to place children away from the parent(s) were based on documented evidence of child neglect.

Court-admissible evidence was most likely to result in placement.[9] Even though the Juvenile Court is a relatively new statutory entity designed, in part, as a parental surrogate, "it is a court first and foremost; an inter-disciplinary instrument for individualized justice and treatment within the overarching need of public security."[10]

No statistically significant differences were found in relation to family size or to age of children in a family as related to court decisions to sustain or reject a recommendation for placement outside the home. The sex of the child was likewise not a factor influencing placement decisions. It had occasionally been alleged by workers in child welfare that court decisions were frequently related to the above practical considerations; the findings of this research failed to support such contentions.

Clear and present danger to the safety and well-being of children was

---

[9] Legal neglect arises out of certain *factual* situations. The word "neglect" as respects custody of children "is the disregard of *duty,* owing to indifference or willfulness." In *re Sweet* (1957) 317 P2d (OKL) 231, 235. We usually speak of parental duties as care, custody, and control. Court interpretations seem to define neglect in reference to the categories of physical abuse, moral atmosphere, desertion, physical health, and work or labor required of the children. The question of neglect is a question of fact. For an incisive discussion of the legal point of view about child neglect, *see* William T. Downs, "The Meaning and Handling of Child Neglect—A Legal View," *Child Welfare,* XLII (1963), 131–134.

[10] Homer W. Sloane, "The Juvenile Court: An Uneasy Partnership of Law and Social Work," *Smith College Studies in Social Work,* XXXV (1965), 225–226.

the principal factor influencing a court decision to remove children from the care of their parents. Evidence of physical abuse or malnutrition, documented evidence of inadequate child care, and police intervention on behalf of neglected children were associated with court action that led to separation of children and parents. On the other hand, psychodynamically based predictions of adverse future emotional development of children resting on casework inferences derived from parental character problems or inadequacies were inversely related to court decisions resulting in placement.

Essentially, then, when requesting placement, caseworkers focused on the current and future needs of children and parental failure to meet these needs. The court focused on legally admissible evidence indicating neglect, and sustained placement where such evidence was most fully presented.

The data allow for inferences about factors influencing disposition of neglect cases in Los Angeles County Juvenile Court. It is not suggested that the generalizations advanced in this presentation are equally applicable to the disposition of neglect petitions in other parts of the country. It seems important that this survey be replicated in a variety of localities so that we can learn more about the working relationships between social agencies and Juvenile Courts and, aided by empirical research, take steps to improve it.

## IMPLICATIONS

The data from this research inferentially suggest that social workers buttress placement requests with supporting material that is based on psychological considerations, such as emotional damage that is likely to result to a child when parental behavior is immature or emotionally disturbed. Although such an outcome may well be the case, predictions of this kind do not constitute factual evidence of neglect in the eyes of the court.

In order to facilitate placement where indicated, it might be worth considering whether social agencies involved with the preparation of neglect petitions might not benefit from legal counsel with the preparation of petitions. This might lead to greater efforts to identify and document court-admissible evidence of child neglect that is undoubtedly available, thus enhancing the likelihood that the court will concur in a social-work-recommended placement request.

A more fundamental and more meaningful step would be to establish a study group composed of representatives of the Juvenile Court, the Probation Department, the Bureau of Public Assistance, and other agencies concerned with the welfare of children whose task it would be to work toward greater consensus on criteria that constitute neglect. In such

an undertaking, there is the possibility of achieving a higher rate of agreement between social work and legal agencies based on improved communication. The need to define child-neglect criteria that are mutually
acceptable to all instrumentalities charged with the welfare of children
is seen as an urgent task in light of the findings of this study.

# 6

([ The following article represents one of the few attempts at systematic
evaluation of the work of protective-service agencies.

## What Protective Service Can Do

*Joseph B. Kelley*

Protective service has been defined as service given to protect children
when there is evidence of their being neglected, abused, cruelly treated,
or in moral danger.[1] In Fresno County, where there has been a Protective
Service Unit under the auspices of the Welfare Department since 1954,
a community screening committee accepts referrals of cases from any individual or agency in the county. This committee, the official "intake"
group for protective services, is presently composed of the probation intake
supervisor, the county child welfare services supervisor, and representatives from the county schools' guidance office, the Family Service Center,
the sheriff's department and the county health department.
    Criteria for acceptance of a case are:

• Existence of a problem involving children which we deem likely to lead
  to neglect.
• Possibility of resources within the family to improve the situation or
  to prevent further deterioration.
• Availability of resources within the community for helping the family.

---

[1] *A Guide to Protective Services for Children*, California Department of Social Welfare, February 1958, Foreword.

Clients of the protective services unit do not voluntarily seek assistance, and in the majority of cases the juvenile court is involved on a neglect or potential neglect basis. Most referrals have come from the schools, public health nurses, the probation department and law enforcement officers. The present staff of the protective services unit consists of three full-time workers, each with case loads of about twenty-five.

The questions with which we concerned ourselves in this study were: With what kinds of problems does our protective services unit help neglectful parents? And how successful have we been? Since most referrals are made because of children's anti-social behavior or problems resulting in harm to children, an examination of success—or lack of success—in working with clients ought to contribute to a possible means of predicting situations we can help. This should sharpen intake criteria, improve treatment, and help to assess the general effectiveness of our program.

## IDENTIFYING PROBLEM AREAS

We chose as the method of approach an analysis of our entire protective services case load as of July 1, 1958. First we listed and categorized the problems in all cases active as of January 1, 1958. Surprisingly, this did not prove difficult. The problems were readily identifiable from intake summaries, periodic evaluations, and other reports in the case record. Low case loads may have accounted for .the ease with which problems were identified and diagnosed. The responsibility of keeping the juvenile court informed of progress in many of the cases and the protective services screening committee in the others may also have been an incentive. Information gained from court, medical, psychiatric, and psychological examinations and official school records, and verified acts of the client were the basis of the diagnosis. The actual tabulation for purposes of the survey was made by the supervisor after examining the case record and conferring with the worker assigned the case.

It is significant that twenty-six problem areas were encountered in all the cases. Situations noted in the case record could be assigned to the proper category with a minimum of difficulty. While the problems presented covered a wide range, it may be helpful to organize them into three main categories; these should not be considered mutually exclusive, since there is a certain amount of overlapping.

## OVERT PROBLEMS

The first group would be that in which problems were overt, where danger of physical harm was often immediate or where a single, specific act or a repetition of the same act was necessary to correct a situation. Because of the imminent danger, these were the problems of greatest concern to other agencies and individuals, professional and lay, in the community. These conditions included:

> lack of proper physical care of children, need for medical care, poor management of finances, inadequate supervision of children or the absence of any supervision, problem created by mother's disappearance, inadequate housekeeping, grossly inadequate housing, and alcoholism. (Alcoholism was included because we have no specific treatment program for it and its most significant aspect was the effect of a parent's condition on children and others in the community.)

All these situations created or threatened danger of physical harm to children.

Problems requiring one specific action or a repeated action to correct a situation were:

> failure of absent parent to contribute; law violation by parents, usually repetition of one previously committed (placed in this category because we have no formal approach to the problem such as in a probation or parole setting); school adjustment and attendance, especially attendance (placed in this category because difficulties were so often traced to such factors as parents' keeping children home to care for younger children, failure of parents to insist that children attend school, lack of clothing, inappropriate or filthy clothing, no lunch or lack of lunch money, or the lack of specialized facilities at a particular school).

## PROBLEMS REQUIRING BASIC CHANGE

The second group of problems were those in which a basic readjustment seemed necessary for basic improvement—some change in personality or feelings in approaching a situation, and often a new relationship or feelings toward another person or persons. This group included problems of employment and rehabilitation, including working relationship with co-workers (attitudes and personal problems were usually more significant than job opportunities), problems involved in reuniting of family and in abandonment of unrealistic plan, parent-child relationships, husband-wife relationships, general adjustment of children, and general adjustment of mother. Problems involving recreational activities were included because they usually were related to the family's approach to its environment, manifested in gross deficiency or mishandling of recreational activities. Arrangement of living plan was placed in this group because this problem often involved a family's "way of life" and the ability or inability to accept assistance from others and to respect necessary limits or standards. Assistance from relatives, also included, usually involved situations in which feelings toward and frequency of contacts with relatives were a potential source both of difficulties and of aid.

The problems present in the third main category caused difficulties inherently impossible to overcome; or at least it was not primarily the protective service workers' job to help the client overcome them. These problems were mental deficiency, mental illness, blindness and incurable ill health. Only one case out of twenty-one in this category showed improvement.

## ASSESSING IMPROVEMENT IN CASES

The methods and procedures used at the beginning to assess the status of problems were also used at the close of the survey period. As much reliance as possible was placed on court, medical, psychiatric, and psychological examinations, official school records, and verified acts of the client. In other words, in a court case where failure to obtain medical care for a child was part of the original complaint, the court would determine at a later hearing whether the parents had acted to provide the necessary care. If they had physically abused the child or ignored his needs, the court would determine whether the parents had taken adequate steps to improve the situation. The evaluation was based on the points of law involved, and reports from the social worker, law enforcement officers or a physician, as indicated.

In a case which had not come to the attention of the court, school records would verify how many absences a child had had, and which were excused absences. For purposes of assessing improvement, the record might include a statement by the school attendance officer about what is considered satisfactory school attendance.

Some problems do not lend themselves to the type of description I have just made: parent-child relationships, for example. With problems of this sort the determination of improvement or lack of improvement consisted in a judgment by the worker based on statements by the parents and children and sometimes others, and the worker's evaluation of whether the parents' behavior in particular situations showed greater understanding and acceptance of a child and his needs (or whether a child made some effort to control behavior particularly upsetting to parents). Refinements in methods of measuring improvement, while desirable, are not absolutely essential in such a study. Determinations can still be made as to improvement or lack of improvement.

## RESULTS OF SURVEY

Following are the tabulated results of the survey on Groups 1 and 2:[2] It is interesting that improvement was achieved in almost one-half the problem areas identified. (Improvement is defined as some significant improvement rather than elimination of problems.) Anyone who has worked with problem-riddled families in neglect cases will appreciate the complex-

---

[2] Group 3 (mental deficiency, mental illness, blindness and incurable health) is not tabulated because only one case out of twenty-one showed improvement.

GROUP 1. **Problems of Overt Behavior**

| Problem | Improved | Not Improved |
|---|---|---|
| Inadequate physical care of children | 2 | 3 |
| Need for medical care | 7 | 1 |
| Poor management of money | 15 | 12 |
| Inadequate supervision of children | 10 | 9 |
| Failure of absent parent to contribute | 2 | 0 |
| Mother's disappearance | 1 | 0 |
| Alcoholism | 7 | 7 |
| Inadequate housekeeping | 7 | 9 |
| Inadequate housing | 5 | 7 |
| School adjustment and attendance | 8 | 12 |
| Law violation by parents | 1 | 3 |
| Totals | 65 | 63 |

GROUP 2. **Problems Requiring Basic Readjustment**

| Problem | Improved | Not Improved |
|---|---|---|
| Problems involved in reuniting family | 17 | 3 |
| Re-employment and rehabilitation | 13 | 8 |
| Arrangement of living plan | 6 | 3 |
| Holding of unrealistic plans | 4 | 0 |
| Recreational activities | 3 | 0 |
| Problems involved in relatives' assistance | 4 | 3 |
| Relationship with co-workers | 3 | 2 |
| Parent-child relationship | 7 | 7 |
| Husband-wife relationship | 1 | 6 |
| Child's general adjustment | 2 | 8 |
| Mother's general adjustment | 3 | 16 |
| Totals | 63 | 56 |

Total of Groups 1 and 2: Problem improved—128 cases; Problem not improved—119 cases.

ity of the assistance and the skill needed to help them effect and sustain even the simplest change.

Although the number of successes and failures for each of the problems varied, the potential for improvement for the cases in Group 1 does not appear to vary greatly. A possible exception is the problem of obtaining medical treatment. This area showed much more success than the others, perhaps because decisive help was often obtained from a source outside the family, such as the Red Cross or the public health department. In general, these are all areas in which the workers in the unit feel more sureness in working. Also, what is not being done and what needs to be done is often fairly clear and understandable to the client.

Our assistance to one-half of the cases with alcoholism, as indicated by the figures, might be questioned, since we have no specific treatment program for alcoholics. Success which was not due to good fortune must have been brought about indirectly by other factors. It does need further study.

The degree of success with problems in Group 2 was approximately the same as for Group 1, but the spread was much greater. First of all "reuniting of family" was the item which improved most often in the whole survey. Part of this success is undoubtedly traceable to the unit's basic approach —to prevent family breakdown and unnecessary foster home placement. In both these goals the protective services unit has the backing of the juvenile court. However, it is striking that within the last six months families were reunited in approximately one-fourth the cases covered in the survey. With the number of problems present in these families, the potential for breakdown would seem to be as great as the potential for reconciliation. In the majority of instances the reconciliation involved the return of children to a parent or parents. Our workers have found that in spite of many negative factors most parents love their children and want to care for them. This is a strength which can be built upon.

The table shows that conditions in Group 2 improved in a number of cases. Most of these successes showed some of the same qualities as the successes in Group 1; that is, clients readily understood the situation and their involvement, as in reuniting of family, employment and rehabilitation, and arrangement of a living plan. In other cases substantial aid was forthcoming from a source other than the client: for example, in problems involving recreational activities, protective services solicited aid from agencies in the community; assistance was asked from relatives for clients who had limited potential, or whom it was very difficult to assist substantially. Arrangement of living plan also involved outside assistance sometimes, when living arrangements with relatives were made for the client, to get help for him with the problems of daily living.

## PROBLEMS SHOWING RARE IMPROVEMENT

Finally, the last three items in Group 2 evidenced a large degree of failure, registering only six instances of improvement and thirty instances of lack of improvement. These conditions often seemed more nebulous and "total," both to workers and clients. Limiting factors may have included lack of sharpened diagnosis or of skill to help the client come to grips with these problems as well as clients' inability to make improvements. Although all the items in Group 1 formed part of a constellation of family problems, the conditions in Group 2 seemed to have a more pervading influence on the potential for improvement of the total family situation.

## SUMMARY AND CONCLUSIONS

In general, improvement or lack of improvement was not directly related to whether a problem situation was located in Group 1 or Group 2, although problems in Group 1 seemed more directly prone to possible improvement—especially those which were overt. In items showing improvement in Group 2, lack of overt behavior problem seemed to be compensated for by the fact that the problem in general seemed reasonably clearcut and understandable to the client. Secondly, and probably more important, the root cause of problems in Group 2—over-all poor adjustment, attitudes, or approaches to the situation—was not necessarily removed from those cases which showed improvement through assistance from resources other than those of the client. Reuniting of family, as noted previously, may have been an exceptional problem because of outstanding motivation on the part of the client and clear-cut agency function.

Group 3 needs no further comment, since treating these problems was not generally within the function or direct treatment skills of the protective services unit. They were included because when present they proved to have even more influence on other aspects of a case than did some of the problems in Group 2. Although this study was concerned only with success in helping clients to effect improvements in various problem areas, it is true that the problems dealt with were component parts of cases involving many other elements. Personality and motivational aspects of the clients themselves need evaluation. Also analysis of the incidence and success of the various problem areas, and their improvement in relation to a case as a whole, might well modify and refine conclusions about work with the various types of problems.

Problem areas in the protective service cases studied did not prove difficult to identify. The same conditions recurred in many of the cases. There appeared to be some success in helping clients to effect improvements in almost one-half the problems during the six months' study period; the condition most often reflecting improvement was reconciliation of parents and children. The problems with which protective service was most often successful were those where *what was not being done* for the children and *what needed to be done* for them was made clear and readily understandable to the parent. Situations in which assistance was forthcoming from sources other than the client were also more prone to improvement.

A number of values in the type of study undertaken seem evident. The preliminary step of identifying and tabulating the problems present seems valuable in itself since problems, goals, techniques, and chances of improvement in neglect and potential neglect cases have been only partially identified. Knowing the results which can be expected with various types of problems is especially important in relation to intake criteria, since existing protective service units undoubtedly have to establish intake priorities. We need further refinement of findings and knowledge of the relationship between specific problems and personality factors. This would increase the chances of evaluating various techniques for working with clients in different situations, and of determining the circumstances in which opportunities for effective service are greatest.

# 7

❲ The following is one of the few articles available which presents details of an experience in use of the group service method with protective-service families.

# Parents' Groups in Protective Services

*Jane McFerran*

/Public agencies can improve their services to neglectful parents through the use of parent meetings./This has been demonstrated by the success that the Protective Service Division of the Jefferson County Welfare Department, Louisville, Ky., has had in conducting discussion meetings for parents who have come to the division's attention on complaints that they have neglected or abused their children./The meetings supplement and reinforce the caseworkers' efforts to help these parents, many of whom tell of having difficulties with their children, but are largely unaware of their own responsibility in this regard. /

Most of these parents grew up in homes that badly prepared them for parenthood. Furthermore, they have not attained any preparation through formal or informal education. They are usually overburdened by childbearing and day-to-day living and lack knowledge of many of the elementary principles of child care.

We recognized that our primary purpose as a protective-service agency is the resolution of the problems behind specific complaints regarding the neglect or abuse of children, and that this would have to be done individually. But we came to the conclusion a few years ago that additional help in the principles of child care might be given to our clients in groups if they would be willing to attend meetings. In such groups the parents would have opportunities to meet others with similar problems, to exchange ideas, and to have a social experience. The practical hurdles of babysitter and transportation expenses were overcome when a local church provided funds for these and for refreshments.

## GETTING UNDER WAY

One of our caseworkers, who had had previous experience in leading group discussions and who understood the problems of families receiving protective service, volunteered to lead the discussions. Arrangements were made for the meetings to be held at a centrally located community settle-

63

ment house. A rather small room, where everyone could sit around the table, provided an informal atmosphere. We planned evening meetings so that the fathers could attend.

The caseworkers explained the purposes of the meetings to the parents. They emphasized that each person had something to contribute to the others because of his own experience as a parent, and that each could gain from the others. No coercion was used, but the caseworkers did revisit some families in order to encourage them to attend. As far as we know, only two families came reluctantly, feeling that attendance was expected of them, but after the first meeting they too attended willingly. Most of the parents who were invited had already overcome any initial resistance toward the agency that they might have had, and they expressed interest in this method of learning more about ways to become better parents.

The parents with whom we come in contact vary in their ability and capacity to change, and in their desire to do so, as well as in the degree of their cooperation with the agency. We have found that most of them do not intentionally neglect their children and really want to be good parents. By assuming this during our initial contacts with them we are usually able to overcome any resistance or hostility, so that the parents become willing to work with us. On the whole, the clients who have attended the meetings have seemed to develop a closer feeling for the agency as time goes on.

The original invitation list consisted of 13 families; this list increased to 24, and it varied throughout the series as new names were added and others were eliminated because of withdrawals. Nine members attended almost all the meetings, which took place every 2 weeks over a 6-month period. A core group of 14 persons consisted of 4 couples; 3 married women whose husbands were not in the home; 1 unmarried mother; and 2 married women whose husbands did not attend. The ages ranged from 21 to 50 years. All the families but one were of extremely low economic status. The intellectual level varied. Both whites and Negroes attended.

## THE CONTENT

As a starting point the group leader prepared an outline of topics to be covered during the series, but she allowed the meetings to be directed to the needs expressed by the group. The members spoke up freely about what they wanted discussed, and the discussions generally extended to topics that the agency considered important for them—such as discipline, normal child growth and development, and parent-child relationships. The group expressed such interest in husband-wife relationships that this subject was discussed at some length, and the members finally related their problems in this area to the problems they had with their children.

The leader used methods such as role playing and program aids such as pamphlets and an occasional film. An additional tool now being considered is the use of resource persons.

Recording was considered essential for group evaluation and for the information of the caseworkers. We have experimented with various methods of recording and, with the approval of the group, now have an additional staff member sitting in as recorder.

At the first meeting, the parents were somewhat aloof but they soon seemed to feel at ease and began to talk freely about themselves and their problems. As the meetings progressed they showed signs of more and more security.

The increasing ability of the group to assume responsibility for the direction of the discussion was demonstrated by the manner in which the meetings changed. The first meeting was opened by the leader, by introducing the members and reviewing the objectives of the series. At the beginning of each of the next two meetings she asked what the group planned to discuss. However, when the group assembled for the fourth meeting one of the members immediately presented a problem she wanted discussed. From then on, the members themselves suggested the topics for discussion.

The effect of the growing security of the members in interacting with the group was illustrated by the changes in Mr. and Mrs. White. When Mr. White joined the group, he apologized for his stuttering. The other members gave him considerable reassurance and acceptance. They talked about how verbal problems could be influenced by emotional problems. This ultimately led to a discussion of stage fright and of speaking in a group. The ability to function better when one felt sure of oneself was discussed at some length. As the meetings progressed, Mr. White's speech difficulty became less and less noticeable. His improvement was noted by the group three meetings later, and the reasons for the improvement were discussed. Mr. White's explanation was, "I can talk better now because you understand me and my problems." Other members said that they too now felt comfortable with the group because they felt accepted and knew what to expect. The leader then helped the members relate these ideas to children and their need to feel safe and comfortable.

Mrs. White seemed embarrassed by many of her husband's remarks during the first meeting, and tears would come to her eyes. By the second meeting she seemed completely at ease, laughed a lot, and entered into the discussion more readily. She also supported her husband's opinions and ideas. The group's acceptance of her husband, as well as of herself, was undoubtedly responsible for this change.

The group quickly identified with the purpose of the meetings, and by the second meeting was actively and enthusiastically engaged in problem solving. The "we" feeling or group spirit was evident during the third meeting and continued throughout the series. All the members took special interest in helping fellow members understand and find solutions to their problems. Each expressed a need to introduce personal problems, but the members were surprisingly willing to subordinate their needs to the needs of their members.

For example, at the end of the third meeting, which had been primarily devoted to teen-age problems, Mr. White, the father of teen-agers, pointed out that while the parents of younger children might profit in the future from discussion of teen-age problems, the next session should be concerned with younger children so that other parents could bring up their current problems. Another member offered to visit a couple who had been absent. On another occasion a member offered to help an unemployed father find a job.

The members of the group soon recognized the helpfulness of knowing that other people have problems and feelings similar to their own. To one member, who had feelings of inadequacy because of his financial situation, this recognition seemed to come as a shock. He said he was amazed to learn that the majority of those present had serious financial problems and that some were worse off than he. The mutuality of the members' problems seemed to produce a bond between them.

## GROUP FEELING

The members expressed appreciation of the meetings and a desire for other parents to have the same satisfying experience. One member wanted his neighbors to know he was part of such a group.

Considerable interest in meetings of this type had been expressed by a number of agencies and individuals in the community, and our agency wanted to share the results of this experience with them. The members of the group seemed pleased with the idea of publicity that might help to interest others in joining future groups sponsored by the agency or in forming their own groups.

When the possibility of inviting a reporter to sit in on one of the meetings was suggested, the members responded enthusiastically, saying that this would be the best way to explain the meetings. We, of course, would not have gone ahead without their approval. They showed their pride in being identified with the group by indicating a willingness to have their names used even when assured that this was not necessary. They said they wanted others to know that they were trying to improve themselves as parents.

In order to protect the members, we talked the whole matter over ahead of time with a reporter whom we selected because of his knowledge of social agencies and his sincere respect for people. He agreed to call the members "parents with problems," who had been referred to the Protective Service Division for casework help.

The following example illustrates the warmth, friendliness and acceptance, as well as the group feeling, that existed in the meetings.

The Martins joined the group for the first time at the fifth session. Mr. Martin had a "chip on the shoulder" attitude. He dominated the meeting, talking in an almost compulsive manner. He was defensive, antagonistic, and suspicious of the acceptance and friendliness of the group. As Mr. Martin dogmatically advocated various methods of discipline for children, the leader attempted to emphasize and utilize any positives in what he was saying. The group attempted to follow suit. For example, as Mr. Martin advocated harsh methods of discipline, Mr. White would attempt to clarify his statements, emphasizing agreement with the need for firm discipline, but distinguishing between firm discipline and harsh measures that reflect rejection. At one time during the evening, Mr. Martin asked the members of the group just what they were trying to do. Their explanation revealed a clear understanding of the purpose of the meetings and showed how they had been helped by them. Typical was the statement: "We talk over our problems and give each other ideas."

When the session ended, several members of the group urged Mr. Martin to return to the next meeting. He said he would probably not come again and expressed doubt about the value of the meetings and his ability to participate in them. Several of the members again explained to him the purpose of the meetings and reassured him about his ability to participate. Their efforts to help Mr. Martin feel accepted and wanted were sincere and friendly.

Later in the week, Mrs. Martin told the caseworker that her husband had had such an enjoyable time that he could hardly wait until the next meeting. The Martins attended every meeting from then on and are currently attending this year's sessions.

## THE EFFECTS

Many members of the group made sincere attempts to apply at home some of the ideas developed in the meetings. One discussion of husband-wife relationships illustrates these efforts:

Mr. Johnson complained that his wife never had time for him, and several husbands and wives said that they had similar problems. Mrs. Johnson admitted that her husband's complaint was valid, but said that she was unable to do things differently because of her many chores. Mr. West told about some similar problems that he and his wife had been able to work out by talking them over. Mrs. Johnson reviewed her schedule and some of the practical problems involved, giving many reasons why she could not solve her problem. Mr. West said, "It looks like you don't want time with one another." This seemed to set Mrs. Johnson back for a moment and she did not respond.

The group then suggested to the Johnsons and the others who had this problem that the husband and wife sit down and discuss the matter, each considering the other's needs and schedule, and find some time they could spend together. Mrs. Johnson, and also Mrs. Roby, whose husband did not attend the meetings, agreed to try. At this point Mrs. Kerwin, whose husband had deserted, interrupted to comment laughingly, "I certainly wish that I had that problem now; I sure would know how to solve it." Although she said this with humor and everyone was amused, it obviously carried home a point to the wives who were fortunate enough to still interest their husbands.

At the next meeting, the leader showed a film entitled "In Time of Trouble," which depicted some of the marital problems discussed at the previous meeting. A lively discussion of wives finding time for their husbands ensued. Mrs. Roby contributed an account of recent improvement in her home which she had brought about by making a point of leaving the dishes in the sink and sitting down in the living room with her husband for an hour or two of conversation. She said she felt that her husband appreciated what she was doing, and she gave examples of how he had become more considerate of her. The Johnsons said they had tried to set aside some time to spend with each other and had found this beneficial, although they still had problems.

The group leader attempted to help the members see that their children's concept of marriage is based on the example set by their parents. In this connection, Mr. White talked about the way his stepdaughter belittled him to his wife and constantly urged her mother to divorce him because of his inability to earn a living. The group members encouraged Mrs. White to tell them how she thought she might handle this problem. She said that she would tell her daughter that her husband is her choice, that it is her marriage, and that her daughter may make her own choice about whom she will marry and the kind of marriage she will have. Mrs. White spoke with sincerity about her feelings of responsibility and loyalty toward her husband and her desire to be a partner in the marriage regardless of the problems that arose. Mr. White was obviously touched by her remarks and asked, "Why don't you say things like that to me at home?" Without embarrassment Mrs. White replied that she thought he knew how she felt. Later, during an interview with his caseworker, Mr. White spoke enthusiastically about the meetings and particularly about the leader's ability to help his wife speak up as she did at the meeting. He had never heard her do this before.

### HELPING EACH OTHER

On one occasion Mr. White described an incident that had taken place when he was out working with his 11-year-old son. He started teasing the boy about girls, particularly about one long telephone conversation the boy had had with a girl. Shortly after that the boy disappeared, and when it came time to go home, he could not be found. Mr. White regarded his son's running away as a case of disobedience. The others in the group disagreed. "You shouldn't kid children," said Mrs. Cook. "It makes them feel small and inferior." Mr. Martin commented, "You teased him about something he was sensitive to. He didn't like it, so he ran off." Mr. White then told about trying to make amends by buying a fishing rod for the boy. Another member then asked, "But why didn't you apologize to him?" "Apologize—to a child?" Mr. White retorted. "I wouldn't apologize to a child unless I was seriously wrong." "But giving him the fishing rod was an apology," said Mrs. Cook. "And I think it was misleading," put in another. "Suppose there comes a time when you can't give him something." After a number of other general comments by other members about teasing, Mr. White admitted, "Well, I've learned this lesson—never to tease my boy about girls."

Some of the participants demonstrated a great deal of insight and understanding. At times they were rather direct in their efforts to help others understand their own behavior better.

On a number of occasions Mr. Johnson had his inconsistencies pointed out to him by another member of the group, who encouraged him to reevaluate his methods of dealing with his children. For example, Mrs. Kerwin said, "You make exceptions for yourself and are able to give many excuses, but you do not do the same thing for others. Surely you can make exceptions for your own children." Mr. Johnson, who had joined the meetings with a rigid set of ideas, at first became confused as he began to question his own methods. He became anxious as he expressed a desire to change, but an inability to do so. He asked, "Is there any hope for a person like me?" His acceptance by the group and reassurance by his caseworker in individual interviews helped to relieve his anxiety as he attempted to assimilate new concepts and methods and incorporate them into his life.

The outstanding example of group feeling occurred when the group arranged a surprise shower for Mrs. White, who was expecting a baby. All were enthusiastic about the plan, and at the next meeting the Whites were overwhelmed by the thoughtfulness of their new friends. Mrs. White had had five children, but had never been given a shower before, and most of the other parents had never participated in such an activity.

## VARIOUS USES

During the period when the first meetings were being held, the caseworkers were occupied with getting people to join and to return. We had not really expected the resultant enthusiasm. As the meetings progressed and our initial fears of failure proved unfounded, we realized that the meetings could be used in several ways to improve our service to clients.

A new service concept emerged as we found that the meetings could supplement our casework efforts with parents whose children were no longer seriously neglected or abused. The following case illustrates this process:

Mrs. Kerwin, a young woman with eight children, whose husband had deserted the family, had been living with her relatives in a dilapidated coal shed. Nineteen people were living in the one room, with insufficient furniture and heat. The children were usually found completely unclothed and dirty. We had worked on this case for several years, persisting in our efforts to help the young mother obtain suitable housing. Our casework service was focused on cleanliness, proper care and supervision of the children, improvement in physical surroundings, and the mother's conduct with men as well as other relationships as they affected the care of the children. When these problems seemed to have been resolved, we could have terminated our contact, for as the worker reevaluated the situation with Mrs. Kerwin, both recognized that the children were no longer neglected. However, the mother was able to see that she needed better understanding of the emotional needs of her children. We felt an obligation to help her with this and suggested that she might benefit from our group meetings.

Mrs. Kerwin joined the parents' group, attended regularly, and participated enthusiastically. Her increased understanding and her desire to apply her new knowledge was revealed through her answers to theoretical questions, as well as her comments on how she handled specific problems at home. She became increasingly aware of the way in which adults can be affected by childhood experiences, and was able to offer personal illustrations of this. For example, she expressed resentment of the extreme criticism she had received as a child and talked about her efforts to be more understanding about what she expected of her children. She told about allowing the children to wash dishes their own way even if she had to do them over after the children went to bed.

When the first series of meetings was completed we closed this case, knowing we had done much more than effect a temporary adjustment. We had been able to reach this mother while her children were still young and to provide her with the opportunity to develop more fully her potentials for being a good mother. This was a truly preventive service.

Another case shows how group participation and individual casework can interact to provide a more effective service to clients. The Andrews family was referred to us on complaint of abuse of a 16-month-old child. Mrs. Andrews was harassed by the care of six children. Over a period of time we found no recurrence of the abuse, but did spend much time trying to motivate the parents to seek necessary medical attention for the family. Mrs. Andrews would appear to accept the worker, and would make plans for obtaining medical care, but later she would change the plans or put them off. At first she was quite defensive about the abuse charges and tried to convince the caseworker that everything was all right. Both parents were finally induced to attend the parents' meetings.

Immediately after the first meeting, Mrs. Andrews kept her first appointment at the agency's office. During that interview she broke down, saying, "That movie at the meeting was intended for Ira and me." The group leader had shown a film concerned with marital difficulties; it depicted a husband going out and getting drunk because of pressures at home. Mrs. Andrews then brought up her concern about her marital problems and her husband's drinking. Up to this point she had defensively denied any marital or drinking problems. Participation in the meetings had helped her to bring out and discuss her need for help.

This paved the way for a better working relationship with her caseworker, who was then able to help Mrs. Andrews develop more understanding of her husband and of her own feelings. The meetings provided an opportunity to the couple for evenings out and stimulated them to plan other activities together. The marital relationship improved as did the relationship with the children. Mrs. Andrews' comments about the meeting were: "We have so much fun," and "The meetings are relaxing. Afterward I am not so tired and irritable with the children."

We closed this case when the couple demonstrated increased ability to assume their responsibilities as parents.

Still another case, the Martins, suggests a way in which parent meetings can assist the caseworker in one phase of her work with a family. The worker was attempting to help Mr. Martin overcome feelings of insecurity, which had resulted in friendlessness, possessiveness toward his wife, and harsh treatment of their children. The fact that the Martins had no social contacts was a source of conflict between them. Mr. Martin's perception of himself in relation to other people was reflected in statements he made to the group at the early meetings, such as "You don't like what I say" and "Everything I say is wrong." The group assured him that they liked him even if they did not agree with everything he said.

The positive responses he received from the group seemed to encourage Mr. Martin to attempt other interpersonal relationships. He made a conscious effort to be friendlier with his neighbors, whom he had ignored in the past. At first this new friendliness consisted merely of speaking to his neighbors. However, Mr. Martin was able to recognize his own positive feelings about his ability to do this and his enjoyment of the responses he received. He then demonstrated his increased security in his relationships with others by inviting some neighbors to visit his home. Later he expressed a desire to form a discussion group in his neighborhood.

The efforts to help Mr. Martin understand himself better and become more socialized are still in progress. The meetings have helped the case-worker toward this goal by providing this man with a testing ground for experiencing a pleasurable relationship with a group and helping him to move on toward others.

## CONCLUSIONS

It should be noted that the members of the group described varied in age, economic status, and intellectual capacity, and included both Negroes and whites, as well as both sexes. This suggests that the major ingredient in selection of the participants is the similarity of their problems. This idea is, of course, open for further observation and study.

We have concluded that such meetings, geared to the intellectual capacity, knowledge, experience, and interests of our clients, can give them an enriching experience and can assist us in our efforts to help them become better parents. At present we do not know how lasting some of these effects may be. In order that these new-found satisfactions might be continued and developed further after the meetings are over, we are considering ways in which the families now participating in our second series of meetings may be helped to move into other community group activities.

We are also considering measurement techniques for making objective evaluation of various phases of such projects.

We sincerely think that the parents gained from the experience. The following are a few direct quotations from the parents' own comments about the meetings:

> • On the way home from the meetings we stop for hamburgers, like a couple of teen-agers on a date.
> • The meetings help me more when I get home and think about them.
> • My wife talks about nothing else. Although she doesn't talk much in the meetings, we discuss everything that happened. This is the first thing she has been interested in that we can talk about together.
> • It is the only time I have to sit down and think.
> • We help each other. One week I get something from the others; the next week they might get something from me.

So regardless of what we think, it is clear that these people are aware of the positive nature of this experience for them. We hope other agencies will form similar groups and report on them so that the use of parent meetings may become an accepted procedure with clients of casework agencies.

# Section II

Homemaker and
Day-Care Services

HOMEMAKER SERVICE and day care are both supplementary child-welfare services; they assume some of the responsibilities of the mother when she is ill or when she is employed. Both programs offer great promise in providing adequate care for the child so that he can remain in his own home. Despite the great potential value of these programs, both are, as yet, of very limited development.

A Children's Bureau report published in 1968 indicates that although some 4.1 million working mothers with children under six years of age were in the labor force, only 265,000 of these children were cared for in a day-care center or nursery school.[1] A nationwide sampling of day-care centers indicated that "only 7% have the regular services of a social worker."[2]

Compared with potential need, day care is in short supply and only a limited number of the limited centers utilize the services of social workers. Similarly, as of January, 1968, there were only 11,500 home-makers throughout the country, only half of whom worked full time.[3] This contrasts with an estimated need of 200,000 homemakers if the country is to be adequately supplied with this much-needed service.

Both day-care and homemaker service should be developed as "social utilities"; like other "social utilities," such as public schools and libraries, they should be made available to all families with or without the supplementary casework service. This would be in line with an "institutional," as opposed to a "residual," orientation toward day-care and homemaker service. Yet even if this were the case it is likely that the child-welfare social worker's responsibility in the day-care center and with the home-maker would have a "residual" focus. Social work would be offered to, and used by, those families who could not make adequate, appropriate use of these services without additional help.

---

[1] Seth Low and Pearl Spindler, *Child Care Arrangements of Working Mothers in the United States*, Children's Bureau Publication, No. 461, 1968, p. 16.

[2] Florence A. Ruderman, *Child Care and Working Mothers*, C.W.L.A., 1968, p. 102.

[3] A *Unit of Learning About Homemaker–Home Health Aide Service*, National Council for Homemaker Service, Inc., New York City, 1968, Table III, p. 13.

# 8

⟪ The following two articles offer some empirical evidence to substantiate the contention that homemaker service, appropriately used, can prevent placing some children outside the home and provide care for the children at substantially lower cost to the community. Both are reports of demonstration projects, one in a private agency, the other in a public agency.

# Nine- to Twenty-four-Hour Homemaker Service Project

*The Staff of the Homemaker Service of the Children's Aid Society, New York*

In August 1958, The Children's Aid Society, in cooperation with the New York City Department of Welfare, Bureau of Child Welfare, completed a study of 229 children in 100 families who were returned to their own homes from temporary care. The findings of this study indicated that 143 children in sixty-one families could have remained at home through a more flexible use of homemaker service. Many of these children were from one-parent families who appeared to be self-sustaining but did not have the resources to provide care for their children during crises. In 1959 a grant from the New York Fund for Children was matched by equal funds from The Children's Aid Society to test the validity of the 1958 findings.

## PURPOSE

The purpose of the project was to prevent the placement of children in shelters by providing homemaker service for more than the usual eight-hour day. It was anticipated that having homemakers respond to emergencies at any time of day or night would (1) enable children to remain in the familiar surroundings of their own homes, schools, and neighborhoods, and thus prevent the emotional shock of abrupt removal from their own homes; (2) enable a father to retain responsibility for his family and remain on his job; (3) hasten the recovery of a mother by relieving her of worry over the care of her children; and (4) keep intact families who otherwise would be scattered. Experience has shown that once the members of a family are separated, it is difficult to bring them together again, and the children linger on in the shelters.

## PROCEDURE OF PROJECT STUDY

Three experienced homemakers were designated to meet emergencies at any time of day or night. In addition, funds for two days of casework time and one day of clerical help per week were included in the project budget.

When an emergency arose, the Bureau of Child Welfare, the police, or the shelter worker was to call The Children's Aid Society caseworker, who would immediately either accompany one of the homemakers to the home or send her there alone. If the caseworker was not able to go with the homemaker, she would visit the home as soon as possible.

The project began in January 1960. Clarification of administrative questions and procedures, however, delayed referrals from the Bureau of Child Welfare for several months. Meanwhile, the service was also opened to applicants from other agencies and to individuals.

During the course of the project 185 applications involving 781 children were received. Of these, forty families with 184 children received extended hours of homemaker service. One hundred forty-five families with 597 children had to be refused because no project homemaker was available.

Twenty-nine children were under two years of age, fifty-nine were between two and six years, eighty were between seven and twelve, and sixteen were thirteen years and over.

## REASONS FOR EXTENDED HOURS OF SERVICE

The basic criterion for acceptance in all cases was that the children would have required shelter care had homemaker service not been available to them for more than the usual eight hours. Twenty-two of the forty families were maintained by one parent. The mothers were either unmarried, divorced, separated, or widowed. In one instance the mother was in a mental hospital and the father had been caring for the children. In three other families the fathers were in the hospital at the time of referral, and in one family the father was in prison.

Fifteen fathers were in the home when the need for extended hours of homemaker service occurred. One of the fathers suffered from severe epileptic seizures and consequently was unable to assume responsibility for his children. The other fathers worked at night or had such long and irregular hours that they could not care for the children while the mothers were absent. Many of them had marginal incomes, and the loss of even a few days' pay was crucial. Several of the fathers had histories of unemployment and were fearful of jeopardizing their present jobs; others had used more than their quota of absences, vacation, and sick leave and were also apprehensive about their jobs.

In fifteen of the forty families extended hours of homemaker service were needed because of childbirth. In ten other families the mothers had entered the hospital for emergency or planned operations—mastoid, gynecological, lung, heart, or other surgery. Twelve mothers were hospitalized for ulcers, hepatitis, Parkinson's disease, pneumonia, cerebral palsy, or infections. One mother had deserted her family, and another mother was at home but too incapacitated to care for her child during convalescence. In the family where the mother was in a mental hospital and the father had been caring for the children, the father suffered a stroke and had to be hospitalized. In eight families referral was a bona fide emergency, and a homemaker was placed on the day of request.

> The three Lewis children, ranging in age from seven to eleven, were without care when their mother had to leave suddenly for the hospital. Mrs. Lewis asked two neighbors to "keep an eye on" the children until the Department of Welfare could work out plans for their care; she did not want her children placed in a shelter, as she was certain that they would be upset and confused if they were separated from each other and from their home. The family lived in a rundown building in a deteriorated and desolate section of the city. When the caseworker and the homemaker arrived that evening, they found all three children huddled together on a bed, clinging to one another and obviously terrified. One neighbor, who lived in the next building, had told the girls to call out across the areaway if anything happened to them. There was no telephone in the apartment, and the lock on the front door was broken. When the children realized that the homemaker was going to stay, their relief was unmistakable and touching. Throughout the time their mother was in the hospital, they related warmly to the homemaker and made excellent use of the service.

The urgency of the request for extended hours of homemaker service was almost as great in thirteen other situations as it was for the eight families that required emergency service. In these cases a homemaker was placed within two days of the application. In the remaining nineteen families plans for extended hours of homemaker service were made in advance, and the homemaker was introduced to the parents and children before the service began.

## TWENTY-FOUR-HOUR SERVICE

Around-the-clock service, five to seven days a week, was needed by 135 children in thirty-one families. Two of these families had eight children, two had seven children, four had six children, six had five children, six had four children, five had three children, and six had two children.

In only ten of these families were the parents married and living together; in the other twenty-one they were either separated, divorced, unmarried, or widowed. Thus, ninety-six children had only one parent, and when anything happened to the parent, the children were completely alone. In twenty-two of these situations the request for twenty-four-hour homemaker service was due to the hospitalization of the mother. Eight other mothers were going to the hospital for confinements. In one family both parents were in the hospital. Eight of the fathers worked at night or had work shifts that prevented their caring for their children. One father was in the hospital, and another was at home physically incapacitated.

The extent to which the majority of the families in this group appeared to be completely estranged from their own close relatives was striking. They also suffered isolation from friends, neighbors, churches, and other groups. Only seven of these thirty-one families had relatives or friends who indicated any willingness to help. The remaining twenty-four families had either lost touch with their own relatives or the inter-family relationships were destructive. In this latter group a number of mothers refused to allow their own relatives or friends to care for their children or to visit in the home during their absence. An equal number of relatives made it clear that they would not involve themselves in any way in the family's problems.

> This kind of family alienation was illustrated by an urgent request for twenty-four-hour homemaker service for a mother of three children who was expecting her fourth child within a few days. The father had been on his way to meet the mother to buy a crib when he collapsed and died of a heart attack. Neighbors called the Children's Aid Society, and when the caseworker arrived, she found the mother in such a depressed and exhausted state that she was totally immobilized. She repeatedly expressed terror about going to the hospital and leaving her children without care. The mother's father and three sisters lived in the city, but relationships were so strained that they neither visited nor offered help in any way. The mother went to her husband's funeral by herself, and although various relatives were there, she also returned alone to her home.

## CHILDREN'S RESPONSES TO
## TWENTY-FOUR-HOUR HOMEMAKER SERVICE

Twenty-two children in six families told the homemakers how upset and frightened they had been during previous placements.

> In the Brown family the father had deserted. The mother kept postponing an urgently needed operation because she dreaded having her seven children placed as they had been when she was previously hospitalized. When twenty-four-hour homemaker service began, however, she left calmly for the hospital. All of the children quickly became devoted to the homemaker and mentioned how nervous and lonely they had been when they were separated the year before. During the months that the homemaker was with them, the children taught her Spanish cooking so that everything would be "exactly like home."

At first all of the one hundred thirty-five children reacted with varying degrees of upset and fearfulness to the emergency that required the homemaker to stay with them on a twenty-four-hour basis. The majority of these children, however, adjusted surprisingly quickly to the changes in their lives and were reassured both by the homemaker's presence and by her efforts to maintain their daily patterns of living. In most of these situations the tears, sleeplessness, and occasional tantrums of the first few nights subsided quickly.

In the King family, with five children between three and eleven, the unmarried mother had to be hospitalized immediately for a breast tumor. The homemaker and caseworker arrived just as the mother was leaving for the hospital, and although the mother tried to reassure the children as best she could, they huddled together in a fearful and suspicious group across the room from the homemaker. The younger ones were crying and calling for their "mommy," and one of the older boys seemed almost mute with fear. The homemaker reported that she could scarcely get any of them to eat. Three days later, when the caseworker returned, all of the children were talking and laughing noisily. Two of them were helping the homemaker make pancakes, two others were busily constructing a zoo out of cardboard, and the three-year-old was happily bothering everybody. They spoke of missing their mother and continually expressed their relief that they had been able to stay at home together.

In one-third of the families the children were not as easily reassured and exhibited disturbed behavior that ranged from natural reactions to the immediate crises to behavior that was obviously a result of severe and long-standing pathology. The children who presented the severest problems were those whose relationships to their mothers were the most troubled. These children had the greatest difficulty accepting or relating constructively to a mother substitute and were upset and threatened by the separation experience.

The most serious signs of disturbance tended to occur during the late evening and nighttime hours. These included severe asthma attacks, aggressive outbursts, attempts at running away, and a variety of sleeping disturbances such as nightmares, sleepwalking and talking, head banging, constant rocking, enuresis, and soiling. In one family the homemaker, at the request of the four young children in the home, agreed to sleep with the brilliant lights of a large mechanical Santa Claus shining in her face. The children were accustomed to the light and became wakeful and frightened when the homemaker attempted to dim the glare. In another family the three small children woke up regularly at 3:00 A.M. and sang hymns until 5:00 A.M. The presence of a comforting, reassuring homemaker was of inestimable value to these frightened, confused, and lonely children.

When service was needed for more than a week, a second homemaker was usually sent to relieve for a day or two. Although these families, particularly the children, were always prepared in advance for the necessity of relieving the homemaker, the change was frequently distressing to the younger children and to those who were most disturbed. In one family the three-year-old daughter had shown almost no reaction to her mother's leaving for the hospital. A week later, when the homemaker was preparing to leave for the weekend, this little girl became hysterical, sobbed, and clung to her, begging her not to leave her "with the new lady and without my mommy." Homemakers went to considerable lengths to reassure and prove to the children that they were definitely returning to them after the weekend or after a few days off. Most of the children seemed to relate with greater intensity and warmth to their first homemaker, who had been with them from the time of separation from the absent parent. A few children, however, related better to the different personality of the relief homemaker.

## PARENTS' RESPONSES TO TWENTY-FOUR-HOUR SERVICE

Approximately two-thirds of the thirty-one families who received twenty-four-hour homemaker service made constructive and appropriate use of it. The attitudes and behavior of the parents in this group ranged from passive, noninterfering acceptance of the homemaker and minimal involvement with the caseworker to families who actively and eagerly involved themselves in every step of planning and worked cooperatively with both the homemaker and the caseworker throughout the period of service.

Initially, many of the mothers, including the more adequate ones, evidenced great anxiety about their own displacement and fearfulness around the homemaker's role and functioning in their homes. Their uncertainty and fearfulness subsided in response to the steady reassurance and support of the caseworker and the homemaker.

In the remaining one-third of the families the combined efforts of the caseworker and the homemaker to help the parents use homemaker service appropriately were almost totally unavailing. This group included the most disturbed and deteriorated family situations. The parents tended to be suspicious and distrustful of the homemakers and frequently telephoned from the hospital or asked neighbors to drop in to "check on" the homemaker. Some of them were fearful that the homemaker would learn too much about some aspect of the family's life that they preferred to keep hidden, such as the whereabouts of the children's father, an illegal source of income, an extramarital affair, or the extent of disturbance in their children. Many of these parents were highly manipulative and demanding in their contacts with the homemaker and became upset and angry when all of their demands were not met. For example, one mother of three very disturbed children called the homemaker daily from the hospital to find out whether she had washed all the walls in the apartment, cleaned the venetian blinds, waxed the floors, and ironed all of the children's summer clothing, which was stored in the basement.

The adequacy of the homemakers seemed to threaten these mothers. Competition with the homemakers was increased by the positive reports they received from thoughtless or malicious relatives or from friends who told them how much calmer and better behaved their children were and how much better organized their households were now that a homemaker was in charge. Not infrequently these mothers attempted to alienate their children from the homemaker or managed to provoke a crisis of one kind or another that greatly added to the homemaker's difficulties in the home.

In some of these instances the problem was resolved by changing homemakers. In three situations the parent's inability to use the service constructively made it necessary to terminate the service following the mother's discharge from the hospital, although further help was obviously needed.

All but one of the eight fathers who were in the home when twenty-four-hour homemaker service was given were helpful and cooperated with the homemakers. These seven men made excellent use of the service. The responsibility the agency assumed for these children, particularly those in one-parent families, required that the casework staff be available night and day. The usual scope of casework service had to be broadened and intensified, and immediate action had to be taken. The first home visit and the arrival of the homemaker often took place on the day the mother left for the hospital. In the first interview and under emergency circumstances, information had to be secured about the children, the household routines, the management of money, where and how rent and utility bills were to be paid, where food was to be purchased, and the locations of schools and churches. A form was used to secure the written consent of the parent for the agency to obtain any emergency medical or dental treatment the children needed during the parent's absence. In some homes immediate arrangements had to be made for installing a telephone during the period of service so that the homemaker could phone in an emergency without leaving the children. If there was no adequate bed and bedding for the homemaker, the caseworker had to purchase a cot and bed linens and arrange for their speedy delivery.

Arrangements were also made with the parents to enable the homemaker to cash relief checks. In these instances the homemaker assumed total accountability for the family income in addition to her regular duties. In a number of the more physically deteriorated homes the caseworker had to enlist the cooperation of the landlord or the health department or call in an exterminating firm to rid the home of roaches, rats, bedbugs, and mice. Occasionally the homemaker was unavoidably involved in arbitration with a landlord who tried to use the single parent's absence to evict the family. When electricity and gas were turned off, the homemaker had to improvise cooking and lighting facilities while the caseworker negotiated with the utility company.

While the mothers were in the hospital, increased casework time had to be spent in working with the homemakers and with the children. Problems that are a part of daily living and of every homemaker situation became magnified when the homemakers were with the children throughout the night. The homemakers felt more alone after office hours, and it was frequently necessary for the caseworkers to keep in touch with them during the evening hours and on weekends. Homemakers were sometimes obliged to protect the children from divorced or separated fathers who threatened to remove the children or who created unpleasant scenes during unprecedented daily visits to the children while the mothers were in the hospital. One putative father picked up his six-month-old daughter and walked off with her.

Because of the children's increased need for support and reassurance, the caseworkers saw them frequently and served as the liaison between them and their mothers. They accompanied some of the children for medical and dental treatment, conferred with their teachers when school problems arose, and attended to unexpected happenings. One family had to move during the period of twenty-four-hour service, and the children in another family were being harassed by the landlady with threats of eviction.

On occasion older children were critical and became aggressively angry at the homemakers. When these children told the caseworkers about their problems and dissatisfactions, their conflicts subsided or were resolved. This was especially true of the more seriously disturbed children. The caseworkers spent considerable time in helping the homemakers understand and cope with the baffling and trying behavior of these children.

Many of the mothers felt isolated from their families and displaced by the homemakers. It was therefore important for the caseworkers to see absent mothers frequently and include them as much as possible in all of the planning. Continuous communication among the caseworker, the parent, and the homemaker enabled the mother to cooperate while she was in the hospital and after she returned home.

The caseworkers also worked closely with the other agencies involved in the welfare of these families. The combined observations of the caseworkers and the homemakers provided these agencies with information about the families' strengths and needs that otherwise might not have emerged. Because of the intensive involvement of the caseworkers and the homemakers in these families, excellent opportunities arose to encourage parents to seek further help for themselves and their children when this was indicated.

## NINE- TO SIXTEEN-HOUR SERVICE

Nine to sixteen hours of homemaker service was needed by twenty-four children in six families. In five of these families the parents were living together. In the other family the mother had moved out, and the father had phoned to ask for help. He worked in the post office from 4:00 P.M. until midnight and had no one with whom he could leave his two young children. Homemaker service was given for ten to fourteen hours a day. Meanwhile, the caseworker got in touch with the mother. Both parents and the family agency to which they were known believed that foster care was the best solution for the children. Homemaker service was terminated when the mother agreed to remain in the home until placement could be arranged.

In three of the remaining five families nine- to sixteen-hour service was needed because of the confinement of the mother. The fathers in two of these families worked long hours, and there were no relatives to care for the children. The father in one family had had a recent heart attack and had been discharged from the hospital the day before his wife's confinement. He was bedridden most of the time, and a homemaker was needed during the daytime and early evening hours to care for the family's four young children. A relative who worked during the day was able to stay with the family at night.

In another family, with eight children ranging in age from one to twelve years, the request for extended hours of homemaker service came while they were receiving regular eight-hour service. The mother was pregnant and had toxemia, and her doctor had recommended complete bedrest during the latter months of her pregnancy. One child was severely disturbed and had been discharged from a state hospital a few weeks before homemaker service began. The father worked ten hours a day and showed little interest in his family when he was home. When the mother entered the hospital for the birth of her ninth child, homemaker service was increased to twelve hours per day to avoid placing the eight children in temporary shelter care.

All six families in this group were enthusiastic about homemaker service. In addition to their expressed relief about the care of their children, there was noticeable improvement in their standards of housekeeping and in their relationships to their children when the service was discontinued.

## EIGHT-HOUR SERVICE

The referrals for extended hours of homemaker service for twenty-three of the forty families were made sufficiently in advance to place a homemaker on an eight-hour basis for a day or two before the mother had to leave the home. This enabled the homemaker to become acquainted with the children and with the normal routines and habits of the family. It cushioned the impact of separation for the children and was reassuring to their parents. The physical condition of several mothers necessitated placing the homemaker on an eight-hour basis prior to the time extended hours of service were needed.

In three families referred for twenty-four-hour homemaker service, plans changed during the period the family was on eight-hour service. One mother, after being admitted to the hospital, told the caseworker she was opposed to twenty-four-hour homemaker service and preferred that her husband care for the children during her absence even if it meant that he would lose his job. In another family, where the mother was expecting her seventh child, the father was able to change his working hours and share the night care of the younger children with the twelve-year-old daughter during the six days that the mother was in the hospital. The social and psychological pathology in the third family was so extensive that the plan to give twenty-four-hour service was changed to a recommendation that the children go into long-term placement.

Following the period of extended hours of homemaker service, regular eight-hour service was given to twenty-eight of the forty families included in this study. In these families although the mother was again at home, she was physically unable to resume complete responsibility for her children and household.

## FINDINGS

### Housing

In the forty families included in this study fifty-seven children in twelve families were adversely affected by inadequate housing. Many of these families lived in buildings and neighborhoods that fell far below minimal standards of health, decency, and safety.

Eight of the families, with forty-two children, were living in dangerously overcrowded quarters. In all of these situations the number of persons living in one, two, or three small rooms constituted a gross violation of the Board of Health's standards. One mother and her four children ranging in age from two months to four and a half years lived in an exceedingly small and incredibly crowded room. Every inch of space was occupied by beds, the baby's crib, and a bureau. Cockroaches were rampant, often completely covering the baby's hands and face. The older children played in a poorly ventilated and dimly lighted hallway. One bathroom was used by all the occupants of the floor. The entire building was decrepit and filthy.

In addition to these eight families who lived where space was desperately limited, four other families, with a total of fifteen children, lived in buildings that were in a state of extreme deterioration and neglect. One family with eight children ranging in age from three to seventeen years lived in a dangerously neglected and acutely decayed apartment house that was scheduled for demolition. They had lived in this building for five years and were one of three families still there. At first sight, the building appeared to be completely abandoned. It stood alone on several square blocks and was surrounded by more than a year's accumulation of rubbish, trash, wrecked cars, and the foundations of buildings that had already been torn down. Over half of the window panes were broken, the front door was off its hinges, and the staircases were rotted. The plumbing and heating systems worked sporadically. Large rats frequented the building in increasing numbers as the other buildings in the neighborhood were torn down; they clawed and chewed holes in the walls of the apartment almost as quickly as the homemaker and the children could board them up. All efforts to rid the apartment of rats were unavailing.

Wherever deficient housing and environmental conditions seriously affected the health and well-being of families, the casework staff in the homemaker service project took every possible step to improve or change housing conditions. They worked with relatives, the Housing Authority, the Health and Fire Departments, the Department of Welfare, hospitals, landlords, other interested agencies, and individuals. One family was relocated, and conditions were improved for three others.

In addition to these twelve families, six families with thirty-nine children lived in fairly adequate housing, but the housekeeping standards of the mothers were so poor that they presented a health hazard to the children. In one home it was literally impossible to walk through the apartment because of the accumulation of torn and unwashed clothing, dirty sheets and bedding, old newspapers, scraps of food, and useless appliances that covered the floor and the furniture. Since this type of extreme neglect, dirt, and disorderliness appeared to be a reflection of severe and deep-seated problems in the personalities of the parents, the efforts of the homemakers and the caseworkers to help them improve their standards of housekeeping were only temporarily or partially successful.

In no instance was homemaker service refused because of inadequate housing. We operated on the principle that if children in our city are allowed to exist under such shocking circumstances, a homemaker could bear these conditions on a temporary basis. These hovels meant home to the children, and it was as important to avoid abrupt placement for them as it was for the children in better housing.

### Severe Emotional Disturbance

In one-fourth of the families one or both parents showed signs of severe emotional disturbance. Most of them appeared to be functioning on a precarious level and had personal difficulties of such intensity that they were scarcely able to meet the minimal needs of their children and households. Without exception they had the most difficulty in making constructive use of the service. They were suspicious, critical, and often openly antagonistic toward the homemakers. At times they made obvious efforts to alienate their children from the homemakers and to sabotage the work of the caseworkers and the homemakers. They usually appeared unaware of their destructive and demoralizing behavior.

In almost all of the families where there was extensive social and emotional pathology, one or more of the children showed serious signs of disturbance. In addition to the wakefulness and temper tantrums described earlier, these children were also stealing, truanting, and fighting.

Other children were acutely depressed and detached. Although they remained in a state of anxiety throughout separation from their mothers, all but one of the children continued to function and remained in contact with the world around them.

## Health

Insofar as could be determined without individual medical examinations, the physical health of the children was good. Many of them attended neighborhood health centers and hospital clinics. Fifteen children had physical illnesses, of which ten were medically diagnosed as psychosomatic. Three children were physically handicapped and retarded in their development. A five-year-old boy in a family of six small children was blind. He was unable to walk and had to have the attention given to a young baby. A three-year-old girl in another family had epileptic seizures and was functioning on a year-old level. In a family of eight children the six-year-old had cerebral palsy. She had to be watched constantly to keep her from injuring herself. She screamed continuously unless she was held by one of her brothers or sisters or by the homemaker. This little girl was up most of the night crying disconsolately or wandering aimlessly around the apartment. Some mornings the homemaker would find her asleep on the floor huddled in a corner of the room. Twelve other children in good physical health were in special classes in school or were noticeably retarded.

## DESCRIPTION OF FAMILIES NOT SERVED

Five hundred ninety-seven children in 145 families could not be served by the project. They were referred by the same sources, and for the same reasons, as families that were served. One hundred eleven families with 452 children were refused service because no homemaker was available. Thirty families with 134 children withdrew, and four families with eleven children were referred to other homemaker services.

## ADMINISTRATION

The original project was designed for 8000 hours of homemaker service by three homemakers available for nine- to twenty-four-hour duty, two-fifths of a caseworker's time, and one-fifth of a secretary's time. Supervisory and administrative costs were to be absorbed by The Children's Aid Society. Shortly after the project began, however, it became apparent that we had underestimated the amount of casework time needed to handle the volume of applications, the assignment and supervision of homemakers, and the extensive help required by the children and their families. Consequently, the project ultimately absorbed the equivalent of one fulltime caseworker. It was also necessary to adjust our estimate of three homemakers, as it required at least three additional homemakers for weekend relief, vacations, illnesses, and other absences of the project homemakers. The original estimate for secretarial service was adequate. The additional casework and homemaker time required was met by the diversion of some of our regular homemaker service staff to the project.

In September 1960, arrangements were completed for the New York City Department of Welfare to reimburse The Children's Aid Society for twenty-four-hour homemaker service on the basis of $2.50 an hour for twelve hours. These payments, plus additional Children's Aid Society funds, enabled the project to provide 13,097 hours of service instead of the 8000 hours originally planned.

Homemakers on twenty-four-hour duty were given full pay for twelve hours of active duty, half pay for four hours of inactive duty, and no pay for eight hours when they would presumably be sleeping.

The families who received extended hours of homemaker service relied heavily on the caseworkers and homemakers. The three caseworkers who carried project assignments were fully trained and experienced in family and child welfare. Our initial intention of hiring new homemakers for nine- to twenty-four-hour duty was abandoned in favor of using three of our most experienced homemakers. Even though these homemakers were well trained, they sought and insisted upon frequent consultations with their caseworkers. The extension and intensification of the caseworkers' function gave support to the homemakers and helped to maintain balance in these families.

If the 184 children in these forty families had been placed in city shelters, they would have required 8173 days of shelter care. At the rate of $13 per day, the cost of shelter care would have been $106,249, as compared with the project cost of $35,972.

## SIGNIFICANT FACTORS IN THE PROJECT

The following factors contributed to the success of the project:

1. The use of experienced casework and homemaker staff.
2. The ability to respond immediately to requests for homemaker service.
3. Flexibility in adapting hours and length of service to the changing needs of families.

4. The agency's assumption of full parental responsibility when the parent in a one-parent family was absent.
5. Giving service when there was only one child in a family.
6. Providing service to fathers who worked nights or irregular hours and whose jobs would be jeopardized by further absences.
7. Willingness to go into any home regardless of the state of its deterioration.
8. Availability of the caseworker-homemaker team at any hour of the day or night.

## CONCLUSIONS

The results of this project confirm the findings of the 1958 Department of Welfare Children's Aid Society Study of Children in 100 Families Who Were Returned Home from Temporary Care. These findings indicated that two-thirds of the 229 children involved could have remained with their own families had homemaker service been available for more than the usual eight-hour day. Therefore, when the present demonstration project was set up, the basic condition for providing nine- to twenty-four-hour homemaker service was that the only alternative plan for the children would be shelter placement. The project did not include children who could be given care, however sketchy or questionable, by neighbors, relatives, or older children. This latter group presented itself as also needing the protection of extended hours of homemaker service, but did not come within the project specification that no plan other than shelter care would be possible.

One hundred eighty-four children were kept at home by the project. Of the 597 seemingly eligible children who were refused because of lack of staff, some are known to have gone to shelters. Others stayed at home with fathers who remained away from their jobs or with mothers who postponed surgery or medical treatment. What happened to the majority of these children is, however, unknown to us.

The economy of extended hours of homemaker service in alleviating the overcrowding in shelters was shown. In addition to the financial saving, the lessening of human distress was immeasurable.

The results of this demonstration suggest expansion of nine- to twenty-four-hour homemaker service and realignment of programs to meet the varying needs of children and their families.

# 9

# A Demonstration Homemaker Project

*Bessie Mae Jones*

Several years ago, the New Orleans Child Welfare Division of the Louisiana Department of Public Welfare became increasingly concerned about the growing numbers of children who were being removed from their homes because of emergencies. Subsequent evaluations in these placements consistently revealed that no true emergency existed but, rather, that the basic problems leading to placement were of long standing. In trying to curtail the emergencies, the agency had used a number of procedures without effect.

Then, the agency's Citizens Advisory Committee recommended a demonstration homemaker project. (The agency is fortunate in having an extremely knowledgeable, interested, and active citizens committee, who invest a great deal of their talents, time, and effort in our activities.) The recommendation was approved by the Commissioner of the State Department of Public Welfare, with the hope that the service would be extended to other areas of the state if the demonstration proved successful.

## OUTLINE OF PLAN

The primary purpose of the project was to enable children to remain in their own homes during periods of crisis when there were no relatives or friends to sustain the family. Using homemaker service, which we defined as "a social service—an integral part of a casework plan to help maintain children in their own homes and to strengthen family life," we felt we could thereby eliminate the trauma of separation, and reduce the anxiety of both the parents and the children. We also thought that, through the service, we could help families to work out their own problems and to develop improved methods of household management and child care.

The program was restricted to families who were in the basic program of the Division of Child Welfare—those with dependent and neglected children. Casework was used to determine the feasibility of the service and the goals to be pursued, and to evaluate its effectiveness. We expected that the success of the project would be contingent on two factors: our ability to locate and train competent homemakers, and the ability of the Department of Public Welfare to evolve flexible and adequate policies to provide essential maintenance promptly for families who lacked it.

## EMPLOYMENT AND TRAINING OF HOMEMAKERS

The recruitment, selection, and orientation of homemakers began in July 1961. Luckily, we found two homemakers who had previously been employed by the Family Service Society of New Orleans, a third who had once been employed by our agency before as a practical nurse for two severely handicapped children, and a fourth whom we recruited from our foster parent applicants.

The orientation and training consisted of six two-hour sessions that the homemakers attended prior to assignment to families, and supplementary meetings were held as necessary through March 1962. The subject matter covered in the meetings comprised (1) agency structure, philosophy, and purpose; (2) policies and procedures; (3) health precautions and first aid; (4) general problems found in children in families served by the Division of Child Welfare; and (5) interpretation of families with multiple problems. Various staff members and persons from other community agencies, such as the Red Cross, the Health Department, etc., presented the material through lectures, discussions, and films. Individual conferences supplemented the group orientation program throughout the training period.

Ongoing individual supervision of the homemakers was given in half-hour weekly conferences, and the homemakers were encouraged to telephone the caseworker if any emergency developed. If indicated, time for extra conferences was made available. The individual supervision proved to be an important part of the program because it enabled the caseworker to offer help with individual problems that could not be dealt with appropriately in group discussion.

## PLACEMENT IN FAMILIES

The placement of homemakers began in November 1961. From that date until October 1962, services were given to 144 children in 29 families, 14 white and 15 Negro. In about 50 percent of the cases, an emergency precipitated the request, and, in a few cases, homemaker service was offered until the family could be approved for housekeeping service through a public assistance grant.

The project was set up to operate on a 24-hour basis, and every attempt was made to place the homemaker as quickly as possible, and, in some instances, a homemaker was placed within hours of the referral. So far, though, homemakers have not been used in response to emergency placement requests made by the Juvenile Police during the night.

A statistical breakdown of the reasons for placement indicates that:

Two placements were educational. These families were known to have multiple problems, the main ones handled by the homemakers being irregular school attendance, inadequate child care, disorganized home management, and inadequate housekeeping. In order that other families referred for a similar purpose might also receive service, a homemaker worked with this kind of family for no more than three months.

In 20 cases, the goal was to provide child care during the absence of the mother for medical reasons or to provide help to an incapacitated parent. Of the 20 mothers referred for medical reasons, 10 had to undergo surgery; three were having babies; two were suffering from tuberculosis; one each from cancer and pneumonitis, and three from mental illness.

In four cases, the placement was effected to help us evaluate the parents' capacities to provide continued care for their children with our help.

## ACCOMPLISHMENTS

By using homemakers in these families, the separation of 142 out of 144 children was prevented, and the 2 children who were placed in foster care had had time to be prepared for the change. In the families in which the children were not placed, family ties were maintained, children attended school regularly, and family patterns of living were improved. In one family, the standards of care improved to the extent that two younger children who had been placed could return home. Since none of the families wanted placement of their children, it was important to them that the fear that this would happen be alleviated. For the sick mothers, their recovery was probably aided by the knowledge that their families were being cared for at home.

More generally, the children's school attendance showed marked improvement, the families' organization of household management improved, housekeeping standards were improved, and children were helped to assume chores consistent with their age level. In a number of families, the homemaker had the secondary function of teaching homemaker skills.

## PROBLEMS

As would happen in any program of this kind, various problems were encountered, which we had to handle as we progressed and gained experience. In early referrals, lack of medical information was a serious problem. We found that we had to have this information in order to determine goals and to assess the incapacitated parent's capacity to take on responsibilities. We found also that resistance to change, particularly concerning eating and cleanliness, was an area of difficulty.

There was an obstacle in the homemakers' need to see progress and change occur rapidly. It was difficult for these middle-class people to learn to tolerate and understand the low standards they found in most of these families. When progress was minimal and exceedingly slow, and when there were periods of regression, homemakers became frustrated. In addition, the homemakers had difficulty in focusing service in accordance with the casework plan; they sometimes wanted to select their own priorities. At times, a homemaker would compete with the mother and her role in the household, or would become involved with the family's personal problems rather than refer them to the caseworker.

When the program was initiated, the responsibility was divided between two caseworkers: one gave services to the family, and another supervised the homemaker. It was found, however, that the worker supervising the homemakers was spending an inappropriate amount of time in conference. This and other problems that were subsequently encountered were alleviated by having one caseworker carry the total service. Even though this was the better plan for us, it may not be practical to use one worker in both capacities in a large program.

In retrospect, it seems that some of the problems we ran into might have been mitigated if, during orientation and training, we had focused less on academic discussions and more on the concrete problems that the homemaker would be called upon to handle. For instance, we now believe that we should have anticipated some of the specific reactions the homemakers might have because of the conflict of standards, and that we should have offered some suggestions about how to handle these. We should have anticipated their identification with the family and the discomfort they would feel when they told the caseworker facts they had obtained about the family.

## COMPARATIVE COSTS

The comparative costs of homemaker service and of care of children away from their own home is also interesting: the homemaker service was less expensive. For example, in a family with eight children, in which the homemaker gave 72 hours of service in 14 days, the homemaker's salary was $86.40 and the ADC payments were $65.00; this makes a combined total cost of $151.40. Foster family care would have cost $265.44 and institutional care $432.32. In another case, homemaking service was given to a family with 12 children for 363 hours in 85 days. The homemaker's salary was $435.60 and the ADC payments were $388.60—a total of $824.20. Foster family care would have cost $2417.40, and care in an institution, $3937.20. Examination of the total cost for the time from November 1961 through October 1962 shows that the total paid in salary to the homemakers was $6726.60 and that the total cash outlay, including ADC payments to 14 families, was $10,339.30. Foster family care for these children would have cost $21,119.07—which is $10,779.77 more than the homemaker program; and institution care would have cost $34,396.46—which is $24,057.16 more than the program.

## RESULTS OF THE PROGRAM

During the past 15 years, public welfare agencies have increasingly been called upon to give services to families variously described as "multiproblem," "hard-core," and "hard-to-reach." In the placement field, we recognize that foster family placement for all of these children is not necessarily the answer and that for some of the children it is certainly *not* the solution. But many of the children now being referred for services come from homes in which the standards of care do not even meet what we describe as minimum for decency and health. Removal of the children, however, does not motivate parents who have themselves known no existence other than emotional deprivation, neglect, and poverty.

A large percentage of the families known to our agency are limited in many areas of their total functioning. They are often suspicious of others, impulsive, use poor judgment, and are easily frustrated. In the project, although a specific crisis such as illness precipitated most of the requests for homemakers, in the course of the service we found many families with real economic need, social isolation, inadequate care of children, etc. Through the homemaker service, then, we were able to assess family strengths and weaknesses more carefully. In each case, the caseworker discussed with the parents the goals that both the agency and the parents hoped to accomplish by using the homemaker. The agency tried to define the expectations for change and to preserve family patterns that were of value and had importance.

The purpose of the service was, of course, to maintain and strengthen the families, but offering it reaffirmed our conviction that education of the parents is an important part of our casework job. The agency's aim was to improve the overall functioning of these families and to help them modify their behavior and attitudes. Since their basic problems were usually not neurotic in origin, the concrete help of providing a homemaker was an important service. It conveyed to them the agency's acceptance and concern in a way they could understand, and the tangible help it afforded with the daily problems of grocery shopping, cooking, and cleaning was perhaps what they needed most.

Services have been continued in 4 of the 27 families in which homemakers have been placed, because the problems in these families are such that continued casework help and support are necessary to consolidate the original gains. There have been no second referrals on any of the closed cases, and we assume and hope that the improvement they showed has carried over.

The Citizens Advisory Committee has now unanimously recommended to our State Commissioner of Public Welfare that a homemaker service be included as a continuing service in our program and that the service be expanded as the need arises in New Orleans and in other areas of the state.

# 10

([ The following article is yet another example of a different kind of use of homemaker service. In this instance it is used to help carry some of the burden of caring for a handicapped child. This article shows the contribution homemaker service can make in enhancing the functioning of any family faced with a child who imposes more than normal demands. The article reports the result of a cooperative demonstration project between an agency offering homemaker service and an agency concerned with retarded children.

## Homemaker Services to Families with Young Retarded Children

*Irene L. Arnold and Lawrence Goodman*

In an effort to bring together two social trends which have been slow to meet—the growing concern for the retarded in our population and the increasing recognition of homemaker services in helping families cope with situations of stress—two voluntary agencies in New York City recently carried out a 3-year project to demonstrate the potential contribution of homemakers and other home helpers toward preserving families of the retarded. Its results may suggest guidelines for the most effective, economical, and efficient utilization of such services in community plans for the retarded.

Established to examine systematically the effectiveness of homemaker and other home-help services to families with retarded children under 5 years old, the project was cooperatively conducted by the Retarded Infants Services, Inc. (RIS), and the Association for Homemaker Service, Inc. (AHS), with support from the Federal Children's Bureau.[1] Behind its establishment was the conviction that such services, perhaps with various levels of integration with casework services, have an important place in the chain of services required by families of the retarded at the various times in the retarded person's life.

How parents respond initially to the fact of their child's retardation will determine to a great degree the quality of their lifelong reaction to their child, whether or not he remains with the family. The shock of learning that their child will not develop normally may cause them so

---

[1] U.S. Department of Health, Education, and Welfare, Welfare Administration, Children's Bureau: The value of homemaker service in the family with the mentally retarded child under five. Child Welfare Demonstration Project No. D-66. 1965.

much inner turmoil—characterized by ambivalent feelings of guilt, sorrow, and disappointment—that they may want to cut themselves off from the offending object by immediately placing the child in an institution or by withdrawing from him emotionally. New and more lasting problems can be created in such a futile effort to regain a semblance of normality.[2] If the child is to be placed away from home, the effect of an insufficiently considered decision can result in later self-blame and other manifestations of unresolved inner conflict. Providing the parents with help at the crucial period following their confrontation with the fact of their child's retardation must be the first phase of any broad program for the retarded.

In planning to help families at such a time, the first concern, of course, must be with the accessibility of comprehensive medical and psychological evaluation of the child and of whatever treatment may be indicated. At the same time the provision of skilled casework counseling to the parents can mean for many of them the difference between workable solutions and destructive ones. But also of vital importance are the associated services which may be able to relieve parents of the overwhelming sense of burden sufficiently to permit utilization of other kinds of help. Here is where homemaker services may play a key role. Our purpose was to demonstrate how.

## PROCEDURES

The project focused on 35 families. All were drawn from new referrals to RIS. Twenty-four had been referred from general hospital clinics, six from the New York State Department of Mental Hygiene, three from clinics for the retarded, two from private physicians. The intake social worker's determination that the family needed homemaker service was the basis of selecting the family for participation in the project. The only criteria were that the family have a mentally retarded child under 5 years of age and appear able to benefit from the presence of a helper in the home.

Of these 35 families, 9 were referred to AHS for a conventional homemaker service in which a caseworker and a homemaker, both on the staff of the agency, work closely together as a team; and 20 remained with RIS for service, which included the help of domestic workers called home aides recruited for the family by the agency and some limited casework treatment. A control group of six families received no service but were put on the waiting list for future service.

A clarification of the two terms, "homemaker" and "home aide," seems

---

[2] Begab, Michael: The mentally retarded child: a guide to services of social agencies. U.S. Department of Health, Education, and Welfare, Welfare Administration, Children's Bureau. CB Publication No. 404. Reprinted 1965.

pertinent. According to the standards suggested by the Child Welfare League of America: "The distinctive elements of homemaker service are (a) placement in the home of a trained homemaker employed as an agency staff member, who works together with a caseworker in carrying out a casework plan to help restore and strengthen parental functioning, or otherwise assure that the child has the care he needs; and (b) use of casework as an integral part of the service. . . ."[3] Homemaker service, as thus described, is closely interwoven with casework.

Home aides, as used by RIS, also are assigned and supervised by case-workers, but the emphasis is placed on their ability to do light cleaning and cooking and their experience in caring for children, rather than on working consciously with the caseworker to help restore parental function-ing. The family may concurrently receive some casework treatment fo-cused on helping the parents reach the best plan for the child's care.

Experienced homemakers from the staff of AHS who were selected for the project participated with the casework staff in a seven-session orien-tation program. These sessions focused on the condition of mental re-tardation; the differences and similarities between retarded children and normal children; and the kinds of parental responses they could expect.

Most of the home aides who took part in the project had had previ-ous experience with RIS. Each was carefully prepared by the caseworker to be aware of the general dynamics of each case situation.

In each case the particular homemakers and home aides assigned to the families were selected on the basis of the caseworker's professional judg-ment.

The two treatment conditions were not set up for the purpose of meas-uring the efficacy of one service over the other, but rather to seek further understanding of the impact on families of direct assistance in meeting the burdens of the family's daily routines, whether or not this assistance is interwoven with continuing casework treatment. If improvement were possible without the close caseworker-homemaker teamwork, this would seem to suggest that homemaker services for families of the retarded might be offered at different levels of casework involvement, depending on the families' need, capacity, and readiness to use total services.

Instruments created for the study included a "family rating form" for measuring the quality of interaction within the family; and a "decision-making form" for evaluating the character and adequacy of the parent's decision about the retarded child at the close of treatment. At the end of the period of service, all participating families were seen by a social worker in a followup interview. In this the interviewer attempted to view objectively the carry-over effect of the treatment received.

---

[3] Child Welfare League of America: Standards for homemaker service for children. New York. 1959.

## FINDINGS

Both the data secured from testing the case material with the measuring instruments and the data from the clinical followup showed improved functioning in the families served by either homemakers or home aides, in contrast to the families which received no service.

The family rating forms indicated that, in contrast to the control group, families served by AHS made important gains in their intrafamily relations as did families served by RIS, though there were some subtle differences between the two groups in the types of changes which occurred. For example, the AHS group showed a greater increase in friendliness among family members than the RIS group, but the RIS group showed greater development in rationality of conduct.

The decision-making forms indicated that families in both serviced groups rated much higher than those in the nontreatment control group in the quality of plans made for the retarded child. Little difference existed between the AHS and RIS groups.

Similarly, the clinical followup of cases indicated a high degree of sustained gain in families which had received service, regardless of which agency had served them. Some parents who had become involved in relatively intensive casework were able to face openly some of their basic conflicts about their child. However, even families in which the parents regarded the casework they had received as superfluous, but who had a high regard for the help they had received from the homemaker or home aide, improved in intrafamily interaction. Also, the families who had had only occasional encounters with a caseworker focused on specific problems showed sustained improvement.

Thus the findings suggest that, in families confronted with the reality of retardation, help from a homemaker or home aide, selected and supported by a casework agency, can in itself be salutary.

The following two cases illustrate how this may be so at different levels of casework involvement.

### THE A FAMILY

Mr. and Mrs. A were referred to RIS by a diagnostic clinic. At the time of referral, their retarded child Amy was 4 years of age. Her brother James, age 9, had normal intelligence. Mr. A was unemployed because of a strike. Mrs. A said she was at the breaking point because Amy was completely unmanageable, could not be left alone at any time, and had proved to be a tremendous burden to James, who was charged with some of her care.

Both parents seemed immature, demanding, and manipulative. A severe marital problem had developed out of conflict around Amy. The mother was particularly anxious, describing herself as confused, forgetful, and fearful of harming Amy. Mr. A and his parents were pressing her to send Amy to an institution; Mrs. A was not yet ready to do so.

RIS referred the case to AHS, which sent a homemaker into the home. She was trained not only to assist the mother in carrying the burden of household management and child care, but also to observe changes in behavior and attitudes. Part of her role was to help find out whether or not Amy was educable.

Under the regular supervision of the AHS caseworker, the homemaker assumed a nurturing, maternal role with both the children and the parents, but she was careful not to encourage lingering dependency. Amy responded well to her special attention and soon began to show remarkable improvement. Mrs. A apparently had been too tense to handle her in a way that could bring out her potentials.

James, too, showed improvement. He had not only been relieved of Amy's care, but was also getting more attention from his parents. Soon he seemed less withdrawn and behaved in a more forthright and appropriately aggressive manner.

Mrs. A seemed more relaxed, since for the first time in years she had some time for her own needs. The tension between the parents also relaxed a little, and both seemed to have less need to reject Amy.

The AHS caseworker kept in regular touch with the staff of the referring diagnostic clinic who soon reported that the homemaker services had helped clarify the condition of the child and the dynamics of the family situation. It was then agreed that the AHS caseworker would take over the family counseling role from the clinic and would attempt to bring about better relations between the parents by helping them both to a better understanding of the needs of their retarded child, of their normal child, and of each other. As a result, it became possible to enter Amy into a special day class for the retarded instead of into an institution.

This case exemplifies homemaker service in its complete sense. The steadying influence of the homemaker, working in close partnership with the caseworker, expanded the understanding on which a diagnosis could be made, thus making possible more appropriate recommendations for the child's management and care.

As is common with organically damaged children, Amy had responded negatively and with hyperactivity to the anxiety-ridden, erratic handling she had been getting from her parents, and thus her true functioning ability had been obscured. The consistent, well-planned approach of the homemaker helped the child function less destructively and on a higher intellectual level. The resulting decrease of tension in the home increased the parents' ability to make use of casework help. Thus, an institutionalization, likely to be harmful to both the child and the parents, was avoided.

### THE M FAMILY

The following case illustrates the provision of home help chiefly to relieve harried parents while they are mobilizing themselves to adjust to a severe emotional blow.

Mr. and Mrs. M were first known to RIS in 1962 after they learned that their 2-year-old daughter Ruth was severely brain damaged and hopelessly retarded. With the assistance of the agency the child had been placed in an institution. Recently the tragedy was re-enacted. RIS received a call from Mr. M, who was crying hysterically. His wife was in a hospital having an operation and he had just been informed by the family's pediatrician that his 7-month-old son John was also severely retarded. Mr. M seemed to be at the breaking point.

The RIS social caseworker made a home visit the next morning and immediately arranged for a home aide to go into the home to assist Mr. M in the care of both the retarded baby and the family's 5-year-old normal child. Within a few days, Mr. M had recovered sufficiently to go back to work.

After Mrs. M returned from the hospital, the home aide, a person of much warmth and sensitivity, remained in the home to help out while Mrs. M recovered from her physical weakness as well as from the emotional shock of the baby's retardation. At the same time, the social worker and the family pediatrician worked closely together to help both parents accept the diagnosis and again prepare for placing a child in an institution. Mrs. M also received help from the social worker in explaining the baby's condition to the 5-year-old.

Throughout our analysis of the project cases, the effectiveness of the help given by the homemakers appeared most clearly when, as in this case, it was extended to families in the early stages of their response to a crisis. By providing instant help with the burdens of daily existence, the home helper often made it possible for parents to begin to regain enough psychic balance to be able to use casework counseling and help with planning for their child's future.

## SOME CONCLUSIONS

The nature of parents' early reaction to their child's retardation—often with the need to deny reality and to isolate all feeling—can block parents from entering into a therapeutic relationship with a social caseworker, as well as from being able to encourage their child's progress or create the kind of emotional atmosphere that can stimulate development. While not all parents respond to a crisis in the same way or experience trauma with the same intensity or duration, many do remain fixed in a state of emotional turmoil for long periods of time. Suppressed anger toward the retarded child, and toward fate in general, becomes internalized and thrust upon the self.

When such psychic turmoil is taking place, the introduction of a homemaker or home aide, who offers warmth and support and provides direct evidence of the community's desire to share their misfortune, can cut through some of the sense of hopelessness. Freed sufficiently to deal with the needs of other family members and to resume activity outside the home, the parents may then be able to perceive the retarded child with sufficient objectivity to consider alternatives in planning and to participate in the kind of continuing casework treatment that can build up the strength in the family. Thus the dynamic potentials of homemaker services go far beyond the practical assistance offered.

We found in the project that most families were enabled to maintain the child at home until a reasoned, reality-based decision about his future had been made. But even when parents proceeded with inadequate planning, the home helper's assumption of many of the responsibilities of the retarded child's care tended to mitigate their guilt and anxiety regarding their child.

Because existing homemaker agencies can obviously play a major role in helping retarded children and their families to a better life, community plans for comprehensive care for the retarded should incorporate such agencies into the overall design and goals of their programing. Ideally, these agencies should be able to provide home help flexibly, according to the varying needs of families of the retarded. Some families can benefit by home help which is not so closely interwoven with casework treatment as is required to help other families. Where such flexibility is not possible, home aide services might appropriately be offered by specialized agencies for the retarded.

While the project described here focused on the needs of families with young children, homemaker service should not be regarded solely as an emergency resource. Actually it is badly needed by many families on a long-range basis. The demands of a severely or moderately retarded child can be so consuming that at least part-time home help may be needed as long as the child remains in the home.

The complex needs of retarded children and their families require bold new planning that includes the creative use and adaptation of existing approaches to families in trouble. Agencies which specialize in service to the retarded must provide the direction that will encourage others to open up a variety of previously unobtainable services to families of the retarded.

# 11

⟨[ The following article reports the use of homemaker service with a particularly difficult group of clients, multiproblem families who neglect their children. The homemaker in the role of a tutor and accepting representative of the community was instrumental in helping these families.

## Use of Homemaker Service in Families That Neglect Their Children

*Miriam Shames*

"The problem of dependent poverty in California is extensive, and increasingly stubborn. It is increasingly specialized and concentrated and self-perpetuating."[1] Judging from newspaper reports it is "increasingly stubborn . . . and self-perpetuating" all over the country, and new ways of meeting the problem will have to be devised if there is to be any hope of reversing the present trend.

The project described in this paper, in which homemakers were placed with seriously neglecting families receiving Aid to Needy Children (as AFDC is referred to in California), had for its purpose a demonstration of what homemakers could do as teachers in homes in which standards of household management were so poor as to seriously jeopardize the health and welfare of the children in the family. What came out of the project was far more than this, and it is with the purpose of describing the project and pointing out some of its implications for work with the multiproblem family and with long-standing dependency that this paper was written.

### SELECTING FAMILIES AND HOMEMAKERS

The "Neglect Unit" in the Los Angeles County ANC program is a unit to which cases in which there is serious and longstanding neglect of children are referred. Case loads in this unit are comparatively small and casework is more intensive than in the regular ANC case load. The unit chosen for this project is located in a part of the city that is predominantly Negro in population, and consists of one supervisor and five caseworkers, with a total case load of 240.

---

[1] Earl Raab and Hugh Folk, *The Pattern of Dependent Poverty in California* (Berkeley, Calif.: Welfare Study Commission, 1963), p. 382.

101

Each worker selected five cases he felt would benefit from a homemaker. A total of twelve cases were included in the project, comprising fourteen adults and sixty-seven children. The first six were selected randomly from the initial twenty-five designated by the workers and the second six were chosen from the remaining nineteen by the ANC supervisor, the ANC worker, and the homemaker supervisor on the basis of the families' apparent ability to make use of the service. Factors considered in selection of the latter group were largely the bases from which the neglect seemed to stem, such as lack of acculturation, absence of standards of care in the mother's own family, or early marriage with no opportunity for learning family and childrearing skills. Also looked for were some evidence of positive feelings and ego strengths on the part of the mother.

Five homemakers were selected from the staff of Homemaker Service of the Los Angeles Region. With one exception they had been with the agency for a period of three or more years. It was felt that in addition to qualifications required of all homemakers in the agency those confronted with the difficult and complicated situations presented by project families needed to have a fairly high native intelligence not necessarily correlated with the amount of their formal education. They must, to an even greater degree than is called for in all homemakers, have the ability to behave in an accepting and nonjudgmental way, an intuitive understanding of human behavior, and some diagnostic ability. They must be outgoing and able to verbalize fairly freely. In addition to being able to accept the limitations of her own agency, the homemaker on a project of this type has to be able to work co-operatively with and be accepting of the limitations of the Bureau of Public Assistance. Since these cases are uniformly difficult, it was desirable that the homemaker have a fairly wide range of life experience herself and a real understanding of the significance of extremely severe economic and emotional deprivation and the limitations this places on the abilities of both mother and children to function well. In actual practice, the selection of homemakers was made on the basis of past performance in the agency, especially with complicated family situations, and on the homemaker supervisor's knowledge of their work and personality.

One of the significant facets of this project was the growth and development of the homemakers. Originally it had been anticipated that the possible impact of the problem situations encountered might necessitate alternating the more simple type of cases usually carried by this agency with project cases. As it turned out, the enthusiasm of the homemakers grew as they developed an increasing understanding—especially of the emotional factors underlying the neglect they encountered—and as they were able to see the many tangible improvements that took place during their duty on a case.

Placed in homes to act as teachers to the mothers, they found conditions that they had never before encountered, and a degree of maternal rejection in some of the cases that could not fail to shock these warm, giving women. The economic problems posed by the ANC budget was the least of their concerns—they were well versed in the art of doing a lot with limited funds and well grounded in nutrition and the physical needs of children.

As had been anticipated, it was found that supervision and education of the homemakers would have to be intensive and continuous. This was accomplished by means of staff meetings and personal conferences with the homemaker supervisor and the ANC worker. Conferences were begun before the actual initiation of the project work, when participation in the project was offered each homemaker and some of the situations she might encounter were discussed.

Staff meetings were held weekly. Of the four meetings held each month, one was a joint staff meeting including the ANC Neglect Unit workers and their supervisor, and another involved participation of the psychiatric consultant, provided for this project by the California State Department of Mental Hygiene. The remaining two meetings were attended only by the homemakers and their supervisor. The purposes of these staff meetings was support and education, the support aspect being essential because of the emotional impact of this type of case on the homemaker. Interpretation of the causes of observed behavior was extremely important, especially with regard to the homemaker's need to understand and therefore accept the reasons for the maternal rejection encountered so frequently. Support was also provided during the course of these meetings by the homemaker's presentation and discussion of her cases and participation of the other homemakers in the discussion. The presence of the consulting psychiatrist was invaluable not only for his suggestions and evaluation of techniques utilized by the homemakers, but also because of his interpretation to them of the background and causative factors of the behavior encountered.

## SERVICES OFFERED

On her initial contact with the family (homemakers were usually introduced by the caseworker), the homemaker did little more than become acquainted with the mother and perhaps meet some of the children. The average period of time spent in the home on the first day was from one to two hours. In the first (random) group of cases there was always some resistance on the part of the mother to the homemaker. This resistance was usually implied and indicated in disguised ways, with the mother verbally expressing delight at the homemaker's coming to help her.

In all cases the following general conditions were found: The children were dirty and unkempt and homemakers had the impression that their hair had not been washed or combed for weeks. Many of these children had been sent home from school by the school nurse because they were too dirty to stay. Dirty clothes were scattered throughout the house—in two cases a whole room was given over to dirty laundry. There was garbage and filth all over the house and the care of food was so poor as to constitute a real health hazard. Budgeting was always a problem, with the family running out of money long before the monthly check was due. In some cases there was neither gas nor electricity turned on. School attendance was sporadic or nonexistent in all but two cases, and complaints from school authorities, neighbors, and sometimes relatives ranged from accusations of neglect to reports about the children foraging in the neighborhood garbage cans for food. Of course each family also had its own special problems in addition to these.

One of the first services the homemaker always gave was to do some of the housework, especially the laundry, for the simple reason that none of the family members had anything clean to wear. Soon after her advent the homemaker was able to engage the mother in working along with her, and through this method techniques of housecleaning, food preparation, child care, and personal hygiene were taught. Through these means the homemaker related herself to the mother, completed some of the preliminary work that absolutely had to be done, and demonstrated what a clean house and clean children looked like.

Direct services also included child care in order to free the mother for tasks that necessitated her absence from the home, such as househunting, clinic attendance, or enrolling a child in school. Isolated as these families were found to be—even in the midst of a highly populated neighborhood—they had not found it possible, or had not had enough motivation, to find such child care for themselves.

Another activity universally engaged in by the homemakers was to beautify the house once a certain amount of cleanliness and order had been achieved. By the time this process was begun there was enough relationship between the homemaker and the mother to engage the latter's interest sufficiently for active co-operation in these efforts. This included hanging curtains, painting furniture and walls, and obtaining some type of floor covering and bedding. At this point the homemaker could introduce the mother to new sources of inexpensive household supplies in the community. Most of them did not, for instance, know what could be obtained in "thrift shops" and, prior to the advent of the homemaker, had felt that everything had to be purchased new and on credit.

Here the basic home management knowledge of the homemaker was brought into play and the mother taught not only about local sources of supply, but also how to do such elementary tasks as hanging curtains, ironing, and mending. Woven into all this and ever present were the homemaker's services to the children in the family—first in the way of direct physical care (to which, incidentally, the children responded with delight). In some cases the homemaker had to introduce the concept that eating was a social and family activity and should have a special place in the home, such as a table with chairs around it. In several families there was no such thing as "meals." The children fended for themselves, with the younger ones often going unfed. Dishes and silverware also had to be introduced in some cases.

Other services to clients included an introduction to community resources for recreation and cultural purposes—community centers, churches, and the like. Often there was some direct interpretation by the homemaker to relatives, and an effort made to re-enlist the interest of these relatives in the family—in two cases with notable success.

## FAMILY CHARACTERISTICS

Families in the project have been receiving assistance in this county continuously from four to twenty years. The average time on assistance is just under nine years, but this tells only a small part of the story, since at this time many of the families have numerous small children and the outlook for independence in the near future is dim. A striking fact is that the cases almost always began with the application of a young unmarried girl (age range at time of application from 16 to 20 years) either pregnant or with one baby. This, of course, would have been the ideal time for active rehabilitation of the mother. The problem becomes much more difficult with each ensuing year and child.

Although each family had its unique features and problems, in the words of one homemaker, "Two things you find in all cases—dirty laundry and depression." Loneliness of the mother was another characteristic. One said that when she first came to Los Angeles she felt that no one would ever talk to her again. When mothers were asked on follow-up visits by the homemaker supervisor how the homemaker had been most helpful, it was her friendship, conversation, and company that were mentioned—not the work she did. "By being here," said one mother. Other answers given were: "She was my first friend." "She was the first person who showed me respect." "She listened to me." "She made me feel like a real human being for the first time." The woman who felt that no one would ever talk to her again said that when she awakened in the morning and looked forward to a day with only the children for company she felt so discouraged that she just went back to sleep again. In this case none of the children—five of them of school age—attended school, partly because no one got them ready or sent them off in the morning. After the assignment of the homemaker, who came daily for half a day, she would look forward to the coming day, and she eventually became "self-starting" in the morning.

The multiplicity of children was also common. One of these families

had only two children, but the others had five or more, the total for the
twelve families being sixty-seven. Efforts have been made in various communities to bring a knowledge of contraception to ANC mothers. The
availability of such information, however, cannot alone solve the problem
of illegitimacy. There are too many and too complex reasons behind the
birth of these children. Expert birth control information is readily available in Los Angeles, but is rarely used by the type of mother found in
this kind of a case load. Many of the encounters that result in pregnancy are unplanned and are but one result of the bitter loneliness of
the mother. One of the mothers, for example, who has had a child a
year for the last six years, is fearful of the prospect of all of them reaching school age. She is afraid that she will "die of lonesomeness." Another
has illegitimate children to punish her own extremely religious and moral
—but severely rejecting—mother. Each time she becomes pregnant she
fantasies that her mother will have to take the new baby and "bring it
up." At the age of 25 she is now in her eighth pregnancy—the possibilities are rather frightening. Her children range in age from 1 to 9, and
it is the 9-year-old boy who assumes the entire responsibility for child
care in the family.

In all but three of the cases in this group (in which there are fathers
or stepfathers present) the liaisons made by the mothers that resulted in
their pregnancies were fleeting, apparently with no thought of a permanent relationship, and were with men who were unreliable and exploitive
—the majority of them had been in more or less serious trouble with
the law on numerous occasions. This pattern reflects in part the dispar-
aging self-image these mothers have.

In some cases the caseworker was able to revise his estimate of a family situation after the homemaker had been in the home for a while. This
was especially true in one case, in which the homemaker had been assigned with the purpose of teaching the grandmother in the family because the mother was considered too retarded to function. After being in
the home a while, the homemaker found that, while certainly retarded,
the mother was also very much afraid of her mother-in-law, who with her
son (the husband) seemed to be terrorizing the family. With casework
help and the adroit encouragement of the homemaker, this mother was
found to be able to function to a much greater extent than had been
thought possible. In another case, in which there was also a father (stepfather to some of the children) present, the homemaker was requested
because it was felt that the extreme disorganization in this family might
break up the (common-law) marriage. The father, while himself quite
immature in many respects, was the stronger parent and was employed
(ANC supplementing for the stepchildren), but was threatening to leave
because of the dirt and neglect of the children.

An interesting observation was that the mothers made of their relationship with the homemakers what they needed. In many cases what they needed was a mother themselves and this was how they viewed the homemaker, without regard either to her age or race. This is a situation similar to the use made of relationship in therapy. The cases that follow illustrate typical family situations and the homemaker's function.

## MORALLY SUPPORTIVE ROLE OF HOMEMAKER

The K family consists of a 26-year-old mother and her six illegitimate children, the oldest of whom is 6. The family first came to the attention of the Bureau of Public Assistance in April 1956 when Miss K, then 19 and pregnant with her first child, applied for assistance. The family was referred to the Neglect Unit in December 1960, but the case record shows neglect long before this. At one time the worker described one of the babies as being so poorly cared for that it hardly resembled a human being. Miss K was highly defensive about her standards of care and seemed unable to improve, although repeatedly adjured to do so by a succession of workers. One child was severely handicapped with cerebral palsy but Miss K had never kept clinic appointments made for him. She herself had a speech defect and severe hearing loss. In appearance she looked like a frightened and defensive teen-ager.

When the homemaker arrived she was met with Miss K's statement that she did not need anyone to tell her how to take care of her children. The homemaker said of course not, but that with so many young children she could surely use a bit of help with the housework. Within a few days Miss K was able to feel that she could trust the homemaker with her children.

The family occupied a tiny, filthy, and inappropriate apartment with no safe play space for the children. Miss K left the house as soon as the homemaker arrived each day and went househunting, until she found an attractive and larger apartment in a quiet, pleasant neighborhood, one that had a large screened-in porch that provided an ideal play area for the children. As soon as the family moved to their new home Miss K resumed weekly clinic attendance for the cerebral palsied child, and no appointment was ever broken.

In her new home she and the homemaker worked together to improve the appearance of the house. It was discovered that she had remarkable energy. She was able to install a pulley clothesline by herself, and the lines were filled early every morning with newly washed clothes. With the helpful suggestions of the homemaker the apartment soon took on an appearance that was comfortable and attractive by anyone's standards.

It was also discovered that Miss K had a talent for sewing, and she made clothing for her children. The homemaker supervisor felt that this talent could well be made the basis for vocational rehabilitation and, in spite of the large number of young children and the severely handicapped child, efforts should be made fairly soon in this direction.

Supportive casework will be needed for quite a while if the long-term plan of rehabilitation is to be successful, but there is a good possibility that this family can become at least partially self-supporting. This should lead to a different feeling about herself on the part of the mother, and might prevent the advent of more illegitimate children.

It is interesting that in this case the role of the homemaker was primarily one of moral support for a long time prior to the case's termination. Once given a good start, the mother was able to continue on her own impetus remarkably well. The last follow-up visit was made six months after termination of homemaker service, and it was found that the house was still clean and attractive, clinic appointments were kept regularly for the cerebral palsied child, and the two school-age children attended school regularly. At the present time Miss K is not pregnant, even though her youngest baby is now over a year old.

### HOMEMAKER AS MOTHER SUBSTITUTE

The L family consists of a mother and six illegitimate children, most, if not all, by different fathers. Miss L has been receiving assistance continuously since 1943. She herself had been reared in numerous foster homes and was often separated from her own siblings. At the time of the initiation of service she was completely cut off from her numerous relatives living in the area, because of their disapproval of her. An attractive woman, she considered herself ugly—a reflection of her low self-esteem. The children were exceptionally attractive but extremely unkempt, and one little girl who was approaching kindergarten age was so extremely shy that she was unable to speak in the presence of anyone outside the family.

This client made of the homemaker a substitute for the mother she never had (in actual fact the homemaker was younger than the client), and wanted very much to please her. She soon took over most of the actual work of running the household, learned much about cooking, and showed great ingenuity in purchasing and mending secondhand clothing for her children. When the house had been cleaned and decorated, she was emboldened to invite several of her relatives to a birthday party for the 5-year-old, using this means to renew her relationship with them.

Several follow-up visits have been made to this home, and six months after the termination of homemaker service Miss L was still maintaining the improved appearance of the house, her children were attending school regularly, and she herself seemed like a different person, efficient and proud of her family. The social worker believes Miss L will probably soon want to seek part-time employment.

Although this case has been discussed here only briefly, Miss L's background includes a great many complex problems that had an effect on her relationship with her own children. This summary is designed only to give some indication of the movement made by the family during the short time it was included in the project.

## CONCLUSIONS

Homemakers were assigned to twelve families, all of whom had been receiving assistance for many years and none of whom had shown any response to efforts on the part of social workers to improve their standards of household management or child care. In addition each family had its own special problems.

All the families showed movement in most problem areas, and gains made during the time the homemaker was assigned are holding remarkably well. Much has been learned about which families are likely to benefit most from the assignment of a homemaker. A surprise to everyone involved in the project has been the amount of improvement made in a relatively short period of time in situations so long standing and in which the mother herself was so severely deprived during her own childhood that it would seem only intensive, long-term therapy could reorient her.

Indications are that the progress made was not so much on the basis of the homemaker's skill and proficiency in homemaking and child care as because of her intuitive ability—strengthened and directed by frequent and careful supervision and professional support—to give the mothers in these families the kind of acceptance, respect, and understanding that in many cases they had not encountered before. The significant result was a real strengthening of the mother or, in some cases, a strengthening of the older children to a point at which there was a realignment of relationships within the family. Of course, the hoped-for result is that the young children in the family will now receive the kind of support their own mothers lacked, and perhaps themselves grow up to become independently functioning members of the community. An indication of this possibility is that in eight of the families in which school attendance was sporadic or nonexistent it has been reinstituted and, at the time of the latest follow-up visits, maintained.

Introducing a professionally supervised homemaker to multiproblem families seems to be one way to start them in the direction of rehabilitation, and suggests that there may be many other possible ways of attacking this difficult problem. The importance of instituting active rehabilitation of the young applicant for assistance as soon as possible after intake also seems inescapable. New ways of instituting change leading to the strengthening of individuals caught up in the kinds of situations in

which the families in this study are involved must be found. Otherwise
the burgeoning load of dependency, which conceivably could result from
the sixty-seven children involved in this study alone, could be staggering.

# 12

◖ There are more mothers working than there are employed mothers.
Mothers work at home, and because many are overworked, children suffer.
The following article calls attention to the value of day care for children
of mothers working at home.

# Day Care Services
# for Families with Mothers
# Working at Home

*John E. Hansan and Kathryn Pemberton*

Day care, either as a commercial service or a social service, generally
denotes supervised care given to children between the ages of 3 and 6
whose mothers find it necessary or desirable to work. For those mothers
who must work but who do not have sufficient income to meet the costs
of a commercial center, day care provided by a social agency is a subsidized service.

Day care should not be confused with nursery school programs that are
directed toward the education and socialization of the preschool youngster. Nursery education is usually for short time periods and is sometimes very expensive. In addition, it differs in the very nature of the
program; although it is desirable for all day care programs to incorporate
the principles of preschool education, it is impossible for them to maintain the same levels of program and participation for eight or nine hours a
day that nursery programs can maintain for their two- to four-hour sessions. Perhaps the most important factor in day care is that the service
offered to children assures them better care than they would receive if
they remained at home.

In Cincinnati, day care as a social service teeters on the edge of community acceptance. Many working women who need this service can afford private centers or, at least, prefer them. Day care for the children of mothers who cannot afford private centers is viewed by United Funds as an expensive form of assistance, especially since existing day care centers are not filled to capacity.

Riverview Neighbors House, a branch of Seven Hills Neighborhood Houses, is located in the East Basin of Cincinnati. It serves a lower-class, racially mixed population that includes a large number of families who have recently migrated from the southern Appalachian area of Kentucky and West Virginia. In an attempt to help this group, our settlement house has been conducting a day care program that differs from the traditional service to children of working mothers. Our program has served children who need day care even though their mothers, and frequently their fathers, do not work.

Our knowledge of the families in the neighborhood indicated that both the mothers and the children had great need of some outside help just to meet the day-to-day demands placed on them. Living in substandard, overcrowded, and unsafe apartments, many of our families were recipients of AFDC (Aid to Families with Dependent Children) and general relief. There were many fatherless homes, mentally ill mothers, and delinquent children, but none of our programs seemed to be effective in preventing more of the same from happening. We could almost predict the pathologies that particular families would develop.

As the character of the neighborhood changed, reducing the enrollment of the children of working mothers in our day care program, we found it necessary to redirect our service. Therefore, we offered day care service to these families for their younger children. And in the 18 months that our new program has been in operation, we have learned to value the day care program as a means of establishing effective relationships with some of the most primitive and hard-to-reach families.

Very few of the adults in the neighborhood had taken any interest in our house groups or activities, and all efforts to involve mothers, especially the rural newcomers, met with dismal results. We found that we were operating a child-centered neighborhood house program. As the day care center reached out to the families, however, there was a marked increase in the number of adults, especially mothers, who began to use our services. The attendance in adult clubs swelled; a nursery parent study group was formed and has continued to meet regularly. Parents began to offer their time and talents to help us with specific tasks: establishing a clothing exchange, decorating the nursery, repairing equipment, and maintaining the building. There was also a noticeable increase in the requests by parents for our help with problems they were having with schools, the welfare department, etc.

This experience is teaching us how day care can be employed as a means of helping families who are, or may become, the hard core of families with multiple problems in every metropolitan area. The program is not meant to be a panacea, nor can it be expected to work successfully in every instance. The success we have experienced, however, gives us hope that day care service extended to the nonworking mother who needs such supportive help can be financially justified by the help it gives to the family and the child.

### MOTHERS NEED HELP

A young mother with several small children, regardless of her socio-economic level, needs assistance from her husband, her family, her friends, or hired help. The ordinary demands on a normal family clearly show the importance of some such assistance. Running errands, keeping appointments with doctors, schools, and other social institutions, marketing, neighboring—all these require the mother of young children to seek help so that she can be free to do what is necessary. At the same time, most women need recreation, socialization, and some creative pursuits—impossible unless they have help with the young children.

If we assume that it is difficult to be a good parent in a normal situation, we can see how difficult it must be to carry the role of both parents. The single parent must be mother, father, nurse, teacher, disciplinarian, provider, and housekeeper. Thus, mere deduction shows us that the mother of several small children without a functioning husband or a larger family needs some *relief.*

If any one of the normal forms of support—husband, family, money— is removed, severe strain is put on the remaining forms. A mother who does not have the assistance of her husband will require additional support from her extended family, or she will have to purchase this assistance. If the larger family of relatives is not available, the husband may be required to shoulder an even greater part of the supervision of children.

Fortunately, most women have the normal forms of support and are able to supplement them with babysitters, nurses, and schools. There is, however, an increasingly large number of families in which the mother is without adequate help. For example:

> The oldest of Mrs. Baker's four children was 4 when this family came to our attention. Mrs. Baker felt that she was going to have to resort to desperate measures to solve her problems, and she told the agency director that she had decided to place her children in foster care. Beset by an inadequate welfare allotment, substandard housing (four children and herself in two rooms), marital difficulties, and full-time care of the children, Mrs. Baker was finding life "too much" for her. The day care center was suggested as a means of relieving some of her child-care burdens so that she could reestablish herself.

When she approached us, Mrs. Baker was trying to manage on general relief. She was always in debt at the local store and completely unable to make ends meet financially. The family lived in a flat overrun with roaches. During our first visit we found two of the children in cribs and two in playpens. Because Mrs. Baker was unable to supervise them when they were about on their own, she decided they were safer there, even though she was well aware that it was very wrong to keep toddlers so confined. The odors that are present when young children live in crowded, unkempt quarters with insufficient care were much in evidence.

Families in slum neighborhoods often live under such conditions. They are caught up in a relationship that becomes like a vicious circle. Troubles pile upon troubles until something gives way. When the family seeks help or assistance, social service often adds to the complex of responsibilities under which they are functioning. Too often, our health and welfare agencies are insensitive to the real needs of the family; instead, they are interested in their eligibility for a particular service—no matter how urgent the family's requirements are. Our program differs, however, in that we offer families assistance in what they are doing rather than requiring them to do more immediately.

Too frequently, community concern is focused on helping the mother to budget a totally inadequate amount of money or on advising her to take better care of her apartment and the clothing, diet, or health of her children. Is this really the help the mother needs? Are any of these tasks so difficult, strange, or repugnant that the woman would not try to do these things by herself if she had the physical strength and emotional health to attend to them? In our experience, these matters are really very *minor* in the face of what she has to cope with daily.

## BENEFITS FOR MOTHERS

Our next assumption is that the mother who lets us take these responsibilities is not going to do so just to have time to indulge her own desires. It has been repeatedly demonstrated that the mother uses this extra time to attend to useful duties such as clinic appointments, shopping, house cleaning, and visiting neighbors.

Mrs. Baker has been able to plan meals more effectively; she has established relationships with her neighbors by visiting and thus, by trading baby-sitting time, has been able to buy groceries at a supermarket instead of at the expensive local store. She has used her time to draw pictures for decorating the day care center, and to read stories and articles from magazines given her by the center. Thus, she is making an effort to become less isolated from the community.

This much progress indicated to us that we should consider the program as a vital part of social service to the AFDC families and general relief recipients. The benefits of the program, however, do not end here; through frequent contacts with the day care director, the mother begins to learn much about the care and rearing of children.

> When Mrs. Baker came to observe the children in the day care center, she noted with some relief that her Joe was not the only child who threw things. She has seen that there are other children who "can't cut on the line," as she has tried to force Joe to do. Mrs. Baker was most interested to learn from the teacher that Joe is too young to be expected to cut "on the line." Since her anxiety over unrealistic expectations for her children has been relieved, the neighbors report that Mrs. Baker doesn't spank her children as much as before.

### BENEFITS FOR CHILDREN

In the program so far, all of our attention has been directed toward assisting the mother or the family as a whole. More lasting and, ultimately, perhaps most important, is the effect that such service can have on the child. Obviously, even children from otherwise normal families living under these circumstances would find it difficult to grow into socially healthy and constructive citizens. Therefore, we believe that any supportive assistance we can give will be beneficial to both the child and the family and that any relief of the ordinary stresses of the family will have a proportional effect on the behavior of the children.

If a child is given the benefit of good preschool education through a day care program, he will be provided with needed support for his healthy growth and development. In reference to the children cared for in the program we are discussing, we have seen great changes take place.

> When we first took little Joe Baker, he stood almost immobilized; he did not know what to do in a group—any place outside his playpen was very, very strange to him. Now, Joe has become the clown of the nursery. He plays with everybody, he enjoys throwing things, he does puzzles better than his sister who is a year older than he, he uses crayons and scissors well, he builds with blocks, he is agile on the climber—in short, he has a wonderful time. He has made an excellent adjustment in the nursery.
>
> His older sister was so unstable that the worker characterized her as "a grasshopper on a hot tin roof" and felt that the nursery just could not tolerate such constant nervous activity on the part of this youngster. The worker was about to ask the mother to take her from the center when all the difficulties of the mother's situation became clear. After several home visits, the worker realized that we could not refuse service to this child, as disrupting as she was to the program.

Here again, the nursery staff, upheld by the total agency purpose, stretched every facility and every bit of energy that they could garner to make room for these two youngsters. We believe that these children now have a good chance to make full use of kindergarten, because they are intellectually healthy enough. What life might have meant for them if the nursery had not been available, is truly hard to say; it seems that they would have been under some kind of institutional care, either now or in the future.

Thus, as they move into school, these children—having become more adjusted socially, more acceptable culturally, and better prepared educationally—will be more able to meet the new, frightening, and challenging, but unavoidable, problems that we must all face in new situations.

### SERVICE TO WHOLE FAMILIES

Our new emphasis has pointed toward further service to whole families. For example, we have made repeated home calls to the Bakers, and now the mother comes to tell us her problems. Since the agency sought her out, she is willing to ask for help. More than once, the director has helped clarify the status of the family with the Welfare Department. Mr. Baker had served six months in the workhouse because of child neglect. Near the time of his release, the day care center initiated a meeting with Mr. Baker's probation officer to help clarify the role of the different agencies after he was released. (This is quite a change from the usual role of day care.)

In this case, the center assumed the care of two of the Baker children so that Mrs. Baker could give what energy she had to the younger two. The center has acted as a sounding board and a refuge; it has been supportive in straightening out difficulties with agencies that often seemed terrifying and threatening to the client. In short, we have remained calm with people with whom almost every other agency is angry and disgusted. Our approach has been positive and hopeful instead of resentful and negative.

### AID TO HEALTHY FAMILIES

Another example of the success achieved by our "new" approach in service to a family with less involved problems is the Carter family. The Carters are a two-parent family with seven children, "living" on take-home pay of $50 a week, out of which $22 a week is paid for rent. The chief environmental problems here, then, are inadequate income, too expensive housing, and too many young children. These problems became so big that Mrs. Carter felt "like jumping off a bridge." She talked out her problem with the director, and, as in the case of Mrs. Baker, he was able to offer the day care center as a means of lightening the load. Recognizing that limited finances were a major difficulty for the Carters, no fee was charged and Mrs. Carter was told that there would be other ways she could help pay for the service later. She accepted the service and two of her seven children were enrolled. The 4-year-old boy made the adjustment rapidly, the 3-year-old girl slowly.

Later, when the mother had herself and her family under better control, we established a small weekly fee. We made it clear, however, that cash was not necessary; Mrs. Carter could earn the fee by mending sheets and, being paid for her service. Because we know that insufficient income is a common block to accepting service, no matter how needed, the agency has been able to find ways for families like the Carters to use their talents and skills as payment for the day care service.

Mrs. Carter has returned the agency's aid a hundredfold, by helping at rest time, cleaning shelves, making doll clothes, and sending her husband to help fix toys. Mrs. Carter has become the rallying point for the nursery mothers' study group, encouraging her neighbors to participate in the program. Thus, she lends strong support to our efforts.

The Carter family is another instance of how a basically sound family whose problems are more environmental than emotional can, with just a little help, be more effective. By offering the resources of the center in a dignified way, by acting as a means of relieving pressures in an atmosphere of confidentiality, and by offering Mrs. Carter opportunities for repayment that undoubtedly gave her satisfaction, we feel we are successfully helping this family.

## CONCLUDING COMMENTS

This, then, constitutes our concept of direct social service in which the day care center works as a part of a larger agency. This service is given where the mother is not working, that is, where she is not holding a job outside the home. In all fairness, however, we cannot really say that this mother is not working. We maintain that she is working very hard. She should not be penalized by a definition that limits "work" to employment outside her home. And *until* we realize that the mother in the home, maintaining her family against incredible deficiencies in housing, income, and cultural advantages, needs and deserves all the support society can give her, we are being unrealistic, evasive, and ineffective. Proper emphasis and evaluation must be given to the role of the woman who stays at home to rear her family in the depressed, slum neighborhood.

# 13

❨ Although it employs methodologically unsophisticated evaluative procedures, the following article is of interest because it is the only one available which attempts a follow-up study of users of family day-care services.

# Followup Study on Family Day Care Services

*Elizabeth K. Radinsky*

In 1952, after careful study by the Federation of Jewish Philanthropies, Family Day Care Service was established as a two-year experimental project to be administered under the joint auspices of the Jewish Child Care Association and the Jewish Youth Services of Brooklyn. The program was limited to 15 Jewish children between the ages of 8 months and 3 years whose parents resided in Brooklyn and Manhattan.

This two-year demonstration program, limited as it was, proved both the feasibility and the value of the service. Since then, with the cosponsorship of the Eisman Day Nursery, Family Day Care Service has gradually been expanded to serve 62 children. With turnover, the service now cares for over 90 children annually, exclusive of intake applications. The area served is limited for financial reasons to two of New York City's boroughs—Manhattan and Brooklyn—although the need is, of course, equally great in other parts of the city. It is hoped that when public funds become available to supplement those now being provided entirely by the voluntary agency sponsors, our service can be extended city-wide.

## REASONS FOR FOLLOWUP STUDY

As we reached our tenth year of operation, we felt it was appropriate to determine, in an organized way, our clients' reactions to the service and its effects on the families served.

A staff group, assisted by a subcommittee of board members and a trained casework volunteer, worked out the study plan and the final report. We devised a relatively simple procedure to bring response from our clients. We hoped to determine from the clients' answers: (1) areas in which the children and parents experienced help, (2) the effectiveness of the caseworker's help in bridging environmental and child-rearing differences in the two home settings, (3) clues to the effect on the young

**117**

child of having two home environments and two "mothers," (4) a comparison of our estimate of the value of the service with that of the client, and (5) gaps and other points of friction needing further consideration, as well as suggestions for improvement.

The followup study was made through a six-point questionnaire sent to a sample group of 60 families who had received at least six months' service terminating between July 1958 and July 1961. The object was to find families who had had a period of service long enough to be significant, and recently enough to remember experiences clearly, but with some time-lapse for perspective. Seventy percent responded—a total of 42 families with 44 children.

## CHARACTERISTICS OF FAMILIES

In social characteristics the respondents closely paralleled the overall experience of Family Day Care Service. One-fifth had needed day care service for economic reasons only. The remainder—35 out of the 42— were families whose homes had been broken or disrupted in one way or another. There were 20 in the group who were divorced or separated, another 11 couples with serious marital problems, and 4 unwed mothers.

Almost half of the 44 children had passed their second birthday but not their third when placed, four were 3 (two of these were older siblings accompanying a younger brother or sister), and the rest were under 2. Eight of the 44 children were in day care placement less than a year, 13 from one to one and a half years, 10 from one and a half to two years, and 13 over two years.

## PARENTS RATE SERVICE

The questionnaire invited both an overall rating and specific comments on the service received and the financial arrangements. It also inquired as to how the child formerly in Family Day Care Service was currently spending his daytime hours and asked for suggestions to make the service more helpful.

The responses added up to a general endorsement of day care service with emphatic recognition of the specific help derived. In terms of economics, there was 100 percent agreement that the service made it possible for the mother to hold or get a job. In personal and family problems, the families acknowledged help in understanding child behavior and in coping with marital difficulties. All agreed that financial arrangements were satisfactory.

In answer to the question, "How is your child who received our service spending daytimes this fall?" we found that 18 were attending school, 10 were being cared for at home by their mothers, 7 were in day care centers, and 2 were in permanent foster placement. This makes a total of 37 children accounted for (7 were not reported on in this regard). It is significant to note that only two were in full-time placement. It is also of interest that the problems that had made it necessary for the mother to work had been resolved in 10 cases, so that these mothers were able to assume full care of their children at home.

## THOUGHTFUL REPLIES

The general impression of the total responses on the 44 children is that they were thoughtful, sincere, and very warm. Most of the clients did more than fill out the blanks; they added comments freely. Even those who indicated that the service was only partially satisfactory also gave positive responses, and those who rated the service as excellent entered criticism or suggestions. There is a balance in the replies that indicates sincerity and thoughtfulness.

Almost all of the early responses contained a warm personal note to the caseworker in addition to the filled-in questionnaire. Almost all who answered indicated they would be willing to discuss the subject further.

Concerning the casework service, many said they had been given helpful marriage counseling that enabled them to resolve some of their marital difficulties. Several said that caseworkers helped them greatly by referral to other agencies, primarily family service agencies.

Many of the replies revealed progress and marked improvement, especially impressive because of the families' initial difficulties. Some indications were comments on the benefits of the service—"help in understanding child's behavior," "relieving tremendous strain," "guidance in adjusting to a new life," "help in getting my child established in nursery school," "the caseworker always understanding in discussing my problems with my child."

The clients who found the service less than "excellent" frequently offered constructive criticisms. One report, fairly negative throughout, said that, nevertheless, the service was indispensable, whatever the conditions, and should be expanded. (This client was critical of the day care mother, acknowledged no help from the caseworker, and wanted to make her own decisions with the day care parents without the caseworker's being involved.) Another said that family day care was not the answer for her, although she found the day care mother helpful. She found her child did better at home.

## DAY CARE MOTHERS

In reference to the day care mother, 75 percent rated the service as excellent. Many indicated a great deal of regard for the day care mother and said they were still in touch with her or expressed the wish that they might have further contact. Some indicated some difference of opinion with the day care mother in such areas as the child's clothing, diet, and opportunity for outdoor activity. The minority who expressed criticism of day care mothers raised questions about the amount of affection shown, hygiene in the day care home, or discipline practiced.

## CASEWORKERS' RATINGS

To round out the picture, Family Day Care Service caseworkers who had served the responding clients independently filled in a duplicate questionnaire for each client, adding descriptive and diagnostic material and a statement of casework objectives. The responses of client and caseworker were then compared, and areas of agreement and disagreement noted.

In the seven instances in which the client checked the service as "adequate," the caseworker agreed in five cases, gave an "excellent" rating to one, and only "fair" to the other. In all, there was agreement between the mother and the caseworker as to the quality of the day care service in 28 situations; the mother rated it higher than the caseworker in 14 situations and lower than the caseworker in 3. (There were 45 ratings because one mother rated her experience twice, since she considered one day care mother "excellent" and the other "poor.")

## CONCLUSION

An added dimension came into review of the original case records, which brought to light two vital points underlining the social value of the service. These points are: First, in ten instances, day care service had prevented imminent application for foster care placement. In nine others, the need for full-time separation would probably have eventuated. Second, in 14 situations, a relief application to the Department of Welfare was prevented.

The percentage of responses to a voluntary mailed questionnaire—even such a short one—was unusually high. Although we had anticipated little difficulty in obtaining client cooperation, the responses, both in quantity and in evidence of painstaking thought and consideration, far exceed our expectations. This would seem to indicate both client approval of the service and a feeling of its social acceptability. Essentially, clients seeking day care see themselves as utilizing a socially approved way out of an economic dilemma that threatens the family unity.

The high percentage of agreement between clients and caseworkers on the quality of the day care service was reassuring. Equally important were the differences of opinion and the suggestions, which emphasize the need to reexamine continually the day-to-day care of the child and the need to be watchful lest concern with family casework problems unwittingly overshadow the close attention to the practical specifics that are basic to the agency's principles of operation. An important byproduct of the study, which has been helpful in all services, was that it emphasized the significance of discussing specifically with the client what the service meant to him. The perspective that time has added and the information obtained about the postservice adjustment of both children and parents made this study especially valuable.

This study cannot, of course, document the full preventive value of the service—its protection of the child against the hazards of unsupervised private arrangements and its safeguarding of the family unit. In this connection, it is worth noting that many of the responses volunteered by the clients indicated a high level of family stability in this postservice period—a stability particularly striking among families who, when they came to the service, were beset by overwhelming difficulties. This, we believe, is significant evidence that many troubled young mothers and fathers can be helped to assume their full role, both as parents and as responsible members of society, when at an early point of their difficulties the community provides sustaining services to meet their needs appropriately.

# 14

⟨[ The following article reviews the experience of a public welfare agency in initiating, developing, and offering a program of family day care. It points to some of the recurrent and frustrating problems.

# Family Day Care for Children

*Frank A. Foley*

In 4 years of operating a family day-care service as part of its public child welfare program, the Division of Child Welfare of the Monroe County (N.Y.) Department of Social Welfare has learned considerably more about the value of the need for a family day-care service in the community and the vicissitudes of getting such a service under way than it did at the outset. Originally begun as a service for mothers in the public assistance program, the service is now offered, on a casework determination of social need, to families throughout the community.

With the industrial city of Rochester as its core, Monroe County has a population of about 500,000. About one-tenth is nonwhite. Employment is relatively stable. The median income for all families is $7,000; but 10 percent of the families have incomes under $3,000 and 1.5 percent are receiving public assistance.

In our community, interest in the need for a service to provide day care for children in family settings originated with the Monroe County Council of Social Agencies, the coordinating body for the community's 99 public and voluntary health and welfare agencies—including two Community Chest supported day-care centers. During the 1950's, the council's Family and Children's Division—representative of 35 casework agencies—had frequently discussed the need for such a service for children for whom group care in a day-care center was not advisable but whose family situation required that they be cared for away from home during the day. The chief concern was for children from families in which the social situation—interpersonal conflicts, illness, or the strain on an overburdened mother—indicated that separation of child and mother during the day might be necessary as a step toward strengthening family life. In the fall of 1961, the council's newly formed Day Care Committee conducted a sample survey among local family service agencies—including the county welfare department's public assistance division—to determine the volume of such need.

The agencies were asked to list families who, in a given period, had been asking for help in making a day-care arrangement for a child or children, and another list of families for whom the caseworker would have chosen family day care if this service had been available, and the reasons why. The replies were startling. Caseworkers in the county welfare department's public assistance division alone reported 450 families who in their judgment could have beneficially used a family day-care service. The two community day-care centers, which had carried out the survey for the council, considered developing family day care as an adjunct to their group-care services, but did not have the funds to do so without additional Community Chest support, and this was not forthcoming.

At that time the county welfare department had no legal authority under State law to provide a day-care service or to use State child welfare services funds for the purpose. However, the imminent provision of Federal funds for day care appeared on the horizon with the introduction of the 1962 Public Welfare Amendments to the Social Security Act,[1] and a change in the New York State Social Welfare Law became a distinct possibility. Therefore, the State Department of Social Welfare encouraged the local welfare departments to plan to provide day-care services. In Monroe County we found that with cooperation between our public assistance and child welfare divisions, we could, with appropriate participation of the State Bureau of Child Welfare, get some family day-care service under way under existing State law and even before the Federal funds, appropriated in 1963, became available.

---

[1] Public Law 87–543.

The plan was for the public assistance program, which already allowed an item for group day care to be included in the budgets of recipient families needing this service, also to allow the inclusion of an item for the day care of children in families approved as day-care providers by the State Bureau of Child Welfare. Family day-care homes would be recruited and studied by the staff of the local child welfare services program and those found promising referred to the area office of the State Bureau of Child Welfare where responsibility for approving or disapproving the home would rest. The final decision would be made after a member of the State child welfare staff had visited the home.

Our initial program was, therefore, confined to providing service to families in the public assistance program. In the beginning it was limited to those who were living in the two census tracts where the council's survey had indicated the need for day care was greatest.

Before we got under way, we had some difficult planning sessions because of differing points of view between our public assistance and child welfare divisions on how the day-care families should be paid for their services. The public assistance division fought hard for adhering to its principle of including funds for all supplies and services budgeted for a family in a direct cash payment to the family head, who is then responsible for paying the vendor himself. The child welfare representatives held firm to the principle that families approved by the agency to provide care to other people's children—whether full-time foster care or day care—should be paid directly by the agency, since the foster mother or day-care mother works under standards and policies set by the agency and not by the child's parents. In the end the point of view of the child welfare representatives prevailed and a system for authorizing direct vendor payments was devised.

## GETTING UNDER WAY

On July 1, 1962, Family Day-Care Service became an established unit within the child welfare division of the Monroe County Department of Social Welfare. It was staffed by an experienced child welfare supervisor with full graduate training. In the early months of the program she handled all its aspects alone.

Initially, the supervisor spent most of her time publicizing the agency's need for family day-care homes and recruiting families to provide daytime child care. She prepared a fact sheet which she distributed widely among groups of social workers, nurses, doctors, clergymen, and laymen, including women's clubs, boards and staffs of character building agencies, and professional organizations. She also began a reference library on day care for use by professional staff members and prospective day-care mothers.

Before long the supervisor became very busy handling inquiries and applications from prospective day-care mothers. But referrals of families for service trickled in slowly.

The first referrals were almost all for the care of Negro children. Just as the agency had always had difficulty in developing boarding and adoption homes for Negro children, so it found difficulty in locating family day-care homes. It had established a rule that every day-care home must be within walking distance of the child's own home. This presented a real difficulty since these children lived in the city's most blighted areas.

The day-care supervisor involved all sorts of people in homefinding—school, church, housing authority, and settlement personnel—and finally succeeded in securing family day-care homes for Negro children. Then came the surprise. She discovered that the families for whom she had been making these plans had not waited for the agency but had found jobs and had taken themselves off the assistance rolls. Since at that time the family day-care service could only be offered to public assistance recipients, the agency could not offer these families the supervised day-care homes that had been found for them.

Another surprise was the scarcity of referrals from the public assistance division. However, this gave the day-care supervisor an opportunity to make thorough studies of each family referred for service and of the prospective day-care home. Then came another frustrating surprise. Many of the families who were referred for the family day-care service did not want it! In many instances the family's public assistance worker, noting inadequacies in the care provided a child in his own home, had apparently thought of day care as a panacea for his problems. Moreover, while referrals for day care had not been made simply to get the mother into the labor market, some of the mothers thought they were. And indeed some of the referrals could have resulted not in helping the mother to provide better child care, but in her abrogation of her child-care responsibilities.

In interviewing many of the mothers referred for the service, the family day-care supervisor found them tense and suspicious. Some of them seemed to think the agency was trying to get their children away from them. When they learned that the service was available only to assistance recipients, they saw it as something not quite respectable.

Another surprise, however, was more encouraging. Some highly disorganized parents who had very damaging relationships with their children but who had resisted suggestions for their placement in foster care accepted the offer of family day care. In some instances this proved to be a successful step toward badly needed full-time separation of parent and child. In other instances, however, the mother lacked sufficient strength to get the child up and dressed and to the family day-care home, although it was in her own neighborhood.

Because so few suitable referrals were made by the public assistance workers covering the two census tracts to which the service was initially restricted, the service was soon opened to assistance recipients throughout the county. Still very few referrals were made.

The discrepancy between what the day-care survey had led us to expect and the number of referrals received obviously arose from the realization of public assistance workers, after the program got under way, that some of the families they had originally thought could benefit from day care were either not able or not ready to use such a service. It became clear that a great deal of casework was necessary to help families benefit from it.

## TYPES OF FAMILIES SERVED

In December 1963, Federal funds for day care became available for the service through the State Department of Social Welfare. We were therefore able to enlarge the day-care staff with the addition of two caseworkers and to extend the service to families needing it, whether or not they were on the assistance rolls. Soon the unit was serving many mothers whose motivation for employment was high but was accompanied by considerable pathology in family relationships. At present the family day-care caseworkers handle intake, homefinding, supervision of the day-care home, and, except in some cases already being served by other child welfare workers, continuing casework with the child's own parents.

Today the families who come to the unit for placement of their children in family day care can, for the most part, be classified into three groups:

1. Young families in which the father is a graduate student in one of the local institutions for higher learning and the mother, the main breadwinner. For example:

> The A's are young parents of a 4-year-old child who are expecting a new baby in a few months. Mr. A is one of several graduate students who have sought family day-care service. Mrs. A is employed as a clerical worker and supports the family. In spite of the fact that these young people did not plan to have children until the husband finished his schooling and that they are deeply in debt and have some difficulties with their own parents, they discuss their problems in a matter-of-fact way and do not express feelings of anxiety about them or about the new baby. Although their 4-year-old little girl has been cared for by numerous substitute mothers since her birth, she is making a good adjustment in the family day-care home provided by the service.

2. Families of divorced parents in which the employed mother carries full responsibility for rearing the children. For example:

> Mrs. B is an attractive, intelligent, warm, and stable 32-year-old mother of two children ages 8 and 2. She experienced a very stormy marriage with an immature husband who acted out his hostilities in a flagrant manner. Both she and the children bear emotional scars. Even now Mr. B uses his

visiting privileges with the children to punish their mother by trying to turn their affections from her.

Mrs. B and the children now live with Mrs. B's parents, who are both employed and who complain that the children make them nervous. Mrs. B's 8-year-old daughter has exhibited some reactive behavior, anxiety, and poor school adjustment, but has improved since settling into family day care. Mrs. B uses her relationship with the caseworker to ventilate her feelings and to plan for her own and the children's adjustment to life with the grandparents, the family day-care mother, and Mr. B's continuing and disturbing visits.

3. Families with rather severe social malfunctioning. For example:

The C's are young 24-year-old parents of a 6-month-old child. Both parents have extremely dependent personalities and have great difficulty in expressing their feelings. Mrs. C uses the baby to hold off her husband's attention. Mr. C acts out his inner stress through excessive activity and busy work. When they applied for family day care for their child, the C's were nearly overwhelmed by financial stress. They reacted to this by further constricting their feelings and by seeking employment for Mrs. C.

In the casework interviews Mr. C was initially hostile, but now pours out his troubles with apparent relief. Mrs. C, on the other hand, strictly controls her feelings and has a very flip attitude toward the caseworker. The baby reflects the family strain by extreme tenseness, constant crying, and demands for attention in the day-care family, as well as by the physical symptoms of allergy and diarrhea.

We also serve families who come to us because they want to "park" their children so that the mother can go to work to bring the family a second salary. We believe that such families need our service, but in offering it to them we ask the parents to involve themselves in goal-directed planning.

In all cases the agency provides casework help to the family not only at the point of admission to the service, but also on a regular basis during the entire time the child is in care.

The caseworkers in the service also provide support to the day-care mothers to help them to understand and withstand the behavior of children who are reacting to problems in their own families and to the daily separation from their parents. We hope to experiment in the future with group meetings for training day-care parents.

## PROBLEMS AND PROMISE

In short, in our 4 years of experience in establishing and operating a family day-care service we have encountered problems requiring difficult policy decisions in four areas:

1. *Administrative procedures regarding certification of day-care homes and methods of payment.* Although the methods we adopted were difficult to work out, they are now operating smoothly.

2. *Recruitment and training of day-care families.* We have stuck by our decision to place children in the same neighborhood in which they live, although this has added to our recruitment difficulties.
3. *Intake.* While we see the family day-care placement as part of a total family casework service, we have had difficulty arriving at a sharp definition of intake policy. In other words, the questions still arise: Should we limit our services to families requesting casework service because of malfunctioning in the family? Or should we also serve parents who resist casework help and wish only to be provided with a reliable day-care home for their children?
4. *The use of the agency's casework staff.* Because of the chronic shortage of professional social caseworkers in a public agency, the question also arises about how much casework treatment the family day-care service should provide. In other words, when the agency receives a request for day care from a family in which there is serious pathology, should the child be placed in family day care and the parents referred to the voluntary family service agency for casework help? Or should the casework treatment be provided by the public agency's family day-care caseworker? We believe that sound practice requires the second alternative for we see the day-care placement as an integral part of a total casework service. However, shortage of professional caseworkers in the public agency makes this level of service difficult to provide. The goal will probably not be fully achieved until the public agency has staffing requirements and salary levels high enough to attract and retain more highly skilled personnel.

In spite of these difficulties we are convinced that the family day-care service is an important addition to our public child welfare program's efforts to strengthen family life. Today we have 27 children from 20 families in family day-care homes, and 21 children awaiting placement. Those in care range in age from 2 months to 12 years, but the majority are under 5 years of age.

All are children who need the service either because being away from their families during the day is a therapeutic necessity, or because their mothers are determined to go to work and without our provision of a supervised day-care family would be likely to fall back on a hit-or-miss, and hence, hazardous child-care arrangement.

Our experience has convinced us that a public agency is performing a real service to children when it sets up a family day-care program, *if* it accepts children for family day care only if this is the best plan that can be made for them, and *if* the agency is able to provide skilled social caseworkers for recruiting and sustaining day-care homes and for working with families to remedy many of the situations which make the day care necessary.

# 15

(| With very few exceptions all the day-care service available in the United States today is designed for children three years of age or older. There is, however, a growing interest in day care for children from six months to three years of age. The hesitancy and anxiety about the desirability of such a program is based on the possible damage resulting from maternal deprivation, despite recognition of the difference between deprivation and separation.

Although we have provided almost no day-care service for the infant, European countries have had a great deal of experience with such care.

The World Health Organization in its publication *Care of Children in Day Centres* (Public Health Paper 24, W.H.O., Geneva, Switzerland, 1964) reported the research conducted by Professor B. Gornicki (Director of the National Research Mother and Child Institute, Warsaw) which compared the development of 900 children from nine months to three years of age. Five hundred of the children were brought up in their own homes, 400 had attended day-care centers from seven to nine hours a day for at least half of their young lives ("The Development of Children in the Family and in the Day-Care Centres in Poland," pp. 112–137, *op. cit.*, W.H.O.). Physical and psychological testing led to the general conclusion that, "The environment of a well organized day-care centre does not markedly retard the child's psychomotor development or, in the majority of children, cause behavior disorders or particular difficulties other than those found in children of the same age brought up in their own homes" (p. 136). The following article is an abbreviated version of another report, this time from France, from the same W.H.O. publication. It reports similar results.

# Day-Care Centres in Paris and Its Suburbs

*F. Davidson*

## THE DAY-CARE CENTRES OF THE DEPARTMENT OF THE SEINE

The French legal definition of a day-care centre, or crèche, is an establishment where healthy children below the age of three years may be left during the mother's working hours.

Such establishments are open from 6 or 7 A.M. until 7 or 7:30 P.M.;

128

they are closed at night and on Sundays and public holidays. In view of the long time the children spend in these day-care centres, it is essential for them to receive in them all the attention necessary for their satisfactory physical and mental development.

Day-care centres are regulated by the Decree of 21 April 1945 and the Administrative Order of 18 April 1951. Without going into the details of these legislative texts, their general provisions are as follows:

1. No day-care centre may be set up unless it is first authorized and then supervised by the public health authorities of the Department.
2. The premises must comply with certain minimum standards in regard to number of rooms, size of rooms, ventilation, heating, etc.
3. The number of staff looking after the children must not be less than a statutory minimum, and the head of the centre must hold the State *diplôme de puériculture.*
4. Finally, a medical practitioner with adequate experience in pediatrics must be responsible for the medical supervision of the establishment.

A survey was carried out simultaneously on 1 October 1961[1] in all the establishments. It covered 115 public and 39 private district centres and 19 factory centres. This investigation brought to light some interesting points. The family situation of the children, their ages, and the occupations of the mothers are shown in Tables 1–4.

TABLE 1. Family Situation of 7,507 Children in Day-Care Centres

|  | Number of children | % |
| --- | --- | --- |
| Living with both parents | 5,627 | 74.5 |
| Unmarried mothers | 774 | 10.3 |
| Widowed or divorced mothers | 324 | 4.3 |
| Fathers in the armed forces | 773 | 10.3 |
| Alone with fathers | 9 | 0.12 |

TABLE 2. Age of 7,507 Children in Day-Care Centres

|  | Number of children | % |
| --- | --- | --- |
| 2–6 months | 936 | 12.5 |
| 6 months–1 year | 1,434 | 19.2 |
| 1 year–18 months | 1,661 | 22.1 |
| 18 months–3 years | 3,476 | 46.2 |

[1] This date was chosen as a time of year when the centres are at maximum capacity; all the children have returned, the new admissions have settled in, and absenteeism is still low.

TABLE 3. Number of Brothers and Sisters in Families of
7,507 Children in Day-Care Centres

|  | Number of children | % |
|---|---|---|
| Only children | 5,135 | 68.3 |
| 2-child families | 1,596 | 21.3 |
| 3-child families | 433 | 5.8 |
| More than 3 children | 343 | 4.6 |

TABLE 4. Occupations of Mothers of 7,507 Children in
Day-Care Centres

|  | Number of children | % |
|---|---|---|
| Office workers and administrative staff | 1,927 | 25.7 |
| Factory workers | 1,712 | 22.8 |
| Secretaries, shorthand-typists, telephonists | 1,299 | 17.3 |
| Paramedical staff: nurses, social workers, puericulturists, family aides | 632 | 8.4 |
| Cleaners, charwomen, general domestic servants | 555 | 7.4 |
| Teachers | 407 | 5.4 |
| Shop-assistants | 345 | 4.6 |
| Students | 300 | 4.0 |
| Chemists, laboratory assistants, radiology technicians | 195 | 2.6 |
| Women working at home, artisans | 120 | 1.6 |
| Liberal professions | 15 | 0.2 |

## MENTAL HEALTH PROBLEMS AND PSYCHOLOGICAL
## DEVELOPMENT IN DAY-CARE CENTRES

The very definition of a day-care centre (a place where infants under three years are cared for during the day) is sufficient to indicate the reasons for the psychological difficulties that may be encountered in them. The prolonged absence of the mother, the difficulty of providing compensation in the shape of another person who must take the mother's place, the routine of life in the centre and the different atmosphere from that of the home—all are factors that cause suffering to the infant, whose age and intense emotional needs make him particularly vulnerable. It is therefore important to recognize the responsibilities assumed by the day-care centre in the field of mental health and to orient the outlook of physicians, and particularly of directresses and subordinate staff, towards prevention of the emotional deprivation that can prejudice the physical and mental condition of a child in the near or distant future.

There is a very considerable demand for day-care centres. Some districts of Paris and some suburban communes are still without them, and at existing centres there was a waiting list of 3396 on 1 October 1961.

On the basis of these various surveys, the situation in the day-care centres in the Paris region appears to be as follows:

1. They are not charitable institutions for social-problem cases; 85% of the children belong to normally constituted families (including those whose fathers are in the military services); "problem cases" are admitted together with these children without any discrimination.
2. Only children—or rather, first children—constitute 68% of the total enrolment. Infants from families with two children constitute 21.1%, but those from families with three or more children are rare. This is easily explained by the legislative provisions in France with regard to family allowances and the single-income family; considerable advantages accrue by the time there is a third child, so that mothers of large families are able to remain at home. The only women in this category who work are those who have a specialized profession or special qualifications or advantages attaching to seniority.
3. The French social legislation whereby women are granted postnatal leave and in some circumstances nursing leave avoids the very early placing of infants in day-care centres in many cases. Nevertheless, the demand for places for first-age-group infants is very great. In the course of our survey we noted that 31.7% of the children admitted are under one year and 53.8% under 18 months.
4. Study of the occupations of the mothers confirms what is stated above. The day-care centres are clearly used in the very great majority of cases by young mothers with stable and even specialized occupations but, like all young workers, with very modest salaries.
5. In order to be really useful, therefore, the day-care centre's tariff must be low. Only public centres can afford to charge low fees; private undertakings are no longer able to meet the enormous deficit entailed in the running of a day-care centre, unless children are to be selected on the basis of the parents' incomes or unless a heavy burden is to be placed on the economically weak families.
6. The demand for places in day-care centres is very great and the needs are still considerable. As stated above, 3396 children were entered on the waiting lists at the time of our survey, but this number gives only a very approximate idea of the real demand, since very often, when informed of the long delay, mothers do not enter the children and endeavour to find some other immediate solution, which is, as a rule, the placing of the child in a family (here it should be noted that in 1961 we kept under surveillance 9554 children under three years placed out with families). Unfortunately, the family placement situation is not very satisfactory in Paris; although it is better in the suburbs, it is always

very costly and the cost must be borne entirely by the families (250–
300 NF per month).

These are the sociological aspects of the day-care centres in the Paris
region. Their social importance emerges clearly from the foregoing and
justifies the studies and measures necessary to ensure their satisfactory
operation so that they may fulfil their social role and at the same time
perform their tasks in the fields of education and health.

So many works of French and other psychiatrists and psychologists during recent years have called attention to the harmful consequences of
emotional deprivation that everyone is convinced of the need to make an
effort to prevent them. However, the backwardness in this field as compared with the progress made in the field of general hygiene is obvious. It
is of course as impossible for any legal text to establish minimum requirements in affective conditions as stipulate compulsory activities and games.
The initiative still rests with the responsible services and persons, and this
would be a good thing if they were not obliged to take into account factors that have no bearing on this problem, especially financial ones.

The provision of optimum conditions for psychomotor development
depends on a number of factors, chief among them being the environment,
the personnel (number and qualifications), the equipment, and the organization of life in the centre.

While in present conditions a satisfactory environment can be obtained,
the number of staff is calculated essentially on the basis of the material
tasks connected with the care and feeding of the children, cleaning, etc.
The time necessary for purely maternal attention is not sufficiently taken
into account, and for this reason there is in practice a shortage of staff per
establishment. This quantitative deficiency is unfortunately allied to a
qualitative deficiency, which it is difficult to remedy by in-service training
because of the numerical shortage of staff.

The equipment, and in particular the games and elementary educative
material, which in general are adequate at the opening of a day-care centre,
rapidly deteriorate and their replacement is expensive. It is difficult to
convince some people that this is not a question of luxury but of basically
necessary equipment.

The organization of a harmonious life in a centre depends on the above-
mentioned factors as a whole; although we are unable to achieve perfection
in all of them, we do everything in our power at least to approach the
achievement of our aims in every possible respect.

The team of psychologists attached to the maternal and child health
service of the Seine has for several years been assisting our service in the
organization of a routine of life in day-care centres based on our knowledge of the psychological development of the child. Their work in the
survey of the environment and the results of the psychological tests they

made during the investigations covered by this report seem to us to deserve mention.

### Psychological Study, 1961

This study covered 11 of our day-care centres and one establishment not attached to our service but considered typical in its organization; this was included for purposes of comparison. We selected centres representing the different types of establishments in our service, some very modern, others less so, and still others very dilapidated. The establishments in question had no special advantages as to either personnel or equipment, and if the results are average they have at least the merit of being in accordance with reality.

These investigations, within their limits, confirm what careful observation of the establishments had already revealed, namely:

1. The day-care centre is not in itself a retarding environment; on the contrary, for children who suffer from a poor home environment the conditions in the day-care centre are more favourable for development.
2. While the architecture of the establishment is not without its importance, the internal layout, the organization of daily life and of the sections, and the equipment are much more important—above all, the toys and playthings.
3. First and foremost, the role of the personnel is paramount. The personality of the directress, the training and natural qualifications and qualities of the subordinate personnel, and of course, their number, will determine whether a day-care centre is good or bad.

### CONCLUSION

We have endeavoured in this report to give an unadorned and frank description of the day-care centres of Paris and of the Department of the Seine and to indicate their virtues and their defects. In other countries we have seen day-care centres different from ours—different in the material arrangements, in their organization and in their operation. No ideal formula seems to have been found, but one point seems generally accepted, viz., the need to divide the centres into small, limited sections according to the children's age and psychomotor development. Unfortunately, multiplication of groups means multiplication of rooms and of personnel and therefore higher running costs. However, this disadvantage may be offset to some extent by increasing the overall capacity of the establishment while maintaining the same general services, the same management, etc. It is with this idea in mind that some of our new centres now being built will have, instead of the three sections described (10 first-age-group, 10 second-age-group and 20 third-age-group children), two sections for the first-age group, two for the second, and one for the third, older group; i.e., 60 children in all. This will make it possible to form more homogeneous groups and at the same time to admit more younger infants, since the demand in this section is greater.

When all has been said, the day-care centre is an unnatural environment for first-age-group infants, whom nature intended to be close to the maternal breast. However, the human child's capacity for adaptation is obviously very great, since he can grow and develop satisfactorily even in the absence of the mother, on condition that he is assured of a daily ration of maternal love and that a certain number of now well-known conditions are provided. The provision of these conditions is the whole problem of the day-care centre.

# Section III

Foster-Care Services

FOSTER-FAMILY CARE is, like adoption and institutional child care, a substitutive child-care service. In each instance someone other than the natural parents takes responsibility for full-time care of the child. Foster-family care is one of the principal service responsibilities of professionally trained child-welfare social workers. The amount of literature written by professionals concerned with foster care exceeds that of any other child-welfare service.

Despite the professional staff time and attention devoted to foster care, the service faces a continual crisis. The need for foster homes is always greater than the number of foster parents available. Not only is there a chronic absolute shortage of foster homes, but the deficiency is particularly great in terms of the needs of physically, mentally, and emotionally handicapped children.

Currently, children needing foster-family care come from situations which are more pathological, from homes manifesting more limited potential for ultimate rehabilitation. Consequently, more of these children tend to stay in foster care for longer and longer periods of time. For such "orphans of the living" more explicit consideration is currently being given to long-term foster care on a planned basis.

Such permanent foster care is a formal contractual arrangement between the foster family and the agency, gives the family greater autonomy in its care of the child, and guarantees the maintenance of the child in the home. Children would thus remain in a particular foster home over a long period of time by design rather than by default.

Despite the difficulties faced by foster-family-care services, the continuing need for a temporary substitute home for many children and the need for a quasi-adoptive substitute-care facility for many nonadoptable children guarantees the persistence of the foster-family-care arrangement for the foreseeable future. The drive is toward improvement of foster-family care rather than its abandonment, toward the development of a continuum of diversified foster-care services which would' include group homes under agency auspices, toward greater subsidization of the foster home, and toward career status for foster parents and a peer relationship with agency personnel. More adequate provision of the resources previously discussed is implicitly designed as primary and secondary prevention procedures to reduce the number of children who might need foster care.

Currently, some 225,000 children live in foster-family homes. It is estimated that the number will increase to 300,000 by 1975. The readings have been selected to include research regarding recruitment of foster parents, the motivation of foster parents, the actual behavior of foster parents as they carry out their responsibilities, the antecedents of children coming into foster care, the variables which relate to the probability of their remaining in foster care, the factors which determine the worker's decision to offer foster care to the child, and foster-care outcome. There is a substantial gap between the image and the actuality of foster care, between the theory and the practice. The readings have been selected to mirror the situation as it actually is, as reflected by the relevant research.

# 16

( What factors account for the difficulties in recruiting a sufficiently large number of foster parents? What factors relate to the likelihood that a family will accept foster children? The following two articles attempt to explore these questions. The first is a study of attitudes toward foster care in households in a large city in the United States. The second is a report of a similar study done in England. The study is a research analysis of the special characteristics of foster families as compared with a random sample of families in the community.

## What People Think About Foster Care

*Kenneth Dick*

The hope of learning something about public attitudes on foster care that would be of value to agencies recruiting homes to board children was the stimulus for a survey conducted by the St. Louis University School of Social Service in 1959. Cooperating in the study were the Children's Services of St. Louis, Family and Children's Service of Greater St. Louis, which suggested the survey, the Catholic Charities, and the Child Welfare Services of St. Louis County. The findings revealed that attitudes believed by the agencies to be inhibiting people from boarding children—disapproval by friends and relatives, visits by the child's parents, and low payment for board—were actually lower in intensity than expected. Rather, the common attitudes were expressed by statements such as "we don't want to be bothered," or "agencies expect too much of people." These replies and the apparent lack of accurate information about child placing agencies present a challenge to agencies planning homefinding activities.

From addresses provided by three of the four co-operating agencies, we plotted the areas in the city and county with a high concentration of boarding homes, separately for white and for Negro foster families. From these areas, a total of 50 blocks were chosen—25 blocks each for white and Negro—and in each block a nonfoster family was selected at random for interviewing. The other half of the sample, also equally divided between Negro and white families, was selected from sections of the city and county in which the four agencies had indicated that their recruitment efforts were meeting with little success. This type of sampling enabled us

138

to analyze racial differences and to compare families with some chance of exposure to agency programs with families that theoretically do not have that chance. In all, 100 persons from 100 blocks were interviewed.

Except for questions about foster parents or foster children, direct questions regarding what they knew about or thought of foster care were not asked the persons interviewed. Instead they were presented with two hypothetical situations—parents needing to place their children and a family boarding a child—around which sets of problems were constructed. The respondents were asked to give their opinions on these problems or tell what advice they would give to a friend faced with a decision in regard to them. From the replies, certain attitudes and knowledge or lack of knowledge about foster care were inferred.

We do not maintain that these responses reflect the attitudes or knowledge in the total community. We recognize the limitations of a sample of 100 and the hazards of public opinion interviewing. The findings may have value, however, as clues to understanding the problems of homefinding.

Some agency publicity was found to be trickling through to the public, but not in the amount or of the kind to kindle a desire in people to become foster parents or to make clear exactly what it is that the placement agencies are doing.

Less than half of the 100 people interviewed had heard, read, or seen any publicity about the agencies' need for foster homes. Furthermore, they were not inclined to believe that the need existed, or that the agencies would have a hard time finding sufficient homes to care for homeless children. Yet these persons were interviewed at a time when special newspaper features, spot radio and television announcements, and special speakers were appealing for homes to place the children who were in the care of these agencies.

## LACK OF RESPONSIVENESS

Another, even more serious aspect of the problem was uncovered. When agency publicity did get through, it did not touch a responsive chord. Not only did the publicity fail to reach half the people but those it did reach often could not remember the name of the agency or the major elements of the publicity. Many interviewees said that not enough was told about either the agencies or the children, and that there was not enough heart appeal to make them want to know more.

On the other hand, nearly half the people interviewed said they would like to hear more about foster home programs or children needing homes. They belonged to clubs, church groups, or PTA's which they thought would welcome a speaker; but, as one woman commented, they "wouldn't know how to go about getting a speaker."

Herein lies the challenge to placement agencies. People want to know more, and at the same time agency publicity is failing to reach or impress them. New methods and a new focus are therefore called for. But will the publicity techniques that sell cigarettes, toothpaste, or nail polish do the job? There is no popular image of the agencies that makes them a "household item." Nor is their work generally controversial or sensational. Newspapers, radio, and television may arouse the public on political, racial, and other "hot" issues, but can they alone achieve the desired results for agencies reaching out for foster homes?

The problem apparently is more complicated than catching eyes or ears. The anxieties or fears of potential foster parents about agencies, as well as their motivations and their understanding, obviously play an important part in their reactions.

In neighborhoods of many foster homes, interviewees who had known foster parents remembered things about the child and his parents but were confused about the agency's part in the picture. They saw little difference between foster children and other children in the neighborhood. When they did see the child as different, the difference they mentioned was usually shyness, lack of self-confidence, or a physical handicap. Few mentioned the acting-out child; most tended to be tolerant of his behavior. Therefore, we might imply that foster children were acceptable in neighborhoods in which an awareness existed of what foster parents do. The opposite was found in neighborhoods of few boarding homes. There the residents often considered the foster child as something apart and potentially a problem.

The respondents were less certain in their thinking about why children need to be separated from their parents and placed in foster homes. This may be a factor that is overlooked in the recruitment of homes. In commenting on the hypothetical situations presented, 16 percent of the sample expressed the opinion that a child should not be placed away from home under any circumstances except for adoption. Among them was a professional woman who commented that "Taking a child from his parents does nothing for him; it only magnifies his problems." Such attitudes are similar to findings in the recent study by the Child Welfare League of America.[1] For the other 84 percent, broken homes, morally unfit parents, working parents, and parents unable to support the child, in that order, ranked highest as the reasons given for separating a child from his parents. To help or treat a child was mentioned by only one person. On the other hand, when questions about the reasons for boarding children were asked directly, "to help the child"—provided he was homeless—became significant.

---

[1] Maas, Henry S.; Engler, Richard E.: Children in need of parents. Columbia University Press, New York, 1959.

## MOTIVATIONS

Most of the people interviewed considered foster parents as having healthy motives for boarding children. The simple love of children was the outstanding reason given, particularly in neighborhoods with a high concentration of boarding homes. Persons who mentioned this also saw foster parents as having a giving nature and a desire to help a homeless child.

The financial motive for foster parenthood, though important, was stressed less often than we had expected. It was greatest in the neighborhoods in which the recruitment efforts of agencies had met with least success. We were also surprised to find that the opportunity to help a child who needed to be separated from his parents temporarily for study and treatment had almost no appeal.

Although the concept of love of children and the willingness to give of oneself may be an oversimplification of the actual motives of foster parents, it is the essence of a positive approach to foster parenthood. Caseworkers assume that positive motivations, though sometimes cloaking negative needs, do exist. A corollary to this is the fact that people derive "healthy" satisfactions from the service they give a child and an agency. More attention to these aspects of recruitment might enable the child-placing agencies to reach more people who have the precious gift of love and understanding to offer a child. There is the need to probe deeper into the meaning of this love to the foster parents themselves and into the conscious satisfactions the experience of foster parenthood brings them. Interest in this subject has led the Family and Children's Service of Greater St. Louis to consider making a study of this among persons boarding children.

When we tried to get at the reasons why it is hard to interest people in becoming foster parents, we found, as might be expected, an opposite set of factors. Selfish motives predominated, such as, "I don't want to be bothered" and "It's too much responsibility; agencies expect too much of people." These comments reflected the attitudes of nearly half of the 57 people who said they thought agencies would have difficulty in recruiting boarding homes. Other important reasons were that people had children of their own to take care of and that board payments were considered inadequate.

Further questions gave some insight into the unwillingness to be bothered. In 40 percent of the families interviewed, the woman was working. Slightly less than a third of this group indicated they might be interested in boarding a child if they were not employed. Two-thirds of all the families had school-age children. In about a fourth of these, the parents said they might like to become foster parents when their children are older. And finally, a third of all the people interviewed might be interested if they had more room.

There may, however, be something more to this unwillingness to be bothered. Perhaps the equilibrium of these people's lives, the solidarity of the family, and the satisfactions achieved in it outweigh the factors that might lead them to want to board children. Herein may lie the dilemma of the agencies: the people with the best potential for foster parenthood are the hardest to motivate. If so, what significance for recruitment programs lies in the combined tendencies of interviewees to feel that boarding children is too much responsibility and that agencies expect too much of people? Do these attitudes indicate that desirable applicants do not take the first step toward foster parenthood because an unwillingness to take on added responsibility or to be bothered outweighs their love for children and any potential satisfactions from boarding children?

## ATTITUDES TOWARD THE AGENCY

The study did not bring out the usual stereotype of the social worker that we sometimes think exists. Nor was a great deal of hostility to social workers apparent. What hostility did exist was occasionally bitterly expressed and was more often directed toward the agency than against the social worker. In discussing the hypothetical foster home situations, only 10 percent of the interviewees said they would object to the visits of a social worker. More significant, a third, composed largely of people tending to be vague and lacking understanding of agency programs, said it would make no difference to them whether or not a social worker visited. The remaining 57 percent indicated they would welcome the visits of the social worker and at times might seek his help.

There was also a disappointing confusion about the role of the agency, especially among people who had seen agency programs in operation. In this group, with more doubts than those in other neighborhoods about what the agencies were trying to accomplish, the point was frequently raised that too much was expected of foster parents. Maybe this was a factor in the widely expressed preference in this group for boarding children independently of a social agency. Undoubtedly a latent anxiety and fear of agencies as well as feelings of insecurity on the part of the interviewees may have contributed to these attitudes. However, it raises the question of how much effort is expended in educating foster parents on the problems and the role of the child-placing agency. In this connection, the Family and Children's Service decided in 1959 to inaugurate a group training program for foster parents.

Slightly more than half of the total sample said they would prefer to board children for an agency. The major reasons given for this preference were that: (1) there would be less interference from parents—"things go smoother"; (2) the agency helps the child and foster parents with their problems; (3) the agency protects the foster family and is more dependable than the child's parents themselves are apt to be.

The people who said they would prefer to board independently based their preference on the belief that taking a child directly from his parents provides better opportunities for: (1) knowing both child and parents; (2) getting along with the parents and the child; (3) inducing the parents to take more responsibility for the child. There was some secondary but direct criticism of agency standards and procedures. Most of these interviewees questioned the wisdom of an agency's interfering with the rearing of a child, and expressed doubt about whether the agency really knew the child and what was important to him. Such doubts indicated a lack of knowledge, not only of the agency's role but also of its responsibilities.

A few excerpts from the interviews throw light on some of the issues:

> For my own, I want to know the family, not the little bit that someone tells me. I want to know what I am getting into.
> I'd rather go see them (the social worker). It would seem less like they're checking up on me.
> The social worker shouldn't visit without the consent of the parents.
> From what I hear from other people, they upset you. Why did you do this? Why did you do that? They don't give you enough to really take care of the child. So why be bothered with an agency too?

Similar attitudes were displayed when we asked what advice the interviewees would give a friend who needed to place his child. However, only 39 percent of all said they would recommend agency placement, although 52 percent said they themselves would prefer to board for an agency. Both groups gave a similar reason: the agency would know what is best for the child and would investigate the home.

The people who would recommend to the friend that he find a home on his own initiative raised questions about the role of the agency. They seemed not so much to dislike agencies as to regard them as third parties intruding in the relationship of the parents and the foster parents. The reasons they gave for recommending that the child be placed independently were that the friend would have (1) a more personal relationship with the child and the foster family; (2) a better chance to know the quality of the foster parents; (3) better care for his child by someone of his own choice; (4) an easier time in placing the child and getting him back; and (5) more trust in the foster parents.

Some of these reasons were expressed in the following ways:

> It is not good for a child to be shifted from one foster home to another.
> It is better to have the child with someone you know or can get to know rather than with strangers.
> The parents should see for themselves where the child is going.

The parents would be better satisfied; the home they choose would not be like the homes used by welfare agencies.

Such comments pose a question that is sometimes overlooked. Does caring for someone else's child make a person a "foster" parent? Or does it, in the eyes of the public, merely provide child care for the parents, who do not thereby lose parental status? The Child Welfare League of America has recognized this difference in one of its documents:

> Adding, no doubt, to the confusion of roles is the myth that these people are foster parents. They well may have been so when most children in foster care were either orphaned or abandoned, but it can hardly be sustained in face of active parental involvement in the case of the child's natural parents, their participation in planning and often financing of his care, and their visits with him in the foster home. Clearly, if these are his parents, then the foster parents are not, yet we persist in calling them foster parents and in selecting them as if they were that to some extent.[2]

## ATTITUDES OF NEGROES

Many of the findings of the survey have implications concerning the social role of the agency and concerning cultural factors in the problem of foster home recruitment. Indirect evidence of this was revealed in the data obtained from Negroes.

Fewer Negroes than whites knew people who had boarded children. This was understandable in view of the great immigration of Negro families to the city in recent years. Many of the Negroes we interviewed indicated that they did not consider taking care of a friend's or relative's child, often without pay, as "boarding." The problem of recruitment of Negro homes, or at least one facet of it, must be viewed with the knowledge that the Negro community is carrying out some of the child care task spontaneously.

Although only about 50 percent of the Negroes interviewed had known someone who had boarded a child, more of them than the white interviewees had talked to foster parents about their experiences in boarding a child. They too regarded foster children as little different from others. Yet they tended not to be interested in boarding children themselves.

Generally, however, the Negroes had a favorable attitude toward the agencies. Almost twice as many Negroes as whites would recommend agency placement to a friend. They stressed the facts that the agency knows what is best for the child and is able to assume financial responsibility. On the other hand, more Negroes than whites were hesitant about ever wanting to board a child for an agency. This uncertainty

---

[2] Wolins, Martin: Proposed research program for the Child Welfare League of America. Child Welfare League of America, New York, 1959.

seemed to be rooted in lack of knowledge rather than in negative attitudes toward children or the agencies.

Eight percent of the Negroes said they did not know of a social agency to which they might refer a friend who needed to place his child, compared with 3 percent of the white people interviewed. Furthermore, 15 percent—almost twice the proportion of whites—did not know whether agencies paid board for children. The Negroes also tended to be less well-informed than the white interviewees about the agencies' needs. Nearly one-fourth—twice as many as the whites—thought that agencies would not have difficulty finding foster homes for children.

However, about the same proportion of each race had heard or seen agency publicity on the need for homes. The Negroes more often had been reached by radio and television and the whites by newspaper publicity and talks before groups such as parent-teacher's or church associations. But the Negroes tended to remember fewer of the details of the publicity. On the other hand, over twice as many Negroes as whites said they thought their PTA, church, or club would like to hear more about children needing foster homes. Whether or not this was the kind of sincere interest that would produce foster homes or mere friendliness could not be determined. Nevertheless, this expression of good will, viewed in the context of the general lack of information, produces a challenge to reach Negroes at the grass roots, in their primary groups.

Another significant attitude among Negro interviewees was that if they were to be paid at all for boarding children they ought to be paid well. Generally they reacted much more negatively than the whites to the current board rates for foster care. Faced with economic realities, and given an alternative, the majority of Negro interviewees apparently would choose that which produced the higher income. This raises the question of whether higher board rates, geared more specifically to the recruitment of Negro homes, would bring results.

In spite of some differences in degree between the races and between the neighborhoods, one common thread ran throughout the interviews: a general fund of misinformation and lack of information about agency programs and the role of the agency in child placement. Slightly less than half of the people interviewed had seen or heard any publicity about the need for homes.

From this it would appear that spot announcements in the mass media of communication and other agency publicity are not effective in making people want to board children and are not correcting misinformation. The people with the least knowledge about foster care thought that such things as low board payments, visits by the social worker, or disapproval by friends would deter them from becoming foster parents.

Increasing knowledge and understanding, therefore, is of crucial importance to recruitment. It is a prerequisite to a more favorable attitude toward foster care itself and to influencing otherwise positively motivated families to take the initial step toward foster parenthood.

On the other hand, the survey also gave many hopeful clues to recruitment. A sizeable proportion of the interviewees indicated that they thought their club, parent-teacher's association, or church group might like to hear more about the needs of foster children. Meetings with groups at the "grass roots" should provide the opportunity to interest people in boarding children and to correct misinformation. Methods learned from working with the "hard to reach" families, such as holding first interviews in the home, might well be adapted to this purpose.

Also significant for recruitment planning was the finding that people who had known foster parents knew little about the agency's role. There was the inference that the use of the impersonal agency in some way removed the child and the foster parents still further from the child's own parents. Apparently agencies cannot take for granted that foster parents themselves understand, let alone can interpret, what an agency is trying to achieve. In the realm of interpretation as in other areas, foster homes are only as good as an agency makes them. The need for a specific, if not formalized, training program for foster parents is implied.

In conclusion, the survey in all its aspects points up the need for focusing attention on the content as well as the direction of foster home recruitment programs.

# 17

# Fostering—A Sociological Perspective

*John Wakeford*

In modern Western society the female role contains two principal requirements. To be a success, a woman feels that she must get married and secondly, she must rear a family. These two ideals dominate our culture in nearly all age groups, social strata and sub-cultures. They are accepted by the majority of the unmarried as well as the married. If a woman remains single, she is encouraged to feel a sense of inadequacy in spite of the several possible alternative goals available. Religious withdrawal, social mobility, positions of power are rarely entirely satisfactory, viz. the seriousness with which she pursues them—out of all proportion to their intrinsic value and economic rewards. Efforts to provide culturally acceptable substitute goals are ineffective, when the pressure of popular culture persuades every adolescent girl that, if she is not a mother in her early twenties, she is a failure. This is only one of the pressures entailed in our increasing emphasis on the nuclear family as the basic social unit in contemporary western society.

Perhaps the principal function of the nuclear family concerns the re-production, maintenance and socialization of children. Due to the division of labour within the family and its typically small size, the female role provides the sole adult responsible for child care. Although the father may not be Margaret Mead's 'tired, and often dreaded, nightly visitor,' his role is mainly concerned with providing economic means and status rather than an adult model for the children. He is not as identified with child-rearing as is the mother. On the other hand, many mothers have no significant role in the family besides mothering. If a married woman is unable to have her own children, she will feel deprived, and look for alternatives. Some women turn to voluntary work, others to a career and some adopt or foster a child.

A recent research project on foster parents illustrates the role of the foster-child in the life of the mother and in the family structure as a whole.

## THE SURVEY

The original problem arose out of a current shortage of foster-homes in a local authority area. It was considered that not enough was known about a family's motives for fostering a child. So a comparison was made of those accepted and registered as foster-parents with a random sample of the whole population.[1] Sixty-six out of the complete list of seventy foster-parents were successfully interviewed. The controls were selected by taking every hundredth name, where it was female, from the Register of Electors in the areas, and then omitting those names where no male elector of the same name appeared at this address. The result was a list of adult women with an adult husband, son, brother or father at the same address. Interviewers then selected names at random from this list and carried out the complete interview when the interviewee was con-firmed to be living with her husband and where both were aged under 65 and in good health. Those who were widowed, single, living apart, over 65 or in poor health would normally be dissuaded from fostering and were therefore eliminated from the comparison. Approximately 30 successful schedules were completed for each of the five districts and only

those found to be out on three occasions were omitted as 'not contacted.'
This analysis of the interviews attempted is given in Table 1.[2]

TABLE 1. The Control Group—Selection

| | |
|---|---:|
| Total names used | 236 |
| Found to be | |
| Unmarried or widowed | 8 |
| Either 65 or husband over 65 | 37 |
| Either in poor health or husband in poor health | 2 |
| Moved out of the district | 16 |
| Not contacted after three calls | 21 |
| Refused interview | 4 |
| Successful interviews | 148 |

## HOUSEHOLD STRUCTURE

For a family to agree to receive children there must have been a pressure to alter the structure of the household. Though to a local authority the problem may be one of finding 'suitable' foster-parents, to the parents themselves the problem would normally be the burden of an extra child. In a comparison of family size a significant difference was found between foster-homes and controls (Table 2).[3] The principal difference was the low number of two- and three-child families among the foster-parents, which showed itself equally when only those children actually living at home were included.

TABLE 2. The Size of the Nuclear Family (Excluding Foster Children)

| Number of Children | Controls, % | Foster Homes, % |
|---|:---:|:---:|
| 0 | 19 ⎫ 45 | 23 ⎫ 61 |
| 1 | 26 ⎭ | 38 ⎭ |
| 2, 3 | 46* | 27* |
| 4 or more | 9 | 12 |
| | N = 148 | N = 66 |

* Chi-squared = 6.5. With two degrees of freedom this is significant at the 5% level.

There is no evidence that this is a class difference. A comparison of both groups with heads of household in the Registrar General's classes IV and V suggests that the contrast exists within this class as well as in the sample as a whole.[4] The foster-mother typically has fewer children than the norm. This means that she is frustrated in her principal status-carrying role. Although she has a fundamental status of being her husband's wife and being responsible for activities concerning the management of the household, she probably *either* has only one child *or* none at all. She has a family which does not fit the normative pattern of our culture and which therefore does not permit her to exercise her traditional role of mothering two or three children.[5]

Foster-mothers showed a prevalence of another unconventional attribute. There was a tendency for them to have married either very early or unusually late in their lives, when compared with the controls. Only half the foster-mothers had married when they were aged between 20 and 34, compared with 78% of the controls, considering present marriage only. This tendency for the very young or middle-aged bride to be a foster-parent suggests an effort to compensate for deviant behaviour. Both teen-age and middle-aged brides hope to have a normal family, but both are forced to turn to adoption or fostering when they are unable to fit in to the prescribed pattern. Both possibly married at this stage because of a strong orientation towards motherhood—the younger in preference to the rewards of adolescence and the older in response to years of unsatisfied ambition, and to compensate for wasted maturity. Both of them are strongly orientated towards normative behaviour and the accepted family pattern. Both desire motherhood and show a tendency to foster.[6]

## HOUSEHOLD STATUS

The position of a family in the social structure affects its members' attitudes to size and function, and this can result in different evaluations of fostering. Occupational status, particularly, is frequently found to correlate with different conceptions of the parental role and techniques of socialization.[7] To the middle-class parent, the child must be conscientiously trained to learn middle-class norms and middle-class standards —approximating to Riesman's 'inner-directed' type. Here the mother's status is measured by the efficiency of her mothering. To the lower-manual worker's family a child must learn merely to adapt, to perform simple roles and to be contented. The mother is less likely to feel guilty if her children are left with their peers. She feels that love, attention to health and happiness are the essentials of the mother's role, and her

TABLE 3. Occupational Classification of Head of Household

| Registrar General's Classification | Controls | Foster-homes, Percentage of Those Known |
|---|---|---|
| I, II | 33 ⎫ 80 | 22 ⎫ 58 |
| III | 47 ⎰ | 36 ⎰ |
| IV, V | 20* | 42* |
| | N = 147 | N = 66 |

* Chi-squared = 11.0. With one degree of freedom this is significant at the 0.1% level. With two degrees of freedom it is significant at the 0.5% level.

status is determined more by the size of the family than by the quality of her training of them.

The survey included one district with a high population of classes I and II, which explains the large numbers in this group in Table 3. Significantly more foster-parents appear in the homes with an unskilled or semi-skilled head of household than would be expected from the controls. Although still a minority, this class of mother seems to foster more frequently than other occupational groups. The high orientation towards the role of mother, and her evaluation of that role in terms of family size, entails an encouragement to foster a child to perform her role adequately. This is reflected too in the economic position of the foster-home. Here too the lower groups predominate in fostering. (The 20% of the controls refusing to answer would probably be in the higher-income group and would therefore accentuate this difference.) This fact has been suspected for some time, and has led to the suggestion that fostering is motivated by a desire to increase income, although allowances do not usually include an element of reward. However our analysis suggests another explanation—that the foster-mother fosters a child *as an alternative* to maximizing income.

TABLE 4. Reported Weekly Income to Household (Excluding Wife's Earnings)

|  | Controls, % | Foster-homes, Percentage of Those Known |
|---|---|---|
| Under £15 | 41 | 61 |
| £15 or more | 59 | 39 |
|  | N = 116 | N = 61 |

* Chi-squared = 15.0. With one degree of freedom this is significant at the 1% level.

The additional child fulfils a purpose that is social rather than economic. The class and economic disparity is explained by the different emphasis placed on the role of motherhood—the middle-class mother is less likely to want another child, since she can concentrate her energies on a smaller number or adjust more easily to alternative prestigeful goals, but the lower-working-class mother needs another child or at least one child to give significance to her role.

Fostering is also associated with working-class housing, more particularly with pre-1914 or post-1919 working-class housing. In the area of the investigation very few houses were built in the inter-war years, and most of these were for owner-occupiers. But under a third of the foster-parents were in middle-class houses, compared with over a half of the controls.[8] The foster-child will typically be placed with a working-class family, with a low income, in a working-class house. He will be a member of a small family. Thus he will be fostered in a home where working-class standards are accepted, but working-class expectations have not yet been fulfilled.

Partly because of the low status position of the foster-home, there is a tendency for the foster-mother to have been downwardly mobile, that is, to have a lower occupational status now than had her parents. Mobility was calculated merely by comparing the occupational classification of father and husband.[9] This suggests that a child, which might normally not be considered an asset in a family concerned with appearances and a higher standard of living, may provide a social reward to a family less concerned with economic advancement. Several studies have suggested that it is only a section of the working class which is concerned with collecting consumer durables and the supposed insignia of status. A large section of the working class still appear at the other end of the continuum—the 'rough' and the 'sociable'—who may well have both fewer alternative goals and be more family-oriented than the 'respectable' and the 'reserved.'[10] Amongst these a high rate of fostering is to be expected. In fact it has been suggested that a high rate of fostering may also be associated with declining *areas.*[11]

## THE ROLE OF THE MOTHER AND THE
## DECISION TO FOSTER

In view of the particular decision to foster, a characteristic ideal of foster-mothers is to emphasize the role of mother. This is reflected in their patterns of work, interest and family ideals. Certain features show no differences. Churchgoing as represented by attendance the previous Sunday is no more evident in foster-mothers than controls (one-third claimed attendance). Work-patterns were similar. The tendency towards part-time rather than full-time work is probably a reflection of the children's department policy rather than actual preference. On the other hand, the foster-mother claimed fewer interests outside her home. She visits less, spends less time shopping, less in social organizations, and, given an extra hour free each day, more would spend it in the home. Compared with the controls, she would be more likely to spend her leisure in her home. This is not a reflection of class differences—interests outside the home were equally distributed in the three classes and a comparison within the lower working class indicates the same contrast in the spare-hour activity as the samples as a whole.[12, 13] This is particularly significant in view of the tendency for the foster-mother to have a smaller family, needing, presumably, less time and attention if needs are similarly defined. The foster-mother seems to concentrate more intensively on the home—it provides her with a stage for the performance of her dominant role—that of mother.

Not only does she concentrate on her family and home, typically she

TABLE 5. Interests Outside the Home (Excluding Work)

|  | Controls, % | Foster-parents, % |
|---|---|---|
| An interest (for 3 hours or more per week) | 54 | 41 |
| None | 46 | 59 |
|  | N = 148 | N = 66 |

* Chi-squared = 3.1. With one degree of freedom this is significant at the 10% level.

would prefer an even larger one. Asked 'how many children would you like in your home (now)?', the most significant difference in the whole study emerged: two-thirds of the foster-mothers (compared with under a quarter of the controls) said that they would like a family of at least three children, nearly a third wanting four or more. A third of the controls had no desire for *any* children in the home. So fostering is clearly linked with family aspirations. Again this is not attributable merely to class differences, because the same picture is shown within each class.[14] Although her family is probably small, the foster-mother not only wants a normal-sized family, in many cases she wants an unusually large one. Her life and aspirations centre round her family and she wants it to be a satisfactory size to perform her role by concentrating on it. She is a dissatisfied wife. Fostering could alter the structure of her household and enable her to achieve her goal.

TABLE 6. 'If you had an extra hour free each day, how would you spend it?'

|  | Percentage of Those Answering | |
|---|---|---|
|  | Controls | Foster Parents |
| Household or family duties | 29* | 45* |
| Classes, clubs, outdoor activities, intellectual pursuits | 30 ⎫ | 18 ⎫ |
| Other, including relax, etc. | 41 ⎭ 71 | 37 ⎭ 55 |
|  | N = 142 | N = 66 |

* Chi-squared = 4.7. With one degree of freedom this is significant at the 3% level. Not significant with two degrees of freedom.

The question that arises next is, why does she choose to foster? There are alternative means to increase family size; normally a wife would have her own children or adopt. A large part of this question must remain unanswered, since the survey did not include questions on her ability to have more natural children. However, some relevant information was obtained. The survey was designed so that 'fostering' was not mentioned until late in the interview. So there was the opportunity to discover

TABLE 7. Concept of the Ideal Size of Family

| Number of Children Desired | Controls, % | Foster Parents, % |
|---|---|---|
| 0, 1, 2 | 77 | 36 |
| 3 or more | 23 | 64 |
|  | N = 131 | N = 64 |

* Chi-squared = 32.6. With one degree of freedom this is significant at the 0.1% level.

whether foster-mothers were the only ones who had heard of fostering. The issue was first raised by asking 'What can be done about caring for children who have no home?', and standard prompting was used to illustrate the question. The proportion mentioning fostering was over three-quarters in both groups, with no significant difference, and few mentioned alternative methods of care (such as adoption and children's homes) without mentioning fostering. And this in spite of few controls having personal acquaintance with a foster-home (14% compared with 33% of foster-parents). So most married women know about fostering, whether they chose to foster or not, and newspaper campaigns designed merely to inform would probably not affect her choice.[15]

In a sense most of the control group had de facto decided not to foster a child in spite of not having made a decision consciously. When the (hypothetical) issue was raised by the interviewer, 87% of the controls firmly said that they would not foster a child, even given an allowance 'of £2 or £3 per week.' Most had reasons for not wishing to foster, and some of those, who were themselves prepared to take a child, had doubts about accommodation or their husband's attitude. In only 10 of the 148 controls was there considered to be any chance of fostering, and in no case did anyone follow up the interview by contacting the local authority. Table 8 gives the 'reasons' for not fostering a child. These probably do not reflect basic motivation to any great extent—for instance, the very inertia of the existing family structure creates its own values. One of the basic reasons may merely be that there is no desire for this sort of change. Any disruption of family patterns and roles would have to be justified in terms of a strong need for another child, especially when it involves the added hazards and responsibilities of a foster-child.

Accommodation is a case in point. Although mentioned in only a minority of cases, the allocation of rooms is the expression of implicit values. In many cases accommodation is insufficient by any standards, but in others the number of rooms is greater than that required on an objective standard. However, each room has a function in the home, whether this is or is not represented by its name. This particularly applies to spare beds and bedrooms—what is to the outsider an empty room, may often

TABLE 8. 'Why would you not take a homeless child into your home?'

|  | Controls only, Numbers |
|---|---|
| Feel too old | 27 |
| Prefer more of own children | 25 |
| Insufficient accommodation | 20 |
| Disrupt family organization | 19 |
| Prefer adoption | 9 |
| Interrupt wife's work | 8 |
| Husband does not agree | 7 |
| Other | 27 |
| (Some gave two reasons) | |

have an important meaning for the household. It may be reserved for the absent son, who is at home for a few weeks each year, or for mother on her frequent visits or just be for any guests or friends who visit the district. Rooms are allocated rather by custom than usage. 'Our kid's room' could not be used for a foster-child since it is, in a sense, a link with a member of the family, which might be broken. Nor could the middle-class guest-room be defined as unused. To be without it would be a disaster. It is only when the motivation to accommodate a child is extremely great that the family will accept this sort of change. In fact only eight wives said that they had a spare bed available, and only six of them had also a spare room.

Foster-parents seem to have no characteristic conscious reason for deciding to foster. Most had a great deal of difficulty in remembering how they came to think of it. In about a quarter of the cases it was the result of a neighbour's or relative's suggestion, but there was no evidence that people living near foster-parents were more likely to foster. This again suggests that information about fostering is available and a part of most wives' general knowledge. Few remembered local press articles or advertisements or television programmes on the subject. One or two had discovered fostering by attempting unsuccessfully to adopt a child, later accepting a foster-child as an alternative.

Once fostering, a foster-mother seems to be almost as loyal to that role as a mother is to motherhood. Three-quarters of the foster-mothers predicted that nothing apart from age and poor health would prevent them from continuing. In spite of general dissatisfaction with their allowance, nearly all claimed to have *enjoyed* spending considerably more than they need on their foster-child. Few had considered the possibility of giving up fostering. The child or children had been accommodated in the structure of the family, and the absence of a child would mean readjustment, normally the loss of an important role and dissatisfaction on the

part of the foster-mother. When asked what *would* make them give up
fostering, they nearly all answered 'nothing.' Any answers given were so
vague that it appears to be considered a most unlikely, or at least un-
looked for, event.

## CONCLUSION

No one will voluntarily apply to take an extra child into their homes
unless it is rewarding in some way. This applies especially to a foster-
child. First, there are all the duties and obligations associated with the
maintenance and socialization of any child. Then there are the particular
difficulties associated with the care of another mother's child, who already
has his own patterns of behaviour. Also there are visits, inspections and
duties, which, however skilful and understanding the child care officer,
can only add to the foster-mother's problems. She cannot have a sense
of complete proprietorship. Moreover she has little assurance of the security of her emotional investment, since, compared with adoption, the
relationship is relatively transitory. The child's main obligations and affections often remain centred on his original home. Fostering holds little
promise of continuity or lasting emotional satisfaction, and in this sense
is not an adequate substitute for parenthood. Economically speaking, it
is a burden. In none of these fields can the decision to foster be a decision for personal gain.

On the other hand the majority of the control group were content,
having no desire to be foster-parents. The majority of foster-parents are
also content, in fact often dedicated to their task. The survey found few
controls prepared to be foster-parents, and none actively desiring to take
a foster-child. Nor did any foster-parent express the wish to be rid of
the child. So the differences must be explained in terms of relative satisfactions, available to many but chosen only by the few.

As we stated at the outset, the major role of the married woman is
that of a mother. She cannot perform this role without children. If she
has fewer children than she would like, she has a problem when she is
unable to have more of her own. One way of solving this problem is to
adopt or foster a child. If her need is mainly to establish or reassert her
position as mother, then it may be unnecessary to have a close emotional
relationship with the child. It might be suggested that the wife who in
addition requires a child for affection would prefer adoption, or only
be satisfied with long-stay fostering. The foster-mother may in some cases
want to *avoid* a mother-like relationship in this sense, and fostering, with
all its attendant problems, may be more suitable than having to lavish
the child with the affection she may not feel. Also, if fostering solves one
of the more important problems of the female role, we should expect,
and do in fact find, that those whose expectations of family size coincide

with reality will rarely consider fostering. Those, too, who have solved
this particular problem by fostering are highly satisfied, irrespective of
obligations and expense.[16] Their claim that they spend more on the child
than the local authority allows supports this suggestion. The existence of
the child in the home is in itself the predominant reward.

Many foster-mothers make considerable sacrifices for their foster-children. They do this as a contribution to their self-respect. The significantly
higher numbers amongst them of wives of unskilled and semi-skilled
workers suggests that here, where the wife's role of mother is particularly highly evaluated, the pressure to foster is greatest. Similarly the
factors of early or late marriage, downward mobility, lack of outside
interests and high family aspirations suggest that the foster-mother is
more family-orientated than average. She values the home; there she
finds most of her satisfactions and employs most of her energies. There
she is in her element. Without children her work is largely pointless. If
she has only one or two, perhaps grown up and away from home, her
importance is diminished. She is unable to perform the traditional role
of caring for children. Some wives, although mothers, are not satisfied
with an average-size family of two or three children; they desire more to
give them greater scope and significance. Particularly in working-class culture the wife has no alternative highly evaluated role to that of mother,
and, if necessary, she will foster a child to assure or emphasize it. The
disadvantages of a large family are, to her, *advantages*. In a life where
the other occupations open to her give her little satisfaction or status,
the work involved in caring for a large family or in fostering a child
gives her the significance that she can obtain in few other ways.

Fostering solves a problem. When a married woman finds that her
translation of these particular cultural demands conflict with her ability
to meet them, the problem may in some cases be adequately resolved
by fostering a child provided by the local authority. The costs, economic
and social, are outweighed by the reward—she is provided with a significant role.

### Notes

1. This investigation was not concerned with the success or failure of foster-
   homes. All those interviewed were generally satisfactory and satisfied in
   order to be on the register of foster-homes at all. Therefore the neurotic
   applicant and the disillusioned foster-parent will not appear in the study.
   For information on this aspect of fostering see G. Trasler, *In Place of
   Parents*, Routledge, 1960.
2. It can be seen incidentally from Table 1 that geographical mobility eliminated at least 16 and possibly 17 of the controls. This in itself suggested
   a factor which could not appear in the results—that relative immobility
   is a necessary precondition of fostering, whether the local authority prefers

the immobile or not. Poor health does not appear to be an important factor.

3. There were no significant differences between:
   (i) the number of members of the household who were *not* members of the nuclear family (about 20%);
   (ii) the number of dependents living with the family or away from home (about 10%);
   (iii) the age structure of the children in the family.

4. The size of the Nuclear Family excluding foster-children. Classes IV and V only.

| Number of Children | Controls | Foster-homes |
|---|---|---|
| 0 | 8 | 13 |
| 1 | 1 | 3 |
| 2,3 | 11 | 5 |
| 4+ | 10 | 7 |
| | 30 | 28 |

5. Cf. T. Parsons, 'Age and Sex in the Social Structure of the United States,' *Essays in Sociological Theory,* The Free Press, Glencoe, 1954, p. 95.

6. Cf. Trasler, op. cit., p. 113, and Hutchinson, D., *In Quest of Foster Parents.* Columbia U.P. 1945. Both writers comment on the frequency of the compensation effect.

7. See for instance Floud, Halsey & Martin, *Social Class and Educational Opportunity,* Heinemann, 1956, or Jackson and Marsden, *Education and the Working Class,* Routledge, 1962.

8.

| House Type | Controls | Foster-Parents |
|---|---|---|
| | Percentage of Those Known | |
| Owner occupied or rented | | |
| Middle class: | 53 | 29 |
| Working class: | | |
| pre 1914 | 13* | 27* |
| 1914–1939 | 15 | 9 |
| post 1939 | 18† | 35† |
| | N = 146 | N = 66 |

* Chi-squared = 6.0. With one degree of freedom this is significant at the 2% level.

† Chi-squared = 7.3. With one degree of freedom this is significant at the 1% level.

The figures are not significant with two or three degrees of freedom.

9. Intergenerational Occupational Mobility of Wife:

| | Controls | Foster-Parents |
|---|---|---|
| | Percentage of Those Known | |
| Downwards | 22* | 37* |
| None | 44 ⎫ 78 | 35 ⎫ 63 |
| Upwards | 34 ⎭ | 28 ⎭ |
| | N = 138 | N = 65 |

* Chi-squared = 4.8. With one degree of freedom this is significant at the 3% level.

10. See Goldthorpe and Lockwood: 'Not so bourgeois after all,' *New Society*, Vol. I, no. 3; L. Kuper, *Living in Towns*, Cresset 1953; Liverpool University: *Neighbourhood and Community*, Liverpool U.P. 1954.
11. See Dyson, *No Two Alike*, Allen and Unwin, 1962, p. 43.
12. The proportion with no interests outside the home—Class I, II: 42%, Class III: 46%, Class IV, V, 54%. These differences are not significant.
13. 'If you had an extra hour free each day, how could you spend it?'— Classes IV, V, only:

|                                | Controls | Foster-mothers |
| ------------------------------ | -------- | -------------- |
| Classes (etc.)                 | 6        | 3              |
| Household or family duties     | 8        | 11             |
| Other                          | 12       | 14             |
| Not known                      | 4        | —              |
|                                | —        | —              |
|                                | 30       | 28             |
|                                | —        | —              |

14. Also the degree of association between fostering and high family ideals is greater than the class difference. The difference with Classes IV, V, is shown by this Table:
Concept of Ideal Size Family:

| Number of children desired | Controls | Foster-mothers |
| -------------------------- | -------- | -------------- |
| 0, 1, 2                    | 17       | 10             |
| 3 or more                  | 11       | 18             |
| No answer                  | 2        | —              |
|                            | —        | —              |
|                            | 30       | 28             |
|                            | —        | —              |

15. The class where the rate of fostering is highest claimed least frequent reading of the local evening paper. Only a third had read one on the previous evening.
16. An omission in this investigation was the ages of the two groups. However it does seem that age-differences would only emphasize the distinction between actual family size and ideal family size.

# 18

❲ The more imaginative approaches to social-problem situations involve efforts to solve one problem situation by using social resources made available as a consequence of the existence of a second social problem. One such approach is illustrated in the following report—an attempt to solve the problem of the shortage of foster-family homes by employing the skills of the AFDC mother. The reported experiment is of further significance in that it indicates a potential employment possibility for the otherwise unemployable poverty-ridden mother.

## Public Assistance Families: A Resource for Foster Care

*Patricia Garland*

For the past few years in New York City, we have been concerned about the continuance of the deplorable situation in which over a hundred babies, mostly under two years of age, remain in the wards of our public and voluntary hospitals while waiting for foster home placement. This problem has persisted despite the efforts of public and private child-caring agencies. In November 1959, with a grant from the Field Foundation, the New York City Department of Welfare initiated its Foster Home Demonstration Project in an effort to provide these babies with foster home placement in selected families which are receiving public assistance.

Our hope that families could be approved for foster care despite their dependence upon public support for their own maintenance was based on the knowledge that financial dependency may result from a complex of interrelated personal, social, physical and cultural factors. In view of the urgent need for more homes for these babies, and the hope that public assistance families would benefit through increased feelings of dignity and self-worth, the State Department of Social Welfare agreed that these families could be licensed. It also agreed that the board would not be counted as deductible income in computing the public assistance budget.

The Foster Home Demonstration Project was initiated, then, because of our conviction that we must put warm, loving arms around the babies who had been languishing in our city's hospitals, and because we felt we could begin to meet this need by drawing on the strengths of a selected group of public assistance families. We have had conviction about the potentialities of this project from its inception. At the same time we have recognized that there are many new concepts and many casework and practical problems inherent in the program. We felt, therefore, that in the fullest sense this was really a "demonstration" project, which needed to be objectively and carefully evaluated.

## HOW THE DEMONSTRATION PROJECT WAS INITIATED

The grant from the Field Foundation made it possible to recruit experienced staff with background and experience in foster care. The unit consists of the Director, four caseworkers and three clerical workers. The Foster Home Demonstration Project is set up within the Bureau of Child Welfare. The Director of the project is responsible to the Director of the Bureau of Child Welfare.

Administrative leadership and organizational flexibility were crucial factors in the initiation of the program. The Commissioner of Welfare and the directors of the Bureau of Child Welfare and of the Bureau of Public Assistance were involved in the policy formulation and in its initial implementation. The administrative officers of the entire Department of Welfare were called upon to adapt procedures to the needs of the Foster Home Demonstration Project. The co-operation and resources of related city departments were utilized. There has been close collaboration with the Department of Health with regard to the medical aspects of the program. The prelicensing medical examination required of all prospective foster parents is given by a Department of Health doctor in a district health center. This function was undertaken by the Department of Health especially for the project.

Commissioner Dumpson appointed a Technical Advisory Committee comprised of representatives from the voluntary and public foster care agencies, the medical and hospital field, and the general community. This committee has met regularly and has participated in the development of the project's program, policies and procedures. Subcommittees have been set up to deal with special problems or areas of work. The Technical Advisory Committee has played a significant role in interpreting the Foster Home Demonstration Project to both professionals and the community.

## POLICIES AND PROCEDURES

Because the Foster Home Demonstration Project was set up to meet the problems of babies who remain in hospitals, and because of some of the problems inherent in the project, babies are placed for interim care while long-term plans are being worked out. The agency responsible for long-term planning carries the responsibility for work with the parents and the total situation. The project's program thus has many of the features of an interim care, grooming, or shelter care program. The procedures and policies reflect this. For example, a panel pediatrician gives not only the initial admission examination but regular follow-up care.

With the exception of single men and families in which the mother is receiving Assistance to the Blind or Aid to the Disabled, any public assistance recipient can be considered for this program. This includes women over sixty years of age, those who are temporarily heads of their households, and those who are separated or divorced. Of primary importance are the stability of the home and the family's emotional and physical ability to provide a child with care that meets the generally accepted standards.

Clients may apply or be referred directly. The majority of referrals come through the individual welfare centers in accordance with the procedure established by the Bureau of Public Assistance. The Foster Home Demonstration Project staff carries the responsibility for "screening in" suitable applicants, interpreting the program to the families, and maintaining the appropriate liaison with the welfare center and other interested agencies.

The project caseworker reads the Bureau of Public Assistance record to determine whether the family meets the "gross criteria." In those cases where the client has not applied directly, the worker initiates contact with the client to explore his interest in foster care. Because temporary shelter care is physically and emotionally demanding, we feel that we must focus on the special demands of the program and the needs of the babies early in the contacts. When the worker has determined the client's interest in the program and finds that the family has potentialities for foster care, an application is given.

When, following a complete foster home study, a home has been licensed, a grant is made to cover the needs incidental to opening a home, such as a crib, a mattress and formula equipment. (A basic equipment guide has been prepared by the Department of Welfare's home economist.) When a child has been selected for a family, board payment for a two-week period is authorized in advance of placement, since the public assistance recipient has no funds of his own to draw upon.

In this initial phase of the demonstration project, the caseworker is responsible for the study and the supervision period. Because the homes are being used for temporary care, there are more frequent supervision visits than are usual in long-term care and the child is under the medical supervision of the panel pediatrician.

## RECRUITMENT OF HOMES

By March 30, 1961, 160 inquiries or self-referrals had been received. Applicants contacted the Foster Home Demonstration Project in response to press releases in the local papers, and a flyer which was distributed in the housing projects, selected churches, and other community organizations where public relief recipients are known. Recently, the most productive recruiters of all—the foster parents themselves—have stimulated referrals of public assistance recipients and of other families as well. More than two hundred Spanish-speaking families responded to publicity about the project in the local Spanish press in December of 1960. Very few of them were recipients of public assistance, but we did take responsibility for following through with referrals to the appropriate agencies.

A total of 264 referrals have been received from social investigators in the seventeen welfare centers of the Bureau of Public Assistance since the procedure was initiated in April 1960. Initially there was a limited and spotty trickle of referrals from the investigators. This seemed to be related not only to the problem of staff turnover and work pressure, but to lack of understanding and confusion about foster care. With the leadership of the administrators of the welfare centers, the Foster Home Demonstration Project staff was given the opportunity to interpret the program to the centers' staff, and by October there was a marked increase in the number of referrals.

We have found that public assistance recipients who are interested in foster care have the same wide variation in their understanding of what is involved in foster care and in their motivation to become foster parents as do other foster parents. We have found that a number are really interested in adoption; some of the Aid-to-Dependent-Children mothers who were deserted find it most painful and difficult to face the possibility that they will not have more children. Money, surprisingly, seemed to be a major motive in very few situations. As a matter of fact, many of the recipients thought that the board money would be deducted from their budget. The families who were referred through their investigators were informed about the project through an "interest letter." It was agreed that for administrative and casework reasons the social investigator would suggest names without discussing the referrals with the family, and that the project worker would assume responsibility for the initial screening. Most of the families responded favorably to the fact that their investigator had recommended them.

We have used a number of direct approaches to some of the families who failed to respond to the initial interest letter. We found that in a number of instances the families were confused or misinterpreted the letter. A few suspected that it might be an ingenious method of checking eligibility. Families who were not interested in foster care were able to express this directly. We had been concerned about the possibility that the social investigator referral might be threatening and anxiety-provoking, or seem coercive, but there are no grounds for such concern when the interest in foster care is explored thoughtfully and sensitively. We do not feel that we have a "captive pool" of families among the 130,000 recipients; like any sound foster home recruitment effort, a direct, clear appeal to prospective applicants must be made.

## HOME STUDY AND PLACEMENT

In announcing the Foster Home Demonstration Project, Commissioner Dumpson spoke of his hope that these babies could be placed with "carefully selected" families who are receiving public assistance. We have found two somewhat contradictory questions or criticisms with regard to the project: Many wonder how public assistance families already overburdened with their own problems can possibly be of service in such a sensitive area as foster care. Others, are impatient because we have opened so few homes when there are more than 130,000 families receiving public assistance.

We have tried to develop a program based on sound and well-tested child care principles. At the same time, creative flexibility has been our keynote in taking a look at a group in the community which was categorically excluded from consideration as foster parents. We have recognized that our staff, too, was hampered by stereotyped concepts of the public assistance recipient and by the experiences of social and community agencies with the so-called hard core, multi-problem family. From January 1960 to May 1961, as a result of studying the first group of self-referrals, we came to know these families, found the answer to some of our questions, posed new questions, and began to develop some dynamic constructs.

Our home study process, our criteria and our focus are now fairly well defined. The home study process begins after the screening of the Department of Welfare record and the home screening and interest interview. The Department of Welfare record, in most instances, is focused on the questions of eligibility for assistance. Problems, facts and more problems, rather than dynamic psycho-social material and evaluation, are characteristic of most of the records. The family as a whole, the parents and children, rarely emerge.

In terms of the kind of accumulated information with which the caseworker is armed before meeting the applicant, the starting point of our home study is rather different from that of most foster care programs. The caseworker has to find the way to identify strengths in a group of families which have failed in one of the most important areas in our culture— economic self-sufficiency. We must try to find strengths and stability when we know that there are many ramifications and reverberating effects of economic dependency upon personality development and family life.

Perhaps by giving you a profile summary of the families we have approved I can best point up the strengths, assets and potentialities we have been able to identify.

Twenty-two families have been approved. Twenty-seven children are in care in project foster homes today. Another seven were admitted and have been discharged. The first three homes were opened in May 1960. Since October we have been able to approve two or three new homes each month.

The majority of these families are Negro Protestant. There are two Puerto Rican homes. In three of the families, the father is in the home. The other homes are ADC families with the mother as head of the family. The majority were separated from their husbands, or even deserted; there are also a widow and two single women in the group. Three of the women are between twenty and thirty, six between thirty and forty, ten between forty and fifty, and one between fifty and sixty. Seven have only one child, the majority have two or three children, and five have four children. Most of the families live in Brooklyn, in housing projects.

The potential project foster mother is an ADC mother whose status has been stabilized for two or three years, and who has school-age children who are making an adequate adjustment in school. The family is integrated into the immediate community. The mother is active in a church or parents' group and maintains close ties with her family or a small group of neighbors.

These families belong to a group of recipients who are able to manage with their grant. They are planful, resourceful and ingenious. They manage their bills and the basic necessities and their homes are adequately furnished; more importantly, their children and they are neatly and appropriately dressed, and they somehow manage the extras that are so important to children. We feel that families who can manage this way in view of the limited grants are pretty adequate people. We are able to separate the managers from the nonmanagers very early in our initial contact with the family. We would be unlikely to proceed in studying a home where we learned that the rent was seldom paid on time, the children were shabby, and the family was overwhelmed by the problems of management.

Our continued work with several of our families has confirmed our early observations. They use the clothing and equipment allowance for the foster child planfully and carefully. Our foster children have been kept beautifully dressed and a number of the foster parents buy extras that are not provided for in the allowance. Several foster mothers have been able to accept emergency placements, which meant stretching their own grant for several days until a check for the baby could be processed.

We have found that the fatherless home should not be categorically ruled out, particularly in a. program such as ours offering temporary care to babies. While there is much variation in the part the mother's personality played in determining her status, and while there is also a great deal of variation in her acceptance of her status, there is one thing that all these women have in common. This is their devotion to their children and their concern and effort to provide a stable, happy family life. Some of them are sacrificing their own personal interests. Because of the conflicting community attitudes towards the ADC mother, some feel guilty about staying home to take care of their own children instead of working.

We have found that many of our families are accepted and respected by their immediate neighbors and in their church. Often they are giving of themselves by dedicated service to their group. Many belong to small church groups where they can be more easily accepted. It is important for social agencies to try to consider the meaning of the church affiliation for each person as an individual, and to guard against over-reaction and over-concern about rigidity.

In a number of instances we have found that the family relationships are especially close and meaningful. Children have been very much a part of the application and study process, and have seemed to sense the significance of this new opportunity for their parents.

## THE PLACEMENTS

Thirty-four babies have been placed through the Foster Home Demonstration Project. An analysis of the twenty-nine children who had been admitted by March 15, 1961 will illustrate the kinds of children most urgently needing care.

Seventeen children had been waiting in hospitals; four were referred from the community—because of emergency hospitalization of the mother, for example; four were referred directly from the court; and four had been waiting in shelter care.

There were eight emergency placements. Eight babies had been waiting less than three months, five from three to six months, six from six to nine months, four others from nine to twelve months, and five from twelve to eighteen months.

Nine of the children had been accepted for long-term plans by other agencies and needed interim or grooming care. Five were unallocated although the long-term plan had been determined. In fifteen, or more than half, of these cases, there was no long-term plan because of the family situation, the child's own problems, or the limitation of services and facilities.

## TWO OF OUR FAMILIES

I would like to tell you about two of the families and the kinds of babies we have placed with them.

Our first home, opened in May 1960, was that of the Robbins family. Mrs. Robbins is a soft-spoken, stable, maternal woman in her mid-forties. She has four teenage children—boys of fourteen and fifteen and girls of sixteen and eighteen. The eighteen-year-old girl had just graduated from high school. She had secured a job and was contributing to the family budget. The father had deserted the family nearly ten years before, when because of his personal inadequacy he found it increasingly difficult to cope with the responsibility for a growing family. Both the mother and the children were hurt by this desertion, but their family remained intact and their feelings for each other were strengthened. Each child has made an excellent school and social adjustment; they are respected in their community and are active in the church, the community center and other local groups. The mother is an excellent and resourceful manager, the home is modest but attractive, and the children are nicely dressed. The family decided to apply to become a foster family in a conference around the kitchen table, after reading Commissioner Dumpson's announcement of the project.

A three-month-old boy was placed in this home. His mother had given birth in a state mental hospital. There were several other babies in this hospital and so the children were given individualized attention. He was a cuddly, responsive and healthy baby at the time of placement, but it would have become increasingly difficult for him to have the necessary attention in the hospital as he grew older. The family and baby took to each other immediately. The children were very much involved in the placement and care of their foster brother. The caseworker observed that she should have brought a baby for each member of the family since each one was so eager to care for the little boy. The sixteen-year-old used her allowance to buy the baby a special dress suit. This family has already cared for three babies.

The Suarez family is another one of our foster families. Mr. and Mrs. Suarez are a couple in their late thirties. They live in a housing project with their four children—girls of sixteen, fourteen and eleven and a boy of four. The family came to this country from Puerto Rico while the youngest girl was still a baby. They came from a rural area and Mr. Suarez first worked under contract on a farm in upper New York State. He then was able to secure an unskilled job in a factory in New York and establish his family in a comfortable though modest home here. He held this job for seven years, when the firm closed. Since then Mr. Suarez has been unable to find a steady, well-paying job. His employment possibilities are limited because of his rural background, scanty education and faulty English. During the past year he has eagerly taken even the most menial job, but his wages have never covered the family budget and the Department of Welfare has supplemented them.

Despite his frustration and disappointment, Mr. Suarez is still the head of his family. Somehow the family has remained intact, warm and stable, with close, mutually satisfying relationships between the family members. The girls are each lovely, feminine and appealing, and devoted to their parents and their lively little brother.

The family has cared for two children since their home was approved in September. The first was an eighteen-month-old girl, badly frightened and developing poorly after months of waiting, first in a hospital and then in a shelter. The second baby was fifteen months old when he was placed on an emergency basis. His mother, who was mentally disturbed and physically sick, was hospitalized that day. Little Robbie was a sickly, asthmatic child, whose disturbed behavior bore testimony to the neglect and frustration he had experienced. The Suarez family was at first bewildered because they had never known children as disturbed and difficult as these two were. But as a family they worked together, patiently and lovingly, and within a relatively short period of time each of these children settled down and seemed more happy and healthy.

Recently Mrs. Suarez underwent surgery. When the caseworker discussed re-placement of Robbie or the use of a homemaker, Mr. Suarez, who had been laid off from his job, was chagrined and hurt. Robbie was a member of the family and they had talked together about the responsibility each of the children and Mr. Suarez would assume during the mother's illness. He proudly showed the worker the menus he had prepared for the first days of his wife's hospitalization. Robbie was, indeed, so attached to the family that a temporary move would have been disturbing. Mr. Suarez and the girls did manage very adequately and were proud and pleased.

I would like to stress again how physically and emotionally demanding temporary or shelter care is for foster families caring for young babies, especially babies who have had a poor start. We feel, therefore, that the agency must actively carry its share of the mutual responsibility for the well-being of these children. One of the most important decisions was to use a panel pediatrician rather than the district health station for medical supervision of the babies. The project also gives concrete recognition of the demands it is making of the foster parents by having a caseworker available and ready to be a part of the day-to-day problems, and by recognizing the service motive of these families and their dedication to the children entrusted to their care.

## SUMMARY

There are a great many questions that remain unanswered. Some of these will have to await formal research evaluation. Others will be answered in the course of our day-to-day experiences.

We feel that there is, and will continue to be, a group of families among the recipients of public assistance who despite their economic dependency and associated problems have a stable, wholesome family life and a capacity to be of service to needy children. Rather than being completely overwhelmed or self-centered because of their own problems, many of these families have a tremendous desire and capacity to *give* because of their closeness to the harsher realities of life. This has been seen not only in the way that they are able to reach out and relate to the children, but also in their sensitivity to, and understanding of, the problems of the natural parents.

We do feel that the public assistance recipient can help meet the urgent need for foster homes. Such a program must be based on an acceptance of these families with their known problems and unexplored and untapped potentialities. It must be set up and staffed so that the most creative and flexible use can be made of this resource. The sensitive, supportive help of a caseworker and the agency is necessary. We feel that we are making a contribution to the needs of the children of this city through this small program.

# 19

❴ What factors are involved when a worker ranks one foster home as more desirable for a child than another home? This research study is concerned with these factors and with the reliability of workers who make such assessments.

## The Problem of Choice
## in Foster Home Finding*

*Martin Wolins*

In their recent book W. Allen Wallis and Harry V. Roberts call statistics a body of methods for making wise decisions in the face of uncertainty.[1] In many respects this describes decisions required of professionals. The professional faces a client who has a problem. The problem must be diagnosed and some kind of prognosis and course of treatment established. The prognosis is a prediction, and the course of treatment one of several

---

* This report is part of a larger study published by Columbia University Press in 1963 and entitled *Selecting Foster Parents: The Ideal and the Reality*.
[1] *Statistics: A New Approach* (Glencoe, Ill.: The Free Press, 1956).

possible means for achieving the desired end. In all of this there is considerable uncertainty and risk. The function of the clinician and of the research structure built around him is continually to reduce the area of risk and therefore increase the extent of certainty with which the professional operation is carried.[2] This requires that decisions and the underlying reasons for them be made explicit. As Meehl has shown, in some instances this can be achieved to a point where clinical predictions may be replicated by statistical methods.[3] Such a state of events may evolve around the decision in foster home selection. As yet it has not occurred. The criteria for decision are not sufficiently explicit, and possibly the workers' mode of operation is not sufficiently reliable—that is, consistent or constant—to permit adequate statistical prediction.

What is it the worker does when he selects a home? The situation may be described schematically as follows: Child welfare agencies continually have a stream of children coming to their doors. These children must be either served at home or placed in institutions or in foster homes. To serve many of them, the agency must keep at its disposal a ready pool (reservoir) of available foster homes. The homes in the pool need not fit the needs of any individual child specifically. Rather, it is composed of a variety of families whose general capabilities fit them to serve the predominant categories of children who come into agency care. On occasion, of course, a child will come for whom no appropriate home is available. However, most of the time the children coming into care will, in some manner, be matched to one or more of the homes in the pool and subsequently placed there.

The pool is filled from among applicants. Ideally, every worker selects only those applicants who ultimately succeed in providing a good foster home for a child in the agency's care. A continuum of homes ranging from those which the workers consider highly desirable to those which they consider highly undesirable may be visualized here. On this continuum homes can be arranged in order of their goodness. The worker must then make the decision where to cut the continuum between rejection and acceptance. If such a continuum does indeed exist, the acceptance-rejection decision is quite easy when the agency has many applicants for every home it needs. The major problem is studying the applicants, but it is not a problem in decision, since the probability is quite good that from among the better applicants several very good ones can be chosen. This, although in much less exaggerated form, is the situation in certain types of adoptions. The agency need only skim the cream of the applicants and reject the remainder. Such a course reduces the possibility of risk enor-

---

[2] The process of developing new knowledge for professional use amounts to loading the dice in the game against fate. See Joseph W. Eaton, "Science, 'Art,' and Uncertainty in Social Work," *Social Work*, Vol. 3, No. 3 (July 1958), pp. 3–10.

[3] Paul E. Meehl, *Clinical Versus Statistical Prediction* (Minneapolis, Minn.: University of Minnesota Press, 1954).

mously, and provides the agency with essentially satisfactory decisions.[4]

What happens when the number of applicants only slightly exceeds the number of needed homes? Then the worker has no choice but to set the cutting point further and further down the continuum. While he has certain criteria of absolute unacceptability which will guide him here—for example, a contagious illness, or highly undesirable quarters, or marital status, and in some instances race or religion—the worker is nonetheless forced into a situation in which decisions become extremely precarious. If he cuts the continuum too close to the good end, he may exclude usable homes. If he cuts it too close to the bad end, he runs a high risk of putting into the pool some undesirable ones. Here the worker indeed faces a problem of decision in the face of uncertainty. How well does he perform?

What has been said so far indicates that three separate decisions are involved regarding each one of the foster family applicants. First is the ranking decision discussed above. The worker arranges families—perhaps not explicitly but certainly implicitly—in the order of their goodness as foster families, putting the very best one first, the very poorest one last, and all the others in the order of their goodness in between. Second, the worker must decide on a cutting point—i.e., the point at which families are no longer good enough to be acceptable for foster care. Third, matching is required of specific child and foster home.

The third decision is not within the scope of research reported here. The second decision varies among agencies and undoubtedly hinges upon criteria other than goodness of homes. When the agency is under severe pressure to place more children, it must of necessity lower the cutoff point and accept some homes which it would previously have rejected. Therefore the cutoff point may well be a function of the supply/demand situation in the agency—i.e., the number of available homes divided by the number of needed homes. The higher this ratio, the more resistant the agency can be to the choice of questionable families.

This paper will report on research restricted to the first decision, namely, ranking. This, it was hypothesized, would be similar no matter what the pressure situations were, provided the gross populations of children needing care were also similar. For this purpose a number of large multifunction child welfare agencies were chosen.[5] Mainly they were public agencies, where the populations of children have very broad characteristics. Thus the pools of homes these agencies accumulate include homes desirable for

---

[4] The effect of such high rates of rejection upon the applicants' and others' perception of the agency may be due for serious consideration and research, but this is not germane to the present issue.

[5] The author is indebted to the Westchester County (New York) Division of Family and Child Welfare; the Nassau County (New York) Department of Welfare; the Jewish Child Care Association of New York; the Sheltering Arms Children's Service, New York City; and the Alameda County (California) Welfare Commission for their participation in the study.

a wide variety of children. In these agencies the first type of decision was studied. Before proceeding to describe and discuss findings, several premises of the study will be repeated: (1) Agencies placing children in foster family care must build up a pool of foster homes. (2) Because of the shortage of applicants, they can reject only a limited number of the poorest homes in developing this pool. (3) To make the fewest possible errors, workers must learn to rank with a great deal of reliability the homes which they study so as to reject the same kinds of homes in all instances. (4) Rank ordering should not differ markedly in agencies with similar needs due to the same broad characteristics of the populations of children they have in placement.

## CONDITIONS OF RELIABILITY

Why should reliable decisions be expected? Why should workers in different agencies be expected to arrange homes in the order of their goodness and arrive at the same, or substantially the same, ranking? The expectation for such an outcome relates to a number of forces which bear upon the worker in the child welfare agency. First of all, workers are subject to similar education. Second, the literature is essentially in agreement on selective criteria advocated. Third, the supervisory process in the agency leads to factors of reliability within the agency itself insofar as the individual supervisor spreads his influence over a number of workers. Finally, the ease of transfer from one agency to another would lead to the assumption that the essential variables along which selection is made are similar, or at least substantially standardized, so that a new worker entering the agency does not require marked retraining.

When the terms "reliability" or "consistency" are used, they are intended to convey the degree to which workers agree about the rank order positions of cases. The extent of such agreement can be measured by a variety of statistical procedures. One such procedure called the Freedman Chi-Square Sub-R ($\chi^2_r$) leads to an expression in a single number of the extent of agreement and allows determination of the probability that it may arise by chance.[6] This same chi-square may also be used to express the degree of perfection which has been achieved in agreement among workers.[7]

---

[6] See Frederick Mosteller and Robert R. Bush, "Selected Quantitative Techniques," in Gardner Lindzey, ed., *Handbook of Social Psychology* (Cambridge, Mass.: Addison-Wesley Publishing Co., 1954), Vol. 1, pp. 319–320.

[7] The value of $\chi^2_r$ is very sensitive to N, i.e., the number of judges involved. When groups of various size are compared for extent of agreement, a descriptive form of $\chi^2_r$ is used which is insensitive to N. This value is called $\dfrac{\chi^2_r \text{ actual}}{\chi^2_r \text{ perfect}}$. The numerator and denominator are both $\chi^2_r$, but the latter is computed on the assumption that perfect agreement exists for all judges on all cases. It happens that $\chi^2_r$ perfect = N x df (i.e., the number of judges times the number of cases minus 1).

The problem now is to find out how well workers agree about the position of an individual home on some kind of goodness scale. Ideally a panel of workers should study the same home and render independent decisions about it. However, this is neither practically nor theoretically feasible. Practically, it is obviously impossible to subject the same family to a barrage of home studies. Theoretically, it is not feasible since the family would undoubtedly undergo marked change in the process of each study; thus the workers would be observing different families, although with the same names and addresses attached. Another possible way of dealing with this problem would be to record the home study on tape and have judges listen to the record and make their decisions.[8] This is very time-consuming. A third alternative is the use of case records or abstracts of records. A number of such abstracts were developed and submitted to the staffs of three public and two voluntary agencies. Each worker was asked several things about the cases he read, including his ranking of the cases in the order of their goodness. Some of the findings follow.

## FINDINGS

1. Workers who actually have to make this kind of decision in an agency, namely, the home-finders, make it with marked consistency $(P < .001)$. Participation in the decision-making process seems to correlate with more consistent decisions. In one agency agreement for this group was at 83 percent of perfection, i.e., there were only 17 disagreements for every 100 decisions. The degree of agreement is even more striking when it is noted that most disagreements are of only one position where one judge ranked a case as second, for example, and another one ranked it as third.

2. Agreement is related to the level of workers' sophistication. When staffs of agencies studied are grouped by level of responsibility within the agency as caseworkers, junior caseworkers, supervisors, and students, the reliability within the groups differs. Contrary to belief, it is not positively correlated with status. High status does not necessarily mean good agreement. What does seem to underlie reliability is the level at which interpretation is being attempted and the sophistication which can be mustered to do so. Thus, social work students in one agency were very unreliable, even though they had all had more education and often more experience in social work than the junior workers in the same agency whose reliability was good. It seems possible to view a case and arrive at a decision on various depths of analysis, but those who attempt deep insight must know how to achieve it.[9]

---

[8] This procedure was followed by Donald Brieland in *An Experimental Study of the Selection of Adoptive Parents at Intake* (New York: Child Welfare League of America, Inc., 1959).

[9] Incidentally, and as an aside, it may be of interest to note that although reliability of decisions differs substantially depending upon the level of interpretation and the

3. Volume is almost completely inversely related to reliability. The more bulk a case contains the less likely it is that workers will agree on its position. This was found in a number of different ways. In some cases 20, 40, 60, and 80 percent of the informational items were randomly discarded. Then the cases were read and ranked by several randomly chosen groups of workers. Cases containing 40 percent of the informational items produced the highest agreement. At the same time the median position of each case remained about the same for the 40 and 100 percent cases. This means that the worker perceives essentially the same image of the case when he receives only a small proportion of the information items contained in the ordinary foster home case record. What is perhaps even more crucial is that by eliminating a substantial amount of bulk, which incidentally also contained information, the reliability of decisions was markedly increased.

4. While a random sampling of information from a case required as much as 40 percent of the content for high reliability, intentional selection of crucial materials led to marked reduction of bulk and simultaneous increase in agreement. By selection, it was possible to reduce material to 14 percent of the original items and at the same time increase reliability to approximately 86 percent of perfection. Again, it is important to emphasize that the median position of cases—that is, the worker's perception of the goodness of a case—did not substantially change from what it was when 100 percent of the material was presented.

5. A grasp of the conceptual issues involved in home study leads to substantial improvement in reliability. When judges were provided with the comments of the worker who had done the original home study, or with our own conceptual framework for home study, agreement among them increased. This occurred in spite of the fact that our framework and/or the worker's comments added bulk to the case. In fact when our framework was introduced, workers were required to read some of the lengthiest and most detailed cases to be found.[10] However, the length of the case itself did not present as serious an obstacle as the lack of an organizational framework. Given the organizational framework, the worker could wade through the lengthy material and could conceptually abstract key information (perhaps the same 14 or so percent), as was done for him in one of our previous experiments.

So far the data seem to show two things. One: that workers who are trained to make decisions make more reliable decisions and that this training comes from experience in making decisions and also from a grasp of the concepts the worker uses in studying the home. Second: that certain attributes of the materials themselves contribute to reliability.

capability of the interpreters, the median position of cases—that is, the average judged goodness of a case—remains approximately the same for all groups.

[10] These averaged more than ten single-spaced typewritten pages.

The second finding will now be elaborated somewhat. Why is it that reduction of material leads to increased reliability? It seems that the entire process of home study involves continuous sampling. The worker makes an appointment with the applicant and this leads to a sample in time. A small piece out of the over-all lifetime of the applicant is chosen, and on the basis of this certain inferences will be made.

Then a second sample is taken—a sample of content. When the applicant and the worker meet, whether at home or in the office, they do not discuss everything. They touch on only certain selected issues. Again, this is a sample—perhaps a sample of episodes. Some of these are retrospective, others are prospective, and others deal with the present. But in any event not everything is discussed.

A third type of sampling occurs when the worker returns to the office and decides which of the materials he has heard or spoken are worthy of recording. Two kinds of selection happen now. Undoubtedly the worker has forgotten some of the interview content. But equally if not more important are his deliberate selections of material worthy of note. Finally, if this material is submitted to a variety of readers—as is done for a case conference—then again sampling occurs in the selective way in which material is read. So home study may be seen as a process of nonrandom selection, which leads to the focusing upon a certain number of key episodes dealt with in the case. On the basis of these episodes a prediction is made regarding the family's behavior in a future situation—one the family has never faced—namely, the foster care of a child. Judging from the findings cited above, only a few episodes are needed for a decision. The addition of others can either reinforce the decision or confuse the judge. The data show that it does the latter. As yet the study reported here has no data on the reinforcing effects of additional material.

### CONDITIONS OF UNRELIABILITY

It should be noted that even when the material is reduced, even when it is submitted to the most competent judges, even when key items are chosen and put before the worker, there is still considerably less than perfect agreement. Why is this so? Undoubtedly some of this is pure chance. Clearly, so many variables enter here that some chance errors may be assumed. However, in addition to the chance factors which undoubtedly operate, four others were found which led to inconsistency.

First is a factor previously mentioned—the lack of guidelines or clarity as to what should be noted when a case is read. When long cases were submitted to a number of child welfare workers and they were asked to make decisions about them, they agreed with each other to approximately 50 percent of perfection. When some workers were instructed somewhat with a conceptual framework, the reliability declined. This was quite a surprise to everyone. Why should instructions—giving the workers some criteria for decisions—make their agreement go down? When another group was instructed with the same framework but over a longer period of time, until the research staff felt quite certain that the concepts were clear to the workers, reliability went up substantially to over 80 percent of perfection. What does this mean? It probably means that the worker is simply lost in the forest of a case. He cannot see the over-all picture because he sees the individual incidents. He cannot see the forest because of the trees. Provided with a conceptual guide, he learns how to encompass the case and his agreement with other workers goes up. However, he must really know the conceptual framework, otherwise it serves only to confuse him.

A second reason for disagreements seems to be time lag. Agency practices and the knowledge from which they stem are put on in layers. Various time periods bring with them certain acceptable professional behavior, and this does not become eradicated as the trend changes and new ideas and new behavior become acceptable. There have been changes, for example, in what is considered an acceptable motive. This is seen in workers' interpretation of items like the following:

> With even five dollars extra a month left over from board rate, we can move to a better neighborhood.

or

> Mr. and Mrs. prefer foster care as a means of supplementation to Mrs. going out to work.

Workers who have different time viewpoints perceive these differently. Some consider these items positively; others consider them negatively. Similar differences in viewpoint occur with regard to appropriate child-rearing practices (which have undergone an immense and almost cyclical change over the past thirty to forty years), with regard to the meaning of individualization, with regard to parental rights, and with regard to the function of a foster home—specifically its limited responsibility, the attachment to the child, and so on. In fact, almost every important variable in a case may be evaluated differently, depending upon the time vantage point from which it is seen. Some workers, although functioning in the present agency, operate on premises from the past; others base their practice on present-day views.

A third major reason for disagreement is the differing organizational vantage points workers possess. Especially crucial here are the differences between home finders and placement workers. Although there is much agreement between these two groups, which in effect testifies to a kind of validity in the agency's decisions—indicating that home finders discover the kinds of homes placement workers desire, there is some disagreement. Such disagreement is evident in the way material is perceived. For example:

Younger boy talked of sharing toys with foster child and showing him interesting places in the neighborhood. He has one toy he cherishes. No one, including foster child, can play with this without permission.

This was an item in one of the cases read by home finders, placement workers, and their supervisors. Home finders considered the item quite irrelevant; they did not pick it up as important at all, but five of the seven agency supervisors who read the same cases considered this item highly important.[11]

This and similar items indicate that the home finders tend to have a general orientation to the case. They view the case globally. They are not too severely concerned about specific items. The placement workers are concerned with the specifics. It is the specifics that, to them, make for the successful or unsuccessful foster home. Similar differences occur in relation to other items which seem to show that the home finders are more theoretically oriented—they consider whether the home would theoretically work out—while the placement workers are concerned with practical implications of specific behavior. For example:

Mrs. —— lets her young nephew walk on the table because he enjoys it.

This was picked up by only one of the seven decision-makers, but six of the seven supervisors considered it important. ($P \le .025$.)

Similar distinctions exist in the orientation of the home finders toward the present and of decision-makers toward the future. For example:

Mrs. —— knows foster children have parents. She thinks she would find it hard to be close to a child's parents.

This item was picked up by two out of the seven decision-makers who read the case. All seven of the supervisors considered it important. ($P \le .025$.) The problem is not in the present. For the moment the family is completely adequate, but the supervisor who looks to the future and to work with both parent and foster parent sees in it a potential issue.

A fourth source of disagreement lies in the essentially idiosyncratic behavior of some workers. Interviews with the workers about the ranks they had assigned to cases produced, in some instances, such statements as "Oh, the mother was reared on a farm, and farm girls make good foster mothers," or "I would be very reluctant to accept as foster parents people who were divorced." These views come through only on occasion, but if they are held by some workers and used in a decision, the resulting action leads to some lack of consistency, since other workers do not voice such views and possibly do not hold them.

---

[11] The probability of such a difference occurring by chance is $\le .025$, Fisher-Yates Exact Probability Test. See Sidney Siegel, *Nonparametric Statistics for the Behavioral Sciences* (New York: McGraw-Hill, 1956), pp. 96–104.

What seems to be transpiring with regard to the over-all question of lowered reliability is that the worker who is deprived of a framework gropes for some guidelines of his own. These he may find in previous practice and previously established appropriate procedures; thus he is fixated at a particular layer of knowledge. Or they may come to him from his own organizational vantage point as home finder or placement worker. Or, if these will not suffice, they come to him purely from his personal experience, which may lead him to decisions completely out of tune with the agency's position.

### PRACTICE IMPLICATIONS OF THE FINDINGS

A recent Child Welfare League of America statement on research policy declares that good social work research begins with questions of program and ends with guides to action.[12] What are some action implications of the findings cited?

1. The key selected materials upon which the workers were able to base reliable decisions (the 14 percent of the cases mentioned previously) contained certain items. What did these items mean? If some meaning could be inferred from them, does this meaning not yield the possible beginnings of a conceptual structure which may provide guidelines for home studies? It is possible, of course, to array such material in various ways. One way of structuring seems to yield five groups of items pertaining to:

a. The goal orientation of the family: what the family seeks, how capable it is of seeking it, how realistic it is in trying to achieve its goals, and what its means are for achieving them.
b. The self-image of the parents in the home. How, and how accurately, do they perceive themselves?
c. Perception and enactment of crucial roles—the roles of parents, the roles of spouses, the roles of foster parents.
d. The extent of cohesion and separability of the family unit. What is its capacity to let people in and to let them out after once having had them in?
e. The extent of reciprocity and flexibility in the family: how much can it give, how well can it lead, and how well can it follow?

Whether one accepts these dimensions or others, it seems clear that some set of dimensions has to be made explicit. This is needed for various reasons: to teach students, to train new workers, and to imbue home studies with some measure of consistency.

---

[12] Martin Wolins, *A Proposed Research Program for the Child Welfare League of America* (New York: Child Welfare League of America, 1959).

2. Piling up of many episodes in a case seems unnecessary. The worker might well be advised to pursue several key developments in the family and study them in detail rather than touch on many issues superficially.

3. With an increase in the clarity of dimensions, the worker should know where, how much, and for what to probe. This may imply a return to the case study outline. Restricted and confined by the outlines of long ago, social workers have discarded the idea of structure along with the specific dimensions it imposed. This is *not* to suggest that we go back to the outline of old—to the static, descriptive procedure of home and neighborhood and furnishings. This *is* intended to suggest the desirability of developing an outline which permits the worker some knowledge of the dynamics he must study in order to produce a consistent and—it is to be hoped—valid decision.

4. Consistency of decisions is related to the level of the practitioner's knowledge. Consistent decisions are made by those people who know what to look for and how to use it. If, however, people are taught what to look for, but not how to use the information, then the reliability of their decisions declines markedly and substantially below the level of those who know neither the *what* nor the *how*. If consistency is important, and it seems to be, then this has immediate implications for training of agency personnel.

5. Although the separation of a homefinding unit from the placement unit of an agency does not seem to lead to substantial maladaptation—that is, to the finding of homes that are not usable and the failure to find usable homes, considerable difference in emphasis exists between placement and home-finding staffs as to what is important in the home. This suggests the need to consider rather carefully the separate home-finding unit and to weigh its administrative advantages against its possible service disadvantages.

6. On the whole, it is quite fair to say that we are not doing badly in the consistency of our professional decisions with regard to the selection of foster homes. This becomes especially apparent when we compare the reliability of these decisions with those of other clinicians in other decision-type situations.[13] While we seem to be doing better than some other professions in similar situations (but not by any means the same kind of situations), we are doing far from well. Furthermore, we know little, if anything, about the validity of these decisions except in the limited sense noted earlier. This has definite research implications.

---

[13] Clinical psychologists, for example, did not agree well when asked to judge adjustment, loyalty, and self-sufficiency. See Frederick Elkin, "Specialists Interpret the Case of Harold Halzer," *Journal of Abnormal and Social Psychology*, Vol. 42, No. 1 (January 1947), pp. 99–111. Also, psychiatrists did not agree well on diagnostic categories of cases seen by two psychiatrists simultaneously. See Philip Ash, "The Reliability of Psychiatric Diagnosis," *Journal of Abnormal and Social Psychology*, Vol. 44, No. 2 (April 1949), pp. 272–276.

7. Having some insight now into the dimensions along which decisions are made, it may be possible to build a screen. A simple interview device may conceivably give enough predictive ability upon which to base some gross decisions.[14] That is, if—by means of a simple, short interview—a decision could be made whether a family is generally acceptable for foster care or generally unacceptable, it can lead to a number of important and fruitful studies. These could relate to ways of bringing in acceptable families to the agency even though they have not previously applied. Specifically, these would be studies of client incentives and agency criteria of selection. In the far more distant future, it may also be possible to compare criteria of selection with some kinds of criteria of outcome of children placed in the foster homes, i.e., to begin an earnest validity test of the processes of selection and matching to see under what circumstances of family, foster family, child, and social work intervention we get the results we wish. And, with patience, we may even learn why.

---

[14] Work on developing and validating the screening device is now sufficiently under way to warrant some very cautious optimism.

# 20

⟨[ The following article studies the relationship between factors of possible significance to the decision regarding the specific substitute-care placement of the child and the actual disposition made. The study was done in Israel and consequently may reflect differences between the American and Israeli substitute-care placement situation. It is included, however, because it attempts a study of the placement situation by an explicit identification of the discrete variables which possibly affect the situation.

## Correlates of Differential Placement Outcome for Dependent Children in Israel*

*Eliezer D. Jaffe*

For quite some time now, a debate has been going on among child welfare researchers, practitioners, and administrators concerning the most appropriate forms of care of dependent children.[1] This question of institutional versus foster care or other combinations of care is indeed a universal issue in child welfare about which, unfortunately, little factual material has been obtained. Much of the research that has been done on this topic often stretches its data for the sake of picking a particular bone,[2] is based on a limited number of cases or a single case,[3] or relates to the mechanics and skills of a specific type of care[4] rather than relating to broader cause-effect situations in the service-delivery system which resulted in the child's getting into a specific placement situation in the first place.

* This study was supported in part by a grant from the International Office, Welfare Administration, United States Department of Health, Education, and Welfare, and from the Israel Ministry of Social Welfare to the Hebrew University of Jerusalem, Israel.

[1] Martin Wolins and Irving Piliavin, *Institution or Foster Family: A Century of Debate* (New York: Child Welfare League of America, 1964).

[2] Zira DeFries, Shirley Jenkins, and Ethelyn Williams, "Foster Family Care for Disturbed Children: A Non-sentimental View," *Child Welfare*, 44 (February, 1965), 73–84.

[3] Reuven Cohen-Raz, *Like All Other Boys: A Case of the Rehabilitation of a Difficult Child in the Kibbutz* (Jerusalem, Israel: Szold Institute, 1963). (Hebrew.)

[4] Jean S. Heywood, *Children in Care* (London: Routledge & Kegan Paul, 1959); and Esther Glickman, *Child Placement through Clinically Oriented Casework* (New York: Columbia University Press, 1957).

The issues concerning care of dependent children are no less acute in Israel than in other countries, since over twenty thousand children in Israel live away from their own homes, and since institutional care in that country has been utilized as a facilitating vehicle for large-scale immigration absorption during the past twenty years.

## THE RESEARCH DESIGN

This study involved the selection of public welfare clients from four local public welfare offices in Israel, two offices representing urban towns and two representing rural, development-type towns.[5] In each of these four offices, we studied intensively over a period of one and one-half years all cases of dependent children who had been newly referred or transferred to a special worker for the express purpose of placement in institutions for dependent children.[6] We included in our sample children from infancy up to the age of fourteen. We excluded children who were organically retarded, delinquent, or severely physically handicapped, since our study related by design only to dependent "normal" children and their families. We chose to study this group because it constitutes the largest category of institutionalized children in Israel. For each case included in the study, a case record was accumulated containing monthly dictation by the social worker, outstanding relevant documents (i.e., diagnostic statements, referrals, correspondence, etc.), especially prepared face sheets, monthly statistical reports, opening and closing summaries, and additional case materials. In this way, we were able to obtain comparable data on all cases concerning particular variables thought to relate to differential placement outcomes and a well-documented picture of the origins, management, and outcome of each case.

The different categories of placement outcome utilized in this study were as follows: (1) institutional care, (2) foster-home care, (3) placement in a kibbutz (communal) setting, (4) placement with relatives, and (5) the child's own home. The latter category included children who, at the end of the eighteen-month study period, were living in their own homes with one or both parents, or had returned to their own homes from a former setting.[7]

The period during which social work service with the clients in this

---

[5] Sincere appreciation is acknowledged to the directors and staffs of the Lydda, Holon, Petach Tikva, and Beersheva public welfare offices, the WIZO Baby Home in Jerusalem, and the Division of Child Welfare of the Ministry of Social Welfare, Israel.

[6] In Israel, institutions for normal dependent youngsters are referred to as "educational institutions."

[7] We realize that in other countries additional "outcome" settings might have been used, such as small-group homes or agency-owned homes, but in Israel the above five categories represent the major types of settings used for dependent children, as testified to by the fact that the above categories were determined *ex post facto*.

study took place extended from December, 1963, to June, 1965. At the end of that period, case files had been collected from the four public welfare offices for a total of 197 families. It should be noted that no new clients were included six months before the conclusion of the study. When the records were completed and extensive checks had been made to see that each contained the appropriate information required for data analysis, their contents were coded on 74 different variables and the codes transferred to IBM cards for statistical analysis.

### Variables Studied

The data gathered and the variables coded for each case fell into five categories of information, as follows:

*Category I: The Referral Situation.* These items included such data as the referral cause, the welfare office setting, type of case (new or transferred), the referral source, type of crises presented, family structure, and professional and educational background of the worker assigned.

*Category II: Objective Background Information about the Family.* Items listed here included (partial listing) the number of children referred for placement, size of family, sex of oldest child referred, age of children referred, family income, source of family income, family housing (quality and ownership), highest educational achievement of parents, ethnicity of head of household, length of parents' residency in Israel, age of head of household, other children ever placed out of home, etc.

*Category III: The Family System—Family Relationships and Problems.* These items included, in part, closeness of family to relatives, recency of family breakdown to the referral period, family intactness at referral, parents' relationship to each other, parents' use of children as weapons, parents' frustration tolerance, parents' problem-solving creativeness, parents' analysis of their problems, parents' use of community facilities, parents' co-operation with social worker, father and/or mother's degree of personality disturbance, parental strictness, parents' attitude to institutional care, parents' attitude to foster care, health of the child-caring person, physical defects of the child, child's personality, child's relationship to parents, intactness of parent-child ties, child's desire to leave home, child's educational level, his relationship to siblings, and the parents' desire to have child home.

*Category IV: The Service System—Services Required and Rendered.* This area included such items as the primary intervention target of the social worker, the intervention strategy, the placement goal for the child, the primary and secondary services given, permanency of the plan required, the intensity of agency-family contacts, the degree of pressure on the family and/or the social worker to act, the length of the service period, the degree of agency activity before placement and after placement, the problem-solving creativeness of the social worker, duration of the child's placement out of home, availability of financial help to the family, availability of a place in an institution, the effectiveness of agency structure and degree of interagency co-operation in providing necessary service, and the number of placements for the child since the original one.

*Category V: Whereabouts of Child at End of Project.* Whereabouts of children at end of the eighteen-month study period (from the time the particular case was accepted until the study period ended) was obtained for the oldest child referred in each family, the second oldest child referred, and the third oldest child referred, although, indeed, three children were rarely referred from the same family.

Before presenting the data obtained in this study, it is important to point out some of the methodological safeguards which were used to achieve reliability of findings. The completed case records were coded by three coders, each of whom had a background of professional training in social work or psychology. By design, the coders had no prior contact with this research and were unaware of the research design and the purpose of the study. They were carefully prepared by the principal investigator to abstract on a summary sheet information for each case concerning the 74 variables investigated, according to the various possible codes listed for each variable. Of the 74 variables studied, 36 were objective pieces of information easily obtained from the face sheet or other sources in the record. The remaining 38 items contained some element of subjective judgment. Several practice training sessions in coding and explicit coding criteria, however, brought reliability between the raters up from 21 per cent error to 9.1 per cent error (i.e., percentage of disagreement among raters when 100 per cent is the total number of identical ratings possible).

## Limitations of the Data

It must be noted at the outset that there may be many additional variables potentially related to placement outcome which we did not elect to study or may have simply overlooked. We believe, however, that we selected some of the more important variables.

One problem encountered was the relatively small numbers of cases in certain outcome categories, which led to our inability to pinpoint correlates of foster-care placement, kibbutz placement, and placement in relatives' homes. Consequently, in our analyses we made either a dichotomy between "institutional placement" and "substitute-home/own-home" outcomes or a three-way division among "institutional placement," "substitute homes" (which included foster home, kibbutz, and relatives), and "own-home" types of outcome.

The probability levels referred to in this report were obtained by chi-square analysis, unless otherwise noted. A 5 per cent level of significance was accepted, unless otherwise noted.

## CORRELATES OF PLACEMENT OUTCOMES:
## THE FINDINGS

### Variables Related to the Referral Situation and Placement Outcome

*Type of Case.* Cases which were new to the agency or former cases which had been closed for several years were significantly more likely to end up in institutional placement than were cases which were active with workers within the agency when the study began. The majority (58.1 per cent) of the "substitute-home" placements, however, were cases which had been transferred during the study period to a special worker within the agency. This finding seems in line with the practice in some public welfare offices of using the "specialist" rather than the "generic" manpower model. Cases transferred to "special" workers were destined for special, usually intensive, family-focused care. It is pertinent to point out, too, that transferred cases went significantly more often to workers with academic, professional backgrounds and supervisory systems than cases which were not transferred.

*Referral Cause.* Children coming from situations in which the referral cause involved marital problems of the parents were either placed in substitute homes (i.e., this referral cause accounted for 65.6 per cent of all substitute-home placements) or remained in their own homes. When the problems presented at referral centered around the child's acting-out or delinquency-oriented behavior, he usually wound up in an institutional setting. Those cases which showed a combination of child-centered problems plus illness (temporary or chronic) of one or both parents resulted in a significant number of institutional placements. In our study, 28.2 per cent of the cases constituted child-centered problems, 24.7 per cent involved physical illness of one or both parents, and 47.1 per cent involved broken homes and marital problems.

*Referral Source.* Children who were referred by their mothers remained in their own homes more often than those referred by their fathers or by various social service agencies. Mothers who requested institutional placement were prone to keep the child at home.

Referrals were made by mothers in 30.5 per cent of the cases, by fathers in 12.8 per cent, and by social agencies in 56.7 per cent of the cases.

*Type of Crisis.* Those situations in which family crises were foreseen and which involved some form of preparation did not differ significantly in placement outcome from cases in which planning was not undertaken and the crisis unforeseen. However, of the cases without preparation, in which children did not remain in their own homes and did not go to institutions, the majority went to live with relatives. Cases for which there was advance preparation, when children were not placed in either their own homes or institutions, were mostly placed in foster homes or kibbutzim. In other words, when a crisis occurred and institutions and own-home settings were ruled out, children whose workers and families anticipated the crisis went to foster homes and kibbutzim, while those who were not prepared went to the closest refuge, relatives.

*Family Structure.* Here we have a series of interesting findings. Children from "broken" families (i.e., minus one parent) most often wound up at the end of the study period in substitute homes and much less often in their own homes than children from two-parent families. Children from intact nuclear families rarely went to substitute homes, but significantly more often stayed at home or went to institutions.

When there were a natural mother and a stepfather in the child's home, children were found at the end of the study to be living in a substitute home or in their own home; however, when there were a natural father and stepmother, the children were found significantly more often in institutions. Children with stepmothers were institutionalized more often than children with stepfathers.

When there was only a mother in the home, the children were found in either a substitute or their own home, but when only a father was at home, the children were significantly more often institutionalized.

*Professional Education of Worker Assigned.* Children whose cases were handled either by social workers with a university (B.S.W.) degree in social work or by students in field work in social work were significantly more often placed in substitute homes and in their own homes than were children whose workers had a social work diploma (two years of semi-academic work or short courses in social work). Children whose workers had diploma backgrounds were significantly more often institution-bound.

## Family Background Variables and Placement Outcome

Of the approximately seventeen variables studied concerning the relationship of various family-identifying data with placement outcomes at the close of the study period, it is interesting to note which of them did not differentiate as to outcome. Among the non-differentiating variables were the following: number of children referred for placement in a family; the sex of the children referred (although male children tended to be placed more often in institutions than females); family income (high or low income did not differentiate); primary source of income (parents, public welfare, insurances, or partial breadwinners did not differentiate); quality of housing (good, fair, slum); location of the home (urban, suburban, or rural); father or mother's highest educational achievement (partial or no primary school, primary school, or higher); ethnicity of head of family (Sephardic–Middle Eastern origin, European-American origin, other); duration of residency in Israel; parents' religiosity (traditional, nonobservant, atheistic); and age of head of household. None of the above variables was associated significantly with the various types of placement outcomes, despite the many combinations of categories analyzed for each variable.

Some of the background variables which did differentiate as to type of placement outcome, however, are noted below.

*Age Group of Children Referred.* Although the older children referred (i.e., age six years and over) were more frequently found in institutional settings at the end of the study period than were younger children, a significant number of older children remained in their own homes, as compared to younger children. Of all the children in their own homes at the close of the study, only 15.7 per cent were under age six.

*Family Size.* Children from large families, i.e., five or more persons, remained in their own homes significantly more often than did children from smaller families. In our study, 33.3 per cent of all the children came from small families, and 66.7 per cent came from larger families.

*Family Housing.* Youngsters whose families lived in public housing projects and whose parents were renting from the government Housing Authority wound up in institutions significantly more often than did youngsters referred from families with privately owned (more often, mortgaged) homes. Children from privately owned homes showed a significantly higher number of own-home "placements" and were placed in substitute homes five times as frequently as the children from public housing.

*Other Children Placed Out of the Home.* Children who came from families where other siblings had not been placed out of the home remained at home significantly more often than did children whose families had already had prior experience with placing children away from home. In our study, 29.8 per cent of the children had siblings in placement. Prior experience of the family with institution placement had left them prone to using this type of care again.

### The Family System: Family Relationships and Placement Outcome

As in the last section, we will note first the variables which did not differentiate among the various placement outcomes examined at the close of the eighteen-month period.

Among the non-differentiating variables were the following: degree of parental dependency and self-determination in child-care planning; willingness of relatives to help and closeness of the family to relatives; recency of the family's breakdown to the referral period; parents' relationship to each other, as described by social worker; parents' use of children as weapons against each other; parents' ability for frustration tolerance; parents' potential for help-taking and use of community facilities; parents' problem-solving creativeness, as seen in attempts to resolve the family's problems; parents' objectivity about their problems; parents' co-operation with the worker; gross personality disturbances of the mother and/or father; the health of the child-caring person (usually the mother); physical defects of the child; gross personality disturbances of the child; the child's relationship to his parents (i.e., rejecting, ambivalent, accepting); the educational level of the child (i.e., in accord with his age, below age expectation, above age expectation); and the child's relationship to his siblings (i.e., conflict, no conflict).

Among the factors which were associated with specific placement outcomes were the following:

*Worker's Evaluation of Family Intactness at Referral.* When social workers diagnosed (rightly or wrongly) that a family was either on the "verge of disintegration" or "disintegrated," the children had a significantly greater chance of winding up in institutions than did children whose families were diagnosed as "having a chance of staying together with help." On the other hand, of the children who had been placed in substitute homes, 77.8 per cent came from families which were "on the verge of disintegration" or "disintegrated." Apparently, the children placed in substitute homes (i.e., foster homes, kibbutzim, or relatives' homes) received intensive care due to (or despite) the difficulty of their home situations. In our study, 43.2 per cent of all the children came from families diagnosed as "able to stay together," and 56.8 per cent came from home situations which were "on the verge of disintegration" or already "disintegrated."

*Parental Strictness.* Children who came from homes in which parents were either extremely abusive or extremely permissive were found at the close of the study significantly more often in institutional placements than were children whose parents did not show extremes in the treatment of their children.

*Parents' Attitude Toward Institutional Care.* Children of parents who valued institutional care as a solution to their problems and the problems of their children did, indeed, receive institutional care significantly more often than did children whose parents were either ambivalent or negative about institutional care. It is interesting to note that 64.6 per cent of the families in our study were positively inclined to institutional care, while 35.4 per cent were either ambivalent or negative about it.

*Parents' Attitude Toward Foster Care.* While there seemed to be no significant difference in attitudes toward foster care among parents of institutionalized children and among parents of children who remained in their own homes, there were a significant number of children placed in substitute homes whose parents were in favor of foster care and were knowledgeable about foster care. Concerning this element of "knowledge-ability," 70.2 per cent of the institutionalized children, 76.1 per cent of the "own home" children, and 27.6 per cent of the substitute-home children had never engaged in a discussion of foster-home care during the course of the contact with the social worker handling the case. For all the families included in our study, a full 67.3 per cent of the case records contained no mention of potential use or exploration of foster-care placement.

*Intactness of Parent-Child Ties.* Children who came from families in which they were "accepted by" and "accepting of" their parents and from families in which the parents and the child were at best mutually ambivalent about each other most often stayed in their parents' homes or were placed in substitute homes. Children who rejected their parents, whose parents rejected them, or who lived in "one-sided acceptance situations" (i.e., accepting child-rejecting parent, accepting parent-rejecting child) were found significantly more often in institutions rather than in own-home or substitute-home settings. It was not easy to identify signs of rejection, but, for purposes of this study, we concentrated on overt rather than on latent or subtle signs of aggressive, rejecting behavior, as noted in the case record as well as in the caseworker's direct comments about, or lack of mention of, evidence of rejection. Despite the grossness of the measure, it is interesting that it did significantly differentiate among placement outcomes.

*Child's Desire to Leave Home.* Children who did not want to leave home or were ambivalent about leaving home usually stayed at home. Many of the ambivalent youngsters wound up in substitute homes; 70.0 per cent of the children in substitute homes at the close of the research period had been either ambivalent or negative about leaving their own homes. On the other hand, children who expressed a clear wish to leave home wound up significantly more often in institutional settings than did children who were reluctant to leave home.

*Parents' Willingness to Keep the Child at Home.* Parents who were unwilling to keep the child at home usually got their wish. Children who came from families unwilling to keep them (for whatever reason) were found in institutions significantly more often than children whose parents were unwilling or ambivalent about placing them out of the home. Children whose parents were positive about keeping them at home were rarely inclined to have them placed in substitute homes.

**The Service System: Services Required or Rendered and Placement Outcome**

The following service-related variables showed no significant association with any of the five possible placement outcomes: the primary focus (target) of intervention (i.e., family focus, child focus, or parent focus as the major client or client group); the strategy or goal of intervention (i.e., ameliorative and one-time efforts versus preventive); the permanency of the plan required for the child (i.e., permanent or long-term, temporary, short-term, and unclear). On this last item, there was a distinct trend for children requiring permanent and long-term placement to be found in institutional settings at the close of the study period.[8]

Another variable which showed a trend, but no significant association with placement outcome, was the degree of "pressure" on the family, e.g., from neighbors, relatives, employers, newspapers, and local government officials. In those cases in which such pressure was cited in the record, there was a strong tendency for children to be placed in institutions. Indeed, such pressure usually urged institutional placement, and, apparently, in a good number of cases this influenced the placement outcome. Children from families in which little or no public pressure was involved tended to be placed in substitute homes or remained in their own homes.

Other variables unrelated to placement outcome were the degree of agency activity before placement, the length of time a child had already been in placement, the availability and timing of financial help to the family (i.e., provided as needed, provided insufficiently or too late, not provided), the number of successive placements made for the child since the original placement, and the major type of social problems found in the child's family. It may be of interest to note that, of the "primary social problems" noted by social workers in the families in our study, 23 per cent of the families were cited as being disabled by mental illness (primarily the mother); 13 per cent cited poverty as the family's major manifest problem; 13 per cent cited marital difficulties as the major problem; 15 per cent cited physical health impairment of one or both parents as the major problem; 15 per cent, educational problems of the children; 12.4 per cent, criminal behavior, drug addiction, prostitution, gambling, alcoholism, and various other problems.

The "service" variables that did significantly differentiate among placement outcomes at the conclusion of the study were the following:

*Child-Care Goal.* Children were generally placed where their social workers originally planned that they should be placed, whether the goal was institutional placement, substitute-home care, or own-home care. There is a very significant association between the worker's original goal at referral and the child's whereabouts at the end of the study period.

*Primary Service Given.* As the focus on personal counseling increases, the number of institutional placements decreases. When the primary service rendered included a combination of home help and personal counseling, the possibility of remaining at home or in a substitute home increased accordingly. Tangible service (e.g., financial aid and goods) or personal counseling was the major service provided to 68.3 per cent of the cases; of these, 70.9 per cent of the children remained either in their own homes or in substitute homes.

---

[8] Probability was at the 10 per cent level.

*Secondary Service Given.* When we investigated the combined effect of primary and secondary services given to the family on placement outcome, the combination of personal counseling, home help, and tangible services to the family showed a significant relationship with children's remaining at home or in substitute homes. Of the children living in their own homes at the conclusion of the study period, 91 per cent had received personal counseling and tangible help as the primary and secondary modes of help offered.

*Length of Service Period to Family and/or Child.* Longer periods of service (i.e., six months or more of contact) by the social welfare worker were significantly associated with home placements. Approximately 43.4 per cent of the children located in institutions upon conclusion of the study period had their cases closed within six months after referral, while only 26.4 per cent of the children in substitute homes and own-home settings discontinued this early. Of the youngsters placed in substitute homes, a full 68.8 per cent were active for at least a year to eighteen months.

*Degree of Agency Activity After Placement.* Follow-up activity by the agency dropped perceptibly for institutional children after their placement, while children placed in substitute homes and children returning to their own homes from institutions showed a significant increase in agency activity after the placement.

*Problem-Solving Creativeness of the Social Worker.* Children whose cases had been handled by "creative" social workers (i.e., with imaginative use of available funds and services versus stereotyped, categorical resolution of family problems) were significantly more likely to be found at home or in substitute homes than in institutions.

*Availability of Institutional Vacancies.* Children for whom vacancies in institutions were not available were obviously least likely to be placed there. On the other hand, 76.4 per cent of the children placed in substitute homes or own homes did have institutional vacancies available, but did not use them. For 23.6 per cent of the children placed in substitute homes or in their own homes, institutional vacancies were not available. This fact may have influenced their placement outcome. However, despite the general availability of institutions (to 82.1 per cent of the children studied) this type of placement was not used as a cure-all (i.e., by 30.2 per cent of the total number of children studied). Even so, institutional placements ranked second highest among the placement settings used for the children in our study. The percentage distribution concerning the whereabouts of the children at the end of the study period is shown in Table 1.

*Local Agency Structure and Its Role in Facilitating Service.* Children who were located in substitute homes or own-home settings came from local public welfare offices which were rated as "partially facilitating serv-

TABLE 1.

| Location of Child | Percentages |
| --- | --- |
| Returned to, or remained in, own (parents') home | 56.8 |
| Placed in institutions | 29.1 |
| Placed in foster homes | 8.6 |
| Placed in kibbutzim | 3.4 |
| Placed with relatives | 2.1 |

ice" or as "handicapping" the worker from carrying out his goals. On the other hand, children located in institutions generally came from welfare offices rated as "facilitating service." There may be a tie here between agency bureaucracy and funneling children into specific types of treatment.

*Interagency Co-operation in Placement Planning.* This item refers to the role of co-operation between the local welfare office and other agencies (e.g., district and national welfare agencies, homemaker agencies, tutors, testing, and other community resources) involved in developing and carrying out a placement or treatment plan. Children who were located in institutional placements at the close of the study period usually came from local offices in which interagency co-operation was rated as effective in achieving this goal. The same was true for children in substitute homes (71.9 per cent came from offices rated as highly effective on interagency co-operation). However, children who, at the end of the study, were located in the "own-home" setting were rated as coming from offices showing ineffective interagency co-operation. We can understand that the public welfare network is well geared for effective co-operation in carrying out institutional placements. It is also clear that use of substitute homes requires, sooner or later, effective co-operation in order to develop and keep these settings. One wonders, however, why there was not as effective co-operation among agencies for the children who remained in or returned to their own homes. One possible hypothesis is that interagency co-operation may be a function of "home-leaving," which by definition involves co-operation of a number of agencies in effecting removal from the home.

## SUMMARY

This report presents some basic findings obtained from a study of 197 families in Israel from which one or more dependent children were referred for institutional placement. A number of variables related to each family's referral situation, social background, family relationships, and services obtained were studied to examine the relationship between these variables and their effect on placement outcome for the children referred.

The five types of placement outcome studied were institutional care, foster-home placement, kibbutz placement, placement with relatives, and returning to or remaining in the "own home." Families were selected from four public welfare offices, located in both rural and urban settings, which were noted for high rates of referrals for institutional placement. Each case was followed (i.e., documented) intensively for a period of eighteen months, at the end of which time the whereabouts of the referred children were noted, thus enabling a search for correlates of placement outcome.

Among the high-risk variables which were strongly associated statistically with institutional placement were delinquent and acting-out behavior of the child, chronic illness of parents, children from households with step-mothers, children living alone with father, cases handled by non-graduate social workers, younger children, children from poor families, children from families from which other siblings had been placed, children from disintegrated families, situations in which parents were openly rejecting of children, and lack of creative planning on the part of the family social worker.

It is our hope that the empirical information presented in this study may be helpful to practitioners in choosing strategies for helping dependent families. There are certainly no "cook-book" recipes for predicting placement outcomes, but only probable results which may occur, given certain situational ingredients. Even so, a knowledge of probable outcomes may be a step ahead of trial and error in child welfare practice.

# 21

❨ The following article attempts to answer a frequently, and often heatedly, discussed question: "What is the most desirable substitute-care situation for the emotionally disturbed child—the foster family or the institution?" The conclusion reached is based on an empirical study of the experience of a group of such children placed in foster-family care.

# Foster Family Care for Disturbed Children—A Nonsentimental View

*Zira De Fries, Shirley Jenkins, and Ethelyn C. Williams*

The care of neglected and dependent children by public and private agencies in the United States has gone through a cycle from indiscriminate substitute parent care, to institution care, and back again to more selective individual foster parent care. Current methods strive to encompass the best aspects of both institution and individual care through the use of small residential centers. These alternating attempts imply that a satisfactory means of nonparental care has not yet been demonstrated.

No single means can answer the needs, since these children vary in degree and kind of disturbance, in age, in reason for placement, and in early background. They all have in common, however, the experience of having been separated from own families and being forced to live in atypical situations. Thus set apart, their subsequent personality development is often impaired. The extent to which this deleterious effect can be counteracted or mitigated is a major concern of those engaged directly or peripherally in the care of these children.

Despite new and enlightened attitudes in child care, problems remain that have defied repeated attempts at resolution, especially in regard to a particular means, namely, foster family care. We need to look more critically than ever at any sanguine proclamations about this method of foster care, and to re-examine its rationale in light of existing situations. Under ideal conditions, foster family care can be an effective substitute for parental care, but when actual conditions depart as radically from the ideal as they do in so many situations, particularly those involving severely disturbed children, antiquated ideals must be discarded and workable substitutes found.

An approach that looks at foster parents and at foster children as separate entities tends to dichotomize the problem. Wolins, for example, has studied the decision-making process in the selection of foster parents;[1] Weinstein has studied the adjustment of foster children and their identity problems;[2] and Maas and Engler have reported on the relationship between a community's structure and organization and the community's ways of providing child welfare services.[3]

A problem that continues to be of major concern, however, is the appropriateness of the use of foster family care as the predominant way of caring for neglected children. Too many studies are concerned with the ideal foster family care situation and the attempts to approximate this ideal, whereas all too few make direct and forthright criticism of the realities of foster family care. An example of the latter is the report by Eisenberg, who, after psychiatric examination of 140 foster children with serious emotional problems, attributable at least in part to foster care experiences, asked, "Is it not time that we re-examine the very nature of foster [family] care itself?"[4]

## THE TREATMENT STUDY

In an effort to evaluate the effects of intensive therapy and casework services on foster children with severe behavior problems, a study was made of disturbed children in the caseload of the Department of Public Welfare of Westchester County.[5] The main purpose was to see the extent to which a total treatment program could ameliorate disturbances and thus prevent institutionalization. At the same time, the procedures used provided an opportunity to study a variety of aspects of foster family care for disturbed children, including background, behavior, attitudes, and social status of foster parents, foster children, and own parents.

The design provided for two groups, one experimental and the other control, each comprising 27 disturbed foster children. The foster parents of these 54 children were also studied. The children were selected in pairs matched for age, sex, IQ, ethnic background, and diagnosis, and

[1] Martin Wolins, *Selecting Foster Parents: The Ideal and the Reality* (New York: Columbia University Press, 1963).

[2] Eugene A. Weinstein, *The Self-image of the Foster Child* (New York: Russell Sage Foundation, 1960).

[3] Henry S. Maas and Richard E. Engler, Jr., *Children in Need of Parents* (New York: Columbia University Press, 1959).

[4] Leon Eisenberg, "The Sins of the Fathers: Urban Decay and Social Pathology," *American Journal of Orthopsychiatry*, XXXII (1962), 15.

[5] The study was developed under a planning grant of the National Institute of Mental Health, which also financed the project from 1961 through 1964. This group of children was selected for study because behavior disturbances among children in foster care have been widely reported. The most comprehensive analysis of problem categories, reasons for placement, and whereabouts of children in care is contained in Helen R. Jeter, *Children, Problems, and Services in Child Welfare Programs* (Washington, D.C.: U.S. Government Printing Office, 1963).

randomly placed in either the experimental or control group. They were all on the caseload of the Department of Public Welfare of Westchester County and were selected from among those presenting difficulties requiring attention over and above that given by the usual casework procedures. The ages of the children ranged from 6 to 15 years; two-thirds were boys, two-thirds were Negro, and over half were born out of wedlock. IQ scores ranged from 70 to 110, and the average number of previous placements was two and one-half per child. Correspondence in levels of adjustment for children in both groups had been validated by outside judges, who rated each child on several variables.

After the initial testing and psychiatric evaluation of the children in both groups, children in the experimental group received special services, including psychotherapy, remedial help, and auxiliary community services. Those in the control group received the traditional services of the Department of Public Welfare, which consisted of visits, approximately monthly, from workers who varied in professional education, in training, and in experience. The children in the experimental group were treated for a period ranging from six months to two years. Treatment consisted of weekly sessions with therapists and direct case supervision by a psychiatrist. In addition, biweekly visits were made by caseworkers to the foster home of each child. All children in both groups were evaluated at the beginning and end of the treatment period in order to estimate the effect of extended services on the experimental group and to compare and contrast this with the control group.

## ADMINISTRATION OF THE PROJECT

The project was administered by the Westchester Children's Association, a private agency and guidance center, which worked cooperatively with the Division of Family and Child Welfare of the Department of Public Welfare. The administrative structure, involving the public agency and the private agency in both policy and practice phases, was made easier by the long cooperative association of these agencies. In addition, the private agency was known traditionally in Westchester County as an initiator of projects with potential for broad application in the total community.

The project was housed in the private agency and was staffed by project personnel. Joint case conferences and consultations were held with public agency staff and supervisors. The project director supervised the psychiatric aspects of the program, special services, the selection of homes; and the co-director administered the program in a capacity similar to that of a unit supervisor in the public agency. Authorization for payment of children's board and clothing and certification of special homes remained the responsibility of the Senior Supervisor of Child Welfare Services in the public agency, which also retained overall legal responsibility for all children.

The structure described both frustrated and enhanced learning for personnel in both agencies. Differences in staff salaries; in staff education, training, and experience; in caseload size, and in therapeutic services available—all these affected attitudes. Project personnel reacted against expediency and compromise in standards, and public agency staff reacted against the luxury of using careful research techniques while emergencies mounted. Despite differences, however, relations between the two staffs remained effective. Public agency staff came to appreciate the advantages of the training sessions, case conferences, and depth of the project's concern with child development and behavior; and the project staff saw, quite vividly, the limitations and pressures of working within the public agency framework, as well as the opportunities for serving a caseload with most urgent needs.

## EVALUATION OF CHILDREN

During the course of the project the children were evaluated in several areas: (1) symptomatology, (2) initial and closing psychological tests, including IQ scores, (3) initial and closing psychiatric interviews, and (4) school reports at the beginning and end of the project. In addition, a followup interview on all institutionalized children was made.

Evaluation conferences held jointly by the public and private agencies during the second and third years of the project to review matched pairs of children gave the following results on 42 children:[6] "improvement"— 10 experimental, 9 control; "about the same"—7 experimental, 11 control; "appear to be worse"—4 experimental, 1 control. There was, however, one problem in the conference procedure: with three times the case activity in the experimental group, these children and their problems were better known than were those in the control group.

Comparable data, however, were available for the content analysis of the initial and closing psychiatric interviews, since outside judges reviewed descriptive statements abstracted in both positive and negative categories.[7] Rating independently, 81 percent of 156 separate ratings of the three judges were found to be identical, and the remaining 19 percent were in adjacent categories. Judgments indicated that a total of 21 children were considered to be "improved"—13 in the experimental and 8 in the con-

---

[6] Children who entered during the last year of the project were excluded.

[7] Positive categories were: pleasant manner, spontaneity, capacity to relate, maturity, aware and realistic, standards and ideals, controls, security, directness, ability to express negative feelings. Negative categories were: blunted affect, anxious, depressed, hostile, inhibited, immature, lack of direction or goal, thinking disorder, negative self-image, need for affection, denies feelings, represses hostility, withdrawn, detached and projects.

trol group, 14 to have experienced "no change"—5 in the experimental and 9 in the control group, and 17 to have worsened—8 in the control and 9 in the experimental group. (One pair was not judged because of the circumstances of institutionalization.) These results show approximately the same number rated as worse, but a tendency for more to be rated as improved in the experimental group. The differences, however, are not statistically significant at the .05 level.

Concerning school, over one-half the children in each group were reported to be failing in work at both the beginning and end of the project, and behavior remained essentially the same for both groups over the study period. Further analysis of both symptomatology and psychological test results reinforced the conclusion that movement in the direction of improved adjustment was minimal. Although some minor behavioral changes were noted, the results in the various categories pointed up an unjustified optimism in the original hypothesis of this study—namely, that a variety of special services could alter to a significant extent functioning and behavior of a group of severely disturbed children in foster home care.

A review of the treatment phase of the project and details of the evaluative criteria used have been published elsewhere.[8] Other pertinent findings not yet reported but obtained during the course of the project contain information on the characteristics and attitudes of the foster parents studied and on the followup interviews of institutionalized children. These will be discussed here.

## FOSTER PARENT STUDY

During the course of the project, data were gathered on three groups of foster parents, a total of 148 foster mothers and fathers. The first group comprised the 27 couples who were foster parents of the disturbed project children who were receiving special services. A second group consisted of the 27 pairs who were foster parents of the disturbed children in the control group. They were not as available for case study as the former group, since their foster children were not being treated, but they were all interviewed in their homes on roles and attitudes concerning foster care.

Studies of these two groups were supplemented by a study of a group of 20 foster parents caring for children who did not present evidence of serious disturbance and who were among the best adjusted of the total caseload of approximately 1200 in the Department of Public Welfare. This group was included for purposes of comparison. Thus, a wide diver-

[8] Zira de Fries, Shirley Jenkins, and Ethelyn C. Williams, "Treatment of Disturbed Children in Foster Care," *American Journal of Orthopsychiatry*, XXXIV (1964), 615–624.

sity of foster parents—those caring for the most disturbed children and those caring for the best adjusted children—was studied, and likenesses as well as differences between the groups were noted.

## BACKGROUND DATA

Information about the foster parents was obtained from a variety of sources—case records, social worker interviews in the home, and, in some cases, psychiatric interviews. The areas studied were interrelationships between children and foster parents, motivating factors involved in the desire to care for foster children, social and educational background of foster parents, assessment of personality structure, rewards and problems of being foster parents, and role perception of foster parents.

The majority of the 148 foster mothers and fathers studied came from a segment of the population with minimal education and income levels. They were older than natural parents and, in many instances, were more like grandparents (the median age was just over 50); they had cared for an average of eight children over a 10-year span and had an average of three children currently in their homes. They were predominantly Negro, and their religious affiliations were Protestant and Catholic. The educational level was low, fewer than one-half having completed high school. The majority of foster mothers who had worked or were working were engaged primarily in factory or domestic work. A few had worked in hospitals or as salesladies. The foster fathers worked primarily in factories, as construction workers, and in domestic or commercial service jobs. Many foster parents came from large families; several had been foster children themselves or had been raised in own families in which foster children were kept.

## ATTITUDES

The emphasis in this study was around parent-child relationships, with consequent concentration on foster parents' feelings and attitudes toward the children. It was found that these varied from accepting, to grossly rejecting, to idealizing, with the greatest cluster centering around ambivalence. Perhaps the clearest idea of the feelings and attitudes can be obtained from representative statements in the different categories. Examples of attitudes are selected in order of the frequency with which they occurred: ambivalent, idealized, completely rejecting, and (least frequent) accepting.

Many foster parents caring for disturbed children showed strikingly similar ambivalent attitudes. One foster mother said about an adolescent girl, "All I do is beg and plead and tell her to try to help herself. I said to her, 'If they put you out of school, you can't stay here.' " A foster mother of a 9-year-old boy complained about him thus: "He's a great liar, he 'destructs' everything he gets; he made a terrible mess of his own room—tore sheets, blankets, hacked away at the furniture. He does a lot of stealing; he is a very lazy child." This foster mother went on to say that she "loves the boy—he has nice ways about him," but many times she has said to her husband in the boy's presence, "I think we should give him up." Often, after being scolded by her, he has said, "Give me up; I would rather go back to my own mother anytime." To this the foster mother replied, "If that's what you want and the state wants that, I will gladly let you go." Later in the interview this same foster mother went on to say there was little difference between her feelings for her own and her foster children. She "just loves to have children around to fuss over."

A foster mother of a pair of sibling boys, 10 and 12 years old, was particularly ambivalent about them. She claimed her own girls and these boys had a wonderful relationship. She felt they were doing her a favor by being part of the family, but they should listen to her and should adjust themselves. They should be glad to be in a family that cares for them—they should show their love and appreciation by doing things willingly. They should do the right things. In contrast, this woman's husband only complained about the boys, and both parents completely overlooked the fact that one of these boys was markedly effeminate to the point of actually wearing girl's clothing.

A foster mother caring for a 10-year-old girl complained about the emotional burdens of caring for foster children and described this child as forgetful, irresponsible, and unaffectionate. This foster mother said she had decided to take in foster children as a way of solving a problem—namely, the neighborhood children often congregated in her backyard, and she was reluctant to tell them to leave because she did not want to deprive her own child of companionship. Now, with a foster child, she can tell them to go without feeling guilty. When asked how long she planned to keep the foster child, she replied, "You never know what tomorrow will bring."

Some foster parents covered their ambivalent or rejecting attitudes by idealizing the children and denying difficult behavior. One foster mother of a schizophrenic child told of his urinating on the walls, but did not find this distressing. She remained unperturbed at the fact that he locked himself in his room for hours at a time, was considered a terror by the school personnel, and made no contact with other children except to strike out aggressively.

In contrast to the idealizing foster mothers were the completely rejecting ones. One mother talked about three sibling boys as fellows: "You break your back to get nowhere." All three boys were described as wanton, wasteful, lying like troopers.

Two foster mothers of the group of 27 children receiving special treatment were considered suitable for the job. They accepted the children.

One of these spoke warmly and positively about a difficult adolescent girl, but did not deny her problems: "She is cute looking, neat, a hard worker, but at times she can be quite moody." She saw fine qualities in this girl underneath her rough exterior.

The foregoing illustrations, except for the last, show the parents' lack of empathy for the foster child's situation and their complete inability to comprehend his needs. Efforts directed toward changing these negative attitudes by means of casework or therapy were entirely unrewarding because there were almost no entering wedges. Since the foster parents had no reason to feel guilty about the children, and, in fact, many self-righteously felt themselves superior to the child's own parents, this frequently used means of gaining access to a parent was closed. Thus, an important rationale for psychotherapy did not exist, because these parents dissociated themselves from the children's problems. This fact, coupled with a multitude of other more mundane reasons, such as lack of time, limited mobility, and low educational level, contributed to the difficulties encountered when attempts were made to work with the foster parents. Still another major obstacle to therapy was the vagueness regarding where responsibility for the child was centered.

## MOTIVATIONS

A most perplexing question, the answer to which remained obscure, concerned the foster parents' motivations for caring for disturbed children. It was difficult to understand why people already burdened with economic and social problems would choose to further complicate their harassed lives with a succession of disturbed, deprived children, particularly when the financial rewards were so small. Caring for foster children in this public welfare agency appeared to be limited to one social class, the majority of foster parents being socially and economically underprivileged.

A possible explanation, but one that is difficult to verify, is that by having a steady supply of challenges and problems, a deprived individual is thereby distracted or diverted from experiencing the overwhelming dissatisfactions in living that might otherwise disturb him, but that do not have to be faced quite so directly when the environment is constantly tumultuous.

Attempts to probe motivations by asking a direct question, such as, "What made you decide to take a foster child?" do not necessarily lead to valid answers. Surprisingly simple replies, however, were elicited from some mothers, who stated they "had the room" or had had experience with children and were used to them, having come from large families themselves. But more often foster parents gave a more complicated response and one more difficult to decipher—their desire "to help poor children." A minority indicated personal needs, such as, "I needed an outlet";

"It's better than going to work"; or "I was frustrated." Loneliness and a desire to enhance feelings of worth were other explanations offered.

The question of money as a motivating factor revealed interesting differences between foster parents of disturbed children and those caring for well-adjusted children. The majority of foster parents caring for disturbed children denied money was a motivation, but only 25 percent of those parents caring for well-adjusted children denied this. Despite the genuine frankness displayed by some foster parents in attempting to explain their motivations for becoming foster parents, true motives were elusive. In all likelihood a multiplicity of reasons can be ascribed to such a desire, some of which are practical, others related to intrapsychic needs of the individual. These latter, unfortunately, require more intensive probing than any in which foster parents in the caseload studied were willing or able to engage.

## OTHER QUESTIONS

In addition to inquiries about current attitudes and feelings toward foster children and motivations leading to caring for them, foster parents were asked about a number of other issues: attitudes toward children's own parents; feelings of responsibility; extent of anticipated care; expectations, pleasures, and rewards in care; problems encountered; and suggestions for improvement. In response to the foregoing items, several differences emerged between the parents caring for the disturbed children and those caring for the well-adjusted children.

Own parents presented more problems to foster parents of well-adjusted children than they did to foster parents of disturbed children. Over one-half of the foster mothers of well-adjusted children thought of themselves as "real mothers." Foster parents of disturbed children pointed out the basic legal responsibility of the Department of Public Welfare. Foster parents of well-adjusted children, on the other hand, emphasized that, since own parents failed to take responsibility for their own children, they should be kept away. Many more foster parents of well-adjusted children stated that they would keep them until they were grown; one-half of those caring for disturbed children said they would keep them "until they are moved."

When asked about pleasures and rewards, there were many positive responses from foster parents caring for well-adjusted children; foster parents of disturbed children were hard put to think of pleasures and rewards. With regard to problems, foster parents of disturbed children reported a significantly greater number of problems in the area of school adjustment. Several foster parents in both groups described the foster children's problem as "living in two worlds."

A suggestion for improvement that was recommended by respondents of both sets of foster parents was to raise board rates. The group of foster parents of disturbed children wanted better service from the Department of Public Welfare and more information on children before they were placed. Adoption was considered by both groups to be the most desirable solution for many of these children, but they were not interested in adoption themselves.

In general, the group of parents caring for well-adjusted children were more direct and realistic, freer to complain and to praise, willing to take more responsibility for making decisions, and more rejecting of agency help. They expressed a greater feeling of permanency about keeping the children.

In contrast, the foster parents of disturbed children did not implicate themselves in the children's difficulties and were unable to empathize. They were detached and objective in their feelings, but did not see the children's unfortunate experiences as the causes of their difficulties, since they were so involved in attempting to cope with the effects on themselves of this maladaptive behavior. They showed little or no insight, and, although they verbalized a desire for help, they did not demonstrate a capacity to use it. They found few satisfactions in their role as foster parents and yet were unwilling to let go of the idea of being a foster parent —in fact many expressed wishes for increasing numbers of children and were not in the least deterred by their continually distressing experiences. The negative feedback between these parents and their foster children exacerbated and accentuated the problems of each, as well as their problems together. The fact that these parents persisted in wanting more and more children attested in part to their pertinacity and to their limitations in assessing and realistically giving up on a problem beyond their power to alter to any significant degree.

## FOLLOWUP OF INSTITUTIONALIZED CHILDREN

An initial goal of the project was to avoid institutionalization of children, but, as the limited and often destructive foster home situations of many children became more apparent, decisions based on individual needs of each child resulted in institutionalization of 17 of the 54 disturbed children. These children were placed in 11 child welfare institutions in Westchester and adjacent counties, institutions that varied in operation, philosophy, and population size (from 25 to 700 children).

These 17 children consisted of 11 in the experimental group and 6 in the control group, and they ranged in age from 10 to 16 years. Of the 17, 5 were girls and 12 were boys; 5 were white and 12 were Negro. These proportions reflect the total population group in the study. The total number of prior foster home placements ranged from one to six, with an average of two and one-half. Diagnostically most children were classified as character disorders, and there were a few who were considered neurotic or psychotic.

At the time of institutionalization, all 17 children were acutely disturbed and several had to be precipitously removed from their foster homes. With a great deal already known about their previous difficulties and with their histories of continuing problems, it was considered important to follow up these 17 children in terms of their adjustment to institution placement. Field visits were made to ten of the institutions, and one was contacted by telephone and a mailed questionnaire because it was several hundred miles from the project offices. In the field interviews, a project social worker reviewed each child's initial and subsequent adjustment in each institution with his therapist. These interviews were conducted a minimum of three months after placement, with the average elapsed time in the institution being one year per child.

In the followup interviews, data were gathered on: (1) initial reactions to placement, including reactions of child to social worker, cottage parents, and peers, adjustment in school, and symptom pictures; (2) changes in these areas up to the time of the followup interview; (3) contacts the child maintained with its own and foster parents during the period of institutionalization; and (4) the short- and long-term goals the institution staff held for each child.

## EARLY ADJUSTMENT

Adjustment to the institutions during the first three months was difficult for the majority of the children in regard to relationship with social workers, cottage parents, and peers. The total number of initial negative comments by workers were two and one-half times the number of positive ones. Some negative comments were that the children were fearful, suspicious, distrustful, defiant, complaining, demanding, and failed to keep appointments. With cottage parents, most children were categorized negatively as disliking cottage parents or fearing them, refusing to do chores, and running away from the cottage. With peers, they were described as predominantly hostile and unrelated. When they entered their institution placements, none of the 17 children was considered by his teacher to have demonstrated a capacity for learning commensurate with age or grade level.

The symptom pictures of the children during the first three months of their institution placements were similar to those observed while they were still in their foster homes. The predominant symptomatology was in the hyperactive, hostile, and aggressive categories, with destructiveness, defiance, stealing, lying, truancy, negativism, rebelliousness, disruptiveness, excitability, and restlessness common. Somewhat less common were neurotic symptoms, including enuresis, excessive masturbation, nightmares, temper tantrums, self-destructiveness, clinging, and excessive affectionateness. A few children manifested withdrawal, depression, or thought disturbances such as paranoid ideation.

## IMPROVEMENT

After a minimum of three months in the institution and an average stay of one year, varying degrees of improvement were noted for 14 of the 17 children by workers in the 11 institutions. Although it was not felt that sufficient time had elapsed to consider any underlying personality changes to have occurred, a noticeable increase in stability and a diminution of tension and anxiety were reported. There was almost a complete reversal in the ratio of positive and negative comments concerning social workers, cottage parents, and peers, the negative comments being reduced by one-half and the positive ones being doubled. There was strong evidence of gradually increasing capacity to fit into the institution routines and become an accepted part of the group, although only one child was described as having made a close friend.

In regard to school, after a period of three months, one-half of the children showed some improvement in their academic work. Eight of the 17 were receiving remedial help, and three children were up to their grade level. In addition, many of the children were participating successfully in non-academic subjects, such as shopwork, jewelry making, and home economics; and 12 were active in extracurricular sports and clubs.

The symptom picture after three months showed a reduction by slightly less than one-half in the total number of symptoms, and there was general reporting that, despite the continued presence of symptoms, their intensity had diminished. One worker, for example, described a child who entered the institution with a diagnosis of borderline schizophrenia as follows:

> He still loses his temper easily, but he shows less depression. There is still withdrawal; he is hostile, eneuretic, and infantile, but all his symptoms have diminished in intensity. He is learning a little in school, beginning to cooperate, and beginning to take an interest in people.

A therapist in another institution reported progress with one child thus:

> There is a good deal of change—he shows more hostility to his worker; he doesn't pretend as much as he used to, and he is beginning to try to control his hostility toward the community and confine it to my office.

When the overall picture is evaluated, 14 children showed improvement. The general picture in these children is one of less anxiety, greater self-control, and even increased self-awareness. In the three children who were unimproved or worse, failure in one case was attributed to the fact that this Negro adolescent in a predominantly white institution felt the color boundary keenly, particularly in regard to dating. The reasons for failure in the other cases do not appear to be as directly related to the placement situation per se as to the severity of emotional problems experienced in their early lives. Since the children requiring institutionalization were those who showed the greatest disturbance of the study population, the results of these placements would seem to be significant.

## CONTACTS

The children's contacts (including visits, letters, and calls) with their own and foster families while in the institution were reviewed from three aspects: (1) the institution's policy in regard to such contacts, (2) the extent of contact that took place, and (3) the institution staff's appraisal of the result of what contacts had occurred. Toward own family contacts, the institutions' policies varied from being discouraging of all contacts, to leaving the initiative to the family, to encouraging contacts.

Visits were made by own parents of eight children. Of these, six were reported to be destructive to the child, one helpful, and one ambivalent. One mother was drunk when she visited; one made an appointment and never showed up; another mother, a patient in a mental hospital, sent a confused and garbled letter to her child.

Comments by workers about contacts with own parents were predominantly negative. For example: "Our efforts with this own family are to keep them away from their three children who are placed here—they are too rejecting and destructive." Another worker said, "This child deteriorates whenever there is contact with the mother. She has a deeply disturbing effect on him." It is interesting to note that there was not a single case in which the institution planned to return the child to the family, and many felt that contact should be nonexistent or minimal.

Ten children had received visits from foster parents, and a few had had letters and calls. Contacts were initiated equally by foster families and by children. None of the institutions encouraged contact with foster families, and in four cases they were actively discouraging.

Concerning plans for return to foster families, four institutions contemplated eventually sending children to new foster homes for long-term care, and, in seven cases, workers emphatically stated that children should not return to foster home care because they required the more impersonal and structured atmosphere of the institution. A few institutions mentioned placing discharged children in "halfway houses" or group homes.

## GOALS

The goals of the institutions differed in a number of ways, but there was a general consensus of wanting to assume long-term responsibility, recognizing that the needs of these children could not be fulfilled by a brief stay. Although therapeutic goals were limited in a number of institutions, the desire to care for the children until they could be self-supporting was stressed. Vocational training figured importantly, and special attention to proper schooling was emphasized.

Some representative quotes from a few institution staff members reflect their attitudes. One staff member said: "We believe in the stability of long-term placement here for children who have no one—we have a special fund to send them to special schools—our goal is to make this boy self-supporting." Another said: "We don't have a short-term plan for this child because he is in need of a structured environment for a long time. We will keep him until he is 18 and then make a plan." The child discussed was 10 years old on admission to that institution.

A worker elsewhere stated about a 13-year-old boy: "He has had so many damaging placements in foster homes. We want him to have a long-range, consistent environment, and this is the best place for him. We would not consider any short-term plan, and we will keep him until he is 18 and train him to support himself."

When the institution workers were asked to describe their general attitudes about foster home versus institution care, most of them favored an institution structure for a disturbed child. They opposed foster family care because they felt that, all too often, the child relived those rejecting experiences that had caused his placement in the first place.

These followup interviews about the effects of institutionalization indicated that, after an initial period of three months, almost all the children showed signs of improvement in their behavior, with definite indication of feelings of greater security and stability in their new environments. Although the institutions varied markedly, staff members were agreed about the need for long-range planning for children. This attitude was in marked contrast to that expressed by foster parents, most of whom did not commit themselves to long-time care, and often not beyond "tomorrow."

### CONCLUSION AND RECOMMENDATIONS

The concept of foster family care, arising from expediency, became entrenched as an antidote to the evils of congregate care. Once this form of care had gained a footing, it spread rapidly and was uncritically employed by well-intentioned child welfare workers. Justification for its continued use came from newly developing theories in the field of child therapy and psychoanalysis. Subsequently, however, the increasing number of difficulties and failures experienced by many workers made a second and critical look imperative. Such a second look at the concepts implicit in foster care reveals a complexity hardly recognized in the early, oversimplified idea.[9]

---

[9] Some of these issues are discussed in Martin Wolins and Irving Piliavin, *Institution or Foster Family: A Century of Debate* (New York: Child Welfare League of America, 1964).

Objections to foster family care for disturbed children have already been registered in vigorous terms. In his Presidential Address to the 1962 American Orthopsychiatric Association Meeting, Fritz Redl stated:

> So many very disturbed children, of the degree, and variety of disturbance we happen to produce en masse in our society, are so far beyond the grip of the old concept of 'foster home care' that we can safely say: As an institution for the safeguarding of the mental health of vulnerable children, the foster home of yesterday is either extinct or not sufficient any more. It is an obsolete answer to a current problem of huge proportions. Why, then, don't we who know this become more vocal about it? Just because we have to hang on to the obsolete slogans that even for a very disturbed child, after the neighbor's dog, a 'foster mother' is still the child's best friend?[10]

The foster family care concept carries with it the sentimentalized view that there is a need to simulate family life for the dislocated, neglected, abused child. This view had been propounded partly in order to counteract the widely proclaimed ill effects of institutionalization on children, often discussed in psychoanalytic literature. That it is possible to simulate a family for the disturbed foster child is an unrealistic and outdated concept, however, that must be critically examined before further progress can be made. At the same time, it is necessary to develop better institutions for those children for whom foster family care is not the answer and whose lives are entirely dependent upon the decisions and judgments of total strangers.

The Westchester project encompassed a four-year period, during which time several hypotheses about foster children and their parents were tested and a great deal of data was collected, sorted, and analyzed. For those children in the experimental group, an "all-out" therapeutic effort did not produce significant results while they remained in inappropriate home situations.[11] Most of the foster parents studied were not amenable to therapy even on an elementary level, and they had mainly negative or ambivalent feelings toward the disturbed children in their care. On the other hand, the majority of children who had been institutionalized during the course of the project improved within the professional and structured environment provided, and institution staff had positive attitudes toward the children in placement.

The study results reinforce previous experiences and concerns about foster family care as a major resource for disturbed children. Recommendations, based on both the project experience and a broader view of problems of disturbed children in foster care, suggest these specific goals:

The first is to *reverse* the current order of ways of caring for disturbed

---

[10] Fritz Redl, "Crisis in the Children's Field," *American Journal of Orthopsychiatry*, XXXII (1962), 775.

[11] For a statement of the theoretical basis of the treatment plan, *see* de Fries, Jenkins, and Williams, *op. cit.*

and neglected children. Presently, children in foster family care outnumber those in institution care. By making institution care serve the largest number of children, and thereby curtailing the number of children in foster family care, a more properly selective use of foster homes would become possible. Adoption services need to be considered more widely as an alternative to foster family care;[12] revising and updating cumbersome legal restrictions would facilitate this.

Needless to say, effecting a rearrangement from the current order of frequency—foster family care, institutionalization, and adoption—to a new order—institutionalization, adoption, and foster family care—necessitates breaking with the status quo, relinquishing outworn attitudes, and dispelling false securities—a big order indeed!

The second goal is to upgrade institutions so that they not only provide numerically for the greatest number of neglected children, but serve as centers to which children coming into care for the first time can be channeled and where they may remain if this proves to be the most appropriate place. Since, in many cases, it cannot be known when a child first comes into care whether this will be temporary or permanent, nor how disturbed a child is at the time of initial placement, it is essential to have this new environment a stable and benign one so that the frightened child experiences the least possible threat in his first separation.

Also, the child can be observed and studied in a structured setting, in which there should be trained personnel and in which uniform procedures for diagnosis and prognosis should exist. The long-range plans for a child could thereby be arrived at in a more consistent fashion, and particular types of care could be used more selectively. Adoption would be the goal for the youngest, least disturbed children. The most disturbed children, young and old, would not be considered suitable for foster family care. Using the institution as the major focus, the choice of care then becomes a matter of more careful and considered selection in which the specific reason necessitating placement, the observed behavior of the child over a period of time, and his own family situation become guides by means of which a final and appropriate goal can be projected.

The final goal is to *deprive* own parents of their "parental rights" when they have been shown to be indifferent to the needs of the children for whom they have relinquished both physical and psychological responsibility.[13] A sharp distinction must be made—and made promptly—between those parents who are legitimately unable to care for their children and

---

[12] Some of the problems of moving children from one type of care to another are discussed by Bernice Boehm in *Deterrents to Adoption of Children in Foster Care* (New York: Child Welfare League of America, 1958).

[13] For a discussion of terminology and draft legislation, see *Legislative Guides for the Termination of Parental Rights and Responsibilities and the Adoption of Children* (Washington D.C.: U.S. Government Printing Office, 1961).

those who are only too willing to pass on the job to a third party, be it foster parent or institution. For example, it is hardly difficult to predict in the case of a mother having her seventh illegitimate child, with six previous children in placement, that this new child will have to be separated and separated permanently. Recognition of the deleterious effects of nebulous or nonexistent parental relationships will militate toward more prompt, forceful, and effective methods of obtaining surrender. Perhaps nothing in foster care is more productive of confusion and conflict to the child than the periodic shunting between own and foster parents or own parent and institution when own parents are ambivalent, rejecting, and unrehabilitatable.

The foregoing suggestions can hardly be considered original—in fact, they may be quite commonplace—but, unfortunately, they are ideas to which it is far easier to give lip service than implementation. The sad fact is that the status quo continues to be maintained under the guise of enlightenment. It is far too hazardous to leave the elucidation of foster care concepts to chance. It is unrealistic to expect that most children—and in particular disturbed children, already burdened with confusion about primary relationships and with poorly developed senses of identity—can sort out their place in the intricacies of foster family care, even with a great deal of help. It is similarly unrealistic to perpetuate the idea that replication of a family situation is the best possible kind of care for disturbed children who have been neglected, abandoned, or abused. The risk of the foster parent rejecting the disturbed child is too great.

Child welfare principles are concerned with presenting the child with a family way of life, representing the best of the "American way of life." Ironically, foster family care in many cases emphasizes rather than minimizes a feeling of difference for foster children in all but the most superficial aspects of family living. The children's more subtle needs and their yearnings for genuine relationships remain unfulfilled, and, thus, the discrepancy between the seeming and the real is intensified rather than diminished.

# 22

❴[ Another confirmation of the fact that what the worker brings to the foster-care situation is a significant determinant of foster-care decision is offered in the following article. Here the central concern is with workers' attitudes as they relate to the decision regarding the acceptability of foster-care families.

# Prediction of Child-Rearing Attitudes

*H. F. Dingman, C. D. Windle, and S. J. Brown*

It seems apparent that for the proper organization and supervision of a therapeutic program the therapists should have insight into the motivations and attitudes of the individuals with whom they are working. There have been studies of the attempts to predict personality traits, and generally, these studies have been inconclusive at best. Much depends on the closeness of the association between the predictor and the predicted, as well as the exact definition of the traits involved. In addition, there must be an opportunity for the predictor to observe the predicted in a situation in which he has occasion to exhibit the trait being rated. An example of this is discussed by Buckner wherein he points out that if raters are able to observe only part of man's behavior under a limited set of conditions, the validity of behavior ratings is not likely to be very accurate for situations in which the rater was not able to observe.[1] This point is demonstrated again in a set of ratings by Windle and Dingman.[2]

The literature indicates that social scientists in general, and clinicians in particular, in spite of their training, do not possess superior ability to judge others. Taft has suggested that these paradoxical results may be due to insufficient experience with a wide range of people, and that clinicians may be too involved with their social relations to rate effectively.[3] Since social workers supervising caretakers are likely to be highly involved in the process of rating their caretakers and also to differ from them in social and educational background, it is reasonable to suspect that their ratings may be

---

[1] D. N. Buckner, "The Predictability of Ratings as a Function of Interrater Agreement," *Journal of Applied Psychology*, February, 1959, pp. 60–64.

[2] C. D. Windle and H. F. Dingman, "Interrater Agreement and Predictive Validity," *Journal of Applied Psychology*, June, 1960, pp. 203–204.

[3] R. Taft, "The Ability to Judge People," *Psychological Bulletin*, January, 1955, pp. 1–23.

subject to substantial biases.[4] The purpose of the present study is to examine the accuracy with which social workers can judge the characteristics of the family caretakers they are supervising. To perform supervision adequately, social workers should have insight into the family caretakers' attitudes about child-rearing practices and should be able to predict them relatively accurately.

TABLE 1. Distribution of Social Workers and Family Care Mothers by Age, Sex, and Race

| Race | Age in Years | Social Workers | | Family Care Mothers |
|---|---|---|---|---|
| | | *Male* | *Female* | *Female* |
| Caucasian | Under 50 | 1 | 6 | 11 |
| | 50+ | 0 | 2 | 12 |
| Negro | Under 50 | 2 | 0 | 10 |
| | 50+ | 0 | 0 | 10 |
| Mexican | Under 50 | 0 | 0 | 2 |
| | 50+ | 0 | 0 | 0 |

## PROCEDURE

All forty-five female caretakers whose homes were used in 1958 to care for mentally subnormal patients from Pacific State Hospital (a California institution for mental defectives) were selected for the study. The characteristics of these caretakers have been described in a previous article.[5] Since the personality characteristics of greatest relevance to caretaking involve child-rearing attitudes, the Parental Attitude Research Instrument (PARI) developed by Schaefer and Bell was employed to assess attitudes.[6] Each family caretaker filled out the PARI while attending a social meeting at Pacific State Hospital. The PARI was also filled out by each social worker supervising one of these homes. These social workers were instructed to answer the PARI in two ways: first as he himself felt and second as he believed each caretaker that he was supervising would answer it. In addition, a global rating of "goodness" of the caretaker was obtained from the pooled subjective rating of two *supervising* social workers responsible for the conduct of the entire extramural family care program. It should be noted that these ratings of "goodness" were made by different

---

[4] C. D. Windle, Sabagh G. Brown, and H. F. Dingman, "Caretaker Characteristics and Placement Success," *American Journal of Mental Deficiency*, May, 1961, pp. 739–743.

[5] In Windle (4) it was shown that the "good" caretakers were like the social workers. In this paper the social workers' predictions were most accurate for the "good" caretakers. Therefore, we state that the predictions were accurate for the caretakers that were like the social workers, although we do not present direct evidence because of the unevenness of the sample and the large number of comparisons.

[6] E. S. Schaefer and R. Q. Bell, "Development of a Parental Attitude Research Instrument," *Child Development*, September, 1958, pp. 339–362.

social workers than those who predicted the caretakers' PARI responses.

Since each caretaker goes through an extensive licensing procedure, it would be assured that all caretakers fulfill minimum qualifications. In order to avoid skewed ratings, these supervisors were requested to rate the caretakers' performance on a continuous scale, and the judgments were forced into a normal distribution.

In order to measure congruence between PARI responses, correlations were computed between the answers of pairs of social workers and caretakers for all 115 items of the PARI. This correlation represents similarity in profile shape or in the order of item acceptance. This measure of congruence, by concentrating upon a particular component of accuracy, avoids many of the difficulties in interpreting social perception scores which Cronbach pointed out.[7]

## RESULTS

In Table 1 we present a comparison between the age, sex, and racial categories for the social workers and the family care mothers. It can be noted that there were no Mexican social workers and that there was only one male social worker. As one might expect, the social workers were primarily under fifty years of age, female, and Caucasian.

In Figure 1 are plotted the correlation between each caretaker's PARI response and the responses predicted by the social worker (verticle axis) and those given by the social worker as his own (horizontal axis). These two sets of coefficients are correlated $r = .69$,[8] which is substantially higher than one would expect by chance ($P < .01$). Caretakers are differentiated in Figure 1 according to whether they received relatively favorable or unfavorable pooled ratings of "goodness" as caretakers from the two supervisory social workers. It will be observed from Figure 1 as well as Table 2 that there was a marked tendency for caretakers who were rated relatively good to have higher correlations between their responses and both the social workers' predictions and the social workers' own responses than the other caretakers.

## DISCUSSION

The caretakers rated as good by the supervising social worker are those whose attitudes correspond rather closely with the line social worker's.

---

[7] L. J. Cronbach, "Processes Affecting Scores of 'Understanding of Others' and 'Assumed Similarity,'" *Psychological Bulletin*, May, 1955, pp. 177–193.

[8] Actually it is preferable to correlate the associated Z values using Fisher's transformation. This value $r_x = .63$ which is also significant at the .01 level. However, it is not as clearly understood as the correlation between untransformed correlation coefficients.

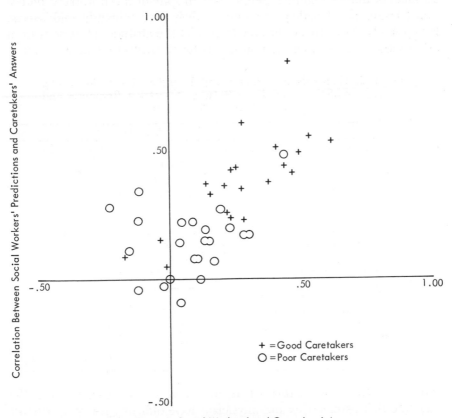

Correlation Between Social Workers' and Caretakers' Answers.

*Figure 1.* Relationship between accuracy of the social workers' predictions of family caretakers' test responses and the degree of agreement between social workers' and family caretakers' test responses.

Furthermore, it appears that social workers are able to predict the responses of caretakers only when these caretakers are responding on the PARI as they did. When the family care mother has attitudes that do not agree with the social worker's predictions of her own attitudes, this disagreement is strongly related to supervisor's judgment about the "goodness" of the home. It was found that objective measures (turnover, return rate, etc.) of patient success did not agree with the supervising social worker's judgments of the home.[9] It may be that the better caretakers were given more difficult cases wherein failure might be more frequently predicted. The social worker's ability to predict responses on the part of the caretakers like themselves is in marked contrast to their abilities to predict

---

[9] Windle, Brown, and Dingman, *op. cit.*

attitudes of different cultural groups.[10, 11] In spite of social workers' professional training and perhaps because of their predominantly middle-class backgrounds, they may not be able to predict the attitudes of persons from other social strata. Exact relationship between attitudes and behavior is

TABLE 2. Comparison of Good and Poor Caretakers Regarding the Degree of Correspondence Between Caretaker Responses and Social Worker Responses

|  | | Caretaker Ratings | | |
| --- | --- | --- | --- | --- |
| Correlation between caretaker responses and social worker responses | | Poor | Good | Total |
| | $r \leqq +19$ | 17 | 6 | 23 |
| | $r > +20$ | 5 | 17 | 22 |
| | TOTAL | 22 | 23 | 45 |

$$\chi^2 = 11.79 \ P < .01$$

Comparison of Good and Poor Caretakers Regarding the Degree of Correspondence Between Caretaker Responses and Social Worker Predictions

|  | | Caretaker Ratings | | |
| --- | --- | --- | --- | --- |
| Correlation between caretaker responses and social worker predictions | | Poor | Good | Total |
| | $r \leqq +19$ | 14 | 3 | 17 |
| | $r > +20$ | 8 | 20 | 28 |
| | TOTAL | 22 | 23 | 45 |

$$\chi^2 = 12.24 \ P < .01$$

another consideration. If this is true, and there is some suggestion in the literature that psychiatrists and physicians have difficulty reaching patients who are quite dissimilar from themselves, then perhaps an essential part of social workers' training, as well as the training in other treatment professions, should be anthropological and sociological in nature so that they can understand their clients well enough to evaluate them more accurately.

In recent years, social workers' education has put more and more emphasis on cultural factors involved in giving a service. This paper indicates that this trend is very much needed.

## SUMMARY

This study investigated the predictions of child-rearing attitudes which were given by social workers who were supervising homes in which the State of California had placed mentally retarded patients. In these forty-five homes the accuracy of the prediction about child-rearing attitudes of family care mothers that were made by social workers seem to depend

---

[10] *Ibid.*
[11] Windle and Dingman, *op. cit.*

upon the congruence between the attitudes of the social worker himself and the attitudes of the family care mother. The implication of this finding is that social workers should receive training which would lead them to understand and deal better with the attitudes and motivations of people whose backgrounds are quite unlike their own.

# 23

❨ Foster parents are not a homogeneous group, nor are foster children. The foster parent who is successful with one kind of foster child may not do equally well with other kinds of foster children. The following report discusses the efforts to examine some of the specifications of the relationship between foster parent and foster child so as to permit greater understanding of what kinds of parents go with what kinds of children.

# Specializations Within the Foster Parent Role: A Research Report*

*David Fanshel*

## PART I. DIFFERENCES BETWEEN FOSTER PARENTS OF INFANTS AND FOSTER PARENTS OF OLDER CHILDREN

In 1956, two social work researchers were asked to review, for the Conference on Research in the Children's Field, the investigations that had been accomplished in the area of foster care of children.[1] After a diligent search, they came up with the finding that there were no recent studies of substance to be found in this field. This was a shocking state of affairs, considering the fact that almost 200,000 children in the United States

* The research reported here was conducted at the Family and Children s Service, Pittsburgh, Pa. under a generous grant from the Field Foundation.

[1] J. Meisels and M. Loeb, "Unanswered Questions About Foster Care," *Social Service Review*, Septmeber 1956, pp. 239–246.

lived in foster family homes supervised by public or voluntary casework agencies and that such care had emerged as the oft preferred form of rearing children who could not live in their own homes. Since that time, child welfare research has made some significant strides forward, but much more is needed.[2]

Without systematic research to test child welfare practice theory, crucial decisions are often made about foster children under conditions of great uncertainty, and sometimes on an almost trial and error basis. Many of these youngsters have already suffered serious trauma by virtue of being separated from their natural parents. Unfortunately, every "trial" that turns out to be an "error"—a placement that does not take—exacerbates an already unhappy situation. Herstein has pointed out that replacement of children is one of the major hazards of foster family care.[3] He calls it "one of the skeletons in the closet of child welfare practice." Herstein's concern is reinforced by data collected by Maas and Engler in their study of children in placement in nine cities.[4] Recent further analysis of their data reveals a close association between length of time in care and turnover in placement. This phenomenon correlates with evidence of considerable confusion in self-identity shown by children in foster care.[5]

The research discussed in this article represents the attempt of one agency, the Family and Children's Service, of Pittsburgh, Pennsylvania, to learn more about foster parents as key persons in the system of foster family care. The decision to take a careful look at the families who were caring for the agency's children was stimulated by the awareness of the casework staff that increasingly the youngsters coming into placement were showing serious emotional disturbance with which only a minority of foster parents seemed able to cope. However, before the special attributes of foster families who could care for emotionally disturbed boys and girls could be identified, there was a need to learn more about foster parents as a general class of people.

Before going on to some of the findings of this study, the reader will want to have in mind the basic sources of the data. They were: (1) structured interviews were conducted with the foster mothers and the foster fathers in the 101 families who constituted the agency's active roster of foster parents in 1957–58; (2) the foster mothers were asked to fill out the

---

[2] Recent significant research dealing with the foster care of children includes: H. S. Maas and R. E. Engler, *Children in Need of Parents,* Columbia University Press, 1959; E. Weinstein, the Self-image of the Foster Child, Russell Sage Foundation, 1960; and M. Wolins, "The Problem of Choice in Foster Home Finding," *Social Work,* October, 1959, pp. 40–48.

[3] N. Herstein, "The Replacement of Children in Foster Homes," *Child Welfare,* July 1957, pp. 21–25.

[4] Maas and Engler, *op. cit.*

[5] Findings being prepared for publication by H. S. Maas and the writer.

Parental Attitude Research Instrument (PARI)[6] developed at the National Institute of Mental Health; and (3) caseworkers who had supervised children in placement in the foster homes were asked to rate the foster parents on a variety of dimensions, including role performance, on an instrument prepared for this purpose, the Foster Parent Appraisal Form (FPAF). The methodological problems entailed in gathering reliable and valid data for this study have been previously discussed by the writer.[7]

### Role Satisfactions

In seeking to develop more basic understanding of foster parents, one might pose a direct question: "Why do individuals choose to take on the responsibility of substitute parental care of children?" It is well known that agencies across the country expend a great deal of effort in foster parent recruitment campaigns with very modest yields of individuals who are willing to take on this challenging role. Practice theory in the child welfare field is still hard-pressed to account for the motivations of the different kinds of people in the foster parent role. Attempting to get at this problem in empirical fashion, the writer developed a list of sixteen role satisfactions which were culled from the agency's records of foster parents. These were presented by interviewers to the subjects of this study who were asked to select the five motivations on the list that most applied to them.

A rather basic dichotomy appeared in the study between those foster parents who cared primarily for infants and those who cared for older children. While this finding will not be of any surprise to most child welfare practitioners, it is well to document the role behaviors that distinguish these two types of foster parents. These differences, if proven to be widespread, would have implications for practice theory about foster family care.

Table 1 sets forth the satisfactions selected by foster mothers of infants and by those caring for older foster children. (There were sixty-two sets of foster parents who had provided care for children whose median age was under one year, and thirty-nine couples who cared for somewhat older children, most of them over three years of age.) There was a significant overlap in the items selected by the two groups of foster parents.[8] Yet an examination of the table reveals some interesting variations in sources of role satisfactions for the two groups which are sufficiently pronounced to warrant further investigation.

---

[6] E. S. Schaefer and R. Q. Bell, "Development of a Parental Attitude Research Instrument," *Child Development*, 1958, pp. 339–361.

[7] D. Fanshel, "Studying the Role Performance of Foster Parents," *Social Work*, Jan. 1961, pp. 74–81.

[8] The correlation of .63 between the rank ordering for the two groups was significantly larger than zero at the .05 level of confidence (two-tailed).

### Private Versus Social Gratifications

To characterize in a general way the difference in satisfactions reported by the two types of foster mothers, one could refer to those caring for infants as being more oriented to *private* gratifications as opposed to the more *social* gratifications of other foster parents. For example, "enjoying a cuddly baby" was the item most frequently selected by the former group but ranked only seventh for the latter. By way of contrast, "knowing I am doing something useful for the community" emerges as the highest ranking satisfaction for those foster mothers who care for older youngsters, while it ranked only seventh for those caring for infants.

Similarly, "I like helping the unfortunate, downtrodden people" achieves a ranking of third for the foster mothers of the older youngsters as contrasted with a ranking of ninth for those specializing in infant care. This "benefactress of children" orientation of some foster parents has previously been shown by the writer to be related to a negative social outlook as measured by Srole's Anomie Scale and to seemingly pathogenic attitudes in child rearing as measured by the Parental Attitude Research Instrument (PARI).[9] It is interesting to find foster mothers caring for infants achieving a ranking of third for the item, "I like the affection I get from children," whereas this is ranked only ninth for those caring for older

TABLE 1. Reported Satisfactions in Being a Foster Mother*

|  | Infant Homes (N = 62) | | Non-Infant Homes (N = 39) | |
|---|---|---|---|---|
|  | Number | Rank | Number | Rank |
| Putting my religious beliefs into action | 29 | 4 | 21 | 4 |
| Enjoying the presence of a cuddly baby in our home | 40 | 1 | 15 | 7.5 |
| Knowing I am doing something useful for the community | 21 | 7 | 25 | 1 |
| Since this makes my spouse happy, it makes me satisfied | 11 | 12 | 15 | 7.5 |
| I like being able to add to the family income | 3 | 15 | 1 | 16 |
| Being a foster parent helps me to continue to feel young | 20 | 9 | 8 | 13 |
| It makes me feel like a *whole* woman | 4 | 14 | 7 | 14 |
| It keeps me from becoming nervous for want of something to keep me busy | 20 | 9 | 9 | 11.5 |
| Satisfies those strong motherly drives of mine | 22 | 6 | 10 | 10 |
| I like helping the unfortunate, down-trodden people | 20 | 9 | 22 | 3 |
| I like being able to meet the challenge of a difficult task | 17 | 11 | 18 | 5 |
| I like being able to put my skills as a homemaker into action | 6 | 13 | 9 | 11.5 |
| I like the affection I get from children | 30 | 3 | 13 | 9 |
| I am fascinated watching children grow up | 36 | 2 | 24 | 2 |
| I get satisfaction out of being associated with an organization such as F&CS | 23 | 5 | 16 | 6 |
| The respect of my neighbors is very gratifying | 1 | 16 | 3 | 15 |

* The foster mothers were asked to select the five items on the list that represented the most important sources of role satisfaction for them. The item which is marked *1* in the "Rank" column was selected most frequenlty by the foster mothers in the group, and the item marked *16* was selected least frequently.

---

[9] D. Fanshel, *op. cit.*, p. 76.

youngsters. Also, "it satisfies those strong motherly drives of mine" is ranked sixth for the former group and tenth for the latter. (It has been found by the writer that the unabashed expression of maternal feeling was positively correlated with superior performance ratings by caseworkers who had supervised children in the foster homes.)

Finally, one other interesting area of contrast between the reported satisfactions of the two groups of foster mothers is with respect to the item "I like being able to meet the challenge of a difficult task," which achieved a ranking of five with those caring for older children and only eleven for those caring for infants. The channelization of aggressive energies through foster parenthood may have some implication for role performance of these subjects with the children who are the target for these drives.

Lest the reader be tempted by these findings to rely solely upon verbalized motivations in the difficult task of screening foster parent applicants, it is well to refer to the admonition of Josselyn that articulated expressions of foster parent applicants can only be the starting point for exploration of deeper motivations.[10]

### The Foster Father's Role

In further support of the concept that foster mothers of infants are oriented to private gratifications is the finding that their husbands tend to share less in tasks related to the care of the foster child than do husbands of foster mothers caring for older children. There is a significant correlation between the age of the foster child and an Index of Sharing. The index is based upon the degree to which the foster father is involved in such tasks as bringing the foster child to the medical clinic, determining whether to board a child at the agency's request, taking care of the child's physical needs, and discussing problems with the caseworker. While it is true that in our culture even the natural father tends to be the "odd-man out" when it comes to infant care, it is nevertheless noteworthy that there are foster mothers who choose to freeze this condition through a steady flow of infant foster children in and out of their homes.

There is a significant negative correlation between the tendency of a home to provide care primarily for foster infants and the foster father's orientation to the agency's caseworkers. In contrast to foster fathers in homes accepting the placement of older children, these subjects tended to more often report that they found that they had very little to say to caseworkers, that they found caseworkers had more to do with their wives than themselves, and that it seemed to them that caseworkers tended to "talk in circles." This is additional evidence of their removal from significant role involvement.

---

[10] I. Josselyn, "Evaluating Motives of Foster Parents," *Child Welfare*, Feb. 1952, 3–8.

The question may arise for the reader as to whether the agency was placing children with the foster parents in accordance with the desires of the subjects. Inspection of our data would show that, by and large, the foster mothers were caring for children who were of an age they preferred. When asked what stage of childhood they had found most enjoyable, more than half of the foster mothers caring for infants reported infancy as the most enjoyable age and 92 percent reported either the infant or the toddler stage, or a combination of both. Only 31 percent of those caring for older foster children reported the infant or toddler stage, or both, as most enjoyable. It is also of interest that the latter group included a much higher proportion of foster mothers who expressed no age preference.

The picture of the foster mother of infants as being more oriented to narcissistic gratifications than her counterpart caring for older children is added to by other findings which show her to be generally more enthusiastic about the role. A higher proportion of these mothers expressed "strong delight" when asked what their reaction would be toward their own children's becoming foster parents some day. Again, when asked to name three things that had given them the greatest satisfaction in life, a significantly higher proportion of foster mothers of infants than of the older group included the foster parent role. Stronger role involvement is also shown by attendance at foster parent club meetings held at the agency; the proportion of infant-care mothers reporting regular attendance was twice that of the foster mothers caring for older children. (It may well be that attendance at foster parent meetings represented one of the few social outlets for those caring for babies. Their tendency to be homebound is reflected by the fact that 49 percent of the foster mothers caring for older children belonged to two or more outside organizations whereas this was true for only 22 percent of those caring for infants.)

### Attachment to the Child

There is also some evidence in the responses of the two types of foster mothers that those caring for infants were more likely to feel separation from the child as loss of an object of personal gratification than those caring for older children. In the former group, 37 percent reported that their reaction to separation from foster children was almost always "very painful." This reaction was reported by only 10 percent of those caring for the older group of children. The need of some foster parents for an almost perpetual symbiosis with an infant is a phenomenon not unfamiliar to many child welfare workers.

This reported greater attachment to infant as opposed to older foster children is perhaps explained by the fact that the infants go into placement without any substantial prior tie to other maternal figures. In a sense the foster mother of infants can indulge in the fantasy that the child is "all mine." Such possessiveness is more difficult with the older child who comes to placement with prior involvements and loyalties to other parent figures.

Comparing the responses of the two categories of subjects with respect to their perceptions of how other persons viewed their being foster parents, some significant differences became apparent. Almost three-fourths of the foster parents caring for infants reported that many people respected them because they were physically able to handle such a responsibility, whereas less than half of the second group reported this. This attitude is evidently not related to the age of the two types of foster mothers, since those caring for older children were not significantly older than those caring for infants. Almost a third of each group was over fifty years of age. That all reactions to foster parents of infants were not ego enhancing, however, is demonstrated by the fact that reports that many people did not seem able to understand why they should want to be foster parents came from 35 percent of this group and from only 15 percent of the other group. Also, 87 percent of the former reported that questions were frequently raised about their being able to stand separation from the foster child, while this was true of only a small percent of the latter.

## PART II. FOSTER PARENTS CARING FOR THE "ACTING OUT" AND THE HANDICAPPED CHILD

In the first part of this article, it was suggested that one plausible way of differentiating among foster parents was to distinguish those occupants of the role who devote themselves to the care of infants from those who were inclined to serve the somewhat older foster child, i.e., the child three years of age and older.[1] Some differences in social adaptation and role orientation of these two groups of foster parents were set forth, and it was hypothesized that foster parents of infants were motivated by rather personal kinds of role satisfactions as opposed to the more social gratifications of the foster parents of older children.

### The Care of "Acting Out" Children

As has been previously pointed out, a challenging task for most child welfare agencies in recent years has been that of recruiting foster homes that can be developed for the care of the apparently increasing number of emotionally disturbed children now coming into placement. Kline has discussed the considerable thought that must be invested in the selection of the foster parents who can tolerate bizarre and unusual behavior in children who, in their young lives, have been buffeted about from

---

[1] Part I, "Differences between Foster Parents of Infants and Foster Parents of Older Children," *Child Welfare*, March 1961.

one home to another.[2] In this connection, it is of interest to examine the manner in which the caseworkers in this study perceived the suitability of foster homes for various kinds of children with special problems who require care outside of their own homes. These perceptions were recorded on the special rating instrument prepared for this project, the Foster Parent Appraisal Form (FPAF).[3]

The caseworkers in this study were asked to rate foster parents known to them in many areas considered important for successful role performance, e.g., methods of discipline, reactions to various types of children, family interaction. The question arose as to what might be the relationship of one variable to another in the rating form. To determine this, some forty variables of the FPAF were intercorrelated and these correlations were submitted to a statistical procedure called factor analysis. This procedure enables an investigator to determine the manner in which ratings tend to cluster together. Thus, it was found that the forty variables on which the foster parents were rated could actually be condensed to six key aspects of their role performance. One of these factors centered about the general ability of foster parents to care for the "acting out" child. Table 1 sets forth the loadings of the variables which were linked together in this factor.[4]

TABLE 1. **Factor Describing Foster Parents' Ability to Provide Care for "Acting Out" Children**

| Variable | Loading |
|---|---|
| 1. Foster family is described as being suited for an aggressive youngster who is reportedly fresh to grown-ups | .53 |
| 2. Foster family is described as being suited for an adolescent girl who is sexually precocious | .52 |
| 3. Foster parent is described as being responsive to child nine to twelve years of age | .45 |
| 4. Foster family is described as being suited for a youngster who shows bizarre behavior | .41 |

Thus, within the same cluster of ratings were those variables referring to the ability of foster parents to provide care for the "fresh" youngster, the sexually precocious adolescent girl, the child who shows bizarre behavior and the older child, aged nine to twelve years.

### A Portrait of Highly Rated Families

Scores were assigned to the 101 families who were included in the study based upon the ratings assigned them on the four variables making

---

[2] Draza Kline, "Understanding and Evaluating a Foster Family's Capacity to Meet the Needs of an Individual Child," *Social Service Review*, June 1960, pp. 23–35.

[3] Discussed in Part I of this article. (*Child Welfare*, March, 1961.)

[4] The "loading" of a variable on a factor constitutes the correlation between the variable and the factor. The higher the loading, the more the variable helps to define the general meaning of the factor.

up the "care for acting out children" factor. A portrait was thus developed of families who scored high in their capacity to absorb this kind of a youngster.[5]

It was found that those subjects who, according to the caseworkers' ratings, seemed able to provide a high level of care for "acting out" children were apt to have had ample experience with children of their own. These subjects also received ratings from the caseworker which indicated, in a general way, what might be referred to as good ego functioning in the parent role. That is, according to the caseworkers who knew them, they demonstrated appropriate warmth, showed understanding of children's emotional needs, had little need to exploit children for neurotic purposes, etc.[6] These families were also seen as being more democratic in their family relationships ($r = .39$) and scored high on a factor measuring their identification with the foster parent role ($r = .25$).

The foster parents who achieved high ratings with respect to their capacity to care for "acting out" youngsters also appeared to be more deeply integrated within their communities than those who achieved low scores. They were more apt to be intimately acquainted with key community figures, to know their immediate neighbors well and to actively socialize with them. The correlation with a Neighborliness Scale developed by an anthropologist on the research team was .30.[7] Upon reflection, it makes sense to assume that if a family is going to accept for placement a foster child who has a propensity for aggressive "acting out" behavior, the members will need to enjoy secure relationships with those in close physical proximity to them in their communities who are apt to become targets of the child's negativistic behavior.

The role of the foster father appears to loom particularly large when caseworkers consider plans for the aggressive foster child. It was found that the foster fathers in high scoring families had relatively little deprivation in their childhood backgrounds compared with fathers in those families deemed not suitable for such children. That is, they were less apt to have suffered the death of a parent or other forms of parental deprivation as youngsters, the economic status of their families tended to be adequate, and they were more apt to report that their parents had been affectionate to them and appeared happily married.

At the same time, the foster mothers in this group were apt to view their husbands in a more positive way, as revealed by their responses on

---

[5] Summated scores were weighted according to the loading of each variable on the factor.

[6] The correlation between the "ability to care for 'acting out' children" factor score and a factor measuring parental ego strength was .52. For this size group a correlation ($r$) of .22 would be considered significant at the .05 level of probability.

[7] Otto von Mering, "The Neighboring Patterns of Foster Parents," presented at the National Conference of Social Welfare, Atlantic City, New Jersey on June 7, 1960.

the PARI scale, Inconsiderateness of the Husband.[8] These women were also apt to avoid harsh attitudes in their child-rearing, as indicated in their responses on the PARI scale, Strictness.

All in all, one is impressed with the fact that the casework staff appears to have identified what might be considered a premium group of foster parents. Being a fairly stable group with little deprivation in their backgrounds and having solid ego structures, they emerge as those foster parents best able to undertake the most arduous kinds of placements.

### The Care of Children with Biological Handicaps

Another cluster of caseworker ratings of foster parents that emerged in this study was one related to the capacity of foster families to absorb physically handicapped or mentally retarded children. The loadings of variables on this factor are shown in Table 2.

TABLE 2. Factor Describing Foster Parents' Ability to Provide Care for Children with Biological Handicaps

| Variable | Loading |
|---|---|
| 1. Foster home is described as being suited for a mentally retarded child | .82 |
| 2. Foster home is described as being suited for a child with severe physical handicap | .76 |
| 3. Foster home is described as being suited for an infant suffering from colic | .55 |
| 4. Foster home is described as being suited for a youngster who shows bizarre behavior | .36 |
| 5. Foster mother is described as *not* being motivated in assuming the role of foster parent by the factor of feeling less feminine with the absence of children | (−) .35* |

* The original sign of the variable in the factor table is indicated in parentheses when the meaning of a variable has been reversed. The negative sign (−) in front of the loading in this instance refers to the absence of a particular condition when the other variables are said to be in operation.

It is of interest to find that the caseworkers' ratings tend to link together the abilities of foster parents to provide care for three kinds of youngsters coming into placement: the physically handicapped child, the mentally retarded youngster and the child who is emotionally disturbed (i.e., shows bizarre behavior). When one also includes the infant suffering from colic, it becomes apparent that the element that links these children together is their essential *dependency*. The inability of these children to fend for themselves—often because of constitutional limitations—in many situations with which normal children can cope, may be the ingredient that appeals to some foster parents. This concept of being oriented toward dependency needs is reinforced by the finding of a sig-

---

[8] Parental Attitude Research Instrument, developed at the National Institute of Mental Health. This was another basic source of data in the study.

nificant correlation of .45 between the factor score based on ability to care for handicapped children and a factor score relating to the usability of the foster home for babies. Furthermore, there is a significant negative correlation between the factor score on ability to care for handicapped children and the median age of the foster children who have been placed in a home, thus indicating that the caseworkers' ratings are supported by *actual* patterns of placement in these foster homes.

The caseworkers' ratings revealed one major psychological variable that was associated with the ability to provide care for the handicapped child: the foster mother's motivation in taking on the role was not related to her need to compensate for feeling less feminine without children around her. Obviously, a foster mother with a vulnerable ego structure might well find the burden of a mentally retarded or physically handicapped child too difficult to carry. The child's disabling attributes might easily loom as a threat for a person whose own self-image is already weak, and who fears that the social stigma suffered by the child will be passed on to herself as the parent figure.

As with those described as being able to provide care for the "acting out" youngster, the foster parents whom caseworkers rated as having the capacity to care for the handicapped child tended to have had the experience of caring for a number of their own children before becoming foster parents. It is interesting to note that foster parents who had not had children of their own showed a tendency to avoid foster children who made unusual demands with respect to their physical care, or because of their behavioral difficulties.

Deserving special attention, however, is the finding that, unlike the foster parents for the "acting out" group, these foster parents were not rated by caseworkers as having high levels of ego-functioning as parents, nor a democratic orientation in their family relationships. This is to say that they were not rated as being patricularly warm or devoid of neurotic qualities, other than in the area of successful resolution of their feminine identifications. These ratings by the caseworkers were validated to some extent by significant positive correlations between the factor scores re handicapped children and scores achieved by the foster mothers on two PARI scales, Deification of the Mother and Suppression of Aggression, which measure authoritarian tendencies in the mother.

The benevolent authoritarianism of the foster mothers in these cases was often associated with ratings of the foster father as suitable for a child in need of a *strong* father figure. It would appear that the ability to care for the physically disabled or retarded child, or the child with bizarre behavior patterns, is often associated in the caseworker's mind with a certain kind of exterior toughness on the part of *both* the foster mother and the foster father. Evidently the care of these children is seen as a task that requires "doing" kinds of people who can take over to some extent, rather than people who are more democratically oriented and who thus tend to "take over" less. Whether this orientation of the caseworkers in this project, as revealed by their ratings, is a sound one is open to question. Warmth and the ability to accurately perceive the needs of the child may be needed more by the handicapped child than by the youngster who is not so afflicted.

It should also be noted that the ratings of the caseworkers regarding the ability of the foster parents to provide care for these children are significantly correlated with self-estimates made by the foster parents. The correlation between the rating score and a scale based upon direct interviews with the foster mothers, Capacity to Cope with Problems of Foster Children, was significant. The scale consisted of seven questions about various kinds of problems of foster children, and the foster mother was asked to indicate whether she felt the problem was of an *easier* kind, *harder*, or of a kind she absolutely could not accept. Thus, it would appear that there is some measure of agreement between these role partners in the placement agency (i.e., caseworkers and foster parents) regarding the allocation of children to the foster homes. The subjects appeared to be getting the kind of children they desired.

### A Sociological Characterization

By way of a sociological characterization of these foster parents, it was found that foster parents who were deemed suitable for handicapped children came from what might be described as clan-type families. That is, their families were large, closely knit, and tended to meet together often for large family occasions—weddings, funerals, etc. Whether the clan-type family provides its members with added social supports, which thus enables them to take on child-rearing tasks which the smaller family units would find more difficult to assume, is a matter for conjecture. It is also possible that the clannish family is one that places value on *all* family members to the extent that the presence of a handicap would not tend to be a factor which would exclude the individual. This value orientation may play a part in the willingness of such individuals to take in handicapped foster children.

In this connection, it was of interest to find that foster parents coming from clan-type families showed greater difficulty in separating from foster children than did those who come from smaller, less extended family systems. The writer had originally hypothesized that the opposite would be the case: that those coming from large family systems would better tolerate the loss of a child because of the lessened sense of intimacy that characterizes large social units. However, upon reflection, the finding seems quite plausible when one realizes that a major dynamic of clannish families is the fact that they need to vigorously hold on to every member, even distant cousins!

One incidental finding about the sociological characteristics of foster parents who in direct interviewing indicated an unwillingness to take care of foster children with handicaps, is of interest. Foster parents who came from rural backgrounds showed a noticeable reluctance to care for the handicapped child. It has been suggested to the writer that perhaps this attitude relates to the economic necessity of farmers to destroy farm animals who are born with physical anomalies, and that perhaps this has helped create a general psychological set against all disabilities of living creatures.

One final element in the portrait of families considered suitable for the disabled child concerns their adaptation to the foster parent role. These families were rated by caseworkers as more strongly identified with the role than those caring for the more normal child. This finding is based upon a number of items in which the foster mother was asked the length of time she intended to continue in the role, the conditions under which she would find it necessary to abandon it, and the centrality of the role within her total life-space.

## The Areas of Specialization

The data reported in both parts of this paper suggest meaningful dimensions along which foster parents can be categorized. These dimensions relate to the characteristics of foster children for whom foster parents appear best suited. A basic division of labor exists between those who can provide care for infants and those who can take older foster children into their homes. While these are not necessarily mutually exclusive categories—some foster parents can provide care for children of diverse ages—the tendency, nevertheless, appears strong for sub-specializations to take place within the role based upon the age variable.

The other dimensions that are suggested by our data indicate two other areas of specialization: care of "acting out" youngsters and care of biologically handicapped children. Foster parents capable of caring for the former are also those who are most often regarded by caseworkers as being able to provide care for the so-called normal *older* foster child. On the other hand, the care of the biologically handicapped child is perceived by caseworkers to be more often the kind of task that is most satisfactorily undertaken by foster parents who care for babies. It has been conjectured that they are essentially attracted to the more pronounced dependency of the very young or of the disabled foster child. Here too, we find that these are not mutually exclusive categories.

Some families are probably so strong in their sense of solidarity and in the ego strength of the individual members that almost any child could be placed with them. These are the small core of almost "professional" foster families that have become visible to agencies. The reasons for their versatility should become the object of further research.

## Discussion

In the research reported here and in other studies of parent behavior, it has become clear that parenthood cannot be studied in isolation from childhood. On the face of it this seems like such a commonplace statement as to be almost banal. Yet, parents and foster parents are very often assessed as if their characteristics can be separated from those of the child under their care. Many of the foster parents in this study showed quite a broad range of behaviors with the foster children placed with them. One kind of child could evoke a positive, nurturing kind of response while a child with different characteristics could bring forth almost rejecting behavior from the very same foster parents. While we would expect that foster parents who have solid ego structures and sound super-ego values would do uniformly well with most children placed with them, their parental capacity must nonetheless be seen as a varying phenomenon.

The aim of high-level casework practice should be to maximize the parental potential through (1) the placement of children who can evoke the most positive response and (2) the provision of supportive help by caseworkers to foster parents to help them withstand the negative and often seemingly unchangeable behavior of upset foster children. The factor analysis reported here appears to point to clusters of traits of foster parents who can care for several types of foster children (i.e., the biologically handicapped child, the "acting out" child, etc.). These findings should be tested further to determine whether they will replicate in other settings.

# 24

❪ What factors are related to the child's need for a foster home? The following study attempts to delineate the economic, social, and psychological factors related to foster-care placement. The data were obtained by intensive interviews with families whose children were referred for foster care.

# Preplacement Situations of Families: Data for Planning Services

*Mignon Sauber*

Concern about the need for a broad spectrum of community services geared toward helping families stay together in their own homes is not new, yet little organized knowledge has been accumulated about the preplacement experiences of families from which children come into care—families who are the potential users of preventive services. The study I am about to report was designed and implemented in an effort to collate systematically information about family situations *prior* to foster care, information that would provide a factual framework for planning the needed community services.

This study, in which we interviewed New York City families whose children had come into social agency foster care for the first time, was conducted under the joint sponsorship of the Community Council of Greater New York and the New York City Department of Welfare, with the aid of a grant from the Children's Bureau. The principal investigator for this study and the senior author of its final report[1] was Dr. Shirley Jenkins; I was the project director and co-author of the final report.

## GOAL OF THE STUDY

The goal of the study was to obtain information that would provide a basis for understanding better the circumstances of children entering placement and those of their families, in particular those children and families for whom care in a social agency foster boarding home or institution was an entirely new experience. The assumption was that a more comprehensive, detailed, and focused picture of this population—new to

---

[1] Shirley Jenkins and Mignon Sauber, *Paths to Child Placement: Family Situations Prior to Foster Care* (New York: Community Council of Greater New York, 1966).

foster care—would be a useful base for planning and developing a range of community health and welfare services that would decrease the need for placement and provide adequate protection for children whenever possible.

## CASE ILLUSTRATIONS

Before reporting in detail the method and findings of our study, I would like to cite excerpts from a few of the stories we heard. I hope they will provide a reminder of the human beings behind the statistics I will be reporting later on. These were some of the replies to the opening question in our interview: "Tell me in your own words what happened that brought about the decision to place —————— in foster care."

One of our respondents, a Puerto Rican woman who was separated from her husband eight months prior to her illness, described the crisis that led to child placement as follows:

> I felt very tired and sick, and I went to a hospital in my neighborhood where they told me I need to be hospitalized immediately since I had hepatitis. I told them I had no one to take care of my children and the doctor took me to Social Service. Social Service called 250 Church Street and the children were placed. I have no friends here in New York and the only one to take care of my children was my mother-in-law and she was in Puerto Rico.

Another case involving the placement of a 12-year-old illustrates a mother's interim attempts to deal with an emotionally upset boy. This mother told her preplacement story as follows:

> I was about to have a nervous breakdown. I had to work all day. Then at night three or four times a week I would get a call from my sister in the Bronx where he was staying telling me that he had run away from home. I would have to get up in the middle of the night and help find him. Nobody could manage him. I tried letting him live with his godmother over a year ago. He would steal from her and run away. Then I boarded him outside, but that lady could only take it for a month. Then he went back to his godmother and she kept him for four more months. Then my sister had him for four more months, then he went to the Children's Center.

The problem of the desertion and abandonment of children can also be illustrated from our interview material. In one case in which it was impossible for us to locate the children's own mother, our respondent, who described herself as a "professional babysitter," told the following story:

> The child was left here by her mother and a man, I don't know if he was the father or not. She was supposed to return to get the child in three days

but she didn't come back. After I had kept the child for a couple of months, I asked a friend who deals with Welfare what to do. She said I would have to take it to the police station. I did and had to sit there a couple of hours until someone came from Welfare to pick up the baby.

One final illustration: this time the neglected child. The paternal grandmother who was our respondent in this case reported as follows:

The mother was going out a lot to beer gardens, leaving the children alone most of the time, neglecting them. She would stay out all night. My son then brought the children over here to me and he went to file a complaint of neglect in the Court. The Court then investigated the house, they found the place filthy and just terrible and then decided it wasn't livable for the children.

These case illustrations may appear weighted or biased, for they involve an emergency, a crisis, or a badly deteriorated family situation. The need for placement in these cases came to agency attention when it appeared to be too late for alternative planning. But these cases were selected deliberately, for if we have learned any one thing from our study it is the inapplicability, in many, many cases, of the notion that placement is necessarily the plan of choice—that it is preceded by a careful assessment of the child's needs and of the family's potential for meeting these needs. But I am getting ahead of my story. Let me briefly outline the method of our study and mention some of the principal findings. This will help place the information about the crisis nature of many placements in its complete context.

## METHOD

The primary method of the study was extensive, direct interviews with the parents or other persons who were responsible for the care of the child before he entered foster care. Utilizing the intake records of the Bureau of Child Welfare of the New York City Department of Welfare (which represent more than 90 percent of all children entering care in New York City), the case selection process was designed to identify for interview all families involved in a first social agency child placement experience between May 1 and August 31, 1963. During that four-month period a total of 1853 children from 1048 families came into care at public charge. Of these, 1069 children from 512 families were experiencing initial placement within the definitions of the study. Families in which the only child placed was an infant under 6 months of age were excluded from the initial placement group, since these infants had not had a one-year familial experience in their own homes prior to placement. Also excluded were families that had had at least one child in foster care previously, and unwed mothers entering maternity shelters.

Of the 512 cases thus classified as initial placements, 425 families with 891 children were subsequently located and interviewed in the field. The primary reason for not interviewing the other 59 families in this group was that the child-caring person could not be located (59 families). Only 17 families refused to participate in the study, while the family court advised against interviewing 11 families.

The study definition of "initial placement" yielded a study group that accounted for 49 percent of all families and 58 percent of all children entering foster care during the four-month period. This initial placement group included relatively more younger children, a slightly larger proportion of minority-group children, relatively larger sibling groups entering care, and a slightly larger proportion of two-parent households than was characteristic of the group as a whole.

Our interviews sought to elicit information about the child's family and home situation during the year prior to placement. The aim was to look at the preplacement experiences and the placement crisis through the eyes of natural parents or parent figures. They were our respondents, and they are the adults who normally would be the primary recipients of preventive services.

These interviews, which were conducted by a staff of professionally educated social workers and social scientists, were held at what had been the child's home as soon after separation as possible in order to obtain responses while the placement experience was still fresh in the parents' minds.

The opening question in the interview asked the respondent to tell in his own words exactly what happened that brought about the decision to place the child, and after a general exploration of the events leading to placement the interviewer explored, retrospectively, occurrences during the preplacement year. Information was obtained on living arrangements of family, housing and neighborhood, sources of financial support, health status of all family members, school experiences, out-of-school activities, and other child care arrangements. In each area, the questioning began with the situation a year prior to placement, traced changes occurring during the year, and determined what, if anything, families did in relation to these changes. Each area of questioning explored in detail the situation at the critical point of placement.

## FINDINGS

### General Characteristics

The typical family interviewed was as likely to be a one-parent family as a two-parent household; just over two-fifths of the cases were in each group. In about one case in seven the children were living with relatives, with unrelated persons, or in other living arrangements. Ethnically, 24 percent of the group were white families, 44 percent were Negro families, and 32 percent were Puerto Rican families.

At least one family in eight contained seven or more persons. A similar proportion of families reported that one or more of the siblings was not living at home one year prior to placement; they were most often reported as living with relatives.

These general characteristics of the group are significant for planning services. As already noted, for example, the standards deriving from our cultural norm of two-parent families cannot be applied to the families requiring foster care: in 41 percent of the families studied the mother was the only parent in the home even a year prior to placement, and the father was the only parent at home in 3 percent of the families. In only 32 percent of the families were both natural parents in the home at the beginning of the preplacement year, and another 10 percent of the couples included one stepparent. In the remaining families children lived with other relatives or non-relatives; neither natural parent was in the home.

These facts are certainly relevant to planning services to help prevent the need for placement. For example, homemaker service as provided by an agency that requires the presence of a responsible adult in the home while the mother is away would not be available as a resource for most of the families in our study.

The study revealed other evidence of the relative lack of stability of these families. More than half—55 percent—experienced a change in the composition of the household during the preplacement year. As a result of many of these changes an even larger proportion of families consisted of only one parent at the time of placement. Of the 137 families with both natural parents in the home a year prior to placement, the mother left in 34 cases and the father left in 42 cases during the preplacement year. Although these breakups occurred throughout the year, the mother's departure brought on placement shortly thereafter, whereas household changes involving the father tended to have a delayed effect.

### Income

The marginal level of income at which many of these families lived is indicated by the fact that during the year prior to placement almost half—49 percent—derived at least some income from public assistance, and nearly half of these recipients had received such aid for at least two years by the time placement occurred. At the same time, however, public assistance was the main source of income at the time of placement for only 38 percent, indicating there are a group of these families—perhaps 10 percent—who move on and off the assistance rolls.

Earnings from the employment of either the mother, the father, or both provided some income during the year for 58 percent of the families; at the time of placement such earnings were the main income of 34 percent of all families. The latter group was probably unknown to the public department when the placement crises occurred. Further evidence of the marginal level of living was the inadequate housing, often at rents that were high in relation to income. Crowded, deteriorated dwellings were often the locale of our interviews. Nearly half of the families—45 percent —moved at least once in the year prior to placement; included were 8 percent who moved at least twice. At the beginning of the year as many as one family in every six lived in rooms—not in an apartment or other complete living quarters—and many of these rooms were totally inadequate for the rearing of children. Changes in housing during the year did not improve the situation, and frequently worsened it.

### Health

During the year before placement the greatest changes occurred in the health area. Although health problems of one or more members of the family existed a year before placement in 55 percent of the cases, this proportion had grown to 71 percent at the time of placement. Acute illness of an adult affected 20 percent of the families at the time the children were placed, nearly a sevenfold increase over the 3 percent with an adult acutely ill a year previously. Twice as many families included a mentally ill adult at placement than 12 months earlier—14 percent as compared with 7 percent. Furthermore, hospitalization of adults for physical or mental illness during the preplacement year occurred in over half of the families studied. These data clearly indicate the importance of health as a factor in the need for foster care of children and may suggest channels for reaching families earlier with needed services.

### Other Characteristics

There were changes in other areas, as well, during the preplacement year. Relatively more children lived and slept away from their own homes at the time of placement than the year before—14 percent as compared with 6 percent of the families reporting such arrangements. But there were no substantial changes in daytime arrangements for children. The majority were cared for in their own homes. Community facilities and resources were not used extensively. Only one in every three families with school-age children reported using community-sponsored recreation facilities. Perhaps most important is that only 5 of the 425 families reported using community-sponsored day care centers during that year. Given the limited number of openings in these centers, it is not clear whether this finding reflects limited resources or a lack of matching between the needs of these families and the kinds of services available to them.

Single-child placements occurred in less than half the cases. Sibling groups of two or more children came into placement from these families in 54 percent of the cases, and in 8 percent the sibling group placed consisted of at least five children. Nearly half of the placed children were of school age.

This overall picture of the year prior to placement shows marginal families. without sufficient resources to sustain themselves in the community when additional pressures or problems were added to preexisting burdens.

### Major Problem Areas

Although it has been possible to make certain broad generalizations about the economic, social, and psychological deprivations of these families, the interviews also revealed a clustering, or grouping, of cases with respect to the major problem areas relating to placement. Further analysis of the interview data confirmed the need for this differentiation in that, with respect to many variables, there were marked differences from one subgroup to another. The five groups and the proportion of all families in each are as follows:

- Children required placement primarily because of physical illness, incapacity, or confinement of the child-caring person—29 percent
- Children required placement mainly because of the mental illness of the mother—11 percent.
- Child placed because of the child's own emotional or personality problems—17 percent.
- Children placed primarily because of serious abuse or severe neglect—10 percent.
- Placements resulting from a constellation of other family problems, including parental incompetence, conflicts in the home, unwillingness or inability to continue care, and desertion and the leaving of children unattended—33 percent.

The study revealed not only that there were these differences in the main reason for placement, but also that there were different contributing factors, as well as differences in the individual characteristics, among the families who made up these five groups.

Families for whom physical incapacity, confinement, or mental illness of the child-caring person was the primary factor associated with placement had as contributing factors the inability or unwillingness of other family members to provide care for the children. On the other hand, conflicts in the family and in the household, unwillingness or inability to continue care, as well as parental incompetence and other family problems were frequently associated as contributing factors to the placement of children who required care because of their own emotional or personality problems. The major contributing factors in cases involving the placement of children for severe neglect or abuse were parental incompetence, desertion, household conflicts and other family problems, and the child's own personality and behavior.

The families whose children were placed because of physical incapacity —including confinement—of the child-caring person tended to have the largest sibling groups enter care, and to be the poorest and most economically dependent. Public assistance was the main income source for 71 percent of the confinement cases at the time of placement. There were relatively more Negro and Puerto Rican families, and relatively more households headed by mothers, with no fathers in the home in this group of cases of physical illness and confinement.

Among families in which child placement was associated with mental illness of the mother, severe environmental pressures were also often noted. This group tended to have somewhat larger and younger families than some of the others, with over a third of them placing only preschool children.

In many respects the families with children placed because of the child's own emotional or personality problems differed from other family groups studied: these were all single-child placements; a larger percentage were white; relatively more of the families were intact and self-supporting; only 20 percent relied primarily on public assistance at the time of placement. As a group, these families placing disturbed children showed greater evidence of the utilization of professional services (including social work) prior to the decision to place the child.

A contrasting picture was evident for families with children who were placed because of serious neglect or severe abuse. These families did not seek placement. They tended either to avoid or to come into conflict with the authorities, or with those professionals whose intervention brought the children into care. This was the group with the second largest proportion of single-child placements and the second largest proportion of two-parent households and self-supporting families. It included the largest proportion of children who had experienced hospitalization during the preplacement year.

In addition to identifying these different characteristics of the families in the five major placement groups, the study yielded information in two other areas relevant to planning services—length of care and voluntary nature of placement.

### Length of Care

Although an investigation of the length of stay in foster care was not a primary subject of this study, information was obtained on the foster care status of the 891 children three months after placement: 16 percent had been discharged to their homes or to other private care within a week. A total of 31 percent of the children were in social agency foster care less than a month. Two-fifths of the children were still in care three months after placement.

Length of care was closely associated with the main reason for placement. For example, 54 percent of the children placed because of the mother's confinement were home within one week, and no child placed for this reason remained in care as much as three months. Placements resulting from the mother's illness were also relatively brief, lasting less than one month for 37 percent of the children and as much as three months for only 23 percent. Even in the neglected, abused group, 17 percent of the children left care within a week. In contrast, only 3 percent of the children placed because of their own personality or emotional problems were back home within a week, and 77 percent were still in care three months after placement.

The very substantial number of temporary placements among all children entering care for the first time indicates the need for planning services that differentiate between the needs of children who require short- or long-term care. These data also suggest that many children might have stayed out of care altogether if suitable alternative short-term services had been available to them in their own homes.

### Voluntary Nature of Placements

One final area explored by the study and especially relevant to the study's findings about the crisis aspects of many placements is what we have called the "voluntary nature of placement." The usual concept of placement is that it is a carefully worked out process, typically involving parental initiative and agreement to placement as the preferred plan for the child. Our study showed clearly that this was often not the case. In our interviews respondents were asked whose idea it was that the child be placed and whether or not they agreed with the placement plan. Of the 425 families studied, 245 (58 percent) said that they fully agreed to the placement. In contrast, the respondents in 16 percent of the cases said the parents did not know the child was being placed, and in 8 percent the parents had knowledge of the plan for placement but placement was carried out against the parents' wishes. For 18 percent of the cases there was not sufficient information on this point to classify the case. Strongest opposition to placement was found in the mental-illness, neglect-and-abuse, and family-problems groups.

An analysis of responses to the above question ("Whose idea was it that the child be placed?") revealed that, except for children placed for their own emotional or personality problems, the police were most often mentioned as the originator of the plan to place the child. From 15 percent to 25 percent of families said the initiative for placing the child came from the police. In less than one family in four was a social worker involved in *initiating* placement planning. Overall, only about half of the families said they had spoken to any social agency or social worker about their problems during the preplacement year, and those who did said they had talked with a hospital social worker or a public assistance worker only.

## CONCLUDING COMMENTS

Despite these gloomy figures, which call upon us to act in improving services for children in their own homes, the study also indicated that, for many children, there were no alternatives to placement. The interviewers were asked to judge, on the basis of their interview and the home setting in which it was conducted, whether or not placement could have been avoided had appropriate community services been available. In the judgment of the interviewers, only 17 percent of all families studied could have kept their children at home even with needed services. This was their judgment for just over a fourth of the group who had children placed due to the physical illness or confinement of the mother, but for only 7 percent of the group with children placed for their own emotional problems. In the other three groups the interviewer's judgment as to the avoidability of placement was that the children might have been maintained at home in only 14 percent to 16 percent of the cases.

The challenge, then, is to develop and implement services specifically geared to meet the needs of those families and children for whom the continuance of the child in his own home *is* possible and feasible. It is hoped that our study has added to our understanding of this group and their needs so that the required actions can be undertaken and the needed services provided in the quantity and quality indicated by our respondents —the potential consumers of these services.

To this task of implementation the Community Council addressed itself when our study was published last spring. Seldom does a researcher have the opportunity of seeing his data applied in this specific manner. This effort undertaken by the Community Council not only provides this high compliment to a researcher, but in my view argues strongly for the appropriateness of a community-planning agency as a locale for research aimed at improving services to people.

# 25

⟨ What factors are related to how long a child is likely to remain in a foster home? The following article is a companion piece to the research by Sauber. It follows some of the same families and, using the data previously obtained, determines what factors are associated with prolonged stay in foster care.

# Duration of Foster Care: Some Relevant Antecedent Variables

*Shirley Jenkins*

Statistics on foster care do not commonly reflect either the duration of care or the factors associated with length of stay, since they tend to be organized in categories that are primarily based on administrative, fiscal, and budgeting considerations rather than on what happens to individual children. Thus "all children in care on any one day" (the most typical prevalence figure) indicates the number of beds in use but has nothing to say about the characteristics of the children using them. Data on intake and discharge rarely take account of the time spent in placement or the extent of reentry, so that turnover figures frequently refer to a changing population base within a budgetary year. To aid in policy planning and allocation of funds, new approaches to data reporting are needed that better reflect the careers in placement of individual children and the antecedent variables relevant to the length of their stay.

## SOURCE OF THE DATA

A two-year followup study of 891 New York City children who entered foster care in 1963 provides data on duration of care and also identifies some variables related to length of care. This population of children was originally studied in a research project cosponsored by the Community Council of Greater New York and the New York City Department of Welfare.[1] That study[2] was concerned with experiences of families in the

---

[1] The New York City Department of Welfare is known as the Department of Social Services, as of July 1, 1967.

[2] See Shirley Jenkins and Mignon Sauber, *Paths to Child Placement* (New York: Community Council of Greater New York, 1966).

year preceding placement. The sample consisted of 891 children from 425 families, and made up the Welfare Department's intake of children for initial placement from May through August of that year. These children had not previously been in foster care themselves and had no siblings who had formerly been in care. Families placing only one child who was under 6 months of age were excluded on the grounds that they represented primarily out-of-wedlock births rather than family breakdowns resulting in foster care. Children in the sample reported on in *Paths to Child Placement* entered care under the supervision of either the family court or the Department of Welfare. By the time data collection had been completed on that study the last child to enter care could have been in care for a maximum of three months, and therefore data analysis included information on the duration of care for time periods of under one week after placement, and one week to under three months.

TABLE 1. Discharge from Foster Care of Initial Placements[a] over a Two-Year Period

| | | Number Discharged | | Percent of Discharge | |
| Time in Care | Number in Care | By Time Period | Cumulative | By Time Period | Cumulative |
|---|---|---|---|---|---|
| At placement | 891 | — | — | — | — |
| One week later | 732 | 159 | 159 | 18 | 18 |
| One month later | 590 | 142 | 301 | 16 | 34 |
| Three months later | 413 | 177 | 478 | 20 | 54 |
| Six months later | 354 | 59 | 537 | 7 | 61 |
| One year later | 290 | 64 | 601 | 7 | 68 |
| Two years later | 227 | 63 | 664 | 7 | 75 |

[a] Excluding infants under six months

In June 1965 the Columbia University Child Welfare Research Program requested access to data, including punched IBM cards, on these 891 cases in developing sampling procedures for another study supported by the Children's Bureau.[3] These data were made available by the Research Department of the Community Council, which cooperated fully in the followup study.[4] The New York City Department of Welfare, which had been a cosponsor of the earlier research, provided further cooperation by making available discharge dates for the 413 children of the original 891 who had still been in care three months after placement. Thus data became available on the duration of care from three months after placement

---

[3] The Child Welfare Research Program is at the Center for Research and Demonstration of the Columbia University School of Social Work.

[4] The data-collection procedures were facilitated by the participation of two second-year students at the School, Geraldine Urbach and Ruth Hellebrand, recipients of stipends from the National Institute of Mental Health. They worked over the summer of 1965 on data collection and prepared tables for the present study under the supervision of the author.

to two years after placement. Since substantial information on the characteristics of these children and their families was already available as a result of the detailed field interviews, the followup study provided an opportunity to reexamine variables associated with placement in terms of the new information concerning the length of time spent in foster care. All analysis of data, however, refers to the original population described in the Community Council study. The followup procedures illustrate the methodological point that supplementary analysis of available data in terms of information collected after completion of the original study may have utility for problems related to a study design but not originally defined in it.

## TRENDS OF DISCHARGE

Table 1 presents the distribution of the number and percent of children still in care at successive time periods. The complementary data on discharge of the children indicate the process of attrition, and the general trend can be clearly seen on the basis of cumulative figures over the time period.

These data show that, of all initial placements (excluding infants)[5] approximately half are short term, or under three months, and half are long term, three months or more. Only 25 percent of all placements in the sample stay in care for two years or more. The decrease of discharge over a period of time for children in the sample is apparent when one compares the percentage leaving care over successive periods. Approximately the same percentage of children leave care during the first week of placement as leave care during the next three weeks, and again during the next two months. For children who remain in care three months or more, approximately the same percentage leave care in the next three months, during the subsequent six months, and again in the final year. The hard core of placement cases—the remaining 25 percent—may well be children who grow to their majority in social agency care.

The trends are illustrated graphically in the figure, which charts attrition first from the base 891 (all children entering care, excluding infants) and then from the base 413 (children in care three months or more). The sharply declining curve A, which shows the drop in children in care in the early weeks, differs from the more flattened and gradual curve B. This indicates that once children have been in care over three months, chances for early return are substantially lessened.

---

[5] The effect of the exclusion of infants cannot be estimated, but since the two factors affecting time in care of infants tend to work in opposition, they might negate each other. These are (1) adoption, which means rapid exit from care, and (2) non-adoption, often involving either lack of surrender, unfitness for adoption, or absence of adoptive homes. For this group, care may mean a lifetime in placement.

## CHARACTERISTICS ASSOCIATED WITH DURATION

There are many categories typically used to classify children in care and their families. Among these are such characteristics as ethnic groups, jurisdiction of case, main source of support, housing circumstances, household composition, and casework judgments on the main reason for placement. The present analysis is designed to determine which, if any, of the selected characteristics that can be determined by agencies at the time of entry may be associated with length of time in foster care. Each of the variables considered will be analyzed in terms of its relationship to time in care: the first group comprises cases in care for under three months, the second group comprises cases in care three months to under two years, and the third group comprises cases still in care after two years.

Ten variables will be analyzed in terms of length of time in care. For four of these—jurisdiction of case, ethnic group, religion, and age—data are available for each individual child in the sample (N = 891). These variables will thus be based on "child data." The other six variables refer primarily to family characteristics. These include household composition, number of children placed per family, parental participation in the

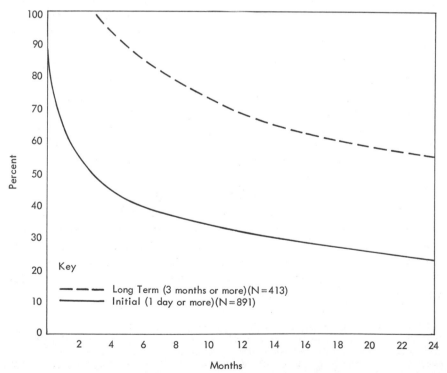

Percent of initial placement and percent of long-term placements in care up to two years after date of entry.

decision, main source of income, type of housing, and main reason for placement. For these variables, "family data" (N = 425) will be the basis of analysis. For each variable, whether child or family, the three periods of care to be compared are: (1) under three months, (2) three months to under two years, and (3) two years or more. Percentage distributions among these periods of care are shown in the tables, but tests of statistical significance have been made on actual numbers in each category by use of chi-square.

### Child Data

The relationships between length of time in care, and characteristics of jurisdiction, religion, ethnic group, and age at placement are shown in Table 2.

TABLE 2. Percent of Children by Length of Time in Care Versus Jurisdiction, Religion, Ethnic Group, and Age at Placement

| Child Variables | Total (N = 891) | Under Three Months (N = 478) | Three Months to Under Two Years (N = 186) | Two Years and Over (N = 227) | |
|---|---|---|---|---|---|
| Jurisdiction | | | | | |
| Court | 19 | 15 | 26 | 22 | $\chi^2 = 12.2$[a] |
| Welfare | 81 | 85 | 74 | 78 | df = 2 |
| Religion | | | | | |
| Catholic | 50 | 51 | 56 | 43 | |
| Protestant | 45 | 48 | 37 | 46 | $\chi^2 = 44.1$[a] |
| Jewish | 6 | 1 | 7 | 11 | df = 4 |
| Ethnic group | | | | | |
| White | 18 | 13 | 25 | 24 | |
| Negro | 47 | 52 | 37 | 43 | $\chi^2 = 25.38$[a] |
| Puerto Rican | 35 | 35 | 38 | 33 | df = 4 |
| Age at placement | | | | | |
| Under six years | 53 | 58 | 51 | 44 | |
| Six years to under twelve | 35 | 34 | 29 | 42 | $\chi^2 = 28.1$[a] |
| Twelve years or over | 12 | 8 | 20 | 14 | df = 4 |

[a] Significant at .01 level

Approximately four times as many children in the sample entered under the supervision of the Bureau of Child Welfare as entered under that of the court. In terms of length of placement, representation of Welfare cases was relatively highest (85 percent) in the short-term "under three months" group, and court cases were relatively highest (26 percent) in the group in care from three months to under two years. With regard to religious affiliation, there was a significant difference in distribution according to time in care. The Jewish children, who represented only 1 percent of the "under three months" group, were 7 percent of the "three months to under two years" group, and 11 percent of all children in care for two years or more. Catholic children represented the highest percentage of the short-term placements (51 percent), and Protestant children were highest among the long-term placements (46 percent).

There were marked differences in the distribution of children by ethnic composition and time in care. The percentage of Negro children in care dropped from 52 percent for the category of children in care under three months to 43 percent for the category of those in care for over two years. The percentage of each group who were Puerto Rican remained the same, whereas the percentage of each category who were white rose from 13 percent to 24 percent.

Relative frequency according to age changed for each of the categories in the sample, from short- to long-term placement. The number of children from 6 months to under 6 years lessened proportionately, dropping from 59 percent to 44 percent of the total. On the other hand the oldest group, 12 years and older, were 8 percent of the short-term group, 19 percent of those in care from three months to two years, and 14 percent of those in care two years or more. Also significant were the changes for the "middle-aged" child, from 6 to 12 years. This group rose from 34 percent in the short-term group to 42 percent in care over two years.

### Family Data

Six variables are analyzed in terms of family data (N-425). Five of these —household composition, number of children placed, parental participation in decision, main source of income, and type of housing—are shown in Table 3. Data on the sixth variable, reason for placement, are presented separately.

For the family variables, the major differences between categories appear to be related to short-term (under three months) as against long-term (three months or more) periods of care. Once a family has a child in care over three months, few variables show important differences between the two longer-term groups (under or over two years in care). Thus one-parent families constitute 51 percent of the short-term placements, but only 36 and 39 percent of the two long-term groups (under and over two years). A comparable shift is seen in the number of children placed, with 59 percent of the short-term category composed of families placing two or more children. For the long-term categories, however, this percentage dropped to 50 percent and 47 percent. The main change in regard to parental participation in the decision to place was for those parents who had no knowledge of placement. This group made up 22 percent of the short-term placements, but only 10 percent and 9 percent respectively of those in care for over three months and over two years.

With regard to income, the main shift among the length-of-care categories was in the relative frequency of families supported by public assist-

TABLE 3. Percent of Families by Length of Time of Children in Care Versus Household Composition, Number of Children Placed, Parental Participation in Decision, Main Source of Income, and Type of Housing

| Family Variables | Total (N = 425) | Under Three Months (N = 214) | Three Months to Under Two Years (N = 87) | Two Years and Over (N = 124) | $\chi^2$ |
|---|---|---|---|---|---|
| **Household Composition** | | | | | |
| Two parents | 42 | 38 | 49 | 43 | $\chi^2 = 8.8$[c] |
| One parent | 44 | 51 | 36 | 39 | df = 4 |
| No parent | 14 | 11 | 15 | 18 | |
| **Number of Children Placed** | | | | | |
| One | 46 | 41 | 50 | 53 | $\chi^2 = 5.1$[c] |
| Two or more | 54 | 59 | 50 | 47 | df = 2 |
| **Parental Participation in Decision** | | | | | |
| Agreed | 58 | 57 | 56 | 62 | |
| No knowldege | 16 | 22 | 10 | 9 | $\chi^2 = 17.9$[b] |
| Oppose | 8 | 6 | 13 | 9 | df = 6 |
| Not ascertainable | 18 | 15 | 21 | 20 | |
| **Main Source of Income** | | | | | |
| Earnings | 34 | 28 | 44 | 37 | $\chi^2 = 9.6$[a] |
| Public assistance | 38 | 44 | 32 | 33 | df = 4 |
| Other: benefits, help | 28 | 28 | 24 | 30 | |
| **Type of Housing** | | | | | |
| Apartment or private house | 78 | 75 | 80 | 81 | $\chi^2 = 12.2$[a] |
| Rooms | 16 | 21 | 13 | 10 | df = 4 |
| Other, not ascertainable | 6 | 4 | 7 | 9 | |

[a] Significant at .05 level.
[b] Significant at .01 level.
[c] Not significant.

ance. Public assistance families constituted 44 percent of the short-term placements, but after three months they were only 32 percent of the total, and after two years 33 percent. Finally, with respect to the type of housing, 21 percent of the families in short-term placements were living in rooms. This dropped to 13 percent for the families with children in care over three months, and 10 percent for those in care over two years.

For the five family variables, there appears to be a common pattern. The combination of characteristics representing typical social problems, such as one parent in the home, dependence on public assistance, and living in rooms tend to be most prominent in the short-term placement group. They persist, but to a proportionately smaller extent, for families with children in long-term care. Thus the urgent environmental pressures bring more children into care, but do not necessarily mean they will remain in care. Situations that result in long-term care may well reflect other variables.

## REASON FOR PLACEMENT

Among hundreds of variables measured in the study of these 891 children from 425 families, the main reason the child entered care appeared to be the most salient factor in terms of grouping of problems and characteristics.[6]

In Table 4, the main reason for placement (based on casework judgment) is presented in terms of the three categories of length of care.

TABLE 4. **Percent of Families by Length of Time of Children in Care Versus Reason for Placement**

| Reason for placement | Total (N = 425) | Under Three Months (N = 214) | Three Months to Under Two Years (N = 87) | Two Years and Over (N = 124) | $\chi^2$ |
|---|---|---|---|---|---|
| Physical illness of mother[a] | 29 | 46 | 18 | 7 | $\chi^2 = 80.4$[b] |
| Mental illness of mother[a] | 11 | 11 | 12 | 10 | df = 8 |
| Child's problems | 17 | 6 | 18 | 35 | |
| Neglect, abuse | 10 | 10 | 12 | 10 | |
| Family problems | 33 | 27 | 40 | 38 | |

[a] Mother or child-caring person
[b] Significant at .01 level.

Three relationships emerge from these data. One reason for placement, physical illness of the mother, is associated with short duration of foster care for the child. These families constitute 46 percent of those with children in care for under three months, but only 7 percent of those with children in care for two years or more. In two categories, those in which children were placed because of their own emotional or personality problems and because of overwhelming family problems such as conflict between parents, incompetence, alcoholism, drugs, or desertion, the families constitute a higher percentage of the long-term than the short-term group. Families with emotionally disturbed children, for example, were only 6 percent of the families with children in care under three months, but made up 35 percent of those in care for two years or more. The third kind of relationship shown in Table 4 includes categories of placement that appear to be unrelated to the time spent in care. These are mental illness of the mother and severe neglect and abuse of the child. Families with

---

[6] See *Paths to Child Placement,* Chapter 4, for the rationale for grouping reasons for placement into the five categories noted.

children placed for these two reasons consistently averaged from 10 percent to 12 percent of all families with children in care in all of the three successive time periods.

## SUMMARY AND CONCLUSIONS

The trend figures on discharge from foster care show that approximately half of all initial placements (excluding infants) left care within three months after placement, and 75 percent left care by two years after entry. A challenge to data-collection-information systems would be the problem of determining variables that could be known on entry, and that would identify children likely to remain in long-term care.

Factors associated with circumstances of living, such as being housed in rooms and being supported by public assistance, tend to be related to a shorter time in care. Demographic variables, age at placement, religion, and ethnic group appear to be interrelated and together can serve as indicators of duration of care. Reason for placement is particularly relevant, and a careful analysis of the situation that brought a child into care may help in making a reasonable estimate of how long he may stay. Although these results cannot be generalized to make predictions about every child in care, the planning process can be improved to the extent that we are more knowledgeable about variables likely to be related to duration.

# 26

⟨[ The concept of role has frequently been usefully applied in social work. The following article is an empirical study of the way foster parents defined their relationship with foster children, and it indicates some differences in the way foster parents and natural parents perceive their respective roles.

# Role Phenomena and Foster Care
# for Disturbed Children

*Walter Ambinder, Laura Fireman, Douglas Sargent, and David Wineman*

Psychiatric treatment for disturbed children originally came in two distinct packages: for severely disturbed children there was the closed residential unit patterned after the psychiatric ward of the adult state hospital. Children less seriously impaired were treated in community outpatient clinics.

Despite the early recognition that the treatment needs of children do not fit easily into this dichotomy of services, many treatment facilities developed over the past thirty years tend to follow the original division. While the need for other units to augment the work of the psychiatric units is accepted (foster homes and halfway houses, for example), with notable exceptions, the "real treatment" is often thought possible only in those facilities whose modes of operation derive from the hospital or clinic.

Many disturbed children live such disorganized lives that outpatient treatment alone will not help them. Yet they are not sick enough, or do not have the right *kind* of illness, to gain admission to psychiatric hospitals. Many of these children are referred to juvenile courts. For want of more appropriate facilities, courts place them in foster homes.

The average foster home is not designed to withstand the impact of impulsive, aggressive children. The same is true of the foster parents who must live with them. After wearing out several placements and a few sets of foster parents, these children gravitate into institutional care as a last resort rather than as a treatment choice.

The need for a wider range of treatment facilities is clear. At the Clinic for Child Study of the Wayne County Juvenile Court we have outlined a pilot project which attempts to explore one way to meet this need by trying to answer these questions:

1. Can we identify aspects of the residential treatment center's therapeutic milieu which, with modification, we can build into a foster home program?

248

2. Can foster parents' attitudes be altered, if necessary, their morale hardened and their uncertainties shored up, so that they can operate in a therapeutic role with some disturbed children?
3. Can foster parents be trained in some techniques that would enable them to function as semiprofessional members of a therapeutic team?

We hope that answers to these questions will lead to the development of treatment facilities for some of the children who fall into the "gray zone" between outpatient and inpatient care, and who, as a result, now get neither.

As background to the pilot project we interviewed 50 foster parents who had cared for "hard-to-place" court wards.[1] Interviews ranged wide over the field of foster parent experience, lasted 1½ hours, and were supplemented by a detailed questionnaire. This enabled us to identify many areas in which these foster parents functioned with anxiety, including some where they were hardly able to function at all.

Two sources of impaired functioning appeared to account for much of the difficulty: confusion or lack of clarity about role; and paucity of knowledge about, and techniques for coping with, normal and disturbed child behavior.

Most foster parents interviewed were vague about the respective roles they, the caseworker, and the agency were to play in the lives of the children under their care. Even more ambiguous was the role the foster child was to play in all of this.

In addition to this lack of role clarity, the foster parents often showed a surprising ignorance about what constitutes normal child behavior. They lacked any conceptual scaffolding (such as causality, for instance), upon which they could erect explanations for the behavior they observed. For coping with normally aggressive behavior they had only a few rigid, pragmatic techniques. Really disturbed behavior left them helpless or forced them to resort to primitive, even brutal methods of control.

This paper will focus on the part role phenomena play in the difficulties encountered in the foster care of disturbed children. Other facets of this work will be reported in a later publication.

## PROBLEMS INVOLVING ROLE PHENOMENA

For clarity, we will first define some terms:

*Role*: the part an individual is called upon to play in a specific social context, in this case, the foster home.

*Role perception*: the performer's image of his own role or that of another participant; e.g., "I am the father."

---

[1] The children fall mainly into the loose diagnostic category "primary behavior disorder."

*Role expectation:* the behavior expected of the performer; e.g., "As the father, I will be the boss."

*Role reciprocity:* the interdependence between roles in the system, functionally linking one to another—father implies child, social worker implies client, etc.

*Role performance:* the enactment of a role; e.g., father does or does not give good advice to an expectant son.

As in other social systems, so too in the foster home, each participant may play several parts. Roles exist in order to gratify *needs* inherent in the social system, and derive their color, shading and intensity from each actor's perception of the system's needs. The ability to discern the needs in a social system is a function of the interplay between each actor's own intrapsychic needs and the extrapsychic forces impinging on him. If role dynamics do not meet the functional demands of the social system, tension leading to breakdown of the system may be anticipated.

## THE DATA

Content analysis of the material obtained from the foster parents yielded these prominent categories of role phenomena: (1) foster parents' perception of own role; (2) foster parents' perception of casework role; (3) role performance of caseworker, as seen by foster parent.

*Foster Parent's Perception of Own Role.* Approximately 25 per cent of the sample explicitly stated their role to be that of a *natural parent surrogate.* This was the most clear-cut category. For example, "Caring for these children would be like bringing up my own." "She thought that these children would be like her own."

We believe this perception to be predominantly extrapsychic in origin, imposed on foster parents by general cultural imagery, by the "type casting" of foster-home finders who look for people who appear to be "motherly or fatherly," and by their own most common role experience with children.

On technical and utilitarian grounds, however, and with an eye to the effect this role perception may have on disturbed foster children, we question the desirability of this image. We know that this role perception implies that the foster child will reciprocate at some level of child-parent interaction. Since many of these children are incapable of responding in the manner expected, the natural parent role is incompatible with the task we believe a foster parent should be expected to perform with them. When these children fail to gratify the foster parents' expectations of reciprocal love and gratitude, the parents may react with hostility.

About 30 per cent of the sample saw themselves as *task-oriented specialists,* selecting a highly specific facet of the natural parent function to epitomize their role. For example:

*Educator:* My husband thought that when he took the boys in he would be able to teach them how to build things, as he is a retired cabinetmaker; and it has worked out this way. We have a workbench and he has been able to teach some boys some things.

*Champion against hostile outsiders:* I have had several bouts with the school because I felt they were abusing and mishandling one of the children in my care. . . . I stood up for their rights.

*Provider of tender, loving care:* You've got to let the children know that you are their friend, and you've got to prove it to them.

The rest of the sample either gave a scattering of replies that could not be categorized or they were quite unable even to attempt a definition of the foster parent role. However, a question on motivation for foster parent work produced replies bearing on role perception. About 40 per cent of the respondents indicated that, as foster parents, *they expected to receive emotional gratification or emotional support.* For example:

She worked in order to allay what she called an "empty feeling." However, in spite of her work she felt lonesome. After reading an article in *McCall's* she called the court and a 15-year-old boy was placed with the family.

Frequently this kind of reply was coupled with overt or subtle indications that when the anticipated emotional gratification did not materialize, the placement broke down. For example, "Boys have to respect me, and as soon as I lose control over them I ship them right out."

Twenty-three per cent became foster parents in pursuit of a *stated value goal.* For instance:

We thought we could help a wayward child. Our own children are good citizens.

I wanted to help children. I felt there was good I could do to help kids in the juvenile detention home.

Some replies to this question suggested that the decision to take in foster children came about accidentally. However, the material hinted that often there were strong unconscious determinants to the "accidents."

Mrs. B said she had been a foster mother for three years. Her own mother is in a state hospital, and one day while visiting her mother she missed the bus home. She got a ride with someone who was a foster mother, who suggested to her that she might like this herself. She called the court and was taken on right away.

This foster parent seemed to have been acting in identification with the lost, motherless foster children whom she cared for.

To summarize the foster parents' perceptions of their own roles, we can say that they derive from a culturally determined image of natural parent surrogate; that they are colored, frequently, by the foster parents' need to receive emotional gratification, either from the children or from acting in conformity with their own value goals; and that the perceptions sometimes are intensified by highly personal, unconscious motives.

*Foster Parents' Perceptions of Casework Role.* Approximately 50 per cent of the sample saw the caseworker as an *ongoing contact person, supervising and helping with problems of the child: a conventional view.*

> The caseworker should come and see how the child is getting along, to find out what more needs to be done and whether or not his needs are being taken care of.

> Workers have a right to tell us what they expect of us. They have a right to come in and see that the children are being fairly treated.

Although we call this a conventional view, we note an emphasis on critical supervisory functioning. Less clear is the view of the caseworker as a helpful assistant to the foster parent, a view that would be more in line with the worker's self-image.

About 25 per cent of the sample elaborated a *highly specific and limited role for the caseworker.* Of these, 12 per cent defined this role as that of a *pastor or good uncle.*

> The caseworker is like a pastor; to speak to people, explain things to me and the children, to take care of things that aren't my place to take care of.

The other 13 per cent perceived the caseworker to be simply a homefinder.

> The caseworker's job is to investigate and find out if we are the right people; also they should bring the children to the home.

An additional 10 per cent saw the caseworker as an *emergency repairman,* available only for trouble calls.

> She felt that the caseworker should just be around if she gets into trouble and can't handle it herself. She said that was the only time she would think of asking for help.

Almost 10 per cent of the sample expressed *frank confusion about the casework role.*

> I didn't know what the caseworker's job was. When things went wrong I didn't call the worker, because *if those children were mine* I would work things out myself. I wouldn't have any worker to go to and I wouldn't want one. I accepted them as my own. If a child knows you are always talking to a worker then he doesn't trust you. They feel you are tattling on them all the time.

Despite the 50 per cent "conventional view" of the caseworker this sampling of role perceptions reveals a continuation of the ambiguous perceptions the foster parents had of their own roles. As long as perceptions and expectations remain in this state we can anticipate that role reciprocity between foster parent, worker and foster child will be subject to periodic disruption.

These data suggest that many foster parents wish to exclude the caseworker from significant involvement in the life of the foster home. We suggest that this is a further manifestation of the foster parent's acting as a real parent surrogate, or seeing the relationship to the foster child as though it were an adoptive relationship, jealously guarding the prerogatives of this role from outside intervention. Other interview material indicates that some foster parents feel competitive with the natural parents of their foster children and try to prove superior to them as child rearers. While this attitude may result in some material benefits to the children, on the whole this attitude has little to recommend it as a basis for rehabilitative work. When the children are aware of this competition for their loyalty, it becomes difficult for them to discuss their feelings about their own parents or the foster parents or workers.

Added to this is the implied threat to the foster parents' continuing emotional gratification offered by a caseworker who is seen as infringing on the foster parent-foster child relationship. The worker who is helpful to the child may take away from the foster parent some of the credit for success.

Further, the foster parent who is identified with the lonely, motherless foster child may experience rejection when the caseworker seems to ignore the parent by focusing attention on the child.

Even the emphasis of the "conventional" 50 per cent on the surveillance aspect of the casework role suggests an anxious anticipation of criticism which may reflect the fear that if foster parents do not "measure up" to the caseworker's standards the child will be removed.

To summarize the foster parents' perceptions of the casework role: The worker is most frequently seen as a helpful supervisor with overtones of criticism. Others view the worker as a child-centered competitor who must be fenced out for fear that some of the gratifications of being a foster parent will diminish significantly if the worker is allowed to come too close.

Many aspects of these role perceptions do not accord with the range of behaviors the professional caseworker attributes to himself or to the agency. Such role distortions resemble transference phenomena, having more relevance to the case history of the foster parent than to the caseworker's self-image. They exist, nevertheless, and their presence may seriously hamper the goal of foster care for disturbed children. The clarification of these role-perceptual distortions will offer an important challenge to an experimental foster home program.

*Role Performance of Caseworker as Seen by Foster Parents.* This material suggests that the hazy perception of the casework role results, in part, from the kind of casework coverage foster parents receive.

Twenty-five per cent of the sample complained of *inadequate preplacement preparation*, in that they were not given sufficient information about the foster child before he arrived.

> They put a child in the home and he has a big problem but they don't tell you about it—they could at least explain his worst problem like stealing or running away. They don't tell you he has a mother, or his mother's address.

About the same number (25 per cent) complained of *inadequate casework coverage* once the foster child was placed.

> The social worker should come to the home more frequently, not merely phone. On the phone we tend to say everything is fine. If she would come to the house, however, we could talk about some of the problems.

> The caseworker should visit the home at least every two weeks. Sometimes we have a problem and don't want to bother them, feel guilty about calling them. However, if they come around they would be able to help you.

Roughly 12 per cent of the sample showed *dissatisfaction with specific casework procedures.*

> He [foster child] called the worker that I was overprotecting him. The worker came to see him and talked to him in the car. I thought it wasn't right—the worker didn't even come in to tell us what she and the boy talked about.

> The worker shouldn't talk to kids unless they talk in front of the foster parents. He told us of one instance where the child complained to the worker, saying he wanted to walk his girl friend home. The worker said he could do this in spite of the foster parents' objections.

Twelve percent of the responses in this category expressed *positive attitudes toward casework performance.*

> I look to the worker to handle problems that come up that I can't understand. He makes me feel free to call him at home too. He has been very helpful. He used to drop by after five at first to see how things were going and help us.

There were, in addition, scattered unclassifiable responses having to do with minor complaints about particular workers or agency policies.

Interestingly enough, most of the complaints about casework role performance came from those foster parents whose perception of the casework role *was not the conventional image,* but from those who seemed to want to limit contacts between the child and the worker. ("Conventional viewers" = 50 per cent of sample; complaining "conventional viewers" = 30 per cent of sample.)

While accepting the importance of fulfilling the unmet service needs explicitly stated in these complaints, we suggest that these same complaints imply that foster parents wish for a deeper, more personal engagement with the caseworker. It is possible to interpret the complaint about inadequate preplacement preparation as a rationalized plea to be *given* something by the caseworker.

## COMMENT

Having identified certain role disturbances that impeded foster home care for "hard-to-place" children, is it possible to remedy them?

Or, must we conclude that "givens" in the situation—aggressive children with disturbed relationship capacities, foster parents with personal needs that are incompatible with goals of foster care, etc.—so mitigate against success as to make foster care for these children a virtual impossibility?

We believe that we should not accept these difficulties as prohibitive without first trying to see if they can be overcome. Not all disturbed children fail in foster care; and the need for alternatives to institutional care for these children is great. It does not appear reasonable to assume that sufficient institutional facilities will be developed within the foreseeable future to meet the treatment needs of these children.

In the competition for admission to hospitals and residential treatment centers they tend to be shunted aside in favor of other children with more classically neurotic or psychotic disorders. And because they are so damaged by the time they arrive, the reformatory types of institution to which they eventually are relegated seem to be able to do little for them.

From the material presented here we can draw several strong inferences about what needs to be done about role issues if a foster care program for these children is to have a chance of succeeding. We know, of course, that simply redefining roles will not do the whole job.

A clear role image must be constructed for all participants in the foster home system. This means that the foster parent must have his role redefined in a manner consistent with the rehabilitative goal of his task. At present we believe that the foster parent falls back on role perceptions derived from a mixture of cultural imagery and inner needs, because a more explicit and functional role has never been defined for him.

A first step, then, would consist of delineating a set of behaviors consonant with the developmental and remedial needs of the foster children, and functionally derived from realistic treatment goals. These behaviors must then be distributed between the foster parent and the caseworker in a manner that leaves no doubt about where the responsibility for various functions lies. The foster parent also must be helped to see the limits and purpose of his and the caseworker's roles in the remedial task.

Next, and we believe even more important, the caseworker must be prepared to give specific and intensive support to the foster parent who performs in the redefined role. At each step in the treatment process, the caseworker must be available to the parent for consultation, advice and active intervention where these activities are pertinent.

Finally, we suggest that there is a need for someone to attempt to *define the role the foster child should play* in the system. Foster care programs run on the assumption that everyone understands the child's role. We doubt that this is true.

We see the role problems outlined in this paper as merely symptomatic of a general need for experimentation in restructuring the concept of foster care for children. The problem has other dimensions.

The following appear to be areas offering possibilities for research experimentation:

1. The application to foster home care of techniques borrowed from the milieu treatment concept: (a) methods for coping with ongoing behavior; (b) methods for verbal handling of symptomatic behavior; (c) exploitation of life incidents for therapeutic ends.
2. Intensified casework coverage to dovetail with recommendations included in item 1; this implies that caseworkers will be "on call" to help with incidents arising in foster homes, school, and community.
3. Utilization of group discussion settings as a vehicle for communicating educational material to foster parents, and as a technique for dealing with ongoing problems foster parents encounter.
4. Experimentation in the application of planned group work services as an integral part of the program for children in foster care.

## SUMMARY

We have presented material from interviews with 50 foster parents who care for "hard-to-place" juvenile court wards. From these data we have selected for discussion disturbances in role phenomena, described how they interfere with the task of foster care, ascribed causes for these role distortions and suggested ways of correcting role problems.

In addition we have related role problems to the general issue of foster care and its implications for casework practice, pointing up areas for experimental research.

# 27

◖ The following research study reports the techniques actually used by foster parents in handling parent-child relationship problems. There may be a greater discrepancy between preferred and actual techniques than we had imagined.

## Foster Parents' Techniques of Management of Preadolescent Boys' Deviant Behavior

*Walter J. Ambinder and Douglas A. Sargent*

The Detroit Foster Homes Project was established to demonstrate the utility of specialized foster family care for emotionally disturbed boys, to develop techniques for training foster parents in caring for such children, to train foster parents in the use of these techniques, and to refine methods for selection of foster parents for this task. The boys who are the subjects of the study form a distinct group of children who occupy a "gray zone" between those children who can "make it" in the usual foster home and those who are so disturbed as to require institution care.

Children selected for the project are wards of the juvenile court. They must have failed in at least two foster homes, be significantly emotionally disturbed (but not overtly psychotic), be not less than 8 nor more than 12 years of age, and be able to attend public school.

The project provides extremely close casework and supervision for the children and foster parents, groupwork services for the children and foster parents, readily available consultation when crises arise, intensive work with the public schools that the children attend, and remedial tutoring when it is required. An attempt was made to select foster parents who have the potential for learning to understand basic dynamics of child behavior and for being helped to utilize this understanding in living with disturbed boys. This understanding should be augmented by techniques of child handling, which the parents could be taught to employ, that enable the child's unacceptable behavior to be controlled without the child or the parent being damaged in the process ("hygienic handling").

Besides the obvious goal of helping foster parents survive, the utilization of adequate management techniques provides an opportunity for strengthening the ego controls of the children. The psychologically hygienic handling of disturbed behavior may promote increased self-knowledge and self-control in the child. Certainly any technique of behavior control used by foster parents should not contribute to the child's insecurity nor make it more difficult for him to relate to the foster parents.

## SURVEY OF TECHNIQUES USED

In order to determine the extent to which special instruction in control techniques was likely to be necessary in the preparation of foster parents, it was important to determine what "homegrown" techniques were employed by experienced foster parents who had no special training in child care, what attitudes seemed to underlie these techniques, and how modifiable these already existing techniques and attitudes might be. Therefore, a survey was conducted.

Fifty foster parents, representing 31 foster families caring for adolescent boys, were interviewed regarding their experiences in the foster care program of a large public agency. The interviews covered many areas, and foster parents were encouraged to discuss all phases of the child care program. Whenever foster parents mentioned a specific example of unacceptable behavior, they were asked how they handled it. This enabled us to learn about their control techniques as they operated in their homes, rather than about reactions to hypothetical situations.[1]

From the 50 parents, we heard about 207 incidents of problem behavior in sufficient detail and clarity to be categorized according to the control techniques used by the foster parents. These incidents were sorted and evaluated by two psychologists and two social workers into three general categories: (1) techniques that seemed unlikely to enhance ego control or stimulate mature development and that were probably harmful (73 percent), (2) techniques that appeared to be likely to facilitate ego controls without trauma (16 percent), and (3) techniques that did not appear to be definitely helpful or harmful (11 percent). Each incident was categorized independently by the raters and then consensus was obtained at a meeting of all raters.

It should be noted that, in the first category, 40 percent of all the in-

---

[1] We recognize that the incidents reported were probably the most provocative and difficult to deal with, but it is through just such critical situations that we have the greatest opportunity to effect change in these children. As Caplan notes: "It is important to realize that during the period of upset of a crisis a person is more susceptible to being influenced by others than at times of relative psychologic equilibrium. This leads some workers to see periods of crisis as a specific opportunity for mental health intervention, in which such members of the community-helping professions as health, education, welfare, and religion may influence large numbers of children and their families to add significantly to their repertoire of reality-based problem-solving techniques and thus improve their crisis-coping capacity for the future." Gerald Caplan, ed., *Prevention of Mental Disorders in Children* (New York: Basic Books, 1961), p. 13.

cidents reported comprised: threats or actions to remove children from the home (15 percent), physical punishment (14 percent), and ridicule (11 percent). Thus, the vast majority of incidents were judged to be positively harmful to the child, and another 33 percent probably did no good.

## REASONS FOR METHODS

The most frequently used control technique was the threat to remove the child from the home. Over half of the foster families reported using this technique at one time or another. Removal of a child from the home should be a measure that is taken only after considerable study, and it certainly should never be used at a threat. In discussing their wards, foster parents indicated, however, that this technique was used more than any other. The significance to the child of this kind of total rejection is apparently not recognized by foster parents. This statement can probably be made for the majority of the techniques used.

Even though, at times, the foster parents knew that their methods were ineffectual and even harmful to the foster children, they attempted to justify their punitive handling by citing its effectiveness with their own children or by stating that they had experienced such punishment themselves ("When I was a child I was whipped and it didn't hurt me any"). They could not understand why the same techniques did not work with these foster children, and they seemed to conclude that they were not being forceful enough or that they simply needed more time to have an effect.[2]

Despite the obvious ineffectuality of these control techniques, foster parents seemed to avoid submitting these measures to logical appraisal. Rather, they continued to employ them in a blindly perservering fashion. One of the greatest barriers to changing foster parents' control techniques is their reluctance to relinquish the unconscious, sadistic gratification that punishment gives and the outlet it affords for the discharge of aggression aroused in them by the foster child's misbehavior. Another, of course, is the apparent absence of effective alternatives.

---

[2] It appears that many of the parents conceived of discipline as synonomous with punishment—an undimensional control technique ranging from sadistic beating to mild scolding. Some of the foster parents felt a kind of moral obligation to punish their charges in order to reform them, and the more offensive the misbehavior, the more severe the punishment. In many cases this moral justification served as a rationalization for acting out underlying sadistic impulses to hurt these troublesome children. Perhaps the moral obligation to punish stems from foster parents' conception of their role as quasi-parents of normal children. If they can be brought to see themselves as quasi-therapists of children with special needs, then they may be relieved of this "moral obligation" to punish or reform these children. The more we relieve foster parents of unreasonably high expectations and goals, the more we can help them handle the inevitable frustration and pain associated with "failure," and the more we can reduce the load of aggression, hostility, and guilt that often obscures their judgment.

Some of the foster parents were vaguely aware that severely deprived, neglected, and "emotionally disturbed" children do not react to discipline in the manner their own children did. They were, however, unable to act on this knowledge by modifying their disciplinary methods, perhaps because there was no genuine, only intellectual, understanding. Also, even with some realization of the ineffectiveness of their control techniques, they had no tools in their repertoire with which to cope with difficult behavior. For the most part, the techniques used by foster parents were not "hygienic." There was an unimaginative, dolorous repetition of measures that were ineffectual at best and damaging at worst.

It might be argued that we have focused on a minor aspect of child rearing by talking about disciplinary techniques; that the overpowering consideration is the "love in the home," or the "atmosphere," or the foster parents' "feeling for the child." Although we readily conceded the importance of atmosphere, it is day-to-day events that make it up, and the child can experience the foster parents' feeling for him only through their overt behavior toward him. And even when a foster parent's motivation is beyond reproach, his disciplinary technique itself may cause additional problems that did not heretofore exist.

## TRAINING IN CONTROL

To be sure, there are some few foster parents who have an intuitive grasp of a youngster's needs and the meaning of his behavior and who can turn a potentially unhappy disciplinary event into a real learning experience. Only 16 percent of all techniques used by this group of foster parents, however, seemed to fall into this category.

If foster family care is to be as effective a method as it might, our findings suggest that much training will obviously be necessary to broaden the foster parents' understanding of how their behavior influences the child and how they can increase their effectiveness through developing a wider assortment of management devices. This will make their job more satisfactory and more beneficial to the child. Simply increasing the range of the techniques at the disposal of the foster parents may do much to alleviate their guilt and impotence.

In many of the interviews, foster parents expressed a clear need for help in acquiring a richer set of strategies and tactics for dealing with both problem and nonproblem behavior of the children. They appeared to be quite eager to relate experiences they have had as foster parents to other foster parents, and they also hoped to learn from professionals about new ways to handle children. The following quotations illustrate these attitudes: "I whipped him several times. I know I'm not supposed to and I feel guilty. I tried to hit him on the arm, and then he moved and I hit him on the head." "Perhaps we could meet with other foster parents and find out how they keep the boys from staying out late."

As a result of this survey, the Detroit Foster Homes Research Project has provided, as part of a broad program, an opportunity for foster parents to learn more adequate techniques of child management through biweekly meetings of foster parents and mental hygiene specialists. At meetings, typical problem incidents have been described, and both successful and unsuccessful control methods have been analyzed in considerable detail. Major emphasis has been on on-the-spot challenges stemming from behavior of the child and on how to develop support and control that is both effective and hygienic. Group leaders also attempt to help foster parents verbalize the subconsciously held theories of child rearing that contribute to their way of handling children's misbehavior.

## CONCEPTS OF DEVIANCE

One of the most common beliefs is that all of the child's behavior is under his conscious control and, therefore, that deviance is always deliberate and amenable to change if the child really wants to change. An example of this attitude is the foster mother who claimed that "he wet his bed because he was lazy and didn't care."

Another common belief is that correct patterns of behavior can be instilled in children through lectures and that they often misbehave because they are unaware of the expectations of society. Teaching becomes telling: "Religion is a real help to a child; it's like Boy Scout oaths—you drill it into them and they start believing it."

A third widespread generalization is that "the children are just born that way." Foster parents pay lip service to the potent effect of early experience; yet in the method of treatment and in the expressed attitudes there is a pervasive belief that the behavior pattern is immutable and to some extent represents "God's will." Given this assumption of a "bad" child, the conclusions about how to treat him follow quite naturally. If the child is left to his own devices, he will perpetrate evil acts. One prevents this by being firm and permitting as few choices as possible. What the child enjoys is evil. A corollary assumption is that the most effective way of exacting cooperation is through depriving him of enjoyment because children learn best through suffering. One woman went so far as to forbid a child to attend Mass because he liked to walk the ten blocks to church.

Early training is perceived to have been lacking. There is a suggestion that in the past, life was too easy. The foster parents' knowledge that the early experiences of the youngsters were marked by lack of discipline and direction is transformed into the notion that their lives were free and easy. There is a widespread misapprehension that lack of controls, guidance, and routines really means happiness, and since the youngsters were "too happy" in the past, they have to make up for it now by suffering.

One woman reported that she attempted to discourage stealing by purposely leaving money around the house, informing the children that it was around and testing their staying power. At a pre-science level, she believed in a "vaccination" approach wherein children are permitted to develop resistance through exposure to temptation. (At a deeper level she may have sought to instigate situations that caused the children to fail. She then could self-righteously punish them for the wrongs they did and the suffering they caused.)

Although the casework offered to this woman will probably never reach the deeper levels of personality functioning that precipitated this behavior, one could hope to point out to her the significance of her actions in terms of the problems they posed for the children and to modify this particularly destructive behavior sequence. This incident could also serve as a vehicle for generalizing about the necessity for helping the youngsters develop controls rather than testing the frail ones they have. One might also attempt to work on the notion of the seductive nature of certain props in the home and the necessity of anticipating and dealing with these. With luck, this woman's harmful behavior and the children's aggressive reactions to this behavior will be reduced, and, thus, her need to find excuses to punish the child will also be mitigated.

## GOALS AND GAINS

The impetus for a particular mode of dealing with children stems in part from a parent's own experiences, values, and needs. Behavior that is central to the foster parent's personality may be difficult to modify. But some destructive ways of handling children are the result of tradition, inadequate information, or thoughtlessness. These patterns of behavior may be modified through training.

In conclusion, we believe that some knowledge of ego functioning, together with a framework for a theory of discipline and concrete demonstrations of how and when to use different control techniques, may be an asset for foster parents. If they can conceive of some kinds of childhood misbehavior as the result of impulses overwhelming the child's ego and, therefore, requiring supportive control rather than retribution and rejection, we would be placing at their disposal a very powerful tool. Not only would their control techniques be enhanced, it seems to us that this would also engender a feeling of professionalism in foster parents. It would give them a set of concepts and tools that make it obvious to them that caring for foster children is a very exacting, special kind of task—that it is not merely babysitting.

# 28

⟨ A more explicit consideration needs to be given to the desirability of long-term foster care. This might amount to a social adoption. The following study reviews instances in which such a resource has been used to the benefit of the child needing substitute care.

# The Legally Adoptable, Unadopted Child

*Alfred Kadushin*

Social agencies are besieged by childless couples anxious to adopt a child. They are also burdened with the care of parentless children who are anxious to be adopted. Yet many of the legally adoptable children never achieve adoption. Such children are different; they are all handicapped, some by their age, some by social background, some by religion, others by physical or emotional disability. These are the children who are hard to place; the children with special problems. No euphemism can vitiate the harsh truth that in the competition of parentless children for childless "parents," these children have been rejected.

There is a rich social work literature on the general problem of hard-to-place children and on the specific categories of handicaps to adoptive placement: race, age, physical disability, mental disability, pathological background. Also there is a growing body of literature which describes successful experiences in placing for adoption children with special problems. There is, however, little systematic discussion of what happens to the legally adoptable child who is not placed for adoption. How are these children cared for after parental rights have been terminated and before they are adopted, if they ever are? Does denial of legal adoption, because of the difficulties these children bring to the adoptive situation, mean depriving them of a meaningful family life? What circumstances are they likely to face in growing up if adoptive homes are not found for them?

## STUDY OF UNADOPTED CHILDREN

The Division of Children and Youth of the Wisconsin State Department of Public Welfare recently made an effort to find an answer to these questions. While the problem of the hard-to-place child is a matter

263

of concern to both public and private agencies, the general practice has been to ask public agencies to take guardianship. Consequently, a study limited to children under state guardianship covers most of the hard-to-place children in the state.

An earlier study had established that the median length of time between guardianship commitment to the Division of Children and Youth and placement for adoption is seven to eight months. It was decided, therefore, to study all children under ten years of age not placed for adoption, who by June 1, 1957 had been under the agency's guardianship for five months or more.[1]

A questionnaire was formulated and tested in consultation with the central office staff of the division. For the selected children it requested reasons for difficulty in placing, a description of efforts that had been made to place them, the results of such efforts, and information regarding the circumstances under which each child was currently living. Questionnaires were distributed to the child welfare workers responsible for the care of these children. After a preliminary review of the completed questionnaires, each was discussed with the worker who had filled it out. In the few instances where workers were unavailable because of illness or vacation the completed questionnaire was discussed with the supervisor.

As a result of these interviews, responses were amplified, clarified and qualified, and with a guided interview form, further information was obtained about the child's current living situation and adjustment.

Following interviews with the children's workers, the records of one-third of the children selected for study were reviewed. This involved reading the last two entries of the record, the last transfer summary and, where available, the latest medical, psychological and psychiatric report. Thus, the data were collected on the basis of a questionnaire, structured interviews with the children's worker and a reading of a sample of the records.

### FACTORS IN DIFFICULT PLACEMENT

Preparations for adoptive placement had not been completed for forty-eight children in the study group. An additional twenty-one were placed for adoption during the two months (June 1 to July 31, 1957) that it took to collect the study data. As of August 1, 1957, 220 children under ten had remained under guardianship to the state for more than seven months. Preparations for placement had been completed but they were not yet placed for adoption.

Five of these children were eminently placeable: all were white, under

---

[1] Children institutionalized because of mental or physical handicaps were excluded from the study.

two years of age, and physically, mentally and emotionally healthy, without hint of pathology in the family background. Delay in their adoptive placement lay solely in the fact that work pressures had prevented offering them adequate service. Since it was confidently anticipated that they would be placed for adoption shortly, without any difficulty, these five children were not further considered.

TABLE I. Factors Responsible for Delaying Adoption*

| Factors | Number of Children | Percent of Total |
|---|---|---|
| Race | 79 | 36.6 |
| Age | 54 | 25.1 |
| Physical | 40 | 18.6 |
| Mental | 24 | 11.2 |
| Emotional | 7 | 3.3 |
| Sibling Ties | 6 | 2.8 |
| Family Pathology | 3 | 1.4 |
| Religion | 2 | 1 |
| Family Social Disorganization (alcoholism, promiscuity, pauperism, etc.). | 0 | 0 |
| Total | 215 | 100 |

* The group included 67 Indian children, 25 Negroes, 1 Puerto Rican, and 1 Mexican.

In each of the remaining 215 cases there is, according to the child's worker, some factor or factors which make adoptive placement more than normally difficult. Table I lists those factors regarded by the workers as of primary importance in contributing to the difficulty in adoptive placement. It should be noted that in 91.5 percent of the cases a limited number of factors—race, age, physical and mental disability—are primarily responsible for the delay in placement.

Table II shows the nature of the living arrangements for these children as of the time questionnaires were answered.

TABLE II. Living Arrangements for Legally Adoptable but Unplaced Children

| Living Arrangements | Number of Children | Percent of Total |
|---|---|---|
| Boarding Home | 198 | 92.0 |
| Relative's Home | 9 | 4.2 |
| Free Home | 1 | 0.6 |
| Orphanage | 7 | 3.2 |
| Total | 215 | 100 |

While adoptive homes have not been found for these children, approximately 97 percent of the group is living with a family. The important question is, however, to what extent these children are considered, and feel themselves to be, a part of the family group with whom they are living? To what degree are they identified with the family, integrated into the family, emotionally a functioning member of the family?

One measure of this is the relative stability of living arrangements for this group of children. Table III shows the relationship between time under guardianship and time in the foster home since guardianship.

The table shows that 152 children, or 73 percent have been living in the same home since guardianship commitment. One hundred and fifty-one have been under guardianship for two years or longer. Of these, 133, or 88 percent, were in the same home for two years or more.

These figures underestimate the stability of family living arrangements for these children. The total period in the home is, in forty cases, longer than the time given in Table III. In some instances the children were

TABLE III. **Relationship Between Time in Guardianship and Time in Foster Home Since Guardianship Began**

| Time in Guardianship | Less than Six Months | Time in Foster Home Since Guardianship Began* | | | | | | | | | | Totals |
|---|---|---|---|---|---|---|---|---|---|---|---|---|
| | | 1 | 2 | 3 | 4 | 5 | 6 | 7 | 8 | 9 | 10 | |
| 1 yr. | 6 | 51 | | | | | | | | | | 57 |
| 2 yrs. | 3 | 5 | 36 | | | | | | | | | 44 |
| 3 yrs. | 3 | 4 | 7 | 24 | | | | | | | | 38 |
| 4 yrs. | | 2 | 2 | 6 | 15 | | | | | | | 25 |
| 5 yrs. | | 1 | | 2 | 3 | 8 | | | | | | 14 |
| 6 yrs. | | | | | | 2 | 2 | | | | | 4 |
| 7 yrs. | | | 1 | | 1 | 2 | 2 | 8 | | | | 14 |
| 8 yrs. | | | | 1 | 1 | 1 | 1 | | 5 | | | 9 |
| 9 yrs. | | | | | | | | | | 1 | | 1 |
| 10 yrs. | | | | | | | | | | | 2 | 2 |
| Totals | 12 | 63 | 46 | 33 | 20 | 13 | 5 | 8 | 5 | 1 | 2 | 208 |

* Time is computed to the nearest six months as of June 1, 1957. "Ten years" means more than nine years, six months, but less than ten years.

placed in the home while under custody commitment to the agency. When this was changed to a guardianship commitment, the child remained in the same home. In other instances the child had been placed in the home by the county and when the State was granted guardianship commitment, the child remained in the same home. The length of time actually in the home was available in twenty of these forty instances. The twenty children for whom such information is available averaged 2.6 years in the home before guardianship commitment.

Stability of living arrangements is a prerequisite for developing social and emotional membership in a family group. The child and the foster parents need time to get to know each other, understand each other, appreciate each other. But while time is necessary it is not, in itself, sufficient. Table III tells us only that in many cases the children have lived with one family long enough to make their incorporation in the family group possible; the children have had the time to develop meaningful relationships in the home. Interviews with the workers and a review of the records tell us that the possibilities for developing meaningful relationships have, for many of these children, been realized.

## EMOTIONAL ADOPTION OF THE UNADOPTED

This is true for children who were hard to place because they are Indian or Negro.

Jimmy, a five-year-old illegitimate Negro boy, has been under guardianship for five years and in the same Negro foster home for four years. The record notes that "Jimmy's adjustment in this home has been good. He identifies with the foster father even to the extent of wanting to dress like him. . . . The foster mother says she wouldn't take a million dollars for this child. The parents talk about him as 'our adopted child.'"

Ted, who is seven years old, of mixed Negro-white descent, has been under guardianship for six years, living in the same Negro foster home for five years. The record notes that "it is questionable that we could provide a more accepting home for Ted. The foster parents have provided him with a great deal of love and security. The child's adjustment in the home has been very good. He is treated like a member of the family."

Barbara, a five-year-old Indian girl, had been so neglected by her parents immediately after birth that it was doubtful that she would live when the agency assumed custody five years ago. Barbara has been under guardianship of the agency for three years and in the same white foster home for five years. Her identification with the foster parents is "quite strong" and the foster parents have "some meaningful relation and affection for her." Aside from some food fads, which the foster parents have handled very well, Barbara has not manifested any problems.

What is true of these Negro and Indian children is also true of children who could not be placed for adoption because of physical disabilities. They have found a family as well as a home.

John, an eight-year-old white, has been under guardianship of the agency for six years and in the same foster home for five years. As an infant in his own home he was beaten, uncared for, and unfed. Just before the agency assumed guardianship John was hospitalized for injuries intentionally inflicted by his parents. He suffered a fractured skull and multiple bruises. He currently suffers from right spastic hemiplegia. John is enuretic and his stammering speech is sometimes difficult to understand. The worker states that the foster parents see him as their son and "never want him to leave." The record indicates that "there seems to be no doubt about the foster parents' acceptance of the child."

Steve is a seven-year-old white, who was born out of wedlock. He has been under guardianship for seven years, living in the same foster home for four years. Steve has a deformed arm and hand. The record notes that "Steve has made an excellent adjustment in this home and is a secure little fellow. His foster parents are extremely capable and have done exceptional work in helping the boy to adjust to his handicap and to reduce it as a limiting factor. It would seem that this home requires only routine supervision." The worker notes, in a transfer summary, that every change of worker "occasions anxiety for the foster parents, since they are afraid that the change might result in Steve's removal from the home."

Four-year-old Ann has been under guardianship of the agency for four years and living in the same foster home for four years. She suffers from marked hydrocephalus and has almost no vision in one eye. The worker states that Ann "is so much a part of this family that taking her away from them would be like taking her away from her own home." The worker "is handling this case as if Ann had been adopted by this family." She states that "we are indeed fortunate that placement was made in a foster home that so meets the child's needs that she may grow up there with or without adoption."

Jimmy is a nine-and-one-half-year-old illegitimate white boy, who has been under guardianship for four years and has been living in the same foster home for four years. He suffers from a paralysis of the right arm and stiffness of the right leg. A recent psychometric exam lists his IQ as 65. He is diurnally enuretic. The record states that Jimmy is a "lovable child who needs a great deal of acceptance and recognition, both of which he has gotten in his home. The foster parents have provided Jimmy with the secure feelings he needs and have done beautifully in helping him to progress without needing to push him beyond his capacity. There is a definite feeling of warmth between members of this family. As far as Jimmy is concerned, this is his home and it is quite apparent that he definitely feels he belongs here."

The following children who could not be placed because they are mentally handicapped are also emotionally adopted but legally unadopted.

Sam, a nine-year-old, has been under agency guardianship for only one year but has lived in the same foster home for seven years. Psychometric examination indicates that Sam is mentally retarded. He is in a specially graded class in school. The boy's father, several uncles and the paternal grandfather have all spent some time in mental hospitals. The record indicates that "in this home the child has received an unusual amount of acceptance and affection." The report of a psychiatrist, consulted in 1956, states that "there are few homes that would so completely accept such a child and give him the warmth and stimulation this family gives. They show complete acceptance of the child as one of their own family group."

Sara, aged nine, has been under agency guardianship for seven years and in the same home for eight years. Her last psychometric examination, given in 1954, shows an IQ of 56. Sara's maternal grandmother, maternal grandfather and a maternal aunt are mentally deficient. The foster parents have one adopted daughter who is now married. They are very much attached to Sara and "wouldn't think of giving her up." The worker states that the foster parents have "given Sara a lot of affection and seem to be able to appreciate her in a very real way. They have a good understanding and acceptance of mental retardation."

Viola, who is nine, and was born out of wedlock, has been under guardianship and living in the same foster home for nine years. Psychometric examination shows an IQ of 63. Her parents are described as "shiftless, ambitionless and dull." Viola's mother has an IQ of 82 and two aunts and an uncle were institutionalized as feeble-minded. Viola is in chronic poor health and now suffers from rheumatic fever. Her foster parents, who have one child of their own, have completely accepted Viola. "They have treated her just as their own child and she has been responsive to them. They are warm, happy people and Viola gives the impression of being a very secure, happy child. . . . She gets along reasonably well with other children and there is no problem in either school or home. The child has the affection and security of a child in her own home."

## "POINT OF NO RETURN" IN FOSTER HOME

Some of the children, despite the handicaps which made them hard to place, have developed such full membership in the foster family that a "point of no return" has been reached. Workers feel that separation from the substitute, albeit non-adoptive home, would entail great pain and hurt and loss for the child. This is a testimonial to the solidity of the emotional ties between child and family.

Pat is a three-year-old Catholic Indian girl whose mother died eight days after giving birth. Her father voluntarily surrendered custody of the child to the agency after deciding that he could not care for her. She has a palsied right arm, the result of a birth injury. Pat has been living with the same family since shortly after birth. A recent entry in the case record notes that "in conversations with the foster mother, the worker learned that Pat continues to be a lovable child. The foster parents are much delighted with her, regarding her much as they would a child of their own. . . . She appears to be a youngster of happy personality development and holds promise of continuing that way. . . . The present placement is most ideal for what it can offer Pat in the way of sincere affection and guidance." The record states that "the fact that Pat is not adopted does not, it appears, detract from the emotional security she is gaining in this home situation. If there is a possibility of adoptive placement in another home at this time for Pat it might be advisable. On the other hand, the possibility should be weighed carefully before decision is arrived at, in view of the security in this home situation."

Theodore, a nine-and-one-half-year-old Indian boy, has been under guardianship for three years and in the same foster home for six years, having been placed earlier by the county. The worker states that Theodore "has become a full and happy member of this home. . . . I have been immensely impressed, in the many months of visits to the home with the great love and understanding given by these foster parents." The foster mother is Indian and the foster father white. The worker notes that she does not feel "that adoption is the answer, particularly when the child's needs are being adequately met in the boarding home. The trauma of a separation would be too great, in spite of the greater accruing securities in an adoptive home."

Ralph is an eight-year-old boy under guardianship for four years. He has been living in the same foster home for four years. Ralph had been neglected by both parents, "tied to the potty chair on numerous occasions, locked in an upstairs room, beaten and not fed."

The mother was relieved when the agency took custody, stating that she was "really afraid she would kill him some time." When Ralph was committed, he was a "bewildered, frightened, pathetic little boy who was afraid of people." The worker notes that Ralph "has progressed very well in the foster home and is strongly attached to the foster parents. It is very possible that, because of strong identification and excellent progress, this foster home may be considered a better long-term home than could be offered the boy through adoption."

William, a nine-year-old white boy who was born out of wedlock, has been under guardianship for four years and in the same foster home for six. He suffers from congenital deformities of feet and legs and had to wear braces until he was five years old. Billy identifies closely with the foster family and they see him as their son. The worker states that the foster parents have "handled the problem of Billy's handicap unusually well. The problem is whether Billy, because of the long time he has been in the home and the fact that he hâs established meaningful relationships here and developed a healthy personality, should be left to grow up in this home or whether further efforts should be made to find an adoptive home for him. This would mean terminating quite a happy relationship."

## ADJUSTMENT OF THESE CHILDREN

Additional data of a somewhat different nature supports the general contention that failure to place a child for adoption does not necessarily mean deprivation for him. In interviews with each worker, the researcher asked specific questions about each child's adjustment in the home, school and community and the extent to which the child was "integrated" into the family group with which he was living—to what extent he saw himself as a family member and to what extent the foster parents and "own" children saw him as such. The questions included a check list of symptoms of maladjustment, such as stealing, truanting, thumb sucking, nail biting, temper tantrums and nightmares. Workers were also asked whether the child was excessively shy, withdrawn, given to day dreaming, or overly hostile and aggressive. The check list was used primarily to give the workers interviewed some idea of what we were looking for.

We do not claim that the analysis of the adjustment of this group of children can meet the standards of a rigorously scientific methodological approach. The analysis concerns itself with overt adjustment and tells us nothing of the inner life of the child. Furthermore, sixty-two percent of the group falls within the latency period age range—six to ten. Theoretically this is a period during which one can anticipate a reduction in difficulties of adjustment.

What we were able to get was the worker's general opinion about the adjustment and integration of the children for whom she was responsible. This is an educated opinion by a professional person, trained to make appraisals of adjustment, who is acquainted with the child's behavior on the basis of a number of contacts.

The worker's opinions were categorized for both adjustment and integration. They were considered good if the worker was moved to make some specific positive comment on the child's adjustment or integration, such as:

The child is "solidly a member of the family," "really one of the family group," "doing very well in this home," "really excellent adjustment," "very happy and relaxed in this home," "has done remarkably well."

They were categorized as fair where the worker stated that there were no behavioral difficulties as far as she could remember, no serious complaints about the child on the part of the foster parents, but at the same time did not specifically commend as noteworthy the child's adjustment or integration. Adjustment and integration were considered poor where some symptoms of maladjustment did exist, such as, temper tantrums, enuresis, negativism, or difficulties with school, or where the child was said to feel like a boarder or a stranger in the home.

Table IV lists the tabulation of the data regarding adjustment and integration.[2] In all except twenty-three cases, the children included in the table had been living in the same home for two years or longer.

TABLE IV. **Ratings of Adjustment and Integration**

| | Adjustment | | Integration | |
|---|---|---|---|---|
| Rating | Number of Children | Percent of Total | Number of Children | Percent of Total |
| Good | 20 | 14.7 | 54 | 38 |
| Fair | 92 | 68 | 79 | 56 |
| Poor | 24 | 17.3 | 8 | 6 |
| Totals | 136 | 100 | 141 | 100 |

The rating indicates that most of the children are getting along well in these homes. Since a rating of poor was given wherever any symptom of difficulty was present, the nomenclature probably does the child's adjustment an injustice. Under a similar system of classification, the adjustment of very many own children would be rated "poor."

The data on integration supports the contention that many of these legally adoptable but unplaced children have found a family. The data

---

2 We were not able to get this data on all the children. In some instances the child had recently been transferred to the worker and her personal knowledge about him was scanty. In yet other instances, the child had been in the home for too limited a period for the worker to venture a valid opinion.

on adjustment inferentially supports the conclusion. It is not likely from what we know about the dynamics of personal adjustment, that so many children would show good and fair adjustment unless they were received with some warmth and affection in foster homes.

### FUTURE PLANS FOR THE CHILDREN

Further evidence of the stability of the living arrangements for the group studied comes from the material regarding future plans for the child, where these have been explicitly formulated. In forty instances (18.6 percent) the child is in the home "with a view toward adoption." The agency and the foster parents have a tacit understanding that the child will be adopted at some indefinite future time. In 119 instances (55.3 percent) while the agency was still supposedly looking for an adoptive home, it was agreed by both foster parents and the agency that the child could remain in the home indefinitely. Thus, in 159 instances, 73.9 percent of the legally adoptable but unplaced group with which we are concerned, some more or less permanent living arrangements have been provided for the child.

What does it all add up to? It is true that social workers have not been able to achieve the very best for these children—adoptive placement in a good home. But the fact that they have not fully succeeded does not mean that they have failed. These children are hard to place for legal adoption, but many have been adopted socially and emotionally. Failure to place for adoption is not necessarily a sentence of deprivation. Children who have "lost" their own parents and have not been adopted may still grow up in the healthy climate of a warm, accepting home.

Legally these children lack a mother and a father. The depersonalized "state" is their parent. Socially and emotionally many do not lack for parents. The legal realities may tend to obscure the social-emotional realities of the situation in which these children live and grow up and develop. Only a legal technicality differentiates many of these hard-to-place children, living in long-time boarding homes, from adopted children.

We are aware of the fact that social and emotional adoption of the child must accompany legal adoption. Can we begin to think in terms of social-emotional adoptions which may not be accompanied by legal adoption? This may be easier for the hard-to-place child to achieve.

Has our focus on legal adoption for hard-to-place children—admittedly the most desirable solution—led us to neglect the possibilities of alternatives for such children?

Perhaps we need to reassess the "respectability" of long-range boarding home care for hard-to-place children. It is wise and right to strive for the very best possible permanent, substitute living arrangement for children who are legally free for adoption if adoptive homes cannot be found for them. But with chronic staff shortages; the public attitude toward the handicapped, the older child and the child of a racial minority group; the economic level of the Negro and Indian which allows them to be subsidized foster parents but not unsubsidized adoptive parents; the crushing burden of medical care for the mentally and physically disabled which makes even economically secure foster parents hesitant to adopt them; the hesitancy of older foster parents who are boarding older children to accept a legal responsibility which, in the case of their death, might fall on their own children—with all of this, and more, long-range boarding home care may be the very best arrangement that can be worked out for many hard-to-place children. And it is an arrangement for which, in many instances, we need not apologize, either to ourselves or to others.

This does not preclude pressing for consideration of a program for subsidized adoptions on a selective basis. The data inferentially support the desirability of such a program.

The data add up to something else. They demonstrate empirically that there are parents who want these children, however different, however handicapped. They may not, for a variety of reasons, want them as their legal sons and daughters, but they do want them, and have accepted them as their own in their minds and in their hearts. To know this is encouraging.

The data finally say that these children, however different or handicapped, can derive satisfactions from family living and can contribute to the satisfactions of family living. To know this means we can confidently offer the hard-to-place child for social and emotional, and ultimately for legal adoption.

# 29

⟨[ There are few follow-up studies of children who spent a significant proportion of their childhood in foster care. The following article is a report
of a recent carefully done study of former foster children as adults.

# Current Circumstances of
# Former Foster Children

*Elizabeth G. Meier*

This paper is based on a followup study of young men and women, aged
28 to 32, who experienced five years or more of foster family care in their
childhood and who had not been returned to their own families while
they were children. As foster children, they had been in the guardianship
of the State of Minnesota. Most of them had been under the direct care
and supervision of public agencies, county or state, but some of them had
been cared for by private agencies.

In a more complete report of this research,[1] a method is described by
which the "social effectiveness" and the "sense of well-being" of the subjects of the study were measured, primarily on the basis of information
obtained in interviews with them. These scores were used to determine
whether the degrees of social effectiveness and sense of well-being were
related to factors in foster family care, such as age at placement, number
of placements, and other factors in the life experiences of the young
people. The full report also describes the subjects' recollections of foster
family care. The materials presented here, describing the current circumstances of these young men and women, are but a small portion of the
findings.

## THE SAMPLE POPULATION

The sample consisted of 82 persons who fulfilled the criteria of age
(28 to 32), length of foster family care (five years or more), and not

---

[1] This research was begun in the summer of 1959, and the findings were used as
a doctoral dissertation. Elizabeth Gertrude Meier, *Former Foster Children as Adult
Citizens*, unpublished (New York: New York School of Social Work, Columbia University, 1962). Readers wishing further information concerning the research methodology or findings may consult the dissertation, available through University of Michigan
Microfilm Library of Dissertations, Ann Arbor, Michigan, Microfilm #62–3699.

having been returned to their own families' care while they were children. In order to fulfill the criterion of age, discharges from guardianship for the period between July 1, 1948, and December 31, 1949, were used for selecting eligible persons. Although 655 children were discharged from guardianship within that period, only 98 fulfilled the three criteria. The sample consisted of all the men who were eligible (34), and a random sample of 48 women from among the 64 eligible. (Information was not obtained from all 82 persons.)

The fewer men eligible for inclusion reflects a factor in foster care during that period and in that locale. Boys who were in foster care were less likely than girls to receive foster family care of a sufficiently lengthy period to be included in the sample; they were more likely to have been in institution care either throughout their period of foster care or for such duration that the length of foster family care did not measure up to the five-year criterion.

Surprisingly, it was found that free home care was used rather frequently. Some children were placed in free homes in early childhood, with the expectation that they would remain in such homes throughout their childhood years. Others were placed in "school homes" subsequent to institution care at an age when it was expected that they would be able to earn their own room and board by helping in the homes and on the farms. These two kinds of care, free homes and work homes, constituted 42 percent of the foster family care experienced by the boys and 35 percent of that experienced by the girls. The balance of the foster family care was in boarding homes.

About half of the group had left their own parental homes prior to the age of 5. The average time spent in living arrangements other than their own homes or the homes of relatives was 11 years 10 months. The average age of discharge from foster care was 18 years 1 month. Between the time of their first foster care placement and their discharge from foster care, these children experienced an average of 5.6 living arrangements, including all kinds of foster family care and institution care. A third of the group had four or fewer living arrangements, 42 percent had five to nine living arrangements, and a fourth of the group had ten or more living arrangements.

Obviously, since all of these children had been in the guardianship of the state, court action had been taken in all instances. It is not the intent of this paper to give detailed data concerning family backgrounds, but it is possible to generalize that, except for those illegitimate children who had been placed in care in infancy and the very few children who were placed primarily because of the death of a parent or parents, they had come from situations in which they had experienced inadequate care.

Almost everyone in the sample was white. There were three Negroes among the 82 persons, but information was obtained from only 1 of them.

Indian children who had been in the guardianship of the state and who had been discharged within the time period specified were not included in the sample because they had not received a sufficient amount of foster family care; most often, they had received only institution care.

## LOCATING AND INTERVIEWING
## THE FORMER FOSTER CHILDREN

As stated, the sample consisted of 82 people, but this does not mean that all of them could be located or that information could be obtained from all of those who were located. Two had died since discharge from guardianship, 75 were located, and 5 could not be located. Of the 75 who were located, 52 had remained in Minnesota or had returned to the state after being elsewhere, and 23 were out of the state. Comparison with U.S. Census reports reveals that, for a comparable age range, approximately the same proportion of the general population born in Minnesota now lives in other states.[2] These 23 persons are in 13 states and 3 foreign countries, 2 of those in foreign countries being in the armed services. The fact that 94 percent of these persons (75 of the 80 now living or presumably living) who had left foster care about a decade earlier could be located may have some value to other persons concerned with followup studies. Whether an equally high proportion of persons could be located from within a population of former foster children reared in more urban settings, however, is not known.

After an address was obtained a letter requesting an interview was sent to the subjects of the research. Sixty-one persons were interviewed.[3] In addition, five young people provided information on a self-administered questionnaire that was sent to them either because they were inaccessible for an interview or because they were willing to give information only in this manner. Nine refused the interview and also refused the questionnaire. The proportion of refusals from men was three times as high as from women.

In the material that follows, the reader will find that different numbers are used for the base figure, because of the different sources of information. Some kinds of information were obtained only in an interview; other kinds were obtained either by an interview or from the questionnaire. In addition, when some subjects refused the interview or the questionnaire, they nonetheless gave some information about themselves in their letters or telephone calls. Also, there were pieces of information *about*, but not *from*, a few other persons.

---

[2] U.S. Census Bureau, *1950 Census of Population, Special Report, Volume IV, Part 4, Chapter A, State of Birth* (Washington, D.C.: U.S. Government Printing Office, 1953), Table 8, p. 15, and Table 23, p. 75.

[3] Sixteen of the interviews were conducted by interviewers other than the author.

## MARRIAGE

The contrasts between the men's and women's experiences, behavior, and attitudes was one of the most tantalizing aspects of this research. A few of these differences have already been referred to above. So, too, in regard to marriage, a contrast emerges. All of the 45 women have been married at least once, but 5 of the 30 men have never married. Only 19 of the men (63 percent) are currently living with a spouse, whereas 38 of the women (84 percent) are doing so. Among the 19 men living with a spouse, 16 are living with a first wife and 3 with a second wife. Nine men are known not to be living with a spouse at the present time, the five who have never married and four whose marriages have been broken by divorce or separation. The remaining 2 men among the 30 have been married at least once, but their current marital status is uncertain.

Among the 38 women currently living with a spouse, 34 are living within a first marriage, 3 in a second marriage, and 1 in a third marriage. Two other women have married at least once, and available information suggests that they are still living in this first marriage.

Of the five women not living with a spouse, two of them have been married once (one is separated and the other divorced). Three have been married more than once. In one of these instances, a very early marriage ended in divorce, following which the woman remarried but lost the second husband in death. The other two women are sisters, who, in all areas of adaptation, were found to be among the least well-adjusted individuals at the present time; they had also experienced tempestuous foster care during which they had continued contact with parents who were a disruptive influence. One of these sisters was divorced from her first husband, whom she married after giving birth to his illegitimate child while she was still in the custody of the institution for delinquent girls to which she had been sent following foster family care. She is currently separated from her second husband. The other sister, who said that she had lived in "more than 50 places" since leaving foster care, claims five marriages. A rather pathetic incident suggests her continuing effort to find something for herself and some goal for the future. She says that she puts aside 50 cents a day for the college education of her 4-year-old son.

Because of the smallness of the sample, it is advisable to regard comparison with the general population as only suggestive. About the same proportion of men subjects and men in the general population of the same age range have never married, but, whereas only 3.8 percent of the general population is apart from the spouse because of separation, divorce, widowhood, or other reasons, this is true of 14.3 percent of the men subjects (using the base figure of 28 men, omitting the 2 about whom information is uncertain).

The sample of women is unusual in that none has failed to marry, whereas, in the general population, 10.9 percent of the women in this age range have not married. In the general population, only 5.1 percent of the women are absent from a spouse because of widowhood, divorce, separation, or other reasons, but this was true of 11.6 percent of the women subjects. Nevertheless, because of the absence of any spinsters among the subjects, a slightly higher proportion of the women are living with a spouse than is true of the general population of women of their age range.[4]

There is a kind of unofficial child welfare myth that foster children often grow up and marry men and women who had also been in foster care. This is not true in this group. Only three of the current spouses had been in foster care, of varying duration, and a few others had been cared for by relatives upon the death or absence of a parent.

The families of spouses are of extreme importance to these individuals. The parents-in-law have become the parent surrogates to whom these former foster children turn for advice and help when needed, and the family of the spouse is the family group with which social and recreational activities are frequent. Some of the most desolate individuals among the sample population are those who are not in close touch with their in-laws either because of geography or other reasons, who are also out of touch with former foster parents, but who continue in conflictual relationships with their own families. In stating this, it is recognized that cause-and-effect relationships between these circumstances and their predicament may be closely interwoven and reciprocal.

## LIVING ARRANGEMENTS

The marital status of these men and women influences the kinds of living arrangements they have made. Eighteen of the 19 men currently living with a spouse is the head of his own household. The other lives with his wife in the home of her relatives. The nine men known not to be living with a spouse are not heads of households—most of them live in some kind of room-and-board arrangement, and two of them have remained with their former foster families. This group also includes a man in prison—the only person in the sample currently institutionalized —and an unmarried man in the armed services. All of the 42 women, on the other hand, whether or not they are currently married, are the mistresses of their own homes, either as the wife of the head of the household or as a currently unmarried person heading her own household.

As might be expected, there are many styles and types of dwellings that

---

[4] U.S. Census Bureau, *1950 Census of Population, Volume II, Characteristics of the Population, Part 23, Minnesota* (Washington, D.C.: U.S. Government Printing Office, 1952), p. 149.

these men and women currently call home. They live in metropolitan communities and on isolated farms, in small towns and in rural areas, in old deteriorated parts of cities and in thriving new developments, in big old houses and in small new houses, in furnished and unfurnished apartments—and two live with their families in shiny new trailers. An artist's sketch of the particular kind of place that would most nearly typify the dwelling places of more persons than any other could depict a small, tidy, well-built house, clean and new, located in a city in a new development in which all the neighboring houses were of a reasonably similar size and shape. The houses would differ from each other in color and details of structure, but seen from a distance it would be likely that the development would present a pleasant blend of pastel colors.

Among the 30 men, 14 were reared on farms, but only 3 are now farmers. Only 2 of these 14 former farm boys now live in metropolitan areas of more than 100,000 population, however, whereas 9 of the 16 men who had not been reared on a farm live in such communities. The other men live in smaller cities, towns, villages, and rural areas, but not farms. Thirty of the 45 women now live in metropolitan areas. Only one lives on a farm. The rest live in towns, villages, and rural areas.

### Number and Quantity of Arrangements

Replies ranged widely to a question about the number of residential arrangements the subjects had had since leaving foster care. One young man had lived in only two places. He had first brought his bride to the farm home where he had been reared, and he continued working the farm with his foster father. Then he bought a farm about half a mile down the road, and he and his family continue to live there. The other extreme was the man in a far western state who said he had lived "in about 200 places." He works for a construction company and moves about from one locality and from one state to another, depending on the company's contracts.

The possible relationship between numbers of living arrangements in adulthood and the continuity or discontinuity of foster care arrangements in childhood was examined. It was found that of the 27 persons who had six or more foster care arrangements, 23 have lived in more than six places since, whereas of the 37 persons who had five or fewer foster care arrangements, less than half, 17, have lived in more than six places since. This difference, tested by the chi-square contingency test, yields a difference significant at the .01 level.

If frequency of moves in childhood is indeed related to frequency of moves in adulthood, then discontinuities in foster care most truly do have a long-term impact upon the individual. If frequent moves in childhood tend to result in the constant seeking after something else in a different location in adulthood, such frequency may not only represent residual effects of emotional damage, but may also in and of itself, generate new problems for the adult person. If the moves are from one community to another, the record of work stability may be affected and interfere with getting good jobs. In some settings, lack of seniority in jobs would also affect wages. Even if the moves are in the same locality, moving is a nonproductive expenditure of money. Children born to a continually moving family have their school progress interfered with and their peer relationships terminated. Should the individual be married to a spouse who did not share the impelling drive to move, marital conflicts might arise.

If the impelling force behind moving about from one place to another is that the individual who was emotionally homeless as a child is attempting to find his "home" and establish for himself an identity based partly upon where he belongs as well as upon who he is, then the behavior becomes self-defeating. The impermanency that characterizes his living arrangements becomes exactly the thing that keeps others from thinking of him as belonging in that neighborhood, that church, or that organization, rooted in a specific locale.

### Indications of "Settledness"

Additional information seems to run counter to the statements above, however. A higher proportion of those persons who experienced many moves (more than six) in childhood are currently buying homes and living with spouses—indicators of settledness—than is true of those who experienced five or fewer moves. Home ownership is very important to many of these young citizens. They speak of their pleasure in owning or buying a place of their own, and several of them who are now renting express their intention to buy as soon as they are able to do so. Among the 65 men and women about whom this kind of information is known, 37 (57 percent) own or are buying their homes, with the women and their husbands (60 percent) doing somewhat better than the men and their wives (52 percent).

Choosing to study persons who had reached the specified age range turned out to be particularly felicitous in this regard, because about half of these 37 persons had begun  to buy their homes within the last three years. Had they been seen earlier or had a younger group been chosen for the sample, they probably would have expressed the hope of home ownership, but such statements might not have been credited as representing an attainable reality.

At the same time, the relative youth of persons within the sample makes it difficult to compare them with the general population in regard to home ownership. Although 75 percent of Minnesota's dwelling units are owner-occupied, this figure is based on a population ranging upward from age 21. It can be estimated that only about 25 percent to 30 percent of this general population of householders is *not* older than the sample population. It would be expected that this older group would have a higher proportion of home owners.[5] Furthermore, comparison is made difficult because patterns of home ownership vary geographically, and, as already indicated, not all of the subjects of this study have remained in the state.

Whatever arithmetical comparisons might be made, given the data to do so, the suggestion is ventured that these former foster children have done very well indeed in this regard. When these young homemakers were married, it is reasonable to assume that one partner in the marriage, the one who had been in foster care, ordinarily had fewer familial resources upon which to count for help in getting the new household underway. They had no family home from which to borrow equipment, and there were no large gifts from that side of the family to help the couple get started.

As stated earlier, it is not the business of this paper to describe the methods used to measure the "social effectiveness" and the "sense of well-being" of these individuals or to state the findings. The data in the full report, however, included evaluations of the quality of housekeeping and, from it, a generalization pertaining to the current living arrangements of the subjects can be drawn. With few exceptions, the homes in which these men and women live show a good quality of housekeeping. There were a very few dwelling places in which the housekeeping standards were so poor that they would seem to have constituted a health hazard for the children in the home, but these were the rare exceptions. Indeed, there were more instances in which the home seemed to be too tidy, suggestive of compulsive neatness.

## EMPLOYMENT AND ECONOMIC CIRCUMSTANCES

Among the 66 men and women from whom such information was obtained, 61 are self-supporting or are living within self-supporting family units; 4 are dependent upon public support, 1 of these being the man in prison and the other 3 being divorced or separated women receiving Aid to Families with Dependent Children; 1 man is heavily dependent upon the bounty of his friends. Among the 61 who are self-supporting, there are a few who, for brief periods of time since leaving guardianship, received temporary help from public funds, usually in instances when the family had excessive medical costs.

On the whole, the women have husbands who are providing a more

---

[5] This estimate is based on data concerning male householders in *Mr. Minnesota, 1958—Continuing Survey of Minnesota Living, 1958* (Minneapolis: National Advertising Department, Minneapolis Star and Tribune Company, 1958), p. 6. We also used data about women from *Homemaker Survey #12, 1959* (Minneapolis: National Advertising Department, Minneapolis Star and Tribune Company, 1959).

comfortable living for them than the men are providing for their families. Forty-eight percent of the men and their families have family incomes of over $100 per week, whereas this is true of 57 percent of the women's families. This reflects the fact that the men subjects are less well educated than the men whom the foster girls married—and the foster girls received better educations than did the foster boys.

Data concerning the occupational ratings[6] of the men and of the husbands of the women are consistent with the findings concerning earnings. Although the actual average rating of the men is about the same as that of the husbands of the women, more of the husbands have jobs in which they are acquiring advanced skills and preparing themselves for higher earnings. Also, among the 29 men about whom such information is known, there is only 1 who is on his way to becoming a professional person. Among the 39 women's husbands, on the other hand, there are 5 professional persons. Three men subjects who own their own businesses—a restaurant, a garage, and a firm that installs heating systems—exemplify the Lipset and Bendix formulation, derived from a large sample of the general population, to the effect that the greatest amount of occupational mobility tends to occur in the shifts to business ownership.[7] For the ambitious person with good native ability but a deficient educational background, business ownership may provide opportunities not open to him elsewhere.

## CHILDREN OF THE FORMER FOSTER CHILDREN

Considering the great differences in the marital circumstances of the men and the women, it is not surprising that comparable differences exist in the numbers of children of whom they are parents and in the proportions of men and women who have their children living in their homes with them.

Of the 24 men who were interviewed or from whom questionnaire data were received, 17 have children, a total of 41 children among them, but only 14 have offspring living in their homes with them, these constituting 33 of the 41 children. Of the other eight children, one child has died and the other seven are the offspring of three divorced men. Six of these children (offspring of two of the men) live with their mothers, and one lives

---

[6] A modification of the Warner occupational rating scale was used to arrive at occupational ratings of the male subjects, the husbands of the female subjects, the male parent at the time of the placement, and the foster father. These ratings were used as means to measure social mobility between the generations. *See* W. Lloyd Warner, Marchia Meeker, and Kenneth Eells, *Social Class in America: A Manual of Procedure for the Measurement of Social Status* (Chicago: Science Research Associates, 1949).

[7] Seymour Martin Lipset and Reinhard Bendix, *Social Mobility in Industrial Society* (Berkeley: University of California Press, 1959), pp. 103, 172–173.

with paternal relatives. There are also three men within the group, however, who have taken on the responsibility of providing for the children of their wives' former marriages.

Forty-one of the 42 women who were interviewed or from whom questionnaire data were obtained have borne children, 129 among them,[8] and 40 of these women are caring for a total of 115 children in their homes. The only two women not caring for children are the one who has not borne a child and the one who lost custody of her two children to a former husband at the time of their divorce. This numerical material is more meaningful when put in terms of family size, particularly if one is considering the child caring responsibilities now being discharged by these former foster children.

We have information on the child caring responsibility of 37 women who are currently living with a spouse. Among them, 2 are not caring for any children, 5 are caring for one child, 8 are caring for two, 9 are caring for three, 10 are caring for four, 1 is caring for five, and 2 are caring for six children. Among the five women who are not living with a spouse, two are caring for one child, one is caring for two children, and two are caring for three children. This accounts for 115 of the 129 children born to the women.

What of the other 14? Two have died, two are the children previously mentioned whose mother lost custody, and ten are illegitimate children, born to seven women, who are being cared for by other families, largely by adoptive families.[9] It must be emphasized, however, that *none of the children of legitimate birth born to the women in the study has been placed in foster care*, a fact of considerable significance in considering the current circumstances of these former foster children in whose behalf guardianship proceedings had been instituted, in most cases because of the neglected conditions in their homes.

Furthermore, for the most part, these are not new mothers whose children are too young for them to have come to the attention of the community if they were being neglected. Most of these mothers have children of school age, and most of them have children who now are older than they themselves were at the time of their removal from their parental homes, sometimes from appalling physical surroundings. Today, their children, with a few exceptions, are sleeping in clean beds. Interviewers saw the youngsters as they dashed in and out of the houses from their outdoor play. They darted into the kitchen to get snacks from sparkling white refrigerators. They wore clean play clothes, and they looked healthy and hearty.

---

[8] This number does not include miscarriages, stillbirths, and neonatal deaths; these occurrences are discussed below.

[9] A few additional illegitimate children born to the women were included in the 115 children now being cared for by them in their homes.

This is not to say that parenting presented no difficulties or that all of the children received excellent care. There were instances in which limited or poor-quality care was observed; some mothers acknowledged behavioral or discipline difficulties; and, in other instances, relationship problems between parent and child were either observed in the interviews or were discussed by the mothers. Some of the mothers clearly felt overburdened by the care of their children and their households.[10] It would be hazardous indeed to predict whether any of the children of these former foster children will ever have to be placed in foster care. The current circumstances of the children of two mothers, each with three children, are such that it would not seem surprising if foster care might be required at some time in the future. This further summary statement may be made: most of these mothers *do* much better than they *think they do*. They expressed more uncertainty and doubt about themselves in their roles as mothers than was warranted by the children's actual behavior and the evidence of their good physical care.

As noted earlier, the numbers used pertaining to the children of these women did not include miscarriages, stillbirths, or neonatal deaths. Among the 42 women there were 15 who had experienced 1 or more such "wasted pregnancies," totaling 32 such instances (6 of the women had such experiences more than once). Again, this is also the kind of information about which it is difficult to make comparisons with the general population, but insofar as such contrasts could be drawn, the number of instances among these women seems excessively high.[11]

High rates of miscarriages and of stillbirths are known to be associated with low economic status, but, given the reasonably decent economic circumstances of these women, this does not offer any explanation. Nor is any other explanation for these phenomena offered—yet the intimate association between body and psyche must always be taken into account in problems of physical malfunctioning. Surely it would be particularly important to do so in trying to understand why, over and over again, the children who might have been "brought forth," the fruits of their parents' bodies and the carriers of their parents' qualities, were instead "cast off."

## SOCIAL BEHAVIOR OUTSIDE THE FAMILY GROUP

### Religious Affiliations

When these subjects were children in placement, boys and girls of Catholic and Lutheran background were likely to have been placed and,

---

[10] The full report of the research includes ratings for "social effectiveness" and for the "sense of well-being" in the area of parenting as well as in other areas of adaptation.

[11] "Study of Prenatal Mortality and Morbidity Programs in the United States, Part 3, Hennepin County (Minnesota), Perinatal Mortality Study," *Journal of the American Medical Association*, CLXVII (1958), 1523–1525.

if replacements were necessary, replaced in homes of the faith of the child's background, but if children were of Protestant backgrounds other than Lutheran, placements and replacements were less likely to have hewn to the denominational lines. Some of the subjects mentioned the diversity of their religious experiences: "I didn't know what I was." Some have solved this dilemma by converting in their adulthood to a faith different from any of the denominations to whose beliefs they were exposed in their childhood.

The extent to which these former foster children who married people of different faiths were converted to or currently attend the churches of their spouses, in comparison with the extent to which the subjects' spouses made the shift when mixed marriages occurred, is of particular interest in testing the strength of religious identifications. Of the 16 situations in which either marital partner (subject or spouse) changed his affiliation to that of the spouse, 10 of these changes were made by the former foster child and 6 were made by the mate who was not a subject of this study. Whether the subject was male or female, a husband or a wife, a greater proportion of the marital partners who were former foster children than of the marital partners who were not former foster children did the shifting and took on the affiliation of the spouse who had been reared in his or her own family home. This is not surprising, since the religious affiliations of some of these persons were very tenuous, having been shifted from one denomination to another upon changes in placement. Furthermore, these former foster children were less likely than their mates to have been subject to family pressure against the relinquishment of a previously held affiliation.

About two-thirds of the group of men and women have retained the religious identifications of their childhood, however. Indeed, for some, these are exceedingly strong. Some of them not only attend a church of the same denomination, but worship in the very church they attended as children.

## Group Memberships

About half of the men stated that they were members of a group or groups; church-sponsored groups were prominently mentioned. There were also sports clubs, unions, card clubs, and other groups formally and informally organized. Four of the men claiming group membership either currently or in the past had occupied some office to which they had been elected or appointed, and another man holds a minor official post in his community. A similar proportion of women are group members. Women, like the men, mentioned church groups, but with them, too, there was diversity of club membership. There were purely social groups, neighborhood service groups, PTA groups, and others. Eleven of the women, either in the present or the past, occupied some position of leadership within their group or groups.

**Other Social Behavior**

Among the subjects, there are men and women who did not claim membership in a group, but said, "Well, no, it's not a club exactly, but there are several couples of us who always get together and go bowling." Or they described other forms of shared recreation. Others reported that social behavior with friends was on a more individualized basis, and some were involved in unorganized neighborhood activities.

There was an inquiry regarding mutual visiting. The question seemed more superfluous on several occasions, when a neighbor telephoned to say that the coffee was ready or actually arrived on the front steps, coffeepot in hand; this was evidence that the presence of the interviewer was interfering with the "friendly neighbor" activities and disrupting the usual routine of the housewife's coffee break.

There were, of course, other persons whose social relationships and social behavior were restricted because of their own feelings about themselves and about other persons, feelings they traced to their childhood status as foster children. One woman, for example, said that she did not like to become friendly with people because, if she did, she might be expected to reveal information about her background.

## STATUS IN THE COMMUNITY

Current literature concerning "multiproblem" families, "hard-to-reach" families, and "hard-core" families points out that these families are frequently isolated from the communities in which they live. They have not been woven into the fabric of shared community activities, and their behavior is not acceptable to community standards. Many of the natural families of these subjects, had they become known to agencies in this era, would be described by such terms.

Case records provided a variety of information about familial circumstances of our subjects at the time of their commitment to guardianship. The preceding materials have already suggested the contrasts between the situations of the parental families and the current families of the subjects, but we should also like to use case record material to contrast the specific ways in which the parents' status in the community differs from that of the subjects.

Within the families of 43 of the 80 members of the sample (excluding 2 of the 82 who had died since discharge from guardianship), one or both of the parents had had one or more of these three experiences while the child was at home: (1) incarceration, (2) hospitalization for mental illness, or (3) commitment to the guardianship of the state as a feebleminded person, with or without subsequent institutionalization and with or without subsequent sterilization. In addition to these three conditions, there were other kinds of social problems, such as illegitimacy, marital discord, economic dependency, excessive drinking, and emotional instability. These three are singled out, however, because of their particular pertinence to the question of social status.

Each of these three experiences has the common denominator of depriving the individual of some of his civil rights. He loses much of his freedom of choice and of movement. As a prisoner, a feebleminded person, or a person declared legally insane, he is deprived of his right to vote. In the case of the parents of the placed children, of course, all of them were also deprived of their natural right of guardianship of one or more of their children.

In drawing a comparison between parental circumstances and those of the subjects, it must be remembered that information was not secured from all of the 80 subjects. Five were not even located. Of the 75 who were located, 9 refused the interview and did not choose to complete a questionnaire. Both the availability of an address for these nine and the absence of social service registrations (as well as information *about* them but not *from* them) indicate strongly that none of the three conditions cited above obtains in their circumstances.

As for the five who were not located, considerable effort was put into trying to find them in the localities (out of state) to which they had gone and from which they had last been heard. In some instances, search included the use of social service clearances, but it is not possible to state that none of these five is hospitalized or imprisoned, somewhere, in some state.

Furthermore, many of the subjects of this study experienced periods of upheaval in late adolescence and early adulthood. Within those years, a considerable number had been arrested and jailed. In some instances, the turbulence of the period subsequent to discharge from guardianship suggested that these young people were experiencing conditions of identity diffusion as they faced the necessity of defining for themselves anew who they were, what they were, and where they were going. But this is a matter for discussion elsewhere.

As of this time, however, now that these men and women are within the age range of 28 to 32 and most of them are parents themselves, *current or recent* incidents of behavior leading to deprivation of civil rights are rare. One man is in prison, and he had also been hospitalized in a mental hospital in earlier years. One man, after being discharged from guardianship as a dependent and neglected child was committed to guardianship as a feebleminded person. Recently, subsequent to sterilization, he was discharged from this status with restoration of his civil rights. One man no longer has guardianship of a child born within a previous marriage, because the child was adopted by the former wife's second husband.

Only one woman lost the guardianship of children born to her within marriage. Under the divorce decree, the children were given into the custody of the husband and later placed for adoption with his relatives. Six women who had each had one or more illegitimate children relinquished guardianship, and the children were placed for adoption. In all but one of these instances, however, these events occurred during their late adolescence or early twenties.

## SUMMARY

Although the title of this article carries the phrase "current circumstances" and these words appear repeatedly throughout the paper, it is likely that many readers will have translated them into: "How well are these former foster children doing?" Or, to paraphrase the classic Sophie van Senden Theis study: "How do foster children turn out?"[12] These questions must be countered with two others: "What were the expectations?" and "As compared with whom?" Other portions of the full report compare subgroups of subjects with each other on the basis of differential kinds of experiences in foster care and by means of their individual scores for social effectiveness and the sense of well-being.

In the full report, comparisons with the general population have also been attempted. As noted, this is difficult, because of the smallness of the sample and sometimes because comparable data concerning the general population are not available. The evidence suggests a higher incidence of marital breakdown than among the general population and a higher proportion of illegitimate births. But more than half of the group own or are buying their own homes, and almost all of them are self-supporting. None of the legitimate children born to the subjects has been placed in foster care.

Comparisons are also drawn between their circumstances and those of their parents. In contrast with the parents, very few of these subjects in their recent adult life have been the targets for interventive acts because of behavior unacceptable to the community. Comparisons of economic circumstances would be somewhat false, since many of these children were removed from the parental homes during the era of the Depression.

The vast majority of the subjects have found places for themselves in their communities. They are indistinguishable from their neighbors as self-supporting individuals; living in attractive homes; taking care of their children adequately, worrying about them, and making some mistakes in parenting; sharing in the activities of the neighborhood; and finding pleasure in their associations with others. They do not always regard themselves as being indistinguishable, however, because they remember that, as foster children, they were different from their peers.

---

[12] Sophie van Senden Theis, *How Foster Children Turn Out* (New York: State Charities Aid Association, 1924).

# 30

⟨[ The following article is a report of one of the few attempts to use a group-work approach with children in foster care.

# Preadolescent Foster Children
# in Group Discussions

*Kenneth W. Watson and Harold Boverman*

Foster care is a way of life for thousands and thousands of children. Even when caseworkers direct their best efforts at preventing the need for children to be placed away from home, at returning children to their own homes, or at finding adoptive homes for them, a large and ever-increasing number of children will be raised in foster care in the next decade.[1] Growing up will be more complicated for these children than for children growing up in their own homes. Children's agencies have a responsibility not only to provide good care for these children but also to help them cope with the particular problems of being foster children.

Although they are aware of these problems, social agencies have not paid them much heed. Unless a foster child has symptoms of emotional illness, his problems as a foster child remain his own. One reason is, of course, the pressure on child welfare workers from large caseloads that leave them little time to do more than meet the child's need for a good place to live. A second reason may lie in the limitations of the one-to-one casework method.

How then can a child welfare worker help the foster child explore his particular problems and at the same time use his skill in casework to help the child resolve these problems? Holding regular casework interviews with the foster child who apparently has no serious problems may seem unnecessary to the child, intrusive to the foster parents, unrewarding to the worker, and wasteful to persons whose money supports the agency. Casework interviews with foster parents may improve the quality of the placement, but it cannot answer the questions that trouble foster children though they do not put them to their caseworker or their foster parents.

The Chicago Child Care Society, a voluntary agency, faced with trying

---

[1] Low, Seth: Foster care of children: major national trends and prospects. U.S. Department of Health, Education, and Welfare, Welfare Administration, Children's Bureau, 1966. (Multilith.)

to meet all the needs of the foster children in its care, decided in 1964 to explore the possibility of using small group sessions as a method of reaching foster children. The agency's decision was based on the speculation that children who share a background of foster care might support each other in discussing openly the problems of their status in a group focused on foster care. It conceived of the project as a way to use a group method to reach a fuller understanding of the unique problems faced by children growing up in foster care and the methods they develop to cope with these problems and to move the children, through their anxiety, to seek out and more effectively use the agency's casework services.

Although at first the agency considered forming groups of adolescent foster children, it decided that the problems normal in adolescence would complicate the task of focusing discussion on problems relating to foster care alone. For this reason, the agency chose children whose ages ranged from 8 to 12 years. Their membership was selected on the theory that the focus could be maintained more easily if the groups contained children of the same age and sex, without symptoms of emotional illness. In 3 years, five different groups were formed with from three to six members each. Each group met for an hour and a half once a week for five to seven sessions. The children in the groups had not known each other before the program began.

The agency's psychiatric consultant and its director of foster care and adoption served as the leaders of the groups. Before they began, the children's regular caseworkers explained to the children and their foster parents that the agency was starting the program because it wanted to learn more about foster children and their problems and that several groups of foster children would be meeting for this purpose. They answered questions about transportation, time, and the names of the leaders, but did not discuss any other details.

### GETTING UNDER WAY

The leaders approached the first meeting without a format, guided only by the wish to keep the content as simple and straightforward as possible. They met with the children around a table on which they had placed a piece of plain paper and a box of crayons, in a small room, unfurnished except for the table and chairs, at the agency.

At each first meeting, the leaders introduced themselves and suggested that the children sign in with the crayons. Then they said directly: "We know that all foster children have certain problems because they are foster children. We would like to know what yours are and how you handle them."

At the first meeting of the first group, soon after the leaders asked this question, Jimmy crossed his arms, leaned back in his chair, and said that he did not have any problems as a foster child. He was, he said, just the same as any other child. He was just as *good* as any other child. The other boys in the group looked relieved and nodded in agreement.

The leaders then said they wondered what kinds of problems Jimmy and the other boys thought a foster child would have if he had problems. Gus, after slowly clenching and unclenching his fists, said softly that a foster child might "get teased."

"But don't all kids get teased?" one of the leaders asked.

"I mean teased because he is a foster child and not living with his family," Gus replied. A tear rolled out of the corner of his eye, and he continued to open and close his fists.

The other boys were silent, but a common chord had been struck. Jimmy now looked to see what the leaders would do. When they made no effort to stop Gus's tears, he gave them a scornful look, quietly fumbled in his pocket, pulled out a dirty handkerchief, and pushed it across the table to Gus, whose face was now wet with tears. The leaders knew they were in business.

Each group had children ready and willing to talk. The leaders' job was to keep them talking about what it was like to be a foster child. If a child started to tell a story about something irrelevant that had happened to him in the last week, a leader would gently interrupt with the question, "What does this have to do with being a foster child?" If a child complained about conditions in his foster home, a leader asked how he thought they would be different if he were not a foster child. If the discussion digressed, the leaders reminded the group that the group had "work to do"; if there was a lag, the leaders would ask a question to get things going again.

Once the children sensed the purpose of the meetings and the direction the leaders were taking, they frequently helped keep the discussion focused on their problems as foster children. At one meeting, for instance, when the group was restless and the talk was diffuse, a boy rapped his hand on the table and said, "All right you guys, let's settle down. We've got work to do. Sooner or later we're going to have to face up to these things, and it'll be a lot easier now than it will be when we're grown."

## SOME COMMON WORRIES

Three questions continually turned up in every group: What is wrong with me that my parents are not raising me? Who will take care of me tomorrow? Who am I and what will I be like when I grow up? Boiled down, they concerned self-worth, dependency, and identity.

Many of the children's problems concerning self-worth centered on why their own parents had given them up. In one meeting, for instance, this exchange took place.

Melvin asked Johnny, "Hey, how come your folks put you in a foster home anyway?"

"What about you? Why did your folks place you?" Johnny retorted.

"I asked you first," Melvin flashed back.

"Well, I don't know," Johnny said thoughtfully. "I figure that I must have done something pretty bad for my mother not to want me. I've tried to think what it could have been. I was only 10 days old when my mother got rid of me. The only thing that I can think of that a 10-day-old baby could have done wrong was to cry too much. I've thought back as far as I can and I don't remember crying *that* much."

In all the groups, the children were concerned about the bad behavior that they thought must have been responsible for their parents' decision to place them in foster care. At one meeting, Larry said: "The only reason that I can think of for my mother not to want me is if there is something terribly wrong with me or something terribly wrong with her. And either way I've had it."

Sometimes a child's concern about self-worth took the form of a defense against admitting that such concern existed. But the children did not hold each other's defenses as sacred. One day Jimmy insisted that a foster child was worth just as much as any other child, maybe more. He himself, he said firmly, was worth a whole lot, maybe a million dollars. As he talked, he nervously played with the box of crayons, carefully peeled the price tag off, and stuck the tag on his forehead. Gus, having listened to Jimmy talk and having seen his actions, said, "Jimmy, if you feel you're worth so much, why did you put that label on your head? It says 19 cents."

The children also frequently discussed the moves they had made and the permanence or impermanence of the foster homes in which they were living. Most of them had lived in more than one foster home. They said a child must find out whether a new home is "for keeps." It became obvious that much of their testing behavior was conscious. Billy told the group about the day he plugged up the wash basin and the bath tub, turned on the faucets, and went out to play. "What happened?" a leader asked. "I got a licking," Billy said. "Boy, I bet you got a good one!" Hank exclaimed. "I sure did," Billy said with a smile. "But it didn't hurt bad, 'cause I knew it meant I could stay."

In another group, a member, Tony, said that he always thought twice before he said anything. That meant he had to talk slowly, but he was sure that he never said anything wrong. A leader asked him what would happen if he did say anything wrong. "I would get punished," he said. The group then asked what kind of punishment frightened Tony so much. "Would you not get to go out to play?" Roy wanted to know. "No TV?" Cy asked. "A whipping?" Roy asked. Tony shook his head to all these questions. Cy spoke up, "I know what punishment he's afraid of. He's afraid he'll have to move again." To this, Tony nodded his head.

In every group, the leaders talked about the agency and asked the children what function they saw it serving in their lives in the years ahead. In reply, one group in particular spelled out the possibilities. Bobby said that all he wanted was to reach 17 so he could quit school, join the Air Force, be on his own, and get the agency off his back. Lonnie said that was not for him. He liked the agency, and he hoped that it would see him through high school and maybe through college. Then he hoped it would help him find a girl to marry, a job, and a house. Joe said that he thought both Bobby and Lonnie were foolish. He did not know how long he would need the agency's help, but he sure would not want to cut it off when he was 17 unless he was sure he could take care of himself. He did not know yet whether he would be able to manage at 17, but he certainly expected to be able to take care of himself some day and not to need the agency the rest of his life.

In all the groups the children talked frequently about their own parents. Some saw their parents regularly or had met with them recently; others drew their ideas from fantasy since they could not remember their own parents.

Although David had never seen his own father, he said that he figured his father was one of the greatest men in the world and that he hoped he would grow up to be just like him. Fred, who saw his father regularly, said that he sure did not want to grow up to be like *his* father. David thought a moment. Then he said he really didn't want to grow up to be like his father because he really did not know what his "Dad" was like.

The leaders asked the group how foster children who had not known their parents know what they will be like when they grow up. Luke said that was easy for him: he just borrowed the characteristics he liked from the various foster fathers he had had and other men he had known and put them together and pictured himself like that when he was grown.

Of course, self-worth, dependency, and identity are subjects that every child is concerned about, but the foster child's concern is usually greater because he is being raised by people to whom he does not really or wholly belong.

## THE GROUP PROCESS

The methods used to lead the groups developed from the leaders' awareness of the purpose of the meetings and from the unfolding pattern of the children's responses to the situation. The process in each group had certain characteristics in common. At first, the children denied there were any problems. Once the group was under way, however, the children shared problems and feelings about being foster children. The talk flowed freely, but as the children continued to talk they became anxious about what they were sharing and the questions the leaders posed. As a result, they were reluctant to get the meetings started on time, their stories became longer and less relevant, their attention spans shorter, and their conversations more diffuse. The increased anxiety led to changes within the groups. The natural leader was no longer the child who could best put his problems as a foster child into words but rather the child who could either keep the discussion away from subjects producing anxiety or who could throw oil on the increasingly turbulent waters.

Another step in the group process came at about the midway point. This was the gradual exclusion of the psychiatrist consultant as a leader. The children realized that the anxiety aroused at the group meetings was not going to be handled within the group but rather within their relationship with the agency. Since the consultant was not a full-time employee of the agency, the children turned to the agency's worker for leadership and the reassurance implicit in his presence that the agency would continue to help them once the group meetings were over. One group told the psychiatric consultant that the other leader was to take over the following session, and at that session they reminded him of this when he made a comment.

## THE MEANING OF THE EXPERIENCE

The final step of the group process was to draw the experience together and make it meaningful for the children. By then, the members of the groups were friends, both inside and outside the groups. Children arrived early for meetings to have time to talk to each other and they left the agency talking and playing together. They were reluctant to have the sessions end, and suggested to the leaders that they hold a final party, a continuing series of meetings, or a reunion at a later date. In the sessions, the leaders attempted to pull together a little of what had happened and to recognize with the children the meaning of the experience.

Helping the children identify the problems involved in growing up in foster care did not resolve their problems, but it did provide both direction and stimulus for their contacts with the agency. The leaders had to guard against the temptation to treat the children as the children's anxiety mounted. Their work was to find the problems, not to treat them. When they began, they did not fully realize the extent to which the children would become available for individual service and did not make allowance for this with the first group.

After the first two meetings of the first group, the leaders noticed that the boys looked for their caseworkers to say "hello." The caseworkers did not grasp the full significance of these "hellos," however, until one day a boy whose worker was on vacation asked one of the agency's other workers if she would be his "worker" that day. She asked him if there was something he wanted to talk over and he said "no," that he just needed to know that he had a caseworker handy. All of the children needed to know they "had a caseworker handy," and many of them were better able to use their caseworker's help after the sessions than before.

Donna's is a case in point. A bright, attractive, 12-year-old girl who had been seeing a caseworker regularly for several months before the group meetings began, Donna barely got by at school and in her foster home. With the agency, she was manipulative and avoided real commitment to treatment. During the time of the group meetings, Donna continued to see her caseworker and talked a great deal about the group and her role in it. As the group sessions neared their end, she expressed her concern about what would happen to her as the previous limited casework had not been enough to help her meet her needs. She insisted that she and her caseworker sign a contract to work together to do something to improve the thing she liked least in her life—herself.

## SOME RESULTS

For one boy, Mark, the group sessions led to adoption. In the meetings, Mark had insisted that most of what the group was talking about was irrelevant to him because he regarded his foster parents as his own. He admitted that he sometimes felt as the others said they felt, but he also said that the degree to which he felt concern was minimal because of the security and permanence he had in his foster home. It was not the only foster home in which he had been, but he had been in this one for several years. The foster parents, too, expressed concern because the agency had failed to see Mark as fully theirs. Mark's caseworker used the anxiety the group meetings released to explore with the foster parents the nature of their commitment to him, and they subsequently decided to adopt him.

For another boy, Roger, the group sessions brought about better understanding between him and his foster parents. Roger had seen his caseworker regularly, usually because of a problem at school or in the foster home. The focus of these interviews had always been a specific difficulty; once the difficulty was past, the interviews seemed of little importance to him. After attending the group sessions, however, Roger asked for an appointment with his caseworker and talked with her not about the school but about the "things that were really" on his mind. Soon, he asked if his foster parents could come in with him since he had to get some things straightened out with them.

As a result of their interviews with the caseworker, the foster parents and the boy lost their ambivalence toward each other, and each was able to make a commitment to the other. Now Roger knows where he will grow up; his school problems have disappeared, and he seldom has to call on the agency for help.

### CASEWORK COORDINATION

The value of the group sessions was in a large measure the degree to which the experience they offered could be incorporated into the regular services of the agency. Some staff members resisted the idea of group services. Although the agency had 35 children aged 8 through 12 in foster care, the caseworkers could not think of a child to propose as a candidate for the first group. They resisted partly because they were confused over the goals of the experiment. Some workers were anxious about the sessions because they thought such a group might stir up quiescent emotions. Some were influenced by the possessiveness that can make caseworkers hesitant about involving "our clients" in unsought therapy.

Once the first group was under way, caseworkers whose children were included became enthusiastic. Their curiosity about what was happening to the children and their wish to be able to tie up their individual work with that of the group spurred their interest. After each group session, a leader would report to the children's caseworkers concerned about what went on and make specific observations about each child.

At first, the caseworkers were unprepared to meet the children's increased need for their help since the agency in planning the program had not given enough thought to how to handle the anxiety the group sessions might release. Once the children made their needs clear, the workers responded. For successive groups, the leaders planned more carefully.

The caseworkers also needed to allow more time for work with the foster parents of the children involved. Some of the parents were reluctant to have their children take part in the groups for many of the same reasons the caseworkers were hesitant. One couple removed their foster child from a group at the last minute and gave many reasons why he could not come. The leaders accepted the refusal but not the reasons. The foster parents' resistance provided an excellent opportunity for the child's caseworker to explore the meaning of foster care with them.

While their foster children were attending the group sessions, the foster parents became more involved with the agency. They called their workers more frequently to discuss the children and sought more casework time for themselves. In some instances, their increased activity reflected only their sense of greater involvement with the agency in working toward common goals. In others, it came as a result of their anxiety over the upsetting of a previous balance.

For example, one couple called to ask what the agency was doing to their foster daughter, Carol. The mother complained that Carol had become a different person, but that they had liked the old Carol better. Carol had been shy, quiet, and compliant. Now she was less withdrawn, more talkative, and self-assertive. In a group session, when one of the other girls had asked Carol why she was so quiet, she had said that she was only quiet on the outside, on the inside she was very noisy. She also said that she only pretended to be sweet and shy to get her own way. The caseworker had to help the foster parents understand the "noisy" Carol.

## WEIGHING THE RESULTS

Evaluation procedures were not set up as part of the project. Therefore, the success or failure of the experience can only be measured by its apparent effects on the children and on the agency. Certainly the problems and feelings of the foster children who took part seemed to be brought into sharp focus and reflected meaningfully through sharing in the groups.

The group sessions helped the agency see the problems of these children with greater clarity and improved its ability to plan effectively. For many of the children, the group was the doorway through which they were propelled to a meaningful relation with their caseworkers by the anxiety the group sessions released. For the staff and board of the agency, the reports from the group sessions underscored and dramatized the fact that a child welfare agency's responsibility must go beyond basic caretaking and planning.

An incident involving a boy named Johnny particularly illustrates this last point. During the final session of one of the groups, the leaders attempted to get the children to draw together and to evaluate the experience. Johnny listened attentively but seemed unable to take part in the discussion. In early sessions, he had been very vocal, but, in later sessions, as other group members discussed their problems, he had grown anxious, withdrawn, and depressed. To involve him in the evaluation, one leader turned to Johnny, pretended to be his caseworker, Miss V, and tried to put Johnny into the leader's role.

"Doctor," the leader said, "as Miss V, Johnny's caseworker, I would like to know how Johnny seemed to feel about the group meetings."

Johnny, responding as the leader, said: "Well, Miss V, Johnny was very quiet in the group meetings."

"Why was that, Doctor?"

"I don't know, Miss V."

"Why do *you* think he was quiet?"

A long pause followed. Then Johnny, still playing the role of the leader, replied softly: "I guess it's because Johnny has so many worrisome things on his mind that he's afraid to talk about them."

"Why is he afraid?" the leader asked gently.

"Because . . . because he's afraid that nobody can help him with them," Johnny answered.

But Johnny was not entirely right. From what she learned about his problems through the group sessions, Miss V was able to help Johnny work out solutions to some of his problems.

The agency has continued to use such group sessions, but because of its small foster-care caseload and the changing ages of the children served, it has expanded its groupwork program and has developed a wider variety of groups with varying focuses.

# Section IV

## Adoption Services

ADOPTION is a sociolegal invention which creates a nonbiological family by bringing together children without parents and parents wanting children. While the rate of adoption has remained almost constant during the past twenty-five years, the number of children adopted by nonrelatives has increased. An increasingly large percentage of such children is placed in adoptive homes by social agencies. In 1967, 83,700 nonrelative adoptions were completed; 74 percent of these were agency placements.

Adoption service, like foster-family care, is the concern of a large proportion of the professionally trained child-welfare social workers.

Earlier in the history of adoption, emphasis was given to providing children for childless parents. More recently the principal focus has been on providing parents for parentless children. Currently the pendulum is moving to a more neutral position, where both the needs of parents wanting children and those of children needing parents are considered.

A changing ratio of adoptive children to adoptive applicants has given impetus to the change in orientation. The total number of children available for adoption exceeds the number of applicants for adoption. We cannot, consequently, be rigorously selective in choosing adoptive parents. What might be required ideally for the very best interest of the child is tempered by what is feasible.

But even if we had a larger pool of adoptive applicants, we are less confident, currently, of the criteria for selectivity which determine adoptive outcome. Hence, adoption workers are more likely to screen in than to screen out, and more likely to see their role as enabling than to see it as evaluative. Rather than spending so much time in selecting the best fit between adoptive child and adoptive parents, adoption workers seek to help the parents and children to use optimally whatever potential they possess to develop a satisfactory relationship between all members of the newly formed family.

Professional interest and attention is shifting from preplacement selection to postplacement help when the adoptive parents and children are involved in the reality of living together.

At the same time greater efforts are being made to increase the pool of adoptive parent applicants by more flexible eligibility requirements regarding age, fertility status, income, mother's employment plans, marital status, length of time married, and so on. Efforts are also being made to use more imaginatively mass media for recruitment, develop regional and national adoptive exchange, and aid applicants so that they can qualify as adoptive parents. As a consequence, agencies are placing more and more children regarded as hard to place. But a substantial gap in need still remains, particularly for black children.

Agencies are seeking to decrease the pool of children needing adoption by more adequate services to the unmarried mother so that she can, without danger or damage, make a home for the child she might otherwise seek to surrender for adoption.

During 1968–1969 four states—California, New York, Minnesota, and Illinois—passed legislation in support of publicly subsidized adoption. After adoption, agencies in these states will continue to pay some families for care of the child. This is one aspect of a trend which, along with long-term foster-care placements, tends to blur the previously clear distinction between foster and adoptive parents. This is further exemplified by increasing acceptance of granting foster parents initial preference in the event that the child boarded with them becomes available for adoption.

Here, as is true for other welfare services, the social agencies are challenged by recipients of the service to justify and validate their claim that they be given clear community sanction to control this sector of human need. Adoptive parents, organized locally and nationally, have raised searching questions about agency requirements, agency service, and adoptive outcomes.

The readings have been selected to reflect the changing process of adoptive parent selection, postplacement activity, research on outcome, and, here as elsewhere, the increasingly frequent use of group activity.

# 31

⟪ Studies by Fanshel ("A Study in Negro Adoption," *CWLA*, 1957), Deasy and Quinn ("The Urban Negro and Adoption of Children," *Child Welfare*, Vol. 41, November 1962), and Fowler ("The Urban Middle Class Negro and Adoption," *Child Welfare*, Vol. 45, November 1966), among others, have attempted to offer explanations for the lack of interest among Negroes in adoption. The following article by Herzog and Bernstein reviews the results of some of these studies and raises doubt that Negroes are, in fact, uninterested in adoption.

# Why So Few Negro Adoptions?

*Elizabeth Herzog and Rose Bernstein*

The lack of adoptive homes for Negro children in need of placement is a problem familiar and painful to persons concerned with the welfare of children. About 70 percent of the white children born out of wedlock are adopted, as compared with less than 10 percent of the nonwhite children.[1]

The painful aspect of these figures lies in evidence about the fate of many children born out of wedlock who are not adopted. No doubt a considerable number are absorbed into the maternal family without serious adverse effects. Some, however, remain indefinitely in institutional or foster family care; and frequent replacements of such children are not uncommon.[2] Some children born out of wedlock remain with mothers who are unable or unwilling to care for them adequately, and who may not have access to the services they need to help them become more effective parents. For example, a mother may need to work to support her child but be unable to provide him with adequate supervision while she is out of the home.[3] Or keeping the child at home may interfere with a young mother's obtaining needed schooling for herself, and so the child becomes caught, with her, in the cycle of poverty and dependency associated with poor education and lack of vocational training.

Thus there are solid grounds for concern about the fact that there are many more Negro children in need of adoptive homes than there are couples wanting to adopt them.

A review by the Children's Bureau of available reports on research and demonstrations relating to births out of wedlock has brought out a number of findings and assumptions concerning the need for more Negro adoptive homes and the effectiveness of efforts to stimulate Negro adoptions.[4-14]

302

## SOME ASSUMPTIONS

One assumption, widely current some years ago, is less widespread today: that Negro unmarried mothers seldom, if ever, wish to place their children in adoption. While many Negro unmarried mothers obviously do wish to keep their children, the large number of Negro infants abandoned in the hospitals where they were born is tangible evidence that many do not. In line with such evidence, the executive director of a maternity home for Negro unmarried mothers said, in an informal interview, that 40 percent of the residents ask to relinquish their babies, and that this would probably be closer to 60 or 65 percent if there were any likelihood of the babies being accepted by placement agencies.

Reports from other sources also indicate that desire to relinquish children born out of wedlock far outweighs desire to adopt them. A participant in a recruitment drive for Negro adoptive homes, launched by several voluntary agencies, commented that the first response to the project was not from prospective adoptive parents, but from unmarried mothers wanting to place their babies. This social worker made a point that is supported by experience as well as by reading between the lines of some research reports: that if unmarried mothers do not believe they will be able to place their children, they do not mention adoption placement when they are asked whether they need or want social services.

Another assumption is still prevalent: that Negro couples are less ready than white couples to adopt children, chiefly because Negroes do not know about the availability of adoption services and of babies to be adopted. A number of projects have attempted to demonstrate the effectiveness of a coordinated communitywide effort to bring to the attention of the appropriate segments of the Negro population the opportunities that exist for the adoption of Negro children. These projects have been based on the premise that the apparent apathy of Negro couples toward the idea of adopting is due primarily to ignorance about the availability of Negro children, misconceptions about application procedures, fear of rejection by prying or prejudiced social agencies, red tape, and the like. Therefore, their major efforts have been directed toward correcting misinformation, or lack of information, and stimulating the interest believed to be latent in the community.

Typically, such projects have used various forms of public education, including spot radio or television announcements, newspaper publicity, speakers' bureaus, bus placards, and informal discussions organized through church, professional, and labor groups in Negro communities. The active participation of Negro community leaders has usually been secured. Direct mailings to members of organizations, and pamphlets and brochures placed in offices of social agencies, doctors' offices, beauty parlors, and barber shops have also been used.

One adoption agency held meetings with Negro couples who had already adopted children, to get suggestions about methods of recruitment based on their experiences. In two projects, mailings were sent to Negro families who were giving foster care to children. In another, meetings were held for Negro adoptive couples and prospective applicants, with the adoptive parents answering the applicants' questions—the theory being that "the best advertisement is a satisfied customer."

In their conclusions, reports of such projects tend to find merit in an organized, consistent, and cooperative community educational program to stimulate interest in the adoption of Negro children. However, some reports are not wholly enthusiastic about the results actually obtained. Moreover, analysis of the figures reported indicates that the numerical increases in applications are modest and suggests that the proportions of dropouts and rejections among applicants are likely to increase during such a drive.

An exceptionally systematic and carefully reported study by Fanshel,[4] based on applications over a 5-year period (1951–55), comments on "the relatively small number of those couples who had come [to the agency] on the basis of newspaper or radio/television [announcements] who went on to adopt a child." Fanshel sees the chief beneficial results of "broad public relations efforts" as indirect and long term, rather than immediate and direct. Like other investigators, he notes improvements in agency morale and "commitment," in interagency communication, and in mutual understanding between agencies and individual professional people, with consequent improvement in referral practices. He reports also that some applicants who withdrew after an initial contact returned later and completed an adoption.

Since most reports are sketchy and since criteria vary from one report to another (and not all give actual figures), there is still room for further inquiry into the sustained effectiveness of such projects and whether it is substantial enough to offset the financial cost, professional time, and community energy they consume. Careful review of the available reports seems to support the comment of Deasy and Quinn: "Social agencies on both the local and national levels have been trying for years to increase the numbers of Negro children who are legally adopted. But the success of such programs seems to have fallen far short of expectations and aspirations."[5]

## REASONS FOR NOT ADOPTING

After a review of relevant studies and demonstrations, Deasy and Quinn concluded that the apparently limited success of such efforts might arise from error in the assumptions on which they are based. Accordingly, they launched a systematic investigation designed to test those assumptions by obtaining answers to the question, "Why don't Negroes adopt children?"[5]

In this investigation interviews were held with 484 Negroes living in two communities—Baltimore (161 respondents) and Washington, D.C. (323 respondents). The respondents were people who, by the usual social agency standards, would be eligible as adoptive parents: partners in intact marriages, between the ages of 25 and 50, either childless (52 percent) or with a child over 5 years of age, and living in neighborhoods that were predominantly stable economically. They were longtime residents of the cities they lived in, more than 60 percent owned their own homes, 60 percent had held their present jobs for more than 10 years. In short, these people had the outer manifestations of stability and security.

The respondents were found to have an understanding, or at least a knowledge, of adoptions and why they become necessary. The majority (89 percent) knew about the adoption work of social agencies, and, although some were articulate in their criticism, they tended to regard these agencies as the best source of adoptive babies; 88 percent knew someone who had adopted a child and, although not interested in adopting a child themselves, appeared to approve the idea of adoption.

The respondents ascribed the shortage of Negro adoption homes to agency practices: "snooping," red tape, overly stringent requirements, and long waiting periods—even though the great majority of those who knew about adoption agencies said they were doing a good job. Most of them said that their main concern about a child would be in regard to his physical health and mental history rather than his birth status, parents' social position, or mother's age at the time of his birth.

The investigators commented:

> . . . it is not . . . for lack of information about adoption. . . .
> Our respondents think of agencies as a prime source of adoptive children and express no great fear of involvement with them. Yet there seems to be a basic lack of motivation to adopt.
> . . . the reasons for this lack of motivation must lie in the values to which successful urban Negroes subscribe. Surely many of the childless respondents we saw were childless by choice. If one chooses not to have a child by the biological process, why adopt one through an agency? . . . Parenthood involves risk. . . .
> . . . We know too well that to attain that state of mind that makes it possible to contemplate the future with any measure of equanimity is difficult for everyone these days—and perhaps more so for Negroes. . . . As the future becomes more trustworthy for them, let us hope that more Negroes can trust and can look to a future that includes children—either born to them or taken as their own.[5]

The same investigators later undertook a similar study in which white couples in the same cities were asked the same questions. It will be interesting to compare the results.

## ARE NEGROES LESS INTERESTED?

None of the studies or demonstrations reviewed raised any question about the assumption that there is, as Deasy and Quinn put it, a "crashing lack of interest among Negroes in the adoption of children."[5] Nevertheless, a question should be raised: Is there really less interest in adoption among Negroes than among whites, or does the scarcity of adoptive applicants merely reflect the relatively larger number of babies available for placement and the relatively smaller number of couples in a position to adopt?

The number of nonwhite children born out of wedlock each year is half again as large as the number of white children born out of wedlock. Yet there are many times more potential adoptive parents among the white population than among the nonwhite. To begin with, the white population is about 10 times as large as the nonwhite. In addition, the white population has, on the whole, far more income annually and far more economic security than the nonwhite. In 1961, for example, nearly half the nonwhite families in the United States had incomes below $3,000 and nearly one-fourth fell below $1,500—as compared with not quite one-fifth and about one-fourteenth of the white families.

Further analysis of Bureau of the Census figures on the characteristics of the white and nonwhite population of the United States, and of Children's Bureau reports on adoption, reinforces doubts about the widespread assumption that Negro couples are, on the whole, more reluctant than white couples to adopt children.

For this analysis we are indebted to Hannah Adams of the Division of Research, Children's Bureau. Miss Adams was hampered in her computations by lack of data from a number of States, and therefore conclusions from them must be qualified accordingly. Even so qualified, however, they call for a new look at an assumption that has been remarkably free of challenge.

She found that for the country as a whole, in 1961—if one considers only husband-wife families with heads under 45 years old—the ratio of nonrelative adoptions was 3 per 1,000 couples for all races combined and also for the white population. For Negro husband-wife families of the same age, it was 2.7, only a little lower.

When income was considered as well as family composition in the analysis, a more striking challenge to the assumption emerged. It seems reasonable to suppose that the great majority of legal adoptions occur in families with incomes over $3,000 a year. If this is so, then families with less than this amount of income ought to be excluded from the base population used in figuring the adoption ratio.

When this was done, the adoption ratio for the United States in 1961, for all races combined, rose from 3 children adopted by nonrelatives per 1,000 husband-wife families with heads under 45 to 3.5 per 1,000 such families. For white families, the ratio rose only from 3 to 3.4. But for nonwhite families it rose to 4.9.

Apparently, either those nonwhite families having higher incomes were *more* likely than white families to adopt children not related to them, or a significant number of nonwhite families with incomes under $3,000 adopted children—or possibly both.

Thus it appears that the lower proportion of two-parent families found among Negroes, and the notoriously low-income levels so prevalent in this minority group, fully account for the dearth of Negro adoptive applicants, without any need to assume different attitudes toward adoption. (It should be remembered also that we are discussing here only legal adoptions, leaving aside informal arrangements of child care which are not legalized.)

The figures are not offered as conclusive. However, even when due allowance is made for the fact that they are based on estimates, they strongly suggest that group differences in the availability of adoption as a resource for child care relate to income and family composition, rather than to differences in attitudes toward adopting. In other words, review of the evidence indicates that coordinated campaigns of public education have been disappointing because they have been based on false premises. Contrary to the frequent assumption, Negroes are *not* less interested in adopting than are whites among those in a position to adopt, nor are they less informed about adoption. Community demonstrations have been expected to cure a condition that apparently did not exist.

Educational campaigns about adoption directed at Negro populations can probably help to some extent, but they cannot be expected to correct the main problems, since they are not directed to the main problems. The test of their effectiveness will be, not whether they can raise the Negro adoption rate as high as the rate among white couples, but whether they can increase still further the amount by which it already exceeds the white rate among couples who are in a position to adopt a child.

## OTHER POSSIBLE APPROACHES

The evidence reviewed does not deny the possibility that adoption rates among Negroes could be increased. It shows merely that the main problem in placing Negro children does not stem from ignorance or apathy ın the Negro population, and that publicity efforts alone are not likely to solve the problem.

It becomes necessary, therefore, to look for other means of solution. The evidence suggests that these should be designed, not for bringing about change in the potential adoptive parents, but rather for bringing about change in the circumstances that, directly or indirectly, encourage or discourage adoption. We cannot here spell out what these changes should be. We can, however, indicate three possible approaches to coping with the scarcity of adoptive homes for Negro children:

1. *To modify some adoption policies and practices* which are criticized in a number of study reports. In the criticisms it is not always possible to separate prevailing misconceptions from actual fact. However, both Fanshel's study[4] and the one conducted by MARCH[6] (Minority Adoption Recruitment of Children's Homes) report high withdrawal rates among applicants for children and document the points at which agency practices (as of the fifties when these studies were made) appeared to alienate prospective adoptive parents. It should be added that a good many adoption agencies—including some of those whose placements were studied—have shown outstanding readiness to look critically at their own procedures and have already introduced modifications that might be expected to reduce the number of applicants who voluntarily withdraw.[7, 8] Other modifications introduced by some agencies might more accurately be called innovations—for example, subsidizing the child in an adoptive home which meets all the requirements except financial ability.

2. *To expand resources other than adoption placement* for children for whom adoptive homes are lacking—for example, increasing payments for foster care and developing good group care arrangements.

3. *To modify the conditions that cause the problem*—a more potent but also a more difficult method than the other two. The large numbers of Negro babies in need of placement reflect the prevalence of lower incomes among Negroes and the high incidence of broken homes and births out of wedlock that are associated with extremely low incomes among both Negroes and whites. The prevalence of these conditions among Negroes reflects, in turn, the low status—both social and economic —of a minority group in an affluent society. Efforts are afoot to improve that status. Success in these efforts could help to reduce the amount of poverty, the proportion of broken homes, and the rate of out-of-wedlock births. In the process it could also help to reduce the discrepancy between the number of babies who need homes and the number of homes ready to receive them.

It is not necessary to wait for major changes in socioeconomic conditions before attempting to increase the number of Negro adoptive homes. On the contrary, every feasible step should be taken. However, it is probably unrealistic to expect a major increase in Negro adoption rates until major changes in socioeconomic conditions are well under way.

## References

1. Adams, Hannah M.; Gallagher, Ursula M.: Some facts and observations about illegitimacy. *Children,* March–April 1963.
2. Maas, Henry S.; Engler, Richard E.: Children in need of parents. Columbia University Press, New York, 1959.
3. Herzog, Elizabeth: Children of working mothers. U.S. Department of Health, Education, and Welfare, Social Security Administration, Children's Bureau. CB Publication No. 382. 1960.
4. Fanshel, David: A study in Negro adoption. Child Welfare League of America, New York. 1957.
5. Deasy, Leila C.; Quinn, Olive W.: The urban Negro and adoption of children. *Child Welfare,* November 1962.
6. Minority Adoption Recruitment of Children's Homes (MARCH): Adoptive placement of minority group children in the San Francisco Bay Area. San Francisco, Calif. 1959.
7. Allen, Alexander J.: A commentary on a study of Negro adoptions. *In* A study in Negro adoption (David Fanshel). Child Welfare League of America, New York. 1957.
8. Hawkins, Mildred: Negro adoptions—challenge accepted. *Child Welfare,* December 1960.
9. Buffalo and Erie County Community Welfare Council: Report and recommendations of the committee for Negro adoptions. (Mimeographed.) Buffalo, N.Y. May 10, 1961.
10. Dukette, Rita; Thompson, Thelma G.: Adoptive resources for Negro children—the use of community organization and social casework in recruitment and development. Child Welfare League of America, New York. August 1959.
11. Foote, Gwendolyn: Report: "homes for children" project—1958–1962. (Mimeographed.) Connecticut Child Welfare Association, New Haven. Sept. 14, 1962.
12. Perry, Martha: An experiment in recruitment of Negro adoptive parents. *Social Casework,* May 1958.
13. Philadelphia Health and Welfare Council, Children's Division: Report of committee on Negro adoptions. (Mimeographed.) Philadelphia. July 7, 1960.
14. Thompson, Gertrude J.: Final report: "homes for children" project, ended Dec. 31, 1958. (Mimeographed.) Children's Services of Connecticut, Hartford. (Undated.)

# 32

◖ If different child-welfare workers had the opportunity of listening to the same adoptive couple throughout an interview, would they come to the same decision regarding the acceptability of the applicant for adoptive parenthood? The following article is excerpted from a research monograph reviewing the results of such an experiment. Using tape recordings of actual adoptive intake interviews, Breeland played these to child-welfare workers in adoptive units throughout the country.

## An Experimental Study of the Selection of Adoptive Parents at Intake

*Donald Brieland*

### HISTORY OF PROJECT

Following the National Adoption Conference held in January 1955, the Child Welfare League of America and the Elizabeth McCormick Memorial Fund sponsored a three-day meeting in Chicago the following September to consider research needed in adoption. The participants included persons from child welfare, genetics, law, pediatrics, psychiatry, and psychology. Conferees agreed that it would be worthwhile to study the decision-making process of caseworkers in selecting adoptive parents from among a group of applicants. As a result, the project reported herein concerning social workers' judgments in selecting adoptive families for home study was planned and carried out.

This research is the first national study in the field of adoption involving interviews with clients. The tape recordings used provided the first opportunity for the workers involved to listen to another worker's interviews.

### STATEMENTS OF THE PROBLEM

The major task of the adoption agency is to find suitable adoptive parents for children. To do so, it must select some couples to become adoptive parents and determine that other couples cannot be served. This study confines itself to the problem of selection of applicants for Caucasian infants, and does not deal with the agency's task of actively seeking couples who will adopt older children or children who are non-white, of mixed race, or physically or mentally handicapped.

In the larger agencies, intake is often a specialized function of one or more workers. Couples to be studied further following the intake interview are assigned to other workers for additional interviews. The specialized intake worker's task is to establish a relationship between client and agency more than between client and worker, since another worker will continue the case if the couple is accepted for study. Since there was not time for the worker-judges to review all the interviews that constitute a complete home study, the focus of this project is on the intake interview as the first occasion for decision-making.

The purpose of this study was to obtain and analyze the judgments of child-placement workers concerning capacity for adoptive parenthood of five couples. While sound motion pictures would have been ideal, maintaining confidentiality of clients' identity would have proved difficult. Therefore, tape recordings were made of complete intake interviews.

## DESCRIPTION OF AGENCY

A private, nonsectarian, statewide agency holding membership in the Child Welfare League agreed to provide the interviews. The agency limits itself to a single function—providing adoptive homes for children under three years of age. Meetings to explain agency function and policies are held for groups of five or six couples. Following the group meeting couples register and make an appointment for the intake interview. After the intake interview the worker dictates the case record and indicates his decision. The couple's qualifications arc reviewed by a case committee. The applicants receive a letter within 60 days indicating whether or not the agency is able to begin home study.

For purposes of the research project the legal counsel for the agency devised a release form which, with other registration material, was presented to applicants:

> The process of learning about the interests and qualifications of adoptive applicants and of making selections of homes for our children makes it necessary to obtain personal information from you. To help us to make a decision with respect to your interest in adopting a child, we will maintain records on information secured and on our contacts with you. The records will be in the form of written records and mechanical recordings. The agency obtains and uses all such information to assist it to make decisions in its selection of applicants, and for purposes of research and training to improve professional practice.
> You hereby give your consent to use all such information for all purposes the Agency considers advisable.
> Signed: _____
>            (Husband)                              (Wife)

The form was used routinely with applicants for over a year. All couples signed it without question. During the course of the research, no client raised any question about the recording or referred to it in any way.

## RECORDING PROCEDURE

Each of the caseworkers in the agency recorded several intake interviews. The microphone was placed inconspicuously in an intercommunication box on the desk in the interviewing rooms. The cord led through the wall to the office where the tape recorder was located. A secretary operated the recorder. Workers were instructed to conduct their interviews as usual. Each caseworker dictated the case record in the regular way. Since intake interviews were assigned to workers randomly, each worker in the agency would be expected at intake to deal with a cross-section of the agency's applicants.

After reviewing the preliminary recordings from seven workers in the agency, it was decided to select as a research interviewer a male caseworker whose trial tape recordings were particularly clear and who seemed to succeed in making clients feel at ease. This decision was made in consultation with the agency and upon its recommendation.

To control selective factors, intake interviews scheduled consecutively with five couples were recorded. Couples who had adopted children previously were excluded from the research group. The recordings were made by professional technicians from a state university audio-visual department.

The five interviews ranged in length from one hour and twenty-seven minutes to one hour and forty-eight minutes. Differences in length were affected by the number of questions raised by the clients and by their verbal fluency during the interview.

The interviews used in the study were more factual than depth-oriented. They were designed to elicit information about the couple and their feelings and attitudes toward children. The interviewer tried to cover a wide range of material and usually did not seek detailed "diagnostic" answers.

The content covered followed the same general order and included these major topics:

1. The couple's interest in a child including sex and age, coloring, and background.
2. First-hand contact with other couples that have adopted.
3. General experience with children (including own children if not childless).
4. Telling the child of adoption and giving the child information about his identity, including any reading the couple has done on the subject.

5. Attempts at having own children, including sterility studies.

6. Development of interest in adoption on part of couple, including which partner's interest is strongest.

7. General sketch of family life experiences, including verbal description of parents and attitudes toward parents and siblings.

8. Educational history, including attitude toward school.

9. Marital interaction.

10. Employment history and attitudes.

11. Social participation in present neighborhood.

12. Religious participation and attitudes.

13. Explanation of agency procedure and promise of notification within sixty days whether a home study would be undertaken.

### THE FIVE COUPLES

The couples were within the age range acceptable to most agencies. Length of marriage ranged from five and a half years to fourteen and a half years, and education from eighth-grade graduation to a post-graduate degree. All of the husbands had permanent employment. None had an income clearly inadequate to support an adopted child. All were home owners, and were covered by some life insurance. All professed an interest in organized religion and attended Protestant churches. In four cases sterility was apparently attributable to organic factors, and in one to functional factors.

Three fixed eligibility requirements of some agencies might have led to rejection of one or more of the couples. A few agencies specify 35 years as the maximum age for applicants for infants. (Couples C and D were older.) Some will not consider applicants with own children. (Couple D had two.) Some sectarian agencies require a definite period of church membership in the community of present residence. (Couple C did not belong to a church in their own community.)

Most agencies, however, would consider the five couples eligible for an intake interview. If a couple would be disqualified because of fixed requirements of an agency, worker-judges were told to assume, nevertheless, that the couples were eligible for consideration but to evaluate them on all other bases as they would if the couple came to their own agency. For example, Catholic agencies do not consider Protestant couples. In this study they did so.

### SAMPLE OF WORKER-JUDGES

The tapes were played on sixteen different occasions to a total of 184 worker-judges—62 supervisors and 122 caseworkers. Seventeen workers were male and 167 were female. Twenty-eight agencies from thirteen states cooperated in providing worker-judges for the project. The number of workers from a single agency ranged from one to seventeen. Eighteen of the agencies used at least 90 percent of their adoption staffs as judges. For the others, some selection resulted because host agencies were encouraged to ask other Child Welfare League members in the same community to participate. When such arrangements were made on short notice, all adoption workers could not be present.

Although an attempt was made to get wide geographic coverage, costs had to be considered. Selection of the agencies was determined in part by proximity to Chicago, where the project was administered. Agencies included all have high standards for personnel and practice. All agencies that were invited agreed to cooperate.

A day and a half were required in each agency for evaluation of the tapes. About 2,500 hours of social workers' time went into the project.

Complete transcripts of the case were distributed before the tape was played. The transcripts made it possible to verify what was heard if a word were missed, and to indicate the portions of the interview that contributed significantly to the judgment of the worker. As they listened to the tape, the worker-judges marked the transcript with plus or minus signs and made brief comments in the left-hand margin, beside the interview content which provided evidence of strengths or weaknesses seen in the applicants. The interviews moved slowly enough so that workers did not have problems in marking judgments and writing reasons as they listened.

The workers were instructed to use the *tape* as a *primary stimulus* and to refer to the transcript when they wished to comment on the clients' responses. They were instructed to avoid evaluating the caseworker and to discuss the couples only after all of the interviews had been judged. The cases were presented in random order to control the effects of order of judgment. In order to insure independence of judgments, the workers were seated behind cardboard screens.

After hearing each interview, the worker-judges wrote a brief summary record and indicated whether they would "begin home study" or "terminate" contact with them. They also rated each couple on a number of specific factors on a check list, indicating whether each was a great strength ($++$), strength ($+$), weakness ($-$), or a great weakness ($--$). If they were unable to evaluate the couple on any one factor or thought it was irrelevant to adoptive parenthood, they were instructed to write in a zero.

The worker-judges gave the couples numerical ratings on a hundred-point scale. In the pilot stage of the study, judges had difficulty ranking the five couples from memory after a day and a half. After making the ratings, the worker-judges transformed them to rankings, and a quality-ordering resulted. Without time to provide training in a rating procedure, use of ranks offered a simple way of approaching relative quality.

How is this experimental procedure consistent with agency practice and how does it differ?

1. Using tape recordings does not make it possible to see the couple. Tapes do, however, provide a better objective indication of the interaction than would a case record.

2. The interviewing method showed a close resemblance to that employed by some of the participating agencies and differed from that of others. Comments of some of the workers indicated areas in which they wanted more information. This is true at the conclusion of their own intake interviews as well. At some points they wished that the couple would have been allowed to pursue a subject at greater length without interruption by the interviewer. The workers were generally agreed, however, that they had adequate data on which to make a decision about studying the couples further.

3. The most realistic task requested of the workers in terms of their practice was to indicate whether or not they would begin home study with the couple. Workers do not ordinarily have to rank families in terms of over-all quality.

4. Whether couples are viewed at intake in terms of suitability for specific children seems to vary from agency to agency. Certain families might be approved for home study because they had qualifications which met the needs of children who are difficult to place, although they might not have as high general quality as other applicants who would be rejected. For this reason, workers were instructed to regard the couples as potential adoptive parents for normal white infants. This was also the way the applicants perceived themselves.

5. Agencies ordinarily have not used check lists to describe characteristics of individual applicants. While such data are not central to the purpose of this study, the method provides an orderly way to get evaluations in a similar manner from each worker.

6. Workers were asked to make decisions immediately following the hearing of each case. Ordinarily such requirements are not imposed. Instead they have an opportunity to dictate the record sometime after the interview has been completed. Under the requirements of the research situation, in order to assure independence of judgments and to make minimum demands upon agency staff, judgments had to be obtained at the end of each interview. However, there is nothing in the research literature of social work or other clinical professions to indicate that the passage of time increases the reliability or validity of such decisions.

The experimental procedure follows the pattern of decision-making in social casework in that the worker is the major decision-maker. The agency must decide, on the basis of the worker's presentation of evidence, whether or not it will begin home study. The experimental method involves responses of judges with similar training to the same stimuli. If it had been possible for each worker to conduct his own interviews or for the interviews of a number of workers to be presented, the results might have been different.

For persons interested in practice in social casework the degree of agreement of workers on acceptances or rejections within the same agency and among different agencies will have the major interest. Ranks and other evaluations of the family are less important. However, the research may attest to the usefulness of some standardization in considering adoptive applicants, both within the interviewing process and in case recording.

## ACCEPTANCES AND NON-ACCEPTANCES OF THE COUPLES

The judgments requested of the worker-judges which are most typical of those made in practice concerned acceptance or non-acceptance of the couples. In this study, there was no chance for the workers to get more information from a subsequent interview—a possible course of action in practice for borderline situations. (Most agencies participating in the study indicated they did not hold a second interview with a couple about whom they had serious doubts.)

Ideally, validity of judgments in this project might have been determined by data on the actual parental performance of the couples, since there are no research data to indicate that performance in pre-adoption interviews can be used as an accurate predictor of parental performance over several years. It was not possible or desirable, however, to place a child with every couple and evaluate what happened over several years. As an alternative, one could have considered as correct the decisions made by the agency actually serving the couple. But then there would have been no chance of knowing if a couple with high capacity for adoptive parenthood had been rejected, since the agency, following typical practice, did not offer such persons a second interview. If serious weaknesses appear in subsequent interviews, couples accepted at intake can still be rejected, but mistakes in judgment that cause "good" couples to be rejected after the intake interview cannot be reversed unless the couple reapplies.

The agency could have been asked to do complete home study on the five couples regardless of their strengths or weaknesses. This would have run the risk of increasing the motivation for parenthood of those who might ordinarily be rejected early.

Thus it was arbitrarily decided to use as the criterion for a correct decision the consensus of the group of 184 worker-judges. If a couple was accepted or rejected by the majority, that decision was considered valid.

The worker-judges accepted:

| | |
|---|---|
| Couple A | 164 to 20 |
| Couple B | 147 to 37 |
| Couple C | 124 to 60 |

and rejected:

| | |
|---|---|
| Couple D | 113 to 71 |
| Couple E | 129 to 55 |

These results for the total sample are statistically significant.[1] Whether or not the amount of agreement they represent is satisfactory to agencies is quite another question, however, since the data reveal considerable disagreement.

The percentages of agreement for the 184 workers for each case were:

| | |
|---|---|
| Couple A | 89.13 |
| Couple B | 79.89 |
| Couple C | 67.39 |
| Couple D | 61.41 |
| Couple E | 70.11 |
| Five Couples combined | 73.59 |

With a decision to accept or reject, chance agreement would be 50 percent.

Table I presents the actual decision of each worker-judge on the individual couples, and the score of "correct" decisions for each worker-judge. To derive the worker score the decisions were scored much as a five-item "true and false" test using the consensus decisions as the key:

| Couple A | Couple B | Couple C | Couple D | Couple E |
|---|---|---|---|---|
| Accept | Accept | Accept | Not accept | Not accept |

Thus, for example, a worker who agreed with the consensus on all five decisions received a score of five; if he differed on one decision, he got a score of four.

Of the 184 worker-judges, 43 workers agreed completely with the majority, 65 agreed on four decisions, 53 on three, 21 on two, and two agreed with the majority in only one of the five cases. Thirty-three workers not only did not accept at least one of the two couples most often

---

[1] $\chi^2 = 196.72$. This result is statistically significant at the .001 level of confidence.

## TABLE I. Decisions on Acceptance*

| Agency | Worker-Judge | A | B | C | D | E | Score | Agency | Worker-Judge | A | B | C | D | E | Score |
|---|---|---|---|---|---|---|---|---|---|---|---|---|---|---|---|
| A | 1 | A | A | A | R | A | 4 | H | 53 | A | A | A | A | R | 4 |
|  | 2 | A | A | A | A | R | 4 |  | 54 | A | R | R | R | R | 3 |
|  | 3 | A | A | R | R | A | 3 |  | 55 | A | A | A | R | R | 5 |
|  | 4 | A | A | R | A | A | 2 |  | 56 | A | A | A | R | R | 5 |
| B | 5 | A | A | A | R | A | 4 |  | 57 | A | A | A | R | A | 4 |
|  | 6 | A | A | A | R | R | 5 |  | 58 | A | A | R | R | R | 4 |
|  | 7 | A | A | R | A | R | 3 | I | 59 | A | A | R | R | R | 4 |
|  | 8 | A | A | R | R | A | 3 |  | 60 | A | A | A | R | R | 5 |
|  | 9 | A | A | R | R | A | 3 |  | 61 | R | A | R | R | R | 3 |
|  | 10 | R | A | A | A | R | 3 |  | 62 | A | A | A | R | R | 5 |
|  | 11 | A | R | A | R | R | 4 |  | 63 | A | A | A | R | R | 5 |
|  | 12 | A | R | A | R | R | 4 | J | 64 | R | R | A | A | R | 2 |
|  | 13 | A | R | A | A | R | 3 |  | 65 | A | R | A | A | A | 2 |
|  | 14 | A | R | A | A | R | 3 |  | 66 | A | A | A | A | R | 4 |
|  | 15 | A | R | R | R | A | 2 |  | 67 | A | A | A | R | R | 5 |
| C | 16 | A | A | A | R | A | 4 |  | 68 | A | R | A | A | R | 3 |
|  | 17 | A | A | A | A | A | 3 | K | 69 | A | R | A | R | R | 4 |
|  | 18 | A | A | A | R | R | 5 |  | 70 | A | R | A | A | R | 3 |
| D | 19 | A | R | A | A | R | 3 | L | 71 | R | A | A | R | R | 4 |
|  | 20 | A | R | R | R | A | 2 |  | 72 | A | A | A | A | A | 3 |
|  | 21 | A | A | R | A | R | 3 | M | 73 | R | A | A | R | R | 4 |
|  | 22 | A | A | A | R | R | 5 |  | 74 | A | R | A | R | A | 3 |
|  | 23 | A | R | A | A | R | 3 |  | 75 | R | A | R | R | A | 2 |
|  | 24 | A | A | R | R | A | 3 |  | 76 | A | R | A | R | A | 3 |
|  | 25 | A | A | R | R | A | 3 |  | 77 | A | R | A | R | R | 4 |
|  | 26 | A | R | A | R | R | 4 |  | 78 | A | A | A | R | R | 5 |
|  | 27 | A | A | A | R | R | 5 | N | 79 | A | A | A | A | R | 4 |
|  | 28 | A | R | R | R | A | 2 |  | 80 | R | A | A | R | R | 4 |
|  | 29 | A | A | A | R | A | 4 | O | 81 | A | R | R | R | A | 2 |
| E | 30 | A | A | R | R | R | 4 |  | 82 | R | A | A | R | A | 3 |
|  | 31 | A | A | A | R | R | 5 |  | 83 | A | A | A | R | R | 5 |
| F | 32 | A | A | A | R | R | 5 |  | 84 | A | A | A | A | A | 3 |
|  | 33 | A | A | A | A | R | 4 |  | 85 | A | A | A | A | R | 4 |
|  | 34 | A | A | A | A | R | 4 |  | 86 | A | A | A | R | A | 4 |
|  | 35 | A | R | A | A | A | 2 |  | 87 | A | A | R | A | A | 2 |
| G | 36 | A | A | A | A | R | 4 | P | 88 | A | A | R | A | R | 3 |
|  | 37 | A | A | A | A | R | 4 |  | 89 | A | A | R | R | A | 3 |
|  | 38 | A | A | A | R | R | 5 |  | 90 | A | R | A | R | A | 3 |
|  | 39 | A | A | R | R | R | 4 |  | 91 | A | A | A | R | A | 5 |
|  | 40 | A | A | A | R | R | 5 |  | 92 | A | A | A | R | R | 5 |
|  | 41 | A | A | A | A | A | 3 |  | 93 | A | A | R | A | R | 3 |
|  | 42 | A | A | R | R | R | 4 |  | 94 | A | A | A | A | A | 3 |
|  | 43 | A | A | R | R | R | 4 |  | 95 | A | A | A | A | R | 4 |
|  | 44 | R | R | A | A | R | 2 |  | 96 | R | A | A | A | R | 3 |
|  | 45 | R | R | R | R | R | 2 |  | 97 | A | R | A | A | R | 3 |
|  | 46 | A | A | A | A | R | 4 |  | 98 | A | R | A | A | A | 2 |
|  | 47 | R | R | R | R | A | 1 |  | 99 | A | A | A | R | R | 5 |
|  | 48 | A | A | A | R | R | 5 |  | 100 | A | A | A | A | A | 3 |
|  | 49 | R | A | R | R | R | 3 |  |  |  |  |  |  |  |  |
|  | 50 | A | A | R | R | R | 4 |  |  |  |  |  |  |  |  |
|  | 51 | A | A | R | R | R | 4 |  |  |  |  |  |  |  |  |
|  | 52 | A | A | A | A | R | 4 |  |  |  |  |  |  |  |  |

* A = accept; R = not accept.

TABLE I. (*Continued*)

| Agency | Worker-Judge | Couple A | B | C | D | E | Score | Agency | Worker-Judge | Couple A | B | C | D | E | Score |
|---|---|---|---|---|---|---|---|---|---|---|---|---|---|---|---|
| Q | 101 | R | R | A | A | R | 2 | V | 139 | A | A | A | R | A | 4 |
|   | 102 | A | A | A | A | R | 4 |   | 140 | A | A | A | R | A | 4 |
|   | 103 | A | A | R | A | R | 3 |   | 141 | A | R | R | R | A | 2 |
|   | 104 | A | A | R | A | R | 3 |   | 142 | A | A | A | R | R | 5 |
|   | 105 | A | A | A | A | R | 4 |   | 143 | A | A | R | R | R | 4 |
|   |     |   |   |   |   |   |   |   | 144 | A | A | R | R | R | 4 |
| R | 106 | A | A | R | A | R | 3 |   | 145 | A | A | A | A | R | 4 |
|   | 107 | A | A | R | A | R | 3 |   | 146 | A | A | A | R | R | 5 |
|   | 108 | A | A | R | R | R | 5 |   | 147 | A | A | R | R | A | 3 |
|   | 109 | A | A | R | R | R | 4 |   | 148 | A | A | R | A | R | 3 |
|   | 110 | R | A | A | A | R | 3 |   |     |   |   |   |   |   |   |
|   | 111 | A | A | A | A | A | 3 | W | 149 | A | R | R | A | R | 2 |
|   |     |   |   |   |   |   |   |   | 150 | R | A | A | R | R | 4 |
| S | 112 | A | A | R | R | R | 4 |   | 151 | A | A | A | R | R | 5 |
|   | 113 | A | A | A | A | R | 4 |   | 152 | A | A | R | R | R | 4 |
|   | 114 | A | A | A | R | A | 4 |   | 153 | A | R | R | R | R | 3 |
|   | 115 | A | R | R | A | R | 2 |   | 154 | A | A | A | A | R | 4 |
|   | 116 | A | A | A | R | R | 5 |   | 155 | A | R | A | A | R | 3 |
|   | 117 | A | A | R | A | R | 3 |   | 156 | A | A | R | R | R | 4 |
|   | 118 | A | A | A | R | R | 5 |   | 157 | A | A | R | R | R | 4 |
|   |     |   |   |   |   |   |   |   | 158 | A | A | R | A | R | 3 |
| T | 119 | A | A | A | A | A | 3 |   | 159 | A | A | R | A | A | 2 |
|   | 120 | A | A | A | R | R | 5 |   |     |   |   |   |   |   |   |
|   | 121 | A | A | A | R | R | 5 | X | 160 | A | A | R | A | R | 3 |
|   | 122 | R | R | A | A | A | 1 |   | 161 | A | A | R | A | R | 3 |
|   | 123 | A | R | A | A | A | 2 |   | 162 | A | A | A | R | R | 5 |
|   | 124 | A | A | A | R | A | 4 |   | 163 | A | A | R | R | R | 4 |
|   | 125 | A | A | A | R | A | 4 |   | 164 | A | A | A | A | R | 4 |
|   | 126 | A | R | A | R | A | 3 |   | 165 | A | A | A | A | R | 4 |
|   |     |   |   |   |   |   |   |   | 166 | A | A | R | A | A | 2 |
| U | 127 | A | A | A | R | R | 5 |   | 167 | A | A | A | R | R | 5 |
|   | 128 | A | A | A | R | R | 5 |   | 168 | A | A | A | R | R | 5 |
|   | 129 | R | A | A | R | R | 4 |   | 169 | A | A | A | R | A | 4 |
|   | 130 | A | A | A | A | R | 4 |   | 170 | A | A | A | R | R | 5 |
|   | 131 | A | A | A | A | R | 4 |   |     |   |   |   |   |   |   |
|   | 132 | A | A | A | R | R | 5 | Y | 171 | A | A | A | R | R | 5 |
|   | 133 | A | R | R | R | R | 3 |   | 172 | A | A | A | R | A | 4 |
|   | 134 | A | A | A | A | R | 5 |   | 173 | A | A | A | R | R | 5 |
|   | 135 | A | A | R | R | R | 4 |   | 174 | A | A | A | R | A | 4 |
|   | 136 | A | A | R | A | R | 3 |   | 175 | A | A | A | R | R | 5 |
|   | 137 | A | A | A | R | R | 5 |   | 176 | A | A | A | R | R | 5 |
|   | 138 | R | A | A | R | A | 3 |   | 177 | A | A | A | R | R | 5 |
|   |     |   |   |   |   |   |   |   | 178 | A | A | A | R | A | 4 |
|   |     |   |   |   |   |   |   |   | 179 | A | A | A | A | R | 4 |
|   |     |   |   |   |   |   |   |   | 180 | A | A | A | R | R | 5 |
|   |     |   |   |   |   |   |   |   | 181 | A | A | A | R | A | 4 |
|   |     |   |   |   |   |   |   |   | 182 | A | A | R | R | A | 3 |
| Workers from three different agencies: |   |   |   |   |   |   |   |   | 183 | A | A | R | A | A | 2 |
|   |     |   |   |   |   |   |   |   | 184 | R | A | A | R | A | 3 |

accepted by the consensus, but also accepted at least one of the couples rejected by the consensus. One worker did not accept Couples A and B and accepted Couples D and E, the reversal of the majority decision on each of these four cases.

There was no difference in the scores of the 62 supervisors and the 122 caseworkers. The mean score for supervisors was 3.688 and for caseworkers 3.682.

The workers who had completed many home studies of adoptive applicants did not differ from those with less experience. The means for various levels of experience are shown in Table II.

TABLE II. Distribution of Workers by Number of
Home Studies Completed and Mean Scores

| Home Studies Completed | Number of Workers | Mean Score |
|---|---|---|
| Over 100 | 105 | 3.64 |
| 51–100 | 31 | 3.84 |
| 50–11 | 25 | 3.56 |
| 10–0 | 23 | 3.69 |

The mean scores of males and females did not differ significantly nor did scores of female workers divided into sub-groups in terms of marital status. Married female workers with and without children did not differ. The male sample was too small to permit comparable analyses.

Various agencies showed wide differences in the decisions to accept or reject couples. These data are shown in Table III.

The majority of workers in no agency rejected Couple A. Agency L (with only two workers) was evenly divided on acceptance and rejection. Two of the agencies, J and K, predominantly rejected couple B and two, I and W, rejected couple C. Five, F, J, P, Q, R, accepted couple D; one agency, Q, accepted couple D unanimously. Four agencies, A, C, O, T accepted couple E. There seems to be little consistency in the pattern. Agency J differed from the majority consensus on two cases but the others did so only on one case.

Among the agencies with over ten workers, at least one worker in each would have enthusiastically accepted a couple for further study who was rejected by the majority of his colleagues. There was less tendency for workers in large agencies to reject the couples who were accepted by the consensus. Agencies D, V, X and Y were unanimous in accepting couple A, X and Y in accepting couple B, and Y in accepting couple C.

## SUMMARY

1. The agreement of 184 worker-judges on the five couples was *statistically* significant, i.e., clearly better than chance, but the amount of

TABLE III. Percentages of Intra-agency Agreement and
Consensus Agreement by Agency

| Agency | Intra-agency Agreement Per cent | Rank | Consensus Agreement Per cent | Rank |
|---|---|---|---|---|
| A | 75 | 16 | 65 | 22 |
| B | 67 | 24.5 | 67 | 20.5 |
| C | 87 | 5 | 80 | 7 |
| D | 67 | 24.5 | 67 | 20.5 |
| E | 90 | 2.5 | 90 | 2 |
| F | 85 | 6 | 75 | 11 |
| G | 73 | 20.5 | 73 | 12 |
| H | 83 | 8.5 | 83 | 4.5 |
| I | 88 | 4 | 84 | 3 |
| J | 80 | 11 | 64 | 24.5 |
| K | 90 | 2.5 | 70 | 14.5 |
| L | 70 | 22.5 | 70 | 14.5 |
| M | 70 | 22.5 | 70 | 14.5 |
| N | 80 | 11 | 80 | 7 |
| O | 74 | 18 | 66 | 22 |
| P | 74 | 18 | 69 | 17.5 |
| Q | 84 | 7 | 64 | 24.5 |
| R | 77 | 13.5 | 70 | 14.5 |
| S | 77 | 13.5 | 77 | 9 |
| T | 73 | 20.5 | 68 | 19 |
| U | 83 | 8.5 | 83 | 4.5 |
| V | 76 | 15 | 76 | 10 |
| W | 74 | 18 | 69 | 17.5 |
| X | 80 | 11 | 80 | 7 |
| Y | 91 | 1 | 91 | 1 |

agreement shown may not be optimal in terms of *practical* significance for adoption practice.

2. The decisions of the majority of the 184 workers to accept or reject were used as the correct decision on each of the couples. 43 workers were in complete agreement with this consensus, 65 differed on only one decision, and 76 differed on two or more. Two of the workers agreed with the consensus on only one decision.

3. Supervisors' scores and caseworkers' scores, computed in terms of agreement with the consensus decision, did not differ.

4. Scores for those worker-judges with considerable experience with adoption home studies were not significantly different from those with less experience.

5. There were no significant differences between scores of male and female workers, nor within the female group subdivided according to marital status. Female workers with children did not differ from those without children.

6. The agencies showed a wide range of intra-agency agreement.

7. Intra-agency agreement and consensus agreement did not show a close relationship. When agencies differed from the consensus they did so typically on only one of the cases, but the particular case on which they differed varied from agency to agency.

8. Agencies did not differ in affirmativeness or leniency, but the five couples differed in their acceptability to the sample of agencies.

# 33

(( The Brieland study employed an experimental procedure to elicit the decision child-welfare workers made regarding the acceptability of adoptive applicants and to clarify the factors which influenced the decision. The following article is a report of a research project which utilized data made available through the ongoing work of the agency to study caseworkers' assessment of adoptive applicants.

## An Exploration of Caseworkers' Perceptions of Adoptive Applicants*

*Trudy Bradley Festinger*

In recent years, adoption agencies in the United States have played an increasingly prominent role in adoptive placements of children with nonrelatives. During 1963 and 1964, about two-thirds of all adoptions by nonrelatives were arranged by social agencies. When compared with national estimates for the years preceding, agency adoptions grew at a faster rate than did nonrelative adoptions as a whole.[1] A study on trends in adoption, published in 1965, stressed the growing importance of social agencies on the adoption scene as revealed in data about the rising number

   * This study was supported by Grant No. R-4(R) from the Children's Bureau, Welfare Administration, U.S. Department of Health, Education, and Welfare.
   [1] *Adoptions in 1963* (Washington, D.C.: Children's Bureau, Welfare Administration, U.S. Department of Health, Education, and Welfare, 1964); and *Adoptions in 1964* (Washington, D.C.: Children's Bureau, Welfare Administration, U.S. Department of Health, Education, and Welfare, 1965).

of children available for adoption, the expanding number of applicants to agencies, and the growth of agency placements completed.[2]

Such an increase is a reflection of society's growing acceptance of adoption as a means of creating families. It also reflects a philosophy that has given the social agency, as an institutional unit of society, progressively more responsibility in consummating the adoptive parent-child relationship. In line with such a responsibility, the adoption field has voiced increasing concern with refining the level of professional practice. One such approach has sought to advance knowledge about the nature of decision making in adoption practice, with respect to both child placement and parent selection.

## PURPOSE AND PROCEDURE OF THE RESEARCH

The focus of the research reported here (carried out under the auspices of the Child Welfare League of America) was on the problem of adoptive-applicant assessment. More specifically, we addressed ourselves to the following questions: (1) What are the implicit perceptual dimensions underlying caseworker assessments of the suitability of candidates for adoptive parenthood? (2) Are these dimensions broad holistic constructs, or are the assessments based on discrete discriminations? (3) Do caseworkers have different applicant models for different kinds of children? Of particular interest here was whether the assessments of applicants considered suitable for hard-to-place children differ in any material way from the ratings of those couples thought to be suitable for the average youngster. And (4), do agencies differ in their assessment tendencies with respect to the underlying perceptual dimensions of applicant evaluation?

This investigator's bias, or what may euphemistically be called "research philosophy," was to look at ongoing practice by tapping the natural setting rather than simulating the adoption situation or using case-record material. The data, therefore, were obtained by focusing on couples who applied for adoption while the research was in progress and by asking adoption workers to complete an extensive rating instrument on each couple they interviewed following the worker's last contact with the couple during the adoption-study period.

Our concern for an adequate description of practice resulted in a number of compromises in selecting our research design and procedures. For instance, we did not devote ourselves to the task of establishing the reliability of caseworker assessments of applicant couples. Rather, we were inclined to accept the fact that judgments in the adoption field tend to be rendered with considerable uncertainty and that the task of assessing applicants does

---

[2] Lydia F. Hylton, "Trends in Adoption, 1958–1962," *Child Welfare*, XLIV (1965), 377–386.

not always stem from a firm knowledge base. Nevertheless, this is how the field has often had to operate, and we wished to lend our effort to building this base by explicating whatever regularities we could find to account for case-workers' judgments of adoptive applicants.

This study—based on social worker assessments of 398 adoptive applicant couples—included eight participating agencies that were all located in the confines and immediate surroundings of a large Eastern metropolitan area. The questionnaire used in the study was devised and pretested during 1962 and 1963, and included ratings that covered a wide range of variables used by adoption agencies in their evaluation of applicants. The data were collected between 1963 and 1965.

In order to gain a picture of adoption practice over a period of time, the research plan called for a gradual, sequential accumulation of the sample of applicant couples until a total of approximately 50 cases had built up in *each* of the eight agencies. All potential applicant couples seen for at least one interview following the starting date of the research in a given agency became part of the study. Our final analysis was based on the 87 social workers' questionnaire assessments of those couples they had seen among the total of 398 adoptive-applicant couples.

From a research standpoint, this project is not an example of a neat and clean design. First of all, we selected these eight agencies because they carried the bulk of adoption practice in this community. We accumulated the applicant sample sequentially over a period of time on the assumption that we would tap a typical applicant group at each agency. Moreover, our major sources of data were such statistically unreliable people as social workers. Yet these same social workers were the very group currently responsible for interviewing and assessing applicant couples, and it was current practice, however unreliable, that was our focus.

One cautionary note, however, must be injected. Any generalizations based on this research are inevitably limited, not only by the quality of the data, but by the passage of time and by the geographical base of the study. We believe that the weight of this study rests on the fact that it is fairly rare in child welfare research to have data based on the experience of eight agencies in a community. And because of this, the size of our sample, and the care with which it was selected, we feel secure about making some generalizations about adoption practices in one Eastern metropolitan area.

In thinking back over the task of carrying out this research, which involved fairly regular contacts with the adoption workers who were assigned to the applicants on our sample, we are struck by two parallel, though somewhat conflicting, impressions. On the one hand, we noted the seriousness with which the caseworkers regarded their responsibility in the applicant-selection process, and the depth of their respect for the couples involved. At the same time, we noted that, although many of the workers

held a strong allegiance to their own agency, they seemed somewhat isolated from the thought and work of other agencies in the field. All too
often, the investigator was placed in the position of channeling information
in response to requests for news from the field and questions about policies
and practices of other agencies in this metropolitan area. Although this
was strictly an impressionistic observation, we did begin to wonder about
gaps in communication among the staffs of agencies and the lack of col-
laborative relationships in the face of a joint task to be done. We therefore
hoped that some of our findings would not only add to general knowledge,
but would serve as a stimulus for better communication among the caseworkers in the field.

## THE ADOPTION AGENCIES AND THEIR APPLICANTS

The majority of couples interviewed in the eight agencies were seen by
one caseworker during the course of their adoption study. It appeared that
most of the agencies tried to maintain continuity of worker in the study
process, a principle that has been stressed in the whole casework field. In
two of the agencies, however, there was a shift between two or three
workers for about 50 percent of the couples in their respective samples.

The median number of interviews per couple was four. Most initial
applicants completed the study process in four to five interviews. The
majority of reapplications were completed in three or fewer interviews.
We noted this with much interest in view of the frequent complaint heard
in the general community that applying for adoption at an agency means
being compelled to submit to interviews *ad nauseum*. Although we can
sympathize with couples who find the interviewing process a strain, this
particular complaint seems to have little merit in light of our findings.

We also noted that the majority of agency interview time was devoted
to initial applicants, who constituted the larger group (approximately five
to seven initial applicants for every reapplicant couple) and who were seen
for more interviews in the study process. We also found that few families
in the total sample had previous private adoption contacts of any sort. We
wondered whether this was due to some reporting error or whether it
meant that agency and private applicants come from different populations
or travel diverse routes in their quest for a child. The latter notion gained
some support from our data on referral sources, which indicated some informal acquaintance system as operative in couples' applying to a particular
adoption agency.

## FINDINGS CONCERNING APPLICANT CHARACTERISTICS

The ages of applicants accepted by the eight agencies ranged from
approximately 20 to 50 years. Although the husband had a better chance

of being accepted if he was between 30 and 39, and the wife had a better chance if she was between 25 and 34 years of age, our data supported the notion of flexibility among agencies—and negated the idea of rigidity of policy and practice—in respect to age.

We were somewhat startled by our finding that, although the number of Negro applicants in the total sample was 41, the proportion of accepted Negro couples was smaller than the percentage among the white group accepted by the agencies. At the same time, the proportion of Negroes who withdrew—yet were judged good prospects for adoptive parenthood—outweighed the proportion of white couples in the same category. These data were troubling in view of the large number of Negro children awaiting adoptive placement, the agencies' outspoken concern about such children, and the general need for recruiting Negro applicants. With more flexible agency criteria for selection, especially among this group, we would have expected to find a larger proportion of acceptances here than among the white couples.

Of equal concern was the sizeable withdrawal rate among those Negroes judged to be good adoptive prospects. When we explored the reasons for withdrawal among this latter group, the single largest category (40 percent) "withdrew: decided to adopt privately." On the other hand, among the white applicants assessed good prospects, the largest single category (39 percent) "withdrew: wife pregnant."

These findings suggest that agencies should take a sharp look at what is happening with Negro applicants, in order to establish the best possible communication with the Negro group and possibly alter certain standards and practices that may be affecting the withdrawal rate.

### Religion

Among the three major religious faiths, there was little variation in the proportion of all couples who were either accepted by these agencies or, although they withdrew, were judged to be good prospects for adoptive parenthood. In other words, couples who had at least one interview had about an equal chance of being selected or positively regarded, irrespective of their religion. This seemed to contradict the notion that Jewish couples have had a more difficult time in the selection process. On the basis of our data, we could only conclude that this idea was incorrect or that it was correct only to the extent that, because of the relative dearth of available Jewish children, the Jewish group does not have as many adoption resources at their disposal. Another possible explanation is that there exists for the Jewish group a more stringent self-selection or screening process *prior* to the first interview.

Our findings clearly indicated that once seen for an interview, none of the applicants identified with the three major religious groups was in a disadvantageous position as far as acceptance for adoptive parenthood. Moreover, the commonly expressed idea that couples of mixed faiths are not acceptable was not supported by our data, although it was true that this group was required to make a commitment about the religious faith in which they planned to rear a child, and there was indication of a some- what higher rejection rate here than if both husband and wife belonged to the same religious group.

### Education and Income

In education, the sample median for husbands was "college, not com- pleted"; for wives, it was "high school graduate," with an overall tendency for applicants to the public agency adoption departments to have attained a lower educational level than private-agency applicants. The acceptance rates bulged at two peaks: the "high school graduate" and the "graduate education" levels, which we tentatively interpreted as reflecting the public- private educational differentials.

Despite such possible differences, the husbands' median total gross in- come of about $8600 remained approximately the same for all the agencies, although a larger proportion of private-agency applicants were at the higher end of the income range than were applicants to public agencies. With respect to husbands' occupational prestige ratings, agency differences were not considered material, and the only differential noted in relation to agency outcome was in the lowest- and middle-prestige categories where rejection and withdrawal rates tended to be higher for couples considered poor prospects for adoptive parenthood.

### Other Variables

For most of the couples in our sample, their current marriage was the first, with the median length of marriage over seven and one-half years. Couples who were married less than 4 or over 16 years had a poorer chance of being accepted, but we suspected that this may have had as much to do with their age as with the agencies' standards pertaining to length of marriage, since the proportion of accepted and withdrawn (but assessed as good) couples at either extreme diminished with respect to couples at the two extremes of the age range.

When we looked at the overall acceptance rates of couples in relation to whether they had children, we noted that couples who had already adopted one or two children were more apt to be accepted than those who had not adopted, and couples with natural children tended to be accepted less often than those couples who had no children of their own. We won- dered—and this was purely speculation—whether this was due to social workers' feeling that the introduction of an adopted child into a house that already included a natural child was a more difficult situation for the adoptive child and for most couples, and, therefore, more stringent stand- ards were applied to this group of applicants. It was also possible that since this was a special group of applicants, i.e., couples who already had children of their own, the social workers were responding to some qualitative difference that made them poorer prospects for adoptive parenthood. We do not know the answer, but we believe that this is an area where further self-scrutiny on the part of agencies might be extremely valuable in order to be sure that they are not excluding a group for reasons extraneous to their potential for filling the adoptive parent role.

When we looked at family backgrounds, we noticed that the majority of applicants came from multiple-sibling family units, and tended not to be the first-born. We wondered whether the size of families meant that such couples were more attuned to children and therefore more likely to be motivated to adopt.

On the medical side, couples were more likely to be accepted by the agencies if the medical prospects of having their own children were deemed doubtful or impossible. Although we are fully cognizant of the possible psychological complexities involved, we cannot help wondering whether there may, at times, be too much stress in this area without commensurate knowledge. For instance, do we know that it is so likely to be detrimental to the adoptee if a couple adopts and then has a child of their own? No doubt the situation has many inherent problem potentials, but would they materialize? Possibly here is another group of potential adopters who are, at present, too liable to be turned away.

The median amount of time between confirmation of inability to have a child and the initial interview with an adoption agency was 16 months. Although these couples had initiated contact by telephone or letter at an earlier date, the time interval seemed to support the idea that a period of time was psychologically necessary in order to come to terms with the inability to conceive and the decision to adopt. An alternative explanation, however, was that agency philosophy on this question had somehow been communicated to couples so that they either tended to be discouraged from contacting agencies too quickly or were not granted an early interview if they did.

When we looked at applicant preferences, we noted that two-thirds of the small fraction of applicants who requested children "over 5 years of age" were considered poor prospects for adoption. We assumed that these ratings were in response to the poorer qualifications of the applicants. Yet, in light of the need for couples who can accept older children, we cannot but wonder if there is some unstated expectation that applicants should want younger children (since most of them do have such a preference). Although purely impressionistic, this is a question that might warrant further examination.

### AGENCY OUTCOME

Contrary to the idea common among many groups in the community that agencies spend much of their time rejecting applicants, we found that, despite some distinct variations among the agencies, in the overall sample 54 percent of the couples were accepted. Another 13 percent withdrew, but were judged good prospects for adoptive parenthood; and we are not in much danger in assuming that a majority, if not all, of these would have been accepted had they not withdrawn. These figures may have been partly accounted for by self-selection and by the screening out of some inappropriate couples prior to the first interview. Nevertheless, most couples who were seen at agencies for at least one interview received a child for adoption. This gave some credence to our suspicion that the myth of agencies busying themselves in the rejection process may be due to the dissatisfied being more vocal than the satisfied.

The continuation of this myth, however, raises some important public relations implications for consideration by the agencies. For instance, in order to counteract the rejecting-agency image, should not more time be devoted to those couples turned away from agencies? To us, this seems to have particular merit in order to avoid discouraging couples from approaching agencies at a time when the field must build applicant resources to match the needs of the increasing numbers of children who need adoptive homes.

We also wonder whether the rejected group of applicants are often those who next turn toward independent sources in their quest for a child. If such is true, it would seem to be an important child welfare service to give more time to this group of applicants and to try to create a better understanding that would encourage this group to turn to agencies for any service that might be needed in the future. Since this group is by and large a disappointed one, with none too kindly feelings toward agencies, it might entail a more aggressive, reaching-out approach, which might well be worth both time and effort.

We used a subsample of cases (those applicants who had been seen for at least two interviews) in order to determine the extent to which the worker's assessments of couples, following the first interviews, was a predictor of the final decision arrived at by the agencies. The correlation between first-interview assessments and final outcome ($r_{pb} = .42$) tended to confirm this expectation of some predictability, but this amount was far from overwhelming. If the correlation had been very high, we would have questioned the usefulness of more than one interview in making decisions on the suitability of couples for adoptive parenthood. On the other hand, the result we obtained seemed consistent with what one could expect in a well-functioning decision operation.

We also examined the trend of workers' assessments over time of those couples who had been seen for at least three interviews. From the very beginning of agency contact, the applicants who were eventually rejected (and here we combined the rejected group with those applicants who withdrew but were assessed poor prospects for adoptive parenthood) received poorer ratings than those applicants who were in the acceptable group at the close of the study period. The data also revealed that, following the first interview, the assessment differential between the acceptable and un-acceptable groups was minimally significant. Following the last interview, however, there was a large differential in the ratings of the two groups. This was the result of a sharp drop in the ratings (following the last inter-view) of those applicants who were considered poor prospects for adoptive parenthood. Many of these ratings probably coincided with, or followed, the final agency decision. The sudden drop in ratings of this group of applicants possibly means that at this late stage in the study process, workers were more willing to render an extremely poor judgment in agree-ment with or in justification of the final agency decision.

## THE ADOPTION CASEWORKERS

Over one-half of the 87 adoption workers who participated in the study were married; their median age was 41. Thirty-seven percent of the group had reared children of their own. Over half of them had master's degrees, but there was considerable variation between agencies in this respect. There was essentially no difference between the public and private agencies in the proportion of workers with graduate degrees, although the public agencies had a larger proportion of staff at the low end of the education range. Despite our awareness of the lack of professionally educated staff in the field at large, it concerned us to note that a number of agencies were using workers without professional education for the specialized, skilled task of assessing adoptive applicants.

In addition to supervisory guidance and inservice training approaches, we suggest two procedures that could help to meet the need for profes-sionally educated personnel. Schools of social work might take a more active role in encouraging students in the direction of child welfare by in-corporating into their education programs a greater emphasis on child wel-fare, and specifically the area of adoption, with special opportunities for training for the public services. Second, adoption facilities might devote more effort to developing fieldwork opportunities that might, in the long run, serve as an indirect recruiting device for those students who have received such training.

Despite sizeable differences with respect to the amount of employment experience in social work, the median fell at about eight and one-half years, with the median number of years in the child welfare field slightly over five, and in adoption about three. We noted considerable variation among the agencies, and a tendency for public agency staffs to have had less adop-tion experience than caseworkers in private agencies. We assume that this reflects the all-too-usual picture of public agencies having greater difficulties than voluntary agencies in hiring and retaining professionally educated staff, the tendency of such staff in public departments to move up the supervisory ladder fairly quickly, and the comparatively recent entry of the public agencies into the adoption field in this metropolitan area.

We also noted that the most experienced adoption workers in our sample had accumulated their experience in one agency. This prompted us to speculate about the existence of a core of agency culture, internal within each adoption facility, that is built up and maintained by a nucleus of long-term staff who serve as transmitters of a particular agency's philosophy and style of operation to any newcomers on the scene.

## THE CHILDREN PLACED FOR ADOPTION

The median amount of time between the first interview and the placement of children in the homes of the accepted initial applicants in our sample was 7.9 months. We found considerable variation among the agencies in this regard, with public agencies tending to take longer in the placement process. Although we do not have data to support an interpretation, we conjecture that this may have been due to heavier caseloads and more administrative details in these agencies. We noted with interest that, on the whole, the lapse of time between initial interview and placement was not as extensive as has been alleged by those in the community who have leveled attacks against agencies for the supposed slowness of their operations. It might also be pointed out that such a time period is shorter than the normal gestation period of pregnancy.

The median age of the children at the time of placement was 4.7 months. We again found considerable variation among the eight agencies, with public placements tending to be above the median figure, whereas private agencies placed children at a younger age. It was encouraging to note that 67 percent of the placements occurred when the child was 6 months of age or younger. This seemed a mark of progress in the agencies' movement toward early placements. On the other hand, we were concerned that only 10 percent of the placements were of children 1 year old or over, of which a mere 4 percent were age 2 or more. Possibly this, too, reflects progress with respect to the placement of older children; yet these percentages seemed disappointingly small, since the need for such placements is great. Our proportions may also have been related to the number of older children referred for adoption from long-term foster care units, because of a traditional exclusion of children from adoption possibilities who have not been considered adoptable.[3]

Prior to their adoptive placement, 91 percent of the children had had only one boarding home experience. In view of the field's concern about

---

[3] See Florence G. Brown, *Adoption of Children with Special Needs* (New York: Child Welfare League of America, 1959).

children being shuttled from one foster home to another, our data were extremely encouraging and seemed to indicate that much headway has been made in this area. The young age of most of the children placed may have partially accounted for this finding, however. After the first glow of enthusiasm, we were also quick to remind ourselves that a selective process may have been operating. That is, we had to question what was happening to those children who had multiple boarding-home placements. Maybe these children constituted the group of children who were either not available for adoption or who were not as likely to be given priority in being selected for adoptive placement. Perhaps, for some reason, they were considered more risky. Therefore, our findings of so few boarding placements may, in large measure, have reflected availability as well as assessments as to which children would be the best candidates for adoptive placement.

Of the more than 200 children placed for adoption with our applicant sample, only 26 were Negro or of mixed racial origins. Although headway has been reported in this area, its movement has been as slow as the progress made in placing children across religious lines. With respect to the latter, it seems unlikely that we will see much change until there are alterations in those laws that largely regulate agency operations or until there is a more child-focused interpretation of the "where practicable" restriction. As for the racial issue, present lags are probably a reflection of agencies' responsiveness to the value orientation of their applicants and the community at large (who, in addition to the race question, may consider Negro children less acceptable because so many more are available), and also of the problems of recruitment and some difficulties in counteracting the sizeable withdrawal rate among Negro applicants. This should pose quite a challenge to agencies, both in the public relations domain and in experimenting with new ways of reaching, communicating, and working with this much needed group of potential and actual adoptive applicants.

## THE DIMENSIONS OF APPLICANT ASSESSMENT

Our major analysis focused on the implicit perceptual dimensions underlying caseworker assessments of candidates for adoptive parenthood. A factor-analytic approach was chosen as the most economical means for an examination of these dimensions. We were interested in determining whether the numerous ratings of the caseworkers were reducible to a few underlying constructs that were basic to the caseworkers' perceptions of applicants, or whether so many ratings were independent of each other. Three factors emerged from this analysis: (1) positive psychosocial appraisal, (2) suitability for a deviant child, and (3) young marriage. We were somewhat surprised that the many variables that caseworkers had been asked to use to assess applicants could be reduced to three dimensions. Nevertheless, even such a minimal yield meant that there was other than a halo operating and that there was an underlying structure guiding caseworker ratings as opposed to a random scatter of responses. Our results showed that workers were discriminating, but that the range within which workers made their judgments was a narrow one, since the repertoire of constructs turned out to be limited.

This finding made sense in light of what Hunt has spoken of as the limits on the capacity of the human being as a processor of information.[4] In a similar vein, past studies of parent behavior have revealed the human limitation with regard to discrete evaluative ratings of perceptual data.[5] This made us wonder whether we have at times made the error of endowing caseworkers in the adoption field with the task of making judgments about parental potential when such a magical capacity should not be the expectation. Possibly the field itself should not carry the burden of predictions about capacities to fill the parental role.

Aside from the limits on information processing, it seems important to ask how workers can be expected to make predictions about parental behavior when, in most instances, they can only be guided by impressions based on observations of couples who are not at that time parents. Of these clinical and perceptual limitations and the resulting limited number of underlying constructs that appeared to be operative in the assessment of applicants, one implication for practice is that a deemphasis of the field's screening ability might be more in keeping with the realities of assessment capacities.

The three dimensions that emerged from our analysis, as mentioned above, were interpreted by us—at the positive pole—as (1) positive psychosocial appraisal, (2) suitability for a deviant child, and (3) young marriage. The first two were highly stable, whereas the stability of the third was of moderate proportions. Therefore, we shall concentrate on the two key conceptual dimensions that were operating in the casework assessments of the adoptive applicants.

The first of these was a major evaluative factor that appeared to be a holistic positive appraisal of the applicants rather than separate or distinct discriminations. Clusters of items that were most highly related to the positive pole of this dimension included the positive quality of the couple's interaction in their marriage, flexible and outgoing characteristics of both the husband's and wife's personalities, the couple's openness, their nonneurotic motivation for adoption, their adequate marital-role performance,

---

[4] J. McV. Hunt, "On the Judgment of Social Workers as a Source of Information in Social Work Research," in *Use of Judgments as Data in Social Work Research* (New York: National Association of Social Workers, 1958), pp. 38–54.

[5] See, for example, Merrill Roff, "A Factorial Study of the Fels Parent Behavior Scales," *Child Development*, XX (1949), 29–45; and Maurice Lorr and Richard L. Jenkins, "Three Factors in Parent Behavior," *Journal of Consulting Psychology*, XVII (1953), 306–308.

and their acceptance of infertility. Positive ratings were also related to the couple's empathy with the problems of and nonpunitive attitude toward unmarried mothers, the absence of difficulty in early social functioning, and the couple's openly spontaneous interview behavior. The wife was rated as undemanding, uncontrolling, and not overprotective in her attitude toward children. This dimension related to couples who were generally rated as good adoptive prospects, good for babies. Yet, curiously enough, these attributes ruled them out for a child who deviated in some way from the so-called normal child.

The four items that stood out most clearly (factor loading of .84 and above) at the positive pole of the second major dimension were all related to a couple's assessed suitability for children who deviated physically, emotionally, by nationality, or racially from the so-called normal child. Among other kinds of clusters related to this dimension was a couple's position in the higher range of the socioeconomic continuum in our sample, which suggests some conceptual association between perceived ability to handle some of the problems connected with child deviance and a couple's economic and educational position.

Our findings here did not agree with those of Maas in his study of a sample of children placed in nine communities across the U.S.A.[6] He noted that the "different" child's adoptive parents tended to be in the lower education and income categories than those couples who adopted the "normal" child. And in another study comparing 91 families who had adopted children with special needs with 91 families who had adopted "normal" children, Kadushin noted a tendency for the latter group of adoptive parents to be better educated, although he found little difference between the two groups as to income level.[7]

We wondered whether some of the differences in our findings were due to regional factors and our dealing primarily with a sample of applicants living in the environs of a fairly prosperous urban community. But, we were more inclined to view the observed dissimilarities as the result of differences in the nature of our study. Our focus was on the social workers' ratings as to their estimate of applicant suitability for the "different" child, whereas Maas and Kadushin examined what actually occurred in practice. In other words, we were tapping attitudinal factors that may not have reflected the couples' preferences or the compromises they were willing to make in order to obtain a child. Possibly, as was true in our study, social workers do feel that higher education and income are associated with a couple's greater suitability for the child who deviates from the normal, even though this association may not prevail at the point of placement.

---

[6] Henry S. Maas, "The Successful Adoptive Parent Applicant," *Social Work*, V, No. 1 (1960), 14–20.

[7] Alfred Kadushin, "A Study of Adoptive Parents of Hard-to-Place Children," *Social Casework*, XLIII (1962), 227–233.

There were other clusters highly related to the second dimension, which we called, at the positive pole, "suitability for the deviant child." Motivationally, the couple was assessed as identifying with the underdog and as nonaccepting of childlessness, whereas motivation based on an intrinsic liking for children was negatively related. Coinciding with Kadushin's findings,[8] the husbands and wives were rated as risky with respect to their health status, the husband's personality was assessed as nonassertive, the wife was assessed as having a demanding and controlling attitude toward children, and they were located at the older age range of our sample (which may, in part, explain their higher socioeconomic position). Their attitude toward unmarried mothers was, on the whole, not seen as positive. They were rated as having matured early psychosocially and as having experienced difficulties in their early socialization. With respect to their agency contact, they were rated as inflexible in their appointment planning and were seen as guarded and nonspontaneous in their interview behavior.

Some of the clusters that related most highly to the first dimension, "positive psychosocial appraisal," such as the positive quality of marital interaction, positive personality description of husband and wife, nonneurotic motivation for adoption, adequacy in marital role performance, and the couple's acceptance of infertility, either had a very low or a negative relationship to the second dimension, "suitability for a deviant child."

In other words, with the exception of socioeconomic status, the second dimension of caseworker assessments tended to focus on the more marginal couples who, as it turned out, were considered more suitable for marginal children.

Thus, our factors pointed to three varieties of couple assessments: (1) the overall positive, (2) the marginal, and (3) the poor or unacceptable. The most striking aspect of these findings was the clear-cut separation between the overall positive appraisal dimension and the factor that related to assessed suitability for children who deviated in some way. Yet both of these were associated with a general positive rating of couples as prospects for adoptive parenthood. In other words, there were two alternative but non-simultaneous routes that led to a positive impression of couples as adoptive prospects, with the "better" couple seen as suitable for the "better" child and the marginal couple assessed as more suitable for the "different" child. At first, this seems to raise an ethical question. It also contradicts some of the practice literature, with its stress on the need for the "better" family to handle the problems that might arise with a hard-to-place child. Apparently what is so voiced may not be followed in actual practice, although we were cognizant that here we were dealing only with worker assessments and not necessarily with what occurred during the final placement decision.

---

[8] *Ibid.*, p. 229.

## DIFFERENCES BETWEEN PUBLIC AND PRIVATE AGENCIES

In respect to the underlying assessment dimensions that emerged, a multiple-discriminant analysis revealed that our eight agencies differed significantly among themselves in their ratings of applicants. The eight agencies could not be separated into two distinct groupings with divergent assessment tendencies. All but one private agency appeared to have different rating tendencies than the public agencies in our sample, although one public agency tended to hold a middle position. The trend was for workers in the public agencies to give, on the average, poorer ratings to couples with respect to suitability for children who differed in some way from the norm and more positive ratings on items that constituted the dimension of an overall positive psychosocial appraisal. In the private agencies, the converse was true.

Although we could not offer any ready explanation for these findings, and the data did not necessarily mean that there were divergent tendencies in overall assessments of couples as prospects for adoptive parenthood or that agencies could be grouped according to different acceptance and rejection tendencies, the data did imply that the caseworkers in the public agencies in our sample (and in one private agency) were less ready to assess couples as suitable for the child who differed from the norm than caseworkers in private agencies. Did this mean that the latter group were more flexible in their ideas about who might be suitable for such a child, whereas in relation to a global psychosocial appraisal, they tended to use more stringent standards? We wonder, for instance, whether public agency workers, on the average, are less willing to risk a positive judgment about suitability for the deviant child and whether this seeming reluctance possibly stems from less agency encouragement of individual initiative and exploration of new methods by individual workers.

If such a reluctant tendency was so, did it, on the other hand, result in a tendency to lean in the opposite direction with regard to ratings of couples on the overall positive appraisal items? Or were there staff differences in the public and private agencies—such as the somewhat larger proportion of public staff at the lower end of the education range and their tendency to have less adoption work experience—that had some bearing? Or did our findings reflect similar rating tendencies, but divergent applicant groups coming to these agencies? In the descriptive material, we did note a few differences in the applicant sample interviewed by public and private agencies, but these did not seem to offer an adequate explanation for the divergent tendencies noted here.

## CONCLUDING COMMENTS

In conjecturing about the implicit dimensions that emerged, the alignment of the "better" couple as suitable for the "better" child, and the marginal couple judged to be more suitable for the "different" child, we could arrive at some tentative reasons for such divergent assessments. Most young couples come to an adoption agency with a desire for a normal, healthy baby. It is certainly likely that caseworkers not only identify with, but respond to, such a preference. We also thought that probably the more workers identified with certain couples (and this was the group receiving the most positive overall appraisal), the less likely they would be to burden such couples with a child who deviated in some way.

In addition, we were aware of certain pressures that the worker-client situation inevitably imposed on adoption workers. For instance, if workers were impressed by certain couples, they were apt to hope that these couples would want to reapply for another child—hence the pressure on the workers to respond to their preferences. We also speculated whether it was psychologically more difficult for a caseworker to place a "different" child in a home that she regarded very positively and, conversely, whether it was easier to do so with a couple considered marginal. There was also the possibility that a marginal couple at some level might, in fact, be better suited for a marginal child.

On the less impressionistic side, we viewed adoption agencies as a product of our middle-class culture, responding to pressures within a community in order to gain its support and also incorporating some aspects of the value system of that environment, which includes values not wholly accepting of the deviant child. Such community pressures may also have influenced the findings we obtained, for it might be more in line with such values to place the marginal child with the marginal family.

In spite of all these possible explanations, reasonings, or what may be rationalizations, we kept smacking up against that most difficult of all words—*why*. In a field that stresses the import of making every effort to meet children's needs in every area possible, the judged alignment of "good" adoptive applicants with "good" children and "marginal" couples with "hard-to-place" children may be thought a strange kind of matching indeed. Despite other advances in flexibility, is this where the field is heading? A good deal of self-questioning and scrutiny, we hope, will result in some compelling answers.

# 34

❪ In response to the need to increase the pool of adoptive-parent applicants for all children, but particularly for the hard-to-place child, agencies have been experimenting with a variety of procedures. The two articles which follow briefly review the experience with some novel approaches. The second article argues for subsidization of adoptive parents; the first is concerned with adoption by a single parent.

# Early Comments on Single-Parent Adoptive Homes

*Velma L. Jordan and William F. Little*

The Los Angeles County Bureau of Adoptions began accepting applications to adopt from single persons in July 1965. This change in our practice was made possible by a revision of the California State Department of Social Welfare Adoption Regulations.

In January 1965, the Department of Social Welfare modified a prohibition against placement with persons living alone by adding the following subsection: "Single parent applications may be accepted only when a two-parent family has not been found because of a child's special needs."

Accordingly, we defined such special-needs children as "Negro children, Mexican children, and children of all races and nationalities with severe medical problems."

We have approximately 275 Negro children available for adoptive placement for whom we have been unable to find two-parent adoptive homes. We also have a substantial number of Mexican babies as well as children of all ethnic groups with severe medical problems for whom adoptive homes are needed.

We have, to the best of our ability, exhausted all possibilities of obtaining sufficient two-parent homes before considering adoption by a single parent for children in a specific group. For example, our best efforts had placed 199 Negro children and over 200 Mexican children in the last calendar year, but it was obvious that others would grow up without homes.

We remain firm in our belief that children both need and desire two parents and that everything possible should be done to obtain a good two-parent home for every child. We are just as determined in our belief that every child needs and deserves a permanent home. But we cannot

338

now provide good, permanent, two-parent homes for all; and we must realistically face up to the alternatives that some of these children face.

For the children for whom single applicants have been accepted, the prospects of continuity of parent figures were bleak. Many of these children would otherwise probably experience a succession of foster homes with, as we know, negative prospects for normal, healthy development.

Entering into a new concept and practice of studying single applicants for adoptive parenthood, we proceeded with caution and, admittedly, some trepidation. Understandably, there was considerable initial resistance on the part of many of our workers to accepting the philosophy that a one-parent home could meet the needs of these children—perhaps not perfectly, but at least as well as the needs of many children in broken homes. The workers who were given these studies were selected on the basis of their maturity and flexibility and their willingness to participate in this project. As to community reaction to one-parent adoptions, acceptance has generally been excellent.

### GUIDELINES FOR SINGLE-PARENT STUDIES

In addition to the usual qualities that we look for in all adoptive parents, we have established some guidelines for use in our single-applicant studies. We believe it important to establish that the applicant is not a recluse who seeks a child for companionship. For this reason, we explore social contacts and activities, and are particularly interested in social activities with couples who have children. It is also our opinion that close family ties and the support of the extended family are most important for the single adoptive parent. We believe, too, that it is important for the single parent to be comfortable in her role as a woman (or his role as a man) and to be accepting of the opposite role. The child should have the opportunity for identification with both roles, preferably in the extended family or with friends on a continuing basis. Because the single applicant must usually work to support herself (or himself) and the child, we carefully explore the child care plan that is presented. We require that the plan have promise of permanency. Usually, a longstanding friend or neighbor, or a relative, has been found to help in this plan. In one placement the adoptive mother's cousin, a young woman with a child of her own, resides in the home and provides care for the children while the mother is at work.

### RESULTS

We have now effected eight adoptive placements with single parents. Most of these were completed in December 1965 and January 1966. Seven of these have involved Negro children; one a Caucasian child with special needs. The children have ranged in age from 18 months to 4½ years. The adoptive mothers have ranged from 37 years of age to 49. Only one adoptive mother had an independent income that permitted her to remain at home with the child. The others were women who work and whose income is sufficient, but in no case exceptionally high.

In every placement thus far, our workers have been tremendously impressed by the positive development of the children and the growing feeling of "good parenting" that the adoptive mothers experience. Some of these mothers have already raised families successfully; others have not had children in their own homes. Some are widowed; others are single or divorced. All have above-average child orientation and ability to give of themselves. In no instance have we found our mothers to be possessive of the children. Instead, there exists a healthy mother-child relationship.

Although we have, of necessity, had to screen out many single applicants, the project has had a total beneficial result that we had not even hoped for. We did not seek publicity for the project; yet we found great interest in it on the part of communication media, which continually demanded information and an opportunity to meet some of these new families. As a result of a highly successful press conference a few weeks ago, which introduced our third and fourth single applicants with their adopted daughters, we have received a large number of applications from couples as well as single persons seeking to adopt. This has included a satisfying number of minority-group applicants whom we so badly need for our children. It is reasonable to assume that, as a result of the single-applicant project, many of these people have been made aware that they stand an excellent chance to adopt and that the presumed unreasonable requirements of adoption agencies do not necessarily exist.

### PLANS FOR THE FUTURE

We have under study at this time—and shall probably approve—single women who look well-qualified to parent on a transracial basis. Needless to say, these women are being studied with the greatest of care. Those applicants approved to date are characterized by a special ability to love and give to a child.

It is our hope to implement group meetings for single parents in order to prepare them, to the extent possible, for some of the more unique situations they may face after the adoptions are finalized and there is no longer a formal relationship with the agency.

To summarize, I would say that our experience with single-parent adoptive placements has, to date, been very promising. In no instance have we observed regression on the part of any of these children. There has been steady progress in the development of the child as a person in his adoptive home, and in several instances, the development has been truly dramatic.

# 35

# Subsidized Adoption

*Chicago Region Child Care Association*

Social Work is facing a crisis in the field of Child Welfare. For more than a decade there has been a spectacular rise in the number of children who are in need of adoptive parents. Adoption agencies have reaffirmed that their primary task must be to find homes for these children.

Recognizing both the scope and the urgency of this task, the Adoption Section of the Chicago Region of the Child Care Association of Illinois has focused its attention on subsidized adoption as one possible way of expanding adoption resources for children.

## DEFINITION

A subsidized adoption is any adoptive plan in which the agency continues financial involvement beyond the point of legal consummation. It differs from other types of agency-sponsored, long-term care (such as quasi-adoption) in that the child is legally adopted.

Such subsidies may fall into three categories: Special services subsidies, time-limited subsidies and long-term subsidies.

1. *Special services subsidy.* This is a contribution from the agency to provide needed services to the child or family. Included would be legal services, medical services, psychiatric treatment, special education, etc. At the time of placement of the child the family and the agency decide the extent of the agency's participation.
2. *Time-limited subsidy.* This is a monthly payment which is continued for a limited time beyond the legal consummation of the adoption. The purpose is to help the family integrate the expenses of the care of the new child into their budget. It may be offered to help a family of temporarily limited means to adopt without delay. At the time of placement the family and the agency decide upon the amount and duration of this monthly payment.
3. *Long-term subsidy.* In some instances, families whose income is limited and fixed, would like to adopt but feel unable to do so solely because of their inability to provide materially for a child. In such cases, the agency may enter into a long-term agreement with the family whereby the agency agrees to a monthly payment toward the child's care until he

is grown. At the time of placement the amount of the payment is decided and a written contract is signed.

## NEED

There is grave concern about the increasing numbers of so-called "hard-to-place" children for whom adoptive parents have not been found. Many of these children have been legally and permanently separated from their natural parents for years. They face a bleak future as they grow up in institutions and agency boarding homes. They are subject to the hazards of multiple placements involving new adjustments and to feelings of rootlessness and being different.

They may have strong emotional ties with boarding parents, but a child needs the permanence, stability and security of legally belonging to a family.

It is also true that many boarding parents do not wish to give up these children, but for socio-economic reasons hesitate to make a commitment to adoption.

The largest single group of hard-to-place children are non-white, of which Negroes comprise the majority. There is a need for Negro adoptive parents, but the Negro population has been subjected to grave inequities in social and economic areas, and there are many families who feel unable to assume the additional responsibility of adopting a child.

There is also a group of children for whom agencies have difficulty finding adoptive homes because of the child's age or physical or emotional problems. Social agencies have not been oblivious and unconcerned about the unfulfilled need for adoptive homes. Despite continuing efforts to secure homes for all of these hard-to-place children by appeals through radio, television, direct community contact, a state-wide adoption resource exchange and the relaxing of eligibility requirements by most adoption agencies, there still exists an urgent need for adoptive parents for these children. In view of the failure to secure enough homes it is obvious that new ways must be tried.

One possibility is subsidizing adoptive families.

The Child Welfare League of America *Standards for Adoption Service* state:

Consideration should be given to supplementing income of families that have the essential qualifications to meet the needs of children for whom there are insufficient homes, but whose income is too low to assume the full cost of care of a child. In this way children who might otherwise never be placed for adoption might be given the emotional security of legal adoption at no greater cost to the community than for long-time boarding home or institution care. A new group of applicants might be reached who do not apply because of limited income. Some boarding home parents to whom a child has become attached might be able to adopt him if financial support were continued.[1]

In *Adoption of Children* the American Academy of Pediatrics recommends certain measures, among which is:

Promoting a system of subsidized adoptions so children need not continue to be deprived of the security of family because of the economic situation. Hopefully this would encourage more adoption in Negro families.[2]

The Joint Priorities Project of the Community Fund of Chicago and the Welfare Council of Metropolitan Chicago states:

Society has assumed responsibility for protecting children who lack families of their own. Adoption is considered the most desirable means of ensuring permanent family ties for children who cannot have the care of their natural parents. A substantial number of children who have never had such permanent family ties present serious behavior and personality problems and require care in correctional institutions, court probation or residential treatment centers for emotionally disturbed children or need other remedial programs. Adoption therefore constitutes one of the genuinely preventive services in the community and it produces savings both in human and monetary terms.[3]

## SURVEY

To explore the interest in subsidized adoptions on the part of adoption agencies in the State of Illinois, the Adoption Section of the Chicago Region of the Child Care Association of Illinois sent a brief survey in March, 1967, to the forty-four agencies within the state licensed to do adoptive placements. *All agencies without exception responded!* We learned that despite the interest in the subject, very few agencies were subsidizing adoptions at that time.

However, many agencies reported a substantial number of children now in foster care who might be adopted by the foster family if monthly payments could be continued.

In response to the questionnaire, some agencies raised thoughtful questions for consideration.

## QUESTIONS

1. *Question:* Is long-term foster care the same as subsidized adoption? *Answer:* No. In long-term foster care the foster parents do not have a

---

[1] Child Welfare League of America. *Standards for Adoption Service.* 1958. Sec. 5.20, p. 36.

[2] American Academy of Pediatrics. *Adoption of Children.* Second Edition. 1967, p. 57–58.

[3] Welfare Council of Metropolitan Chicago. *Joint Priorities of the Community Fund of Chicago and the Welfare Council of Metropolitan Chicago. Part II: Profiles of Forty Fields of Human Care Service in Chicago.* Profile A05. April, 1967, p. 1.

direct legal tie to the child, only a surrogate parental tie through delegated authority.

In subsidized adoption the child is legally adopted by the substitute parents and by this legal process they have all the rights, privileges and responsibilities of parents generally. The subsidy which attaches by arrangement with the agency which placed the child continues to provide financial support in whole or in part for the child on the basis that this otherwise well-qualified adoptive family would not be able to adopt this child.

2. *Question:* Why is subsidized adoption advocated as preferable to long-term foster care?

*Answer:* Subsidized adoptions are not advocated in all instances as being preferable to long-term foster care. In instances where the child continues contacts with his biological relatives, but is unable to live with them, long-term foster care may be the only answer for him. However, if the child has no contact with biological parents or other relatives for a prolonged period of time as defined by statutes, the possibility of adoption, subsidized or otherwise, should be seriously considered.

3. *Question:* To what extent does subsidized adoption involve agency contact and supervision? "Who will watch our money?"

*Answer:* Continuing contact with the subsidizing agency will be a matter to be decided mutually between the adopting parents and the agency on a casework basis. It is the intent of the program generally to permit the adopted family members to function as autonomously as they are capable of doing in the interest of promoting healthy family life. If the agency's evaluation of the adoptive family is sound, there should be no need to approach the family at any time in the spirit of "watching our money."

4. *Question:* Is subsidized adoption a "poor man's adoption?" Will this not bring a stigma to the child?

*Answer:* The families taking hard-to-place children for adoption may not necessarily be "poor" families within the usual meaning of that term. Conceivably they may be self-supporting middle class families, and yet be unable to assume life-long responsibility for treatment of a physically or emotionally disabled child. In other instances, their income may be marginal enough to preclude adding another family member, despite the rich family values available in the home. Perhaps in these latter situations, "poor man's adoption" would involve less social status than the usual adoption. We believe, however, that implicit in the subsidized adoption program is the need for interpretation to the community of the plus contribution being made by families in the program. Our second thought is that a child in foster care usually feels far more deeply stigmatized than would seem expected in the instance of subsidized adoptions.

It is not uncommon for a child to be supported by funds derived from outside his immediate family circle. For instance, many children are supported at least in part by Social Security funds, Veterans pensions, insurance, etc. There have been no indications that children in these circumstances feel different about their status from children being supported solely by parent figures.

5. *Question:* In many cases the child does qualify for hospitalization or other medical care even before the legal adoption. Therefore the circumstances to warrant subsidy would have to be carefully considered.

*Answer:* We agree. Our assumption is that the implicit question is whether subsidizing funds should be made available in addition to other assistance for handicapped children. We believe that such additional subsidized funds should be made available if the child would otherwise not have an adoptive home.

6. *Question:* Has any agency made up a projected budget on one or more of these situations?

*Answer:* Yes. However since these situations are decided on a casework basis it is not relevant for our purposes to try to arrive at average costs. It seems to us that a more meaningful framework of reference is the contrasting cost of supporting a child in a boarding home or institutional setting over a long-term period. In dollars and cents, the costs of the subsidized adoption program will be less than the foster care costs. Far more important in our thinking is the expected decrease in subsequent welfare costs as a result of the adopted child's greater sense of security, identity and self-worth.

7. *Question:* What criteria are available for the determination of which foster parents would make good subsidized adoptive parents? How does one determine whom to approach?

*Answer:* The same criteria for determination of parenting potential are available and usable in considering adoptive families who may need financial subsidy as we use in considering any adoptive applicants. In addition, when we may be considering foster parents who have had a child in their home on a boarding basis and who may be available as adoptive parents for that child if financial subsidy can be provided, the consideration of the parent-child relationship already existing is of paramount importance.

8. *Question:* How can a state tax-supported program, dependent on periodic legislative appropriations, commit the state to financing subsidized adoptions?

*Answer:* When a tax-supported agency accepts responsibility for a dependent child, it implicitly commits its resources to that child for the period the child needs substitute family care. Subsidized adoptions can be seen as one expression of this commitment.

Perhaps existing patterns of federal support could be utilized in the case of subsidized adoptions.

9. *Question:* Will subsidized adoptions attract new adoptive applicants?

*Answer:* We expect so. There is wide community interest in the limited number of subsidized adoptions which have been made to date, and some indication that these placements have already stimulated new applications.

10. *Question:* Many families face difficulties rearing children born to them who are handicapped in the same ways as the children with whom we are here concerned. Direct financial subsidies are not available to them. Why should they be to adoptive families?

*Answer:* This can best be answered by another question. Would these families have assumed this responsibility by choice?

## SUMMARY

Adoption agencies can do nothing more important than strengthen their capacity to meet the problem of an increasingly alarming threat to the maintenance of sound family life. Subsidized adoption may be an essential part of the solution.

We believe, along with others, that a child legally free for adoption has the right to be given adoptive parents who will provide a home in which he can enjoy parental love, security and an opportunity to develop mentally, educationally and physically. He should not be deprived because of lack of economic resources in his own right or on the part of potential adoptive parents otherwise qualified to be good parents to him and eager to have him as their legally adopted child.

Public funds are available in one form or another for large numbers of children in foster care. We suggest that subsidized adoptions would enable large numbers of children now doomed to live as foster children to have the essential security represented through legal adoption.

We are convinced that there is a strong probability that a program of subsidized adoptions would in the long run represent a considerable saving in community money now being expended in efforts to repair the damage children sustain when deprived of permanent family ties.

In view of the urgent necessity to find adoptive homes for the children described, it is our conviction that consideration must be given through all channels to establish a system of subsidized adoptions!

# 36

⟮ The social agency's study of the adoptive applicant can at best predict in a general way how the prospective parent will react to living with the adoptive child. Such a study can "differentiate between potentially good prospects and more or less poor risks." The period following placement of the child imposes on the adoptive couple the necessity of dealing with the living reality of the child. The period following placement, then, is viewed by the agency as a critical opportunity for helping the adoptive parents adjust to the adoptive child in vivo. The following article reports a research project concerned with the relationship between caseworker and adoptive parent during the vital period between placement and legal adoption.

# A Study of the Caseworker— Adoptive Parent Relationship in Postplacement Services*

*Harvey L. Gochros*

Considerable casework effort and time are expended in services to adoptive families following placement. Caseworkers employed in adoption agencies are among the best trained in the social work field. But how successfully is this professional time being utilized? Social work practitioners[1] and adoptive parents[2] alike have questioned the effectiveness of postplacement services as traditionally practiced.

This article is a report of a research effort, the goal of which was to evaluate adoptive parents' and caseworkers' perceptions of the functions of postplacement services and their effectiveness. The point of departure for

* The study reported on in this paper was conducted under the auspices of the Minnesota Department of Welfare, Division of Child Welfare. The author acknowledges the assistance of Dr. Bernice Boehm, who was Director of Research of the Division at the time the study was conducted.

1 See Florence G. Brown, "Supervision of the Child in the Adoptive Home," *Child Welfare*, XXXIV (1955), No. 3, 10–16; Lloyd Conklin, *et al.*, "Use of Groups During the Adoptive Postplacement Period," *Social Work*, VII (1962), No. 2, pp. 46–52; Inter-Agency Discussion Group of New York City, "The Process of Supervision in Adoptive Placements, *Child Welfare*, XXXI (1952), No. 9, pp. 8 ff.; Charles Olds, "Services for Adoptees and Their Parents After Legal Adoption," *Child Welfare*, XLIV (1965), 321–326.

2 See Harry Bell, *We Adopted a Daughter* (Boston: Houghton Mifflin Co., 1954).

the study was an exploration of the major stated functions of the services and the problems inherent in the caseworker-adoptive parent relationship.

## FUNCTIONS OF POSTPLACEMENT SERVICES

Adoption literature generally describes two major purposes of the requirement that a period of time must elapse between the placement of a child in an adoptive home and the final legal adoption decree, and the requirement of a series of casework interviews during that period.[3]

### Probation

The adoption agency retains the custody of a child while it determines the adequacy of parental care and establishes that the child is developing normally and adjusting satisfactorily in the adoptive home before it gives its consent to the legal adoption. It also provides a trial period for the adoptive parents to determine whether the adopted child has any chronic, congenital, or incurable illness that may alter the couple's feeling about the adoption.

### Giving Help

The postplacement caseworker is seen as providing help on several different levels. He can provide support and reassurance to the adoptive parents who may be anxious about their ability to raise an adopted child adequately. He can also help the parents work through problems inherent in adoption, such as feelings about natural parents, illegitimacy, and inability to have children biologically. Insights bearing on their adoption gained by the couple in the adoption study can be applied to their present living experiences, which may have stirred up dormant problems. Through educative techniques the caseworker can help the couple plan their explanations about the adoption to family, friends, and child. The caseworker can also offer service regarding problems inherent in *any* parent-child relationship, and can help with the development of a sense of "entitlement" and of "kinship" or "belonging" between the parents and their child.

The two functions of probation and the giving of help tend, of course, to intertwine. Activities that the caseworker may intend as protective may be perceived by the parents as probationary. Furthermore, if the caseworker's intent is to protect the child and the adoptive parent, he will naturally do everything in his power (i.e., give help) to insure that the ultimate goal of achieving a successfully integrated family is realized.

---

[3] *See* Brown, *op. cit.*; *Adoption of Children* (Evanston, Ill., American Academy of Pediatrics, 1959); Michael Shapiro, *A Study of Adoption Practice* (New York: Child Welfare League of America, 1956); *The Social Worker's Part in Adoption* (Washington, D.C.: U.S. Government Printing Office, 1958); *Social Workers Look at Adoption* (Washington, D.C.: U.S. Government Printing Office, 1958).

Despite the best intentions of caseworkers, however, the postplacement period has been found by adoption workers to be generally stressful and often a threat to adoptive parents who view the adoption agency with mixed feelings. They feel positively toward it for the gift of a child, but once the child is placed they may be eager for the agency to withdraw and allow them to take over the child as their own. Despite possible interpretations by the caseworker that the purposes of the postplacement period are primarily helpful ones (and as found in this study, these interpretations were generally not clearly made), many couples see the agency and their caseworkers as uninvited authority figures acting as benevolent probationers with the implicit power to remove their child for any reason the agency deems appropriate. In this respect the postplacement worker operates with some of the same difficulties as caseworkers in authoritative settings, serving the dual role of enabler and agent of social control.

There are some important differences, however, between adoptive parents and clients served in authoritative settings, and, for that matter, almost all other clients seen by caseworkers. Being an adoptive parent is the occupation of a favorable status, and not a problem. The common denominator of adoptive parents is their lack of success in having their own biological children, and their application to take someone else's as their own. Although there may be various aspects of adoption that give rise to problems, none are necessarily present in all cases and there may be mature, relatively healthy couples who can successfully resolve these problems with no more outside intervention than would be needed by natural parents. Also, since an agency has been convinced during the adoptive study of the relative health and desirability of the adoptive parents, it could be argued that many of these couples are even more well-adjusted and capable of problem resolution than biological parents.

## DIFFICULTIES IN THE POSTPLACEMENT WORKER–ADOPTIVE PARENT RELATIONSHIP

The postplacement period is perhaps the most crucial and stressful time in determining the future role integration of the adoptive couple as parents. Their role during this period is preparatory and transitional to their future role as legalized or "naturalized" parents. During this time they are in many ways not yet parents. It is in this atmosphere that the postplacement caseworker is expected to offer his services.

The set of expectations that accompanies the adoptive parents' role is often quite vague.[4] It is supposedly part of the caseworker's function to help clarify the parents' roles. The caseworker may, however, be vague

[4] See H. David Kirk, "A Dilemma of Adoptive Parenthood: Incongruous Role Obligations," *Marriage and Family Living*, XXI (1959), No. 4, pp. 316–326; H. David Kirk, Kurt Jonassohn, and Ann D. Fish, "Are Adopted Children Especially Vulnerable to Stress?" *Archives of General Psychiatry*, XIV (1966), No. 3, pp. 291–298.

about the rights and obligations of the adoptive parents to the child and to the agency during this period, or he may communicate them poorly. Sometimes these rights and obligations may even be contradictory. For instance, during the postplacement period adoptive parents do not have rights of natural parents. They usually do not have the right to sanction major surgery, or to take the child out of the state without agency permission, yet they are expected to act and feel toward the child as if he were their own and to convey this attitude to their caseworker.

There can be confusion in the postplacement worker-adoptive parent relationship if there is a lack of consensus on the overall goals and purposes of their contacts. The caseworker may view his role as that of a problem solver and may feel that it is his right and the parents' obligation to reveal problems in the parents' role adaptations so that they can be solved. He might take it as a sign of resistance if he senses such problems but finds the adoptive parents unwilling to discuss them. On the other hand, if the caseworker is viewed by the adoptive couple as a probationer who is judging the advisability of the couple's keeping the child, or if they do not consider him capable of solving the problem, they may try to withhold information in the hope that he will not recognize that the problem exists.

Even the implication that the postplacement caseworker is there to help the adoptive parents may be disabling. A couple's inability to have children biologically often tends to produce feelings of inadequacy. The implication that parents may draw from the presence of the postplacement worker (and from the very existence of postplacement services) is that they are thought by the agency to need help during their first year of parenthood and are not recognized as being able to function as parents without assistance until after the year's "probation." This may tend to reinforce their sense of inadequacy.

It would seem that the ambiguous legal status and lack of commitment of the child to a family during the postplacement period may impair or delay role integration of the adoptive family. How valid is it to expect adoptive parents to act or feel like real parents when, legally and in their own minds, they are not yet parents?

Furthermore, the adoptive couple may feel that they are "chosen people," having been selected by the agency for the placement of their child, and that there are therefore high expectations of them. As a result, they may avoid revealing what they feel are inadequacies for fear of disappointing the caseworker or the agency.

Finally, in terms of the content of the postplacement visits, one may question how practical it is to have intensive discussions with new parents about such potential problems as how to tell a child about his adoption when the problem could not emerge in reality for several years (in the case of infant adoption). Would this discussion be more helpful and practical in individual or group interviews offered by the adoption agency on a voluntary basis when the child is a few years older?

Although such questions as these may frequently be asked by adoption workers, most workers could not seriously consider doing away with postplacement services. Rather, there seems to be a growing concern as to how to guide practice during this period to make it maximally useful to adoptive couples while reducing any needless and debilitating stresses. A number of agency studies of the means by which the postplacement services could be practiced more effectively have been reported.[5] No intensive study of the postplacement period, involving direct interviews with a large representative group of adoptive parents and their caseworkers, has been made.

## METHODS OF APPROACH

The present study was initiated to examine the postplacement period intensively, with particular emphasis on the interaction of postplacement caseworkers and the adoptive couple. It was an empirical, exploratory study of a fairly homogeneous group that shared the common stresses and experiences of adoptive parenthood for the first time. In addition to semistructured interviews, tests and schedules were used to elicit parents' and caseworkers' perceptions of the function of postplacement services, the number and intensity of problems as perceived by parents during the postplacement year, the resources parents would choose for help with these problem areas (with particular emphasis on the relative rank of the postplacement caseworker), and parents' evaluation of the helpfulness and stresses of the postplacement period.

Data was obtained from interviews and pencil-and-paper tests secured from 114 adoptive parents (57 couples) and their postplacement caseworkers. The following criteria were used for selection of the adoptive parents included in the study:

• Adoption of their first child was completed in 1961. Parents were not included if they had children of their own prior to adoption, so each family faced its first experience of parenthood.
• Residence in Hennepin or Ramsey Counties in Minnesota. (This included the large urban areas of Minneapolis and St. Paul.)

---

[5] *See* Catherine R. Collier and Anne Campbell, "A Post-adoption Discussion Series," *Social Casework,* XLI (1960), 192–196; Betty Woodward, "After Adoption: A Community Workshop," *Children,* IV (1957), No. 4, pp. 140–142; Lois R. Beemer, "Supervision after Adoptive Placement," *Casework Papers 1955* (New York: Family Service Association of America, 1955), pp. 101–108; Edith Zober, Elizabeth S. Turner, and Katherine B. Wheeler, "Post-Placement Services for Adoptive Families," *Child Welfare,* XL (1961), No. 4, 29–31; Sylvia E. Biskind, "Helping Adoptive Families Meet the Issues in Adoption," *Child Welfare,* XLV (1966), 145–150.

• The caseworker who provided postplacement services must have been available for participation in the study.

Three agencies were selected for this study. These represented the three major types of agencies placing children for adoption: public, private sectarian, and private nonsectarian. The agencies selected were those placing the largest number of children in the area. In addition, the level of casework practice in these agencies seemed representative of better adoption practices throughout the country. All cases of the agencies that met the above criteria were selected for study.

Letters were sent to the adoptive parents by their adoption agencies advising them of the study, urging their cooperation, and reassuring them of the confidentiality of their responses. It was made clear that the study was to be conducted by the State Division of Child Welfare, and that responses of the individual parents would not be made available to the agencies. Each of the parents (both father and mother) was then interviewed in his own home. The parents' interviews all took place approximately a year following granting of their adoption decrees. The caseworkers who supervised each of these placements were subsequently interviewed concerning their services to the particular family and their general opinions about postplacement services.

## FINDINGS

### Parents' and Caseworkers' Perceptions of the Function of Postplacement Services

There was marked disagreement between caseworkers and adoptive parents concerning the function of the postplacement period.[6] All the caseworkers in this study felt that the primary function of postplacement services is to help in the successful integration of the adoptive family. Activities relating specifically to the giving of help were ranked highest by the caseworkers when they were asked what they were trying to do during the postplacement visits. Parents, on the other hand, ranked the activities relating to probation highest when asked what they perceived their caseworker trying to do; and when asked what they thought the primary purpose of postplacement visits was, the most common single response was "probation."

### Problems Experienced by the Adoptive Parents During the Postplacement Period

None of the parents reported being free of concerns in relation to adoption during their postplacement period. On the other hand, none of

---

[6] Unless otherwise noted, significance was determined by chi-square tests, using a .05 level of significance.

the parents seem to have been overwhelmed by a number of disabling problems. Rather, the majority of parents reported having several areas[7] connected with adoption that concerned them "occasionally" or "often" during the postplacement period.

Although the caseworkers felt that their primary function during the postplacement period was to give help, the majority of caseworkers believed paradoxically that most adoptive parents do not have problems that require help. They also generally underestimated the number and intensity of concerns experienced by their own clients. This apparent confusion of the caseworkers between their role expectations and role performance is reflected in the report of a majority of parents that their caseworker's interpretation of the purposes of the postplacement services was either vague or nonexistent.

In the interviews with the adoptive parents, the concern most often reported was the possibility of loss of the child through removal by the agency, through the reclaiming of the child by the natural mother, or as the result of the death of one of the parents. Other areas that concerned at least half of the parents on a paper-and-pencil check list were how to tell their child about adoption (96 percent); that they were spoiling their child (84 percent); how they would go about answering their child's questions about his background (80 percent); and the possibility that some day the child would try to find his natural parents (60 percent). In rating the same families, caseworkers significantly underestimated these concerns. One of the few areas in which caseworkers overestimated the problems was in relation to the parents' feeling of inadequacy connected with the adoptive parents' status.[8] Almost universally, the parents felt that their concerns were normal for adoptive parents and estimated that the average adoptive parent is concerned about far more problem areas than they themselves were.

### Parents' Perceptions of the Caseworker as a Resource for Help

Based on the comparative rankings of the caseworker as a resource for help in hypothetical situations occurring during the postplacement period, caseworkers were generally seen by the adoptive parents as a good resource for help with a wide variety of problems. They ranked overall between second and third as a choice for help in a field that included spouses, doctors, clergymen, relatives, and friends.

Although the majority of the parents stated they would not be likely to contact their caseworker for help with a child behavior problem after the adoption decree was granted, those who felt they had been helped most during the postplacement period were significantly more likely to

---

[7] A median ranking of six areas.

[8] It is possible, however, that this discrepancy may be partly attributable to the parents' tendency to deny the existence of such emotionally loaded problem areas.

do so than those who were not. Caseworkers with master's degrees were not ranked significantly higher as a resource for help by their clients than caseworkers with only a bachelor's degree. Caseworkers with only some graduate social work courses, however, were ranked significantly lower by their clients than either those who had completed their degree requirements or those who never attempted graduate courses.

In a similar test taken by the caseworkers, the caseworkers tended to rank themselves significantly higher as a resource for help than did the parents. In fact, the caseworkers ranked themselves higher in seven out of the eight hypothetical problem situations. Caseworkers ranked themselves highest in a situation in which one parent became moody and short-tempered following the placement of the child. The parents, however, ranked the caseworker highest as a resource for help in a hypothetical situation in which they could not decide when and how to tell their child that he is adopted. It would appear that caseworkers tend to see themselves as being most helpful in counseling situations, whereas the parents perceive them as being most helpful in situations that call for educative assistance.

## Amount of Help Received by the Parent

Of the 112 parents who were present at at least one of the postplacement interviews, 40 percent felt that the interviews had "not been particularly helpful," 41 percent felt that they had received "some help," and 19 percent felt that the visits had been of "substantial help." It should be noted again, however, that most of these parents probably did not have severe or disabling problems at the beginning of the period. Moreover, a number of the parents commented that the reason they were not helped substantially or at all by the postplacement visits was because many of their problems had already been resolved with the help of the worker during the adoption study.

The caseworkers significantly overestimated the helpfulness of their services to the families as compared to the parents' own estimates. The caseworkers thought that they had helped 90 percent of the parents who felt "somewhat helped" or "substantially helped." They also felt that they had helped 73 percent of the parents who reported they had not been helped by the postplacement services.

## The Nature of the Help that the Parents Received

Parents reported being helped in two general areas: reassurance (such as reassurance that they were doing a good job, that their child was developing properly, or that the agency would not take their child away) and problem solving (such as the provision of child care and developmental information, legal procedural information, or help with specific adoption problems such as how to tell their child about adoption). As the level of help reported by the parents increased (from "no help" to "some help" to "substantial help"), the greater was the likelihood that the help reported by the parents came in the form of problem-solving assistance rather than in reassurance alone. The single area of service that the greatest number of adoptive parents considered the most helpful, however, was reassurance that they were doing a good job as parents. It was observed in talking to many of the adoptive parents that there is a great deal of anxiety on their part about their adequacy as parents. Many talked about the great responsibility that parenthood involved—about their concern that their child should develop into a healthy, emotionally adequate individual. There were several parents who commented that they recognized that they were overindulging their child or "spoiling" him more than they thought they would a natural child. In view of the anxiety that these parents showed, it is understandable that any reassurance from the caseworker was generally welcome.

When the caseworkers themselves were asked what services they considered to be most helpful to the parents, the most common answer, again, was in the area of reassurance. Very few caseworkers stated that they had offered substantial help in the area of problem solving in their postplacement cases. The caseworkers tended to feel that most of the problem solving and resolution of conflicts about adoption were successfully accomplished—if needed—during the adoption study. Yet there was some inconsistency on the part of the caseworkers. When they were asked to rank those activities they carried out with each of their adoptive families, the activity that had the highest median rank was "helping adoptive parents with their feelings connected with adoption."

### Factors Associated with Parents' Perceptions of Being Helped

Four factors within the adoptive family itself were significantly related to helpfulness. A significantly higher number of those parents who had a lower level of educational attainment (not beyond high school) reported being helped than those who had a higher level (at least some college). Those parents who reported being the most helped by the services were those whom the caseworkers had rated as the healthiest and best-adjusted, with the highest potential for being good parents. Also, a significantly higher proportion of parents who already had a second child placed with them by the time of the study reported being helped than parents who had applied for, but had not yet received, their second child.

A test was administered to determine general attitudes toward the acceptance of outside persons or resources as sources of help, and it was found that those parents who reported having been helped by the postplacement services had more underlying attitudes compatible with turning to others—particularly to their caseworkers—for help with problems than those who were not helped.

Several factors regarding the caseworker or casework services were also tested to determine if they had any influence on the helpfulness of the postplacement services. No significant relationship was found between the helpfulness reported by parents and the age, experience in social work or adoption, or the marital or parental status of their caseworkers. There was also no significant difference in the helpfulness reported by adoptive parents adopting through the private nonsectarian, private sectarian, or the public agencies.

There were two factors in casework services, however, that did have a significant relationship with the helpfulness perceived by the parents. A significantly higher number of those parents who had four or more postplacement interviews reported being substantially helped than those parents who had three or less interviews.[9]

There was also a significant relationship between the helpfulness of the postplacement visits and the parents' rating of the clarity of the caseworkers' interpretation to them of the purpose of these visits. A significantly higher number of those parents who recalled the interpretation being clear felt helped than those who felt the interpretation had been vague or nonexistent.

Some of the factors described in adoption literature as having an association with the effectiveness of postplacement services were found in this study to have no such association. It has been suggested, for example, that the postplacement period be seen as only one part of the whole of adoption services, and that there is a need to carry over diagnostic formulations and treatment plans from the study period to the postplacement services. In the present study it was found that in the cases of 43 parents there was no such carryover according to their caseworkers. In 21 cases there was a simple, positive diagnostic impression carried over, to the effect that a parent was relatively healthy and would probably have no problems in adjustment to parenthood. Finally, there was a group of 48 parents for whom a problem-focused treatment plan was developed. No significant difference, however, was found in the helpfulness reported by those parents for whom a treatment plan had been made and those for whom no such plan had been formulated.

---

[9] The median number of interviews per family according to the caseworkers was 3.83 and according to the parents was 3.16. The great majority of interviews were in the parents' homes. The number of visits for each family seemed more often dictated by general agency policies than by individual case diagnosis. There was a significant difference in the number of visits per family arranged by the workers in the three agencies, with those in the public agency generally having the most interviews, those in the private sectarian agencies having the second most, and those in the private nonsectarian agencies having the least. Fathers were less involved in the postplacement interviews than were mothers. According to the caseworkers, only 16 of the 57 fathers were present at all the postplacement interviews. When asked whether they felt left out of the visits, almost a fifth of the fathers said that they did—even when they were present. Many felt that the conversations were mainly intended for the mothers.

Another concept found in the literature is that, whenever possible, the worker who carries the adoption study should continue to work with the family during the postplacement period. The present study would seem to indicate, however, that no significant relationship exists between the helpfulness reported by the adoptive parents and whether or not they had the same worker for the postplacement visits and adoption study. Furthermore, only half of those parents who had different workers stated that they had any difficulty at all in making the change, or even that they had a preference for having the same worker.

### Parents' Reaction to Caseworkers in the Postplacement Period

Generally, the caseworkers were well liked, with few criticisms from the parents. For instance, 84 percent of the parents replied that their caseworker created an atmosphere that was conducive to the discussion of personal problems during the postplacement visits. Nineteen parents, however, said that they consciously withheld information pertinent to the adoption from their caseworker.[10]

The parents usually characterized the postplacement visits as anxiety-provoking, although almost a third of the parents thought that the visits were more relaxed and less "official" and that their caseworkers were less critical than they had anticipated. Some of the comments of the parents are illustrative of what they expected the visits to be like. One mother said that she "expected the unexpected." Another said that she did not know what to expect: "I worried about whether I was doing a good enough job and that it might show up if I wasn't." A father stated that he was "somewhat apprehensive at first, because we did not know what to expect." Another father said, perhaps only in part facetiously, "I thought the caseworker was coming to see whether our child was all covered with bruises." Finally, one mother commented, "I didn't know what to expect, I just accepted it."

Thus, while most of the parents perceived their caseworker as a friend, at the same time they perceived the visits as a threat. The caseworkers, however, were able to some extent to handle parents' anxiety regarding the postplacement visits. Nearly half the parents reported that they felt more relaxed and less on probation as the series of interviews with the caseworker progressed.

A final question asked of the parents to assess their reaction to the postplacement period was about their feelings on obtaining their adoption decree. Well over half of the parents commented that when they got their decree they felt for the first time that their child was really theirs

---

10 The kind of information withheld was related to a variety of problems. One mother became very depressed after placement. Another couple experienced marital friction following the placement. Several mothers started working part-time and did not think the worker would approve, and one father lost his job.

to keep, or expressed relief that it was all over with. Some of the comments of the parents are again illustrative: "I was very relieved; I had had a nagging fear that maybe I would lose the child, and now the child was mine to keep." "It was a great day—a real relief—now the whole thing was sewed up." "Now I was safe." "Now the child was really ours—we were really parents." "It was like burning the mortgage."

Although parents were threatened by postplacement visits, they (as well as the caseworkers) usually felt that the services were necessary. Parents felt postplacement contacts were needed to protect adoptive children, and felt that these visits should be compulsory as a "social responsibility." About half of both the caseworkers and the adoptive parents felt that a postplacement period of six months rather than a year (as was the case in Minnesota) would be adequate to carry out the purposes of a postplacement period.

Although most parents stated that they would not feel it appropriate to return to the adoption agency following the completion of the adoption should they run into a behavior problem with their child, there was a great deal of interest expressed on the part of the parents in agency-sponsored discussion groups for adoptive parents planned for several years after adoption. Sixty-five of the parents were interested in groups for the parents of 5-year-old adoptive children. Even more parents (74) were interested in a group for parents of adolescents.

## SUMMARY AND IMPLICATIONS FOR CASEWORK PRACTICE

The adoptive parents in this study were concerned about a number of real or threatened problems in their adjustment to the adoptive-parent role. Although the postplacement caseworker may sometimes be seen and successfully used as a resource for reassurance and support, his effectiveness may be handicapped by the differences of perception of the caseworker's role by the caseworker and the adoptive parents. Although the helping and probationary roles of the caseworker intertwine to some extent, the caseworkers tended to see themselves primarily in the helping role, whereas the parents tended to see them more as benevolent probationers. This lack of consensus in role definitions is compounded when the caseworker does not adequately interpret his function and the purpose of the postplacement period, as was frequently seen to be the case in this study.

Although caseworkers perceived their primary function as helping the adoptive parents during the postplacement year, paradoxically, few thought that it was usually necessary. Furthermore, the caseworkers usually failed to develop a substantial diagnosis and a treatment plan based on their study to guide them in working with the family during the postplacement year. They also tended to underestimate the extent to which their clients were concerned about real or potential stresses, and although there was a significant relationship between the number of postplacement visits and their usefulness, it appears that the number of visits is determined more often by agency policy or tradition than by diagnostically determined need.

Although most adoptive parents have a number of areas that concern them during the postplacement period, they are not necessarily in need of intensive treatment. In fact, it is noted that in this study those parents who felt they were being helped most by postplacement services felt least that their caseworker was trying to help them with their feelings. During the postplacement period, adoptive parents are in the honeymoon stage of their adoption with its concomitant pleasures and stresses. They may not yet have encountered any specific problems and they may be unable or unwilling to focus on any incipient problems. They may, in fact, perceive delving for problems at this time as dangerous. Appropriate reassurance and education as diagnostically indicated would seem to be the treatment of choice in some cases. Furthermore, overseeing the adoption and merely being available as needed may be the legitimate professional activity as well as social responsibility of the social worker in many cases.

Agencies might explore the possibility of more frequent, more closely spaced interviews, and caseworkers might work on developing those skills necessary to use the home visit effectively for evaluation and, if needed, as a therapeutic tool. If there is a limitation on the number of visits that can be economically offered to each family during the postplacement period, further exploration might be made of the possibility of providing the same number of interviews in a shorter postplacement period.

Adoption workers might reexamine some basic assumptions regarding effective practice. For instance, this study casts some doubt on whether the professionally trained worker in present practice provides the services needed by adoptive parents more effectively than an agency-trained worker. Furthermore, is it really necessary, or even more effective, to have continuity in workers from the adoption study to the postplacement period? Instead, would a change of workers at the time of adoption placement enable adoptive parents to make a new start, avoid a carryover of the investigative aspects of this study, and help them make more effective use of the postplacement services? Would different talents and experiences be indicated for study workers and postplacement workers?

There would seem to be a need for continued exploration of how caseworkers can most effectively help adoptive parents with some of the normal problems inherent in adoption. For example, how can we help adoptive parents most successfully interpret adoption to their children? It would appear that this enigma, about which most of the parents were concerned, remains unresolved by most at the completion of the postplacement period.

Although the services that are provided by adoption agencies after a child is placed are already plagued with a multiplicity of names, a new one that would not carry the vagueness of "postplacement services" or the authoritarianism of "supervision" would seem desirable. The name "transitional period" may better describe the purpose and goals of this period, implying movement and direction for the services. The name implies both the transition of responsibility for the child from the adoption agency to the adoptive parents, and the transition of the adoptive parents themselves from an entity separate from their child to an integrated family.

Adjustment to adoption does not stop magically at the time of the adoption decree when agency contact usually terminates. Rather, problems often just begin. Agency-initiated contact should terminate at the point of the adoption decree, and parents should emphatically be reassured of the agency's confidence in them as parents and of its willingness to relinquish all supervision of the adopted child. Effective service can, however, be offered to adoptive parents on a voluntary basis in the form of postadoptive groups, of which many of the adoptive parents in the study were in favor.

Finally, postplacement services in adoption were established when the bulk of adoptions were independent and there was reason to fear for the well-being of the children. Over the years both the ratio and quality of agency placements has improved, and with this there has been a theoretical change in emphasis in the postplacement period. It is questionable, however, whether practice has caught up with theory. Many caseworkers now seem trapped in a no-man's land between probation and help-giving, all too often providing little of either. Often parents do not know the purpose of postplacement visits. Several parents said to the researcher in reference to the postplacement period: "It's for the agency—not us." They think of the period as probation and then are surprised at the lack of strictness and focus in the visits. It would seem necessary for social workers to decide what the purposes of postplacement visits are and then interpret them clearly to parents. Caseworkers should not compound adoptive parents' anxiety, leaving them with a vague feeling that the only purpose of the visits is to put them on trial, if in reality it is not. To do so would be delaying the provision of society's sanction to the parents' early assumption of their parental roles.

# 37

⟨[ Adoptive parenthood is, in its genesis, different in a very crucial way from that of biological parenthood. The following article attempts to spell out the consequences of this difference. At the same time it suggests the relationship between adoptive parenthood and social-work practices which support the parents' efforts to deal with the problems of adoptive parenthood.

## A Dilemma of Adopted Parenthood: Incongruous Role Obligations

*H. David Kirk*

This paper is to serve a two-fold purpose. Its primary objective is to show the existence of incongruous role obligations in the situation of adoptive relations, and to indicate the likely consequences of current modes of dealing with the dilemma which the incongruity produces. Secondarily, in terms of methodology, this paper is meant to help demonstrate the applicability of structural-functional analyses to the strategies of welfare practice.

Reference to the adoptive situation is here restricted to a single type of it. Throughout the discussion which is to follow, the reader should bear in mind these characteristics of our special case:

1. The adoptive parents are non-fecund, that is, they have never had a child born to them.
2. The child adopted by them is biologically unrelated to either spouse.
3. The child has entered the adoptive family unit in infancy or babyhood.

Before the proper task of this paper is begun, it is pertinent to discuss the cultural meaning of adoptive parental non-fecundity. Conception, pregnancy, and birth involve more than biological and social facts: they represent important cultural goals which, at least in the context of marriage, are furthered by powerful positive sanctions. We have research evidence to suggest that the biological foundations of normal parenthood are widely considered a necessary condition for optimal parental role performance.[1] Moreover, there is reason to believe that public sentiments of

---

[1] H. D. Kirk, *Community Sentiments in Relation to Child Adoption*, Unpublished Ph.D. thesis, Ithaca, N.Y.: Cornell University Library, 1953 (see p. 165). (The pilot studies which the above dissertation reports were supported by a predoctoral research

this order tend to enter the self-perceptions of non-fecund adoptive parents themselves. Acceptance of values which are inappropriate to the adoptive situation may occur the more readily because adoptive parental roles as alternatives to those of biological parenthood are at present neither adequately defined nor fully sanctioned.[2] In the absence of institutionalized learning patterns concerning adoptive family roles, biological parenthood provides the most readily available frame of reference for the self-perceptions and role definitions of adopters. For the purpose of the forthcoming analysis it is important to keep in mind, however, that the cultural role supports[3] which accrue *ipso facto* to biological parents do not enter the picture for the adoptive parents as a result of their autistic perceivings. Therefore, without clear definition of the adoptive situation, without adequate sanctions, and without the concomitant role supports, it should not be impossible to conceive of non-fecund parenthood as involving a deprivation of elementary cultural goods.

Of course fecundity values are learned well in advance of the occurrence of these deprivational experiences. When one considers that sentiments related to fecundity tend to enter the standards by which adoptive parents estimate the meaning of their situation, it becomes reasonable to suppose that their estimation frequently implies devaluation.[4] On the level of interpersonal behavior, the conditions of deprivation and self-devaluation are subsumed under the concept of *role handicap*.

Whether or not the preceding ideas concerning the meaning of non-fecund parenthood appear plausible as presented, the reader is asked to accept them as presupposed for the purposes of this paper. If that is done, it will be possible to move on to the exposition and analysis of the incongruity involved in adoptive parental role obligations.

## OUTLINE OF PROCEDURE

The presentation will be in the following order and will involve the exposition and analysis of:

---

fellowship of the National Institute of Mental Health, United States Public Health Service.)

———, "Values Related to Adoption—An Aspect of the Adopted Child's Heritage." Address to the National Conference on Adoption, Child Welfare League, 1955, Mimeographed, Montreal: McGill University School of Social Work.

[2] Evidence for this contention will be furnished in another paper entitled: "Situational Discrepancy and Role Handicap."

[3] By "role supports" I mean all those intra-psychically, inter-personally, and collectively derived gratifications which aid in the enactment of role expectations. The "good conscience," the reputation of "good parent" among neighbors, and the "Mother-of-the-Year" award are types of parental role supports on these three levels respectively. Conscience, reputation, and award each draw the actor's attention to the normative expectations involved and support his readiness for further acts in the required direction.

[4] In other contexts, this phenomenon has been variously noted under the concepts of "identification with the aggressor" and "self-hate."

1. Certain normative requirements (role obligations) which the contemporary nuclear family system entails for the parent couples, and which adoptive parents share with biological parents.

2. The direction in which adoptive parents tend to modify the expected response to these requirements as a result of their initial role handicap.

3. A special requirement for adoptive parents which derives from the professionalization of adoption services, and the peculiar incongruity which this special requirement introduces into the adoptive parental role system.

4. Current modes of parental behavior which are here identified as mechanisms of adjustment to the conflicting requirements of the adoptive situation.

5. The implied meaning of these would-be adaptive patterns for their users.

6. The relationship between current adaptive mechanisms and the child-placing policies of social agencies.

7. Finally there will be an assessment of the utility of current modes of adaptation in terms of the likely consequences which their employment has for the parent-child system when the parents seek to satisfy both of the incongruous role requirements.

## USE OF RESEARCH MATERIAL

At several points in this paper, the points of view of adoptive parents will be given. These statements derive from material supplied in response to a mail questionnaire in which more than 1,500 adoptive couples furnished information concerning their attitudes and experiences.[5]

## THE REQUIREMENTS OF INTEGRATION AND SUBSEQUENT PROGRESSIVE DIFFERENTIATION OF THE CHILD

All family patterns involve some emphasis on, and at least partial realization of, the integration of new members with the existing unit. In

[5] H. D. Kirk, "Rationale for a Study of Attitudes and Experiences of Adoptive Parents," mimeographed, Montreal: McGill University School of Social Work, 1955.
Cynberg, et al., Insights Into Adoption—A Systematic Content Analysis of Mail Questionnaire Content, Montreal: McGill University Library, 1958 (MSW group thesis produced in connection with the Adoption Research Project).
Acknowledgment is hereby made to the following for financial and other aid rendered this study: McGill University; The Harry M. Cassidy Memorial Fund, University of Toronto; The Children's Service Centre, Montreal; Children's Aid and Infants' Homes of Toronto (now the Children's Aid Society of Metropolitan Toronto); The Catholic Children's Aid Society of Toronto; The Spence-Chapin Adoption Service, New York City; Children's Services, Cleveland; The State of California Department of Social Welfare; The County of Los Angeles Bureau of Adoptions.

the companionate type family, as we know it, this pressing toward integration tends to be counterbalanced by an emphasis on individuation. Integration is thus expected to lead to an evolving autonomy through increasing opportunities for the acquisition of independence. But if the contemporary middle class family gives at least lip-service to this balance in child rearing between integrational-participational value and those of individualism and autonomy, I suspect that the "good family" and the "adequate parent," in the sense of public reputation, can afford to err more readily on the side of over-emphasizing integration than differentiation. Certainly the clinician sees more of the results of persons made "over dependent" than of the reverse.

The norms of the nuclear, companionate family system appear to require of the parent figures that they initially do everything to make a newcomer into a member, that is, to integrate him or her. These norms further require that the child be in time allowed to move outward, to find companions outside the family circle, to develop alliances with, and allegiances to, other groups as well. *The norms require progressive differentiation on a firmly established base of integration.*

In the biological family this progressive moving from integration to increasing autonomy is facilitated by the ascription to the members of a blood-familial status. Members know that, within wide limits, they are free to do as they please since their place in the family group cannot be readily forfeited. And biological parents know that the child, for all his growing up and out of the protective familial situation, always belongs by this very ascription of membership.

## ADOPTIVE PARENTAL RESPONSE TO THE INTEGRATION—
## DIFFERENTIATION REQUIREMENT

In the absence of such biological bonds and of family line continuity, the emphasis of the non-fecund adoptive couple appears to be on integration rather than on the differentiating forces of autonomy. While the normative role obligations of *biological* parents also apply to adopters, the latter are probably more threatened by the differentiation aspect. Adoptive parents can be expected to respond by greater-than-ordinary protectiveness of the child and by trying, with all means at their disposal, to make inviolable the integrity of their familial unit.

In principle it would seem that they might achieve this most directly by hiding the fact of the adoption from the child as well as from others, and by simulating as completely as possible the conditions of the natural family. As long as their secret were to remain undiscovered, the couple could move toward integration with their adopted child as any other family. Most likely they would pay such psychic penalties as tend to be exacted for successful deceit in our culture, but the move toward integration would otherwise be uninhibited. As it is, however, complete secrecy is probably seldom to be achieved. Not only will those who attempt to practice it live under the cloud of the fear of discovery and the subsequent loss of their desired *quasi* biological-parent status, but they will live in further fear of being rejected by the child if someday he were to find himself deceived in his identity. Adopted persons who were told by others, or who were confronted by the adoptive parents with the fact of adoption at times of crisis such as adolescence or just before marriage, are reported subsequently to have had serious identity problems.

## A SPECIAL REQUIREMENT FOR THE ADOPTIVE PARENT—CHILD SYSTEM

Considerations of this order have for several decades made mental health specialists emphasize the importance of candidness between adoptive parents and children concerning the adoption status of the latter. Such practitioners have counseled that the child should be told from the very start, and that "adopted" should be a word of common usage in the adoptive family.[6]

If the advice is followed, the child's familial membership and reference group focus may be blurred. Ordinarily a child has but a single focus of membership and reference within his family of orientation. For the adopted child, however, there is the clearly visible one of the adoptive situation, with the unseen and ordinarily little known reality of his biological forbears hovering in the background.[7]

It is not surprising then that the requirement of informing the child of his adoptive status is problematic for adopted child *and* parents. One particularly perceptive parent put it this way:

> We have missed [in the mail questionnaire] a reference as to how parents are approaching the problem of the natural acceptance by the child of his unique position in the family and society. This may not be of apparent importance at first but will no doubt be the one single factor which will determine the future relationship between the child and his or her parents and society in general.

---

[6] Lee M. Brooks and Evelyn C. Brooks, *Adventuring in Adoption*, Chapel Hill: University of North Carolina Press, 1939, p. 183; Ethel D. Eppich & Alma C. Jenkins, "Telling Adopted Children," in *Studies of Children*, edited by Gladys Meyer, New York: King's Crown Press, 1948, p. 121; Louise Raymond, *Adoption and After*, New York: Harper, 1955, Chapter 4; Kurt Lewin, "Bringing Up the Jewish Child," in *Resolving Social Conflicts*, New York: Harper, 1948, p. 173.

[7] It is sometimes said that children are prone, at some point in their growing-up process, to imagine that they were adopted. One might note, however, that for children reared in their biological families, it would demonstrably be a fantasy while the adopted child who knows of his adoption and dwells on his dual orientation, also knows that his imaginings are *not* of the order of fantasy.

Through the eyes of this parent one can see something of the significance of the special requirement. In complying with it, adoptive parents in effect set the child apart, giving him a "unique position in the family and society." The requirement of an early and ongoing "revelation"[8] (my shorthand term for informing the child about his adoptive identity) thus conflicts with the requirement for basic familial integration.

Apparently to compensate themselves for their deprivation of given familial role supports, adoptive parents may be inclined to strive for family integration with particular intensity. Under such circumstances, the special requirement to engage in the differentiating act of revelation is bound to confront the adoptive parent with a well-nigh insuperable conflict. This conflict seems unavoidable as long as adoptive parents are subject to the push and pull of incongruous role obligations.

The next step in our analysis will be an identification of current modes of adjusting to the frustration of efforts to satisfy the conflicting requirements of the adoptive situation.

### SOME MECHANISMS OF ADAPTATION

A number of phenomena, more or less commonly associated with adoption in our culture, appear related to adoptive parents' aspirations for family integration and for role supports. In Table I, these patterns are presented in the approximate order of their occurrence in the evolution of adoptive family living. The left-hand column lists ten such phenomena which have been identified in direct observation, in the literature on adoption, and in the material obtained from our mail questionnaire study. The right-hand column lists suggested explanations of the observed phenomena.

A brief discussion of the items in this table will help to identify the underlying pattern of their meaning.

1. Physical resemblance and the knowledge that the adopted child shares the adopters' ethnic background seems to be reassuring to many adoptive parents, in part perhaps because they can thereby pass the more readily for just a family.

2. Whatever other satisfactions they may derive from adopting an infant as against an older child, adoptive parents are helped by this means also to "pass."

---

[8] The suggestion has been made that I replace the term "revelation" by "telling" which is the term in social work usage. It is felt that the term "revelation" has misleading connotations by suggesting a single, drastic, and highly charged event. While it should be made clear that the concept of revelation does not imply a single event but a recurring one (as is the case in the ongoing revelations of juvenile sex education), I believe that for our analytic purpose "revelation" is preferable to "telling" because the former makes explicit in the emotive weighting which is part of the situation of telling but which the term "telling" does not imply. I suggest that the conceptual requirements of mental health education and of sociological analysis may be different.

3. Some 90 percent (1,373) of the mail questionnaire respondents said that at least once outsiders have asked them some questions like: "Do you know anything about this child's background?" Of those to whom this had happened, only 3 percent report that they felt pleased about the inquiry, and only 7 percent say they felt amused by it. Many wrote in to say that they consider such inquiries from other people to be uncalled for and that questions like these show how misinformed people really are on the subject of adoption. Some of the adoptive parents report having replied as politely as they could: "It's none of your business."

4. Adoptive parents who seek to have more than one child seldom can get a child "on short order." Since they usually have to wait for several months, or even years, this situation helps them to simulate the spacing between biological family arrivals.

5. Such multiple adopters generally follow the pattern necessarily set by biological family units in that subsequent arrivals tend to be younger than the children who preceded them in the family.

TABLE I. **Some Phenomena Associated with Adoptive Parental Aspirations for Family Integration and Substitute Role Supports**

| Observed Phenomena | Suggested Explanation of the Phenomena in Terms of Adoptive Parental Aspirations |
|---|---|
| 1. Simulation of appearance, race, and ethnic background. 2. Infancy adoption. 3. Fending off the inquiries of outsiders. 4. Simulation of the biological family's arrival spacing. 5. Simulation of the biological family's age constellation. | Mechanisms serving to keep differentiating adoption factors from outsiders. |
| 6. Minimizing the impact of social problems which gave rise to adoption. 7. "Ignoring" the child's biological parents. 8. Myths of origin of the adoptive family unit (with the child as principal focus). | Mechanisms serving to keep differentiating factors from the child. |
| 9. Myths of origin of the adoptive family unit (with the adopter as principal focus). 10. Repressing the dilemma of identity (forgetting the adoption). | Mechanisms serving to keep differentiating adoption factors from the adopters' self-awareness. |

*By means of these five mechanisms, adoptive parents are enabled to keep differentiating factors in adoption from the gaze of outsiders. The following three phenomena operate within the confines of adoptive relationships:*

6. The parents who reveal the child's adoptive status to him are certainly under considerable pressure to play down the differentiating meanings of the information. One such couple suggests that

Adults accept adoption well but seem to find it difficult to explain to their children in a comfortable way. This is upsetting for the children.

An adoptive father makes clear that the adoptive parents try to minimize the impact of the situation not solely for their child's sake but also their own:

> There are the feelings about explaining to the child early about adoptions, particularly a very small child so that he learns it first from us. There is the fear of confusing him and also involved is the wish that we really were his parents.

7. Minimizing the impact of "revelation" for the child involves the disappearance, as it were, of the natural parents. This is done by depersonalizing them through reference to them as "the lady and the man who brought you into the world," or by avoiding references to them altogether. One need not be surprised that adoptive parents who seek to have the original parents disappear from the familial scene find it difficult to explain the meanings of adoption to their children. Generally, adoption is made possible by the relinquishment of a child on the part of a first parent or a guardian, as a result of death or some problem of living. The majority of non-familial adoptions—that is, adoptions made outside the child's original family line—come about as a result of the relinquishment of their children by out-of-wedlock mothers. By ignoring the existence of the original parents, the adopters can thus avoid discussion of the social and personal problems which made the child available for adoption in the first place. But these problems remain to plague the adoptive parents, for they must ask in what context the revelation about the adoptive status is to be made to the adopted child. Some such parents write:

> Would it be possible for suggestions or thoughts relating to the answers we shall be called upon to give our children as they grow up, in connection with their natural parents? We are somewhat apprehensive about this.
> We are not quite sure how to answer our children's questions [when they arise] concerning their background—why they were given up, brothers, sisters, family, et cetera.
> There is the problem of how much to tell the child about the child's natural parents—should he ever know about his being born out-of-wedlock? Are parents going to tell the children the complete truth about their [natural] parents or will they make up a story which will please the child?

8. Adoptive parents who strive toward integration but who also feel impelled to reveal this adoptive identity to the child may seek to minimize the impact of revelation through assurances of their love. Here enters the use of myth. The story of the adoption is made into a myth of family origin. In an indigenous version of it the parents chose the child above all others. In a social-work approved version, the parents chose the child after

the agency had judged that these parents and this child might suit each other. The adoptive parents, in telling the myth, try to deal with the reality without touching its painful aspects. One woman writes:

> I probably wouldn't tell them if I knew they'd never find out. But if we didn't [tell them] they would some day know. So they know they were "chosen" because they know we love them more than anyone else in the whole wide world.

However much the "chosen baby" myth may minimize the differentiating impact of "revelation" for the child, the adoptive parents still have to reckon with the impact of such telling on themselves:

> I used to force myself sometimes to say "Mommy's chosen baby," but now I can answer questions without showing emotions.

*Mechanisms six through eight appear then to serve primarily in keeping the differentiating adoption factors from the child.*

Through the mail questionnaire respondents, two other mechanisms have come to our attention. These help in the quest for integration by allowing the adoptive parents to affirm their parental identity.

9. In this instance a myth is created about the origin of the adoptive parent's own position:

> We were very elated that our daughter accepted us as Mother and Father from the very first day she came to live with us. She was 3½ years old and we believe that she was meant for us and that God had a hand in bringing us together.

In this myth, fate had meant the adoptive parents and the child to be the real family so that the biological parents are simply discounted. In this particular version, there is a special twist in that the child "acknowledges" the situation created by the myth. The child accepts the adoptive parents from the first as if he also were saying "of course, we really were meant for each other."

Some years ago I interviewed several university students who had been adopted. One of these made references to her adoptive family along lines of myth. She spoke of her older sister who was also adopted into the family but who is no blood relation. She said: "Olga is sloppy where I'm fastidious. My mother is a good housekeeper as far as she goes, but I'm quite different from her in my insistence on order. I have an aunt, however, who is very much like me." This aunt turned out to be the adoptive father's sister. This respondent's myth consisted of the implicit assumption that the similarity between her's and the adopted aunt's trait of neatness constituted a special familial link.

We have suggested that myths of origin in the adoptive situation serve as aids in the striving for integration between the members. In this connection, we may want to recall Malinowski's observations concerning the circumstances associated with the existence of myths of origin in Trobriand culture:

> It is clear that *myth functions especially where there is a sociological strain*, such as in matters of great difference in rank and power, matters of precedence and subordination, and *unquestionably where profound historical changes have taken place.* [emphasis added.][9]

This paper was begun by pointing to nonfecundity as the basis of cultural deprivation and role handicap in the adoptive situation. Additional strain was shown to arise from the conflicting expectations of integration simultaneous with revelation. Interestingly, we find in our analysis, as did Malinowski in his, that the myths are allied with profound historical changes. Here the changes occur in the life histories of persons, and are profound because potential fecundity is presupposed for normal adults so that its absence is both unexpected and unprepared for.

10. We now turn to the remaining mechanism, repression. One couple writes:

> We are telling our daughter she is adopted but it is hard for us to realize this ourselves. We feel almost as though we were telling her an untruth.

Such "forgetting" closes the gap between myth and reality. The myth sustains at the beginning and supports through certain crises. But finally the troublesome reality is most conveniently dealt with by it being removed from one's awareness.

*The last two mechanisms operate on the level of the self and are thus true defenses in the psychological sense of the term. They appear to serve the adoptive parent who employs them in keeping differentiating forces in adoption at arm's length.*

## A PROPOSED EXPLANATION OF CURRENT MECHANISMS IN TERMS OF THEIR PROBABLE CONSEQUENCES

It has already been suggested that these mechanisms, aside from other consequences, may serve adopters in keeping the differentiating aspects of adoption from coming to the surface too noticeably. These several[10] phenomena may then be conceived of as mechanisms of adaptation.

Like everyone else, the adoptive parent is in need of a role pattern sufficiently defined and sanctioned to support the actor in carrying out cul-

---

[9] B. Malinowski, "Myths in Primitive Psychology," in *Magic, Science and Religion*, New York: Doubleday Anchor Books, 1954, p. 126.

[10] We have no way of knowing whether the listing here given is exhaustive either of the possible or actual universe of such phenomena.

turally required behavior. In the absence of well-defined substitute-parental role patterns and in the absence of a readiness to invent and pioneer novel roles, it is understandable enough that adopters will attempt to minimize or to deny the difference between their position and that of biological parents. The role pattern, created by the use of such denial mechanisms of adaptation will from here on be referred to as rejection-of-difference orientation, or rejection orientation in short.

## THE ADAPTIVE MECHANISMS IN THE LIGHT OF SOCIAL WORK PRACTICES

Two tasks of analysis remain to be accomplished. In a final step, we will assess the probable utility of these would-be-adaptive mechanisms as the context for revelation. Before doing so, it is appropriate to make a brief detour and to look at the phenomena of Table I in the context of current social work practices. Table II lists the observed phenomena in relation to the child-placing patterns of adoption agencies.

In Table II the previously enumerated mechanisms are examined in the light of the policies and practices of child-placing agencies. We find that each would-be adaptive mechanism has some reinforcing counterpart in the setting of social work practice. The adoptive parents are thereby given the sanction of professional authority, not only for the employment of the mechanisms themselves, but *indirectly* also for a rejection-of-difference orientation. This latter consequence of social work practice is probably *unintended* which makes it, of course, nonetheless real.[11]

## FUNCTIONAL ANALYSIS OF REVELATION IN THE CONTEXT OF CURRENT ROLE SUPPORT MECHANISMS

We are now taking the final step in the analysis of incongruous role obligations in adoption. As was pointed out, the role patterning in response to the incongruous requirements of integration and revelation is typically of the order of rejection-of-difference, reinforced by professional practice patterns. The question must now be raised how revelation affects the adopters' parental aspirations under conditions of rejection orientation.

The scheme of analysis is mainly that set out by Merton.[12] Table III

---

[11] The position I am taking involves refusal to impute motivations to social agency policies other than those overtly expressed by child welfare policy makers. At the same time, it is interesting to note that Brenner feels that individual adoption workers involved in her study have their own tendency toward "rejection-of-difference." "Workers tend to be happier if they can think of it [the adoptive relationship] as exactly like the usual parent-child relationship and without special problems in a home where families really love and accept children." R. Brenner, *op. cit.*, p. 23.

[12] Robert K. Merton, "Manifest and Latent Functions," Chapter 1, *Social Theory and Social Structure*, Glencoe, Illinois: Free Press, 1949, especially pp. 48–61.

lists the assumed consequences of revelation for the adoptive parent-child system.

The functional-dysfunctional dichotomy aids in visualizing and sorting out certain believed consequences of revelation in the context of rejection orientation. Consequences are regarded as "functional" if they are plausibly

TABLE II. Parental Role Support Mechanisms and Social Work Practices in Child Placement

| Adaptive Mechanisms | Supportive Social Work Practices |
|---|---|
| 1. Simulation of appearance and background. | "Matching" of children and parents. |
| 2. Infancy adoption. | Recent orientation toward early placement (given special impetus by the Bowlby Report).* |
| 3. Fending off inquiries. | Confidentiality of agency and court records insures the adopter against the intrusion of others into the privacy of their family. |
| 4. Simulation of the biological family's arrival spacing. | Insistence that a suitable period elapse before additional application can be accepted. |
| 5. Simulation of the biological family's age constellation. | Reluctance to place children outside the common age sequence pattern. |
| 6. Minimizing the impact of problems related to the child's availability for adoption. | Confidentiality of agency and court records insures the adopter against the child's stumbling on, or otherwise becoming acquainted with, matters not revealed by parent. |
| 7. Ignoring the natural parent(s). | The agency's role as mediator obviates direct dealings between natural and adoptive parents. |
| 8. Myths of origin: (child as principal focus). | Indoctrination through social work literature and contact with agency. |
| 9. Myths of origin: (adopter as principal focus). | The agency initiates the revelation but does not offer means of solving the incongruity between it and the normative requirement of integration.** |
| 10. Repression: forgetting the fact of adoption. | The agency "leaves the scene" after the legalization of adoption. |

* J. Bowlby, *Maternal Care and Mental Health*, Geneva: World Health Organization, 1952.
** It is pertinent to quote in this connection from Brenner's excellent study: "Often workers said that parents would need to feel comfortable about discussing [adoption] with their child before they could do it, *but there is no indication in the records that workers themselves had understood the full complexity of the problems for parents and child alike*." Ruth F. Brenner, *A Follow-Up Study of Adoptive Families*, 1951, pp. 72–73 [emphasis added].

operating in the direction of fostering and maintaining the equilibrium of the adoptive parent-child system. Similarly, consequences are regarded as dysfunctional if they would appear to threaten this equilibrium. In addition to the functional-dysfunctional distinction between objective consequences, another conceptual dimension enters Table III, namely the dimension of subjective aims and perceptions. Merton distinguished between *manifest* and *latent* functions:[13]

---

[13] R. K. Merton, *op. cit.*, p. 51.

TABLE III. Some Consequences of "Revelation" for the Parent-Child System in Adoption When Parental Attempts at Role Patterning Are Primarily Oriented Toward Rejection-of-Difference

| | A<br>Consequences Which Appear Functional | B<br>Consequences Which Appear Dysfunctional |
|---|---|---|
| C<br>Intended consequences (Merton's "manifest functions") | 1. Avoidance of long-run identity problems for the child.<br>2. Avoidance of long-run difficulties (arising from 1) for the parent-child relationship and thus also for the parents. | |
| D<br>Consequences which are *un*intended but which may be recognized. | 1. Partial identity for the child: "adopted child" symbol and reference category. | 1. Likelihood that revelation will obstruct the drive for integration.<br>2. Periodic self-induced recall when "forgetting" is desired.<br>3. Revelation will make public the couple's situation of "sterility." |
| E<br>Consequences which are unintended and probably remain unrecognized (Merton's "latent functions"). | | 1. Revelation by itself is incapable of supplying the child with complete adoptive identity since the situation usually lacks role models.<br>2. No identity for the adopter: neither adequate symbol nor role model. ("Adoptive parent" not in common usage.) |

*Manifest functions* are those objective consequences contributing to the adjustment or adaptation of the system which are intended and recognized by participants in the system;
*Latent functions*, correlatively, being those which are neither intended nor recognized.

To Merton's reference points of intended-and-recognized (manifest) consequences and unintended-and-unrecognized (latent), a mid-position has been added: we are interested in consequences which are unintended but which may be recognized by the participants.

Two consequences are visualized as belonging in cell AC (functional and manifest). It has already been suggested that early and on-going candidness with the child regarding his adoptive status probably secures him against certain psychic disasters later on in life. If the child is thereby being protected from this particular source of possible disintegration of the adoptive family relations, it is evident that the maintenance of the system itself and the correlative psychic security of the parents *qua* parents will also be secured. In cell AD the suggestion is made that revelation gives the child a symbol for naming himself. As a result, he knows that he belongs to a recognized category of persons, the adopted. This consequence of revelation, though possibly recognized, is probably unintended.

Among the dysfunctional consequences, item BD 1 draws attention to the strong possibility that the act of revelation will raise further questions by the child. In that sense, revelation is likely to disturb the child's sense of belonging and to frustrate the parental aspirations for family integration.

Item BD 2: In speaking of the adoption to the child the parents are also addressing themselves. For those committed to a rejection orientation, this periodic recall means the uprooting of forces which they seek to leave quietly repressed or forgotten. Thus, in the very act of helping their adopted child, the adoptive parents necessarily destroy a desired psychic equilibrium for themselves.

Item BD 3: In the context of rejection orientation, revelation affects the self-regard of the adoptive parents in yet another sense. At the beginning of this paper, it was suggested that fecundity represents an important cultural goal. Concomitantly, infertility is regarded as a handicap. As long as the non-fecund couple's adoption remains a secret, their non-fecundity does likewise.[14] But once it is known that the child or children they have are adopted, this information necessarily suggests that they were unable to produce their own and thus it publicizes their particular deprivation.[15]

In cell BE (latent dysfunctional), item 1 points to the fact that revelation by itself does not supply the full requirement of an identity, for which symbol *and* cultural model are required. As long as most adopted children are not members of groups of such children, few knowing other adopted children intimately, revelation must in that sense be assumed to have dysfunctional aspects. It supplies only half a loaf, where a whole one is wanted. In this connection the report of a young woman, who had been adopted in infancy, is particularly pertinent. She told the interviewer that three of her most intimate childhood friends had been adopted. She said that this was a great comfort to her when she first learned of it, and that it remained a help throughout her growing years.

Item BE 2: If the parents' revelations give the child a partial basis for an adoptive identity through the symbolic referent "adopted," the revealing parents do not receive even that. While the adopted belong to a reference category understood in the vernacular, no terms such as "adopter"

---

[14] Some adoptive parents appear inclined to postpone informing their children of the fact of their adoption until such time as the parents consider them "old enough" to keep the information to themselves.

[15] I am indebted for this salient point to Mr. V. Hartman. See his contribution in Bramble, *et al.*, *An Exploration into Some of the Attitudes in the Community Surrounding the Adoptive Family*, Montreal: McGill University Library, 1957 (MSW group thesis produced in connection with the Adoption Research Project).

or "adoptive parent" exist in common usage. When we listen to the manner in which people, adopters included, refer to adoptive parents, we hear references to the Browns "who have adopted a child" or "who have an adopted child." In other words, for adoptive parents there exists no commonly employed symbolic referent to suggest the nature of their adoptive identity. In common usage they are adopters, identifiable solely by references to the *means* of substitute parental role gratification, that is, *having adopted*, or to the *ends* of the gratification, *the child*. It is as if a teacher's role were not identifiable by the referent "teacher," but only by pointing to the activity of teaching, that is, "the man who teaches" or by the social objects dealt with, "the man who has students." This phenomenon is illuminated by associations of adoptive parents in California. These associations originally came into being as pressure groups to initiate changes in the state's adoption laws and they now serve a variety of educational and mutual aid interests. When Professor Brooks[16] first wrote to me about these organizations, he noted that they seemed *mis*named "Adopted Children's Associations" since they are associations of parents and would-be parents rather than of children. On the basis of the foregoing discussion, it can now be suggested with some plausibility that the misnomer appears to have arisen by necessity because the proper symbol has not yet become part of the vernacular.

Our language patterns thus give a clue to the present condition of child adoption. The symbolic lacuna noted is apparently related to the lack of cultural definition of the adoptive situation. In addition to other handicaps inherent in their situation, adoptive parents may thus be considered symbolically "short-changed."

## SUMMARY, CONCLUSIONS, PROSPECTS

1. The adoptive family system has been shown to operate under incongruous parental role obligations of *integration plus revelation*.
2. In the process of trying to adjust to the frustrations involved in satisfying both of these requirements, adoptive parents appear to have developed a number of distinct patterns of behavior.
3. These patterns were identified as mechanisms of adaptation which also serve as role supports.
4. The mechanisms described in this paper all help the adopters who use them to deny or reject the differences between the adoptive and the biological family situation. This pattern has been called "rejection orientation."
5. Present child-placing policies and practices in social work appear to reinforce this rejection orientation on the part of adoptive parents, even

---

[16] Private correspondence with Dr. Lee M. Brooks, at that time visiting professor at Whittier College, Whittier, California.

though this result of professional activity is probably neither intended nor recognized.

6. When the rejection oriented mechanisms are assessed for their utility as means of adaptation to a situation involving incongruous role obligations, we note a preponderance of dysfunctional consequences.

In addition to its idea content, this paper was intended as a demonstration of the applicability and use of functional analysis to the strategies of welfare planning. The mental health professions in general, and social work in particular, concern themselves with the optimization of certain conditions of living. In the establishment of substitute families, social workers are principally interested in the potential viability of these interpersonal systems as the milieu necessary for child-personality development. Through the application of a systematic structural-functional analysis to forces already well-known to professionals in child-placing work, it was possible to identify actual or potential trouble spots. These trouble spots represent the dysfunctional consequences of attempts to satisfy requirements of the situation without due regard for the context provided by the mechanisms of adaptation which are used. The consequences were regarded as dysfunctional from the point of view of the long-term goals of child-placing agencies, namely the establishments and maintenance of viable family systems.

The analytic procedures employed in this paper were meant to answer these questions:

1. What are some of the crucial strains in this particular situation (adoption) of interest to the mental health professions?
2. What types of common adaptations are at present discernible in the situation?
3. How do the observed adaptive patterns operate relative to the ultimate goals of (a) the participants and (b) the professionals?

These questions pertain therefore to the diagnostic phases of professional helping activity. Is functional analysis primarily applicable to diagnosis then? In forthcoming writings I hope to be able to show that structural-functional analysis is helpful to a much wider range of mental health planning. Specifically, this analytic method should be able to help practitioners in seeking answers to the following questions:

1. What alternative means of adaptation (alternative to those presently patterned) are in view or can be hypothetically projected?
2. Which among the available or imaginable alternatives is functionally most conducive to the establishment and maintenance of the end-in-view (that is, the desired system)?

# 38

⟨[ A sizable number of research studies have been devoted to the question of the number of adopted children referred for treatment and the particular nature of the symptomatology of the adopted child. Kadushin reviewed many of these studies in "Adoptive Parenthood: A Hazardous Adventure?" (*Social Work*, Vol. 11, July 1966, pp. 30–39). Reece reviewed some of the more recent studies in "Psychiatric Disturbances in Adopted Children: A Descriptive Study" (*Social Work*, Vol. 13, January 1968, pp. 101–1113. Despite the number of studies the questions of both the rate of need for psychiatric care and the uniqueness of symptomatology are still unanswered.

The following article is a carefully designed attempt to determine whether or not adopted children are disproportionately represented in the case load of a community mental health center.

## Adopted Children Brought to a Child Psychiatric Clinic

*Jerome D. Goodman, Richard M. Silberstein, and Wallace Mandell*

During the past three years reports have appeared suggesting that parents of adopted children apply for psychiatric care of their children many times more frequently than nonadopting parents. These reports have aroused interest and concern among child welfare agencies. Prompted by this concern, the Staten Island Mental Health Center undertook a review of 593 cases studied at that child psychiatric clinic between 1956 and 1962. In this sample of cases only a small difference could be discovered between the rate of applications for adopted versus biological children and the proportions of such children living in the community.

The sample of children studied at the Staten Island Mental Health Center differed from the children studied in two reports which have generated much discussion. Dr. Schecter[1] reported a high rate of adopted children admitted to his private practice of child psychiatry in Southern California between 1948 and 1953. He did not include data about the income levels of the families applying to him for the care of their children. Dr. Toussieng[2] reported a high rate of application for adopted children in the children's service of the Menninger Clinic between 1955 and 1960. Neither the geographical distribution nor the income levels of the families were discussed in that report. It is assumed, however, that many of these children were drawn from areas beyond the metropolitan area of Topeka, Kan., in keeping with the policies of that service. The Staten Island study includes only those children whose families were residents of Richmond County. Our clinic policy limits service to families of lower income, usually less than $8,000 per year. The Staten Island Mental Health Center is a community clinic offering the only voluntary service for children of Richmond County families. Because of the location of this insular borough of New York City, it is rare for families to secure medical care in other areas. When psychiatric evaluation and treatment are sought for children of lower income families in Richmond County, it is likely that these children will be brought to the Staten Island Mental Health Center.

This study attempted to extend Dr. Schecter's and Dr. Toussieng's findings by determining the proportion of children who were adopted by families living in the community from which the studied children would be drawn. Dr. Schecter had used an index of incidence of adopted children in the general population which may not have been representative of the area from which his practice evolved. He compared: (*a*) the number of children in 29 states for whom adoptive petitions were filed, and (*b*) the child population for those states in 1953. Comparing the rate of adopted children seen in his practice to this base, Dr. Schecter claimed that he was seeing a "100-fold" over-representation of adopted children. Dr. Toussieng did not consider another base rate, nor did he draw conclusions (about whether or not) "adopted children are more prone to serious emotional or personality disorders." Rita Dukette, in her discussion of Dr. Toussieng's findings,[3] proposed that a more appropriate base rate for the existence of adopted children would be comprised of ". . . the total number of adopted children and nonadopted children in the general population of the age range represented by the children known to psychiatrists and mental health clinics." This study set out to determine such a pertinent base rate. Specific data about adoptions were obtained from the Richmond County Surrogate's office.[4] There were found to be 1,917 adoptions by Richmond County residents during the period 1945–1960. During these 15 years, an average of 113 children were adopted annually. Utilizing census figures for children under age 21 in 1950 and 1960 (61,084 and 84,530), an annual rate of adopted children per 10,000 children residing in the county was calculated. This rate of 15–16 children adopted annually per 10,000 child population compared with a nationwide estimate of 14–15 annually adopted children per 10,000 child population for the corresponding period.[5] Table 1 illustrates Richmond County's relatively high annual rate of adoption.

Not all adoptions carry with them the same psychological and social implications (e.g., the adoption of a step-child at age 18 versus the adoption of the newborn child of a stranger). The Staten Island Mental Health Center therefore separates adopted children into two categories. When a

TABLE 1. Adoption Rates in Richmond County, New York State and USA

| | Annual Rate of Adoptions Per 10,000 Children Under Age 21 | Extrafamilial Adoptions as % of Total Adoptions | Proportion of Adoptions Agencies Sponsored, % |
|---|---|---|---|
| USA | 14–15 (1950–1960) | 54 (1960) | 59 (1960) |
| New York State | 10–11 (1959) | 65 (1954–1957) | 35 (1954–1957) |
| Richmond County | 15–16 (1950–1960) | 61 (1954–1961) | 36 (1954–1961) |

Sources: 1. Child Welfare Statistics (5).
2. Surrogate's Association of the State of New York Adoption Statistics (10).
3. Surrogate's Court of Richmond County (4).

child is related to one of the adopting parents, such a child is termed intra-familially adopted (IFA). When the child is related to neither of the adopting parents, that child is termed extrafamilially adopted (EFA). The data from the Surrogate's Court for the years 1957–1961 indicated that 61% of all adoptions by Richmond County residents were extrafamilial. If an average of 113 children were adopted annually, it can be estimated that of those children, 70 were not related to either parent. Having determined the proportion of extra-familially adopted children to all adopted children, it became possible to calculate the probable number of EFA children in the community. There are two ways of doing this.

One basis for determining the prevalence of EFA children in the community would be a determination of the EFA children adopted annually as compared to the number of children born in the community (mean annual live births). There was a mean of 400 live births per year during the period in which there were 70 EFA children adopted annually. Thus, of the yearly increment of children, 1.75% would represent extrafamilial adoptions.* A second approach would involve a comparison of the total EFA adoptions over a 15-year period to the census of children age 15 and under living in the community. The span chosen was 1945–1960, and the census was for 1960. There were a total of 1804 children adopted in this time span, of whom an estimated 1,100 children were extrafamilially adopted. The census of 1960 recorded a total of 66,549 children living in Richmond County. From these data, it is found that 1.66% of the children living in the community and of the age range known to the Staten Island

---

* The number of children born in Richmond County, who were adopted by parents outside of the county, is known and was subtracted from the mean annual live birth total.

Mental Health Center were extrafamilially adopted. The calculated prevalence of EFA children as determined by the two approaches is similar (1.75% and 1.66%). Both methods do not include a factor of population shift resulting from moves in and out of the community. Even without that factor, which would favor influx of population, it can be assumed that 1.7% of the children in the community is a useable estimate of the existence of EFA children in the pool from which this study's sample was taken.

The charts of children seen at the Staten Island Mental Health Center during the seven-year period 1956–1962 were examined. All closed cases were included in the study except those in which there had been insufficient study to produce necessary data (usually withdrawals or cancelled applications). When more than one child in a family was studied, the children were counted in this study as a single unit. A total of 593 family units constituted the sample. Of these 593 case units, 16 were found to include adopted children. Fourteen of the 16 cases were EFA children while the other two were related to their adopting parents. It is possible that additional adopted children remained "hidden," chiefly IFA cases as represented by adopted step-children. This report focuses on the EFA group because those children are less likely to remain "hidden" and because EFA children are of most interest to child welfare agencies. Of the 14 EFA children found among the sample, 7 were privately placed and 7 were agency-guided. The group was made up of eight boys and six girls, a sex ratio in keeping with the over-all experience of the sample. There were siblings in 6 of the 14 families. These siblings were also found to be adopted children in three of those six families. The mean age when these extrafamilially adopted children were brought to the clinic for study was 10.5 years. The children came from families whose average annual income was $5,185, as compared to the average annual family income of $6,836 as determined for Richmond County in 1959.[6] The mean age of these EFA children at the time of their adoption was 30 months. This is older than the estimate of 2.1 months as the mean age at adoption for all adoptions throughout the USA in 1960.[5]

During the seven-year span covered by the study, there was yearly variation in the ratio of adopted to total children examined at the clinic. The annual percentage of EFA children brought to the clinic ranged from 0% to 5.6%. Table 2 lists the yearly number of these children seen. During the period of the study, 2.4% of the total children brought to the Staten Island Mental Health Center, who were studied in sufficient detail, and whose cases were closed, were found to be EFA children.

Dr. Schecter had reported that reasons for referral of adopted children in his private practice were "without specificity." There was similarity as regards presenting difficulties among several of the children we studied. Eleven of the 14 children were referred with complaints of a behavioral

TABLE 2. **Annual Rate of Extrafamilially Adopted Children Studied at Staten Island Mental Health Center for Each Year 1956–1962**

| Year | Ratio Adopted Children to Total Number Children Studied | Adopted Children Studied, % |
|------|---------------------------------------------------------|-----------------------------|
| 1956 | 1:68  | 1.5 |
| 1957 | 1:53  | 1.9 |
| 1958 | 1:69  | 1.5 |
| 1959 | 2:92  | 2.1 |
| 1960 | 0:96  | 0   |
| 1961 | 6:108 | 5.6 |
| 1962 | 3:107 | 2.8 |

disturbance. Stealing was a primary symptom in six of the children. Aggressive behavior and hyperactivity were among the presenting complaints of seven of the children. A learning disturbance was among the symptoms for which six children were brought to the clinic. The learning disturbance was found to be part of a behavioral complex rather than a "primary learning disorder" for five of these six children. Enuresis was a referring symptom in one child, diuresis in another. The parents' impression of the child as conveyed by presenting complaints in the social histories was consistent with most of the final diagnoses. One case was diagnosed as a psychoneurotic reaction, and that child was living in an acute situational disturbance. One child was found to be mentally deficient without known cause, and achieved a full scale IQ of 67. A personality trait disturbance appeared in the diagnosis of 10 of the 14 children. Six of the children were found to be living in disturbed situations. Table 3 lists some of the characteristics of these children. The social histories reported by the adopting parents revealed that the locale of adoption was distant from Staten Island in 10 of the 14 families. Most of these 10 families had moved to Richmond County shortly after the adoption of their children. With only 4 of the 14 cited families adopting locally, it appears that the rate of extrafamilial, locally adopted children being brought to a child psychiatric clinic within the community of their adoption may be lower than that for biological children.

The rate of diagnostic study of EFA children at the Staten Island Mental Health Center was 2.4% of the total children examined at that facility over a seven-year period. The rate of EFA children residing on Staten Island was 1.7% during that period. These data are based on the best available local records for the prevalence of adopted children in the community. The socioeconomic segment of the population from which the applications for psychiatric service came is more clearly specified here than it is in reports presented by Drs. Toussieng and Schecter. A comparison of

TABLE . Characteristics of Adopted Children Seen at Staten Island Mental Health Clinic 1956–1962

| Age at Adoption, Month | Year of Adoption | Age at Referral Year | Private Agency | Income | Where Adoptions Took Place | Sex | Siblings | Presenting Complaint | Diagnoses |
|---|---|---|---|---|---|---|---|---|---|
| 0.13 | 1946 | 11 | P | $4,250 | Local | M | 1 | Sexual advances toward sister | Obsessive-compulsive reaction; situational disturbance, acute |
| 0.25 | 1950 | 12 | A | 3,500 | Distant | M | None | Stealing, migraine | Brain syndrome of unknown cause, chronic; situational disturbance, chronic |
| 3.0 | 1957 | 5 | P | 7,500 | Distant | M | 1 | Slow in learning | Idiopathic mental deficiency |
| 5.0 | 1948 | 9 | A | 3,500 | Local | F | None | Poor schoolwork, aggressive behavior with children | Passive-aggressive character disorder |
| 8.00 | 1949 | 11 | A | 4,500 | Distant | F | None | Temper tantrums, poor schoolwork | Passive-aggressive character disorder |
| 24.0 | 1947 | 16 | P | 7,000 | Distant | M | None | Stealing cars | Inadequate personality |
| 24.0 | 1946 | 15 | P | 6,500 | Local | M | 2 | Stealing, lying, poor schoolwork | Passive-aggressive character disorder; situational disturbance, chronic |
| 24.0 | 1947 | 15 | A | 6,600 | Distant | F | None | Temper tantrums, poor schoolwork, poor peer relations | Oral depressed character; situational disturbance, chronic |
| 32.0 | 1958 | 7 | A | 5,200 | Distant | M | 1 | Thumbsucking, nailbiting, enuresis | Passive-aggressive character disorder; special symptom formations |
| 36.0 | 1953 | 8 | A | 4,000 | Distant | M | None | Nervous, stubborn, aggressive, cruel, fire-setting | Passive-aggressive character disorder; special symptom formations |
| 42.0 | 1958 | 6 | A | 4,750 | Local | M | 3 | Hyperactive, poor schoolwork, disruptive behavior | Situational disorder, chronic; special symptom formation with passive-aggressive features |
| 60.0 | 1953 | 11 | P | 3,200 | Distant | F | None | Stealing, screaming, poor peer relations and diuresis | Passive-aggressive character disorder |
| 69.0 | 1959 | 8 | P | 8,000 | Distant | F | None | Lying, stealing, cannot tell right from wrong | Situational disturbance, chronic; special symptom formations |
| 84.0 | 1955 | 13 | P | 8,000 | Distant | F | 3 | Lying, stealing, poor school behavior | Passive aggressive character disorder |

this study's findings with theirs is given in Table 4. An attempt to understand the strikingly lower rate of EFA children brought to this clinic as compared to another clinic and a private practice would have to consider the difference of income of the families bringing their children for care. The Richmond County families studied in our sample were representative of lower income groups, and it is possible that higher income families seek psychiatric attention for their adopted children more readily. Locale of adoption may also be a determinant for choosing locale of sought psychiatric help. Private treatment or geographically distant clinic settings may provide for enough anonymity to overbalance an adoptive parent's reluctance to seek aid for his children, but such reluctance is common to all parents. While this study reports the relative incidence of psychiatric clinic service for adopted versus nonadopted children, it does not attempt to assay the adopted child's vulnerability to emotional disorders. The prediction of vulnerability to psychiatric illness in adopted children is best determined by other methods such as longitudinal investigations. In the past, authors have differed in theoretical and clinical predictions of the adopted child's emotional outcome. Lilli Peller[7] has written that a higher proportion of adopted children than natural children develop emotional problems which require psychiatric help. Dr. Powers, on the other hand, has stated: "Clinically speaking, the adopted child shows no different symptomatology or diagnostic variations from any other child."[8] Dr. Bernard has wiped the slate clean. She has written that "Reports from guidance clinics, agencies, and physicians about disturbed adoptive children cannot measure adoptive outcome in general since these sources have but a one-sided view. They do not see the many well-adjusted adoptive families as well, and thus lack access to the total picture. Furthermore, there are no reliable figures as yet, though some have been ventured, for comparing

TABLE 4. Findings of Three Studies of Adopted Children in Psychiatric Settings

| Study | Length of Study Period | Income Group Served | Sample Size | Number of Extra-familially Adopted Children in Sample Studied | Extra-familially Adopted Children in Sample Studied, % | Agency Sponsored Adoptions as % of Total Adopted Cases Reported | Ratio of Girls Boys |
|---|---|---|---|---|---|---|---|
| S.I.M.H.C. (Goodman; Silberstein; Mandell) | 1956–1962 7 yr | Low-Middle | 593 | 14 | 2.4 | 50 | 6:8 |
| Menninger Clinic (Toussieng) | 1955–1960 6 yr | Middle-High | 357 | 39 | 10.9 | 54 | 11:28 |
| Private practice (Schechter) | 1948–1953 6 yr | Middle-High | 120 | 16 | 13.3 | — | — |

the rates of emotional maladjustment for nonadoptive and adoptive children."[9]

The review of the Staten Island Mental Health Center cases was sparked by child agency concern as to whether or not agency-guided adopted children were being seen at high rates in psychiatric offices, whether private or clinic. On the basis of their existence in the community of this study, adopted children were seen in a clinic only slightly more than biological children. The over-representation of extrafamilially adopted children in our clinic caseload (2.4%) as compared with their rate in the community (1.7%), is of a magnitude which, though statistically significant, is not believed sufficient to warrant social consequence. Our findings suggest that child care agencies might postpone their anxieties pending further investigations.

## SUMMARY

The charts of 593 children seen at the Staten Island Mental Health Center were reviewed. Of this total, 14 cases or 2.4% were found to be extrafamilially adopted children. Among the small number of adopted children seen in the sample there was a preponderance of personality trait disturbances. The studied children were brought to the clinic 1.4 times as frequently as would be expected on the basis of their existence in the community. The rate at which they were brought to a low income, community clinic was found to be much lower than the rates reported in a higher income clinic or in a private practice. Extrafamilially adopted children who had been adopted in the community of the study, and who had remained there, were seen less frequently than were non-adopted children. Sampling and choice of base rates for assessing emotional morbidity of adopted children were thought to explain higher rates found in other studies.

*References*

1. Schecter, M. D.: Observations on Adopted Children, *Arch. Gen. Psychiat.* 3:21–32 (July) 1960.
2. Toussieng, P. W.: Thoughts Regarding the Etiology of Psychological Difficulties in Adopted Children, *Child Welfare* 41:59–65 (Feb) 1962.
3. Dukette, R.: Discussion of "Thoughts . . . Children," *Child Welfare* 41:66–71 (Feb) 1962.
4. Personal communication to the author, Surrogate's Court of Richmond County, Hon. Frank Paulo, Surrogate.
5. US Department of Health, Education and Welfare, Child Welfare Statistics, 1961; Children's Bureau Statistical Series No. 66, 1962.
6. Census Tracts for New York City, Final Report PHC (1)—104, Part 1, US Department of Commerce, 1960.
7. Peller, L.: About Telling the Child of His Adoption, *Bull. Phila. Ass. Psychoanal.* 11:145–154 (Dec) 1961.

8. Powers, P.: Adopted Children Seen in a Child Guidance Clinic, *Catholic Charities Rev.* 44:10–13 (April) 1960.
9. Bernard, V.: Adoption, *The Encyclopedia of Mental Health*, New York: Franklin Watts, Inc., 1963, vol. 1, pp. 70–108.
10. Surrogate's Association of the State of New York, Adoption Statistics Table II: Percentages of Total Adoptions, 1959.

# 39

([ Follow-up studies of adopted children are frequently made. There are follow-up studies on placement of infants, older children, foreign-born children, and handicapped children. The studies vary widely in the level of research sophistication. Perhaps the most comprehensive and rigorous of these studies is *Independent Adoptions—A Follow-Up Study* by Helen Witmer et al. (Russell Sage Foundation, New York City, 1963).

The following research report also attempts to apply careful research procedure to the question of adoptive outcome. The child's adjustment at follow-up is related to antecedent factors in the child's history, to factors in the adoptive application study, and to the postadoptive experience.

# A Follow-Up Study of Adopted Children*

*Lilian Ripple*

Over the years the practitioner in the adoption agency has faced a growing dilemma: our aspirations for healthy living have increased, and our certainty about the components of healthy living has decreased. In all aspects of human relations we know a good deal about pathology but relatively little about normality.

* This study was undertaken by the Research Center of the School of Social Service Administration of the University of Chicago at the request of the Illinois Children's Home and Aid Society. The research was supported in part by a grant (WA-CB-R-92) from the Children's Bureau of the Welfare Administration, Department of Health, Education, and Welfare. The author acknowledges the contributions of all members of the study staff, but special thanks are given to Joan Foster Shireman, research associate, for her assistance in the planning and execution of the study.

The objective in adoption is to provide good parenting so that children may achieve normal development. The two concepts central to adoption practice—"good parenting" and "normal development"—are stated almost entirely in terms of high-level aspirations. The dilemma is that as soon as the terms are explicated the components emerge, not as dimensions of "good parenting" or "normal development," but as the absence of the elements in "bad parenting" or "disturbed development." Furthermore, the list of specifics grows as we discover new sources, or new descriptions, of disturbance. The coverage embodied in the typical "adoption study outline" has become so extensive that it has precluded intensive assessment, except on a highly selective basis. But there have been neither empirical data nor a coherent theory to help in this selection. It was hoped that the present study could contribute to an understanding, and reduction in the quantity, of these specifics.

## STUDY METHOD

The investigation dealt with the preadoptive evaluations and selected aspects of postadoptive experiences of one hundred and sixty children placed in infancy by the Illinois Children's Home and Aid Society. The specific purpose of the study was to identify factors associated with "good" and "poor" adjustment of the children at the time of follow-up. Three types of factors can be postulated: (1) those known to the agency at the time of placement; (3) those which, although unknown to the agency at that time, could have been known, i.e., were of such a nature that their existence can be presumed; and (3) those which did not in fact exist before placement, e.g., death of one of the adoptive parents. Obviously, if adoptive placements are to be improved, the first two sets of factors are those about which agencies could take action.

*Sample.* The study included children seven through ten years of age at the time of the 1965–66 follow-up who had been placed in adoption during the years 1955–58, with certain exclusions. The most important exclusions were children placed in families already having their own or an adopted child (63 cases) and children placed in families living more than three hundred miles from Chicago at the time of follow-up (49 cases).[1] The latter exclusion was necessitated by the expense of follow-up. Exclusion of families with a child already in the home was deemed desirable in the interest of achieving homogeneity, because quite different assessments are involved in making decisions about couples with no experience as parents. The year 1955 was chosen as the starting date for selecting the sample both because infants placed during or after that year would be in the de-

---

[1] The other exclusions were children of races other than Caucasian or Negro (10), children twenty-four months of age or older at placement (7), and "confidential file" cases (4).

sired age range at follow-up and because in 1954 the agency had re-examined its practice and developed a revised guide for adoption studies. In the opinion of agency staff members, general procedures and basic criteria remained essentially the same during the years in which the study children were placed.

The Illinois Children's Home and Aid Society provides service through a Chicago area office and downstate districts. Because of differences in resources, operations, and clientele between these two major divisions of the agency, it was desirable to sample the two units separately. Because of possible differences in placements of white and Negro children and of children of different ages, the plan called for random sampling of these subgroups.

For white children a random sample of 60 cases, stratified by age of the child at the time of placement, was drawn from the Chicago area and another sample of 60 cases from downstate districts. Substitutions necessary because families could not be located (11) or refused to participate (6) were made by continuing the random process (through use of a table of random numbers). For Negro children, all eligible cases were included and, in addition, the sampling period was extended through early 1959. Even so, it was not possible to reach the goal of 60 interviewed families. There was a loss of 31 families; 16 that could not be located and 15 that refused to be interviewed. The final sample included 30 Negro children placed by the Chicago office and 10 placed by downstate districts.

In 50 of the interviewed families, the baby's age at placement was under two months; in 55 it was two but less than six months; and in 55 it was six but less than twenty-four months. At the follow-up, the children were seven through ten years of age, distributed fairly evenly over the four years. White boys outnumbered white girls by almost two to one (78 boys and 42 girls). This disparity may reflect some stereotyping in placing a boy as the first child, in the expectation that a second child may be placed. Among Negro families, however, the study group was evenly divided (19 boys and 21 girls). By the time of follow-up, almost half the Negro children and 80 percent of the white children were in homes with a second (and, sometimes, a third) child—adopted or biologic.

Characteristics of the families, especially in the white sample, resemble those of the "typical" couple seeking to adopt a first child. Among white families, all but eight of the prospective adoptive parents were twenty-five but less than forty years of age when the baby was placed. None of the couples had been married less than two years, and only one-fourth had been married ten years or more. In only seven of the white families (6 percent) had either partner been married before. Negro couples generally had been married longer, and a much higher proportion (42 percent) had had previous marriages. Educational background and economic status covered wide ranges for both white and Negro families. Although the general level was higher for the white families, both groups were well above the average.

Between placement and follow-up, most of the families had substantial improvement in economic conditions.

*Data Collection.* Essentially, the method of study involved comparing data for several points in time. The major comparison concerned data from the case record of the original adoption study and the supervision period and from follow-up interviews.[2] The items in the Case Record Schedule dealt with the factors whose association with "outcome" was under investigation. The factors were drawn primarily from the adoption study outline used by the agency and from discussion with agency staff members. These factors generally coincide with those stressed in the literature and included in other studies of adoption.

The ratings were made by experienced caseworkers,[3] but each set of ratings was made independently; that is, no rater worked on material for more than one time period for the same family. The case records were separated into portions so that assessments of the adoption study material were made before the "supervision" record was read. Any material subsequent to the original adoption was removed from the case folder for this stage of data collection.

Interviews were arranged by the Research Center after the family received a letter from the executive director of the agency explaining the purpose of the research and its auspices. The family was given an opportunity to refuse an interview but was informed that, if the agency or the Research Center did not receive a response within about a week, an interviewer would telephone to arrange an appointment. This letter also made it clear that no reference to adoption would be made in the child's presence.

The interview with the adoptive mother, held in the home, usually took about two and one-half hours. The child was seen for about a half hour, usually after he returned from school. The father was interviewed at his place of business, in the home (usually in a separate visit), or at the Research Center; this interview typically lasted about an hour. One schedule, covering some "factors" and some "criterion" data, was filled out during the interview with the mother, and an abbreviated version was used in the interview with the father. Subsequently, the interviewer completed two additional schedules.[4] One contained certain items parallel to those in the Case Record Schedule to note changes since the adoption and the status at the time of follow-up, as well as items for assessment of the handling of

---

[2] When it was found that in many situations material was available from intervening contacts with the agency, a few additional assessments were made from the case records. These intervening contacts were almost all connected with application to adopt another child.

[3] Mary Baker, Dulcine Chapin, Sharon Moynihan, Marjorie Richard, and Audrey Smith. Reliability tests were conducted on the ratings of the case records.

[4] Interviewers were Marianne Elkisch, Joan Foster, Philip Hovda, Lucille Levitan, Louise Marks, Lilian Ripple, Dorothy Warton, and June Yoxall.

adopted status per se and of parental satisfaction. The final schedule, the Criteria of Adjustment, provided for rating the child's behavior at the time of follow-up.

For many of the factors that received attention in the study, there are generally accepted "predictions." In relation to infertility, for example, mutual supportiveness in handling disappointment is considered favorable, while blame of the "responsible" partner is considered unfavorable. For a child to have had many placements before going into the adoptive home is considered unfavorable, compared with a single placement in which he received good care. Expectations about associations of particular ratings with outcome were stated. Analysis of the data consisted of examination of the distribution of ratings for each item in the light of these predictions.[5] For a number of items no such predictions were involved, and the only analysis consisted of examination of the frequency distributions for descriptive purposes.

*Criterion Measure.* The purpose of the criterion measure is to divide the study children into two or more groups, by level of adjustment at follow-up, in order to ascertain whether there are differences for these groups in the various factors investigated. The intent of the study, that is, is to make comparisons for the various factors within the sample studied, and not to draw conclusions regarding the level of adjustment of all adopted children, or even about all the children placed by the study agency during the period covered by the study. The sample was drawn to provide a basis for certain kinds of comparisons, rather than to represent the adoption work of the agency. It will be recalled that the same sample was restricted to first placements in the particular adoptive families and to families living within three hundred miles of Chicago at the time of follow-up. Differences in the number of children in the "eligible pool" for the sample and in the number of refusals or families not located result in some overrepresentation of white infants placed at less than two months of age and underrepresentation of Negro infants placed at less than six months of age.

Data on the children's adjustment at follow-up represent assessments by the research interviewers on the basis of information from the parents and limited observation of the children. Attention was directed toward those life-tasks whose mastery is the primary job of the latency-age child. These include successful completion of the tasks of earlier developmental periods; development of relationships; acceptance of controls; and learning, that is, the development of skills. The child's apparent functioning in relation to a number of specific components of these four major aspects was rated, followed by an assessment of over-all adjustment.

Assessment of handling of these four specific aspects of task-mastery

---

[5] The chi-square test was used to assess differences, and the significance level was set at .05.

showed some variation in extent of disturbance. For 31 percent of the 160 study children, difficulties were noted both in completion of earlier developmental tasks and in learning. For 45 percent there had been difficulties in acceptance of controls, and for 50 percent, in the development of relationships.

The study children were grouped according to four levels of adjustment: (1) serious emotional or behavior problems; (2) some problems in adjustment; (3) within the "normal" range, but showing some symptoms; and (4) within the "normal" range, and showing no symptoms. The first of these groups is the purest, in that the sharpest distinction was made between it and the next category. To place a child in this first category required considerable evidence of disturbance in a number of aspects.

Twenty-four percent of the children were assessed as showing serious problems, and another 29 percent were showing some problems. The problems noted more often reflected internalized conflict than acting-out behavior. It should be noted that the criteria used for assessment of disturbance probably differed considerably from those used in the community in general. We undoubtedly noted as problem behavior many aspects of internalized conflict that would not be so classified by "the man on the street" or that would not come within the purview of child guidance or psychiatric facilities.

Virtually by definition, children rated as having serious problems were showing marked disturbances in most, if not all, aspects of adjustment. In fact, only 6 of the 38 children showing "serious" problems seemed to have even one problem-free area of functioning. Children in the "some problem" group tended to resemble these more disturbed children with respect to relationship and control difficulties and to resemble the "normal, but with some symptoms" group in mastery of tasks of earlier phases and in learning.

A possible alternative criterion measure is parental satisfaction. Although this variable was not directly assessed, follow-up interviewers rated the extent to which parental expectations were being met by the child in his behavior in the home, in the school, and in the community. Exactly 70 percent of the children were meeting parental expectations to a high degree. Association between the degree to which parental expectations are met and the level of adjustment of children is to be expected. These two measures were linked not only theoretically but also in data collection. After all, the data came mainly from parents, so their reporting would be influenced by their views of the child. Therefore, disagreement between these two ratings is of more interest than agreement. Sixty-seven of the 75 children in the "normal" group were meeting parental expectations to a high degree. Of greater interest is the finding that 33 of the 47 children with some problems and 12 of the 38 children with serious problems were also meeting parental expectations to a high degree.

Case material for the most deviant group—the 12 children with serious problems who met parental expectations to a high degree—shows three distinctly different kinds of situations. Three children met expectations that had been lowered because of the child's limited capacity. Four children with high academic achievement and nondisruptive behavior had combinations of serious symptoms of internalized conflict. In all instances, parents were highly pleased with the academic achievement and the conformity, and they minimized or were gratified by the symptomatology. Five children were so caught in family pathology that they were being abetted in acting out the parents' own unacceptable impulses, or were used in the parents' acting-out. One mother, for example, used the child as the point of entry for her repeated assaults on community institutions.

The follow-up interviewers also rated the parents' affect toward the child. In 51 percent of the families, the affect of both parents toward the adopted child was assessed as strongly positive and in 19 percent as at least moderately positive. The remaining 30 percent of the families were almost evenly divided between those in which one parent showed at least moderately positive affect and neither parent showed negative affect and those in which the affect of one or both parents had strongly negative elements.

Parental affect is associated both with the child's meeting parental expectations and with the child's level of adjustment. In 86 families the parental affect was highly positive and the child was meeting parental expectations to a high degree; adjustment at follow-up was rated within the "normal" range for 70 percent of these children. Either parental affect or the child's meeting of expectations was lower in 45 cases; adjustment of only 30 percent of these children was rated "normal." In 29 families parental affect toward the adopted child was ambivalent and the child was meeting parental expectations to a moderate, or even low, degree; adjustment for only two of these children was assessed as "normal."

Theory postulates continuous interaction between parental affect, a child's meeting of parental expectations, and a child's adjustment. The issue here is not that of cause-effect connections. Rather, the question is whether the appropriate measure of outcome is the adjustment of the child or parental satisfaction, or both. We took adjustment of the child as the criterion measure because of the danger of attributing "good" outcomes to situations, such as those described earlier, in which favorable ratings on parental expectations apparently reflect situations involving considerable pathology.

## THE CHILDREN BEFORE ADOPTION

Agency practice when the study children were placed was based upon the assumption that adoptive parents seek children who are relatively normal. The agency's adoption studies emphasized three types of information relevant to assessing potential risks to normal development: (1) the baby's family background; (2) the baby's health, including any problems during the mother's pregnancy or at birth; and (3) experiences and development of the baby from birth to placement in the adoptive home.

No significant association was found between various preadoption factors and the adjustment at follow-up. On the whole, however, the background and health history of these children did not indicate potential risk to development. For only 18 children did family background suggest potential risks to health or intellectual development (although for another 64 information regarding the natural father was meager), and difficulties during pregnancy or at delivery were noted for only 30 children.

More surprising was the lack of significant association between the child's adjustment at follow-up and the age at which he was placed in his adoptive home, the number of preadoptive placements, the apparent quality of care in those placements, or the early behavior of the child himself. For a few of those factors the association with adjustment at follow-up was in the expected direction, although it was not statistically significant.

*Placement Experiences.* The factors most amenable to agency influence are the placement experiences of the baby, since with rare exceptions the children come into agency care at birth. How vulnerable children of different ages are to separation remains an unanswered question. Almost universal condemnation of maternal separation for young infants, following Bowlby's 1951 report,[6] has given way to a more moderate view and to efforts to understand the concomitants of separation and their effects upon the child. Research findings to date can at best be described as inconclusive, but there is consensus that re-placements present increasing risks as the infant becomes older. Those before six months of age—and especially before two months—are believed less damaging.[7]

Only for the very young infants was the expected association with outcome found. Of the 50 children placed in their adoptive homes at less than two months of age, only 14 percent showed serious problems at follow-up, compared with 28 percent for the other age groups. This difference disappears, however, when both problem groups ("serious" and "some" problems) are compared with the normal group. For each age-at-placement group, about 50 percent of the children showed at least some problems at follow-up.

Placement in the adoptive home was, of course, not necessarily the first separation from former caretakers. In fact, 56 children (35 percent) had

---

[6] J. Bowlby, *Maternal Care and Mental Health* (Monograph Series, No. 2 [Geneva: World Health Organization, 1951]).

[7] For an excellent review of the issues and findings see Leon J. Yarrow, "Separation from Parents during Early Childhood," in *Review of Child Development Research*, Vol. 1, ed. Martin L. Hoffman and Lois Wladis Hoffman (New York: Russell Sage Foundation, 1964), esp. pp. 89–99, 121–130.

two or more placements before going into their adoptive homes. For 41 children the foster-care re-placement occurred at less than two months of age, and for only 2 children was any re-placement made at six months of age or older. No differences in later adjustment are associated with the number of preadoptive placements.

Quality of care—physical and emotional—provided before adoptive placement was examined. For the very young infant, it is often difficult to assess quality of emotional care, particularly when the observer—in this instance the worker on the case—sees the infant relatively infrequently and for brief periods, and the research ratings are further diluted because of being made from case record material. In any event, the ratings in the present study tended to be similar for physical and emotional care, and for 85 percent of the children care was rated as at least of moderate quality throughout the placement experience. The quality of care in the preadoptive placements was not associated with subsequent level of adjustment of the children.

*Preadoptive Development and Behavior.* Evidences of serious disturbance in the baby's behavior before adoption tended to be associated with ratings of problematic behavior at follow-up. Difficulties in adjusting to preadoptive placements, indicated by persistent symptoms of distress that took the form of motor discharge (restlessness, irritability, hyperactivity, excessive crying), were recorded for 19 children, of whom 9 were showing serious problems at follow-up. Other symptoms of distress—disturbances in eating or sleeping, lethargy, or lack of responsiveness—were recorded for 18 children, but showed no association with outcome.

Developmental pace was considered questionable—being either definitely slow or markedly erratic—for only 12 children, 7 of whom were showing serious problems at follow-up. Twenty-six children showed problems in task-mastery at the time of adoptive placement, but these problems were associated with unfavorable outcome only when found in combination with other preadoptive disturbances. The tendency toward association with outcome, thus, is limited to difficulty in adjusting to preadoptive placements through motor discharge reactions and/or questionable developmental pace. Although 12 of the 27 children with these difficulties showed serious problems at follow-up, and another 5 showed some problems, in comparison with children showing little or no difficulty in preadoptive behavior the difference is not statistically significant.

## ADOPTIVE APPLICANTS

Preadoptive studies of families are directed toward assessing the applicants' motivation to adopt and their potential capacity for parenthood, that is, their apparent ability to provide nurturance and, as the infant develops, to permit appropriate independence and separation. While health and economic conditions are not ignored, the crucial and more difficult decisions concern psychological considerations.

As indicated above, the agency selected predominantly a particular kind of white adoptive family: couples in their late twenties or thirties, for whom this was a first marriage, and who were well above average in education and economic circumstances. Negro families were not so concentrated in a modal group: 40 percent had had a previous marriage; a substantial number were more than forty years old; only about one-half had completed high school or were in better than moderate economic circumstances.

Most of the economic and social factors examined showed no association with outcome. Small but persistent differences in the white subsample showed higher education and economic status to be less favorable. This finding, common to several adoption researches,[8] has been interpreted as reflecting the more frequent errors in judgment, both by practitioners and by research raters, about better-educated, more sophisticated, and more articulate clients. Interestingly, for Negro applicants, higher education and economic status were favorable factors.

Only two other findings about social factors showed associations with the child's adjustment. In the white sample, children placed with younger applicants (both under thirty) who had been married less than six years were more likely to be in the "serious problem" group at follow-up. In the Negro sample, the unfavorable factor was previous marriage of either adoptive parent. Although the differences in proportion of children showing problems or serious problems were statistically significant compared with children placed in families with other marital situations, only 17 children were involved in each of these two groups.

*Motivation.* Motivation has been defined as the person's goal and the strength of drive toward his goal. In assessing motivation to adopt, agencies generally attempt to answer three major questions: Why do the applicants not have their own child? What needs are they trying to meet through having a child? Can a child, and specifically an adopted child, meet these needs?

Exploration of childlessness involves aspects of capacity in relation to the maturity with which feelings were handled, but it also touches importantly on motivation. If the reason for childlessness is not organic, there is always uncertainty about whether failure to conceive reflects unconscious aversion to parenthood.

There is considerable speculation in adoption literature regarding the relationship between various causes of childlessness and the outcome of adoption. Only with respect to one reason, however, did we find fairly

---

[8] See Child Adoption Research Committee, *A Follow-up Study of Adoptive Families* (New York: The Committee, 1951), and Ruth Medway Davis and Polly Bouck, "Crucial Importance of Adoption Home Study," *Child Welfare*, 34 (March, 1955), 20–21.

general consensus. If the reason for childlessness is health hazard—inability to carry pregnancy to term, danger to the mother's health, possible deformity of the child—the association with adoptive outcome is expected to be favorable. The data tend to support this hypothesis, but health hazard was the reason for childlessness in only 12 cases.

On the important issue of interaction in relation to childlessness, 131 couples had the hypothesized favorable rating of "mutual supportiveness in dealing with a disappointment," and only three had the unfavorable ratings of "mutual feeding of disappointment" or "depreciation of the partner at fault." Obviously the hypotheses for this item could not be tested.

Concentration of ratings was not quite as heavy for assessment of the mode of handling feelings regarding childlessness. In approximately one-third of the cases, both applicants were judged to have worked through their feelings to a substantial extent. The proportion of children in the problem group at follow-up was just as high in these families as in the ones in which feelings were recognized but not worked through or were repressed. Feelings about childlessness were rated as being "acted-out" when the applicant seemed not to have handled or contained the affect and to be demanding recompense. The hypothesis was supported for the small group of 7 couples in which either applicant was rated as "acting-out" feelings; in all instances the adopted child was showing behavior problems at follow-up.

Direct assessment of motivation consisted of ratings on the strength of desire to adopt and the specific nature of the motives. It was hypothesized that either a very strong or a weak drive would be unfavorable. An unusually intense desire might be expected to reflect pathological needs with too much energy channeled into this single solution. At the other extreme, defined as minimal willingness to go along with the application for a child, it might be expected that there would be unwillingness to be inconvenienced or actual resentment of the child.

While a weak drive to adopt was unfavorable, a strong drive was not. In 6 of the 8 families in which one or both applicants appeared to have a weak drive to adopt, the child was showing problems at follow-up. In contrast with this small number at one extreme, 101 women and 90 men (a total of 80 percent) were rated as having a very strong drive. There were no differences in outcome associated with moderate through very strong drives in the white sample. In the Negro sample, however, a very strong drive on the part of both adoptive parents was favorable: in the 10 such families, 7 children were in the "normal" group at follow-up and only one child was showing serious problems.

Among the specific motives for adoption,[9] the desire to express parental

---

[9] The categories used were adapted from Irene Josselyn, M.D., "Evaluating Motives of Foster Parents," *Child Welfare*, 31 (February, 1952), 2.

feelings was hypothesized to be favorable. Evidence of enjoyment of children, but without the indication of parental feelings, was thought to be a relatively favorable motive. There was some uncertainty about a third category, "conformance to an accepted family model," but it was seen as more favorable than not. It should be noted that this motive is distinguished from a desire to remove external pressure in that it is the applicant who has accepted (or internalized) the model.

All other motives were seen as undesirable or presenting potential risks. For example, the wish to remove pressure from the spouse, relatives, or friends is likely to mean that the child is not valued for himself but because he will make his adoptive parent more acceptable in the family, in the neighborhood, or to himself. Motives of a narcissistic nature contain obvious potential risks. The desire for a child in order to perpetuate one's self is probably an element in much of childbearing and adoption. If it is the predominant motive, however, the child is frequently permitted little chance for growth and individuation. Another motive—the wish to give to a deprived child because of identification—may have elements of altruism, but has great risks because the capacity to give to a child is believed to be nourished by the very elements of which the applicant himself was deprived. The attempt to fill a void in the person's own life is frequently involved in adoption requests. The applicant may be trying to withdraw from the marital partner and seeks to replace the unsatisfactory spouse with a more pliable child. Perhaps more often, the attempt is to replace a lost child. In either instance, the adopted child is unlikely to fill the bill of specifics fantasied by the applicant.

Attempts to assess motives of adoptive applicants, in actual practice as in research, are enormously complicated by the context in which the relevant material is obtained. Unless the effort to adopt is greatly pathological, the applicant necessarily makes considerable effort to "put his best foot forward" and to suppress, or repress, any ambivalence. It is not surprising, then, that unfavorable motives were identified in the study group only infrequently. We must recall, however, that our research concerned only families in which children were placed. Many applicants are rejected because of unsuitable motives.

Parental feelings were judged to be the major motive for the majority of white men and women, whereas among Negro couples enjoyment of children was more often judged to be the major motive. The distinction between these two motives is, however, a slim one and may reflect primarily the sophistication and articulateness of the applicants. These two motives taken together account for about 80 percent of the white and 70 percent of the Negro couples. The only other category accounting for as much as 5 percent of the sample is "conformance to an accepted family model."

Most of the specific motives for adoption (and the strength of drive, considered earlier) could apply as well to the desire to have an own child.

Motivation to adopt involves additional issues centering around the ability to accept someone else's child. The essential question is whether the applicants have faced and accepted adoption, neither fantasying the child as their own and denying the fact of adoption nor overemphasizing adoption. This question can probably not even be explored adequately until after the child is placed with the family, yet decisions to place involve some assessment or guess as to whether the child can be accepted for what he is: an adopted child.

Among the measures used to assess the "reality" of the motivation to adopt were the applicants' attitudes toward inheritance of traits, talents, and behavior patterns and their attitudes toward telling the child of his adoption. Obviously, it was hypothesized that strong belief in the inheritance of personal traits would indicate attitudes inimical to the acceptance of the child (particularly should he show any undesirable traits) and be associated with unfavorable outcome. Unwillingness to tell the child of his adoption would also be unfavorable because of its possible indication that the goal of having a child requires denial of adoption as the means to this goal.

Only a few of these prospective adoptive parents indicated a belief that negative factors in heredity would influence a child's development, and in the white sample all said they planned to tell the child of his adoption. Although only one Negro applicant did not plan to tell of the adoption, 10 other families expressed such uncertainty that it was doubtful that the agency's recommendation to tell was being accepted. In these 11 families, 9 children were showing problems at follow-up. The issue here, of course, is not whether in fact the child was told of his adoption, but the implications of the uncertainty on the part of the applicants.

Only negative aspects of selected motivational factors seemed predictive of later adjustment of the child. In 12 families raters noted at least one partner whose drive to adopt was weak or whose predominant affect about childlessness was anger at a cruel fate or an implicit demand for "restitution" for loss. In 10 of these families the child was showing problems at follow-up. In another 26 families there were signs of unfavorable motives, mainly extreme narcissism or non-acceptance of the fact of adopting. Children in 17 of these families were showing problems at follow-up. These "predictors" account, however, for only one-fifth of the 85 children in the two problem groups at follow-up. The great majority of adoptive applicants were assessed as having moderate to very strongly positive motivation. No significant differences in adjustment of the children were found to be associated with these varying levels of positive motivation.

*Capacity.* Child development theory postulates two requisites for good parenting: the capacity to provide physical and emotional nurture and, then, as the child develops, to permit separation and independence. It is immediately obvious that motivation and capacity interlock, perhaps espe-

cially in their negative aspects. Narcissistic motives of competitive posses-
sion, for example, are hardly compatible with providing nurturance, or
altruistic "giving," to an infant or with permitting the gradual separation
necessary for the child's subsequent growth. Generally positive motivation,
however, may accompany a fairly wide range in capacity for parenting.

There is a considerable body of theory regarding the requisites for
development of capacity for sustained nurturing relationships, for creating
appropriate role models, and for permitting individuation. According to
these theories, however, the evidence required for meaningful assessment
involves comprehensive material about experiences and reactions to experiences. The issue, then, is whether the kind of data obtained in the
usual adoption investigation permits the depth of assessment necessary for
determining the person's potential for parenting. Even when assessment
is viewed primarily in terms of current behavior, rather than personality
development, the issue arises as to whether capacity for parenting can be
appraised in the absence of observation of performance in parenting. In
other words, can capacity for functioning in any role set (in this instance,
parenthood) be estimated from functioning in other role sets and, if so,
from which ones?

Adoption agencies, whatever the uncertainties, daily face the need to
make decisions about potential parenthood. From applicants' reports of
past experiences and current functioning, inferences are drawn regarding
the applicants' future functioning as a couple and as parents. In the
present study, we perforce had to take the same approach, both because
of the nature of the material available and because of the lack of any
better organizing scheme.

Capacity for parenthood was assessed in terms of the kind of family
model reflected in current functioning of the couple, their interpersonal
relationships, selected aspects of personality, and evaluation of early
familial experience. The family model presented by the applicants seems
almost the stereotype of the suburban or smalltown young couple, especially for the white families. Husbands were vocationally stable and
satisfied with their chosen occupations, wives enjoyed homemaking, relationships with the extended family were cordial but not suspiciously intense, meaningful social relationships prevailed. The lack of variation in
most of these data precluded finding differences with respect to outcome.

Analysis of various facets of marital interaction provided no useful data,
partly because the material generally presented such undifferentiated
"good" pictures. Attempts to assess ego functioning were equally fruit-
less for the same reason. Efforts at indirect measurement by assessing
responses to children the applicants had known produced similar concentrations of favorable ratings. Further indirect evidence was sought
through examining the applicants' early familial experiences. Again, however, homogeneity and absence of unfavorable situations were the predominant features.

A few factors of a more directly observable nature provided some discrimination. In 20 families the adoptive mother was rated as less than high in health and energy at application, and in 16 of these the child was showing problems at follow-up. Among 27 downstate couples (including both white and Negro) in which neither partner had had much contact with children, 21 children were showing problems at follow-up. The latter finding did not hold true for the Chicago sample in which, on many items, the distribution of ratings and the association with outcome differed substantially from those for downstate cases. In fact, it was often found that factors expected to be favorable, according to child welfare literature, were unfavorable for the Chicago sample.

*Relationship Between Applicants and Agency.* The final set of evaluations for the preplacement study concerned interaction between the applicants and the agency. Ratings were made of the applicants' verbal activity in the interviews, participation with the caseworker in the adoptive study, and affect toward the worker; and of the caseworker's affect toward the applicants. These aspects of participation reflect capacity, both for relationship and for involvement, and motivation to adopt, in that inappropriate behavior might suggest at least an unconscious wish to be denied a child. They also influence importantly the material that is produced in the adoption study.

The adoption studies which provided the basis for the placement decisions varied considerably in time span and number of contacts—from two months to three years and from three to fifteen interviews with the applicants. Most of the studies were conducted in a context of sharing between applicants and agency. While applicants differed in verbal facility, in only 5 cases did both partners appear to participate in the adoption study to a low degree, and in only 4 cases did both seem to engage in excessive verbal outpouring. Moderately positive affect was judged to characterize the interaction between most applicants and caseworkers, but in one-fifth of the cases one or both applicants seemed ambivalent, weakly negative, or fearful toward the worker. Two observations for the Chicago white subsample may be relevant to other findings for these cases. First, in 20 cases in which the adoption study period exceeded one year, only 6 children showed problems at follow-up (30 percent compared with 62 percent in the other 40 cases). Second, in the Chicago white cases in which affect of both applicants and the worker toward each other was moderately positive or higher, problems in adjustment at follow-up were more likely (about 60 percent) than in cases in which the worker's affect was more muted (only 21 percent).

*Selection and "Matching."* During the years when the study children went into their adoptive homes (1955–58), selection and placement were influenced by several important agency policies. In the main, handicapped children and those with significant potential risks to development were not placed in adoption. "Matching" of adoptive parents and child was considered important to establishment of identity as a family. Very few children went into their adoptive homes without a prior period of foster care,[10] so that a "placement process" was involved which varied with the age of the baby and other circumstances in the situation.

Opinion has been by no means undivided regarding the two major aspects of selection—the adoptive applicants' preferences and the issue of "matching." Strong specific preferences about the age, sex, appearance, etc., of the child they would like to have are usually regarded with suspicion as reflecting rigidity of the applicants, but lack of—or fear of stating —preferences has been almost as suspect. In any event, no hypotheses regarding association between applicants' preferences and outcome could be tested. These adoptive applicants often indicated some preference, but almost no instances of a pattern of strong preferences were noted.

On the subject of "matching," there are two contrasting opinions. One is that similarity between the adopting parents and the child in appearance, ethnic background, and temperament is conducive to identification and, hence, to "successful" outcome. The other holds that such similarities are not merely unimportant but present the risk of playing into adoptive parents' wishes to deny the reality of adoption.

For the white subsample the extent of matching of coloring (hair, eyes, complexion) and of ethnic background was examined in detail.[11] Several facts of interest emerged. The less the adoptive parents resembled each other in appearance or ethnic background, the higher the proportion of "matching" placements. In other words, a dark and a fair applicant were more likely to be given a child whose own parents were a combination of dark and fair. An initial match on appearance was no guaranty of later resemblance. Of 111 children for whom complete information was available at placement and at follow-up, 70 had a substantial shift in appearance —at the later date, 29 children looked less like their adopting parents, 26 had a stronger resemblance, and 15 looked less like one but more like the other parent.

None of the evidence showed matching to be a favorable factor. The only associations, in fact, were in the opposite direction. Families in the "very high" match group on physical resemblance and ethnic background had more children in the problem groups at follow-up, and those in the "very low" match group had fewer children showing problems. Adopting parents in the "very high" match situations tended to have less favorable ratings on various aspects of capacity. While intensive efforts at matching

---

[10] In the sample, only 6 children were placed directly from the hospital nursery; in addition, the sample was selected to have about two-thirds of the children two months of age or older at placement.

[11] Information in the case records was too sketchy to permit analysis of body or intellectual potential. For the Negro subsample, too many contradictions in descriptions precluded classification.

sometimes involved the search for parents for a child with an "unusual" combination of ethnic backgrounds, such efforts often seemed designed to compensate for limitations in the adopting family's situation.

*Placement and Supervision.* The few days, or week or two, covered by the placement process are exciting and happy ones for most adopting families and their caseworkers. The goal toward which they have all been working has finally been reached and, unless there is some major upset, the decision will not now be reversed. Questions or doubts of the couple or the staff are not easily raised at this point, and are even less likely to be raised after the child has gone into the home. Although some impetus to sharing problems comes from the worker's availability and the un-likelihood that the child will be removed, in the context of "supervision," the weight is probably on the side of minimizing problems. In any event, during the placement and supervision period, what difficulties there are merit attention and relatively little differentiation is or probably can be made between various gradations of positive reactions and adjustment.

Evidences of difficulties during the placement process or the supervision period augur poorly for favorable later adjustment. In this study, signs of difficulty were a less-than-positive initial reaction to the child, negative reaction to the former foster parents, or absence of the adoptive father on the placement day. During the supervision period, problems noted for the child were general difficulty in adjusting to the adoptive parents, re-peated minor illnesses, and slow or erratic pace of development. For the parents, difficulties were evidenced by lack of enjoyment of the child; the mother's low competence in physical care of the child; reactions charac-terized by ambivalence, depression, or anxiety; failure to take on a parental role; or serious strains introduced into the husband-wife relationship.

For 49 families, problems were noted in the placement or supervision period. In only 8 was the evidence confined to the placement process; in 19 there were difficulties in both the placement and the supervision period; and in 22 difficulties were noted only in the supervision period. Children in 40 of these 49 families (82 percent) were showing problems at follow-up—evenly divided between "serious" and "some" problems—compared to 42 percent of the 111 families in which no problems were noted during the placement and supervision period. To put it another way, among the 85 children in the two problem groups at follow-up, diffi-culties had been noted in the early period in 40 cases, while among the 75 children in the "normal" group at follow-up early difficulties had been noted in only 9 cases.

## THE POSTADOPTION PERIOD

The research interview with each parent covered considerable material about experiences of the family and child since adoption, and ratings were made of various attitudes and behaviors of the parent.[12] The more inferential these judgments are, the more they must be regarded with caution. Our theories regarding child development can lead to the trap of assuming that pathology in the parents means problems for the child or that if there are problems in the child there must be pathology in the parents.

The ratings of discipline, together with the assessments of the child's adjustment, illustrate one of the possible difficulties in rating or, perhaps, illustrate the connection between theory and observed behavior. Disciplinary methods described by the parents were assessed to be consistently moderate and realistic in 83 families. In the other 77 families, discipline was considered harsh in only 11 and light or inconsistent in the remainder. More children were rated as having problems with controls—either accepting external controls or developing internal ones—than with any other aspect of adjustment. Does this reflect the apparently light and/or inconsistent discipline? Or, in the face of the apparent minimal discipline, did we conclude that children must be having trouble with accepting and/or developing controls?

Assessments of the parents' attitudes and behavior at follow-up showed a high association with the child's adjustment. In addition to the contamination problem noted above, this finding is of somewhat limited value for another reason. There was little association between the assessment of these qualities that was based on the case record of the original adoptive investigation and the assessment at follow-up. In other words, we found little evidence that potential for good parenting can be assessed with confidence.

Considerable information was sought in the follow-up interview about various facets of the adoption experience. The accuracy or the meaningfulness of the responses is questionable. Almost all children had been told about their adoption, but often at such an early age or in such a *pro forma* manner that their understanding of the meaning of "adoption" was dubious. Most children were reported to be uninterested or only slightly interested in the fact that they had been adopted. Only for a few children with marked reactions did there appear to be an association with adjustment. Ten children, for example, showed much preoccupation with adoption, and eight of them were showing problems. Adoption, however, was only one aspect of general anxiety shown by these children.

Only a small group of parents seemed to overstress adoption. Generally, limited information had been given to the community, with restriction of knowledge more common among Negro than white families. A moderate

---

[12] In addition, material was available from interim contacts with the agency: 108 families initiated one or more contacts to apply to adopt another child; in 88, placements were made; 14 were rejected because of problems; and 6 withdrew their applications. Help was subsequently sought by 5 of these 108 families and by another 3 whose only contact with the agency was for this purpose.

to high degree of acceptance of adoptive parenthood seemed to describe the feelings of the majority of parents. Either a "very high" (defensive?) or "very low" acceptance of their status was unfavorable. Most parents felt adequate in handling problems of adoption, fathers more so than mothers—who up to this point in the children's lives had done most of the "handling."

Relatively specific non-inferential material from the follow-up interviews provides a significant finding. Forty-two families had experienced some form of breakup at some time since the adoption, through divorce or death. (5 families each), serious illness of one or both parents (15 families), or some other kind of marked disruption in the family's living pattern (17 families). Children in 37 of these 42 families (88 percent) were in the two problem groups at follow-up. Before concluding that events beyond the control of agency or family are "responsible" for a large number of problem outcomes, we must note the possibility of "disruption-proneness." The particular type of disruption was not associated with specific earlier events (the divorced parents, for example, had not been identified as showing marital problems), but for only 4 of these 42 families had there been no previous indicators of some kind of disturbance.

*Cumulation of Unfavorable Factors.* Major difficulties and disturbances rarely occur singly. As just noted, for 38 families earlier difficulties were followed by marked disruptions in family life between the adoption and the follow-up interviews. In another 49 families, unfavorable ratings had been given to more than one aspect of the parents' behavior or to both the parents and the child. In 14 families, for example, both parents had had little or no contact with children before the adoption, and the adopted child had had developmental problems before the adoptive placement. For 69 families there had been no signs, or only one minor indicator, of possible difficulty. For example, in 8 cases the only negative was "short marriage of young couple," that is, they had been married less than six years and both were under thirty years of age when the baby was placed with them. Incidentally, only one of the children in these families was showing serious problems at follow-up, and 6 were in the "normal" group. This particular factor, thus, showed up as negative only when combined with other unfavorable factors, mainly questionable motivation for adopting.

For the 38 children in the "serious problems" group at follow-up, there was a concentration of negative factors or the presence of a few very serious ones. In the "some problems" group concentrations followed a similar pattern, but were not quite as great. Conversely, for two-thirds of the children in the "normal" group, no substantial difficulties were reported for the preadoption period, nor were there notable disruptions in the family following adoption, compared with about one-third of the children in the "some problems" group and one-tenth of those in the "serious problems" group (see Table 1).

TABLE 1. Extent of Negative Factors, by Adjustment at Follow-up for Children Placed at Less Than and More Than Two Months of Age

| | | ADJUSTMENT OF CHILDREN | | | | | | | |
| | | Placed at Less Than 2 Months | | | | Placed at 2 Months or More | | | |
| NEGATIVE FACTORS | Total | Total | Serious Problems | Some Problems | "Normal" | Total | Serious Problems | Some Problems | "Normal" |
|---|---|---|---|---|---|---|---|---|---|
| Total | 160 | 50 | 7 | 18 | 25 | 110 | 31 | 29 | 50 |
| Both preadoptive difficulties *and* postadoptive family disruptions | 38 | 10 | 4 | 6 | — | 28 | 16 | 9 | 3 |
| Either preadoptive difficulties *or* postadoptive family disruptions | 53 | 13 | 1 | 5 | 7 | 40 | 13 | 12 | 15 |
| No known negative factors | 69 | 27 | 2 | 7 | 18 | 42 | 2 | 8 | 32 |

Age of the child at placement relates in an interesting way to these findings. First, more of the younger children were in families in which there were no known negative factors. Second, when there were no major negative factors, the proportion of children showing problems at follow-up was about the same for those placed before two months of age and for those placed later. Third, when there was a heavy cumulation of pre- and postadoptive difficulties, age at placement was not related to problematic behavior at follow-up, although babies placed in the earlier months were more likely to be in the "some" than the "serious" problem group. Finally, the age at which the baby was placed in adoption seems to make a difference in the "middle" group, in which there were difficulties in either the pre- or postadoptive periods, but not in both. In the "middle" group, children placed at the age of less than two months were more likely to be in the "normal" group at follow-up and only one of the 13 children was in the "serious problem" group, whereas among children placed later 37 percent were in the "normal" group and 32 percent in the "serious problem" group.

In sum, these findings seem to indicate that certain minor "negative" factors (such as low child-care experience or early marriage of young couples) are unimportant provided they "stand alone." When these factors are combined with negative factors or uncertainties relevant to motivation or to the child's need for special attention, they become strongly unfavorable. Other negative factors—in motivation, acceptance of adoption, low health and energy of the adopting mother, major difficulties in the baby's development, or marked disruption in the family following adoption—rarely are found singly, but whenever found they show an association with unfavorable outcome. The presence of these negative factors does not seem to be counterbalanced by any number of other positives. As a consequence, we return to the conclusion that "good" parenting could not be predicted, but that a few major indicators of "bad" parenting can be identified.

## IMPLICATIONS

The study findings lend support to some of the shifts in practice that have occurred since the children were placed in their adoptive homes, and they bear upon other less firmly established developments in practice. The implications derive more from the nature of the findings than from their specific content. The main tenor of the findings may be summarized as follows:

1. The associations found were between "negative" factors and "unfavorable" outcome, rather than between "positive" factors and "favorable" outcome. The only exception was that infants placed in their adoptive homes before two months of age were less likely to be in the "serious problem" group at follow-up.

2. In general, factors pertaining to the child, and particularly those used to assess potential risk to development, did not prove discriminating.

3. None of the factors believed to be important to realistic integration of the adopted child into the family—"matching" and handling the facts of adoption—showed the expected association with favorable outcome.

4. For most factors, the children and the adoptive applicants were given favorable ratings. The most favorable rating on a particular factor, however, was not always as closely associated with good outcome as was the "next best" rating. In particular, children for whom some minor difficulties were noted in the preadoptive or supervision periods were less likely to show problems at follow-up than were children for whom no difficulties at all had been noted.

5. Those factors that were associated with outcome concerned specific factual information or directly observable behavior from which only very limited inferences had to be drawn.

Three of the findings are relevant to changes in adoption practice in the years since the children were placed. These changes are the shift to placement of infants at much younger ages than formerly and the reduced emphasis upon "matching" of adoptive parents and child, both of which would be supported by our data. The third relevant finding, that health conditions suggesting risk to development were not predictive of outcome, might not be found in more extreme cases because, during the period in question, the agency sought to avoid placement of children with serious handicaps or health risks.

The remaining findings, which are interrelated, bear upon the type of data that can be obtained in the usual adoption investigation and the kind of interpretation that can safely be given these data. The important considerations that link our findings with possible implications for practice may be summed up in a few basic propositions: (1) We know very little about the elements of "good" parenting—that is, the relative merits of adequacy or superiority. (2) Adoptive applicants wish to present themselves in a favorable light; they do not readily admit to themselves or reveal to the agency their weaknesses or their doubts about adoption. (3) We know a good deal about the elements of "bad" parenting and have considerable skill in identifying them. (4) Adoption practice in general calls for far too many assessments of far too much attitudinal and inferential material. (5) In adoption theory and practice there remains the issue of whether adoptive parenthood is markedly different from biologic parenthood or whether adoptive parenthood is essentially similar to biologic parenthood. In any event, taking on and carrying the roles of parenthood—biologic or adoptive—presents a formidable task.

The conclusions to be drawn for practice appear to be very simple to state, although very difficult to implement. First, those negative factors believed to present the greatest potential risk to adequate parenthood and to be the least amenable to modification should be identified. It is believed that the list of such negative factors would be fairly small. While "investigation" is hardly the most favorable context within which revealing material is obtained and assessed, some means must be found for applicants and agency together to reach a decision about the presence or absence of serious impediments to satisfying and satisfactory parenthood. If such impediments are not found, the "exploration" should terminate and attention should be turned to the placement process. In other words, the position taken here is that applicants cannot go on exploring and re-exploring their readiness for parenthood while trying to win approval. Rather, agency work should be focused on decision about what help applicants need and can be given by the agency in preparing to be parents and, especially, in actually experiencing parenthood during the early months after placement.

# 40

⟦ Despite all the supposed and real difficulties, adopted children seem to be resilient enough to adjust successfully to their situation. The following article reports success for one group of hard-to-place children—older children—and reviews reversibility of trauma in other children provided with substitute care.

# Reversibility of Trauma: A Follow-Up Study of Children Adopted When Older*

*Alfred Kadushin*

A common supposition, which has been elevated to the status of an axiom, is that children emotionally damaged in early childhood are likely

* The research on which the report is based was conducted with the support of a grant from the Children's Bureau, U.S. Department of Health, Education, and Welfare.

to be scarred for life. In order to determine whether reversibility of damage is possible, a follow-up study was conducted of a group of ninety-one children who were placed for adoption when they were at least 5 years of age or older and who had suffered considerable trauma before adoptive placement. At the time of the study most of the children were in early adolescence, the average age of the group at follow-up being 13 years and 9 months.

The group of children included forty-nine boys and forty-two girls. They were white, of average intelligence, and without physical handicap. They had been removed from their own homes at an average age of about 3½ years, had been placed for adoption at the average age of 7 years and 2 months, and had experienced, on an average, 2.3 changes of homes prior to adoptive placement.

## EARLY DEVELOPMENTAL DATA

In all instances, the children in this study group became available for adoption as a result of court action to terminate parental rights because of neglect and/or abuse. The families from which they came were atypically large, 52 percent having five or more children. They had lived, during their infancy, in socially deprived circumstances, in substandard housing, with families whose incomes were most often below the poverty line. Natural parents had limited education, only 2 percent of the fathers having completed high school. When employed, they worked in unskilled or semiskilled occupational categories. The marital situation in the natural home was, in almost all instances, conflicted. In addition, the natural parents presented a picture of considerable personal pathology compounded of promiscuity, mental deficiency, alcoholism, imprisonment, and psychosis. The average number of specific social and personal pathologies exhibited by each of the natural families from which these children came was 5.7

The relationship between the natural parents and these children was most frequently characterized by physical neglect, although 31 percent of the group were described as having experienced an emotional relationship that was "normally warm and accepting." Physical abuse was encountered with only 4 percent of the mothers and 10 percent of the fathers. In the largest percentage of cases physical neglect was accompanied by emotional indifference or emotional neglect and, less frequently, by emotional rejection. In 70 percent of the cases the child was physically neglected by the mother, in 40 percent the child was emotionally neglected (mother indifferent, showed no affection, recognition, encouragement, or approval), and in an additional 7 percent the mother was emotionally punitive (active disparagement of child, overt expressions of hostility or rejection).

In about 48 percent of the cases there was some relationship with parental surrogates prior to the first foster placement. In 23 percent of the cases this relationship was with grandparents; in 11 percent it was with older siblings.

Data on the backgrounds of these children were derived from the records of the agency that placed them for adoption, the Division for Children and Youth of the Wisconsin State Department of Public Welfare. In each instance there was a separate voluminous record available on the child, the natural parents, and the adoptive parents.

Categorization of the record data was done by a graduate social worker. A 10 percent sample of the records was independently rechecked by another trained worker. As a result of this procedure reliability of categorization for items requiring some subjective interpretation was satisfactorily determined.

Of principal concern to this particular report is the confirmation of the fact that these children lived at an early age during a prolonged period under conditions of serious deprivation. The worker's categorization of the record data is confirmed by the court action.

The courts in the United States, as elsewhere, are reluctant to terminate parental rights and do so only when it is clearly established to the satisfaction of the court that the living situation presents a real danger to the child. Often, even when such danger is clear and immediate, the courts tend to temporize by maintaining the child in the home and assigning a social agency to supervise the family in the hope that they can be helped to change. It is generally only in the most egregious circumstances that a child is removed from the home and parental rights terminated. The fact that all of these children were removed from the home by the courts and parental rights terminated corroborates the social worker's negative characterization, based on record data, of their early living situation.

## CRITERIA OF OUTCOME

Follow-up interviews were conducted jointly with the adoptive father and mother, using a semistructured interview form. The interviews were conducted by graduate social workers, were tape-recorded, and lasted 2–2½ hours on the average. 

The focus of the interview centered on the parents' satisfactions and dissatisfactions with the adoption, the problems they encountered, and the adaptations they made. Consequently, the child was not contacted and no attempt was made at a direct assessment of the child's functioning. The presumption was that parental satisfaction is related to the child's functioning. A child who is showing poor achievement in school and demonstrating behavioral difficulties in the home and with his peer group is not likely to have parents who express satisfaction in the relationship. A high correlation between parental satisfactions and outcome measures that include the child's adjustment has been established empirically in other adoptive studies (8, 31).[1]

All of the taped interviews were transcribed, the typescripts averaging about fifty double-spaced pages of type. The researchers had available a total of some 4,300 pages of interview transcription. Each typescript was read and scored independently by three readers, all of whom were graduates of a school of social work and two of whom were working, at the time they engaged in this task, in the adoption unit of a public agency. Two of the three readers had no knowledge of the background material with regard to the family or the child whose interview they were reading.

Since the principal concern was with adoptive parent satisfaction and dissatisfaction in the adoptive experience, the primary outcome criteria of adoption "success" derive from this focus. Two measures of this were obtained. One was a ratio of satisfactions to dissatisfactions articulated by the parents during the course of the interview. Independently, the three typescript readers checked off on a prepared form that listed eighty different satisfactions and dissatisfactions the particular satisfactions they perceived the parents as having expressed explicitly or implicitly. An item was tabulated only when the same item for the same parent was checked by at least two of the three readers.

TABLE 1. **Ratio of Expressed Satisfactions to Dissatisfactions**

| Ratio | Number | Percentage |
|---|---|---|
| 5 or more to 1 | 60 | 66 |
| 4–1 | 2 | 2 |
| 3–1 | 4 | 4 |
| 2–1 | 1 | 1 |
| 1–1 | 8 | 9 |
| 1–2 | 4 | 4 |
| 1–3 | 5 | 6 |
| 1–4 | 1 | 1 |
| 1–5 or more | 6 | 7 |
| Total | 91 | 100 |

A ratio was computed for each case based on the total number of satisfaction-dissatisfaction items that appeared in the interview and were checked by two or more of the readers. Table 1 shows the distribution of such ratios. The ratio was computed to the nearest whole number so that a ratio of 1–1.4 appears as a ratio of 1–1 and a ratio of 1–1.6 appears as a ratio of 1–2.

---

[1] Numbers in parentheses refer to the numbered references at the end of this article.

The second outcome criterion measured was a composite score of parents' over-all satisfaction in the adoptive experience with the child. This was derived from a checklist completed independently by each of the parents at the end of the interview and from judgments made independently by four graduate social workers—the worker who interviewed the parents and the three typescript readers. The method of scoring applied the corrective of the social workers' objectivity to the parents' more subjective judgments. Once again a preponderance of responses fell in the upper end of the scale, some 87 percent of the parents being judged to be either "extremely satisfied" or "more satisfied than dissatisfied" in the adoptive experience with the child.

The two criteria of outcome were correlated with each other at a very high level ($r = .89$, $P < .001$). The two different kinds of criteria give similar kinds of outcome data—the composite ranking criterion indicates 78 percent of the adoptions as successful, 13 percent unsuccessful, and 9 percent that might be regarded as neither successful nor unsuccessful. The ratio of satisfactions to dissatisfactions criterion for these categories indicates 73 percent, 18 percent, and 9 percent, respectively. A comparison of these results with other adoptive outcome studies, the subjects of most of which were children adopted in infancy, indicates that the outcome of the group studied here was only slightly less successful.

The general conclusion indicating a considerable level of success is somewhat unexpected and raises a question of great interest. The data on the background factors and developmental history of these children indicate that almost all of them lived, during early childhood, under conditions of great social and emotional deprivation. The families into which they were born and from which they were removed by court action after the community had recognized the dangers of such an environment for healthy child development were characterized by considerable social and inter-personal pathology. Given the conditions under which these children lived during their most impressionable years—in poverty, inadequately housed, with alcoholic, promiscuous parents who frequently neglected them, sometimes abused them, and only rarely offered them the loving care that is the prerequisite for wholesome emotional development—how can one explain the generally favorable outcome of these adoptive placements? A successful adoptive experience might have been anticipated for the 31 percent of the children who had a good relationship with mothering figures, but the general success level is closer to 82–85 percent.

It would be easy to dismiss the conclusion out of hand by suggesting that the interview material presented by the parents had little relationship to the actual experience. The social workers who conducted the interviews rated each of the parents on the basis of their involvement, defensiveness, sincerity, and the like in the interview. The overwhelming impression was that most often most of the parents were being honest.

Whenever possible information obtained from parents was checked with earlier record material; this check revealed few discrepancies. The material was also consistent with a projective technique used at the end of the interview, a sentence completion form filled out by each of the parents. It seems that the question raised needs to be answered on its own merits.

## OTHER STUDIES

Before attempting an explanation, however, it might be well to point out that other studies have shown the same unexpected results with similar expressions of surprise on the part of the researchers. In each instance the children studied turned out to be more "normal," less "maladjusted," than they had any right to be, given the traumata and insults to psyche that they had experienced during early childhood.

Theis, in summarizing her impression derived from one of the first large-scale follow-up studies of foster children, expresses gratification at the adjustment of the group, 80 percent of whom came from "bad backgrounds." She says:

> Our study of the group as a whole, in so far as the subjects have demonstrated their ability to develop and to adjust themselves to good standards of living, and perhaps even more strikingly, our study of individual members of it, leave us with a distinct impression that there exists in individuals an immense power of growth and adaptation. (26, p. 163)

Roe and Burks did a follow-up study of thirty-six young adults who had, as children, been removed from their homes and placed in foster care because their own parents were chronic alcoholics. Other types of deviant behavior were associated with alcoholism; 81 percent of the fathers and 44 percent of the mothers of these children "were guilty of mistreatment or neglect of their children" (23, p. 38). The authors note that since most of the children

> became dependent as a result of court action—this means that the first few years of life of these children were spent in a home situation which left much to be desired—and that they were probably subjected to traumatic experiences during the early years of their lives. (22, pp. 382–383)

As adults, at the time of the follow-up interview, "most of these subjects have established reasonably satisfactory lives, including adequate personal and community relationships and most of them are married" (22, p. 388). The authors are prompted to ask:

> How did it happen that these children turned out as well as they did? How did it happen that in spite of these [adverse] factors many of them have become not only useful citizens but reasonably contented persons working adequately, with pleasant family lives and sufficient friends? No one who has

read the records of some of these lives and pondered on them can escape a profound sense of awe at the biological toughness of the human species. (22, p. 391)

Maas conducted a follow-up study of twenty children who had been removed from home during infancy and early childhood and placed for at least a year in a residential nursery. He reviewed agency records, interviewed parents, and saw the children themselves, who, at the time of the follow-up study some twenty years later, were young adults. Maas reports:

> Although these twenty young adults may have been seriously damaged by their early childhood separation and residential nursery experiences, most of them gave no evidence in young adulthood of extreme aberrant reactions. . . . To this extent the data support assumptions about the resiliency, plasticity and modifiability of the human organism rather than those about the irreversibility of the effects of early experience. (16, pp. 66–67)

In a follow-up study of independent adoptions conducted by Witmer, a group of fifty-six children were identified as having lived under "possibly traumatizing conditions" prior to adoption. These children had lived under adverse physical conditions and the psychological situation "was even more pathetic." At follow-up there was little difference in the adjustment ratings achieved by this group of children as contrasted with other adoptees placed at a similar age and in similar adoptive homes but who had not experienced such "possibly traumatizing conditions" (31, pp. 286–287).

Meier completed a follow-up study of sixty-one young adults who had grown up in foster care. All of the group had experienced five years or more in foster care and none had returned to his own family. About half of the group had been removed from their own homes before the age of 5. Between their first foster placement and their discharge from foster care at 18, these children had experienced an average of 5.6 living arrangements. Most of them had been removed by the courts from their own homes "in which they had experienced inadequate care" (18, p. 197).

Based on lengthy interviews with the group—now young adults—Meier concluded:

> The vast majority of the subjects have found places for themselves in the community. They are indistinguishable from their neighbors as self-supporting individuals, living in attractive homes, taking care of their children adequately, worrying about them, and making some mistakes in parenting, sharing the activities of the neighborhood and finding pleasures in their association with others. (18, p. 206)

In a later report Meier says:

> Child welfare workers are continuously baffled, as well as heartened by the fact that over and over again they see children removed from impossibly de-

priving circumstances who, by all the rules "ought" to be irrreparably harmed, who, nevertheless, thrive and grow and learn to accept love and affection and respond to it. (17, p. 21)

Lewis followed up 240 children who had been studied at a children's reception center following removal from their own homes. Seventy-one of these children came from problem families "characterized by gross neglect and squalor" (15, p. 84). On follow-up two years later 64 percent were doing "good" or "fair," 36 percent were assessed as "poor" (15, Table 71, p. 120).

Rathbun reported on a follow-up of thirty-three foreign children who, after having suffered considerable deprivation in their own countries, were placed for adoption in the United States. Interviews by caseworkers with the adoptive parents six years after placement, supplemented by contact with the schools, showed that "the adjustment of the majority was judged adequate and in some cases notably superior" (20, p. 6). The report concludes by noting:

> The consistency of the ratings for all categories in which assets outweigh liabilities, points in the direction of a considerable degree of reversibility of the effects of early psychic damage. (20, p. 131)

Another research group studied twenty-two Greek children institutionalized during the first two years of life and subsequently placed for adoption in the United States. Testing and interviews five years after adoption rated only two of the children as "poorly adjusted." The researchers concluded that "despite early deprivation the children have done remarkably well" (9, p. 19).

Welter studied seventy-two children placed for adoption in the United States when older than 5 years of age. Thirty-six of the group were children born outside the country and transferred to it for adoption. Some 85 percent of the children were judged to be showing "good" to "excellent" adaptation on follow-up (29, Table 40, p. 126). Welter notes, in summary:

> Perhaps the single most important implication may be drawn from the fact that according to the social workers [responsible for working with the children] both of these groups of older adoptive children . . . , despite extended exposure to massive deprivation, have indicated a degree of responsiveness to a restitutive environment and a reversibility of early psychic damage which seems to exceed even the most optimistic assessments of the studies on maternal deprivation and separation we have seen thus far. (29, p. 164)

A somewhat different series of studies helps to support the general contention we are trying to substantiate here—the contention that childhood trauma can be overcome and an initially adverse developmental history does not, necessarily, inevitably, lead to subsequent incapacity for social functioning.

Victor and Mildred Goertzel, both psychologists, raise this question in their study of the developmental history of eminent people. Using published biographies of four hundred prominent people, all of whom "lived into the 20th century," they codified material available on the nature of the childhood experiences of these people. They established that the greatest majority of the group came from homes that demonstrated considerable pathology and that the childhood experiences of many of the group were replete with potentially psychogenic factors. "Only 58 of the 400 can be said to have experienced what is the stereotyped picture of the supportive, warm, relatively untroubled home" (11, p. 131).

Renaud and Estess conducted a typical clinical history interview with "100 men whose functioning could be described as distinctly above normal by all ordinary standards" (21, p. 786). The findings of the detailed interviews indicated that this group of men who

> . . . functioned at above average levels and who were substantially free of psychoneurotic and psychosomatic symptomatology, reported childhood histories containing, seemingly, as many "traumatic events" or "pathogenic factors" as we ordinarily elicit in history taking interviews with psychiatric patients who are in varying degrees disabled by their symptoms. (21, p. 796)

Having been exposed to such "traumatic events" and "pathogenic factors," these men, who never would have come to the attention of mental health clinicians, have been able to reverse the expected developmental direction.

Similar findings are noted when one seeks to differentiate, on the basis of background factors, an essentially normal group from a group manifesting emotional pathology. Schofield and Balian matched a group of 178 schizophrenic patients with a group of 150 people who had never manifested any psychiatric disturbance. Matching was in terms of age, sex, and marital status. A comprehensive clinical life history interview was conducted with the normal group and a comparative item analysis was made. In general, there was a surprisingly great degree of "overlap of the normal subjects and schizophrenic patients in the distribution of the personal life history variables" (24, p. 222). While it is true that about 35 percent of the schizophrenic patients had a pathological relationship with their mothers as against some 19 percent of the normals, the question is raised as to why the 65 percent of the schizophrenics who had an essentially normal relationship with their mothers broke down and why the 19 percent of the normals who had pathological relationships with their mothers did not. The question as it stands of course, puts too much of a strain for causation on one isolated factor, but the question can be repeated for a variety of supposedly significant explanatory items and it can be repeated for configurations of items that supposedly "explain" emotional maladjustment. The authors conclude by stating:

The finding of "traumatic" histories in nearly a fourth of the normal subjects suggests the operation of "suppressor" experience or psychological processes of a immunization. (24, p. 225)

Similar kinds of studies by Munro (19) and Brill and Liston (5) show considerable traumá in the childhood backgrounds of psychiatrically normal populations.

In the studies reviewed by Bowlby (3) in his widely disseminated and influential report on the dramatic negative effects of early trauma, it might be significant to call attention, in this context, to the fact that, as Yarrow reminds us (32, p. 20), a sizable proportion of the children in each of the studies listed did not show the predicted negative reactions to separation and deprivation.

One might, for comprehensiveness, cite Bowlby's later modification of emphasis on an irreversibility in his study of sixty children who had experienced prolonged institutionalization in a tuberculosis sanitarium early in life (4). Contrasted on follow-up with a control group of schoolmates who had not experienced early separation, there seemed to be only a 20 percent greater incidence of maladjustment in the sanitarium group as compared with the control group. For most of the sanitarium group, then, the effects of early trauma seem to have been reversed.

The work of Clarke and Clarke showing cognitive recovery from severe early deprivation is also relevant here (6). Adolescents and young adults coming from backgrounds in which they had experienced cruelty, neglect, separation, and long periods of institutionalization were able, in a benign environment, to achieve significant increases in IQ test scores. Clinical reports also support the contention of reversibility of trauma in response to special psychotherapeutic effort (1, 2, 12).

## FACTORS RELATING TO REVERSIBILITY

Does all of the above then imply a contradiction of the most important tenets of child rearing—namely, that continuous contact with one set of loving, accepting, understanding parents providing the proper emotional as well as physical environment is the best basis for healthy biopsychosocial development? Actually not. The writer is not suggesting that neglect, abuse, and physical deprivation are not harmful. As a matter of fact, each of the studies cited shows that a more detailed contrast within the follow-up group invariably favors those sub-sets of children who were provided with a more benign environment prior to separation. For instance, while most of the children in the Maas study and in the study by Roe turned out reasonably well adjusted, those who came from less pathological backgrounds did better than those who had been subjected to greater trauma (16, p. 67; 22, Table 1, pp. 381–382). In the present study of adoption of older children outcome is positively related to natural mother's acceptance. The data do not argue for a rejection of the generally accepted tenets but rather for recognition of at least the partial reversibility of the effects of deprivation.

Explanation for reversibility lies with biological, social, and psychological factors. There is much empirical evidence indicating that constitutional factors play a part in differing levels of vulnerability to deprivation and resiliency in recovering from deprivation.

Studies of differences among children immediately after birth, before one can postulate differences owing to the effects of variations in their surroundings, indicate that children differ in many ways that have significance for the result of interaction between themselves and their environment. Thus, Thomas studied 130 children from the first months of life onward. From the moment of birth children differed in terms of activity, adaptability, distractability, persistence, mood, intensity of reaction to sensory stimuli, threshold of responsiveness, and so on. He notes:

> Given constancy of environmental factors the reaction will vary with the characteristic of the child upon whom the relatively constant stimulus is brought to bear. . . . This holds true for all aspects of the child's functioning . . . including reactions to situations of special stress, such as illness, radical change in living conditions or abrupt shifts in geographic environment. . . . This view of the child stands in contrast to the assumption that environmental influences as such have determinative effects. . . . Our findings suggest that exclusive emphasis on the role of environment in child development tells only part of the story and that responses to any regimen will vary in accordance with primary patterns of reactivity. (27, pp. 84–85)

These conclusions are supported by additional research that points to the same fact—that children are different at birth in ways that are crucial for personality development (7, 10, 30).

If biological determination of individuality, as contrasted with environmental or experiential determination, is given greater consideration, the resiliency of the children in this study group may be more explicable. One child's trauma, which makes future positive adjustment very improbable, may be another child's inconvenience, the effects of which, given reasonable opportunity, may be reversed.

There may, however, be another general line of explanation somewhat more sociological in nature. These children adopted when older made two important shifts in moving from their own home to the adoptive home. They made the change referred to above, from a home that offered little in the way of meeting their needs in terms of affection, acceptance, support, understanding, and/or encouragement to the adoptive home, which offered some measure of these essential psychic supplies. They also made a change from a lower-class, multiproblem, generally disreputable family living in a slum-ridden area in the community to a middle-class, reputable home in an area of the community that had some status.

A child's self-concept is developed as a result of his experience in the intense relationship with significant others within the intimacy of the family group, particularly in relation to the most significant of all others, the parents. A child who perceives himself as acceptable to the parents perceives himself as acceptable to himself. But however important this factor is in building the child's self-concept, it ignores the impact of the wider world, which soon begins to transmit messages to the child relevant to his conception of self that he cannot ignore. The Negro child has to have a much stronger positive self-image, initially, to withstand the corrosion on this image of the thousands of overt and covert cues that come from the predominantly white environment, all of which say black is bad, white is better, black is down, white is up, black is subordinate, white is supraordinate.

This problem operates along class lines as well as along color lines. The same kinds of messages are received by subsets within the white community. The standard-bearers of the white community behave toward the lower-class, multiproblem, disreputable white family in such a way as to transmit the message, loudly and clearly, that the family is unacceptable. The child identified with such a family, carrying its name and associating with its members, inevitably begins to be affected by this pervasive negative labeling.

The child is then removed from this family, placed in a decent-appearing, middle-class home in a nice-looking neighborhood, identified with a well-organized family of father and mother who act in a responsible, respectable manner. He now receives messages that proclaim his acceptability, that support, reinforce, and strengthen whatever components of self-acceptance—however limited—he has been able to develop within the family. Burks and Roe, in attempting to explain the better-than-anticipated outcome in foster care of children removed at the median age of 5 from homes in which the parents were alcoholic and/or psychotic, point to this as a factor that needs consideration:

> Had these children remained with their own outcast families, they, too, would have been, in a sense, outcasts. They could react only by identifying with their families and rejecting the community and all its customs, or by rejecting their families and striving ceaselessly somehow to achieve membership in the group which had despised them. (23, p. 116)

The children having been removed from such homes and placed in acceptable ones, the authors note:

> It seems very probable that residence in a home which is a respected part of the community, and the child's acceptance as a member of that community, make possible the formation of an organized ideal derived from the attitudes and forms of behavior of the community which can function as an integrating force. . . . (23, p. 116)

Srole, in his report of a large-scale effort to assess the level of "mental health" of people in midtown Manhattan, reports that mental impairment is related to socio-economic level. More of the "poor" in his study were apt to be "mentally impaired." In attempting to explain this, the report points to the factor of community rejection of the lower-class child, which intensifies tendencies toward maladjustment.

> In many areas of his experience the lower class child encounters the contempt, implicit but palpable, in the non-verbal behavior of others who think of him in the symbolism of such words as rubbish, scum, dregs, riff-raff and trash. These devastating judgments inevitably force their way into his own self evaluating processes. (25, p. 198)

Thus, in moving the child from a lower-class home and social environment to a middle-class adoptive home and social environment, the agency has "rescued" him from a situation that intensifies the problem of adjustment to one that assists the child in making a positive adjustment.

Supporting these two factors that dispose toward reversibility of trauma for children adopted when older—the biological factor of constitutional resiliency and the sociological factor of upward displacement, which reinforces self-acceptance—is the more important factor of making a therapeutic milieu available to such children. Adoption is not psychotherapy, but its psychotherapeutic potential is like a good marriage, a true friendship, a new and satisfying job, an enjoyable vacation. It can help to repair old hurts.

What is involved here are different approaches to an explanation of what is psychotherapeutic. The rationale that is basic to the traditional approach to therapy (specific remedial measures) suggests that the behavior itself is not of primary importance since the behavior is merely a manifestation of some underlying intrapsychic conflict. Since behavior is merely symptomatic of underlying disturbances, these inner causes, rather than the behavior itself, should be the focus of attention. The behavior itself is purposive and beyond rational control or simple re-education, exhortation, persuasion, or the like, since the individual is motivated to act in this way in response to a conflict that he cannot resolve because its nature is not fully available to conscious awareness. Changes in behavior may be achieved, but unless the basic conflict is resolved, other, equally disabling, symptoms may be substituted for the symptom that is no longer manifested.

It would consequently be futile merely to seek to change behavior and/or relieve symptoms without attempting to trace and resolve the conflict, the "real" problem from which the symptoms originate. It follows then that effective therapy is directed not toward changing behavior but toward achieving understanding, toward an "expansion of consciousness" so that it includes the hidden sense of conflict.

If the client can be helped to understand why he behaves as he does or to recognize and understand the origin of his neurotic tactics that continually defeat him, he will gradually abandon the inappropriate behavior and substitute therefor more rational tactics in the management of his life. (13, p. 474)

The promotion of self-understanding, of insight, is the most effective approach toward helping people with their problems and all strategies—reassurance, universalization, desensitization, catharsis, clarification, interpretation—are valued because they free emotional energy or change the balance of intrapsychic force in such a way as to maximize the possibility for self-understanding. Even environmental manipulation—reducing, modifying, or mitigating external stress infringing on the client—is regarded as a desirable tactic primarily because this, too, frees ego energy (previously devoted to struggling with the environment) for dealing more effectively with the basic intrapsychic conflict. These postulates are fundamental to one view of what is psychotherapeutic deriving primarily from psychoanalytic psychology.

Another view of therapy derives from the learning and conditioning psychologies. Here the primary concern is with the behavior itself without concern for underlying "causes." The behavior is viewed as the result of some unfortunate learning, conditioning experiences that have taught undesirable, unadaptive approaches to interpersonal relationships. The concept of symptoms as a response to an underlying conflict, in this view, is unnecessary and superfluous (28, p. 8).

The therapy is primarily focused on the behavior itself and is concerned with providing an opportunity for unlearning the unadaptive behavior and learning new, more adaptive modes of behavior. The therapy seeks to identify "unsuitable stimulus-response connections," to dissolve them and to teach more desirable ones. It seeks to identify the specific environmental conditions through which the undesirable behavior is controlled and sustained and to change these. The stress is on immediate experience and specific behavior.

The view expressed here regarding what is therapeutic about adoptions is closer to the second rationale for therapy outlined, the learning-conditioning rationale, than it is to the first, the psychoanalytic psychology rationale. The child's previous living experiences may have "taught" a view of parents and parental surrogates that resulted in neurotic, unadaptive behavior. Defenses were developed and behavior manifested that was in response to the nature of the situation to which the child was subjected. Moving into the adoptive home meant moving into an environment that was set up to condition the child to a change in behavior. Previously learned, now inappropriate, behaviors went unrewarded or were actively discouraged; new, more appropriate, more adaptive behaviors were rewarded and actively encouraged. Without any explicit effort to resolve whatever underlying intrapsychic conflict may or may not have been present, without any explicit effort to have the child develop insight or self-understanding into his distorted perception of himself in the parent-child relationship and/or his distorted expectations with reference to the parents' behavior toward him, the living experience provides the corrective in day-to-day learning. The living experience teaches new ways of relating to people and new ways of perceiving oneself. In this sense, the adoptive home is a therapeutic milieu—a healthy restitutive living experience. It acts as a large-scale conditioning matrix that stimulates and supports changes in the child's feeling and behavior.

Psychotherapy is, in effect, a condensed, systematic attempt to imitate curative, real-life situations and assure the availability of such a curative configuration to the patient. Environmental therapy—therapy that actually affords the child the opportunity to live in a healthier family situation and experience the possibility of successful interaction with parents—is, as Josselyn notes, "the least artificial form of therapy" (14, p. 120). And, like all therapies, it is grounded in the supposition that experiences in the present can free us from the past and that the effects of such earlier experiences are reversible.

*References*

1. Alpert, Augusta. "Reversibility of Pathological Fixations Associated with Maternal Deprivation in Infancy," in *Psychoanalytic Study of the Child*, Vol. 14. New York: International Universities Press, 1959. Pp. 169–185.
2. Appell, Genevieve, and David, Myriam. "Case Notes on Monique," in B. M. Foss, ed., *Determinants of Infant Behavior*. New York: John Wiley & Co., 1963. Pp. 101–112.
3. Bowlby, John. *Maternal Care and Mental Health*. Geneva, Switzerland: World Health Organization, 1951.
4. ———, and Ainsworth, Mary. "The Effects of Mother–Child Separation: A Follow-up Study," *British Journal of Medical Psychology*, Vol. 29, Part 3 (1956), pp. 211–244.
5. Brill, Norman, and Liston, Edward. "Parental Loss in Adults with Emotional Disorders," *Archives of General Psychiatry*, Vol. 14, No. 3 (March 1966).
6. Clarke, A. D. B., and Clarke, Ann. "Recovery from the Effects of Deprivation," *Acta Psycholi*, Vol. 16, No. 2 (1959), pp. 137–144.
7. Escalona, Sibylle, and Heider, Grace. *Prediction and Outcome: A Study in Child Development*. New York: Basic Books, 1959.
8. Fanshel, David, and Jaffee, Benson. "A Follow-Up Study of Adoption— Preliminary Report." Unpublished paper, New York, N.Y., 1965. Mimeographed.
9. "Final Report to Children's Bureau on Study of Adoption of Greek Children by American Foster Parents." New York: Research Institute for the Study of Man, November 1964. Mimeographed.
10. Fries, Margaret E., and Woolf, Paul Y. "Some Hypotheses on the Role of the Congenital Activity Type in Personality Development," in *Psychoan-*

*alytic Study of the Child*, Vol. 8. New York: International Universities Press, 1953. Pp. 48–62.

11. Goertzel, Victor, and Goertzel, Mildred George. *Cradles of Eminence.* Boston: Little, Brown & Co., 1962.

12. Hellman, Ilse. "Hampstead Nursery Follow-up Studies: 1. Sudden Separation and Its Effect Followed Over Twenty Years," in *Psychoanalytic Study of the Child*, Vol. 17. New York: International Universities Press, 1962. Pp. 159–174.

13. Hobbs, Nicholas. "Sources of Gain in Psychotherapy," in Warren G. Bennis, Edgar H. Schein, David E. Berlew, and Fred I. Steele, eds., *Interpersonal Dynamics.* Homewood, Ill.: Dorsby Press, 1964. Pp. 474–485.

14. Josselyn, Irene M. *Psychosocial Development of Children.* New York: Family Service Association of America, 1948.

15. Lewis, Hilda. *Deprived Children.* London, Eng.: Oxford University Press, 1954.

16. Maas, Henry. "The Young Adult Adjustment of Twenty Wartime Residential Nursery Children," *Child Welfare*, Vol. 42, No. 2 (February 1963), pp. 57–72.

17. Meier, Elizabeth G. "Current Circumstances of Former Foster Children," *Child Welfare*, Vol. 44, No. 4 (April 1965), pp. 196–206.

18. ———. "Former Foster Children as Adult Citizens." Unpublished doctoral dissertation, Columbia University School of Social Work, 1962.

19. Munro, Alistair. "Childhood Parent-Loss in a Psychiatrically Normal Population," *British Journal of Preventive and Social Medicine*, Vol. 19, No. 2 (April 1965), pp. 69–79.

20. Rathbun, Constance, McLaughlin, Helen, Bennett, Chester, and Garland, James. "Later Adjustment of Children Following Radical Separation from Family and Culture." Paper presented at the annual meeting of the American Orthopsychiatric Association, Chicago, Ill., 1964. Mimeographed.

21. Renaud, Harold, and Estess, Floyd. "Life History Interviews with One Hundred Normal American Males: 'Pathogenicity' of Childhood," *American Journal of Orthopsychiatry*, Vol. 31, No. 4 (October 1961), pp. 786–802.

22. Roe, Anne. "The Adult Adjustment of Children of Alcoholic Parents Raised in Foster Homes," *Quarterly Journal of Studies on Alcohol*, Vol. 5 (March 1945), pp. 378–393.

23. ———, and Burks, Barbara. "Adult Adjustment of Foster Children of Alcoholic and Psychotic Parentage and the Influence of the Foster Home," *Memoirs of the Section on Alcohol Studies*, No. 3. New Haven: Yale University Press, 1945.

24. Schofield, William and Balian, Lucy. "A Comparative Study of the Personal Histories of Schizophrenic and Nonpsychiatric Patients," *Journal of Abnormal and Social Psychology*, Vol. 59, No. 2 (September 1959), pp. 212–225.

25. Srole, Leo, *et. al. Mental Health in the Metropolis: The Midtown Manhattan Study.* New York: McGraw-Hill Book Co., 1962.

26. Theis, Sophie Van Senden. *How Foster Children Turn Out*, Publication No. 165. New York: State Charities Aid Association, 1924.

27. Thomas, Alexander, Birch, Herbert, Chess, Stella, Hertzig, Margaret, and Korn, Sam. *Behavioral Individuality in Early Childhood.* New York: New York University Press, 1963.

28. Thomas, Edwin J., and Goodman, Esther. *Socio-Biological Theory and*

*Interpersonal Helping in Social Work.* Ann Arbor: University of Michigan, School of Social Work, 1965.
29. Welter, Marianne. *Adopted Older Foreign and American Children.* New York: International Social Service, 1965.
30. Witkin, H. A., *et al. Psychological Differentiation.* New York: John Wiley & Sons, 1962.
31. Witmer, Helen, Herzog, Elizabeth, Weinstein, Eugene, and Sullivan, Mary. *Independent Adoptions—A Follow-up Study.* New York: Russell Sage Foundation, 1963.
32. Yarrow, Leon J. "Maternal Deprivation—Toward an Empirical and Conceptual Reevaluation," *Psychological Bulletin,* Vol. 58, No. 6 (November 1961), pp. 459–490. Reprinted in *Maternal Deprivation.* New York: Child Welfare League of America, January 1962. Pp. 3–41.

# 41

❲ Group services for adoptive parents have been imaginatively employed at different stages of contact. Groups of parents have met with agency representatives at the time of application, immediately after placement, and some years after placement. The following two articles review such group service efforts after placement of the child.

# A Post-adoption Discussion Series

*Catherine R. Collier and Anne Campbell*

The discussion series described in this paper was the result of co-operative planning by the Children's Aid Society and the Catholic Children's Aid Society of Vancouver, which offer adoption services, and the Extension Department of the University of British Columbia.

Over the years, the caseworkers who were making adoptive placements had been aware that much pertinent material discussed with adoptive parents during the first year of the child's placement seemed to have fallen on deaf ears. Parents seemed unable to absorb some of the information the caseworker gave them that had a bearing on the child's future adjustment. Although it has been the practice for adoptive parents to sever connections with the agency when legal adoption has been completed, some parents have subsequently returned to the agency for help with a specific problem. The need for help became evident only after the parents had had the actual experience of living with the child as he grew older. Parents asked for help with such problems as how to tell the child that he was adopted, what to do about questions concerning the natural parents, how to handle a school problem or the young adolescent's feelings of personal worth in relation to his adoptive status.

The discussion series for parents was regarded by the agencies as a means of their learning more intimately and directly the challenges and difficulties faced by adoptive parents as well as the joys and satisfactions of creating a family through adoption. It would also offer the parents an opportunity to share with each other and the agency some of their particular concerns about adoption and the ways in which the parent-child relationships were developing. It was decided that the discussion series would have an educational, rather than a therapeutic, emphasis. The hope was that the adoptive parents, through the modification of attitudes inherent in the group discussion procedure, would achieve better understanding of family and environmental situations that might be creating difficulty.

## SETTING UP THE SERIES

The discussion series was conducted in five weekly meetings of one and one-half hours each. Meetings were held in the evening so that fathers, as well as mothers, could attend. The registration fee was five dollars for a couple and three dollars for one parent. A brochure, "Family by Adoption," printed by the Extension Department, gave the information that the series was being planned especially for adoptive parents; that the content of discussion would depend on the members' interests and might include such questions as, "What is the normal pattern of development for all children?"; "Do adopted children have special needs?"; "When and how should we tell a child he is adopted?"; "What is the impact of adoption on a family through the years?"

Experienced workers in the adoption field led the group discussions. The chairman was a worker with fourteen years of experience in a child placing agency; the recorder had had ten years' experience. The parents to whom letters of invitation were sent were those whose adopted children were from four to six years of age. Thirty-four parents registered; of this number, twelve couples and six individuals attended. The number of attendants at the five meetings was 27, 28, 26, 23, and 29 respectively. Participants arrived punctually for each meeting.

Most of the participants were in their late thirties or early forties, and had been married an average of ten years before applying to adopt a child. All had had some medical exploration regarding their inability to have children. In the case of eight couples, the reasons for childlessness had not been determined; two couples had both natural and adopted children. Nine of the men in the group were white-collar workers—a doctor, an optometrist, a chartered accountant, a forest ranger, an insurance executive, two business executives, and two salesmen. The remainder were skilled and unskilled workmen.

The sessions were planned as straight group discussions because it was thought that these persons would benefit most from active participation. Since we envisioned the series as the parents' own forum, we wanted them to set the group goals according to their own needs. So that we could have some idea of the areas that would be of most interest to the parents, and in order to stimulate them to reveal their particular concerns, space was available on the application form for listing suggested topics. We wanted to help both the parents and the agencies to identify which problems were directly related to adoption, and which were related to the parent-child relationship in the broad sense. We wanted to offer these adoptive parents an opportunity to express their feelings about being adoptive parents, and about their own adopted children. As far as we knew at the beginning of the series, the individuals in this group had only one common interest—having adopted children of about the same age. Moreover, to our knowledge none of these parents had sought help for the child, nor had any of these children had special difficulties in school.

## FIRST MEETING

After introductory remarks by agency and university representatives, the leader opened the discussion by mentioning the question most frequently indicated on the application forms as being of concern to those present: "How and when do you tell a child he is adopted?" There was an immediate positive response to the idea of telling a child that he is adopted. Only one mother took exception to this by saying that the answer depended on the child and the circumstances. This opinion drew strong disapproval from the group. It was interesting, however, that as the series progressed, it was discovered that other parents had also delayed telling the child but evidently had not been free in the beginning of the discussion to acknowledge their hesitancy and anxiety.

Some of the typical comments made were: "If you do not tell a child early, you multiply the difficulties." "It is impossible for a child not to discover from some source that he is adopted." "What you grow up with is never as great a shock as a sudden revelation." "One must feel right and comfortable about telling, and this is tied up of course with adoptive parents' acceptance of their own inability to have children." One of the discussants poignantly remarked, "It is the fear within ourselves because we had such a shock when we first discovered we could not have natural children." One of the members described the devastating effect on a boy of nineteen when he had discovered at the time of his enlistment into the armed forces that he was adopted. He had rejected his parents for a long time thereafter because of their deception.

## MAJOR TOPICS DISCUSSED

The group leaders were concerned lest the mother who had had the courage to acknowledge at the first meeting that she had not told her child about adoption might fail to appear at the second meeting because of the group's strong negative response to her. She did come, however, and whispered to the leader that she was not going to speak any more but that she had talked over with her husband what had happened in the meeting and that they were definitely going to tell the youngster. She participated actively in later discussions.

Certain topics seemed to hold a great deal of interest for these parents and each one will be discussed in some detail.

*Telling a Child:* This topic was discussed on many occasions. One parent commented: "I think a child should be told he is adopted from the first day on. If you associate the word 'adoption' with loving and put real meaning into it, children think they have heard it forever and you teach them in an unembarrassed way."

"What do you do when a child doesn't ask about adoption?" was a question asked by several people. The question, "Is it that he doesn't understand what you have told him?" brought forth this interesting response from one mother: "We bring fear into the situation. There is a sadness in telling, and some people just can't do it. I left it to Daddy to tell." Another mother mentioned the extreme anxiety of a woman friend who had not told her 12-year-old son that he was adopted. She had said, "I don't know how to tell my child or where to begin." The group suggested that this mother might talk to her son about other children in the neighborhood who are adopted, and that she and the son might visit families in which there was an adopted child and discuss the situation afterwards. Then she might move on to telling him about his own adoption. A father in the group thought that over-emphasizing adoption would make the child think he was "somebody apart" or "an odd ball." "In this, as in all areas, one should travel the middle road."

*Natural Parents:* The discussion about natural parents was opened by one of the participants who said that her 8-year-old child inquired, "Will the lady who borned me want me again? Will we ever meet her?" Another group member remarked that "The child's age and his capacity to absorb information should determine what is told the child." The leader stressed that it was not so much the words that are used as the parents' feelings and attitudes that are important. The group members were divided on what they wanted to know about natural parents. Some of them did not want to know anything at all, so that they could answer truthfully that they did not know, should the child ask them. Others thought that the adoptive parents should know the child's possible inherited talents. Still others wanted "to know everything and have it in writing."

Toward the end of the series, the group became more comfortable in discussing natural parents. Some members apparently were not as comfortable as their discussion made them seem since, as the discussion proceeded, their deeper mixed feelings of resentment, and a desire to deny the existence of the biological parents became evident. One member revealed that she could not think of the natural parent as the child's mother. She called her "that lady" in speaking to her adopted child. Another called the natural mother the "blood mother" or the "other woman." One member felt it was better to call the natural mother "the first mother," rather than calling her "the lady." One father mentioned his wonderment and worry when once his daughter said, "I've got two Daddies." This alarmed the parents until the child went on to explain "I've got God, and a Daddy here." Another father said that he felt that giving up a baby must be a sacrifice. His experience with the social worker had led him to feel that if the surrender could be handled by anyone it could be by a social worker who had real confidence in her ability to help the mother.

A doctor in the group thought that the passage of time was an important factor in building parent-child relationships and that bearing a child did not make a mother. It was brought out often that parents, in their anxiety, do not "listen with an understanding ear to a child's questions." It was suggested that before answering what seems to be a difficult question, a parent might well say, "What made you think of that?" or "Why do you ask?" This approach should help the parent not to go beyond a child's needs at the time. One 5-year-old boy in responding to a playmate's query as to why he had not "grown in his Mummy's tummy" settled it by saying comfortably to his friend, "That's just one of God's secrets."

Another father reported that his 9-year-old adopted boy had been playing with some of the neighborhood children and they had begun to quarrel. The father was lying unobserved on the patio. He heard a neighbor's boy say to his son in a moment of anger, "You're nothing but a bastard." The father's heart had seemed to stop until he heard his son quickly reply, "Well, my Daddy loves me more than your Daddy loves you." The discussion group seemed to accept the idea that parents cannot protect children from all pain, but they can try to build the child's inner resources which will make it possible for the child to meet difficult life situations which are inevitable.

*Illegitimacy:* The subject of illegitimacy was introduced by the leader who suggested that in the light of the fact that the group members had come from various cultural backgrounds and family settings, it might be useful for the members to share with each other what they had been brought up to think about girls who had borne children out of wedlock.

The participants responded quickly. "There's a stigma attached to it." "It reveals a lack of training in the home." "As one grows older he realizes that anyone can make mistakes." "It's the wrong thing to do." "Society is severe on the girl but it has to be that way; if illegitimacy is taken too lightly, society may break down." "The unmarried mother of today is not looked upon as she was twenty years ago. Twenty years from now there will be a different approach." "A mother must feel guilty at not looking after her own." "Many young people have to get married. Is the unmarried mother any different when for some reason or other she and the father of the baby were unable to get married?" "Their misfortune is our good fortune." "The word illegitimate should never be used." The discussion on this subject was lively and the group seemed to want to share their ideas. Although some of the remarks were obviously judgmental, the group's interest in the subject indicated that this was an area in which deeper understanding was needed.

*Probation Period:* Many persons in the group were confused about the purpose of the probation period. "The suspense of that year is hard." "I felt I was under surveillance; I thought it was a challenge and that we had to prove ourselves." "The fear that the child might be removed hovered over me." "We lived in absolute fear of the mother's reclaiming the child." Some expressed opposite views. "It is of benefit to both the child and the adoptive parents to have an open year." "It is a waiting period for assessing the child and the parents after the child is in the home." "There were worries in that first year, and the social worker would reassure me."

The group leader discussed the three R's in adoption: (1) responsibility to the child; (2) responsibility to the natural parents; (3) responsibility to the adoptive parents. The leader also stressed that social workers are not infallible in their assessment of individuals. The probationary period provides an opportunity for the social worker to give help, to the end that the child may become integrated into the family group with as little worry and difficulty as possible. The creation of a family by adoption is not, and cannot be, the same as biological creation. It can, however, be a satisfying and happy experience, if the parents have resolved their feelings of disappointment and inadequacy and their resentment toward those who can have children. The parents must be able to accept a child as he is, whether born to them or not, and must feel that he is special and precious to them.

## GENERAL OBSERVATIONS

In planning this series, we had kept in mind that feelings and attitudes relating to adoption were to be explored on a conscious level. In the actual working out of the program, the group members set up their own framework for discussion and seemed comparatively free in bringing out their concerns and questions. This method, by and large, was acceptable. There was some feeling, however, that using a combined lecture and discussion method during some sessions might have been more stimulating.

With the exception of one member, the entire group participated in varying degrees. The member who did not participate in discussion wrote in her evaluation, "I was interested to learn the time-tested methods. I enjoyed and benefited from the talks and the summation of the social workers." She was also interested in being a member of a similar group in two or three years. No one emerged as the leader of the group, and no one attempted to dominate the discussion, but the men tended to be more vocal than the women. Five of the fathers shared the spotlight in group participation. It was said of one father who spoke calmly and thoughtfully that "he should have been a minister," and his opinion seemed to carry considerable weight with the group. Members apparently felt free to question each other's opinions, and only on one occasion was a member of the group dealt with harshly.

The ease with which the participants became a cohesive, spontaneous group was evident almost from the first session. The members' spontaneity, warmth, and willingness to share with one another pervaded the series, and increased as they felt safe in bringing out the more subtle aspects of their own parent-child relationships. For example, in the third session, a mother was able to tell of her son's difficulties and the help she had received from a mental health service in the community.

Although it is difficult to assess the extent to which individuals in the group gained something from this experience, it is our impression that the majority benefited to some degree from the series. It seemed obvious that all members were seeking help with some aspect of adoption. Some members wanted help with specific problems such as telling the child about his being adopted or discussing with him his natural parents or his having been born out of wedlock. Others were more interested in considering how best to deal with the community, the school, relatives, and so on. Two-thirds of the members mailed to the agency a written evaluation prepared at the conclusion of the series. Two direct referrals of prospective adoptive parents were made to the agency as a result of the series, and there were several telephone calls for clarification of some of the points raised. The members were unanimous in expressing an interest in further group meetings, perhaps a series to be held every two or three years. All of them requested a written summary of the discussions, which was provided by the University at no extra cost.

A few excerpts from evaluations written by group members are worthy of note. "Even at first meeting the members were eager to express their ideas and problems. Perhaps we might discuss definite problems and then have professional help from our leaders." "We were all seeking reassurance. In the group discussions we found that our situations were normal. Do most adopting parents to some degree lack self-confidence?" "Perhaps if specific questions were assigned for discussion, we could assemble our views better, or contribute more to the discussion." "The course has given me more confidence and I feel I will be more relaxed in dealing with situations." "The fact that the fathers' viewpoints and interests were solicited rather than just the mothers' was of mutual benefit to my husband and me. I'd suggest a slightly more rigid program with topics laid out ahead of time and given out at an introductory meeting when the group could change the plan if it so desired."

## CONCLUSION

From the reactions of various group members, the agency gained a number of important suggestions for improving adoption services. More visits in the probationary period would be welcomed. Adoptive parents should be informed that the end of the probationary period does not necessarily mean the complete severance of ties with the agency. The legal aspects involved in adoption should be made clearer to adoptive parents. The child's medical history is important, since pediatricians often ask for more details than are available, and these should be supplied by the agency.

The two agencies concerned and the University Extension Department are convinced that many adoptive parents are eager to discover more and better ways of understanding and fulfilling their roles as fathers and mothers through the medium of group discussion. We are also convinced that various post-adoption services have an important place in a good adoption program.

# 42

# Adopting Couples Come to Grips with Their New Parental Roles

*Edith M. Chappelear and Joyce E. Fried*

When a husband and wife learn that their application to adopt a child has been approved, it is for them as though their fondest dream has come true. But when the child is actually placed with them, questions that ought to have been resolved through the home study process may arise. However, their reluctance to share anxiety with a caseworker after placement often makes it difficult to help them prepare for the special problems they may face as parents of adopted children. The Montgomery County (Md.) Department of Public Welfare has found the group discussion method an effective way of breaking through such reluctance.

The agency has had professionally trained social workers on its adoption staff for the past 4 years. During this time it has emphasized the preparation of applicant couples during the home study for the problems they may face as adoptive parents.

Over the years, the agency found that the early period of placement is the most crucial to the quality of parent-child and child-parent adjustment. Unfortunately, it also found that this was the period when social workers face the greatest difficulty in finding a meaningful relationship with adopting parents. At this point, parents were usually most unwilling to discuss or come to grips in any way with the problems they might have with their children. The caseworkers felt effectively shut out by couples who had participated actively during the home study and preplacement period. For the adopting parents, once they had the baby, the focus seemed too narrow to include only themselves and the child. In talking with the caseworker, they tend to gloss over their problems and to make only platitudinous observations such as "It is as though he had been with us always."

Knowing that initial parent-child adjustment is rarely so idyllic, the adoption unit considered the following possible reasons for the failure to get a true picture of what was going on in these homes.

1. The worker's visits in the supervisory period seemed threatening to adoptive parents. The couples felt that since the agency still retained guardianship over the child it might use its authority to remove the child if the social worker thought the placement was not proceeding satisfactorily. Parents, therefore, felt a great need to emphasize the positive.

2. The couples unconsciously felt that discussion of the strangeness, fears, and changes involved in the new experience of adoptive parenthood would sharpen their awareness of the differences between adoptive and natural parenthood. They preferred to avoid the pain of speaking of something they would like not to exist. It is easier to deny an unpleasant fact than to face it, particularly in talking to a person vested with authority.

Realizing that both these reasons were probably operating to a certain extent, we wondered whether the parents might be able to help one another. We, therefore, instigated the program of group meetings to supplement the social workers' individual interviews with the parents. Under the plan each couple was to attend two group meetings in the office in the supervisory period: one, 6 weeks to 2 months after the placement, and the other, 1 week after that. One home visit was made by the caseworker within 2 weeks after placement.

The new program got under way in October 1965. Each meeting was attended by five or six couples and lasted about an hour and a half. Discussion was led by a caseworker, who encouraged the couples to participate and gradually turned the meeting over to them as much as possible, intervening only with occasional guidance. No two meetings were exactly alike. They varied with the group's composition and the leader's experience in stimulating discussion.

The only bases for membership in specific groups were the date the couple had received a child and the age of the child. Parents who were adopting children over 4 years of age met in separate groups. Some couples were having their first experience with parenthood; some already had one or more adopted children; some had children who had been born to them in addition to one or more adopted children. The age range among the couples was wide: from the early twenties to the forties.

The only common denominator among the couples was the similar situation they were in: they had all undergone a home study and had a child placed in their home by an agency—usually the Montgomery County Department of Public Welfare, but sometimes an out-of-state agency for whom the department was carrying the supervisory responsibility.

The discussions were always concerned with the adjustment involved in becoming an adoptive parent, the kinds of problems that could be anticipated, and how they might be met.

### THE MEETINGS

The first of the two meetings each couple attended was focused on the subject "Being Adoptive Parents"; the second, on "Being an Adopted Child." The discussions covered the following aspects of adoption:

1. The difference between adoptive and biological parenthood.
2. Helping a child to an acceptance and understanding of his adoptive status.
3. The adoptive parents' feelings toward the child's biological parents.
4. The adoptive parents' feelings about illegitimacy.
5. Letting persons outside the family know that the child has been adopted.

The group leader always opened the first of the two meetings by explaining the purpose of having them—giving the couples an opportunity to discuss a common experience and problems of common concern. She pointed out that the agency's workers were always ready to be of help, but that in a way they were on the outside looking in and that the agency believed the participants as new adoptive parents might have something to say to each other. In almost every group, the parents in their first meeting began to discuss questions their friends, relatives, and acquaintances had raised—questions they resented and did not know how to answer. Almost all had been asked what they knew of the child's background. To this, many of them had given angry, evasive answers such as "none of your business." Some had even been asked if they could really love an adopted child as they would a child of their own.

Often during the first meeting a parent would express concern about how his adopted child would look on him and whether the child would feel he had no need to respect or obey him because adoptive parents are not "real" parents. In discussing this possibility, the group members usually decided that it might happen, but then someone—sometimes the group leader, sometimes one of the parents—would point out that even children living with their "real" parents often had moments of rebellion, and examples would be cited of such children who had accused their parents of not being their "real parents."

The parents were nearly always unanimous in feeling that they would have difficulty in discussing the subject of adoption with their child. In the first meeting, the group leader did not usually make specific suggestions in regard to this problem but, rather, suggested that the parents think a lot about what they might do, read about what others had done, and plan to discuss the subject again in the second meeting.

The second meeting usually started with a reading of the minutes of the previous meeting after which the group leader would ask whether the participants had any questions they would like to discuss further. Often the first question raised was whether it is important to discuss the fact of adoption with the child. All of the parents had been encouraged to explore the subject in their individual interviews with the social worker before a child had been placed with them. The questions of "when" and "how" usually elicited much difference of opinion. In one group, for example, a man who had adopted four children from different agencies said he felt he could tell them all that their parents were dead.

"To me," he said, "They are dead. If the children believe they are living they will go to the ends of the earth to find them."

His wife did not agree with him. Other couples said they understood his wish to "bury the parents" but tried to explain to him why this would not "work." They said that they could not in good conscience falsify the facts, that it would be easier for them to help a child face and accept the facts behind his placement than to live with a lie. Some parents said they felt that "truth will out" anyway, that as the child got older and learned more about the frequent association between illegitimacy and adoption, he would begin to wonder if his adoptive parents had been entirely truthful with him. All of the parents in the group indicated they felt they could not comfortably repeat an earlier falsification, nor did they wish to jeopardize their relationship with the child by admitting they had lied originally to protect him.

The group leader always encouraged the participants to talk about why it would be difficult for them to bring up the subject of adoption with their child. Usually it turned out that their difficulty was closely related to their feelings about the child's out-of-wedlock birth. As one participant expressed it: "It's hard enough to talk about sex without having to talk about birth out of wedlock." Some parents tried to reassure themselves that out-of-wedlock birth would have no stigma by the time their children were old enough to ask questions.

The leader would then encourage the participants to discuss their feelings about illegitimacy in general, how these feelings were affecting their feeling about the natural mother of their child, and what other feelings they had about this "unknown" (as far as they were concerned) woman or girl. The reactions were as varied as the personalities of the participants. There was usually at least one parent who said the mother "didn't care" that she had "dumped the baby with the welfare." This was always countered by others with compassion—"She will always remember," "The birthday will be terrible for her." "She tried to give the baby what she couldn't give by herself—a family."

When the discussion revealed the parents' negative feelings about unmarried mothers and even some fear that their adopted children might become as "irresponsible" as the women who bore them, the group leader would ask the parents why they themselves had come to the agency and then would try to help them see that an unmarried mother who has released her baby to an agency for adoption has shown the same sort of responsible concern for the child's future as has the couple who has come to a social agency to secure a child for adoption. When the group leader asked what kind of information about the mother of their child might be helpful to them, the parents would usually respond that they did not want to know very much.

While the major part of both meetings was spent discussing the effects of adoption on the parent-child relationship, the group leader would always make a point of bringing the discussion around to the danger of over-emphasizing the fact of adoption both in the parents' direct dealings with the child and in their search for causes of whatever behavior difficulties may arise.

The leader always closed the second meeting by expressing the agency's belief in the ability of adoptive families to become closely knit, loving families.

Because only two postplacement meetings were held with each group, we did not attempt to do anything more in these meetings than to raise questions and to help adoptive parents talk about them together so that they might become more comfortable in their new parental role.

After nine series of meetings, we sent a letter and a questionnaire to the 44 couples who had attended them in an attempt to evaluate the program. The couples were not asked to sign the questionnaire. The letter explained that the meetings had grown out of the agency's desire to help the parents discuss problems of concern to all of them. Thirty of the couples filled out and returned the questionnaires.

## PARENTS' OPINIONS

The following is a list of the questions with a summary of the parents' responses:

1. We did (or did not) find the postplacement group meeting helpful— 21, did; 7, did not; 2, "somewhat helpful."
2. Did the meeting evoke any new questions in your minds concerning adoption? If yes, what are they?—1, yes; 25, no; 4 returns showed no response to this question. A specific question was not mentioned.
3. Did you find the subject matter stimulating?—14, yes; repetitive?—5, yes; moderately interesting?—7, yes; not pertinent?—2, yes; a waste of time?—none; no response—2.
4. Did the questions raised cause you to worry? If yes, which ones?—1, yes; 28, no; 1, no response. (The respondent who answered "yes" did not explain.)
5. Please check which, if any, of the following subjects seemed appropriate to your present experience and worth talking over in a group: (*a*) Adjustments involved in becoming a parent—7; (*b*) difference between adoptive and biological parenthood—4; (*c*) helping a child to an acceptance and understanding of his adoptive status—23; (*d*) adoptive parents' feelings toward child's biological parents—5; (*e*) adoptive parents' feeling about illegitimacy—3; (*f*) sharing knowledge of child's adoption with outsiders—12.
6. Did you feel free to express your opinions and feelings at the meetings? —26, yes; 4, no response.

Twenty couples offered suggestions of topics they would like to discuss in future meetings. Most frequently mentioned was the desire to speak with a couple who had been adoptive parents for some time.

The four caseworkers who conducted the meetings regarded them as varying in their effectiveness. In some of the sessions, the discussion was very lively; in others, the leader was hard put to stimulate any kind of discussion. In general, we found that couples whose ages and family situations were analogous and whose adoptive children were of similar ages seemed to have more to say to each other than to couples whose family situations were markedly different from their own. We found, too, that the couples were often more interested in exchanging pictures of and pleasant anecdotes about their children than in thinking out loud about the problematic and emotional aspects of adoption. Several parents said at the meetings that the problems seemed "so far in the future" that they found it difficult to theorize about how they would meet them when and if they occurred.

Nevertheless, the answers to the questionnaire showed that 23 of the 30 responding couples found topic 5c—helping a child to an acceptance and understanding of his adoptive status—the most "appropriate to their present experience and worth talking over in a group." This, of course, is the crux of the problem.

What of the 14 couples who did not answer? Since we did not require the returns to be signed, we have no way of knowing who responded and who did not. Perhaps in some instances the questionnaire was not received because of changes of address. For the majority of those who did not respond, however, one or the other, or both, of the following assumptions may apply:

1. The couple was reluctant to indicate a negative response and, therefore, did not reply.
2. The child seems to have become so much a part of the adoptive family that the parents have not wanted to be reminded of the adoptive status.

In either case, it is difficult if not impossible to tell whether the meetings were of value to these couples.

Some of the agency's caseworkers who have not been directly involved in the group meetings have expressed some skepticism about their value. They have not relished the possibility of being exposed to criticism from a group of parents who by and large have resisted their efforts to be of service in individual interviews. The agency has, however, come to the conclusion that it is better to help adoptive parents in a group situation than in a one-to-one relationship. It is, therefore, continuing to carry on group meetings, and at the same time it is seeking ways to improve its service to adoptive parents through a combination of individual and group approaches.

# Section V

## The Child-Caring Institution

T HE SHORTAGE of foster homes and the changing ratio of adoptive applicants to children available for adoption has precipitated a re-evaluation of the institution as a substitute-care resource. The re-assessment has been supported by more recent research regarding the effects on children resulting from institutionalization—research which tends to question the previously accepted axiom that institutionalization is invariably and irrevocably harmful.

Group care is beginning to be accepted as merely another possible way of caring for children, with its own particular advantages and with weaknesses which might be mitigated by proper safeguards. There is a growing appreciation of the fact that children may be successfully cared for in a variety of different ways and that for some children the institution may be a satisfactory alternative.

Child-care institutions, sensitive to the criticism that institutionalization deprives children of affectionate care and adequate stimulation, have responded by providing more frequent, personalized contact between adult caretakers and children and by trying to plan an enriched environment. They have been assisted in this by recently organized programs, such as the foster-grandparent program, which make available a larger number of adults to care for the children.

Although it is clear that the institution can provide individualized contact and adequate stimulation, it has not as yet been able to give the child continuity of care—a person with whom the child forms a close attachment and who remains in contact with the child over a significant period in the child's development. High turnover of staff and the movements of children in and out of institutions make it difficult for the institution to meet this significant need.

Because of the general disrepute of the institution as a substitute-care resource among child-welfare workers only a small percentage of professionally trained workers are employed in child-care institutions. They tend to be concentrated in the residential treatment centers for emotionally disturbed children. Such institutions are a relatively small proportion (8 per cent) of all institutions. The largest single group, 40 per cent of all institutions, is that serving the dependent and neglected child.

In 1967 some 80,000 children were living in institutions because they were dependent and neglected or because they were emotionally disturbed. Specialized institutions for the mentally and physically handicapped and for delinquent children are not generally included in statistics of child-welfare institutions.

The readings selected reflect primarily the particular interest of child-welfare social workers in the residential treatment center and the special problem involved in meeting the developmental needs of the institutionalized child.

438

# 43

⟨[ Acceptance of institutionalization for a child is a difficult decision for parents to make. Frequently the social workers help the parents resolve their ambivalence regarding this step. The following research study is concerned with the variables which differentiate those parents who accept a recommendation for placement of a child in a residential treatment center from those parents who refuse such a recommendation.

## Some Social-Psychological Variables Influencing Parental Acceptance of Residential Treatment for Their Emotionally Disturbed Children*

*Anthony I. Schuham, Rodney M. Coe, and Naomi I. Rae-Grant*

### INTRODUCTION

When a child is sufficiently emotionally disturbed to warrant the recommendation for residential psychiatric treatment, it is apparent that the final decision for or against admission rests largely with the child's parents. Since the child does not act for himself, parental perceptions and attitudes thus become the critical factors in determining the disposition of such cases. The time interval between a recommendation for placement and admission (or its rejection) constitutes the crucial decision making period when parents are grappling with the emotional implications of placement. Denial of the severity of the child's disturbance, criticism of the possible benefits of treatment, and the feeling that acceptance of placement would be an open admission of their own incompetence, are but a few of the common parental attitudes in such situations. Dittmann (1962) has recognized the importance of parental resistance to placement by noting that when a child is placed in an institution, it is usually the last remedy for an overwhelming problem which has confronted the family.

While it is recognized that parental attitudes are not independent of the

* This study was supported by the Children's Research Foundation of St. Louis, Missouri and the Medical Care Research Center, a joint agency of the Social Science Institute of Washington University and the Jewish Hospital of St. Louis, under funds granted by USPHS, Division of Community Health Services (Research Grant CH-00024).

child's condition, the correspondence between these variables may nevertheless be distorted. A factor such as guilt, for example, has been shown by Zuk (1959) to be critical in determining the level of parental acceptance of retarded children. Zuk noted that religious faith resulted in mothers being more accepting of their retarded children because of the apparent absolution of guilt through explicit religious practices. Other studies have sought to demonstrate the significance of variables in similar areas. Wolff (1961), for example, in studying a sample of pre-school children attending a child guidance clinic, stressed the pathology of the children's parents and reported that they showed a significantly high degree of psychiatric disturbance and deprivation in their own childhood. Similarly, Creak and Ini (1960), working with psychotic children, noted that there appeared to be a preponderance of cases in families where the mother was emotionally cold.

Waltuck (1962) has pointed out that the placement process should be understood from the point of view of family dynamics, the need for placement being seen as the symptom of a deeper family emotional illness. Families considering placement were classified by Waltuck into groups described in terms of certain interactional phenomena, e.g., the family in which the child threatened with placement is the family scapegoat, or the family where a symbiotic tie exists between mother and child. While classifications such as Waltuck's seem justified on the grounds of global description, they do not do justice to the more specific variables which might be operative in determining the course of the placement process.

The present study attempted to determine the significance of three social-psychological variables in the placement process by a comparison of a sample of children admitted for residential psychiatric treatment with a control group of children recommended for admission, who were not admitted. It was thought that only by reducing the 'family dynamics' concept to more specific variables could the influence of parental attitudes and behaviour be ascertained.

The three variables selected were: (1) parental attitude toward the child, (2) social relationship of parent to child, and (3) parental guilt feelings over the child's condition. It was hypothesized that parents who had accepted residential treatment would be more likely to have been rejecting in both attitude and social relationship, and to have experienced more intense feelings of guilt, than parents who rejected residential treatment. Of particular interest was the manner in which parental attitudes were translated into overt behaviour in terms of the characteristic social relationship observed.

## METHOD

Two samples of children recommended for residential psychiatric treatment were selected. The first sample, drawn from the closed records of the Ellen Steinberg Division of Child Psychiatry, Jewish Hospital of St. Louis for the years 1958–1962, included cases in which the recommendation had been accepted. The second sample was drawn from the closed records of the Washington University Child Guidance Clinic for the years 1954–1961 and included children for whom the recommendation for residential treatment had not been followed.

The criterion for inclusion in the placement-acceptance sample was admission with the intention of treatment; thus, cases admitted for diagnostic or evaluation purposes only were not included. Since the duration of the evaluation period was usually 30 days, this figure was utilized as a cut-off point below which no case was considered for possible inclusion in the sample. It was occasionally found that parents would accept admission only for the expressed purpose of evaluation but then decide to undertake treatment near the end of the evaluative period. Such cases were included.

The criterion for inclusion in the placement-rejection sample was a recommendation by the clinic to the parents for residential psychiatric treatment and failure to obtain such admission within two years. This was sufficient to allow parents actively seeking placement to achieve admission after possibly being forced to consider several alternative facilities, usually for reasons of limited financial resources, failure of a given treatment center to provide an opening, or a judgement on the part of the treatment center that the child was not suitable for treatment. The limit was computed from the date of the clinic's diagnostic conference with the parents at the time the recommendation was made. Parents rejecting the suggestion for placement at the clinic but referred to another agency for placement planning were included if the time limit had expired. Cases rejecting residential treatment but accepting outpatient treatment were also included.

In addition, several selection criteria were established in both groups to aid in insuring that parental attitudes and behaviour were minimally influenced by extraneous factors. Cases in which referral had been occasioned under duress, e.g., court or judicial referral, were excluded from both samples. Referrals clearly motivated by forces within the family, but not by the parents *per se*, were likewise eliminated. These included several cases where impetus for the original referral was provided by grandparents living within the home. Finally, an effort was made to include only totally intact families, although this criterion was later altered to families in which two parents were present, but not necessarily the natural parents. The distribution of cases for the combined samples for this variable of family intactness was as follows: families where both natural parents had been present from birth of the child (74 per cent), families where there was one natural parent but one foster or adoptive parent (18 per cent), and families where both parents were foster or adoptive (8 per cent). In the families where there was one or more foster or adoptive parent, there had occurred no change in the family constellation less than five years prior to referral.

After preliminary selection, the total samples for the placement-acceptance and placement-rejection groups were 73 and 60 cases respectively. The samples were to be matched on the basis of four variables: (1) diagnostic category, (2) age at referral for residential treatment, (3) sex and (4) socio-economic class. Classification by socio-economic class was based on a multiple index of parental income, education and occupation devised by Warner and associates (1960). In instances of mixed or multiple diagnoses, the primary diagnosis was utilized as the basis of categorization. While the preliminary selection yielded no significant differences on the first three matching variables, socio-economic class did reach significance ($\chi^2 = 8.43$; $df = 3$; $p < 0.05$). The placement-rejection group was weighted heavily in favor of families from the working and lower classes with 57 per cent of that sample so classified. On the other hand, 62 per cent of the placement-acceptance sample were rated as coming from upper and middle class families.

Previous research, e.g., Hollingshead and Redlich (1958), has indicated that certain parental behavioral patterns tend to be highly associated with various levels of socio-economic class. It was therefore apparent that the variable of socio-economic class required control and this was carried out by further eliminating 25 cases from the combined samples, 19 and 6 cases from the placement-acceptance and placement-rejection samples respectively. This matching process was accomplished by eliminating from the placement-acceptance samples cases of upper socio-economic status patients which would not alter the non-significant differences on the other matching variables. Similarly, cases of patients from low socio-economic status in the placement-rejection sample which did not disturb the relationship between the other variables were also eliminated. The resulting distribution of both samples over the matching variables is presented in Table 1. Each sample now totaled 54 cases. It should be noted that discrepancies still appeared (e.g., the proportion of psychotics in the groups was 16.7 per cent vs. 22.2 per cent) but these differences were minor and none reached statistical significance.

The three variables of experimental interest were defined as follows:

(1) *Attitude of parent towards the child.*

This variable was defined along an acceptance–rejection continuum with four levels:

(a) *Complete acceptance*—The parent maximized the child's problem, saw him as incapable of caring for himself and as being in need of constant protection from the environment.

(b) *Qualified acceptance*—The parent minimized the child's problem, tended to tolerate his behavior but did nothing about it. The severity of the disturbance was often denied. The parent may have recognized that the child was different from other chil-

TABLE 1. **Distribution of Matched Cases in Placement-Acceptance and Placement-Rejection Samples on Selected Variables**
(N = 54 in Each Sample)

| | Sample | | | |
| | Placement-Acceptance | | Placement-Rejection | |
| Variable | N | % | N | % |
|---|---|---|---|---|
| (1) *Diagnostic category* | | | | |
| Psychosis | 9 | 16.7 | 12 | 22.2 |
| Neurosis | 16 | 29.6 | 15 | 27.7 |
| Personality disorder | 16 | 29.6 | 14 | 26.0 |
| Brain damage or mental deficiency | 13 | 24.1 | 13 | 24.1 |
| (2) *Age at referral* | | | | |
| 3–5 years (pre-school) | 7 | 12.9 | 7 | 12.9 |
| 6–8 years (primary) | 15 | 27.7 | 13 | 24.1 |
| 9–12 years (pubescent) | 21 | 39.0 | 22 | 40.8 |
| 13 years or older (adolescent) | 11 | 20.4 | 12 | 22.2 |
| (3) *Sex* | | | | |
| Male | 42 | 77.8 | 41 | 75.9 |
| Female | 12 | 22.2 | 13 | 24.1 |
| (4) *Socio-economic class* | | | | |
| Upper | 5 | 9.2 | 4 | 7.4 |
| Middle | 29 | 53.8 | 28 | 52.0 |
| Working | 16 | 29.6 | 15 | 27.7 |
| Lower | 4 | 7.4 | 7 | 12.9 |

dren in some areas and may have attempted to cope with these differences.

(c) *Qualified rejection*—The parent tolerated the child's behavior for the most part but was very pessimistic about the chances for improvement. The parent readily admitted that the child was his responsibility but may have given up trying to cope with him. The parent would not have been disappointed if someone else were to have taken over management of the child.

(d) *Complete rejection*—The parent had not only given up hope, but did not want the child in the home and would have been relieved if someone else were to have taken the child or if he had been institutionalized.

(2) *Social relationship of parent towards the child.*

This variable was defined along an approach–avoidance continuum with the following levels:

(a) *Overprotective*—The parent excessively limited the child's behavior in a non-punitive manner and was overly concerned with his well-being, giving the impression that he was very delicate and had to be protected from a potentially harmful world. The parent was unable to permit the child any freedom or independence and was reluctant to leave him with others. Physical care was often extended beyond an appropriate age.

(b) *Indulgent*—The parent was unable to frustrate the child's demands and usually gave in to his every request. This may have
been expressed by attempting to anticipate the child's every
desire, giving up any attempts to control or manage the child, or
merely complying with the child's every wish.

(c) *Inconsistent*—The parent alternated ways of responding in an
ambivalent manner, or erratically mixed various behavioral patterns so that no systematic approach could be observed, e.g., the
parent may have punished the child for minor misbehavior and
was then immediately indulgent afterwards.

(d) *Aloof*—The parent exhibited only nominal interest in the child
because it was 'expected' of him. There was minimal interaction
between parent and child; warmth and spontaneity were missing.
Physical care tended to be mechanical with no emotional warmth.

(e) *Alienating*—The parent was essentially rejecting in behavior,
made efforts to avoid contact with the child. This category implies the greatest amount of social distance between parent and
child. Since the child may have still attempted approach behavior
even in the face of avoidance by the parent, attempts at dis-
tancing by the parent may have included punitive or restrictive
measures.

(3) *Parental feelings of guilt.*

(a) *None*—The parent did not feel personally at fault, blamed other
persons or forces for the child's condition, or did not see guilt as
being relevant to the situation. Included here were cases where
parents may have projected guilt on to external agents of cause,
e.g., God, faith, etc.

(b) *Moderate*—The parent may have blamed others but felt that if
he had acted differently, the child's condition might have been
avoided. Ambivalence concerning guilt feelings was often evident.

(c) *Marked*—The parent attributed the child's condition solely to
his own inadequacies. The parent may have blamed his own behavior or else uncontrollable situations in which he felt personal
implications, e.g., 'bad genes,' etc.

Data on the above-mentioned variables for both parents were abstracted
from each case record in both samples by four raters using a previously
prepared data collection form. Primary sources were social histories and
pre-admission psychiatric and psychological interviews with the parent and
child. It was recognized that the 'pure case' of parental behavior is so rare
as to be practically nonexistent so that raters focused on what appeared to
be recurrent themes and patterns in the data. Since the data were of the
'judgemental' variety, continuous effort was exerted to insure that the
percentage of agreement among the raters remained high. First as a pre-

test, each of the four judges rated ten cases not in the sample. On the cases in the sample, one rater rated all the cases while the other judges independently rated the same cases on one-third of the total sample. Reliability coefficients ranged from 0.87 to 1.00 with an overall average of 0.95.

## RESULTS

There is a significant trend ($p < 0.05$) for families accepting placement to be characterized by mothers who are less accepting in attitude, while the reverse is true of families who rejected placement. It should be especially noted that the overwhelming majority of mothers in both samples tended toward some form of qualification in attitude. The analysis of data for the father's attitude towards the child did not produce significant results.

At first glance, it appears that the parents' decision to accept placement is associated with the mother's rejecting attitude. Supporting this conclusion is the fact that twice as many mothers in the placement-rejection sample were completely accepting of their children. On the other hand, a

TABLE 2. **Attitude of Mother Towards Child and Parental Acceptance or Rejection of Residential Treatment (N = 108)**

| Maternal Attitude | Placement-Acceptance | Placement-Rejection | Total |
|---|---|---|---|
| Complete acceptance | 9 | 18 | 27 |
| Qualified acceptance | 15 | 20 | 35 |
| Qualified rejection | 22 | 11 | 33 |
| Complete rejection | 8 | 5 | 13 |
| Total | 54 | 54 | 108 |

$\chi^2 = 8.05$, $df = 3$, $p < 0.05$.

further analysis of the data showed that the relationship was not so simple and that other variables were found to be highly associated with maternal attitude. For example, maternal acceptance varied significantly as a function of both the age and sex of the child. Female children were accepted a significantly greater proportion of the time ($\chi^2 = 9.87$; $df = 1$; $p < 0.01$) as were children within the age range of three to five years ($\chi^2 = 8.25$; $df = 3$; $p < 0.05$).

The finding that mothers in both samples tended toward some form of qualification of attitude is open to a number of interpretations. One is that a qualified attitude is equivalent to ambivalence toward the child and/or the need for residential treatment. Ambivalence toward the child, at least in terms of the actual behavior observed, would not be supported by the results presented in Table 3. A significant difference on the variable of social relationship of mother to child is evident between the two groups ($p < 0.05$). It should be noted that whereas mothers tended to qualify their attitudes, they tended to react at the extremes of behavior. Only 12 cases in the combined samples total (11 per cent) were rated as inconsistent, the category which included cases of marked ambivalence.

TABLE 3. Social Relationship of Mother to Child and Parental Acceptance or Rejection of Residential Treatment (N = 108)

| Maternal Social Relationship | Sample | | Total |
| | Placement-Acceptance | Placement-Rejection | |
|---|---|---|---|
| Overprotective | 10 | 17 | 27 |
| Indulgent | 8 | 4 | 12 |
| Inconsistent | 4 | 8 | 12 |
| Aloof | 6 | 11 | 17 |
| Alienating | 26 | 14 | 40 |
| Total | 54 | 54 | 108 |

$\chi^2 = 9.53$, $df = 4$, $p < 0.05$.

The most noteworthy feature of the data presented in Table 3 is thus the manner in which cases in either sample tended to be concentrated at the extremes of the continuum. While the cases were spread somewhat more evenly along the continuum in the placement-rejection sample, almost one-third of them were rated as overprotective. Conversely, almost one-half of those mothers in the placement-acceptance sample were alienating in social relationship. It should be pointed out that data on the father's social relationship to the child again failed to reach significance.

Since information about the manner in which maternal attitudes were associated with social relationships was one of the primary objectives of inquiry, a further evaluation of the apparent disparity between these variables seemed necessary. A measure of consistency between the mother's expressed attitude and observed behavior was derived by plotting attitude against social relationship for each sample separately. It was found that mothers in both samples tended to act in accordance with their basic attitude, but that placement-rejection mothers were significantly more consistent than were mothers in the placement-acceptance sample. Using a technique described by Zelditch (1959), the measure of association for placement-rejection mothers was $\gamma = +0.91$ while for placement-acceptance mothers, $\gamma = +0.60$. More importantly, the consistency was in opposite directions for the different samples, placement-acceptance mothers tending to be rejecting and alienating but placement-rejection mothers being accepting and overprotective.

Table 4 reveals a strong tendency for mothers in both samples to express little or no guilt over the child's condition, although the difference between the groups is significant ($p < 0.05$). Comparison between samples shows that the trend is even more pronounced in the placement-rejection group where 38 mothers (70 per cent) expressed no guilt feelings and only three (6 per cent) displayed marked guilt feelings. Again, analysis of data on the father's feelings of guilt produced no significant results although the trend was in a similar direction.

TABLE 4. Maternal Guilt Feelings and Parental Acceptance or Rejection of Residential Treatment (N = 108)

| Maternal Guilt Feelings | Sample | | Total |
| --- | --- | --- | --- |
| | Placement-Acceptance | Placement-Rejection | |
| None | 26 | 38 | 64 |
| Moderate | 19 | 13 | 32 |
| Marked | 9 | 3 | 12 |
| Total | 54 | 54 | 108 |

$\chi^2 = 6.41$, $df = 2$, $p < 0.05$.

Any discussion of the significance of guilt feelings should take into account the variable of socio-economic class, and it should be borne in mind that although the samples were matched on this basis, the within sample distribution of cases showed a marked middle class bias in both groups (53.8 per cent and 52.0 per cent in placement-acceptance and placement-rejection groups respectively). It is a generally accepted finding that social pressures are much greater in middle class families, and this, coupled with the fact that the children of parents in the present case showed severe enough psychopathology to call for a referral for inpatient treatment, made it surprising that the parents failed to express much guilt.

At least part of the reason for this result can be traced to a lack of sensitivity in the measurement of parental guilt feelings. The evaluation of data was based on the parent's spontaneous verbal report and this report was taken at face value. Thus, cases in which guilt might have been present, but successfully defended against, were usually rated as evidencing no guilt. For example, a parent who constantly and vehemently denied any guilt might actually have been displaying a reaction formation against anxiety caused by unconscious guilt. Since in the ratings of data it was considered unwise to make such psychodynamic inferences, it is highly likely that a number of cases of marked guilt feelings were not classified as such and the intensity of guilt feelings was probably consistently underestimated in this study.

Another factor to be considered was the possibility that the exclusion of the 25 preliminary selection cases had significantly distorted the data on the guilt variable. In order to check this possibility, the omitted cases were again added and a second $\chi^2$ value for the distribution was computed. It was found that although the value of $\chi^2$ was raised ($\chi^2 = 7.14$; $df = 2$; $p < 0.05$), it was not a significant increase, but one to be expected with a concomitant increase in N.

It should finally be noted that while a general underestimation of the intensity of guilt feelings may have occurred, it may be assumed that this underestimation was equally operative for both samples. Thus, while most mothers in both samples expressed little guilt, the result remains that mothers in the placement-rejection group expressed feelings of guilt in significantly fewer cases than did mothers in the placement-acceptance group.

## DISCUSSION

There are a number of classes of variables which probably have significance for parents considering inpatient treatment for their children. Factors relating to the parents themselves, the child, the institution, and the interaction between them, all have an important bearing on the course of the placement process. This study attempted to isolate and determine the significance of three variables pertaining to one of these areas, the relationship of the parent to the child.

On a predictive basis, the results obtained would indicate that the greatest probability of a family accepting placement is associated with an increase in (1) maternal attitudes of rejection, (2) maternal social relationships of alienation, and (3) strong maternal feelings of guilt. The probability of maternal rejection is in turn increased when the child is male and is between the ages of 9 and 12 years. Finally, the probability of acceptance of residential treatment seems to vary directly with the degree of disparity between the mother's expressed attitude towards the child and the actual behavior she exhibits towards him, i.e., the greater the degree of disparity, the more likely the acceptance of residential treatment.

It should be emphasized that we are not necessarily positing a causal relationship here. For example, the significant frequency of alienating social relationships in the placement-acceptance sample implies a maximal amount of social distance between these mothers and their children. The implication for placement might be that if a family is moving towards the acceptance of residential treatment, the existence of such a relationship simply makes it easier for the mother to separate from the child. Similarly, the more rejecting attitude might make it easier for the mother to arrive at an intellectual acceptance of placement.

The role of the guilt variable is more difficult to evaluate. In the simplest sense, guilt might be thought of as being a motivational factor which impels the parent to seek an outlet for his anxiety. If a great deal of guilt is present, then the parent is likely to feel some relief through the knowledge that placement constitutes a positive action, i.e. that they are at least 'doing' something which might alleviate the child's condition. This interpretation might have been more compelling had there been, in the present instance, a higher incidence of cases of marked guilt in the placement-acceptance sample. Although the samples were significantly differentiated by the guilt variable, the differential was caused more by negative than positive evidence, i.e., a great preponderance of no guilt cases in both samples but significantly more in the placement-rejection sample. A possible artifact in the measurement of guilt has already been noted.

While guilt may serve as a motivator for some parents to seek placement, it is also possible that the parent's perception of what constitutes treatment may serve to increase resistance to placement through the expectation that latent guilt feelings will be aroused. For example, the parent may feel that the child will reveal 'family secrets' during the course of psychotherapy, that they may be 'found out,' or that the blame for the child's condition may be placed by the agency on them. In any event, the precise role of parental guilt feelings in the placement process remains obscure and would be a suggestion for future research. Rather than measuring the intensity of guilt feelings only at referral, the more cogent question would be the level of guilt feelings at referral, admission, and discharge. In this way, the therapeutic effects on both the parent and child might be evaluated.

One of the most striking findings of this study was the absence of any significant results on the father's attitude, social relationship, or expression of guilt, while all these variables significantly differentiated the groups of mothers. From one point of view, this might be indicative of the more usual peripheral involvement of fathers than mothers with their children in any family. Various authors have thought of American culture as becoming increasingly matriarchal with the influence of the father only secondary. Parsons (1951), for example, has claimed that in the socialization process, the participation of the father is important, but his participation in the routine care of the child is minimal. The child's security rests largely in his attachment to the mother, and the adult masculine role is generally less implicated with detailed child care than is the feminine role.

Again, the importance of socio-economic class cannot be overlooked and the middle-class bias in the present research should be re-emphasized. Kohn (1963) has reported that in most middle-class families the roles of the mother and father are not sharply differentiated. Middle-class mothers want their husbands to play an essentially supportive rather than a directive role. Kohn further notes that most middle-class fathers agree with their wives and play a role close to that which the wives would have them play.

While the father's specific social relationship to the child may be of secondary importance, this does not imply that he is not a primary agent in the placement process. This may indeed mean, however, that he does not become a significant figure until a point occurring later in time in comparison with the mother. Even then, the nature of his interaction with the mother may be more critical than his relationship with the child.

In terms of placement, the picture would thus be one of the mother-child relationship being the focal point at first, the father entering later, and the focus then shifting from parent-child to parent-parent interactions. The health of the child has traditionally been largely the mother's sphere of influence. Although the mother and father may reach a mutual decision to seek help (the initial referral), the mother is usually the one who accompanies the child to the clinic and is involved in the diagnostic work-up, e.g., giving the social history. Once the question of treatment, and especially placement, has been raised, the father more fully enters the picture. However, his impact is still primarily a matter of communication with the mother. Questions to be discussed may center around the entire issue of placement; if accepted, the method of financing it, etc. Thus, if the 'family dynamics' of the placement process may be conceived of as being a series of communicative links between three persons, the mother, father and child, then the weakest link probably exists between the father and child.

## SUMMARY

The samples of parents whose children were recommended for residential psychiatric treatment, differing only in terms of acceptance of the recommendation, were compared on the basis of parental (1) attitude, (2) social relationship, and (3) guilt feelings toward the child. Every variable significantly differentiated the samples for mothers while none reached significance for fathers. The probability of acceptance of residential treatment is significantly increased under conditions of (1) maternal rejecting attitudes, (2) maternal alienating social relationships, and (3) strong maternal guilt feelings. It appears that rejecting attitudes facilitate the mother's intellectual acceptance of placement, while alienating social relationships enable her to more easily separate physically from the child. Marked guilt feelings may serve as a motivational factor to seek placement. The non-significance of data on the father's relationships was interpreted as reflecting his more usual peripheral role in the family as compared to that of the mother.

*References*

Creak, M., and Ini, S. (1960) Families of psychotic children. *J. Child Psychol. Psychiat.* **1**, 156–175.
Dittmann, L. L. (1962) The family of a child in an institution. *Amer. J. Ment. Def.* **66**, 759–765.
Hollingshead, A. B., and Redlich, F. C. (1958) *Social Class and Mental Illness.* Wiley, New York.
Kohn, M. L. (1963) Social class and parent-child relations: an interpretation. *Amer. J. Sociol.* **68**, 471–480.
Parsons, T. (1951) *The Social System.* Free Press, Glencoe, Ill.

Waltuck, M. (1962) Diagnostic criteria and treatment methods in averting child placement. *J. Jewish Comm. Serv.* **38**, 376–384.

Warner, W. L., Meeker, M., and Ellis, K. (1960) *Social Class in America: An Evaluation of Status.* Harper Torchbooks, New York.

Wolff, S. (1961) Social and family background of pre-school children with behavior disorders attending a child guidance clinic. *J. Child Psychol. Psychiat.* **2**, 260–268.

Zelditch, M. (1959) *A Basic Course in Sociological Statistics.* Henry Holt, New York.

Zuk, G. H. (1959) The religious factor and the role of guilt in the parental acceptance of the retarded child. *Amer. J. Ment. Def.* **64**, 139–147.

# 44

⟨[ In attempting to help the client to change, the treatment institution finds that it must deal with the social systems of the client group within the institution. The following article, based on research in a residential treatment center, attempts to clarify the important elements of the client subculture and to indicate how the staff might deal productively with the client system.

# Changing Delinquent Subcultures: A Social-Psychological Approach

*Howard W. Polsky*

In increasing numbers, psychologists, anthropologists, and sociologists are turning their attention to the interpersonal dynamics of juvenile delinquent groups.[1] One important source for investigation has been the training schools and residential treatment centers.[2] We have come to realize after

---

[1] This sociological tradition in America goes back at least to 1930–1931 with the publication of Clifford R. Shaw's *The Jack Roller* and *The Natural History of a Delinquent* (Chicago: University of Chicago Press, 1930 and 1931). Recent cross-cultural work in this vein can be found in Herbert Bloch and Arthur Niedenhoffer, *The Gang: A Study in Adolescent Behavior* (New York: Philosophical Library, 1958).

[2] See for example Richard D. Trent, *An Exploratory Study of the Inmate Social Organization*, Vol. 5 of Warwick Child Welfare Services Project, 1954–1957, ed. Bettina Warburg (New York: State Board of Social Welfare, 1957). (Mimeographed.)

considerable trial and error that it is no easy matter to intervene effectively in the delinquent subcultures established by aggressive adolescents. This paper is a contribution to an understanding of delinquent social structures and the bearing this has upon group intervention and individual rehabilitation. Our fundamental source is an intensive participant-observation analysis over the period of a year in a cottage containing the oldest, toughest, and most delinquent boys in a residential treatment center.[3]

The sociologist attempts to find the mainsprings for human behavior within the matrix of interpersonal relationships in which the individual functions. He tries to determine the significant people in the delinquent's life and how they are influencing him. To be sure, the press of the environment—the external frame of reference—has as its counterpoint the individual's internal reference structure. We must evaluate the pathology inherent in the psychic structure, lest we overestimate the extent to which group norms influence individuals. This must be carefully assessed in any intervention program. Our primary focus in this paper, however, is to delineate some of the social and cultural forces that shape delinquent group life and individual "careers" within it.

The theory of delinquency as a subculture has left many gaps in the analysis of its organizational character. We know little about how delinquent boys interrelate between antisocial outbreaks. What are the normative interpersonal relationships in a delinquent subculture which periodically spill over in the form of aggression against society?

An organized delinquent peer group is not merely the sum of hostile projections of disturbed boys who are externalizing intrapsychic conflicts. A large variety of diagnostic types can be found to "fit" the alternative roles the delinquent culture assigns its recruits. An important need today is a better understanding of the *system of norms and statuses* which delinquent groups create and the interpersonal soil in which antisocial acts, values, and personalities are nurtured.[4] "Economic" principles appear to operate not only in the individual, but in the group as well; delinquents are able to articulate a highly stylized social and cultural organization to which all its members must contribute and respond—often at great personal risk and deterioration.

Thus far sociologists have tended to concentrate their fire on the accommodation patterns by way of which the leaders and activists in the delinquent gangs gain recognition by adults in the community.[5] But this

---

[3] Howard W. Polsky and Martin Kohn, *Progress Report: Analysis of the Peer Group in a Residential Treatment Center* (Hawthorne, N.Y.: Hawthorne Cedar Knolls School, 1957, mimeographed); "Participant-observation in a Delinquent Subculture," *American Journal of Orthopsychiatry*, Vol. 29, No. 4 (October 1959).

[4] Albert K. Cohen, "The Study of Social Disorganization and Deviant Behavior" in Robert K. Merton, Leonard Broom, and Leonard S. Cottrell, eds., *Sociology Today* (New York: Basic Books, 1959).

[5] For an excellent summary and analysis of new developments in this approach see

is akin to describing American society only by analyzing its international relations. We need more empirical studies of delinquency as a social system, emphasizing the sources of strain and anomie generated by "internal" social and cultural normative processes. As long as this approach is lacking, we shall have a distorted concept of the emergence and maintenance of delinquent groups as viable organizations.

For example, we analyzed a runaway which culminated in the theft of an auto in a town near the institution. Two boys, an introverted isolate and a rebellious scapegoated newcomer, combined forces to escape from *both* their peer group and adult authorities. The significant precipitating cause was the rejection of both boys by the cottage peer group. The sources of stress within the peer group on this microscopic level can be multiplied many times.

In our analysis we shall stress the "internal" systemic aspects of delinquency, which means that our focus will be upon the normative interpersonal relationships and processes within the group, and the values upon which they are based.[6] At a minimum four questions must be posed: (1) What is a delinquent subculture? (2) To what do we want to change it? (3) How can we change it? (4) How can we evaluate culture and individual change?

## THE AGGRESSIVE SOCIETY

Every social system consists of ideal or expected patterns of action and statuses and is stratified so that power, prestige, and income are differentially distributed among its members. The recruitment for positions and their consolidation vary with the character of the group and its stage of crystallization. The criteria which distinguish the superior and inferior strata depend upon the core norms of the group. The rigidity of the delinquent social structure is formed by underlying sanctions of brute force and manipulation which are used by the top clique boys and filter down through the entire social order. The boys in Cottage 6 believed that no other boy had a right to enter their cottage, but if they suspected someone else of taking something from their cottage, they felt they had the unqualified right to ransack other cottages.

Within the cottages, there are several variants of a stratified social struc-

Richard A. Cloward, "Illegitimate Means, Anomie, and Deviant Behavior," *American Sociological Review*, Vol. 24, No. 2 (April 1959).

[6] Our analysis of the social structure of the delinquent group has been observed by others who have described juvenile gangs. See William Poster, "T'was a Dark Night in Brownsville," *Commentary*, Vol. 9, No. 5 (May 1950); Dale Kramer and Madeline Karr, *Teen-age Gangs* (New York: Henry Holt & Co., 1953); Stacy V. Jones, "The Cougars—Life with a Brooklyn Gang," *Harper's Magazine* (November 1954), pp. 35–43; Harrison E. Salisbury, *The Shook-up Generation* (New York: Harper & Brothers, 1958).

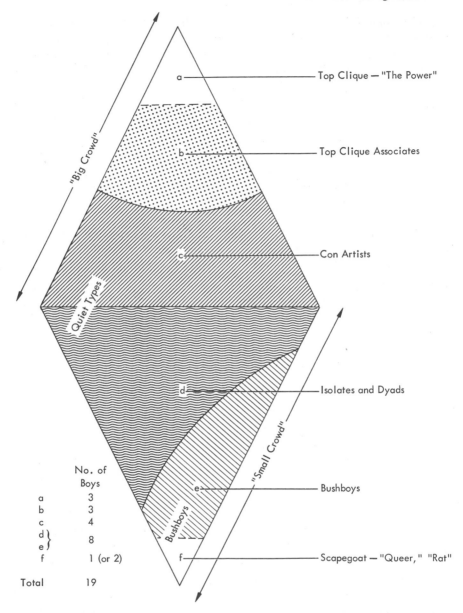

| | No. of Boys |
|---|---|
| a | 3 |
| b | 3 |
| c | 4 |
| d }<br>e } | 8 |
| f | 1 (or 2) |
| Total | 19 |

ture based on toughness, "brains," deviant activities, and status-deflating, rigidly controlling interpersonal processes. In some groups the tough boys —the "power," "big men," or "take"—maintain absolute hegemony and assign the "con-artists" subsidiary positions. In other groups, the gamblers and con-artists unite with the tough leaders and maintain a pressing rule over the "punks" or "bush-boys"—the weak and less able boys. In any case, muscles, brains, and deviant activities are united in one form or another to insure a flow of psychic and material services upward to the boys in the upper half of the status hierarchy. Brute force maintains the rigid pecking order and is exemplified in violence, manipulation, exploitation, "ranking," and scapegoating. These processes occur not only between delinquent groups, but are the essential dynamic of social control *within* the delinquent group.[7]

This paradigm was vividly corroborated by a perceptive cottage leader and has been verified by detailed independent observation:

Q: Well, who ran the cottage when you first came into 7?
A: Hank Shade, Frankie Gorman, Spiffy Weiner. You see, a cottage is never actually run by one guy. One guy has brains, the other guy has muscles, but always four or five, or three guys are the power in the group. They might not be the roughest guys, these three together, but they are the power of the group. What they want to do mostly is what the group does, and a lot of smart guys don't actually want to become the leader, they want to be the guy in back, they want to become the *power* of the group. And then the cottage guys clique up, you know, they fall into certain groups where they hang together and they stay together. And these groups, you know, are your power.
Q: Well, when did you become a power in 7? I know you did. It was one of the reasons they changed you. Right?
A: Well, that's true. But I came about power in a different way than a lot of other kids. I like to gamble and I'm good at it, and through the fact that you can win, well, then you have money. That automatically makes the group have to come to you at one point or another.
Q: That's right.
A: Guys are going AWOL, they got to come to you to get money. So what they try to do is when you get money and they're looking out for themselves, they try to get you to like them. And in order to get you to like them, when you make a suggestion they follow it, because there is no reason to antagonize the hand that's feeding you. So that's how I came into power. Guys owed me money, so guys were afraid to get me mad because they'd have to pay. I had my own strong-arm boys that were willing to collect for me. . . .
Q: Like who?
A: Like Foster, and Simon, like myself. You see, I mean I wasn't . . . the whole point is that I never had to use them. I'd collect my own debts, but yet everybody knew that these guys would help me collect my debts if it ever came to something like that, and it never did.
Q: Well then, were you the three guys who were sort of the top guys up there?
A: Yes.[8]

We have found in several cottages a diamond-shaped social system which persists over time as old leaders leave and middle- and low-status boys rise

---

[7] Delinquent interpersonal processes are discussed in detail in *Cottage 6: A Study of Delinquency as a Social System* (New York: Russell Sage Foundation, 1962).

[8] Howard W. Polsky, *A Treatment Center Alumnus' Own Story* (Hawthorne, N. Y.: Hawthorne Cedar Knolls School, 1958). (Mimeographed.)

in the hierarchy.[9] Delinquent status positions are useful in predicting the boys' interrelationships in the cottage. This is why we view their behavior as a social system. Every stratum combines a cluster of privileges and duties. The translation of each clique's norms into concrete action is the function of the diverse roles in the cottage.

The top clique is the "power"; within it boys of inferior status were ranked and exploited by the tougher boys; the former attempted to take over the cottage when the toughs left. Below the top clique are the "con-artists," who are not afraid to fight, but more typically employed their manipulative abilities and skill at deviant activities to exploit boys further down in the hierarchy. The "quiet types"—or "regular guys"—have abandoned gross delinquent activities, but are not typed "punks"; several are regarded as mentally or socially retarded by the older boys and have a long history of foster home and institutional placement. The bottom stratum consists of "bushboys" or "punks," the targets of the boys above; they carry out the menial tasks in the cottage, are looked upon as "dirt" or "sneaks," not to be trusted, and frequently singled out for violence and ranking. At the very bottom are the scapegoats—the "queers"—who are the focal targets for the entire cottage; some break down under the pressure and run from the institution; others compulsively ingratiate themselves with higher-status boys or accept the minimum duties required at this station and, biding their time and using violence and ranking upon boys arriving after them, eventually climb up the status hierarchy.

Social distance between the cliques within a cottage is quite large. The cliques are ranked and each person recognizes to which one he belongs, and its relationship to others. Clique members share common activities and outlooks. They reinforce each other in opposing "out-cliques" and exert social control throughout the group.

The statuses are unusually "frozen." A new boy coming into the cottage must identify with the lowest stratum. He is put into the "punk bedroom" and undergoes a period of severe manipulation and testing. This includes social ostracism as well as performance of menial duties for older boys. He learns how to take it and if he survives, how to dish it out too. One of the chief ways a boy can change his status is through physically challenging higher-status individuals. This frequently culminates in a fight or "stand-off." The outcomes of these fights are burned into the boys' memories and can drastically change one's status and horizons in the cottage.

The delinquent social system is essentially inequalitarian. Individual boys become alerted, sensitized, and preoccupied with power relationships; it is to each according to his status, from each according to his status. This

---

[9] Howard W. Polsky, *Continuity and Change in a Delinquent Sub-culture* (Hawthorne, N. Y.: Hawthorne Cedar Knolls School, 1959). (Mimeographed.)

colors the most incidental interactions. I have observed unbelievable anxiety in the simplest request for milk on the part of a low-status member who was addressing a high-status boy. It is our feeling that this authoritarian type of social structure organizes and controls the major portion of the boys' lives, inculcates delinquent norms, defends them from facing threatening problems—school, girls, jobs, community disgrace—and blocks involvement in constructive activities.

Among the boys hostility is so pervasive that after a while it becomes the automatic response and is displaced readily upon any available target. The stultifying process works as follows: when violence is used against individuals within the group (and they are always around), it creates an intense need on the part of the perpetrators to rationalize their behavior. Thus they condemn those against whom they commit violence by citing the latter's "queerness," "sneakiness," and "grubbiness." This justifies increased violence and manipulation against them, which in turn reinforces stereotypes. The omnipresence of the strong-weak continuum, the followers' identification with power figures, and the lack of *alternative identifications* exaggerate the importance of toughness. The vigilant alertness for potential "pretenders to the throne" leads to projection of hostility in situations in which it does not actually exist.

The analysis of delinquency as a social system enables us to view the developmental phases of the group. With each turnover in the cottage, especially when the leaders leave, a crisis is precipitated. The boys then subject one another to a period of intensified manipulation and testing until each recognizes where he stands in the total system. Out of this interregnum of testing and manipulation new alliances and out-groups are formed. New members become extremely vulnerable because of their function as targets for the other boys to gain prestige. The punk "invites" his oppressors to harass him. The scapegoat's fears are monitored by his tormentors as they stimulate one another to exclude him from their midst. Thus by examining the total social system we have a better understanding of its hierarchical components. All the group members must learn how to orient themselves to one another.

There is another dimension to cottage social control based upon personality factors. Within each clique there are pecking triangles which are miniature reproductions of the larger social organization. Regardless of the extrinsic characteristics of each clique we believe that there are intrinsic personality factors which predispose individual boys to fulfill specific roles. Psychodynamically, a high-placed punk in Clique I has more in common with a punk in Clique IV than he does with a dominant member of his own clique. What specific personality traits huddle together with each role is now being explored. We want to emphasize that the complementary role sets in each clique that fulfill the requirements of the aggressive society can be understood fully only if we are flexible enough to shift from group to personality variables when the analysis demands it.

Several sociologists have asserted that delinquents pursue "malicious, negativistic, and non-utilitarian" goals.[10] However, this appears to be a cultural bias. If one evaluates their culture according to society's value system, their actions appear nonutilitarian. Looking at the delinquent social system from within, however, our perspective changes. The drastic restrictions for achieving status within a delinquent group lead to exaggerated conformity with the group's norms. If one can gain prestige by showing defiance against adults, this is not a negativistic activity from the point of view of the boy who is attempting to gain recognition within his group. Thus before we conclude that a boy trying to swing from one of the trees is trying to kill himself because he cannot control repressed conflicts, we have to analyze such an act in the context of his strivings in his primary group.

Group participation shapes personality organization; the latter partially determines role incumbency. Peer interpersonal patterns are crucial for the development of the boy's attitudes and philosophy of life, his aspirations for the future, the kinds of activities in which he will excel, and the form and content of relationships he will make with adults. In short, we must challenge the delinquent subculture as well as its individual constituents.

## CONTROL VERSUS CHANGE

Staff members who have to deal with these boys on a day-to-day basis learn to accommodate themselves to the delinquents' system of social control. Counselors will assign a bushboy to a "regular guy's" bedroom and thereby help him avoid extreme forms of ranking and violence. Social workers have been known to prod their charges to fight in order to change their social status. The "pro-academic" youngster is removed from an "anti-academic" cottage. Top delinquent leaders are accorded community-wide prestige; one "tough boy," a dictator who exercised rigid control over the other boys in a cottage, inadvertently was given the top award for the most improvement.[11]

In order to maintain a state of equilibrium the cottage parent "strikes a bargain" with the delinquent leadership. The latter "agrees" not to cause disturbances within the institution outside of the cottage. The price that the staff pays is "restricting" the aggression and hostility to the cottage.

---

[10] Albert Cohen, *Delinquent Boys: The Culture of the Gang* (Glencoe, Ill.: The Free Press, 1955).

[11] We have analyzed the relationship between the cottage culture and the institution in a paper entitled *Why Delinquent Subcultures Persist—The Double Standard "Interaction" Hypothesis* (Hawthorne, N.Y.: Hawthorne Cedar Knolls School, 1959). (Mimeographed.)

The unintended consequence of such compromises is reinforcement of the authoritarian social structure. Our observation of the cottage parents in the senior unit indicates that their background, their isolation from the professional staff, and the dense interaction with twenty disturbed delinquents results in a role adaptation which alienates them from the relevant structures of the treatment institution and its philosophy.

Many of the inequalities institutionalized in the peer group are reminiscent of the boys' typical family situations in which we find the incipient cause for delinquent acting out. Many of these boys are in revolt against highly unstable, controlling, narcissistic mothers and weak, indifferent fathers with whom they are unable to identify. These parents and delinquent gang leaders have served as the chief models for the boys' superegos. The natural inequality between parents and child is further exploited in the peer group so that "the whole relationship is not one of universal goodness but of arbitrary power."[12]

It is important to point out that we not only have to change the stereotyped ideology upon which the boys' social structure is based, but modify their interrelationships as well. The leadership in the delinquent group we analyzed frequently verbalized democratic and laissez-faire principles:

> Observer: Did you stay in the same bedroom with Red Leon and Stein?
> Steve: No, when I first came, I roomed with two other guys. Then I started buddying around with Red Leon and I finally moved into the end room. It was me, Red Leon, and Wolf. Then it was the big room.
> Observer: Then it was the big room? What do you mean by that?
> Steve: Well, what I mean by the big room is that we were about the only guys in the cottage who were considered big around the campus—me, Red Leon, and Wolf. We were considered the biggest on the campus.
> Observer: By biggest, you mean toughest? Because you certainly weren't the tallest or heaviest.
> Steve: Well, all the guys considered us the toughest, me and Leon especially. But we never really looked for trouble. The only time we'd fight was when trouble came to us.

This vocabulary has to be challenged in concrete situations. The toughest boys claim that "they never look for trouble." Yet they are the chief controllers and perpetrators of the delinquent orientation. How does this occur? Steve Davis, the undisputed leader in the group, talked about Ricky Kahn as follows:

> Well, Rick Kahn, when he first came up, he was a bushboy. I got that slang word from the gang. They call a guy a bushboy when he does another guy's clothes for him, or runs errands for him. Another guy tells him to do

---

[12] Eric Homburger Erickson, "Growth and Crises of the Healthy Personality," in Clyde Kluckhohn and Henry A. Murray, eds., *Personality in Nature, Society and Culture* (New York: Alfred A. Knopf, 1956), p. 209.

that and do that, and he runs and does it. That's what we mean by bushboy.
But he used to do a lot of that for me and we got along.

In other words, "getting along" with the top delinquent leader is conforming to his expectations for behaving as a bushboy. In turn, the latter
internalizes the delinquent leader's image and practices the same kind
of exploitation with new boys who enter the cottage after him. Thus the
delinquent cycle is perpetuated.

We have discovered that these very disturbed ("maladaptive") delinquents are able to create a well-organized social structure. Critical
questions in an institutional setting concern not only individual pathologies, but the ways in which they are mutually reinforced in the peer group
and between it and the staff. Therefore we believe that to maximize the
therapeutic influence we must go beyond the concept of accommodation
with the intact delinquent social system and think in terms of penetration
and change.

## WHAT KIND OF CULTURE SHOULD BE PROMOTED?

The foregoing presentation has stressed the concept of group delinquency in terms of authoritarian interpersonal processes, fascistic values,
and deviant activities. We want to change the boys' activities, goals, and
interpersonal relationships. Gambling, liquor parties, and "kangaroo
courts" are gross activities that we agree should be prohibited; what is
less stressed is changing the boys' interrelationships.

Social work is committed to a democratic ideology.[13] We would like to
influence delinquent groups toward democratic rather than authoritarian
relationships. Each individual has a right to participate in the decision-
making process. Might is not right. Activities should fulfill rather than
negate human dignity and integrity. The stress upon *democratic* procedures
is crucial because we know that the boys can become involved in many
nondelinquent activities using authoritarian methods. (This is why spotless
cottages in institutions are suspect.) The boys must be enabled to formu-
late realistic goals and handle frustration constructively. We would emphasize the boys' acceptance of each other even though they may differ
about the criteria of acceptability. High evaluation of other human beings
should be stressed, apart from their social status. Basic social rights should
be so institutionalized that all have an equal chance to gain satisfaction
on bases other than authoritarian. The group worker and other adults
should strive to promote consensus for *democratic procedures* as the
ground rules under which individual interests may be pursued.

---

[13] See among numerous writings Herbert Bisno, *The Philosophy of Social Work*
(Washington, D.C.: Public Affairs Press, 1952); Gisela Konopka, "The Generic and
the Specific in Group Work Practice in the Psychiatric Setting," *Social Work*, Vol. 1,
No. 1 (January 1956), p. 72.

We have found that intragroup (and outgroup) aggression and manipulation alternate with long periods of apathy, boredom, aimlessness, and depression:

> "It's boring around here. We're around all day, then stay up all night shooting the shit, just shooting the shit, and playing with *Oscar.*" The guys chimed in in agreement: "The trouble is, there isn't anything to do around here all day, it gets boring. In the morning we have a couple of details and work . . . imagine on our vacation [recorded during Christmas]. Spend a little time in the gym in the afternoon and then there's nothing to do until we eat and then we come back and look at television, play a little cards . . . and just sit around shooting the shit."

This is the cottage milieu which is structured by the boys' aggressive tendencies. One of the key tasks of the professional worker responsible for the cottage is motivating the boys toward goals which are realistic in terms of individual and group achievement and which are meaningful *to them.*

## THE BASIC INSTITUTIONAL CHANGE

The boys do become aware of positive values and goals in their individual casework interviews. However, the pressure encountered in the daily cottage living situation can be so overwhelming that it counteracts values which are and could be engendered in the social worker's office. The first step necessary for change is to acknowledge the existence of the delinquent subculture with all its ramifying importance for individual and group rehabilitation.

The next step is to fashion an institutional arrangement whereby we can place at the center of the cottage a professional person who works directly with the boys on a cottage level. This residential worker, together with cottage parents, caseworker, and other adults who come in contact with the boys, must begin thinking creatively about supplanting the aggressive vicious cycles in the cottage with positive relationships, activities, values, and goals. No longer satisfied to react merely to the boys' internal delinquency, we propose that they take the initiative to plan a viable cottage program which unites the group's propensities for health and all the available resources in the institution. Only by constant feedback with a professional (or professionally oriented) residential worker responsible for the boys' collective living situation do we create the possibility of continuous and cumulative development rather than having to start all over with every major turnover of boys. This resident worker is a middleman between the boys and the administration. We assume he will be primarily a social group worker, but with experience and background in working with disturbed individuals.

One way of conceptualizing our approach is by visualizing the delinquent culture as being "invaded" by the culture of the group worker. He will be resisted as he tries to maintain his standards. Increased social tension is inevitable. The boys will try to resolve the situation by making the intervener conform to their values. They may be enraged at the threat to the system that has served them. Thus we have to evaluate carefully the investment of the different strata in the cottage violence, ranking, and manipulative patterns. We must know not only each boy's role but his attitude toward it, and carefully assess his actual behavior vis-à-vis members of his own status and above and below it. The crux of the group worker's problem is focused in emphathizing with the boys' gripes, constantly challenging them to resolve their collective problems, and at the same time retaining adult standards. One cannot underestimate the amount of pressure in the form of testing and seduction to which the worker will be exposed.

We view remotivation as confronting the boys with constructive alternatives to achieve satisfactions articulated with meaningful realizable goals. As long as the conduct routines in the peer group remain unchallenged, the boys will continue to elaborate authoritarian roles via delinquent interpersonal processes. If we present the cottage with other expectations, then we introduce the element of choice and "constructive conflict" which can lead to new self-images.[14]

## ASSUMPTIONS UNDERLYING INDIVIDUAL
## AND CULTURE CHANGE

There are two ways of looking at maladjusted adolescents. Above we have emphasized delinquency as a social system. We have to go further. We have to ask ourselves what childhood compulsions force individual boys to behave destructively and reinforce authoritarian group adaptations. We have to pinpoint the specific intrapsychic processes that lead them to fashion this way of life. We believe that an adequate social-psychological formulation must comprehend intrapersonal and interpersonal approaches —with varying degrees of emphasis on each.[15] Thus a boy who is a punk but also a paranoid may need special supports beyond revamping the group's standards and changing his role. Youngsters with severe neurotic pathology benefit substantially from a close relationship with an individual therapist or caseworker. It provides a transference experience on the basis of which neurotic delinquents can acquire insight and new identifications.

The conflicts arising out of changing peer group relationships and be-

---

[14] George H. Grosser, "The Role of Informal Inmate Groups in Change of Values," *Children,* Vol. 5, No. 1 (January–February 1958).

[15] Talcott Parsons, "Psychoanalysis and Social Science," in Franz Alexander and Helen Ross, eds., *Twenty Years of Psychoanalysis* (New York: W. W. Norton & Co., 1953), pp. 186–215.

tween the standards of the boys and the group worker will tend to heighten intrapersonality conflicts. Pressures stemming from interpersonal and intrapsychic stresses increase the possibilities of reactive deviant behavior. For extremely defensive, irrational, emotionally disturbed youngsters the group worker will have to call on his caseworker colleague. An important contribution can be made here by a combined group work and casework attack upon juvenile delinquency in the residential treatment center. Each has a unique contribution to make toward helping the disturbed delinquent; learning about each other's perspective and skills by working together with specific groups and individuals will result, we believe, in more effective treatment.

This leads us to one of the major problems which the group and "island culture" therapists have not as yet posed for themselves. How much real personality change is effected through group participation? Sociologists involved in group treatment claim that delinquents for the most part are normal boys reacting to abnormal situations. Change the culture and individuals will change by assimilating new roles and values. However, the implication here is that *basically* the character structure of these youngsters is sound. Nevertheless, a contradiction remains—when the delinquent boy returns from a physically or psychologically removed therapeutic milieu to a disorganized neighborhood, should he not, according to the theory, after a short period resume his delinquent way of life?

Apparently the sociologists fall into an obsolete "imitation theory" of personality. Psychological processes are oversimplified. The boys are perceived as nuts and bolts which have been pressed into a cultural mold. In order to understand the complex interplay of personality and social and cultural forces, we must incorporate into our thinking dynamic explanations of personality; the impact of the milieu upon the personality must be detailed in light of clinical experience. We shall not be able to do this until we welcome into our interdisciplinary family psychoanalytically oriented practitioners who are trained to diagnose the manifest and latent intrapsychic factors in personality structure. Once this is done we can then seek to explore how the "role expectations of the social system" become the "need dispositions of the personality."[16]

### THE TECHNIQUE OF CHANGING
### DELINQUENT SUBCULTURES

The theory for changing individuals by changing the group's norms and structure can be summarized briefly:[17]

---

16 Talcott Parsons, *The Social System* (Glencoe, Ill.: The Free Press, 1951).
17 Kurt Lewin, *Resolving Social Conflicts* (New York: Harper & Brothers, 1948), chap. entitled "Conduct, Knowledge and the Acceptance of New Values."

1. People are influenced to behave antisocially in much the same manner as they are conditioned to behave in socially conforming ways. The basis for change is that the individual will accept new values, perspectives, and modes of conduct if he will accept a new group as an instrument in which to achieve satisfactions. Boys "out of step" with society strongly feel their peculiarity and alienation from socially conforming peers and adults. By affording them an opportunity to express their hostility in a permissive setting, they learn that they are not as "queer" as they imagine people think them to be.

2. It is also assumed that delinquents have, in addition to a great storehouse of negative and distorted values, positive strengths. They will be manifested only if the boys have a feeling that they are not being attacked.[18] Given an opportunity to make constructive choices, they will do so if they are properly guided. Two prerequisites are freedom to make meaningful decisions (this does not mean the absence of limits) and confidence that adults are there to help them *achieve, individually and collectively*—not only to restrict them.

3. It is indispensable to this approach to have attached to the cottage a professional practitioner who would (a) be able to serve as a socially ideal model in his transactions with the boys and (b) be able to use himself as a link to the administration and community to enable boys to release pent-up emotions by affording them constructive outlets for resolving problems which emerge in the institution and which come out of their group interaction.

4. It is assumed that with continued positive interaction and successes in resolving problems, the group can become a positive instrument which the boys want to utilize in order to achieve further satisfactions and rewards. Prestige is allotted to group members not because of antisocial behavior, but according to the contribution made toward the achievement of collective goals which rise out of the boys' interaction in the group. Prestige is added to a boy's stature as he fashions a role which helps the others achieve recognition and group goals. Conversely, individuals who obstruct the group's goals are pressured to conform. Authority begins to inhere in the consensus of the group, which now has a more positive orbit and is gaining a more constructive self-image.

5. In addition to these social dynamics within the group, its relation to outside groups and individuals is critical. Part of the group worker's job is protecting the boys from delinquent-prone adults. He must help his charges graduate from the group if consistent improvement is demonstrated; a feeling of direction is helpful, and the knowledge that the others

---

[18] Gordon W. Allport, "A Psychological Approach to the Study of Love and Hate," in P. A. Sorokin, ed., *Explorations in Altruistic Love and Behavior* (Boston: Beacon Press, 1950).

have been instrumental in helping him to gain the maturity he needed to strike out on his own.

6. The extremely disturbed youngster in the cottage will need special support at every phase of the group intervention; this can be given only partially by the resident worker in the cottage situation. The one-to-one social worker-client relationship appears to be the ideal setting for the youngster to "explode" or reveal *privatissima* which are disabling him from satisfactory interpersonal relationships. In his special setting the psychiatric caseworker may be able to give the kind of support the extremely disturbed youngster needs in order to survive in the cottage without disrupting the group.

It is important to conceive of the total therapeutic approach to the boys and evaluate its steps in relation to the sum process. The over-all goal is to move the boys to a level of collaboration in which they feel free to (1) raise all kinds of questions—concerning family, sex, peer group, work, school, recreation; (2) become accustomed to having the group, or cliques, including the intervener, discuss these issues constructively; and (3) develop an action program in which they can carry out the decisions they reach as a result of democratic discussion. Only when these criteria are met can the group become a constructive source of authority, new roles develop, and socially acceptable values form the norms of the group's activity.[19]

## ONE STEP BACKWARD—TWO STEPS FORWARD

Dynamically, the attempt to change delinquent subcultures is similar to the process of Western colonialism, which sometimes leads to native movements that rally the most reactionary elements to ward off all change.[20] This is sparked by the invested leadership. Our intentions, materially or spiritually, are not exploitative, but can be so defined by delinquents.

The presentation of new rewards and tasks to the boys is the opening tactic. The first step is to convince the boys that by cooperating they can undertake new activities which they cannot engage in now. If the boys accept new ways of relating on a superficial level as *conditions* to receiving concrete rewards, we may ultimately move toward a point where they will co-operate without such "bribes." If they can be persuaded to conform to new values and conduct on utilitarian terms, we might then explore how these changes can be incorporated permanently into superego structures. We believe that this "superficial" manipulation is an important inter-

---

[19] Lewin, *op. cit.*

[20] A. Irving Hallowell, "Sociopsychological Aspects of Acculturation," in Ralph Linton, ed., *The Science of Man in the World Crisis* (New York: Columbia University Press, 1950).

mediate step for delinquents from actively *opposing* to *internalizing* new norms of conduct.

Psychodynamically, there are important gains for each member if he can overcome his initial resistance. The aggressive leader rests uneasily with his power because of its tenuous foundation; the manipulator constantly seeks opportunities for exploitation, not only because of satisfactions he gains, but because of his own fear of being a sucker; the bushboy must develop a whole strategy of distasteful ingratiating tactics in order to survive. A permissive peer group environment would free these boys to expend their psychic energy in ego-strengthening pursuits rather than in futile efforts to dispel anxiety through delinquency.

We feel that if the group worker "sticks" to the boys during this rough period of mutual adjustment and active opposition, they will come to realize gradually that he is there not to "do them in" or to assume the role of the unconditional giver, but to help them. We need much more experience in learning how to work through "group transferences," with specification of the important group and individual variables in the process.[21]

## MEASURING CULTURE CHANGE

Any evaluative program for gauging change in a group in a natural setting offers tremendous problems for those who are sticklers for reliability and validity. The fact is, we have little systematic knowledge of successful intervention in a delinquent group as an ongoing social system. Although there have been more than seventy years of experimentation with these strategies, little work has been done to date to validate their therapeutic influence. Empirical experiments are sorely lacking in the field.

The measurement of change from a delinquent social structure to a less delinquent one involves focusing upon the boys' interactions, the group norms and roles, and the extent of involvement in nondeviant activities. Each one of these realms of group process can be defined in operational terms. In our studies we have focused primarily on peer group interactional processes as a basic criterion of change.[22] In any culture, norms, activities, and interactions are all interrelated and the researcher can select one or several key variables to evaluate change as a function of intervention.

The process of intervention is dynamic and dialectical; it includes not only stages of peer group development but, concurrently, stages of acceptance of the adult—the purveyor of socially acceptable norms. Once he

---

[21] Harold Esterson, Martin Kohn, and R. Magnus, *Countertransference in a Clinical Group* (Hawthorne, N.Y.: Hawthorne Cedar Knolls School, 1957). (Mimeographed.)

[22] Howard W. Polsky and Martin Kohn, *A Pilot Study of Delinquent Group Processes* (Hawthorne, N. Y.: Hawthorne Cedar Knolls School). Paper read at American Sociological Society Meeting, Seattle, Wash., August 1958. (Mimeographed.)

is accepted, he must be cautious about the issues he can raise with the group. At first he may take up general issues. Only later when the group begins to crystallize and gains a positive identity will it feel secure enough to explore individual or group problems of a more threatening nature. Regression and rebellion may occur at any stage and will have a different meaning each time.

Methodologically, the next steps in research in group treatment can be summarized as follows:

1. Measurement of group processes so that we can objectively state: *Group X has moved so far from a negative hostile aggressive orbit to a positive one.*[23] We have begun to approach this problem in our utilization of Bales's interaction instrument to determine the extent of delinquent processes in one group of extremely aggressive boys.[24]
2. Measurement of individuals' attitudes toward peers, adults, themselves, school, work, and so on.
3. Measurement of the role performances of group members.[25] (This is revealed by Bales's instrument.)
4. Finally we must try to quantify the highly qualitative dynamic clinical diagnoses of psychiatric practitioners; this must be done before and after group treatment, so that we can determine whether members have ·changed fundamentally—internalized nondelinquent outlook and conduct—or are merely superficially adapting to a new behavioral setting.

When these four methodological prerequisites have been fulfilled adequately, we shall be in a much better position to shed some light on the effectiveness of group treatment for fundamental personality reorganization, and *how* new role and value assumptions become part of and change group members' basic character structures.

In the foregoing we have tried to conceptualize delinquency as a peer group authoritarian social system with terrifying internal conflicts as well as anticommunity outbreaks. We have outlined the difficulties of introducing a group worker amidst the boys in their daily lives. We have anticipated the boys' resistances and how best to overcome them by *not controlling* but *changing* their culture. This cannot be done by remote control; our best professionals with maximum support of the institution have to

---

[23] Harold L. Raush, Allen T. Dittman, and Thaddeus J. Taylor, "The Interpersonal Behavior of Children in Residential Treatment," *Journal of Abnormal and Social Psychology*, Vol. 58, No. 1 (January 1959).

[24] Robert F. Bales, *Interaction Process Analysis* (Cambridge, Mass.: Addison-Wesley Press, 1950).

[25] Norman A. Polansky, Robert B. White, and Stuart C. Miller, "Determinants of the Role-image of the Patient in a Psychiatric Hospital," in Milton Greenblatt, Daniel J. Levinson, and Richard H. Williams, ed., *The Patient and the Mental Hospital* (Glencoe, Ill.: The Free Press, 1957).

learn how to create truly therapeutic day-to-day cottage living situations. Speculation is now momentarily suspended and the larger complexities of experimentation begin. In this way theory and practice never cease building upon each other.

# 45

(( Cottage parents and caseworkers comprise two of the principal staff groups in child-care institutions. Consequently, they frequently have to work closely with each other in discharging their responsibilities. The following research reports on some of the actual strains and stresses in the relationships between cottage parents and caseworkers.

# Conflict Between Cottage Parents and Caseworkers

*Irving Piliavin*

It has been frequently observed that the achievement of therapeutic goals by institutional-care programs is greatly dependent upon the degree to which the efforts of personnel within these settings are integrated. The need for integrated effort has been particularly stressed in relation to the work of personnel providing individualized treatment and those responsible for the day-to-day care of people in institutions.[1] Yet, analyses of institutional programs have indicated only a minimum of co-operation and

---

[1] Norman Lourie and Rena Shulman, "The Role of the Residential Staff in Residential Treatment," *American Journal of Orthopsychiatry*, XXII (October, 1952), 801–4. Similar views have been expressed by a number of writers. See, for example, Hershel Alt and Hyman Grossbard, "Professional Issues in the Institutional Treatment of Delinquent Children," *American Journal of Orthopyschiatry*, XIX (April, 1949), 279–94; Maurice Harmon, "The Importance of Staff Teamwork in a Training School," in *Selected Papers in Group Work and Community Organization Presented at the National Conference of Social Work*, 1952, pp. 109–17; Swithun Bowers, "The Social Worker in a Children's Residential Treatment Program," *Social Casework*, XXXVIII (June, 1957), 283–88.

co-ordination among workers providing these services. Specifically, within institutions for delinquent and/or emotionally disturbed children, in which these roles are generally performed by caseworkers and cottage parents respectively, reports reveal that working relationships of these employees are often characterized by resentment, differences of opinion, and lack of mutual respect.[2] Most writers concerned with institutional care agree on the gravity of the cottage-parent–caseworker conflict problem but do not agree in their beliefs about its causes. Perhaps the dominant view is that these disputes stem from cottage parents' resentment of the accurate perception of the professional workers that resident staff members fail to perform in a manner consistent with therapeutic dictates. Writers have attributed this failure in turn to a variety of factors, including cottage parents' lack of allegiance to program aims,[3] their lack of training for therapeutic endeavor with disturbed children, as well as their emotional inadequacies and problems.[4] An alternative formulation, however, sees conflict between cottage parents and caseworkers as a product of competition among these workers for the affection and loyalty of children under care,[5] while a third explanation is that the conflict results from caseworkers' unrealistic expectations of cottage staff.[6]

---

[2] George H. Weber, "Conflicts between Professional and Non-professional Persons in Institutional Delinquency Treatment," *Journal of Criminal Law, Criminology, and Police Science*, XLVIII (June, 1950), 26–43; Eva Burmeister, "Training for Houseparents," *Child Welfare*, XXXVI (January, 1957), 27–31; Robert A. Cohen, "Some Relations between Staff Tensions and the Psychotherapeutic Process," in *The Patient and the Mental Hospital*, ed. Milton Greenblatt, Daniel J. Levinson, and Richard H. Williams (Glencoe, Ill.: Free Press, 1957), pp. 301–8.

[3] This inability to secure allegiance has been accounted for by the failure of institutions to provide cottage staff adequate status, compensation, and promotional opportunities. See, for example, Mayer Zald, "The Correctional Institution for Juvenile Offenders: An Analysis of Organizational Character," *Social Problems*, VII (Summer, 1960), 63.

[4] References to either or both of these possible sources of cottage-parent malfunctioning may be found in Burmeister, "Training for Houseparents," *op. cit.*, pp. 27–31; R. L. Jenkins, M.D., "Treatment in an Institution," *American Journal of Orthopsychiatry*, XI (January, 1941), 85–91; Jerome Goldsmith, "The Communication of Clinical Information in a Residential Treatment Setting," in *Casework Papers, 1955* (New York: Family Service Association of America, 1955), pp. 43–52; Howard Polsky, "Changing Delinquent Subcultures: A Social-Psychological Approach," *Social Work*, IV (October, 1959), 3–15; Ella Reese, "The Professional Child Welfare Worker: Institutional Child Welfare Worker," *Child Welfare*, XXXV (December, 1956), 8–10; Elliot Studt, "Therapeutic Factors in Group Living," *Child Welfare*, XXXV (January, 1956), 1–6; Child Welfare League of America, "Report of the Committee on Standards for Group Care" (undated, mimeographed).

[5] Goldsmith, "The Communication of Clinical Information . . . ," *op. cit.*, p. 48.

[6] These unrealistic expectations, it is asserted, derive from the failure of caseworkers to appreciate the range of tasks and problems faced by cottage parents in performing their roles. See Lloyd Ohlin, "The Reduction of Role Conflict in Institutional Staff," *Children*, V (March–April, 1958), 65–66; Robert Vinter and Morris Janowitz, "Effective Institutions for Juvenile Delinquents: A Research Statement," *Social Service Review*, XXXIII (June, 1959), 118–30.

The above views have served as bases for a wide variety of proposals for mitigating relationship problems that occur between cottage parents and caseworkers. Examples of such remedies include attracting more mature and emotionally secure cottage personnel through provision of higher salaries and promotional opportunities, insuring better resident staff performance by means of training programs and professional supervision, and increasing the flow of communication between professional and non-professional staff members to develop better understanding. While many of these recommendations have been put to use within institutional settings, systematic assessment of their effect has yet to be reported. This is the intent of the present paper. Specifically, the research on which it is based sought to furnish data on three questions: (1) How do the treatment ideologies of cottage parents in institutions employing procedures to reduce cottage-parent–caseworker conflict differ from those of cottage parents in settings not utilizing such procedures? (2) How do cottage parents and caseworkers evaluate one another in these two types of settings? (3) What are the implications of these evaluations for cottage-parent-caseworker relations and programs in these facilities?

### DESCRIPTION OF SETTINGS

Because of limitation of funds, it was necessary to restrict the study to two institutions, one voluntary and one state-supported.[7] The settings were roughly similar in that they were large, cottage-based correctional institutions for boys.[8] However, as suggested by the staffing patterns presented in Table 1, the agencies differed widely in their provision of services.

The model within which Institution A most readily fit was that of a residential treatment center. All clinic personnel were professionally trained social workers, and all had small caseloads. Each cottage, manned by a husband-wife team, housed at most twenty boys. Psychiatric consultation to program staff was liberally provided. Finally, the agency took a number of steps to insure the adequacy of performance of cottage parents and the integration of the efforts of these workers with those of caseworkers. These steps included the following: (1) providing comparatively high remuneration to cottage parents in order to attract better applicants; (2) financing cottage parents' attendance at training institutes given by nearby social work schools;[9] (3) furnishing professional supervision for

---

[7] Hereinafter referred to as "Institution A" and "Institution B."

[8] Although the organization of services for the care of delinquents may differ in some respects from that for non-delinquents, sufficient similarities exist in the two forms of care to suggest that the findings of this study may be relevant to settings serving non-delinquent youth.

[9] About one-third of the cottage parents had attended at least one such institute.

cottage staff;[10] (4) instituting formal, weekly case conferences for clinic and cottage personnel; and (5) narrowing the range of "communication partners" among caseworkers and cottage parents by organizing the cottages into four autonomous units, each with its own complement of clinic and resident staff workers.

The institutional model most resembled by Institution B was that of a so-called custodial institution. Its caseworkers, three of whom had no social work training, had little time to provide direct service. Its cottage parents,[11] although better paid than those at Institution A, had no access to staff-training programs, were supervised only in administrative matters, and had to care for cottage populations half again as large as those at Institution A. Finally, formally arranged contacts between cottage parents and caseworkers were virtually non-existent. They occurred only when some crisis event, such as a runaway, took place.

## STUDY METHOD

The data on which the study was based were obtained in "focused interviews" with cottage parents and clinic workers.[12] Preliminary interviews revealed that many of the resident staff workers were reluctant to be interviewed individually.[13] Consequently, rather than risk high refusal rates, couple members were interviewed together.

TABLE 1. Selected Staffing Characteristics of Institutions A and B

| | INSTITUTION | |
| CHARACTERISTIC | A | B |
| --- | --- | --- |
| Approximate average population | 320 | 500 |
| Clinic program: | | |
|    Total budgeted casework positions | 19 | 7 |
|      Budgeted administrative and supervisor positions | 5 | 1 |
|      Budgeted practitioner positions | 14 | 6 |
|    Mean caseload per practitioner position | 23 | 83 |
|    Mean caseworker-youth contacts per month | 3.3 | 0.8 |
| Cottage program: | | |
|    Total cottages | 16 | 16 |
|    Mean number of children per cottage | 20 | 31.2 |

Job vacancies, the desire to limit respondents to those workers with at least six months' experience in their present agency, and the refusal of

10 Of the four supervisors of cottage parents at this institution, two were graduate social workers, one held a Master's degree in psychology, and the fourth had obtained a bachelor's degree in education.

11 As at Institution A, cottages were under the supervision of married couples.

12 Robert K. Merton and Patricia Kendall, *The Focused Interview* (Glencoe, Ill.: Free Press, 1956).

13 These objections were largely based on workers' resistance to give time to the study, as well as some anxiety about being interviewed without partners.

one couple at Institution A to be interviewed made it necessary to limit the number of respondents to fourteen caseworkers and fourteen cottage couples at Institution A and seven caseworkers and fifteen cottage couples at Institution B.

While no systematic assessment of response reliability was made, replies to several "trap" questions suggested that, with the exception of one Institution A couple, workers' replies were valid. The responses of this couple were omitted from the analysis.

Responses were coded by the writer. Twenty-five percent of the interviews were subsequently recoded by another worker, whose codings were in agreement on 86 per cent of the replies.

## FINDINGS

*Workers' Treatment Ideologies.* All respondents were asked two questions designed to ascertain treatment orientation. The first query was intended to tap their beliefs about the primary purpose of the agency, while the second sought to determine, in a general sense, their opinions about the means necessary to fulfil this purpose. Responses to the first question revealed no differences among workers. All stated that helping boys to become law-abiding was the primary concern of the program.[14] This unanimity did not carry over, however, in relation to workers' conceptions regarding the proper means to achieve this aim. While all caseworkers agreed that meeting individual needs was the appropriate approach for effecting their agency's aims, cottage couples' opinions showed strong agency-related differences. Eleven of the fourteen cottage couples in Institution A and only three of the fifteen couples in Institution B believed that an individualized treatment approach was the preferred pathway to rehabilitation of delinquent boys. The remaining couples in the two agencies believed this goal could be achieved only by training and exercise of discipline. These differences are in accord with the previously cited commentaries on institutional staff relations and make plausible the inference that the efforts put forth at Institution A to improve cottage parents' operations did tend to develop among these workers a treatment ideology congruent with that of professional social workers.

*Mutual Evaluations of Cottage Parents and Caseworkers.* Unexpectedly, however, the degree of similarity among the treatment ideologies of cottage parents and caseworkers apparently had little bearing on the evaluations these workers made of one another. At both Institution A and Institution B these mutual assessments were essentially negative.

Thirteen of the fourteen caseworkers at Institution A found fault with

---

14 While this question may seem superfluous, it was asked because of the possibility that staff members believed other goals, such as punishment or community protection, directed their day-to-day activities.

the operations of their cottage-parent colleagues. Their criticisms covered one or more of the following areas: the cottage parents' emphasis on control, their intrusion into caseworkers' responsibilities by counseling youth, and their failure to carry out treatment plans developed by clinic workers and agreed upon in case conferences. Significantly, 71 per cent of the professional staff members regarded these presumed inadequacies in the performance of cottage parents as the result of psychological or training limitations. Portions of assessments of cottage parents made by two caseworkers suggest the flavor of the dominant professional point of view:

> The cottage parents do what they please and what they need to do out of their own particular personality situations. . . . Further, most of them are not even high-school trained. Supposedly they are equal to us administratively, but everyone knows they are not. And this is why they cannot take direction—because they are so threatened. I think direction should be given to cottage parents, but around here you are constantly barking up an impossible tree.
>
> Sometimes cottage parents recognize what I am trying to explain to them. They see the therapeutic value of it, but they find themselves emotionally blocked from implementing my plan.

The above assessments found some parallel at Institution B, in which five of the seven caseworkers noted specific shortcomings in the cottage parents' operations, and three regarded these shortcomings as the consequences of the individual inadequacies of the cottage parents. Significantly, these complaints were confined to the presumed overemphasis of cottage parents on control. The lack of concern about cottage parents' possible treatment ventures[15] apparently stemmed from the marginal position of the professional workers in the agency's rehabilitation program. One caseworker described the situation as follows:

> The cottage parent gives the boys something they receive from no one else on the grounds. The rest of us deal with the boy cursorily. The cottage parent deals with him directly and knows more about him than anyone else.

The attitude of Institution B cottage parents toward caseworkers was essentially one of indifference. Thirteen couples professed ignorance about caseworkers' activities and expressed, further, the belief that clinic workers had insufficient contact with youth and resident staff to affect the actions of either. But, if the stance of these workers toward clinicians was one of insouciance, that of the Institution A cottage parents was one of anger and resentment. Ten of the thirteen couples interviewed held that caseworkers were either unrealistic in their treatment of youth or in their appraisal of the possibilities of program implementation within cottages.

---

[15] While five Institution B caseworkers stated that counseling inmates was an appropriate cottage-parent function, none of the Institution A caseworkers voiced this belief.

In addition, eight of these ten couples, and one other, voiced resentment about the depreciating appraisal of them by clinic personnel. Also, while cottage parents did not deny that they at times departed from established treatment plans or counseled members of their cottages, their rationale for these actions was at variance with that of the clinicians. First, all the cottage parents stated that maintaining order within their cottages was one of their primary responsibilities and that when implementation of treatment plans interfered with control this implementation had to be postponed. Furthermore, eleven of the thirteen couples believed that counseling or advising the boys was an appropriate cottage-parent function. They defended this practice on the ground that caseworkers were not always available to youngsters who desired help and/or on the assumption that they, and not the caseworkers, were the most important treatment personnel within the institution.[16]

*Consequences of Staff Conflict for Institution Programs.* Although two major lines of inquiry were followed in an attempt to analyze the impact of cottage-parent–caseworker relationships on institutional operation, only one of these, the analysis of informal-communication[17] patterns among cottage and clinic personnel, can be discussed here.

The significance of informal-communication networks among organization personnel has been discussed in numerous studies.[18] Perhaps the major function of such networks lies in the fact that they do not involve either formal outlets or "going through channels." Consequently, they offer workers opportunity to exchange essential information much more quickly than do formal-communication networks.[19] Obviously, the importance of informal networks depends on the tasks assigned to workers. When only one individual is responsible for turning out a product, or when activities of personnel are routine, the need for communication with co-workers becomes minimal. At the opposite pole, however, when workers' actions are highly varied and require collaboration, the use of informal communication becomes essential.[20] It is at this latter pole that correctional settings, mental hospitals, and children's institutions are most

---

[16] Twelve Institution A cottage couples believed resident staff to be more important than clinic workers for purposes of treatment; eleven of the caseworkers held the diametrically opposite view.

[17] The term "informal communication" refers to that communication taking place among workers as a result of voluntarily "getting together."

[18] Herbert A Simon, *Administrative Behavior* (New York: Macmillan Co., 1958), pp. 160–64; Peter M. Blau, *The Dynamics of Bureaucracy* (Chicago: University of Chicago Press, 1955), p. 142; Philip Selznick, *TVA and the Grass Roots* (Berkeley and Los Angeles: University of California Press, 1949), pp. 251–52; Alfred H. Stanton and Morris S. Schwartz, *The Mental Hospital* (New York: Basic Books, 1954), pp. 234–43.

[19] The concern here for the merits of informal-communication channels is not to denigrate those of formal communication, which are necessary in the development and communication of official agency decisions and policy.

[20] Simon, *op. cit.*, p. 156.

appropriately located. To the extent that these settings are concerned with rehabilitation, the activities of staff must be sufficiently flexible to respond to the changing needs presented by inmates. Without the communication links between workers such as are provided by informal-communication networks, staff performance becomes less responsive to the various manifestations of inmate needs, and program achievements are reduced.

Given, then, the importance of informal communication in institutional settings, the findings of this research are striking, for they reveal that such communication was rare between cottage parents and caseworkers at both of the institutions studied. At Institution B, cottage couples, by their own estimates, averaged one informal contact with a casework practitioner every eight weeks, while the average of casework practitioners' estimates of their informal contacts with cottage parents was once in five weeks.[21] At Institution A, these contacts, as reported by resident and clinic personnel, averaged once in six weeks and once in four weeks, respectively.[22]

This mutual isolation was explained by most workers at Institution B on the ground that clinic staff, because of their lack of contact with inmates, could provide little assistance to the efforts of cottage workers. This, however, did not furnish the basis for the estrangement found at Institution A. As shown in Table 2, cottage-parent "isolates" placed the responsibility on the intractability of the caseworkers. The assumed disinterest of the professional workers in cottage programs and their mistrust of cottage parents were seen by most couples as the reasons why case-

TABLE 2. Primary Reason Reported by Staff for Limited Informal Contacts Between Caseworkers and Cottage Parents by Institution*

| | INSTITUTION | | | |
| | A | | B | |
| REPORTED REASONS | Case-workers | Cottage Parents | Case-workers | Cottage Parents |
|---|---|---|---|---|
| Total | 9 | 11 | 5 | 15 |
| Intractability of cottage parents | 4 | | 2 | |
| Pressure of other duties | 5 | 2 | | 2 |
| Intractability of caseworkers | | 8 | | |
| Marginal position of caseworkers | | 1 | 3 | 13 |

* Asked only of non-administrative personnel who reported that informal contacts took place less often than once in two weeks.

---

[21] The contact rates of the two groups are in fairly close agreement since there were approximately twice as many cottage parents as clinicians in the institution.

[22] Since there are approximately as many caseworkers as cottage couples at the private agency, these rates as given by the two groups show considerable disparity. Nevertheless, at best, the informal contact rate was low.

workers did not visit cottages and why they, the resident staff, had little inclination to talk to clinic personnel.

Institution A caseworkers, on the other hand, saw their failure to have more informal contact with cottage personnel as due either to the pressure of other clinic duties or to the intractability of non-professional staff members. It must be noted, furthermore, that four caseworkers who attributed their meager contact with cottage parents to the higher priority of other tasks had also described the resident workers as inadequately prepared for their jobs. The neutrality of the responses of these clinicians may have been more apparent than real.

In any case, at both agencies studied, the co-ordination of clinic and cottage services relied mainly on formal-communication channels. The negative effects of this reliance may have been limited at Institution B, in view of the marginal position of clinic workers in the agency's treatment program.[23] Such was not the case, however, at Institution A. Both clinic and cottage personnel of this agency had frequent contacts with inmates. Presumably, these contacts supplied insights having important implications for treatment. Yet, because of antagonisms and mistrust, communication regarding these insights was so infrequent as to put into question the efficacy of this agency's program.[24]

## DISCUSSION

In brief, then, the major finding of this study is that staff conflict as well as its dysfunctional consequences can endure in treatment-oriented institutional-care settings despite the use of measures generally advocated for its reduction. In the present section, an attempt will be made to identify some reasons for this persistence.

It is possible that, as most caseworkers in this research argued, cottage parents were simply not capable of carrying out their assigned responsibilities. This explanation, however, ignores a potent source of conflict among organizational personnel, namely, specialization itself. Two means by which specialization can lead to interdepartmental conflict are of particular relevance to the findings of this research.

First, because workers with different specializations have responsibilities and problems unique to their respective positions, they typically differ in the degree to which they emphasize various organizational goals and

---

[23] This is not intended to imply that the program of Institution B was adequate. Rather it is to recognize that, whatever the level of adequacy of the program, clinic personnel were not in a position to influence it significantly.

[24] Because of the mistrust between several caseworkers and cottage parents, some of this information was not exchanged even in formal conferences. One clinic worker said: "I just feel that basically they do not have 'it,' the minimum amount necessary to give those kids a healthy living situation. All my fancy explanations usually fall on dead ears. . . . I have to be very guarded in what I discuss, for I am not sure how these cottage parents would use it."

tasks.[25] Second, in seeking to attain their assigned goals, workers are led on occasion to expand the scope of their activities into realms regarded by others as reserved only for them.[26] It is only a brief step from these structurally induced practices to staff conflict itself. Disputes about these concerns are generally controlled in organizations largely through use of such conflict-neutralizing mechanisms as communication, supervision, value infusion, and selective recruitment. However—and this is the crucial point of this discussion—it is likely that these mechanisms are òf limited utility in organizations of the type examined in the present study. This point is dramatically demonstrated by comparing institutional-care settings to commercial organizations.

In commercial enterprises, as a rule, organizational goals are well articulated;[27] the tasks of workers, particularly those of lower-echelon staff, are standardized,[28] and the appropriateness of workers' operations for achievement of organizational goals has been demonstrated.[29] Thus, to the extent that workers share organization goals, their expectations of one another are likely to have considerable congruence. Second, because of relative clarity in the means-goal chain, obstacles to efficient performance resulting from organizational defects, workers' failure to share goals, or interdepartmental disputes can be either controlled or accounted for, thus helping to stabilize workers' activities and expectations.[30]

In institutional-care settings, however, these conditions do not apply. Although service goals may be shared among workers, their implications for performance have not been empirically established or even clearly implied. Moreover, workers' roles have yet to be satisfactorily articulated.[31] Thus, in the absence of a demonstrable link between workers' activities and long-range treatment goals, no criteria are available to determine the

---

[25] Alvin Gouldner, *Patterns of Industrial Bureaucracy* (Glencoe, Ill.: Free Press, 1954), pp. 233–36; Neal Gross, Ward S. Mason, and Alexander W. McEachern, *Explorations in Role Analysis* (New York: John Wiley & Sons, 1958), pp. 183–92; Peter Blau and W. Richard Scott, *Formal Organizations* (San Francisco: Chandler Publishing Co., 1962), pp. 173–74.

[26] Gross, *et al.*, *op. cit.*, pp. 123–26; Marshall E. Dimock, "Expanding Jurisdiction: A Case Study in Bureaucratic Conflict," in *Reader in Bureaucracy*, ed. Robert K. Merton *et al.* (Glencoe, Ill.: Free Press, 1952), pp. 282–91.

[27] Thus, according to Simon, commercial organizations are concerned with obtaining the greatest net money return. "This goal is relatively easily measured and thus can serve as a criterion for assessing the adequacy of workers' operations" (Simon, *op. cit.*, pp. 172–73).

[28] Peter Blau, *Bureaucracy in Modern Society* (New York: Random House, 1956), p. 18.

[29] *Ibid.*, p. 32.

[30] James G. March and Herbert A. Simon, *Organizations* (New York: John Wiley & Sons, 1958), p. 145.

[31] These problems as they exist in social work practice are discussed in Joseph W. Eaton, "A Scientific Basis for Helping," in *Issues in American Social Work*, ed. Alfred J. Kahn (New York: University Press, 1959), pp. 270–92; see also Alt and Grossbard, "Professional Issues in the Institutional Treatment of Delinquent Children," *op. cit.*

validity of either professional or non-professional workers' conceptions of the scope of the cottage worker's treatment role. Similarly, no empirical justification is available for the applicability of the caseworker's treatment norms in a group-living situation, in which not only control problems exist, but in which therapeutic actions are carried out in a group rather than dyadic situation. Finally, the lack of programing involved in the cottage parents' organization roles suggests that, regardless of their appropriateness, treatment-plan prescriptions given to these workers will lack operational clarity. That is, their specific application in concrete situations will not be well defined.

These conditions permit institution workers to have objectives, role conceptions, and operating procedures frequently in conflict with and yet unaffected by one another's expectations. In fact, the possibility cannot be discounted that not only may communication between personnel fail to resolve their disputes, it may serve also to increase the visibility of their discordant views and further amplify their conflict.

The above considerations, in brief, lead to the inference that conflict between caseworkers and cottage parents may be an inescapable feature of residential treatment centers as well as of custodial institutions, as these facilities are currently organized. Assuming this inference to be valid, what steps might be taken to resolve the dilemma that follows? While the current state of organization theory does not permit definitive answers to this query, two possible approaches deserve brief mention.

The first approach involves the relocation of caseworkers from their relatively isolated clinic offices to cottages. This move would increase informal communication opportunities among professional and non-professional staff members, would provide a common exposure to the daily activities of the institution, and presumably would enable professional staff members to develop clearer understanding of the responsibilities and problems faced by cottage workers in carrying out their assigned roles. A second, more radical, innovation calls for the assignment of both cottage-parent and caseworker responsibilities to one professional worker. Such action obviously removes the opportunity for conflict between cottage parents and caseworkers. It also offers increased assurance that cottage staff performance will be based on the needs of those being served.[32]

The above courses of action certainly do not exhaust the possible means by which conflict among institutional personnel can be reduced. Furthermore, the feasibility of these, as well as of alternative approaches, still

---

[32] Advocacy of this dual responsibility of professional staff members can be found in other writings. See, for example, Lloyd Ohlin and William C. Lawrence, "Social Intervention among Clients as a Treatment Problem," *Social Work,* IV (April, 1959), 3–13; and Howard W. Polsky, "Changing Delinquent Subcultures: A Social Psychological Approach," *Social Work,* IV (October, 1959), 3–15.

needs to be assessed. However, to the extent that the findings of this research are applicable to institutions generally, introduction and appraisal of such measures must be regarded as among the major needs of the institutional-care field.

# 46

❪ The following article reports some empirical research on the changes that children manifest as a result of institutionalization in a residential treatment setting.

# Behavior and Its Changes in the Residential Treatment of Children: A Preliminary Report

*Armin Klein, Ellin Kofsky, and William Klein*

This pilot study attempts objective measurement of the interpersonal behavior of children in an integrated psychotherapy-milieu treatment and to assess changes in that behavior. The primary aim was to develop a method to study behavior and the effects of different kinds of therapies. The preliminary findings, however, raised some interesting questions about personality and therapy in themselves.

Behavioral studies to evaluate treatment in inpatient facilities have the advantage that the subject's life space is almost completely available to the researcher. As reviewed (Zax & Klein, 1960), most studies reported in the past have measured only symptoms or highly specific bits of concrete behavior that were thought to be crucial for the pathological picture of the individual. Such studies do have the advantage of being able to measure symptoms reliably.

But, the atomistic descriptions of symptoms omitted the context in which the behavior occurred as well as broader descriptions of the patients' non-symptomatic behavior. The generalizability of findings was limited, because without sampling the contexts in which the behaviors occurred, we cannot be sure whether the same behaviors would occur in the world outside the treatment milieu. Moreover, since most symptomatic descriptions are not interpersonal, we have no way of comparing directly the interpersonal behavior of the patient with the interpersonal behavior of normal individuals.

One important exploratory effort which moved toward a field approach in sampling interpersonal behavior was the work of Raush, Dittman, and Taylor (1959) at the residential treatment project of NIMH. Following the tradition of Barker and Wright (1951), they observed and described samples of behavior in broad and interpersonal terms. Their observations were coded, using the Freedman, Leary, Ossorio, and Coffey system (1951). The coding was based on two polar coordinates: love (affiliate, act friendly)—hate (attack, act unfriendly); and dominate (command, high status action)—submit (defer, low status action). The NIMH research team observed one child at a time in several kinds of settings (e.g., meals, arts and crafts) for as long as they felt they could remember all of whatever interactions occurred and then they dictated a factual report to which the codings were later applied. Their subjects were a group of six impulse-ridden, hyper-aggressive boys. They found that they could describe the distribution of general kinds of behavior and evaluate changes in that distribution. They found that the unmanageable children's most frequent interactions with adults were friendly and compliant. During the course of treatment, the friendly acts increased and the hostile dominant behavior decreased.

Dittman & Goodrich (1961) more recently reported a study comparing the behavior of the above Ss early in treatment with a group of nondisturbed boys of the same age in the same setting. There was considerable similarity between the groups, except in one area: the nondisturbed boys showed more hostile submissive behavior, while the disturbed boys showed more hostile dominant behavior.

The present study is an attempt to improve the basic approach of behavioral sampling and coding and to explore its applicability to a heterogeneous group of disturbed children. An attempt was made to elaborate on the Rausch et al. method by increasing the meaningfulness of the observations and the generalizability of the findings. The present researchers thought that the most meaningful observations might come from the most natural participant observers. The child care workers, or sociotherapists, were part of the children's life rather than being outside observers intruding on the milieu. They collaborated with skilled interviewers who helped clarify their observation and who helped them to make strictly behavioral-descriptive, non-inferential reports.

Interviewing sociotherapists at the end of their shifts was a major change in method. Interviewing allowed a thorough and sensitive sampling of many different interpersonal situations. An interview was developed to inquire into the observed behavior of children in reaction to what the staff of the center considered the significant interpersonal situations throughout each whole day. Only school time and the time between retiring and rising were omitted.

## METHOD

### The Setting and Subjects

The Residential Treatment Center of the Convalescent Hospital for Children is an intensive treatment, training, and research setting for a small group of disturbed children between 5 and 12 years of age. The observations were made on the first six children admitted, all boys between the ages of 10 and 12 years old. The group included one psychotic and one neurotic boy, and four boys with mixed hyperaggressive and psychotic features.

### Research Design

Three series of interviews were carried out, the first series one year after admission, the second and third series five and thirteen months later. At the time of the first interviews, the boys were living in an old urban children's hospital. A week before the second interviews, the boys were moved into new cottage quarters in the suburbs and were joined by 11 other children. At the third and last administration, two boys had been discharged, so that four Ss were the basis for the principal data analyses.

### The Interview

At 3:00 P.M. and 10:00 P.M. a psychologist interviewed the two shifts of sociotherapists who had just finished their workday. They had been with the children since 6:45 A.M. or 1:30 P.M. The sociotherapists were told of the interviewer's interest in only the children's behavior, and they knew nothing of the design and the purpose of the project. The interviews were tape recorded, and the interviewer confined his participation to presenting the series of questions for each child, clarifying the responses, and keeping the reporter to a factual account of the child's behavior. Since the observations came to the tape recording through the eyes of a person rather than photographically, it was important to vary the reporting sociotherapists (the observers) each day. In seven days of interviewing each of six sociotherapists was used two or three times to report about the children on that shift. In other words, the block of data covering seven days for each administration contained a sampling of all observers.

The interview contained the following questions:

1. How did (child) react to people when he was getting up this morning? What did he do? (A.M. shift)
2. During the day there is usually some time when you have to stop someone from doing something he isn't supposed to do. Can you think of a time today? What did _____ do when you tried to, or did, stop him?

3. Can you remember a time when there was a switch from one of these activities: skating or some other sport, TV, or arts and crafts, and you had to call a halt to one and begin another? What did _____ do when you told him it was time to finish what he was doing?
4. What did _____ do when he saw a change in shift of sociotherapists when someone, for instance you, came on or were leaving?
5. What was _____ reaction to a reminder about performing a routine like taking a bath or brushing his teeth or doing his job?
6. Was there a time today when _____ was told he would have to wait a while to do something he wanted to do? How did he react to this?
7. What did _____ do at the table when dinner was being served?
8. Was there a time today when another boy attacked or teased him? What did he do then?
9. Was there a time today when he tried to do something but failed or was having a hard time doing something? What did he do?
10. Did anything unusual happen today?

**Data**

Since each S's behavior was described in 10 situations in each interview over the course of 14 interviews, there were approximately 140 observations for each boy in a given interview series. Two judges listened to the tape recordings of each interview and independently assigned each behavior to one of the 16 categories of the Freedman, et al. coding system which is described in fuller detail in Fig. 1. Some modification of the scheme was made in octant BC. The frequency of some of the behaviors falling into some categories was so low that it was decided to combine

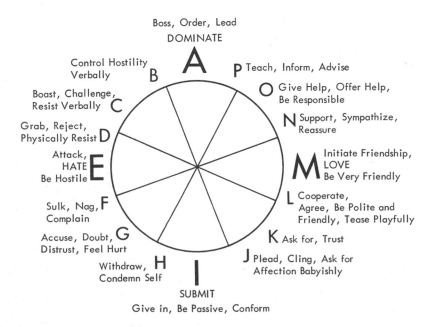

*Figure 1*

data. The 16 categories were grouped, therefore, into 8 pairs, or octants, as suggested by Leary (1957). An inter-judge reliability check was done on a sample of two interviews from each S. On these 120 observations, the judges were in the same octant 90 per cent of the time. At the end of the coding, their judgments were pooled and disagreements were discussed and decided on by consensus.

## RESULTS

The major analysis of results was a three-way analysis of variance consisting of the four boys × three sets of interviews × eight octants of the descriptive scheme. The results are presented in Table 1. Two of the F ratios are particularly important; the pattern of behavior for each child (O × C) is significantly different from other children $(F = 42.82, df = 21/42, p < .01$. There was a shift in behavior (O × T) among the administrations $(F = 10.69, df = 21/42, p < .01)$. Table 2 is a more detailed analysis of the Octant × Time interaction. It appears that the frequency of behavior falling in most of the categories changed significantly over the 13 month period of the study. The most prevalent behaviors were those classified as affectionate-cooperative, and verbal-aggressive. The least frequent were helping and directive behavior. The greatest absolute amount of change occurred in two octants. The passive-aggressive behaviors increased and the verbal-aggressive behaviors decreased.

## DISCUSSION

In comparing these results to the previously mentioned findings of Raush *et al.* we must remember that they used quadrants rather than octants. Nevertheless, the basic distribution they found was similar to that found in this study, i.e., high affectionate-cooperative and low physical-aggressive behavior. It is interesting to note that one of the least frequent behaviors is that which is one of the most frequent referral complaints.

TABLE 1. Analysis of Variance for Repeated Observation of the Frequency of Behaviors of Children Coded in Different Octants

| Source | df | Mean Square | F |
|---|---|---|---|
| Octant | 7 | 1242.078 | 7.40* |
| Time | 2 | 28.197 | 5.71* |
| Child | 3 | 6.817 | ns |
| Octant × Time | 14 | 41.912 | 10.69* |
| Octant × Child | 21 | 167.827 | 48.82* |
| Time × Child | 6 | 4.941 | ns |
| Child × Time × Octant | 42 | 3.914 | ns |

* p < .01.

However, the changes in behavior took a different direction in the present study. Raush *et al.* found a decrease in their hostile-dominant quadrant and an increase in their friendly-compliant quadrant with no changes in their hostile-submissive quadrant. *The present results showed a decrease in the verbal-aggressive octant (hostile-dominant quadrant), with a concomitant increase in the passive-aggressive octant (hostile-submissive quadrant) and no increase in the friendly-affectionate octant (friendly-compliant quadrant). The data suggest that the children in the present study showed not so much a drop in hostility as a change in the way they express these feelings and relate to other people.*

TABLE 2. Changes in Proportions of Behaviors Coded in Octants

| Octant | | 1960 | 1961 |
|---|---|---|---|
| BC: | Controlling Verbal Aggression | 24.0% | 17.0%* |
| DE: | Physical, Active Aggression | 1.6 | 6.2* |
| FG: | Passive Aggression | 6.8 | 12.6* |
| HI: | Withdrawal | 18.6 | 15.5* |
| JK: | Passive Dependent | 8.3 | 8.5 |
| LM: | Affection Cooperation | 32.7 | 31.2 |
| NO: | Support, Help | 6.9 | 3.7* |
| PA: | Direction | 1.1 | 2.3 |

* $p < .01$ based on tests of the mean differneces.

It is of interest to consider this pattern of change in relation to the previously mentioned finding of Dittman and Goodrich. Their matched group of non-disturbed boys showed more hostile-submissive behavior than the hyperaggressive subjects. Dittman and Goodrich also employed quadrants, but the octants within them which are responsible primarily for the quadrant frequencies are those which in the present study were named verbal-aggressive (for hostile-dominant) and passive-aggressive (for hostile-submissive).

An understanding and evaluation of any of these results requires some knowledge of the expectations of the staff, their personal stereotypes of each child and disturbed children in general. Actually this raises complex problems of the interpersonal treatment process, at levels deeper than those of conscious expectation. However, expectations seemed the most pressing question. Were the children learning to live up to staff expectations? Were the adult observers, in their reporting, biased by their own stereotypes of the children?

A survey of attitudes was carried out, after the data of the main study had been collected (but not reported). Five of the sociotherapists participating in the main study and four of the professional staff were asked to estimate on the rating scale shown in Figure 1 the percentage distribution of behaviors of the total group of children at the times of the first and last administrations. The results of the survey are shown in Figure 2.

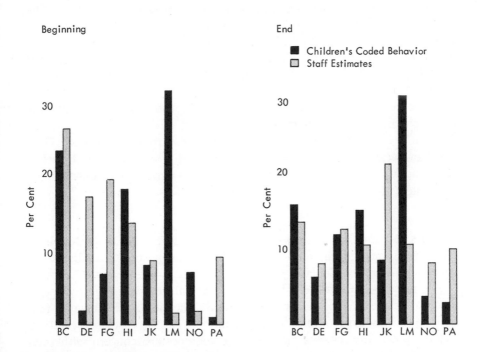

*Figure 2.* Comparison of staff estimates with actual frequencies of children's behavior at beginning and end of study.

The staff group rather uniformly saw the children's behaviors as predominantly aggressive at the beginning of treatment. They saw as most prevalent verbal-aggression, passive-aggression, and physical aggression. They judged that there was very little affectionate-cooperative behavior. The main study (through the eyes of the observing-reporting sociotherapists) had found only verbal-aggression high, and found the highest proportion of behaviors to be affectionate-cooperative.

When it came to expectations or estimations of change, the staff group described a much more nearly even distribution of behaviors. Friendliness was estimated generally to have increased and aggression decreased. They estimated a drop in verbal and physical aggression and passive-aggressive behavior, whereas the main study had found a drop in verbal but a small rise in physical aggression and a marked rise in passive-aggressive behaviors. They estimated a rise in passive-dependent, cooperative, and helpful behaviors. The main study found no change in the first two and a decrease in helpful behaviors.

Summarizing the results: there was a difference between the staff group's perception of the boys' behavior and the more objective description of their behavior derived from the coding of the concrete, descriptive reports. The staff group exaggerated the frequency of aggressive behavior among the boys and minimized the frequency of friendly interactions. The staff's expectation of change and the actual direction of the change were also at variance. The staff's ideas (but not the main study) about the nature of the boys' progress support the outcome of Raush *et al.* that hyperaggressive behavior was supplanted by cooperative behavior in the course of 18 months of observation.

Yet, according to the results of the present observational study, the children remained as frequently aggressive, but dealt with the aggression differently through more passive and more controlled channels. Their behavior became similar to that of Dittman and Goodrich's non-disturbed boys who were as frequently aggressive as the disturbed group but handled their aggression in indirect, controlled ways (passive-aggressive).

### Limitations

The small number of subjects in this pilot study makes the findings only suggestive; indeed, we are comparing findings of one small sample study with another similarly small.

The present study risked a bias of the natural observers who were ego-involved as sociotherapists for the children. The side study suggests that their conscious expectations, at least, did not distort their observation. Yet the possibility remains that the observer-reporters' concern with their adequacy as sociotherapists may have led them to describe the children as being more cooperative than they actually were, since a cooperative child may reflect a skillful sociotherapist. The correspondence with the high cooperative frequency in the NIMH study, however, where non-involved observers were used, does not seem to support this explanation.

### Implications

Why did the staff's estimates of the children's behavior differ so much from the observations of the behavior?

It seems likely that we tend to forget the degree of socialization and adaptation which disturbed children possess, so that we underestimate their ability to cooperate. Secondly, it seems likely that we are particularly sensitive to physical aggression. The physical saliency of a direct attack makes for an impact which increases estimates of its frequency. Finally, the perception of low cooperation might serve to justify a therapeutic social role, and to exaggerate the difference between the "patient" and the "doctor" by stereotyping the "patients." It reminds us of Nunnally's (1961) finding that the general public tends to exaggerate the undesirable qualities of people with emotional problems.

The staff's estimates of the direction of changes may have been wrong because the higher frequency of passive-aggressive behaviors into which the children's behavior moved may be threatening for therapeutic workers to notice.

Although passive-aggressive behaviors are not socially desirable or consciously expected by the staff, it does not necessarily follow that passive-aggressive behaviors are deeply unacceptable. The pragmatic contradiction remains that the people who mistakenly estimated a decrease in these behaviors were the very same people who did the discharging of these children as improved. It may be that although passive-aggressive behaviors are actually and concretely accepted, they are not willingly admitted into conscious concepts of a normal behavioral repertoire.

The discrepancy between the findings of the present study and those of Raush *et al.* regarding the direction of change may be due to the broader range of inter-personal situations sampled in the present study. The distribution of behavior may actually be different under these circumstances. The difference in the nature of the two small samples of subjects may also be quite significant. Not only may the qualitative differences in disturbance be significant. The heterogeneity of disturbances in the present sample versus the homogeneity of the sample of impulse-ridden children would most likely have created different contexts within which treatment took place. Homogeneous and heterogeneous groups would be experienced differently by a child. However, despite population differences, the findings of both studies are quite similar in the early part of treatment.

Differences in the institutions should also be considered. Subjects in the present study were subjected to a change in environment during the course of the study when they moved from an urban hospital to a suburban cottage setting where more children were added to the group.

Finally, the differences in the direction of change may be affected by differences in the kind of treatment.

The present method suggests itself as a productive approach to further research, and may provide more surprises for therapeutic workers. Further research should also be done to explore the influence of *different* expectations on the actual direction of behavioral changes.

The findings of the present study about the direction of behavioral change suggest that the influence of the therapeutic workers is very similar to that of the socializing agents of the general culture.

Finally, the most important hypothesis this pilot study suggests for further research is that what distinguishes the disturbed child may not be the kinds of feelings he has, but the way in which he relates these feelings to other people. Disturbed children would not, then, be characterized as different regarding these basic feelings, but as having difficulty in relating their feelings to other people. A movement, or growth, into passive-aggressive behaviors must, after all, allow, and probably reflects the accomplishment of, closer emotional interchange with other people than the more distance-producing active-aggressive behaviors.

## References

Barker, R. G., & Wright, H. F. *One Boy's Day*. New York: Harper, 1951.

Dittman, A. T., & Goodrich, D. W. A comparison of social behavior in normal and hyperaggressive preadolescent boys. *Child Develpm.*, 1961, **32**, 315–327.

Freedman, M. B., Leary, T. F. Ossorio, A. G., & Coffey, H. S. V. The interpersonal dimension of personality. *J. Pers.*, 1951, **20**, 143–161.

Leary, T. F. *Interpersonal Diagnosis of Personality*. New York: Ronald Press, 1957.

Nunnally, J. C. *Popular Conceptions of Mental Health*. New York: Holt, 1961.

Raush, H. L., Dittman, A. T., & Taylor, T. J. The interpersonal behavior of children in residential treatment. *J. abnorm. soc. Psychol.*, 1959, **58**, 9–26.

Zax, M. & Klein, A. Measurement of personality and behavior changes following psychotherapy. *Psychol. Bull.* 1960, **57**, 435–448.

# 47

⟨[ The controversy around the adverse effects of institutionalization was settled for a time with Bowlby's comprehensive survey of research regarding maternal deprivation as reported in his study published by the United Nations —*Maternal Care and Mental Health* (World Health Organization, Geneva, 1951). The verdict against the child-caring institution seemed to be a conclusively negative one. Yet ten years later the United Nations–World Health Organization published a series of papers (*Deprivation of Maternal Care—A Reassessment of Its Effects*, W.H.O. Geneva, 1962) which indicated that the problem was far from settled. Lawrence Casler's monograph *Maternal Deprivation: A Critical Review of the Literature* (Society for Research in Child Development, Monograph, Vol. 26, No. 2, 1961) was one of a number of additional reviews which reopened the question of the adverse effect of the child-caring institution. The following article is one example of the continuing controversy. It reports an interesting follow-up study of young adults who had experienced institutionalization as children.

# The Young Adult Adjustment of Twenty Wartime Residential Nursery Children*

*Henry S. Maas*

This is a report, necessarily condensed, of a study* of 20 young adults who, as pre-school children in London during World War II, were placed for their physical safety by their parents in British wartime residential nurseries for at least one year. The purpose of the study was to clarify some questions about a working assumption in child welfare practice—that the preschool child who is separated from his parents and placed in any group care residence suffers irreversible psychosocial damage.

The literature on the problem of "maternal deprivation" and, more spe-

* This study was done with the help of a small grant from the Institute of Social Sciences, University of California, Berkeley. During the data-gathering phase, 1960–61, the writer was studying on a Special Research Fellowship from the National Institute of Mental Health, U.S. Public Health Service, as a Visiting Member, The London School of Economics and Political Science, University of London. His indebtedness to his sponsor, Professor R. M. Titmuss, and the many others in England who helped to make this study possible obviously cannot find adequate expression in this note.

cifically, on the separation of the young child from his natural family has grown to almost overwhelming proportions since the 1930's.[1] A systematic review of this literature is obviously impossible here. Regarding the substantive complexities of the separation problem, Mary D. Ainsworth and John Bowlby wrote, in one of the latter's most cogent if least accessible contributions:

> . . . it has become increasingly clear that 'separation' is not a simple aetiological factor, and that the term refers to a wide range of events and an intricate complex of associated conditions, which in different constellations may have different effects on the course of development.[2]

Probably the clearest expression of child welfare's present working assumptions regarding separation and group care and their effects on the child is the review of research John Bowlby wrote for the World Health Organization over a decade ago.[3] While subsequent studies, including Bowlby's own investigations, have somewhat modified formulations found in the WHO publication, in essence the ideas of this report still echo through the halls of practice. It is here that we read:

> ". . . the infant and young child should experience a warm, intimate, and continuous relationship with his mother (or permanent mother-substitute). . . ." If not, we may expect to find "anxiety, excessive need for love, powerful feelings of revenge, and, arising from these last, guilt and depression." "In the second and third years of life, the emotional response to separation is . . . just as severe . . ."; ". . . vulnerability between three and five is still serious, though much less so than earlier." "Deprivation after the age of three or four . . . still results, however, in excessive desires for affection and excessive impulses for revenge, which cause acute internal conflict and unhappiness and very unfavorable social attitudes." ". . . sceptics may question whether the retardation is permanent and whether the symptoms of illness may not easily be overcome." "The long-term after-effects . . . can sometimes be calamitous . . .," with such results as "superficial relationships; no real feeling . . .; deceit and evasion, often pointless; stealing; lack of concentration at school." To the professional world of child care workers, the prescription is unequivocal: "To sum up, then, it may be said that group residential care is always to be avoided for those under about 6 years, that it is suitable for short-stay children between 6 and 12, and for both short-stay and some long-stay adolescents. It is also indispensable for many maladjusted children. . . ."[4]

---

[1] During 1961, two critical reviews of this extensive literature were published: Leon Yarrow, "Maternal Deprivation: Toward an Empirical and Conceptual Reevaluation," *Psychological Bulletin*, LVIII (1961), 459–490; reprinted in *Maternal Deprivation* (New York: CWLA, 1962), pp. 3–41; and Lawrence Casler, "Maternal Deprivation: A Critical Review of the Literature," *Monograph of the Society of Research in Child Development*, XXVI, No. 2 (1961), 1–64.

[2] Mary D. Ainsworth and John Bowlby, "Research Strategy in the Study of Mother-Child Separation," *Courrier*, IV (1954), 105.

[3] John Bowlby, *Maternal Care and Mental Health* (Geneva: World Health Organization, 1951).

[4] *Ibid.*, pp. 11, 12, 23, 26, 57, 15, 25, 31, 137.

Bowlby drew these conclusions from a review of his own research and that of Goldfarb, Spitz, and others. Effects were seen as permanent, though Bowlby noted in passing that ". . . the studies of Theis and of Beres & Obers show that many such children achieve a tolerable degree of social adaptation when adult."[5]

Also warranting observation are certain problems in study design. In regard to such problems, a recent Social Science Research Council report states:

> Two animals—or children—exposed to the same stimulus probably will not respond in the same way because the sum of their experiences previous to the stimulus differ, as do experiences intervening between the observed stimulus and measurement of the desired response. This old dilemma in research is particularly troublesome in studies of the effects of deprivation, for the behavioral changes of greatest interest are those that are shown to be stable over time, and the greater the lapse of time, the greater the opportunity for different intervening experience. Mason [William A. Mason, conference participant] suggested that much parametric investigation is needed, on different ages at which separation occurs, the duration of the deprivation, and the reversibility of the apparent disorders developed.[6]

In the designs of the studies reviewed, some problems are common. First, while the question for investigation was the effects of separation, there was usually no control over the children's preseparation experiences. The children coming out of disintegrated family situations that necessitated their placement might have been damaged before they were separated from their parents. Could not one study children who were separated from intact families, free from gross pathology, so that preseparation experiences might be assumed to be noncontributory to whatever subsequent damage was found?

Second, the children studied had often been placed in what we would now agree were "bad" institutions, understaffed or staffed by persons influenced by the child care standards of their day and, consequently, more concerned with physical hygiene than with human feelings and responsiveness to the children. For others, as in the case of Bowlby's 60 former tuberculosis sanitorium children, the institutional experience involved much more than separation and residential group care, for these youngsters, under four years old, were "confined to cots for rest much of the time" and given gastric lavages, etc.[7] (Clearly, studies of ill children using medical facilities are not studies of simply childhood separation and group care.) But might not one control for institutional effect by study-

---

[5] *Ibid.*, p. 39.

[6] Francis H. Palmer, "Critical Periods of Development: Report on a Conference," *Items*, XV, No. 2 (1961), 16.

[7] John Bowlby, Mary Ainsworth, Mary Boston, and Dina Rosenbluth, "The Effects of Mother-Child Separation: A Follow-up Study," *The British Journal of Medical Psychology*, XXIX, parts 3 and 4 (1956), 213, 215.

ing children from different *kinds* of parent-substitute institutions, run according to different specifiable principles of child care, and compare the results?[8]

Third, children studied in followup investigations were sometimes selected from the caseloads of clinics and social agencies. For example, the 38 persons between the ages of 16 and 26 studied by Beres and Obers were "all taken from the Youth Service Department," set up for young people who, after early years in an infant home, later years in foster care, and then perhaps a cottage school, required "additional care." Obers and Beres note the "factor of selectivity" in their study and that "the degree of pathology in our series of cases is greater than might have been found if all cases . . . had been followed. . . . [but] it would have been altogether impossible to trace these."[9] Perhaps one could do just this—trace children in the community after they had left institutional care. Though they might well be found to be clients of mental health or welfare agencies, at least they would not have been located through a source that, by their presence in an active caseload, marks them as troubled people or people in trouble.

Fourth, the study of persons whose placements were in many different living groups encompasses the effects of considerably more than merely separation and early group residential care. A multitude of changes in living groups for children has been found to be associated with confusion about identity.[10] In trying to assess damage incurred by separation and group residential care alone, one should plan to study persons who have undergone just that—separation and placement in a single children's center. And, as a corollary criterion, early separation should not be equated with permanent severance from own parents. One should thus focus the study on children who have lived in a single group residence and who subsequently returned during childhood to their own families.

Fifth, it seems clear that the child's age at placement is a significant variable in separation research since the meaning of the experience to the child theoretically depends upon his stage of development at its inception. It is obviously possible to select persons age-grouped by separation age for comparison of the effects.

Finally, most of the research has been on the short-term effects on chil-

---

[8] Heinicke's comparative study of six residential nursery children and seven day nursery children is of this order. Christoph M. Heinicke, "Some Effects of Separating Two-Year-Old Children from Their Parents: A Comparative Study," *Human Relations*, IX, No. 2 (1956), 106–176.

[9] David Beres and Samuel J. Obers, "The Effects of Extreme Deprivation in Infancy on Psychic Structure in Adolescence: A Study in Ego Development," *The Psychoanalytic Study of the Child* (New York: International Universities Press, 1950), V, 214–215.

[10] See Factor II-a, p. 128, and Factor III-b, p. 134, in David Fanshel and Henry S. Maas, "Factorial Dimensions of the Characteristics of Children in Placement and Their Families," *Child Development*, XXXIII, No. 1 (1962); reprinted by CWLA, 1962.

dren. Irreversibility of damage is assumed, although there are a few conflicting reports concerning long-term effects on adults. Using a battery of interviews and tests, and drawing other observations from home visits and agency records, one could examine the present adjustment of criteria-meeting young adults. The separation literature indicates what to assess—certain aspects of their feeling life, inner controls, relationship patterns, role performance, and intellectual functioning—if theory on irreversibility of damage is to be tested.

## BRITISH WARTIME RESIDENTIAL NURSERIES

Some of the problems cited seemed manageable if one chose to study young adults who had been separated from intact families, apparently free of gross pathology, and returned to their families during their childhood years after a stay of at least one year in a British wartime residential nursery. (The civilian evacuation scheme in wartime Britain involved about 400 residential nurseries before the war's end.) Richard Titmuss and colleagues have described the problems in launching and operating this program.[11] A reading of their publications and others on the evacuation of British children suggested to me that, in 1960 or 1961, one might study young adults who, as preschool children, had been separated from their parents, not because of the disintegration of their families, but as part of a large-scale movement to send children to places that were, hopefully, remote from enemy bomb targets.

The Ministry of Health assumed from the start that ". . . separation might involve greater risks than did air-raids."[12] Psychiatric clinicians at a 1941 Tavistock Clinic meeting predicted:

> There is in this situation a very real danger that the seeds of neurosis will be sown in an increasing number of children, and apart from the immediate distress and disability arising from this, there is the wider question of what these children will go through as adolescents and adults.[13]

But parents in London streets in 1939 were reading large black- and red-lettered London County Council posters announcing registration and meeting places for the evacuation of children. When war broke out in September, 1939, there were plans for children's flight. Earlier than this, there had been a brief trial-run evacuation of school children, including some from day nurseries. Of the wartime scheme for children, Susan

---

[11] R. M. Titmuss, *Problems of Social Policy* (London: His Majesty's Stationery Office and Longmans, Green and Co., 1950); also S. M. Ferguson and H. Fitzgerald, *Studies in the Social Services* (London: Her Majesty's Stationery Office and Longmans, Green and Co., 1954).
[12] S. M. Ferguson and H. Fitzgerald, *op. cit.*, p. 234.
[13] "War Strain in Evacuated Children," *British Medical Journal*, Issue No. 4177 (January 25, 1941), p. 129.

Isaacs remarked in the *Cambridge Evacuation Survey:* "The parents who parted from their children, far from having failed them, were acting from a sense of duty, often at great sacrifice."[14] Here, then, was a "natural experiment" to study separation without the necessity of prior intrafamily trauma.

*Young Children in Wartime* and *Infants without Families,* by Anna Freud and Dorothy Burlingham,[15] made clear that within the British wartime residential nursery program there was at least one child care center that differed radically from the literature's model of the understaffed and impersonal institution of prior separation research, and finally, advance correspondence assured me that some, if not many, of the former residents of at least two quite different wartime nurseries might be found in London in 1960 and 1961. But not until my early field work in London was completed could I be sure of what was feasible.

In fact, three quite different wartime residential nurseries provided alumni for the group of 20 adults in this study. The three nurseries will be called Nursery N, Nursery E, and Nursery S. To characterize and compare them, three dimensions will be used. (It must be remembered, however, that nurseries, like the children in them, change over time, and only a capsule presentation can be made here. Fuller documentation of the bases for my inferences, drawn from both contemporaneous reports and interviews with staff, will appear in a fuller report on this study.) The three dimensions are: (1) numbers of children and staff; (2) children's relationships with their parents; and (3) staff orientation to the children.

In brief, Nursery N is the middle-sized one in terms of numbers of children, with the most generous supply of staff members to children. Each staff person had at least one child assigned to her. A common pattern among the three- to five-year-olds was the assignment of living groups of about five children to one staff helper. Parents could visit at any time

---

[14] Susan Isaacs, ed., *Cambridge Evacuation Survey: A Wartime Study in Social Welfare and Education* (London: Methuen & Co., 1941), p. 14.

[15] Anna Freud and Dorothy Burlingham, *Young Children in Wartime* (London: George Allen & Unwin, 1942), and *Infants without Families* (New York: International Universities Press, 1944).
  Note, additionally, that in the mimeographed "after-care" newsletter from the Hampstead Nurseries, circulated through Foster Parents' Plan for War Children, Inc., New York, one finds the following observation as reported "by Mrs. Hansi Kennedy, a former worker in the Hampstead Nurseries." "Bridget came to the Nursery in 1941, when she was 9 months old, and returned home shortly before her 5th birthday. . . . She . . . suffered acutely by Nursery life and the separation from her mother. . . . In Bridget's case, the absence of normal family-life in the first 5 years has so far shown no unfavorable after-effects; she has settled down well in her home surroundings and developed normally during the 6 years since her return home. It is however important to see whether this progress will be maintained during pre-adolescence and adolescence." *Hampstead Nurseries After-Care Ninth Half-Yearly Report, April, 1951* (New York: Foster Parents Plan for War Children, 1951), pp. 1 and 6.

and there were "strong contacts with parents."[16] In a time of gasoline shortage, the fact that Nursery N was physically closer to London than either of the other two nurseries is important. With the older children in Nursery N, "we talked about parents, wrote to them. We had pictures of parents. Sunday nights were always exciting. There was a bus every Sunday. Some were very sad when Mummy had gone. Perhaps we can write a letter. We didn't put any child to bed who was upset. We took them in our rooms and talked to them. They could talk about it." This was a key to the Nursery N approach to children—the expression of feelings was encouraged, guided by a depth of psychological understanding of young children that was not present in either of the other two nurseries.

The second nursery, E, was the smallest, able to accommodate only about 20 children. Its staff consisted of a professionally untrained woman, Mrs. E, and her physiotherapist daughter, Miss E, with occasional part-time domestic help from the nearby Welsh village. Thus, the ratio of staff to children was about ten to one. Deep in the Welsh countryside, Nursery E was the most inaccessible to the London parents whose children were routed to Mrs. E and her daughter through an East End settlement house. Interviews and the log book of Nursery E indicate that parents' visits were most infrequent. The alien nature of the East End culture to Mrs. E's stern Welsh world and her approach to the children are best suggested by her own words: "Those were very interesting days and I personally loved every one of them! Bedwetter, sleep walkers, lively heads, and sores. We got the better of the lot, and P was our only failure, and a doctor at the London hospital said he was incurable [as a bedwetter], poor lad. They were all fairly undisciplined—but very soon 'fell in' and we really were a very happy family—no friction anywhere." Nursery E was in marked contrast to the psychologically oriented Nursery N.

The third of the nurseries, S, was eventually the largest and had the highest ratio of children to staff. Nursery S had been a model day nursery school for the children of working mothers. Those who had been attending the school were evacuated as a unit like other school classes—starting out with 47 children who knew one another, their head teacher, and her three helpers. There was "no domestic help at first." Parents visited Nursery S at Christmas or Easter time, in a bus they arranged for themselves, and a festive spread was miraculously provided by Lady X, in whose home Nursery S was billeted. Many anecdotes suggest the teachers' possessiveness regarding the children in their charge during their country's time of crisis. The teachers were trained nursery school educators, not psychologists, as the head teacher remarked, "with their psychological

---

[16] All direct quotations regarding the nurseries are from interviews with the persons in charge.

jargon, their observations, and their graphs." These teachers told their children that they had left London because the King had wanted them to. Children's songs and games, spiritual values, God and country, and the wonders of nature were central themes. The time that the busload of parents was getting ready to leave and the geese were let loose to distract the children was described with delight. In Nursery S, I was told, weeping at parting occurred among the parents, but not among the children. (The statement, not the fact, is important.)

In brief contrast, then, substitute parenting at Nursery N was open and expressive; at Nursery E somewhat firm, if not stern, and suppressive; and at Nursery S, with its faith in God, King, and denial, rather inspirational and repressive, and quite possessive.

## THE YOUNG ADULTS FOR STUDY

In addition to comparisons by type of residential nurseries, the plan for this study was to compare young adults grouped by age at separation. I wanted 20 persons, five from each of four different age-at-separation groups: the Ones, separated in the first year of life; the Twos, separated at about 2 to 2½; the Threes, separated at about 3 to 3½, and the Four-pluses, separated between 4 and 5. For obvious reasons, I wanted each age group to be composed of representatives of all three nurseries and, thus, each nursery group to span the age groups. Finally, relatively equal numbers of men and women seemed desirable.

### Where the Subjects Were Found

Procedures for selecting the young adults for study were quite different for the three nurseries. For 23 young adults who had been residents for at least one year, Nursery N provided a roster of names and addresses, together with age at placement. The addresses were derived from their own 1958 letter survey of former residents. Six of the 23 were eliminated as ineligible because they were illegitimate children, over age (well past fifth birthday) at placement, or from gross-pathology family situations, involving death or institutionalization of parent. Of the 17 letters I mailed, six were returned "not known at this address," six did not reply, and five replied agreeing to see me, but one was a British soldier stationed in Germany. The final group of seven Nursery N young adults in the study comprised four of the responders (one of the four being a young woman whose sister had written for her as well as for herself) and three of the six nonresponders. Because the ages at separation of these three fitted my design needs, I chose to make repeated home visits until I found them in. (The unchosen three of the six nonresponders were a sibship of three sisters, and I already had three pairs of sibs in the study.)

Nursery E gave me a roster of 20 names and the ages at placement of all children who had spent a year or more in Wales. There were London (East End) addresses, as of World War II, for 15 of them, and for five there were only names. Using the Register of Electors (dated 10 October 1959) for the Metropolitan Borough of Bethnal Green, I found two of these families still at the same address. One of them proved to be a major source of leads—which new housing estates others had moved into, whose brother ran which pub, who had boxed recently at a settlement house that would know his address. By sole-wearing footwork, I discovered the addresses of nine persons on the list. Had I needed them, I probably could have located all but three of the others. Two of these, however, would have been eliminated from the study. The seven I approached, selected first according to my design needs for age at separation and second for a relatively balanced sex distribution, all agreed to participate in the study; no one I visited refused.

Nursery S, the former day nursery school located in a stable working-class neighborhood, had had as its head teacher a woman who lived where she taught and who was still in casual contact with the parents of some of her former charges. Having obtained their addresses from their parents because she herself was eager to see them grown-up, she invited eight of them, with their spouses, to a party at her house to meet me. Four came, and the other four telephoned or wrote apologies. Three of those who attended the party and two who did not constitute the Nursery S study group. The twentieth young adult had been a resident of a nursery, called Nursery O, directed by a woman now affiliated with the psychotherapeutic group that ran Nursery N. Since no other adults who had been separated and placed during their first year of life were available to me from Nurseries E and S, and I already had three in this age group from Nursery N, I included him.

### Description of the Young Adults

Since the findings of our study concern the adjustment of these 20 young adults, some data on their backgrounds should be reported. Of the eight women and twelve men, aged 19 to 26 years, just half were 21 years old or less when they were studied in 1960–61 (Table 1). They grew up primarily in working-class families, nine of them in London's East End. About a third were in families headed by unskilled workers—e.g., a stoker, a dustman (garbage collector)—another third were the children of bus or lorry drivers or tailors, and the final third were in families another notch or two up the occupational ladder—a grocer who owned his shop, a clerk-salesman, a teacher.

There were three pairs of siblings—two sisters, two brothers, and a brother and a sister. My tabulation of numbers of siblings in their families and the ordinal position of the persons studied indicates a range from two only children to the third of nine children. The 20 occupy 13 differ-

TABLE 1. The Twenty Cases, by Separation Age and Residential
Nursery

| Age Group at Separation | Case | Nursery | Sex | Age at Interview (Years) |
|---|---|---|---|---|
| The Ones | A | N | m | 19 |
| | B | N | f | 19 |
| | C | S | f | 21 |
| | D | N | m | 19 |
| | F | O | m | 20 |
| The Twos | G | S | f | 23 |
| | H | N | m | 21 |
| | J | N | f | 21 |
| | K | E | f | 21 |
| | L | E | m | 22 |
| The Threes | M | E | f | 20 |
| | P | E | m | 22 |
| | Q | S | m | 24 |
| | R | N | f | 23 |
| | T | E | m | 23 |
| The Four-Pluses | V | N | m | 23 |
| | W | E | m | 24 |
| | X | E | m | 27 |
| | Y | S | m | 26 |
| | Z | S | f | 26 |

ent sibling statuses.[17] When interviewed, all but one of the subjects were living either with their parents or with their spouse and children. In 16 cases both parents were still alive, and 15 couples were still living together.

[17] As the sibling statuses and family size happen to be quite evenly represented among the four age-at-separation groups and the three nursery groups, so, I assume, are many other less readily describable family variables. Specifically, in reference to sibling status among the 20 persons, there are two only children (A,V); three who are the first of two (F,H,W); four who are the second of two (C,K,T,Z); two who are the fourth of six (G,J); and one each of the following: first of three (Q), second of three (B), third of four (M), fourth of four (Y), fifth of five (D), second of six (P) third of six (R), second of nine (L), and third of nine (X). Defining small families as one- or two-child units and large families as those having three or more children, we find that each age-at-separation group has two or three small and large families, except for the Threes, who split one and four. Nursery N splits three and four; Nursery E, three and four; Nursery S, two and three. Similarly, top, middle, and bottom statuses are quite evenly distributed among age and nursery groups.

There is, however, one aspect of family life not evenly distributed. All four parents who were widowed by 1960–61 were confined to the Ones. A's father died when he was twelve, C's when she was eleven, and B has no memory of her father, who died during the second year after her return home. B grew up with her mother and two siblings, however, in a house owned by the maternal grandparents, and the grandfather was described as an attentive and indulgent father surrogate. Also among the Ones is F, whose father's date of death is unknown. By the time of the interviews, his mother was remarried, with a "new family," and F was completely alienated from her.

The subjects' ages at separation and placement ranged from 2 months to 61 months, clustered, by design, in the four age-at-separation groups previously described. Overall length of placement in the nurseries ranged from 12 months to 50 months, with just over three years as the mid-point. As might be expected, the younger the child at placement, the longer his stay was likely to be, though in a few cases this relationship was violated (e.g., a Two who stayed just 12 months and a Four-plus who stayed over 50 months).

While all of these young adults returned to their families during their growing-up years, two of the Ones and one Four-plus spent four or more years in a boarding school, a training school, or an institution for deprived children subsequent to their wartime placements, and one other Four-plus, before returning to her family, finished out the war years in a series of nonrelative family billets. In summary, three of the Ones, all of the Twos, all of the threes, and three of the Four-pluses, that is, 16 of the 20, grew up with their families without interruption after their wartime nursery school stay.

### Reasons for the Absence of a Control Group

Finally, I must comment on the absence of a control group in this study. A control group in an investigation of this type and size should, ideally, be matched with the persons being studied, like them on all relevant variables except the independent variable of early childhood separation and placement in a wartime residential nursery. But children who were not evacuated and stayed in London with their families were exposed for many years to the horrors of aerial attack upon London, and children who were evacuated with their mothers experienced the difficulties of being billeted in someone else's house, often as unwelcome guests, often with many changes of billet.

In addition to these two variations, there was another fundamental difference between possible "controls" and the persons studied. In the case of the nursery school children, the parents *had* decided—admittedly under the force of circumstances—to place their children in a nursery. Our earliest interviews with parents suggested that this fact possibly had multiple and dynamic implications reflecting on the parents as personalities and as members of a family group, and especially on their feelings about parental roles. Any control group would have had to have been matched on this criterion, too. Young adults in such a control group would have to have parents who had decided to place their children for their safety, but for some reason did not. Ignoring this variable would have meant that the children's growing-up years in their own families were spent with parents whose orientations to parental roles, at least in the children's preschool years, were probably different in crucial, although difficult to specify, ways.

We discovered one city where an evacuation nursery was planned and applications were filed, but the scheme was not realized. This seemed at first to answer our needs for a control group, but it became clear that growing up in this city after the war was not really similar to growing up in any of the London boroughs in which our 20 persons lived. At this point we abandoned the search for controls.

The plan for study, then, provided four comparison age-at-separation groups and three comparison nursery groups. It seemed to me that the basic questions we asked could be answered by rating against assumed norms for an urban population. Other controls, such as the blind analyses of some of the data, were built into our procedures for study.

## METHODS OF DATA COLLECTION AND ANALYSIS

I used a direct approach with these 20 adults. I explained that I was a visiting American interested in the care of small children who had had to live away from their parents. Since, for their physical safety, they all had been evacuated during the war, I thought that some things could be learned about such early childhood care if I had a chance to talk with them, primarily about how they were getting along now. Many of them replied in essence that if their participation would help children, they would help us. There was only one exception, a Four-plus who was married and the mother of two children. She completed a first session with my interviewer colleague, Leslie Bell, of The London School of Economics, and then, ostensibly because she was moving and starting a new job, etc., could not arrange a second appointment with me. Confronted with our time limits, she readily agreed to our getting a substitute for her. Our substitute, a Four-plus mother of one child, six months pregnant with her second, was an alumna of the same nursery school. She and all the others kept every appointment, in one case as many as five.

The questions we asked about the adjustment of these young adults were formulated in the light of the literature on early childhood separation. This literature predicts that damage would be manifest in five areas: First, *feeling life* would suffer—apathy, inability to express feelings, narcissism, depression, and/or low self-esteem would be more apparent than their opposites on each continuum. Second, assessment of *inner controls* would reveal extremes of impulsiveness or overcontrol; lack of manifest anxiety or an excess of this; antisocial proclivities or overconforming rigidity; and/or extremes in orientations to pleasure, achievement, and short-term goals. Third, *relationships with people* would be characterized by lack of emotional attachment, social isolation, shallowness, short duration, receptive dependency, distrustfulness, noninitiating passivity, and/or sexual inappropriateness. Fourth, *performance in key social roles*, as, for example, son, daughter, husband, wife, parent, employee, friend, would be characterized by lack of involvement and/or inadequacy. Fifth, *intellectual functions* would tend to be low and/or unstable. (Chart 1).

### Interview Methods

To provide data for rating each of the 20 adults on a five-point scale for each of 24 items dealing with the five major variables, Leslie Bell and I interviewed and tested the young adults, interviewed their parents, and consulted collateral agency records. A case folder on each participant was then submitted for rating to James Robertson and his wife, of the Tavistock and Hampstead Clinics, respectively.

Using a minimum of structure for the interviews, we asked for certain case-sheet data and facts about the chronology of living arrangements, and then for material on work history, leisure-time interests, most recent school experience, and family life (both family of origin and marital family). We cut across these life areas with our questions about the areas of predicted failure listed above. In addition to the interview, each person was asked to tell stories in response to 14 Thematic Apperception Test (TAT) cards, and ten, five men and five women, completed the California Psychological Inventory.[18] The number of interview sessions with each person, the hours for each session, and the informal situations in which we met varied considerably. We saw 14 subjects interacting with their own parents, four with spouses and own children or fiances. We had an informal dinner, tea, or a pub snack and bitters with about half of them. With 15, we walked from office to home or from either to the underground station. Observation as well as tests and interviews seemed important as sources of data.

We also arranged visits with the parents of all but two of the 20.[19] We hoped that their memories would provide us with useful data on the children's earliest days, their leavetaking, and homecoming, but these hopes were rarely fulfilled. Asked to tell what her son was like when he returned home, one harried East End mother of six replied, "He'd had a haircut," and nothing more could be evoked. A less pressed and better educated mother had more vivid recollections of her own reactions at her son's departure than of his. After the bus left, she said, "I went cycling all day long—not to be back in this empty house." Home visits to the parents did, however, provide independent evidence of the young adults' current adjust-

---

[18] The CPI's had not been analyzed when the case folders were submitted for rating. Therefore, the CPI data are not included in this report.

[19] In F's case, he was the only one of the 20 alienated from his mother. For this reason we did not arrange an interview with her, but drew as extensively as possible upon medical and social agency collateral material. The other parents not interviewed were Z's, who was the late substitute for the Four-plus we "lost." We did, however, interview Z's husband, and obtained a picture of Z's relationships with her parents and sibling that was documented by recent photographs. Although Y's parents were separated (the father moved out when Y was about 17), they still saw each other and we interviewed them both.

## Chart 1
### CASE RATING SHEET

_____ (Case)                    (Rater) _____

1. *Feelings* (Write X on one of 5 dashes, or circle ? for "Don't know")
   a. apathetic (lacking feelings)      — — — — —  ? vital (alive)
   b. repressive (unable to express)   — — — — —  ? spontaneous (free)
   c. narcissistic (self-centered)      — — — — —  ? altruistic (outgoing)
   d. pessimistic (depressive)          — — — — —  ? optimistic (happy)
   e. low self-esteem                   — — — — —  ? high self-esteem
2. *Inner controls* (X one of 5 dashes, or circle ? for "Don't know")
   a. impulsive, acting out             — — — — —  ? overcontrolled
   b. no anxiety, guiltless             — — — — —  ? anxiety laden, guilty
   c. antisocial                        — — — — —  ? over conforming
   d. low achievement orientation       — — — — —  ? high achievement orientation
   e. high pleasure orientation         — — — — —  ? low pleasure orientation
   f. short-term goals                  — — — — —  ? long-range goals
3. *Relationships with people.* (For relationship with mother, write *m;* father, *f;* sib, *s;* husband or fiance, *h;* wife or fiancee, *w;* child(ren), *c;* employer, *e;* friend, *fr;* other, *o.* Write appropriate letter, wherever evidence permits.)
   a. emotionally unattached            — — — — —  ? emotionally attached
   b. socially isolated                 — — — — —  ? socially belonging
   c. shallow                           — — — — —  ? deep
   d. short-term                        — — — — —  ? long-term
   e. receptive (dependent)             — — — — —  ? giving
   f. hostile, distrustful              — — — — —  ? friendly, trusting
   g. passive, non-initiating           — — — — —  ? aggressive, initiating
   h. sexually inappropriate            — — — — —  ? sexually appropriate
4. *Role performances* (For role of son, *s;* daughter, *d;* husband, *h;* wife, *w;* parent, *p;* employee, *e;* friend, *fr;* recreation time, *r;* citizen, *c.*)
   a. uninvolved, unmotivated           — — — — —  ? involved, identified in
   b. sees self as inadequate in role   — — — — —  ? sees self as adequate
   c. seen as inadequate by others
      in role                           — — — — —  ? seen as adequate by others
5. *Intellectual functioning* (X one of 5, or circle ? as in 1 & 2 above.)
   a. low functioning (manifest)        — — — — —  ? high level functioning
   b. uneven functioning                — — — — —  ? stable functioning

ment. In addition, these were invaluable opportunities to observe family life and the behavior of parents and siblings together. But if any early damage had occurred, we got essentially no evidence from the parents to describe it.

A final source of information was the records of social and medical agencies and the nurseries themselves. Nine of the 20 adults grew up in the East End. The district office of the Children's Department that had full records on all dependent and delinquent children in its area screened the nine names provided and made folders available. These folders amplified details of the material previously given by the young adults and their parents, but in no case did they reveal any inaccuracies. Specifically, four of the nine had told me in the interviews of episodes that led me to believe the Children's Department would have a file on their family, but the other five described no such episodes. These five were unknown to the Children's Department. Records on the other four essentially corroborated what they had told me: in one case a bicycle theft at age 11, and in the others facts about the dependency or sexual or other delinquencies of siblings in their families. Records from another social agency and from two medical facilities similarly substantiated what our subjects or their parents had said. All this confirming evidence suggests the validity of the interview data. It seems that an American visiting for a year is a safe recipient of London secrets. Or, perhaps an opportunity to talk honestly about one's self in our times is still all too rare to miss.

### Analysis Controls

As another control on the data and their analysis, each respondent's TAT stories were sent for blind analysis to George A. De Vos, a psychologist on the University of California faculty and a specialist in projective tests and in the fields of personality and culture, and delinquency. He was given no more information about each case than age and sex. Although he knew of the problem for investigation, he knew nothing about the sources of cases, their separation ages, or which might be "controls" or "experimental" cases.

Since ratings of case material may, of course, prove unstable even when made consensually, as the Robertsons worked, by co-rating, a table of random numbers was used to draw five cases for rerating. Norma Haan, of the Institute of Human Development, University of California, Berkeley, rerated them. There were two women and three men; one One, two Twos, one Three, and one Four-plus; one from Nursery N, two from Nursery E, and two from Nursery S. The analyses were examined for agreement in the same dichotomous intervals that were used as the basis for findings in this report, and the ratings agreed on a case-by-case basis in a range from 69 percent to over 90 percent. For the five variables, agreement was 76 percent on *feelings*, 75 percent on *inner controls*, 76 percent on *personal relationships*, 92 percent on *role performance*, and 80 percent on *intellectual functioning*.

One procedure for analyzing the ratings is to compare them with a typical metropolitan population. It was arbitrarily assumed that clinicians would rate a typical population on five-point scales in a 5 percent-20 percent-50 percent-20 percent-5 percent distribution. Thus, references to this metropolitan population are to persons for whom 50 percent of the ratings fall in the central interval, with lower and upper quartiles below and above. We tested the observed rating frequencies against this expected distribution (Table 2). Our findings include comparisons of the four age-at-separation groups, on each of the five psychosocial variables studied, and contrasts of the three nursery groups.

## FINDINGS

We are now ready to consider some of the findings and to offer a few interpretations and some questions for further study. We found:

1. Although these 20 young adults may have been seriously damaged by their early childhood separation and residential nursery experiences, most of them give no evidence in young adulthood of any extreme aberrant reactions. There are no ratings at the extremes for 12 of the 20, and 15 have fewer than 10 percent of their total ratings at the extremes.[20] To this extent, the data support assumptions about the resiliency, plasticity, and modifiability of the human organism rather than those about the irreversibility of the effects of early experience.
2. Where there is evidence in individual cases of aberrancy in the adjustment of these young adults, in almost every case the data on their families seem sufficient to explain it. Although our design called for the inclusion only of persons from intact families without gross pathology, as the families became better known, so did their disabilities. In the final section of this paper, the nature of some of these families, in relation to their surrender of preschool children, is described. At this point, however, it should be noted that far from permitting the reversibility of early damage, growing up in some of these families might well have given reinforcement to it; and that, seen against their family and neighborhood backgrounds, a few of these young adults give vivid testimony to the strengths that are either inherent in them or were initially developed during years that included their nursery experiences.
3. The data do support the prediction that children placed in residential group care during the first year of life will show evidence of damage in their young adult years. Every test shows that this age group fared the worst of the four groups. (Details on the Ones appear later in this paper.) The family data, however, indicate parenting problems in this group that cannot be ignored in explanations of these young adults' adjustment.
4. None of the evidence from the Four-plus group supports the prediction that separation and group care starting at this period are followed by enduring damage that is evident in young adulthood.[21]

---

20 More specifically, there were no ratings at the lowest extreme on *intellectual functioning* for any of the 20, no ratings at the extremes of *feelings* or *inner controls* for 19 cases, on *role performance* for 14 cases, on *relationships* for 12 cases. Compare Yarrow's summary statement of findings—albeit largely "clinical impressions"—on the social and personality disturbances of institutionalized children: ". . . characteristics described are usually at the extreme end of the scale, reflecting exaggerated pathology or a complete lack of capacity, rather than a relative deficiency." Yarrow, *op. cit.*, p. 468.
     21 This finding is not a function of shorter periods of separation from family for this

5. The Twos fared quite well, better than the Threes, differing from our metropolitan population on only one of the five psychosocial variables. Possible explanations for the difference between these two age-at-separation groups are offered later, since this fact raises questions about the assumed linear relationship between age at separation (and group residential care) and the extent of enduring damage. In other words, these findings do not support the assumption that the earlier the child is separated, the more permanent is the damage to the child.

With these basic findings as a background, some facts about work and love in the total group are relevant. When interviewed, 17 of the 20 were gainfully employed in the London labor market, two were married women and mothers who had good employment histories, and the twentieth was a university student in her last year of training as a teacher. In four or five cases, at most, could job histories be characterized as unstable. Occupations for the men ranged from an industrial engineer who was graduated from Oxford to a dustman. Half of the 12 young men were employed at trades for which they had begun apprenticeships on leaving school at age 15, and five were employed in unskilled jobs. The unmarried women's jobs were file clerk, typist, switchboard operator, waitress, and tailor. Work seemed important to the young people, and it was an obvious source of satisfaction to most of them. It was manifestly a drain and merely a means of income for only four, and one of these had applied and been accepted at a university after three and a half years of secretarial work, which she had found tedious. Out of a total of 43 ratings made by the Robertsons and Mrs. Haan on involvement and feelings of adequacy at work, "normal and above" accounted for 35 ratings, or 81 percent. To this extent, the group made an occupational investment and a socially responsible contribution.

Love seems more difficult than work for a research person to assess. (The data on *feeling life* and *relationships*, to be presented shortly, bear on this topic.) Two of the women and one of the men were enjoying marriage and had parented a total of seven children. Another six of the 20 had set dates for their marriages. Three had what American teenagers call "steadies." Only four seemed at the time of interviews to be "unattached" by plan, and four others were between attachments. In a country where, as of 1959, the average age at marriage for men was 25 years, and women, 23 years,[22] this group of 19- to 26-year-olds seems well on schedule.

---

age group, since V was in the nursery for 50 months, and two others, Z and X, had subsequent periods of separation from family of five and seven years.

[22] *The Registrar General's Statistical Review of England and Wales for the Year 1959*, Part II (London: Her Majesty's Stationery Office, 1960), Table L, p. 72.

TABLE 2. Distribution of Ratings on Five-Step Scale, by Psychosocial Variable and Age Group

| Age Group | Five-Step Frequencies | | | | | Dichotomies for Testing* | | |
|---|---|---|---|---|---|---|---|---|
| Variable 1: Feelings | | | | | | Low | Normal & Above | Probability |
| I | — | 20 | 5 | — | — | 20 | 5 | p < .001 |
| II | 1 | 5 | 14 | 5 | — | 6 | 19 | n.s. |
| III | — | 15 | 8 | 1 | — | 15 | 9 | p < .001 |
| IV | — | 2 | 17 | 5 | — | 2 | 22 | n.s. |
| Variable 2: Inner Controls (a) | | | | | | Low | Normal & Above | Probability |
| I | — | 15 | 5 | 5 | 1 | 15 | 11 | p < .001 |
| II | — | 7 | 16 | 7 | — | 7 | 23 | n.s. |
| III | — | 5 | 11 | 10 | — | 5 | 21 | n.s. |
| IV | — | 6 | 21 | 3 | — | 6 | 24 | n.s. |
| Variable 2: Inner Controls (b) | | | | | | Normal & Below | High | Probability |
| I | — | 15 | 5 | 5 | 1 | 20 | 6 | n.s. |
| II | — | 7 | 16 | 7 | — | 23 | 7 | n.s. |
| III | — | 5 | 1 | 10 | — | 16 | 10 | n.s. (p ≅ .10) |
| IV | — | 6 | 21 | 3 | — | 27 | 3 | n.s. |
| Variable 3: Relationships | | | | | | Low | Normal & Above | Probability |
| I | 21 | 47 | 13 | 3 | — | 68 | 16 | p < .001 |
| II | 7 | 37 | 75 | 9 | — | 44 | 84 | p < .02 |
| III | 17 | 48 | 66 | 4 | — | 65 | 70 | p < .001 |
| IV | — | 29 | 70 | 9 | — | 29 | 79 | n.s. |
| Variable 4: Role Performance | | | | | | Low | Normal & Above | Probability |
| I | 9 | 9 | 8 | 1 | 1 | 18 | 10 | p < .001 |
| II | — | 12 | 21 | 9 | — | 12 | 30 | n.s. |
| III | 5 | 9 | 22 | 1 | — | 14 | 23 | n.s. |
| IV | — | 8 | 21 | 10 | — | 8 | 31 | n.s. |
| Variable 5: Intellectual Functioning | | | | | | Low | Normal & Above | Probability |
| I | — | 5 | 2 | 1 | — | 5 | 3 | p < .02 |
| II | — | 1 | 5 | 1 | 2 | 1 | 8 | n.s. |
| III | — | 3 | 4 | 3 | — | 3 | 7 | n.s. |
| IV | — | 1 | 7 | 2 | — | 1 | 9 | n.s. |

* Tested against expected distributions of 5%, 20%, 50%, 20%, 5%, or, as dichotomized, 25% and 75%, with values smaller than those required for .05 level considered non-significant (n.s.).

## Ratings on Variables by Age at Separation

Analysis of ratings on the five variables is, however, more revealing.

1. *Personal relationships* present some problems in three age groups, but not for the Four-pluses. That is, ratings on this variable differ significantly from the normal metropolitan population for the Ones, the Twos, and the Threes, but not ratings at the very bottom extreme for the Twos.
2. *Feeling life,* for the Ones and the Threes is less vital, spontaneous, and

outgoing than it is for more normal groups, such as the Twos and the Fours.

3. The evidence that is available on *intellectual functioning* fails to indicate retardation or instability for any group but the Ones.
4. The *role performance* ratings indicate that all but the Ones are performing key social roles with involvement and feelings of adequacy that lie within the expected distribution.
5. Problems with *inner controls* fail to appear in the pattern predicted by the separation literature for any group but the Ones. The Twos and the Four-pluses are rated within a normal distribution for inner controls. The Ones alone present a group picture of somewhat greater impulsiveness. The Threes also show a group tendency to differ, approaching the .10 level of significance, but in the direction of above normal control and conformity.

In summary then, the ratings indicate that relationships are some problem for all but the Four-plus group. The other variables present a scattering of age-differentiated findings that principally involve the Ones, who emerge as the lowest rated group on all variables. The Four-pluses pass on all tests, and the Twos are a better adjusted group than the Threes.

### Ratings by Nursery

There are also findings on these young adults as alumni of the three quite different wartime nurseries. For this analysis, the Ones were eliminated because Nursery E is unrepresented and Nursery N is over-represented in this age group. This leaves only 15 cases, but there are 176 to 277 ratings for each nursery group (Table 3). Examination of these ratings by nursery group reveals that the graduates of the somewhat firm, if not stern, and suppressive small Welsh Nursery E appear as young adults to be essentially no better or worse adjusted than the graduates of the psychologically sophisticated and much larger Nursery N. The group that is

TABLE 3. Comparison of Three Nursery Groups by Summated Frequencies of Ratings on Five-Step Scale

| Nursery | Rating Frequencies | | | | | Total |
|---|---|---|---|---|---|---|
| N | 11 | 54 | 78 | 31 | 2 | 176 |
| 4 cases | 6% | 31% | 44%* | 18% | 1% | 100% |
| E | 19 | 116 | 126 | 16 | — | 277 |
| 7 cases | 7% | 42% | 45%* | 6% | — | 100% |
| S | — | 18 | 175 | 32 | — | 255† |
| 4 cases | — | 8% | 78%* | 14% | — | 100% |

* 50% of ratings expected in "normal" central step.
† There are a larger number of ratings per case for Nursery S than for the other two nurseries because the three married adults in the study, all parents, were in this group. They thus had more "relationships" and "roles" to rate, and therefore more ratings.

clearly the best off is the one from the day nursery school evacuated as a unit—Nursery S, with its faith in God, King, and denial and its rather inspirational, repressive, and possessive approach to the children.

## SOME QUESTIONS AND INTERPRETATIONS

A study of only 20 persons, though relatively intensive, cannot provide a sound base for contributions to agency program planning. Rather, such a study may help sharpen questions about assumptions that underlie practice. Therefore, I shall further examine three issues: the superior adjustment of Nursery S graduates, the better adjustment of the Twos than of the Threes, and the matter of family background, especially among the Ones.

### Superior Adjustment of Nursery S Group

The procedure of group residential placement following a period of day care, where children come to know the other children involved and the adults in charge, is unusual. At a day care nursery school, teachers and working mothers meet to discuss child-rearing and child-care problems, and some awareness of each others' values is communicated. Continuity in way of life and in personal relationships for the children between their day care and their residential group is provided for. "For the infant and young child," as Yarrow says, "changes result in a loss of environmental predictability. The degree of stress involved is likely to vary with the degree of unpredictability."[23] The Nursery S placement plan seems to reduce the unpredictability of residential care. Whether this arrangement alone induces results such as the superior adjustment of Nursery S children would seem to warrant further study.

### Superior Adjustment of the Twos

Why should the Twos have fared better than the Threes? The range and average number of years they were separated are similar, mid-points of just under three years. In both age groups, coincidentally, there are three persons who had older siblings present at their residential nursery, and in each group there is one sibling who was the elder sibling at the nursery. During the study the data suggested that younger siblings fared well to the detriment of elder sibs, but later analysis failed to support this proposition any more than it supported the proposition that children placed as sibling units do better than children placed apart from their siblings. Developmental theory suggests that 2-year-olds are closer to the autonomy phase, to use Erikson's term,[24] than are 3-year-olds, who are beginning to be more involved in Oedipal alignments with parents. The Threes also seem

[23] Yarrow, *op. cit.*, p. 481.
[24] Erik H. Erikson, *Childhood and Society* (New York: W. W. Norton & Co., 1950), pp. 222–226.

cognitively better equipped to understand—and misunderstand—the whys of separation than are the Twos. These developmental differences probably contributed significantly to the findings of this study, but we have no data available that help to indicate just how.[25]

Another plausible explanation, however, involves the manifest disturbance in three of the five families in each of these two age groups. Did earlier removal of the Twos than of the Threes give them a sounder base for coping with familial strife upon their return home? Since, in the families of both age groups there are unevacuated younger siblings who seem more troubled than the once-separated persons in this study, questions about the families as causal agents are appropriate. The inference is that separation from such troubled families at age 2 may be preferable to separation at age 3 because by that time greater damage has been inflicted on the child. This proposition might be tested on sibling groups in institutional or foster family care.

### Home Life of the Ones

If the Twos fared better than the Threes because of earlier separation, why then did the Ones not fare better still? They were the earliest separated of all and from troubled parental situations in every case. As young adults, however, the Ones fared the worst of the four age groups. But here the issues of when the damage first occurred, its irreversibility, and its reinforcement seem hopelessly confounded. When did it first occur? Nursery N's longitudinal records, written while the children were in residence, describe three of the Ones. They tell vividly of A's slow motor, language, and social development (because of congenital defect, birth injury, or separation?); of B's growth from a peaked, birdlike 2-month-old at arrival into a willful, active child; of D's excellent physical development and voracious eating, and other not unusual behavior. Except for A's retardation, which is of unknown origin, there is no evidence of gross pathology in any of these records. Only a nursery staff member's memories of F as a wild, unmanageable under-5 foreshadow reports on his later markedly regressive behavior at about age 8. During the intervening years he had returned home to what is probably the most aberrant family situation among the 20 persons studied.

Why are the Ones the worst off as young adults? They were not only

---

[25] Findings that the Threes included some of the most overcontrolled and overconforming of the young adults studied suggest that identifications occurred in the course of early development among these persons although the parent figures present were not their own parents. The extent to which these more rigid ego controls were patterned after nursery staff adults, or developed in response to the institutional children's groups with whom they spent their early years—from about 3 years until school age—is a nice question for study. Are children who begin residential group life at about age 3, among age-mates with whom they pass through the Oedipal period, more likely to be overcontrolled and conforming than children who do not spend these years in group residential life or who begin it much earlier or much later?

the earliest separated, but also, except for C, the earliest to return to their own parents. What can be said about the families in which the Ones grew up? I present just a few observations on four of the families to indicate why I question whether the Ones are the most damaged group by far because they were irreversibly scarred during early separation, or whether their multiple adjustment problems were induced or reinforced by their post-nursery school lives in their relationships with such parents as these.

A's mother, widowed since A was 12, lives in a tiny East End flat, sharing a bedroom with the boy, now 19, her only child. She had kept her husband waiting as a suitor for 12 years before they married, ostensibly because of her relationship with her own mother. She reminisced, "But from the moment we were married, it was wrong from the first time." The symbiotic bond between Mrs. A and her son today follows upon Nursery N's early descriptions of her regular weekend visits. But despite requests that she take him home because he was such a slow developer, she did not do so until Nursery N closed down. The role of mother to infant and preschool child seems to have been impossible for this simple, immature woman to have performed effectually, as was the role of wife. She could not engage in either of the differing kinds of mutuality required for each role.

For Mrs. A, her son in his infant and preschool years was a body to be fed and protected by someone else. A spoke of his growing-up years in terms of illness, outpatient visits to the hospital, and physical impediments to relationships with his peers. Mrs. A's attentions in those years were constantly focused on an unable body. Mrs. A still devotes herself to feeding and protecting this body, although A at 19 is a large six-footer.

B grew up with her immediate family in a house owned and occupied by maternal grandparents. A brief excerpt from Nursery N's wartime records read: "When Mrs. B arrived, B started to cry immediately. Her mother picked her up but B cried more and more. Perhaps the ill baby who vomited so easily could not stand the mother's rocking; perhaps B felt her mother's anxiousness. B got restless each time her mother came to see her. . . . It was hard to feel the disappointment of the kind, shy woman who never complained."

Leslie Bell's impressions of Mrs. B, almost 20 years later, were that she was "very naïve and unintrospective in her observations of her children," and that her early difficulties in feeding B before she placed her in Nursery N at 2 months could not have been a matter merely of her being simple. Even though she is deeply indebted to Nursery N, Mrs. B still feels B became spoiled and willful there, and accounts for the difficulties in their relationship with this idea.

C's mother, an extremely intelligent woman, was outspokenly troubled by her inability to reach or understand her daughter from her birth to the present day. Mrs. C returned to work soon after C's birth and placed her in a wartime nursery at 5 months. In talking of C's undemonstrativeness,

Mrs. C said that she had not had a mother herself and that, consequently, she found it difficult to show her feelings and to give physical affection. C was kept at boarding school until she was 9. Her father died when she was 11, but she remembers most vividly his scolding her for not getting better school reports. The distance from each other that characterizes the members of this family seems to be a model for C's own underlying remoteness from people.

D's parents, superficially warm, had three repeatedly delinquent children with approved school (correctional institution) histories. D, the youngest, seemed to have escaped such a career by acceding to his obese and hypochondriacal mother's demands and by avoiding a close relationship with his father. Mr. D emerged quite accurately in the blind analysis of D's TAT stories as "a rather passive individual who has borderline conformity to the law . . . a corrupter of the young." In the D family, one finds again parents interested in feeding the child's body but too preoccupied with themselves to be able to give much more than food. The fact that D does not more closely resemble Bowlby's descriptions of the "affectionless character"[26] may be because he was in placement for 40 months so early in his life. His older siblings, who spent more of their earliest days with these same parents, have far more aberrant histories than D.

Are the shallowness and the restricted nature of the young adult relationships of these Ones and the flatness of their feeling lives an irreversible result of infant separation and early group care? Or have these parents contributed appreciably during the children's growing-up years to these conditions? The available facts provide no basis for conclusive answers.

They do, however, suggest that parents who voluntarily place a child away from home in the first year of life, albeit in a program sanctioned by society and in a time of national crisis, often have limited or distorted feeling lives and relationship capacities for caring for their children. Even in the families of some of the children separated at an older age, parental roles seem ego-alien. Therefore, the effects of separation cannot be considered apart from the family life from which the children were separated and, in the case of the group under study, to which they were returned.

## CONCLUDING COMMENTS

With these facts in mind, the good adjustment made by many of these young adults—who grew up in a time of war and unsettling postwar years —is worth pondering. As a group, they attest to the plasticity of human personality and, perhaps, also reflect favorably on their early nursery parent substitutes. Finally, they assure us that, at least from about age 2, early

---

[26] John Bowlby, *Forty-four Juvenile Thieves: Their Characters and Home Life* (London: Ballière, Tindall, & Cox, 1946).

childhood separation and preschool residential care are not themselves *sufficient* antecedents to a seriously troubled or troublesome young adulthood.

# 48

❨ The foster-grandparent program is an imaginative attempt to solve two social problems simultaneously—the need for a greater number of caretakers in child-care institutions and the need to provide the aged with a useful, income-producing activity. Several attempts have been made to evaluate the effects of the program on institutionalized children. The following is an excerpt from one evaluation research report concerned with the foster-grandparent program in an institution for dependent and neglected children.

# Evaluation of a Foster-Grandparent Program

*Rosalyn Saltz*

## INTRODUCTION

The Foster-Grandparent Program was initiated in 1965 by the U.S. Office of Economic Opportunity and the Administration on Aging of the Department of Health, Education and Welfare as a part of the "war on poverty."

The "foster-grandparents" are elderly persons with poverty level incomes who are employed to work with children in institutions for about 20 hours per week. Their function is a unique one within the institutional setting. They are required to play a family-type role of a "special friend" or substitute grandparent for the particular children to whom they are assigned and they are encouraged to develop very close relationships with "their" children.

The findings here presented are based on a study by the Merrill-Palmer Foster-Grandparent Research Project[1] of the first year's operation of one

---

[1] This Merrill-Palmer Research Project was separately funded by the CAP Evaluation Branch of the O.E.O. in December, 1965.

Foster-Grandparent Demonstration Project, initiated at the beginning of 1966. The aim of the Research Project has been to evaluate the impact of foster-grandparents on: (1) the social, emotional and intellectual functioning of institutionalized infants and young children; (2) the emotional and physical well-being of the older people involved.

The Program which our Merrill-Palmer Foster-Grandparent Research Project has been studying is administered by the Catholic Social Services Agency of Wayne County and is in operation at the Sarah Fisher Home, a children's institution in Farmington, Michigan. The foster-grandparents were introduced into the Sarah Fisher Home on February 7, 1966. By April, 1966, all children in the institution who were in the appropriate age groups (birth through 6 years) were assigned to a "foster-grandparent"; most share one foster-grandparent with one other child. The foster-grandparents come to the institution for four hours a day, five days a week, and divide their attention during the four hours of work between their two assigned foster-grandchildren.

### Role of the Foster-Grandparents

Considering the relatively short period of time the foster-grandparents have been actively involved in the institution we have studied, their impact has been marked enough to suggest that they have succeeded in playing their unique role within the institution. It will be remembered that this role was to establish a "special relationship" with one or two individual children, rather than to serve as an additional aide to a whole cottage.

The need for this type of "special relationship" can be better understood by reviewing the literature regarding the deficiencies of typical institutional environments from the point of view of the optimum development of young institutionalized children. It has been found that even in modern, progressive institutions (as, for example, both the experimental and "control" institutions we have been concerned with in this evaluation), childhood institutionalization is associated with detrimental effects on development, including the following:

> . . . retardation in certain aspects of development, such as language development, and deviant patterns of social behavior.. . . These detrimental effects of institutionalization may tend to be progressive with longer-term stay.[2]

Further, it is generally assumed that these detrimental effects are associated with the absence of the kind of *emotional commitment* a child ordinarily receives from parents or parental substitutes in a home environment. Yarrow goes on to report that:

---

[2] Yarrow, L. J. Separation from parents during early childhood. In M. L. Hoffman & Lola W. Hoffman (Eds.) *Review of Child Development Research*. New York: Russell Sage Foundation, 1964.

. . . institution care seems to have certain limitations which are difficult to overcome. Rheingold (1961) gives impressive evidence that even in "good" institutions there is less contact with mother-figures than in "good" homes. David and Appell (1962) indicate that, even under the experimental conditions of intensive, individualized nursing care, the quality of emotional interchange remains limited.[3]

In the case of the foster-grandparents, it is exactly this quality of *emotional involvement* that is the most obvious characteristic of their relationships with their individual children. The emotional interchange between the typical foster-grandparent and his or her children is far more intense than that commonly associated with or even desired from other institutional child-care workers. The elderly people seem to find this "special relationship" aspect of their function particularly compatible with their own needs. They take this "quasi-family" concept very seriously and make it work. As one of the foster-grandparents says, "To me it brought out love I never thought I would possess again, as a love for young children. My children are grown now, and the younger ones I don't see frequently."

Thus, the unique "special-relationship" concept appears to be a practical one and to be associated with sometimes remarkable therapeutic effects for both the children and the elderly people involved. At the same time, however, its very potency dictates that those supervising the operation of the Foster-Grandparent Program in an institution have an unusual responsibility to provide guidance in connection with the establishment, management, and termination of these relationships.

## I. DESCRIPTION AND BACKGROUND OF THE CHILDREN IN THE FOSTER-GRANDPARENT PROGRAM

The children involved in the Foster-Grandparent Program's first year at the Sarah Fisher Home in Farmington, Michigan, ranged from newborns to six years of age. Administratively, the children are divided into four cottages with about fifteen children per unit, according to age groups as follows: (1) infants (under one year); (2) toddlers; (3) pre-schoolers; and (4) kindergarten age (5–6 years.). The enrollment in these four units averages about 60 to 70 children at any one time.

In the nursery group, there is a rapid turnover of very young babies, most of whom are eligible and placed for adoption before the age of ten weeks. Some babies who are admitted after early infancy, or who, for some reason, are difficult to place (because of health, physical disability, race, etc.) remain at the Home most of and occasionally a few months past their first year. However, as a matter of institutional policy, a baby is rarely "promoted" from the nursery to the toddler unit; instead, a boarding home or other arrangement is found.

---

[3] *Ibid.*, p. 102.

Thus, the toddlers and pre-schoolers living at the Sarah Fisher Home represent a *different* group of children than the Nursery group. For the most part, these children have been admitted to the Sarah Fisher Home for the first time when they were anywhere from ten months to five years of age. Most of them are either legally ineligible for adoption, or, if eligible, are children for whom adoptive homes and even foster-homes are difficult to find.

### Home Backgrounds

In many cases, *both* financial and emotional deprivation have been involved in the children's pre-placment home situations. For example, agency records on children residing in the foster-grandparent cottages at the Sarah Fisher Home in January, 1967, show that more than half of the children for whom such information was available had at least one parent with a history of severe alcoholism; almost one-third had one parent with a history of mental illness; and the incomplete notations regarding parental incomes and occupational status suggest that many, and perhaps the majority of these children come from poverty level homes.

The following summary of home factors leading to admission gives a vivid picture of the type of traumatic home situations that have led to the

| | |
|---|---|
| Motherless (Deserted or Deceased) | 25% |
| Mental Illness in home | 24% |
| Neglect | |
|     Refusal to support | 15% |
|     Abandonment | 12.5% |
|     Battered | 10% |
| Imprisonment of one or both parents | 5.5% |
| Long-term alcoholic parents | 4% |
| Marital discord–custody problem | 4% |

children's placement at the Sarah Fisher Home. These figures represent reason for admission information on seventy-two children in the Foster-Grandparent Program, aged 4 months to 7 years.

## II. METHODS FOR EVALUATING EFFECTS
## ON THE CHILDREN

The Research Project's techniques for evaluating the effects of the Foster-Grandparent Program on the children included:

1. The administration of appropriate standardized tests, including: (1) the Cattell Infant Intelligence Test, (2) Stanford-Binet, Form L-M, (3) the Vinel and Maturity Scale, and (4) the Draw-A-Man Test.

2. Administration of research instruments in the process of standardization (e.g., Pre-School Inventory).[4]
3. Periodic observations, using both highly structured, categorized "timed observations" and less rigid "anecdotal" methods for reporting observations.
4. Regular interviews with institutional staff concerning each of the children in the Foster-Grandparent Program, according to our "Child Description Interview" Schedule.

Assessments of the children's emotional, social and intellectual functioning were made of: (1) Sarah Fisher experimental children before and after a period of foster-grandparent care; (2) a small group of "control" children from the St. Vincent Infants Home, Timonium, Maryland, matched on crucial variables with a group of Sarah Fisher children. St. Vincent is very similar to the Sarah Fisher Home in all respects except that it is *not* utilizing foster-grandparents. (The St. Vincent Infant Home is administered by the Associated Catholic Charities of Baltimore, Maryland.)

### ABSTRACT OF FINDINGS CONCERNING THE CHILDREN

The addition of foster-grandparents to an institutional staff cannot, of course, provide a magic wand whereby all negative effects on the children of institutionalization and of traumatic life situations can be avoided or erased. Nevertheless the overwhelming weight of the evidence we have gathered indicates that the foster-grandparents have had a definitely beneficial effect on many aspects of the children's adjustment and development.

The major effects on the children in the Foster-Grandparent Program in the Sarah Fisher Home can be summarized as follows:

1. Foster-grandparent care appears to have positive effects on the social behavior and alertness of infants as young as one to seven weeks of age, manifested by:
   (a) decreased fretfulness;
   (b) increased alertness to their environment; and
   (c) earlier evidence of vocalizing attempts.
2. There were indications that foster-grandparent care had beneficial effects on certain aspects of motor and social development of the children from 4 months to 2½ years of age.

---

[4] The Pre-School Inventory was developed by Betty Caldwell, State University of New York, Syracuse, N.Y., in connection with the United States Office of Economic Opportunity's Head Start Program. At present, only an unpublished research version of this is available, but it is being utilized and standardized by Head Start Program projects throughout the country.

3. The addition of foster-grandparents, even to an already "good" institutional environment, appears to help create a favorable climate for certain aspects of institutionalized children's language, skills and intellectual development.
   (a) There is some evidence to suggest foster-grandparents can contribute to the maintenance of a "normal" rate of intellectual development in the institutionalized children.
   (b) There are indications that foster-grandparents can have a favorable effect on the language and skills development of institutionalized children.
4. In their cottage unit settings, the children manifested improved overall social and emotional adjustment after foster-grandparent care. The most striking beneficial effects appeared to be:
   (a) Improvement in the children's *social behavior*. Children were seen as more outgoing and as having improved relationships with both peers and authority figures.
   (b) Evidence of the children's *increased self-confidence*, with a decrease in instances of fearful, insecure behavior.
5. In the pre-school setting, the children showed the same types of improvement as in the cottage units. In addition, foster-grandparent care appeared to have a "settling" effect on the behavior of the children in the pre-school. The children were better able to function appropriately and to make constructive use of the materials and training offered by the pre-school setting. Comparing the children *before* and *after* time in the foster-grandparent program they evidenced:
   (a) Less hyperactive and/or destructive and aggressive behavior;
   (b) An increase in cheerful and even-tempered behavior and a decrease in fretful, sullen behavior;
   (c) improved social skills; better relationships with peers and acceptance of teacher direction;
   (d) Improved language readiness skills, such as recognition of colors and letters, etc.

The extent of the foster-grandparents' impact on the children, as summarized above, may seem less surprising when it is remembered that the children with whom we are concerned are in their youngest and most formative years, and their need for special care and affection is unusually great. Because of their extreme youth, any defensiveness the children may have developed against forming relationships with others as a result of previous hurts can still, in most of them, be overcome by the efforts of loving caretakers.

# 49

⟪ The child's adjustment to the child-care institution frequently reflects the parents' attitude toward the institution. The following article reports the use of group psychotherapy in an effort to help the parents develop a more accepting attitude toward the residential treatment center in which their emotionally disturbed children have been placed.

## Group Therapy with Parents of Children in a Residential Treatment Center

*Alvin E. Winder, Lindo Ferrini, and George E. Gaby*

The practice of psychotherapy with the parents of children with emotional problems has received wide recognition in the child welfare field. Many such parent programs have been reported in the literature. These programs have been carried out in a variety of settings and with parents whose children come from a variety of clinical populations. This paper will deal with a specific population—the parents of emotionally disturbed children; a specific setting—the residential treatment center; and a specific therapeutic procedure—group psychotherapy.

The literature on residential treatment centers for emotionally disturbed children indicates that psychotherapy with parents is accepted both as philosophically sound and as good practice.[1] A recent report of 21 major centers reveals that parent counseling or psychotherapy on a regular basis is a part of the treatment program in all the institutions surveyed.[2]

Group psychotherapy with parents, however, is much less often reported. (Group psychotherapy is distinguished in this paper from group guidance, the former belonging to therapeutic processes, the latter to processes of parent education.) It has most generally been used with the parents of children in outpatient settings or with the parents of children suffering from a variety of specific disabilities.[3] Very rarely has it been reported as

---

[1] Herschel Alt, *Residential Treatment for the Disturbed Child* (New York: International Universities Press, 1960).

[2] Lydia F. Hylton, *The Residential Treatment Center: Children, Programs, and Costs* (New York: Child Welfare League of America, 1964).

[3] Edward G. Colbert, "Group Psychotherapy for Mothers of Schizophrenic Children in a State Hospital," *International Journal of Group Psychotherapy*, IX (1959), 93–

being used in the settings of a residential treatment center. The Hylton survey reports that only one out of the 21 centers studied uses group psychotherapy with parents.[4]

Furthermore, this center had only one group with seven members. It should be added, however, that the literature is frequently a year or two behind actual practice. Recently, the authors heard that the Sweetser-Children's Home is using a group approach in working with parents.[5]

This paper is concerned with reporting the experience of two psychotherapy groups of parents of children with severe emotional disturbances who are resident in the Children's Study Home, Springfield, Massachusetts. This program was set up to meet several difficulties that had manifested themselves in the parents' relations with the Study Home. First, even though the parents were in individual casework treatment, they showed little motivation and strong resistance to change. Secondly, the agency staff felt that the parents had not accepted the help the agency was offering their children and that they had strong inner reservations about the value of the agency's help. Because of these reservations, there seemed to be some parental sabotaging of efforts to help the children. Therefore, the broad objective of the program was to help the parents identify the agency as being therapeutically valuable for their child. Specifically, the Study Home staff hoped for greater cooperation from the parents during the children's stay at the center. They further hoped that, through contact with the agency, the parents would improve their functioning as parents and increase their empathy for the needs and feelings of their children. Change in both the parents and the children could eventually make for successful return of the children to their family homes.

## DESCRIPTION OF THE PROGRAM

The group psychotherapy program was set up for two closed groups, which met separately for 12 sessions each. Group I met for an hour on Wednesday evenings, and Group II for an hour on Sunday evenings.

Group members were selected on the basis of parents' geographic

98; Helen E. Durkin, *Group Therapy for Mothers of Disturbed Children* (Springfield, Ill.: Charles C Thomas, 1954); Mark Eshbaugh and James Walsh, "A Group Approach to Parents of Children in Trouble," *Children*, XI (1964), 108–112; Ruth Rothman, "Group Counseling with Parents of Visually Handicapped Children," *International Journal of Group Psychotherapy*, VI (1956), 317–323; S. R. Slavson, "Steps in Sensitizing Parents (Couples) in Groups Toward Schizophrenic Children," *International Journal of Group Psychotherapy*, XIII (1963), 176–186; Alvin E. Winder, "A Program of Group Counseling for the Parents of Cerebral Palsied Children," *Cerebral Palsy Review*, XIX, No. 3 (1958), 8–10.

[4] Hylton, *op. cit.*

[5] A personal communication from Eleanor L. Dotter, Social Work Supervisor, Sweetser-Children's Home, Saco, Maine; and Nicholas Fish, "Some Statistical Ramblings through Group Psychotherapy," unpublished paper (Saco, Maine: Sweetser-Children's Home, 1964).

proximity to the center, their willingness to participate in the group psychotherapy program, and the possibility of involving both parents in the group process. An initial letter was sent by the Study Home director to all parents residing within a 25-mile radius of the home (the home is located in the geographical center of the city of Springfield, Massachusetts). The letter expressed the goals of the group meetings, in the following terms:

> The Children's Study Home in our interest in serving the children and their families is initiating a series of parent group meetings for the purpose of working on the problems that parents have in relation to their child placed in the Children's Study Home. We know that you are interested in helping your child and that you are concerned about ways in which you can do this. This series is intended to work on this.

Later on, the letter stated:

> A number of parents with whom we have discussed this have already expressed interest in it, and I strongly recommend this program to you. You would be a member of one of these groups. Talk to your caseworker about it sometime before March 1st. We look forward to a helpful and interesting experience.

In almost all cases, it was explained to the parents that the group would not be a substitute for their individual meetings with their assigned caseworker. Twelve parents, seven mothers and five fathers, were selected for the group psychotherapy program. All were white, in their 30's, and belonged to either the upper-lower or the lower-middle socioeconomic class. Most had completed high school, and one of the fathers was a college graduate.

As might be expected, all of the parents manifested marked longstanding, firmly entrenched personality problems and defects. Of the seven mothers, three were grossly infantile, narcissistic, acting-out character disorders; two were rather fragile borderline psychotics (one with strong covert paranoic trends and an angry, phallic orientation; the other with clear-cut cyclothymic tendencies and a somewhat passive, fearful orientation), one suffered from a severe neurosis anxiety, and one is best described as passive and severely schizoid (there being no real suggestion of a potential or likely ego breakdown).

The five fathers all exhibited major problems relative to passive-dependent longings and needs. Three are best categorized as inhibited, markedly passive-dependent, and somewhat schizoid. One is passive-dependent and, unlike the schizoid, capable of appropriate and genuine affective response. He tends, however, to be fearful of emotional intimacy, preferring to withdraw and isolate. The remaining father, out of his pervasive need to deny and defend against his strong underlying passive, homosexual propensities, is assertive (counterphobically intrusive), controlling, and hostile. He is very often difficult to deal with and, clinically, appears to be a "passive-aggressive personality, aggressive type."

The seven children of the 12 parents, four boys and three girls, ranged in age from 9 to 11. Four (two boys and two girls) were clearly schizophrenic. Another girl fluctuated between an acting-out, character-disorder orientation and a confused, hypomanic-like psychotic state. One boy was a severe impulse-ridden character disorder, and the remaining boy presented the multiple problems of a nonspecific aphasia, a significant but not clearly delineated hearing loss, and noteworthy passive-aggressive personality trends.

Two rules governed the assignment of parents to either the first or the second group. These were, first, placing husbands and wives in separate groups and, second, balancing the groups so that there would be approximately an equal number of men and women in each group. Each group met with a therapist and an observer. The therapist in the first group was a clinical psychologist with experience in working with parent groups. The therapist in the second group was a caseworker with experience in counseling parents in the residential treatment setting. A social group-worker was the observer in both groups. The two psychotherapists and the observer met weekly to discuss the group process and the progress of the parents. Agency staff were informed of the effects of the group psychotherapy on the parents through the caseworker's and the observer's reports at staff meetings.

## METHOD EMPLOYED

The group psychotherapeutic approach that was used relied on the interpersonal relationship as the medium through which change was effected. Two levels of interpersonal relationships were present in the parent groups. These were the interaction of each member with the therapist and the interaction of the various members with one another. The major role of the therapist was to make selective use of these interactions, sometimes to encourage and sometimes to discourage them. In order to make selective use of the interactions, he had to understand the basic dynamics of group treatment. These involve the various ways (verbal and nonverbal) in which group members express their tensions. The communication of feelings by the group as a whole sometimes occurred in symbolic form, which is referred to in this paper as a group theme. The therapist also had to be able to understand and respond to nonverbal communications.

## GROUP ATTENDANCE

Initially, six parents attended each group meeting. Group I had four members who attended regularly and two who attended sporadically.

Group II had three whose attendance was regular and three whose attendance was irregular. Our experience indicates that regularity of attendance does not seem to be related to marital pairs.

In only one family did both husband and wife show poor attendance. The partners in two families had equal attendance, even though each member had to appear at a different time for his group session. In two families, one member attended regularly and the other irregularly. The member who was present in each of these families spoke of wishing that his or her spouse would attend. In both situations, the present members spoke of attempts by their spouses to actively dissuade them from group attendance. These attempts at dissuasion were unsuccessful in both cases. The force of the group seemed strong enough to reinforce the attending parents' motivations to make use of the group process.

Absence from the group sessions, but not from the casework sessions, was frequently felt by the staff to be the parents' way of asking the caseworker whether he approved of their participation in the group. Sometimes this was stated directly; one parent said, "I don't want to go to the group; I just want to see you." Sometimes it was stated indirectly. Another parent told her caseworker, "I talk about enough in the group; I have nothing really to say to you." Caseworkers were prepared to expect this kind of reaction. They understood that when the question arose, they should explore the feelings of the parent concerning group participation and that they should be careful to support the parent's participation in both the casework and the group programs.

## GROUP THEMES

Three major group themes—involving mistrust, loss, and defiance—have resolved themselves out of several questions the parents put to the therapist and to each other during the course of the 12 sessions. They asked the therapist and indirectly, through him, the agency: Are you honest in your stated wish to help us? Are you strong enough to withstand our demands? Will you retreat from helping us when you encounter our angry insistence that our demands be met? Do you have competitive values (as we do), which will lead you to reject us for producing an inadequate child?

To their fellow group members, the parents posed the following questions: Can you accept my expression of feeling over a continuous failure to have my demands met? Can you tolerate my criticism of how you handle your child, your family, the agency, me, the other group members, and the therapist? Finally, they asked each other: Can you understand if I become frightened and must stay away from the group meetings?

Initially, parents were very unsure of either the group's or the therapist's acceptance of them in relationship to their child. One parent summed up this theme and then showed his anxiety about whether he had presented an adequate image to the therapist:

I saw George on a recent visit. Since January, his classwork has improved. He has done especially well in his figures and writing. Since he was little, we have accepted any improvement, even if he gained only an ounce. You're doing well for him, he likes it here. His flareups are less. I hope he continues to pick up. I don't know if that's what you want to hear about.

This initial theme of mistrust lingered through several sessions until it became clear that the therapist was not going to give advice defensively, lecture on child-rearing practices, or develop any punitive responses. As the group became more secure with the therapist's, and therefore the agency's understanding and acceptance, they were able to test each other. Are we willing, they asked, to tell each other our thoughts and feelings about our children? Midway through the group sessions, this problem was brought up through the medium of a television program.

Mrs. Hogan asked, "Did you see the Eleventh Hour last night?" Mrs. Quinn had, and she said, "It was about an autistic child. Is that what they are really like?" Mrs. Jones said, "People want to know if that's how Carole is." "You mean they want to know if she is a nut?" asked Mrs. Quinn.

Thoughtfully Mrs. Jones said, "He does a lot of things that Carole does, but he is further into another world. She doesn't really laugh or cry." Mr. Illing said, "I remember when George first cried." Mrs. Quinn countered, "Alice never did." "Carole has had tears in her eyes, but never cried," Mrs. Jones said.

This discussion of feelings about the child who shows no emotion led to a first admission on the part of these parents that their families gained some advantage in placing the child who did not feel. This represents a first handling of the theme of loss.

A few minutes later, in the same session a parent said, "Sara was afraid she would be sent away also. Sometimes I'm happy that Carole is not home." Mr. Illing agreed: "It's easier for David to get along with George here. George used to knock the stuffings out of him." Mrs. Quinn said: "My mother said I never disciplined Alice enough. I think Donald is improving now that Alice is here."

Having spoken about their feelings and experiences concerning the placement of their children, the group seemed to develop a sense of cohesiveness. For the first time in these sessions, they began to express dissatisfaction with the agency. This criticism required a willingness to challenge the group therapist. The excerpt below shows that one of the parents, Mr. Illing, held back, but could not stem the tide of challenge and defiance. The theme of defiance is best illustrated in this material from the 11th session.

Mrs. Treynor said, "My son didn't have trouble at home." Mr. Illing suggested, "Maybe he gained something being here." Mrs. Hellweg interposed, somewhat sharply, "I don't know, I'm no nut; the caseworker did not believe me when I told him." Mrs. Quinn said, "Alice wouldn't tell her caseworker the truth; she really wants to come home now." Mrs. Hellweg agreed, "They are always picking on the kids here: don't do this, don't do that. The housemothers are too old. People that old shouldn't do that kind of work, they are too rigid."

## ADMINISTRATIVE EVALUATION

Since the inception of the program to serve emotionally disturbed children, the professional staff of the agency have had as a major goal rehabilitation of the parents through casework, so that the children might be returned home as quickly as possible. It was considered most fortunate that the physical plant of the center was located in the city proper with easy access to public transportation. In assigning caseloads, emphasis was given to work with parents. In the agency's eagerness to preserve family ties, visiting policies were somewhat permissive, and visits took place as often as the parents wished. Few limits were set.

It soon became apparent that the goals the agency set for these parents were overly ambitious. The parents became increasingly hostile, and, in many instances, they sabotaged treatment. In two cases, the visiting pattern was destructive, and the consultant psychiatrist was able to show that the caseworker's guilt at having taken the child away from the parent was unresolved. It was because of concern over failure to rehabilitate parents and over the resulting lack of success in returning the children to their own homes that the agency turned to another treatment tool—group therapy.

At the conclusion of the first series of 12 sessions, we did a preliminary evaluation. During the group meetings, no evidence of treatment sabotage by the parents was detected. There was a diminution of overt hostility to the agency. These two highly encouraging changes in parent behavior can best be explained by an *esprit de corps* that the parents participating in the groups developed. For example, while the group therapy program was in process, the staff was able to put into effect new visiting policies designed to lessen the destructive impact of erratic visiting. The first two visiting days occurred during this period. Most of the administrative and professional staff were on hand for these visiting times. Refreshments were served. Parents, children, and staff participated in informal group games, and there seemed to be a relaxed atmosphere of friendliness and good will. The positive way in which parent group members responded to each other was especially noteworthy.

There was a change in the attitude of agency staff (possibly a lessening of the guilt of individual staff members), which could be seen when

major shifts in treatment goals necessitated even further separation between the children and their parents. Staff members were able to take a
forceful stand based on the needs of the child. Thus, it seems clear that,
by providing a new vehicle to help parents, the staff of the Children's
Study Home became able to deal with the parents in a much more constructive way.

It seems quite certain that the group therapy project will continue. The
parents themselves sought and obtained a commitment from the agency
for this. Much still needs to be worked through, however, and casework
and group therapy goals need to be redefined and a method of communication developed between the therapists and the caseworkers. At this point,
the staff is convinced that parental acceptance of treatment will be a
necessary criterion for admission of a child.

### CASEWORK EVALUATION

Caseworkers assigned to the parents report a major change in the parents'
perceptions of them. Before the group therapy, some of the parents viewed
the caseworker as a powerful authority with complete control over their
relationship to the agency and to their children. The parents frequently
responded to this perception by either being very submissive or very dependent. This behavior has a parallel in the initial group theme—mistrust.
At first, the parents tried to tell the group therapist what they thought
he wanted to hear.

Coincident with the change in parental attitudes in the group, the caseworkers reported that parents began to shift their emphasis in their meetings with the workers. One worker noticed that the parents seemed less
clinging and less complaining. Another noted a change in the parents' use
of the casework session. She observed that these parents spent less time
unburdening their own problems on the worker and more time on joint
planning for their children. A third worker reported that the parents
assigned to him were more aware of themselves as persons and began responding as individuals and not just as parents. He felt that, through
this change, their relationship to him was expressed less in stereotyped
"parent" questions and became both more professional and more real.

### CONCLUSION

The record of the 12 sessions reveals quite clearly that these parents
were able, through the group method, to become involved with each other
and with the agency to a much greater extent than they had through their
previous agency contacts.

Their involvement seemed to stem, first, from their opportunity to test
the group therapist to see whether he (as the agency's representative)

could tolerate their ambivalent feelings toward themselves, their children, and the agency. Second, involvement developed out of the group identification that was the result of their successful testing experience. Third, it came out of the expression of negative feelings that they felt toward the agency's "inadequate" mothering of their children.

The caseworkers felt that both the stimulation the parents experienced in the group psychotherapy and the parents' increased involvement with the agency made their own contacts with the parents more realistic and more satisfying. The agency administrator noted decreased sabotage by parents of the treatment processes and signs of increased cooperation by them.

Because of the initial success of the program, group treatment will be further explored as a means of working through the parents' feelings about placement of their children, their identification with the treatment process, and their reactions to the improvement of their children's condition.

# 50

⟮ The attitude toward the child-care institution as a group-care facility differs in many countries. The following article reviews some of these differences in attitude toward group care and suggests some of the social and economic reasons for such differences.

## Another View of Group Care*

*Martin Wolins*

It is a commonplace of basic texts in anthropology to point out that in many cultures children are initiated into their adult society by elaborate puberty rites. The more naive student often assumes that the child's society has taken none but these formal steps to assure a satisfactory adult performance. But this is, of course, untrue—the process leading up to the

* The materials used in this report have been developed as part of a project on group care supported by the Ford Foundation and by Grant MH 1430 01 of NIMH, USPHS, HEW.

focal moment greatly exceeds the initiation in importance. Without a long and intensive period of learning, becoming an adult would be a risky venture, which the person's milieu can ill afford. His society prepares him, then, by providing rules and examples, settings and judges. Some of these are comfortably unpremeditated, others carefully planned.

Because it has been in the American tradition to extol laissez-faire solutions in child rearing as well as in commercial and industrial activity, we find it surprising and even discomforting to encounter formalized societal intervention in what may well be the most important function of society —child rearing. Confronted by the existence of such programs abroad, we deny their utility or ascribe them to the unusual needs and problems of societies very different from our own. In actuality, though, the group child-rearing structures found abroad are pinch-hitting for the family in a most crucial way.

The *shkola-internat* (Soviet boarding school) and the group care facility of Youth Aliyah in Israel, for example, are intended to assure satisfactory adult performance. They exist to enhance and promote socialization—the process of acquiring the socially necessary attitudes, values, and behaviors. But they attempt to accomplish their aims through group care rather than families, and that makes us uncomfortable. Our discomfort with these processes is increased when we learn their objective—primary concern for the collectivity, for the social matrix, and not just the individual alone.

Our approach has been markedly different. It has always been parent-child oriented, although the roles of parents and children and outside agents have undergone considerable change.

## EPOCHS OF CHILD REARING

American child-rearing techniques have been described as falling into four major epochs, each with its own objectives.[1] Prior to the Civil War, the emphasis was on breaking the child's will, as if the parents wanted him to accept the dictates of superego and reject the demands of id. Gradually this approach drifted into a recognition of the rights of children to have lives of their own. Perhaps the most outstanding symbol of this new perception of the child was the first White House Conference in 1909. Upon the rather general acceptance of this position, the goals of child rearing shifted again. Self-sufficiency and independence became the new objectives. And these, in turn, yielded a central position to individualization. But, whether the goal was breaking the child's will or creating a self-sufficient and fully expressed person, the parent was charged with the responsibility

---

[1] *See* Daniel R. Miller and Guy E. Swanson, *The Changing American Parent* (New York: John Wiley & Sons, 1958), pp. 3–28, for a detailed review of these periods and their goals.

for achieving it. His were the pleasures of accomplishment and the sorrows of failure. Society was an interested but distant and often uninvolved bystander intervening only when the parent and the child had failed —often beyond repair.

By and large, societal aloofness may have been justified. The child-rearing structures and values of the day may well have produced the adults desired. Attributes wished for in the child fitted comfortably with actual or, lately, historic "rugged individualism." A man who could conquer himself could subdue the West. He who was self-sufficient and independent could survive the competitive pressures of an entrepreneurial society. The individual propensities that developed, when insightful and sufficiently deviant, distinguished the Edisons and the Jesse Jameses, the Fords and the Capones.

Less spectacular changes involved the "average man" as well. Wrapped in the cocoon of family conservatism, he slowly changed from one generation to the next. But even now he finds comfort in the myths that were yesterday's reality. He speaks of individualism and self-sufficiency and personal independence. He may even keep a shotgun for an annual rabbit hunt. But his groceries come from the store and are paid for with a salary check. Virtues of yesterday's entrepreneurial life may ill serve him in the "welfare bureaucracy" of the present. With good intent or without, his parents may have reared him to live in the preautomation age. Socialization may not have kept pace with changes in our society. In any event, the object of socialization, in the last century at least, has not been the creation of new men, but the retention of a strong sense of the past in generations of the future.

But what if change must be more rapid? What if the goals of a society are not to link with the past; what if the society aims at breaking with many values of the past? The Soviet Union and Israel were faced with exactly this situation.

### RUSSIAN GOALS

The Russians have attempted to move a backward people—who, at the time of the Revolution, were only 50 years removed from serfdom—into a leading industrial society. That, to accomplish this task, they have chosen the ideological vehicle of communism may be of lesser significance to the present discussion than the fact that high pressure for change has led them to other than laissez-faire principles, not only in industrial and commercial life, but also in psychosocial enterprises such as child rearing and education.[2] At first, the major objective appears to have been the attainment of general literacy.

---

[2] This should not be surprising to us. After all, we too have been experiencing a continual expansion of compulsory public education—an idea that first took hold in the

Literacy has been achieved,[3] but the other, often newer, goals that have been set are far more difficult to reach. Among them, the most universal seems to be a new objective: the ultimate, consolidating step assuring that "this generation will live in communism." To that end, they need devoted *stroitieli kommunizma*—builders of communism. We have many descriptions of this personality type. One of the clearest comes, interestingly enough, from a new journal called *Shkola Internat*. On page 1 of the first issue in 1963, they say that their task is "to develop minds in accordance with communist ideology and thus create great people. . . . Any and every . . . activity consists of facilitating the development of ideological maturity to better form their communist convictions, sense of duty and a feeling of responsibility of each individual with respect to the collective."[4]

## ISRAELI AIMS

Modern Israel, whose aims antedate the state itself by some half a century, also required a drastic break with the past. A culture of messianic hope and Hassidic escapism, of urban mercantilism and paternal autocracy, could not be functional in a new and barren land. As Spiro had noted, much of the movement into the early Jewish settlements of Turkish and then British colonial Palestine was accompanied by a rejection of the "old man" and the old values.[5] The poet of this movement, the spirited voice that spoke with an understanding of both the old and the new, was unquestionably Bialik. And his most telling phrase, "We are the last generation of bondage and the first of salvation," is a commonplace in Israel today.

From bondage to freedom, from archaic Diaspora to modern Israel is a big leap. Focal points of the change have been *Zionut, chalutziut, avoda* —Zionism, pioneering efforts, labor. The acculturative task has been to convert immigrants of the most disparate backgrounds to national allegiance, enlightened innovation and self-sacrifice, and hard physical work.[6]

---

United States in the second half of the nineteenth century, when the balance between agricultural and industrial society was shifting to favor the latter.

[3] The change has been most remarkable among rural women, whose literacy rate is said to have climbed from 9.6 percent in 1897 to 35.4 percent in 1926 to 79.2 and 97.5 percent, respectively, for 1939 and 1959. See *Zhenshchiny i Deti v SSSR* [*Women and Children in the U.S.S.R.*] (Moscow: Statistical Publishing House, 1963), p. 53.

[4] "Uchit', Zhit' Po Kommunisticheski" ["To Teach Living in a Communist Manner"]. Editorial, *Shkola Internat*, I (1963), 1.

[5] Melford E. Spiro, *Kibbutz: Venture in Utopia* (Cambridge, Mass.: Harvard University Press, 1956).

[6] How diverse the immigrant children's backgrounds have been is reflected in the statistics of Youth Aliyah—the youth immigration agency of Israel. In 1956, for example, 30 percent of the children under Youth Aliyah care came from North Africa, 32 percent from the Middle East, 14 percent from Eastern Europe, 4 percent from Asia, and smaller proportions from other parts of the world. See Hanoch Reinhold, *Youth Aliyah, Trends and Developments* (Jerusalem: The Jewish Agency, 1957), p. 10.

Although their political ideology was largely different from Soviet Communism, the Israelis dealing with immigrant youth also ascribed a central position to the collective. They call it *chevra*, which, incidentally, means both society *and* group. They hold that allegiance and responsibility to *chevra* are the ingredients upon which successful acculturation is built. *Chevra* is the background against which the goals of patriotism, socially oriented innovation and self-sacrifice and an appreciation of hard work are created.

Given these objectives and the familial child-rearing environments at hand, the two societies under consideration had to make a choice. They could have been swayed by tradition and by the overwhelming psychological arguments in favor of a family-based socialization, or they could have chosen to strike out on a new course—child rearing in group settings. They have leaned cautiously in favor of the latter. Interestingly, the Israelis have gone farther in this direction than the Russians, even in the face of considerable (perhaps ill-advised) pressures from well-intentioned Western, mainly American, professionals.[7]

## IDEOLOGY AND REALITY PRESSURES

Why has this development of group care taken place in the two countries under discussion? Although ideology has undoubtedly played an important role in the acceptability and the justification of group care, this pattern of child-rearing was obviously not an indispensable requirement for the societies' development. The number and proportion of children in such programs at any given time, or for that matter the totals who have been so reared, is not very large. Israel's Youth Aliyah has about 100,000 graduates. All of the collective educational facilities of the *kibbutz* movement have reared no more than that number. At most, less than 10 percent of Israel's adult population has been reared in group settings. Comparable proportions for the Soviet Union at this time are much lower.

The explanation for group care of children in these countries lies, it appears, in the belief that certain families were unable to function as

---

The Youth Aliyah statistical report for the second half of 1962 shows 1632 "graduates" who originally came from 45 countries. Although most are still from Eastern Europe, North Africa, and the Middle East, some have come from such disparate cultures as Poland, Yemen, Turkey, France, the U.S.A., Brazil, Ethiopia, China, and the Congo, to name but a few. (Data from Youth Aliyah statistical report for the period 7-1-1962 to 1-1-1963, mimeographed.)

[7] Perhaps there is a direct relationship between the proportion of the population that is seen as requiring change and the rate at which these changes must take place and the recourse to group care. This is completely aside from any ideological reasons that would propel decisions in that direction. Israeli society has been under extreme pressures. The State has been actually or technically at war with *all* its neighbors since 1948. During that time it has also absorbed an immigration exceeding its total inhabitants in the year of independence *and* (along with Japan) has had the highest rate of economic growth in the world.

transmitters of rapid change. Such incapacity may be due to several qualities of family life, outstanding among which are maternal employment
outside the home, scarcity of good housing, and, most important, cultural
lag.[8]

In the Soviet Union, a very high proportion of the female population
is employed, presumably outside the home. Of the 115 million women
of all ages in the Soviet population in 1959, about 61 million were within
the age range of 20 to 69 years. Data for the same year show 47,605,000
women employed. Thus, the rate of employment among women is about
three-fourths of those in the employable age groups. Even more impressive
as an indicator of the rate of women's employment is that they form 48
percent of the total employed labor force.[9]

Housing is another problem. Both the Soviet Union and Israel still face
substantial housing shortages in spite of heavy construction. For example,
in Israel in 1957, 26 percent of the families lived in housing with a density
of three or more persons per room.[10] The recent immigrants, from among
whom most Youth Aliyah children are drawn, still probably live in more
crowded quarters than the average even though they are given priority
for housing.

Employment of women and tight housing obviously predispose toward
child care outside the home. Sometimes they compel such action. The
Soviet Union has been expanding the necessary facilities very rapidly, but
they are still far from adequate to provide for the total or even most of
the child population. In 1961 preschool establishments had a capacity of
about 3½ million children,[11] and schools with extended-day programs
about another million or million and a half.[12] In effect, then, many a
Russian child is reared at home, where he cannot be cared for either by
his mother or by a person of her age group. It is the *babushka*, the grandmother, or a member of her age group who is the major child-rearing
substitute. And *babushkas* in the Soviet Union, as elsewhere, are not of
the generation most amenable to changes in ideology. If the children are

---

[8] Similar concerns with acculturation motivated Jane Addams in the founding of Hull
House, an arrangement for spanning the gap between immigrants and American society.
See her *Twenty Years at Hull-House* (New York: The New American Library, 1961).
*See also* Ann Fischer, "Culture, Communication, and Child Welfare," *Child Welfare*,
XLIII (1964), 161–169.

[9] See *Zhenshchiny i Deti v SSSR*, pp. 36, 82, 83.

[10] M. Smilansky, *et al.*, eds., *Child and Youth Welfare in Israel* (Jerusalem: The
Szold Institute for Child and Youth Welfare, 1960), p. 32.

[11] *Zhenshchiny i Deti v SSSR*, p. 113, shows 3,622,500 children in creches and
kindergartens in 1961. This is a threefold increase over the 1950 population in these
establishments. The estimated urban child population, ages 1 through 6, is about 12
million.

[12] *Ibid.*, p. 138, shows 2 million children in *internats* and extended-day schools as of
the 1962–1963 school year. In all probability more than half of this number are in
extended-day schools.

to be builders of communism, then, it is more likely that they will be educated for it in the boarding school than at grandmother's knee.

In Israel one need not even go back to the grandparents. There, the immigrant parents often are several generations removed from their own children. A Moroccan Jew from the Atlas Mountains who arrives in the modern port of Haifa may well be five centuries behind in social outlook, attitude toward work, and views of women's position in the family from the young *sabra* (native-born Israeli) stevedore who is unloading the ship. Within months the Moroccan's children move ideologically a few hundred years. Can he also? Or, more important, can they do so freely when attached to him?

If rapid acculturation must take place, who should be the agent? *Babushka* and her daughter, who, at best, live in the present, can only impart the ideology of the present—they may even be incapable of conveying the currently expressed motto of the party, "This generation will live in communism." Similarly, the Moroccan Jew and his wife often cannot comprehend and impart the ideals of Zionism, pioneering, and labor— the ideological fundamentals of the new state.

What then are the alternatives? Other families? But their mothers are just as employed, their housing no different, and their *babushkas*, fathers, and mothers no more in the wave of the future than the children's own. In the Soviet Union, foster family care does not exist.[13] In Israel, it is a minor program with little prospect of substantial growth.[14]

In both the Soviet Union and Israel, major emphasis is placed on group care. The *shkola-internat* and the youth group in the *kibbutz* and in the children's community institution are seen as the best media for rapid acculturation. As a consequence, Youth Aliyah has about 95 percent of all children under its care in group facilities of some kind. The Soviet Union has been expanding its boarding schools at a rapid rate, and heavy investments are planned in this area for the next several years. Their goal is to accommodate 2½ million children in such facilities by 1965, which would constitute about 7 percent of the school population at that time. Even more telling evidence of the favor group care has achieved is the recurring assertion made on the highest levels of the Soviet Government that boarding schools are to be "greatly developed as a major form of rearing the growing generation."[15]

---

[13] *See* Bernice Madison, "Welfare Services for Children in the Soviet Union, 1945–1963," *Child Welfare*, XLII (1963), 324.

[14] Youth Aliyah has somewhat more than 100 children (about 1 percent of the population in care) in foster homes. These are mostly disturbed young people who are treated with great perceptiveness and warmth and in the opinion of staff, with considerable success. But this is not seen as a substitute for the massive acculturative job of the group placements offered by the agency.

[15] See N. S. Khrushchev, "Control Figures for Development of the U.S.S.R. National Economy in 1959–1965," *Pravda*, November 14, 1958. *See also* Effie Ambler, "The

## RELEVANCE FOR AMERICA

Granted, then, that the Russians and some of the Israelis approve of group care or even heartily endorse it,[16] what relevance does this have for us in America? As a nation we do not aspire to communism or to Zionism. Our society is markedly different in its aims and makeup from either Israel or Russia. Nor do we as a nation feel a particular urge for rapid change and a sense that the family as we know it cannot keep up with the child-rearing needs of our times. Our overall orientation predisposes a reliance upon the family as the source of values and attitudes that will fit the child into the adult society. Our psychologists, psychiatrists, social workers, and teachers bolster this view with theoretically derived and, at times, even empirically grounded pronouncements.

I do not intend to review here in any detail the capability of the American family as a socializing enterprise. My focus will be on the population most at risk—certain categories of AFDC recipients. But some questions about all families lead to concern about their present and future coping ability. As in Russia and Israel, our interest could well be centered on mothers' employment, housing, and cultural appropriateness. Increasingly, the mother of young and school-age children in America goes out to work. (Of all women employed in 1959, 29 percent had children under 18 years of age.[17]) Who, then, cares for the children when mother is at work? We know some answers—publicly operated school systems and day care facilities, private child care arrangements with commercial establishments, "sitters," or no one.[18] We cannot even fall back on the American version of *babushka*, since it is most unlikely that grandma lives with the family or even nearby.

And housing? Speaking of housing, Michael Harrington names it as "one of the greatest single domestic scandals of postwar America. The statistics have all been nicely calculated; everyone knows the dimensions of the problem; and articles appear regularly predicting the next catastrophe that will come from inaction. But nothing is done to attack the basic problem, and poor housing remains one of the most important facts about the *other* America.[19] Statistics from the 1960 census substantiate Har-

---

Soviet Boarding School," *The American Slavic and East European Review*, XX (1961), 237–252.

[16] One should add here that group care is viewed positively in other countries as well. Poland and Yugoslavia are some additional communist examples, and Austria, Switzerland, and Italy are examples of capitalist societies that have accepted it.

[17] *Special Labor Reports*, No. 7 (Washington, D.C.: U.S. Government Printing Office, 1959).

[18] For example, 99 percent of day care arrangements are of informal types. Florence A. Ruderman, "Day Care: A Challenge to Social Work," *Child Welfare*, XLIII (1964), 121.

[19] Michael Harrington, *The Other America: Poverty in the United States* (New York: Macmillan & Co., 1962), p. 139.

rington's views. A third of a nation ill housed is still a reasonably accurate though shocking statement, just as it was in Franklin Roosevelt's time.

But the major problem here, as in the two countries discussed earlier, is not in the physical ability of families to care for their children. If we focus on that group least able to provide good physical care—presumably certain recipients of AFDC funds—our third area of concern, acculturating ability, becomes clearly the most important. Theoretically, at least, the AFDC mother has been freed from outside employment. Presumably, also, her grant can be made large enough to buy better than substandard housing—although that rarely, if ever, has been so.

Given these conditions, will all be well? In *some* cases there is room for a great deal of doubt. The mother is asked to rear children to a culture she has not experienced and, most likely, does not value. And it is not only the one mother's view that needs to be counteracted. The social outlook, the value systems of an entire environment, have to be overcome in the child in order to permit his evolution away from the culture of "relief recipients." Or to put in a newer, perhaps less stigmatizing, more euphonious way, the "culture of poverty" must be replaced by a culture of achievement.

Can there be much question that such a culture of poverty exists; that it has values of its own with their antecedent causes, their justifiable existence, and their consequences for behavior? Is there much doubt that this culture is geographically concentrated and that it exerts a powerful influence on the children in its midst? Are we not asking for the impossible when we attempt to change the values of children and their adult guardians while continuing to leave them immersed in a culture that denies the validity of the very values to be acquired? All of the evidence available up to this point permits little optimism about the success of this venture. Although our programs for the poor have been urgently needed and useful in sustaining life and, to a limited extent, in preserving the human dignity of recipients and donors (i.e., taxpayers) alike, they cannot be said to have made an evident and substantial impact on the *culture* of poverty or its inhabitants.[20]

It seems unreasonable to expect that a family overcome by financial problems, immersed in a culture of deprivation, and substantially at odds with the dominant values of America will, given some money and a thimbleful of professional help, rear future standard-bearers of the "American way of life."

---

[20] *See* M. Elaine Burgess and Daniel O. Price, *An American Dependency Challenge* (Chicago: American Public Welfare Association, 1963). Forty percent of the families currently on public assistance have had one or more parents or grandparents on assistance.

## WHAT ALTERNATIVES?

What, then, are the alternatives open to us? Other families and institutions. Our reaction to the first of these alternatives is generally that it is impossible and, to the other, that there must be caution and concern. Both views have reasonable historical antecedents.

The foster family answer has been tried to some extent. Of course, in most instances, it is used only as a last resort—or a nearly last one—when the capability of the child, the perseverance of the parent, and often the patience of a judge were worn thin. In many instances it has worked— occasionally, very well. But all over America today there is a shortage of foster homes, and many of those that are available fall short of being good. In fact, the pressures upon child welfare agencies are such that workers may not be able to choose in accord with their perception of what is good.[21] We have in all some 150,000 foster homes, surely an inadequate number even for their present tasks.

Even this small number of foster homes presents serious problems. The identity of a child in such a home is often unclear,[22] his stay is uncertain. He will probably find himself a wanderer, packing his affections, if any, and his problems and transferring them to at least several foster homes before he matures.[23] Although the outcome for some foster children has been favorable,[24] the overall effect of the program is unknown.

Group care, which might be an alternative, has until recently been rejected as a possibility. As late as the 1950's, the American professional considered a group care facility—no matter how good it may have been—in one of two ways: as a treatment setting for the emotionally disturbed or as an old fashioned orphanage that had no right to exist. The "respectable" settings had, with a few notable exceptions, worked overtime since the 1920's to convert their facilities and their public images from the latter to the former. It became exceedingly fashionable to have a "residential treatment center" and to minister to those whose parents, and often foster parents as well, had failed.[25]

---

21 See Martin Wolins, Selecting Foster Parents: The Ideal and the Reality (New York: Columbia University Press, 1963).

22 See Ibid., pp. 8–33; and Eugene A. Weinstein, The Self-Image of the Foster Child (New York: Russell Sage Foundation, 1960).

23 See Henry S. Maas and Richard E. Engler, Jr., Children in Need of Parents (New York: Columbia University Press, 1959). Their study shows that as many as a third of the children move four or more times while in foster family care. Table 36, p. 422.

24 See Elizabeth G. Meier, Former Foster Children as Adult Citizens, unpublished doctoral dissertation (New York: New York School of Social Work, Columbia University, 1962).

25 For a description of such centers today, their activities, aims, populations, and costs (which, incidentally, run up to $17,000 per child-year), see Lydia F. Hylton, The Residential Treatment Center: Children, Programs, and Costs (New York: Child Welfare League of America, 1964).

## CONDITIONS OF INSTITUTION LIFE

The move away from institution care was not new to the present century—and it has already gone beyond the period of greatest impact.[26] Even in the last century there were voices that cried out against this form of care. Eighty years ago, a speaker at the National Conference on Charities and Correction indicted the whole program in a single forceful sentence: "I should like to see every single institution in the country for *dependent* children closed tomorrow, if they could be."[27] Many professionals agreed with this sentiment. Most do today. To support their views, they cite extensive studies on the damaging effects of separation and institutionalization.[28] But the argument in terms of acculturation was made most tellingly by an old-time clinician. Homer Folks, an early leader of the social work profession, summarized the case against institutions by comparing them with family life.

> In the family there is ever-changing variety of interest; in the institution there is comparatively unbroken monotony. . . .
>
> In the family, there is a gradual transition from the complete dependence of infancy to a larger measure of freedom and independence. . . . In the institution, on the other hand, there is of necessity a measure of restraint and repression which tends to obliterate individual distinctions, to discourage originality and inquiry.
>
> In the family . . . the child develops local relations and attachments. . . . The [child] suddenly transferred from an institution . . . is an isolated unit.[29]

If we continue to think about group care as Folks did in his time, then all the qualities ascribed by him to the institution are undoubtedly still to be found. The bad institution program still suffers from monotony,

---

[26] See, for example, Donald L. Loughery, Jr., "The Heirs of Disorganization— Where Do They Go?" Child Welfare, XLIII (1964), 170–174, which describes the work of certain California institutions.

[27] Clara T. Leonard, statement in "Debate on Placing Out Children," *Proceedings of the National Conference of Charities and Correction, 1881* (Boston: A. Williams & Co., 1881), p. 302.

[28] Particular reference is made to the works of Spitz, Goldfarb, and Bowlby, all to be found incorporated in John Bowlby, *Maternal Care and Mental Health* (rev.; Geneva: World Health Organization, 1952). A more recent review of the issues and research in this field has been made by Mary D. Ainsworth, *et al., Deprivation of Maternal Care: A Reassessment of Its Effects* (Geneva: World Health Organization, 1962). More cautious in its conclusions, the later book may well have affected the very tentative current explorations in group care for the "normal" child.

[29] Homer Folks, "Why Should Dependent Children Be Reared in Families Rather Than in Institutions?" *Charities Review*, V (1896), 140, 141. For a more modern, extreme expression of views on this subject, *see* Abram Kardiner, "When the State Brings Up the Child," *Saturday Review*, August 26, 1961. For a modern view favoring one form of group care, *see* Bruno Bettelheim, "Does Communal Education Work?" *Commentary*, XXXIII (1962), 117–125.

restraint, lack of individualization, and isolation. But it is improper to continue treating these as unavoidable qualities of group care. Israeli, Russian, and, to a limited extent, our own programs prove otherwise. This does not mean, of course, that, aside from occasional overenthusiasm, the Soviets or Israelis claim group care, as each has developed it, to have solved all problems. The leaders of Youth Aliyah, the institutions, and the *kibbutzim* in Israel can still point to many problems in this form of child care. Similarly, Russian pedagogues are experimenting and changing many aspects of the *internat*. Admission of possible defects in these programs and changes being made in them is accompanied, however, by a reaffirmation of their basic soundness.

Whether these programs are as good as seen by their supporters still needs much painstaking research investigation. What evidence there is on the 100,000 graduates of Youth Aliyah is largely positive. Similarly, observation of *internat* children by Western child care specialists has produced favorable impressions. More study in these and other group care settings will be needed to reveal details of success and failure. Meanwhile, the very existence of these programs permits us to question the elaborate mythology that our own unfortunate experience has caused us to build around institution care.

Is is true, for example, that individualization is impossible in group care? Here is some contrary evidence.

M. G. Bylanovski, a teacher at Shkola-Internat No. 12 in Moscow relates:

During the first two months of work with the class, the teacher and the upbringer[30] visited almost all the pupils at home. Consequently, the majority of problems that arose as we got to know the pupils were answered. We were interested, for example, in why Vilya K. was untidy, did not want to wash in the morning, was malicious, apprehensive toward others, expecting only harm, and why he repulsed any of the upbringer's attempts to talk with him, always bristling up like a porcupine. The situation was clarified through visits to the family. It became evident that many negative features of the boy's character were the result of an abnormal home atmosphere.

We attempted to give the boy much care and attention in school, to be affectionate and fair with him. We established an atmosphere in class that allowed him to feel that his friends were all well-meaning. This changed the boy's attitude noticeably. He made friends with the other children, became polite and confident with adults, and his former alienation disappeared.[31]

And here is an example from Youth Aliyah:

---

[30] The Soviet boarding school has personnel specifically charged with educational tasks and other charged with "child care." The two staff categories, *utchitel'* and *vospitatel'*, have about the same status and academic preparation.

[31] E. I. Afanasenko and I. A. Kairov, eds., *Pyat' Let Shkol-Internatov* [*Five Years of Boarding Schools*] (Moscow: R.S.F.S.R. Academy of Pedagogical Sciences Press, 1961), p. 35.

A girl who had just returned from vacation to her place of training asked permission for further leave. After much importuning she, at length, agreed to divulge the reason for her application. She had been given an "evil eye" at a certain spot she had travelled through, and her mind could only be set at rest by going back there and scattering some earth.[32]

Surely, no organization in which children are cared for *en masse* would report cases of this type.

It also does not necessarily hold that group care must result in isolation. A child in the youth group of a *kibbutz* is very much a part of things. He not only is among his peers, but the chances are that he works, eats, and sings alongside of regular members of the *kibbutz*. It is very likely that the *kibbutz* staff assigned to the Youth Aliyah group will call each member in it *chaver*—friend—a most intimate and relevant designation.

It is not true that a program oriented around the peer group necessarily ignores the parents. On the contrary, there is evidence in the literature and from observation that an attempt is made to reach (socialize) the parents through the children.[33]

## TWO NOTIONS

It may well be that group care need not be possessed of the negative attitudes usually ascribed to it—providing, of course, that we accept two rather crucial notions. First, we must accept the position that individual competitiveness is not necessarily the most ennobling of human relationships; that self-in-society may be a greater achievement than self-and-society and certainly more acceptable than self-against-society. We have slowly been heading in that direction for a good many years, but still are reluctant to acknowledge the decline of the entrepreneur and the advent of a welfare bureaucracy and the gray flannel suit. Since the change appears inevitable, should we be so fearful of rearing a child who is better accustomed to group than to personal enterprise? And can we try it along with other programs for those whose prognosis at the moment is social failure in personal *and* group enterprise?

Second, we must remember about self-fulfilling prophecies. It is amazing that we professionals who are so sensitive to the operation of predictive statements in individual cases fail to note the import they have for institutions. We carefully avoid publicizing diagnoses on the grounds that they have a tendency to propel the individual toward their realization. But for some 50 years we have pronounced group care bad and have sat

---

[32] Reinhold, *op. cit.*, p. 29.

[33] I. Sotnikov, "Parents' Activity is Essential," *Semya i Shkola*, Vol. X (1959), translated in *Soviet Education*, Vol. II (1960). See also *Chanichei Aliyat Hanoar B'chaim Atzmaiin [Graduates of Youth Aliyah in Independent Life]* (Jerusalem: The Jewish Agency, 1962).

back to wonder why it was so. Well, the Russians and the Israelis of Youth Aliyah (and the Swiss and the Italians, and the Poles and . . .) pronounce it good. Should we not, at the very least, find out whether and when it is a really useful form of care for them and possibly for us?

# Index